World Facts In Brief

Rand McNally
World Facts
In Brief

Rand McNally & Company
Chicago • New York • San Francisco

World Facts In Brief was produced and edited by the staff of Rand McNally & Co. The views expressed are the authors' and not necessarily those of the publisher.

Editorial
Jon M. Leverenz, *Managing Editor*
Susan B. Keating, *Editor*
Elizabeth G. Fagan, *Assistant Editor*
Marga Levy, *Production Editor*
Christine DiThomas, *Assistant*

Statistical Research
V. Patrick Healy, *Department Manager*
Susan K. Eidsvoog, *Research Coordinator*
Dean Westmeyer, *Research Geographer*

Art and Design
Gordon Hartshorne, *Art Director*
Mary Jo Schrader, *Designer*

Information in **World Scoreboard** is derived from current United States government publications and Rand McNally data.

Photo Credits
Cover J. B. Cuny/FPG International (flags outside of United Nations headquarters, New York City)
9 UPI (street scene, San Salvador, El Salvador)
89 Abu Hander/Int'l Stock Photo (annual pilgrimage, Mecca, Saudi Arabia)
129 UN photo 150,094 by Milton Grant (United Nations headquarters, New York City)

Copyright © 1986 by Rand McNally & Company
All rights reserved
Library of Congress Catalog Card Number: 85-43073
Printed in the United States of America
by Rand McNally & Company
SBN: 528-83188-7
      528-83189-5 (pbk.)

Contents

World Gazetteer: Profiles of Nations and Places

World Atlas

Hot Spots and High Tensions

The United States and Canada

The United States and Canada are so bound together economically and agriculturally that they tend generally to share the same economic problems. When the United States is in an economic downturn, Canada is too. When Canada has a bumper crop of wheat and finds it difficult to locate a buyer, it is generally because the United States has generally harvested a bumper crop the same year.

Socially, however, the two countries have separate but related problems. In the United States, the overwhelming social problem has historically been racial, most particularly the status of blacks and, more recently, Third World immigrants. In Canada, the major social problem has always been—and continues to be—the friction that has grown between the segment of the population with a British background and that of French extraction. Since so much of the French-speaking population lives in the province of Québec, the French-English problem has tended to be concentrated there. In fact, the problem in Québec has become so bitter that a large segment of the French-speaking majority (and Québec is the only Canadian province with a French-speaking majority) has demanded that Québec separate from the national government of Canada and assert its complete independence. Although the differences between the French-speaking and English-speaking Canadians are primarily ethnic and social, there is a religious aspect to the problem, since Canadians of French extraction are almost wholly Roman Catholic, while those of British background are mostly Protestant.

In the United States, a religious controversy of a different character is emerging. Unlike such disputes in most parts of the world, it is not a conflict among various religions and sects. Rather it revolves around what role, if any, the government should play in the religious life of the citizenry. Since the United States Constitution—and most state constitutions—prohibit the establishment of religion, it has generally been held that there exists a "wall of separation" between the state and the church. In recent years, that wall has been tested by two highly emotional issues: prayer in schools and the legalization of abortion.

Support of or opposition to these two issues has coalesced in interesting combinations: Roman Catholic, Orthodox Jewish, and fundamentalist Christians have been in the forefront of those demanding the prohibition of abortions. They have called for a constitutional amendment if all other efforts fail to outlaw abortions. On the other side of the issue are more liberal Protestant and Jewish religious leaders and such secular organizations as the National Organization for Women (NOW) and the American Civil Liberties Union.

Fundamentalist Christian churches have been the chief opponents of Supreme Court decisions that have judged official prayer in school sessions as unconstitutional. They too look to a constitutional amendment to remedy what they regard as a triumph of atheism. Opponents of organized prayer in schools have been for the most part the same groups that support legalized abortion.

Québec: Separatism and the Future

Perspective

1534	*French explorer Jacques Cartier lands at Gaspé, claims land for France.*
1763	*French-British wars end with Treaty of Paris.*
1783	*British Loyalists settle west of Ottawa River, in present-day Ontario, starting geographical division between French- and English-speaking people.*
1841	*British Act of Union joins Upper and Lower Canada.*
1867	*British North America Act creates Dominion of Canada.*
1960	*Prime Minister Jean Lesage installs Liberal government and begins Quiet Revolution.*
1968	*Parti Québecois is founded.*
1976	**November 15.** *René Lévesque is elected premier of Québec.*
1977	*Bill 101, legalizing supremacy of French, is passed by Québec's legislature.*
1982	*Canada's constitution is ratified.*
1984	**September 4.** *Brian Mulroney is elected Canada's prime minister.*

A large percentage of French-Canadians live in the Canadian province of Québec, where they constitute over 80 percent of the population. These Québecois strongly resent the anglicization that has been imposed on all of Canada, including Québec, by the majority of Canadians, who are of English or Scotch-Irish descent. Historically, that resentment has manifested itself in several ways: Québec's insistence that French be the official language of Canada on an equal par with English; that the old Canadian flag, closely resembling the English Union Jack, be replaced by the Maple Leaf flag; and, most radically, the demand that Québec form its own independent republic.

Issues and Events

The separatist movement reached its apex in 1976, when the separatist Parti Québecois became the majority party in the provincial legislature. But the heady days of separatism quickly faded. The 1984 elections dealt severe blows both to the national Liberal party (traditionally more sympathetic to French claims) and the provincial Parti Québecois. The Progressive Conservative party, or Tories, were swept into office behind the new prime minister, Brian Mulroney, in a landslide. The Tory triumph could be attributed to Canada's stagnant economy, which the voters blamed on the incumbent Liberal party. Québec had been particularly hurt by the economic slowdown, an issue that obviously loomed larger for many Quebecer voters than the issue of separatism.

Polls indicate, however, that Quebecers' support for independence has dropped independently of the economic issue. In 1980, 40 percent of Quebecers polled favored independence; by 1985, the percentage had dropped to 19.

Nevertheless, the Parti Québecois in 1984 again voted to make secession its major issue. René Lévesque, the premier of Québec and leader in the Parti Québecois, went on record as favoring a moderation of that platform. His position is that the economic issue should be stressed. With a more conservative government in office at the national level, it is reasoned, a radical secession stance by the party would be counterproductive. Hard-liners within the party, however, continue to work for a confrontation on the issue.

Background

Francophones, as the French-speaking majority is known, make up 82 percent of Québec's 6.5 million people. French-Canadian nationalism, as a reaction to many years of discrimination by English-speaking leaders, took seed in the early 1960s. The Liberal party, then led by Jean Lesage, began a movement known as the Quiet Revolution, pointing toward provincial autonomy and national bilingualism. The Parti Québecois was founded in 1968 by René Lévesque as a peaceful vehicle for the separatist movement, opposed to the violent tactics of the Front de Libération Québec.

The passage of Bill 101 in 1977 declared French to be Québec's official language. The process of removing the English language from Québec began by renaming towns, rivers, and mountains; by requiring all professionals to pass a French proficiency test; and by closing or adapting English-speaking schools. New French language regulations proved unrealistic for many businesses, and between 1976 and 1981, an estimated one hundred major company headquarters moved out of Montreal alone, costing the city fourteen thousand jobs. In 1982 Canada's new constitution dealt another blow to separatism. It in effect mandated bilingualism in all provinces; later the Québec superior court declared Bill 101 in violation of the national constitution.

The United States: Religion and Politics

Perspective

1636	*Rhode Island is founded on principle of religious toleration.*
1791	*States ratify Constitution's First Amendment; federal government is prohibited from establishing a religion or interfering with "free exercise thereof."*
1833	*Massachusetts stops Congregationalism, thereby ending all officially established religion in America.*
1843	*Know-Nothing party, an anti-Catholic political movement, is founded.*
1928	*Alfred E. Smith becomes first Roman Catholic to be nominated for presidency by major party.*
1940	*Supreme Court rules that free exercise clause of First Amendment applies to states as well as to federal government.*
1960	*John F. Kennedy becomes first Roman Catholic to be elected president.*
1962	*Supreme Court rules that even voluntary prayer in public schools constitutes establishment of religion and is therefore in violation of First Amendment.*
1973	*Supreme Court strikes down all state laws banning abortions.*
1984	*Prayer in public schools and abortion become major issues in presidential campaign.*

Considering its great religious diversity, the United States has historically been a country of few serious religious divisions; most people would credit the "high wall" of separation between church and state guaranteed by the United States Constitution and the various state constitutions and by the long American tradition of religious toleration.

This is not to claim that the mixture of religion and politics in America has always been totally tranquil; quite the opposite. Furthermore, there are indications in the 1980s that the nation is headed for more religious dispute than the country has seen in the twentieth century. This new religious dissension is not for the most part a division along sectarian lines. Rather it is a clash between those adhering to "fundamentalist" beliefs (in both Christianity and Judaism) and

practices and those who adhere to a more "liberal" or "modernist" viewpoint. Thus, the more conservative Protestants, Roman Catholics, and Jews find themselves lined up together against their more liberal brothers and sisters (and those who hold to no religious beliefs).

Issue and Events

The two issues that have done the most to polarize fundamentalists and liberals are prayer in school and abortion. The prayer-in-school issue arose after 1962, when the Supreme Court first ruled that organized prayers in public schools represented a form of established religion, which is prohibited by the Constitution. Fundamentalist Protestants have been in the forefront of opposing that decision (and others that followed), but they have been joined by conservative Roman Catholics and Jews.

Abortion became an issue after the Supreme Court ruled, in *Roe* v. *Wade* and *Doe* v. *Bolton*, that state antiabortion laws violate a woman's right to privacy, finding that right "broad enough to encompass a woman's decision whether or not to terminate her pregnancy." The court went on to assert that the fetus is not a person whose right to life is guaranteed by the Fourteenth Amendment. These rulings were particularly at odds with Roman Catholic doctrine, which teaches that life begins at the moment of conception and that abortion is, in effect, murder. The so-called right-to-life movement was joined by fundamentalist Christians and conservative Jews. Their eventual aim was to have federal legislation passed that would give back to the states the right to legislate on the question of abortion or a constitutional amendment stating unequivocally that life begins at the moment of conception, which would have the effect of equating abortion with murder.

Opposed to the right-to-life movement were women's groups, liberal religious bodies, civil-rights groups, and public-health organizations. In the early 1980s the abortion issue turned violent as radical "right to lifers" began bombing abortion clinics and harassing women entering and leaving such clinics.

School prayer and abortion were injected into the 1980 presidential election, but they did not become major issues until 1984, when Ronald Reagan ran for reelection. His fundamentalist supporters were led by the Reverend Jerry Falwell, who heads a group called the Moral Majority. Reagan's political conservatism was matched by his religious conservatism. Styling himself a reborn Christian (as had his predecessor, the politically more liberal Jimmy Carter), Reagan allied himself firmly with the right-to-life movement and the fundamentalist, evangelical Christian movement. His support from conservative Jews was somewhat lessened by what many Jews regarded as his lukewarm support for Israel. Reagan, and the Republican party in general, received vast amounts of campaign money from the political action committees (PACs) set up by the various fundamentalist groups. Reagan's reelection was openly supported from many pulpits across the country. One evangelical minister, George Otis, was quoted as saying that the reelection of Reagan "could make a difference in the timing of Jesus' return."

Democrats and political and religious liberals protested that this open alliance of the Republicans and the fundamentalists violated the spirit of the high wall of separation between church and state—particularly because the fundamentalists made no effort to conceal their hopes of having their religious beliefs enacted into laws. The fundamentalists contended in turn that religious leaders had always been involved in serious social issues, such as the civil-rights movement of the 1960s.

Reagan's victory in November 1984 would have seemed to be an indication of victory for the religious conservatives as well. However, in early 1985 complaints were already being voiced that the Reagan administration was not giving the priority to abortion and school-prayer legislation that Reagan's supporters had been led to expect. There was little movement toward constitutional amendments outlawing abortion or permitting school prayer, and Congress did not seem eager to address itself to such controversial issues.

Background

Religious diversity came to the United States with the earliest European colonists. The Puritans who colonized New England were fleeing persecution in England, as were the Roman Catholics who settled Maryland and the Quakers who settled Pennsylvania. Religious diversity was not always accepted in the American colonies, however, especially in Massachusetts. The Puritan theocracy established there in the early seventeenth century permitted no religious dissent. Persons transgressing the accepted theology were dealt with severely. Rhode Island was settled in 1636 by Roger Williams, a Baptist whose religion was anathema to the ruling fathers of Massachusetts. Rhode Island's charter explicitly confined the government to civil matters, thereby setting a precedent for religious liberty in America.

The Puritan theocracy in Massachusetts came

to an end in 1692, when a new charter stripped all religious tests from the requirements for public office. Thus, the eighteenth century began with the English colonies in America basically tolerant of religious diversity, a fact made evident by the widespread movement of religious sects to the colonies: Quakers, Methodists, Scottish Presbyterians, Baptists, Mennonites, Jews, Roman Catholics, Moravians.

The original Constitution of the United States, as adopted in 1789, does not call for separation of church and state. Only in Article Six is the religious issue addressed. It states that "no religious test shall ever be required as a qualification to any office or public trust under the United States." It is generally held that the framers of the Constitution believed that the principle of separation was so well established in the states as to require no specific guarantee.

The colonies held enough advocates of a specific guarantee, however, that it led the list of those contained in the Bill of Rights. The First Amendment, consequently, declares that "Congress shall make no law respecting an establishment of religion, or prohibiting the free exercise thereof...." When ratified in 1791, the First Amendment specifically added religious diversity as one of the guaranteed constitutional rights of the American people.

The guarantee of freedom of religion applied only to the federal government, however. The state governments were not required to live up to its strictures. Many state constitutions, however, contained similar clauses.

During the first half of the nineteenth century, there was a large influx of Roman Catholics into the United States. They became the target of attempts by nativist groups, whose intention it was to preserve the Protestant character of American society. The largest of these groups, the Native American party, better known as the Know-Nothings, briefly flourished in the 1840s and 1850s.

Later in the century, the Mormons created a problem for the doctrine of separation of church and state. When Congress passed a law outlawing polygamy, the Mormons claimed that it interfered with their religious beliefs. The Supreme Court approved the legislation in the 1870s, however, and the Mormons outlawed polygamy. In later years, the government became more accommodating to unusual religious beliefs. The Jehovah's Witnesses were finally allowed not to salute the flag, and male members of various pacifistic religions were generally permitted to become conscientious objectors to military service. Most of these accommodations took place in the twentieth century.

The Caribbean and Central America

The nations of Central America and the Caribbean are generally small, underdeveloped countries and territories. Their economic growth, historically slowed by European colonial exploitation, depends in part on developmental programs sponsored by the large industrialized nations, primarily the United States and the Soviet Union. Most of the region's political upheavals reflect this competition between the two superpowers.

The island nations of the Caribbean are less economically self-sufficient than the Central American republics. Except for Haiti, which has been nominally independent since 1804; the Dominican Republic, which achieved independence in 1844; and Cuba, which gained its independence as a result of the Spanish-American War, all are former colonies made independent since World War II. Most still depend largely on historic economic ties for their livelihood.

Puerto Rico is affiliated with the United States as a Commonwealth. For many years, the United States has maintained a policy of letting that island's people decide what its status should be. In referenda and in public opinion polls, the people have voted to maintain their present status. However, there are strong political movements for both statehood and complete independence.

Cuba's close economic, political, and military ties to the Soviet Union have been a subject of great concern to the United States since the early 1960s. The United States holds that much of the political unrest in other Caribbean and Central American nations is due to Cuban interference, which seems to many a front for Soviet involvement. It was allegedly to thwart the spread of Cuban influence that the United States invaded Grenada in 1983, and United States opposition to the rule of the Sandinistas in Nicaragua is based in part on the Reagan administration's claim that the Sandinistas are, or soon will be, agents of Cuba and the Soviet Union.

In El Salvador, the United States has backed the moderate president, José Napoleón Duarte, against the right-wing elements who support Roberto D'Aubuisson, and the various left-wing guerrilla groups. Again, the United States government maintains that Cuba and the Soviet Union are supporting those left-wing factions.

Mexico, by far the largest and richest Central American republic, is close to economic self-reliance because of rich petroleum deposits. In the late 1970s, this potential income caused Mexico to embark on an ambitious economic program entailing large-scale international loans. These loans, however, became a cause for concern in the international economic community in the early 1980s when a worldwide oil glut seriously reduced petroleum income, which when combined with balance of trade deficits, severely hampered Mexico's ability to make payments.

The countries of Central America and the Caribbean recognize the superpower confrontation being played out, as it were, by proxy in their lands. In this struggle they must maintain a delicate diplomatic balance, accepting aid from any potential source in the search for stability and peace.

Puerto Rico: Statehood, Commonwealth, or Independence?

Perspective

1493	*Christopher Columbus claims Puerto Rico for Spain.*
1511	*Arawak Indians begin revolt against Spanish; importation of slaves is begun.*
1869	*Puerto Rico is made Spanish province.*
1898	*Spain cedes island to United States after Spanish-American War.*
1900	*Congress passes Foraker Act, by which most political power is exercised by Washington.*
1917	*Congress passes Jones Act, which gives United States citizenship to all Puerto Ricans and extends political autonomy of island.*
1930	*Nationalist party, advocating complete independence, is founded.*
1952	*Puerto Rico becomes United States Commonwealth.*
1967	*Puerto Rican voters in plebiscite favor retaining island's Commonwealth status.*
1984	*Rafael Hernández Colón, supporter of Commonwealth status, is elected governor.*

On November 6, 1984, while United States voters were reelecting Ronald Reagan president, Puerto Rican voters were turning out their governor, Carlos Romero Barceló, in favor of Rafael Hernández Colón. Romero Barceló is head of the New Progressive party, which wants United States statehood for Puerto Rico; and Hernández Colón represents the Popular Democratic party, which is in favor of Puerto Rico remaining a Commonwealth of the United States. It was the third time that the two men had faced each other. In 1976 Romero Barceló defeated Hernández Colón, then the incumbent governor, in a surprise victory. In 1980 the two men met again; Romero Barceló retained the governorship, but his victory was by a small margin. And then in 1984 the Popular Democrats put their man, Hernández Colón, back in office. This seesaw movement between the two parties is indicative of the Puerto Ricans' continuing wrestling with the problem of what the political future of their island is to be.

Issues and Events

Polls indicate that Puerto Ricans are about evenly divided between those who want Puerto Rico to become the fifty-first state in the Union and those who want the island to retain its status as a Commonwealth within the United States. Commonwealth status, in effect since 1952, has offered tax incentives for investors and other financial advantages to Puerto Rico.

Advocates of statehood see the future in terms of full political, economic, and social equality with the other fifty states. Some who theoretically favor statehood caution that the United States could not be counted on to admit Puerto Rico under the special conditions deemed necessary if the island is to retain its cultural identity. For example, both Spanish and English are at present official languages; whether Congress would officially recognize Spanish is highly questionable.

There is a third political movement in Puerto Rico: those who wish to see the island become a republic completely independent of the United States. In recent years the Puerto Rico Independence party, which represents the movement, has polled only about 5 percent of the votes in national elections. Despite that small percentage, most political observers believe that there is a much larger undercurrent of independence sentiment and that a worsening of the Puerto Rican economy or an increase in anti-Americanism could see that percentage rise quickly.

Despite the financial involvement of United States companies in Puerto Rico and the island's strategic importance to the United States military presence in the area, the official position of the United States government is that it is up to the Puerto Ricans to decide their political future. That remains United States official policy, but any change in the status of the island would still have to be approved by Congress.

Background

Puerto Rico was claimed for Spain by Christopher Columbus in 1493, and Spanish colonization began early in the sixteenth century. Black slaves were imported from Africa to work on the sugar plantations after the Spanish virtually eliminated the indigenous Arawak Indians.

Despite sporadic efforts over the next two centuries by both the English and the Dutch to seize Puerto Rico from Spain, the island remained firmly Spanish, and its population developed into a racial mixture of Spanish, black, and Indian. In 1898, at the beginning of the Spanish-American War, the United States invaded Puerto Rico, and Spain ceded the island to the United States at the end of the war.

Cuba: Crossroads of the Caribbean

Perspective

1898	*Cuba is occupied by United States during Spanish-American War.*
1902	*Cuba gains nominal independence from United States.*
1934	*Fulgencio Batista comes to power with assistance from United States.*
1953	**July 26.** *Fidel Castro leads unsuccessful revolt against Batista dictatorship.*
1956	*Castro lands on Cuban coast with small band of guerrillas.*
1959	**January 1.** *Batista flees Cuba; Castro comes to power.*
1961	**April.** *Bay of Pigs invasion by exiled Cubans with United States support fails.*
1962	**October.** *Presence of Soviet nuclear missiles in Cuba brings United States and Soviet Union to brink of nuclear war.*
1980	*In Mariel boat lift, 125,000 Cubans migrate to United States.*
1984	*Negotiations between Castro and Reagan administration address problem of Cuban immigrants to United States.*

P ressure mounted in 1984 for a thaw in relations between Cuba and the United States, which have been particularly strained since the 1980 boat lift that brought thousands of Cubans to the United States. In December, negotiations between Fidel Castro's government and the Reagan administration led to the return of 2,700 Cuban felons to Cuba. In return, the United States agreed to accept up to 20,000 Cuban immigrants per year. At the same time, the two countries, which are so close geographically (about 90 miles, or 145 kilometers), remained far apart on many political issues.

Issues and Events

The drama began in April 1980, when a large crowd of Cubans flooded into the Peruvian embassy in Havana. After a short delay, Castro allowed the refugees to leave Cuba.

Within hours, boats from Florida headed toward Cuba's Mariel Harbor, where 125,000 refugees waited to leave. President Carter's administration soon learned that there were numerous convicted criminals and mental patients among the refugees. In addition to calling the

boat lift an attempt to humiliate the United States, the Reagan administration, which took office in January 1981, accused the Castro government of aiding the spread of communism.

Background

During the early nineteenth century, the United States tried unsuccessfully to purchase Cuba, a Spanish colony with a thriving slave trade. The abolition of slavery in 1886 in Cuba was followed in 1895 by a rebellion against Spain. The rebellion was nearing triumph in 1898 when the *Maine*, a United States ship in the Havana harbor, mysteriously exploded. War between Spain and the United States was soon declared, and the United States gained Cuba by treaty.

The United States set Cuba free in 1902, retaining the right to intervene in case of an "emergency." Such intervention took place in 1934, when Fulgencio Batista, with American aid, overthrew the liberal government of Ramón Grau San Martín. The United States eventually grew impatient with the corrupt Batista regime and in 1958 withdrew its support.

Castro had begun his struggle in 1953, when he led an assault upon an army barracks. He failed and went into exile. Three years later, he landed with eighty men and started a guerrilla war. His triumph on New Year's Day 1959 was hailed by Communist and Western nations alike, but only two years later the United States broke off diplomatic relations with Castro, who had declared himself a Marxist-Leninist, nationalized American businesses in Cuba, and strengthened his ties with the Soviet Union as American aid was withdrawn.

On April 17, 1961, a force of exiled Cubans seeking to overthrow Castro was routed at the Bay of Pigs. When it was learned that the United States government had played a role in the invasion, Castro appealed to the Soviet Union for protection, and Russian nuclear missiles arrived in Cuba in October 1962. The thirteen days of the Cuban Missile Crisis that followed saw intensive negotiation between the United States and the Soviet Union and the eventual withdrawal of the missiles.

Fidel Castro—Cuban revolutionary leader and prime minister (1959–   ). Born in 1926 . . . became law student at University of Havana (1945–1950) . . . failed in attempt to overthrow Cuban dictator Batista (1953) . . . succeeded in defeating Batista (1959) . . . foiled Bay of Pigs invasion by United States–backed Cuban exiles (1961) that resulted in Cuban Missile Crisis (1962).

Grenada:
Revolution and Democracy

Perspective

1498	*Christopher Columbus arrives at Grenada.*
1674	*Grenada is annexed by France.*
1762	*Britain captures Grenada.*
1783	*Treaty returns Grenada to British.*
1795	*French commandant leads uprising, killing British governor and forty-seven others.*
1834	*Slavery is abolished. Crops turn from sugar to spices.*
1958	*Grenada joins West Indies Federation.*
1967	*Grenada assumes status of associated state of United Kingdom.*
1972	***February 28.*** *Eric Matthew Gairy and Grenada United Labor party (GULP) are victorious in general elections.*
1974	***February 7.*** *Grenada attains full independence amid strikes and demonstrations protesting Prime Minister Gairy's use of secret police.*
1979	***March.*** *Leftist Maurice Bishop overthrows Gairy's government in coup, installing himself as moderate Communist leader.*
1983	***October 19.*** *Bishop is assassinated. Sixteen-member military council led by radical Marxist Hudson Austin takes over government.*
	October 25. *United States soldiers and marines, joined by troops from seven Caribbean nations, invade Grenada. Seven hundred United States citizens and students of St. George University are evacuated.*
	December 15. *Last combat troops leave Grenada. Three hundred noncombat troops remain.*
1984	***December 3.*** *New National party, led by centrist Herbert Blaize, wins first general election since 1976, defeating comeback bid by GULP leader Eric Gairy.*
1985	***February 8.*** *United States president Ronald Reagan's administration announces that all foreign troops, including 250 United States military personnel, will be withdrawn from Grenada by early fall.*

On October 25, 1983, the United States, accompanied by a small contingent of troops from other Caribbean nations, invaded the island of Grenada, dramatically propelling this small country in the Western Hemisphere onto the world scene. It represented a climax in the efforts of the island to achieve political stability in the face of problems that had beset it ever since independence in 1974.

Issues and Events

The United States intervention was a manifestation of the policy of President Ronald Reagan and his administration of frustrating what they regarded as a major push by Cuba (backed by the Soviet Union) to extend its influence and that of Marxism to other countries in Latin America and the Caribbean basin. The immediate cause of the invasion was the chaos that followed the ousting and later assassination of the Marxist prime minister of Grenada by a more radical Marxist faction. In defending his action, President Reagan cited the need to protect American residents of the island, many of them medical students, and a request from the Organization of Eastern Caribbean States that the United States intervene. Specifically, the United States had formal requests for intervention from the governments of Antigua and Barbuda, Barbados, Jamaica, St. Lucia, and St. Vincent and the Grenadines.

The United States action was generally criticized abroad. The British regarded it as an incursion into their sphere of influence, as Grenada is a member of the British Commonwealth. British prime minister Margaret Thatcher told Parliament that she had expressed "very considerable doubts" about the invasion to President Reagan. The Soviet Union condemned the invasion as "an act of undisguised banditry and international terrorism." Both the UN and the Organization of American States passed resolutions condemning the invasion. The Latin American nations were particularly critical, looking upon the action as an extension of the gunboat diplomacy of nineteenth-century United States Latin American policy. In the United States itself, there was a mixed reaction; conservatives generally supported the president, whereas liberals opposed the action. There was also criticism of the almost complete news blackout of the invasion; for the first time in United States history, news reporters were not allowed to witness and report on military actions and had to depend on government news hand-outs. It was not until October 28, three days later, that a limited press pool was permitted to visit the island. The Defense Department's decision to prohibit news coverage was later upheld in federal court. After considerable debate, both houses of Congress invoked the War Powers Resolution, which required that all United States troops be removed within two months. Many Grenadans, however, supported the invasion.

The invasion began when six hundred marines flew by helicopter from the aircraft carrier *Independence* and landed at Pearls Airport on the eastern shore of the island. The main body of the invasion force soon followed, parachuting onto Point Salines Airport on the southwestern tip of the island. The Grenadian army and Cuban construction workers put up a stiffer resistance than had been anticipated; although the airport was secured in two hours, sporadic fighting continued for the next four days. United States troops quickly spread throughout the island and occupied the medical school where the American students were enrolled.

In all, nineteen hundred United States troops and three hundred soldiers from the eastern Caribbean nations came ashore during the initial strike. By late in the day, United States troops had captured Fort Hale, believed to be the headquarters of the military council. Over the next few days, the number of United States combat troops swelled to six thousand as Grenadian resistance continued, mostly at Richmond Hill. The Pentagon reported that 42 United States soldiers were killed, 1 was reported missing, and 86 were wounded and that an estimated 160 Grenadians and 71 Cubans had been killed. Twenty Grenadian civilians were killed when United States planes accidentally bombed the mental ward of Grenada's hospital.

General elections were held on December 3, 1984, thirteen months after the invasion. Despite United States fears of a resurgence of Marxist support, the winner (with 59 percent of the vote) was the centrist New National party (NNP), led by Herbert Blaize, an economic conservative. Blaize had been a member of the colonial parliament in 1957 and had led the government in the 1960s. His campaign had the at least implicit support of the United States.

The island continued to face overwhelming economic problems. The island's infrastructure—schools, hospitals, roads, communications, electricity, and water and sewage systems—was in a shambles. Any appreciable improvement of these facilities would require a capital outlay beyond the capacity of the island's fragile economy. Unemployment remained at about 30 percent, creating a large, volatile segment of the population ripe for political upheaval from both the right and the left. The tourist industry, always an important factor of the island's economy, required rebuilding after thousands of would-be visitors were frightened off by the island's upheavals.

The new government made immediate plans for a massive public-works project to be funded by foreign aid and low-interest loans from international banking organizations, such as the World Bank.

Background

Christopher Columbus landed on Grenada in 1498 and claimed it for Spain. Throughout the sixteenth century and later, the island was fought over by the European maritime powers chiefly because the secure harbor at St. George's made it an important stopping-off place on West Indies trade routes.

In 1674 Grenada was annexed by France, and French settlements sprang up. In 1762 it was captured by Admiral George Rodney for the British. During the American Revolution, Grenada was regained by France, only to be returned to the British in a treaty four years later. In 1795 a bloody French uprising resulted in the death of the British governor and forty-seven others. The revolt was subsequently put down by the British navy. With the abolition of slavery in 1834, the emphasis on sugar production shifted to the growing of spices, earning for the island the name "Isle of Spice."

The island remained a British colony until 1958, when it became a member of the West Indies Federation. In 1967 Grenada became an associated state of the United Kingdom. General elections were held in 1972, sweeping Gairy and his party to power as the major backers of an independent course for the island. Despite widespread protests against Gairy's policies, the island achieved full independence on February 7, 1974.

In March 1979 the Gairy government was overthrown in a coup led by Maurice Bishop, a charismatic Marxist and the leader of the New Jewel Movement ("Jewel" being an acronym for "Joint Effort for Welfare, Education, and Liberty"). On October 19, 1983, Bishop was assassinated after having been ousted from office by a hard-line Marxist faction supporting his deputy minister, Bernard Coard. The United States looked upon this development as a clear indication that the influence of Communist Cuba was on the rise in Grenada. The United States also claimed that a large airstrip being built on Grenada by Cuban engineers and workers was in fact a military facility rather than a commercial airport. It was at this point that the Reagan administration ordered the invasion of the island, leading to the new government installed in 1984.

Haiti:
Poverty and Repression

Perspective

1492	*Columbus arrives at island of Hispaniola.*
1804	*Independence from France is won.*
1915– 1934	*United States occupies Haiti under Monroe Doctrine.*
1930	**October.** *First National Assembly is elected.*
1957	*François "Papa Doc" Duvalier is elected president.*
1971	*Papa Doc dies; Jean-Claude "Baby Doc" Duvalier succeeds as president.*
1983	**March.** *Pope John Paul II visits Port-au-Prince.*
1984	**February.** *Two-thirds of National Assembly is replaced in national elections.*

H aiti is one of the poorest nations in the Western Hemisphere. It has a per capita gross national product of only $300 per year, and half its wealth is held by 1 percent of its population. This elite is determined to maintain its political and economic control, despite widespread discontent and international criticism. Haiti is also a country with a long history of brutal political repression. Under these circumstances, it is not surprising that about 800,000 Haitians in the past few years have sought refuge in other countries—the favored one being the United States.

Issues and Events

In March and May of 1984, President-for-life Jean-Claude "Baby Doc" Duvalier guaranteed freedom of the press and greater respect for human rights. On May 10, after the release of the first two opposition newspapers, Duvalier halted all political activity except that of his own political party. The editors of the two papers were beaten and imprisoned.

In late May two days of rioting by peasants fighting over food ended in the dismissal of five cabinet members and most of the local government officials where the riots had occurred. In September five men who had been missing since a 1983 bombing were admitted by government officials to have been in police custody. The men were then sentenced to life in prison.

The military strength of the Duvalier government has been sufficient to control the Haitian people to date; but for most people, the real struggle is survival. A 50 percent unemployment rate, a lack of natural resources, poor land management, and limited and overcrowded agricultural areas make for little opportunity.

Wages in Haiti are extremely low, and Duvalier has granted up to fifteen years of tax exemption to foreign businesses. Over three hundred companies, mostly American, have been attracted to the island in recent years. However, due to a woeful transportation system, the factories, which employ some sixty thousand Haitians, must be located in urban areas. Thus poor rural areas have received virtually no help.

The second leading source of income in Haiti has traditionally been tourism, but the island has lost appeal due to widespread publicity of the acquired immune deficiency syndrome (AIDS) epidemic, which cites Haitians as an abnormally high-risk people. While officials struggle to prove that AIDS is prevalent only among the country's homosexual and drug-abusing population, the formerly $80 million-per-year industry has been severely cut.

In the face of the continuing poverty, the Duvalier government points to reforms it has enacted, such as improved tax collection and a crackdown on corruption in government. Despite human-rights violations, considerable foreign aid, much of it American, continues to come into the country.

Background

Christopher Columbus landed on Hispaniola in 1492. In 1697 the western third, which was to become Haiti, was deeded to the French, while the eastern two-thirds would become the Dominican Republic. After a struggle for freedom by the slaves, who made up 90 percent of the population, Haiti gained its independence in 1804. A mulatto elite ruled the country for the next century. The government was reinforced by United States intervention in 1915, and American influence remained strong until 1941. In 1957 François "Papa Doc" Duvalier was elected president and changed the constitution to extend the president's term to a lifetime.

Papa Doc's reign became synonymous with brutality and torture; dissenters were often murdered. His regime lasted until his death in 1971, when his nineteen-year-old son—Jean-Claude, known as "Baby Doc"—became president-for-life. While Baby Doc is considered more liberal than his father, his use of violence and the secret police to control a discontented but politically apathetic populace echoes the previous regime.

El Salvador: War Games in Central America

Perspective

1525	Spanish conquistadores establish city of San Salvador.
1821	Central America becomes independent from Spain.
1823	Monroe Doctrine asserts United States hegemony in Western Hemisphere.
1838– 1840	As Federation of Central America collapses, member states become independent.
1871– 1882	Concentration of coffee-producing lands into hands of minority landowners is aided by abolition of Indians' communal lands and by establishment of rural police force.
1931	General Maximiliano Hernández overthrows popularly elected president in coup.
1932	After failure of peasant rebellion led by Farabundo Martí, Hernández's troops massacre twenty thousand to thirty thousand peasants over period of several weeks.
1972	Generals seize power after slate of moderates is elected. José Napoleón Duarte is exiled.
1979	Moderate generals come to power in coup; they form military-civilian junta, which collapses by year's end.
1980	Major leftist guerrilla groups unify; right-wing death squads roam country.
	March. Archbishop of San Salvador Oscar Romero is assassinated.
	December. Bodies of four United States Catholic missionary workers are discovered. United States threatens to withdraw military aid until deaths are investigated.
1982	**April.** Elections give far-right candidate Roberto D'Aubuisson's party majority in Constituent Assembly, but under United States pressure, moderate-right candidate Alvaro Magaña is appointed president.
1984	**May.** Moderate candidate José Napoleón Duarte is declared winner in new elections; United States promises him largest aid package to date.
	October. Duarte and guerrillas begin first round of peace talks.

The current civil war in El Salvador reflects the decades-long struggle between the have-nots—landless peasants demanding a more equitable distribution of wealth—and the haves—entrenched interests in the landholding aristocracy and the military. Leftist rebels demanding change are opposed by the centrists and rightists in control of the government.

United States involvement in El Salvador's five-year-old civil war increased in 1984, with more than $700 million in military and economic aid given by the year's end. During that year the United States also added to its number of advisers in El Salvador and carried out a series of military exercises in neighboring Honduras. The victory of moderate politician José Napoleón Duarte, who was openly supported by the Reagan administration and most members of Congress, contributed to the administration's willingness to increase its commitment to the Salvadoran government. Another factor was the strength of about twelve thousand left-wing guerrillas who continued to control approximately one-third of the country's territory.

Issues and Events

The current conflict in El Salvador dates from early 1980, after the collapse of the moderate-left, civilian-military junta and the unification of the major guerrilla forces into the Democratic Revolutionary Front–Farabundo Martí Front for National Liberation (FDR-FMLN). The resignation of Social Democratic politician Guillermo Manuel Ungo from the junta provided a major impetus for the unification. Ungo and other moderate leftists now represent the FDR, the political arm of the guerrillas, while the more militant FMLN carries out the war in the countryside.

In the chaos that followed the breakup of the civilian-military junta, right-wing paramilitary groups known as death squads began to roam the countryside. Led in part by army colonel Roberto D'Aubuisson, the death squads terrorized the population by kidnapping and brutally murdering those suspected of leftist sympathies. Archbishop Oscar Romero, an outspoken advocate for the rights of the poor, became a death-squad victim in March 1980. In December of that year three North American nuns—Ita Ford, Maura Clarke, and Dorothy Kazel—and Catholic lay worker Jeane Donovan were found dead in a shallow grave.

After the election of Ronald Reagan in 1980, assistance to the Salvadoran government increased. Such aid, Reagan asserted, was necessary to combat an alleged Soviet-Cuban-Nicaraguan presence in the country. In the meantime, death-squad violence spread in rural and urban areas. The unemployment rate crept even higher as refugees filled San Salvador and the border camps. The elections in 1982 promised to bring democracy to El Salvador after fifty years of military rule. However, the FDR boycotted the election, fearing for the lives of its candidates. The party of far-right candidate Roberto D'Aubuisson won a plurality in the Constituent Assembly, but the Reagan administration pressured leaders to appoint as president the moderate conservative Alvaro Magaña.

United States aid to El Salvador topped $300 million in 1983. Under the direction of United States advisers, the government began a series of counterinsurgency offensives against the guerrillas' control zones. These offensives, which were stepped up in 1984, consisted primarily of aerial assaults that took a heavy toll in terms of lives, livestock, and property without reducing significantly the strength of the guerrillas. By the end of 1984, an estimated fifty thousand Salvadoran civilians had lost their lives during the war, with hundreds of thousands more forced to flee their homes.

In March 1984, another election was held to choose a president for a five-year term. The Reagan administration made no secret of its support for the moderate candidate Duarte, whose presence at the head of the government would gain bipartisan support in Congress for increased assistance to El Salvador. It would have been difficult to amass support for far-right candidate D'Aubuisson. Duarte emerged victorious in a bitter runoff election in May, in which D'Aubuisson claimed vote fraud. Immediately, Duarte promised peace negotiations with the guerrillas and embarked upon a tour of the United States, Latin America, and Western Europe to seek support and monetary aid. Despite threats from the military, Duarte opened talks with the FDR-FMLN in the guerrilla-controlled town of Las Palmas in October 1984.

Background

A Spanish colony since 1525, El Salvador achieved its independence in 1821, and in 1823 became part of the Federation of Central America, an unsuccessful attempt to unite Spain's former Central American colonies. The union was in a state of virtual collapse by 1838, and as the federation dissolved, its members became independent. In the late nineteenth century, the expanding world market for coffee accelerated the concentration of land into the hands of a few wealthy landowners. The Indians' communal landholdings were broken up, and a rural police force was established to quell the protests of the newly deprived peasants.

The support of the peasants contributed to the election of Arturo Araujo as president in 1931. Almost immediately, however, he was overthrown by General Maximiliano Hernández. The military coup sparked an armed revolt in the following year. This revolt, led by the peasant hero Farabundo Martí, was crushed, and in the interval of several weeks, perhaps as many as thirty thousand Salvadorans were killed by Hernández's troops. For the next half century, a succession of military governments ruled El Salvador.

During this period, conditions continued to worsen for most Salvadorans. By 1970, the wealthiest 10 percent of landowners held almost 80 percent of the nation's arable land. Virtually half of those living in the countryside owned no land at all but worked as tenant farmers and migrant wage laborers. Industrialization, while it brought little advantage to the ordinary Salvadoran, continued to concentrate wealth into the hands of the few. Infant mortality remained high, and the rate of unemployment hovered between 35 percent and 50 percent throughout the 1970s. Labor protests in San Salvador and sporadic guerrilla activity generated increasingly brutal repression by the government.

In 1972 a liberal coalition led by Duarte and Ungo won the first election in El Salvador in many years. Charging massive vote fraud, the military stepped in once again. Ungo fled the country, but Duarte was captured, imprisoned, and tortured before being forced into exile. With United States support, the government began a land-reform program that raised many expectations but was rendered virtually ineffective by landowner opposition. A 1977 coup led by the right-wing general Carlos Humberto Romero ended the land-reform program. His widespread human-rights abuses also led the United States to halt aid temporarily. In 1979 a group of liberal military officers overthrew General Romero. Ungo returned from exile to take part in the civilian-military junta, and the land-reform program was again initiated. Progress toward peace and a more equal society turned out to be very short-lived, however.

The civil war in El Salvador threatens to continue for many years and to involve the United States to an even greater extent. It is a conflict rooted in the historical patterns of poverty, concentration of wealth, oligarchy, and political repression rather than in the geopolitical division between East and West. Although Duarte enjoys the support of the Reagan administration, the administration's fear of a leftist takeover and an increasingly intransigent right within Duarte's own country hinder his ability to negotiate an end to the war.

Nicaragua:
Contras Versus Sandinistas

Perspective

1821	Nicaragua gains independence from Spain.
1856	United States adventurer William Walker invades Nicaragua with private army and sets up his own empire.
1893	Liberal president José Santos Zelaya comes to power.
1909	Zelaya government, opposed by United States, falls.
1912–1925	United States marines occupy Nicaragua to protect United States canal rights and to prop up Conservative party government.
1926	Marines withdraw; peasant army organized by Augusto César Sandino takes up arms against government.
1927–1933	Sandino gains wide support among impoverished peasants; marines return and then leave again after growing criticism within United States.
1934	Sandino is assassinated, probably at command of Anastasio Somoza García, head of National Guard; Somoza forcibly disbands peasant cooperatives.
1936	Somoza ousts president, taking power himself.
1961	Sandinista National Liberation Front (FSLN) is organized to fight Somozas.
1972	Earthquake levels center of Managua, leaving 15,000 dead and more than 170,000 homeless; Somoza family and supporters appropriate millions of dollars in relief money.
1979	**July 19.** Series of popular uprisings throughout Nicaragua results in triumph of Sandinistas.
1981	Reagan administration cancels loans and grants to Sandinistas and begins to give aid in secret to counter-revolutionary contras.
1984	**February–April.** Central Intelligence Agency plants mines in Nicaragua's harbors; Nicaragua sues in World Court. **November.** Sandinistas win 63 percent of vote in national elections.
1985	**January.** World Court agrees to hear Nicaragua's case; United States walks out.

February. Reagan and Secretary of State George Shultz declare publicly that they seek removal of Sandinistas.

April. Nicaraguan president Ortega visits Soviet Union seeking economic aid; President Reagan calls for economic embargo against Nicaragua.

June. United States Senate approves $38 million over two years in nonmilitary aid for contras.

In 1979 the dictatorship of Anastasio Somoza Debayle was overthrown by the Sandinistas, a left-wing revolutionary group that had long opposed the United States–backed right-wing Somoza regime. Shortly after the Sandinistas came to power, a counterrevolutionary group, known as the contras, began operations in the provinces of Nicaragua and across the border in Honduras and Costa Rica. The contra forces comprised former members of Somoza's National Guard; some disaffected former Sandinistas, who opposed the increasing Marxist slant of the Nicaraguan government; and mercenaries reputedly paid for by the Central Intelligence Agency (CIA) of the United States.

The contras found a strong new ally in the Reagan administration. United States aid to the contras, previously covert, was openly admitted, and United States pressures against the Sandinista government increased. The Reagan administration accused the Sandinistas of being the pawns of the Soviet Union and Cuba, while the Nicaraguan government accused the United States of attempting to overthrow a legitimately elected government—an act that violates international law and numerous treaties to which the United States is a party.

There was considerable disagreement in the United States Congress with the Nicaraguan policies of the Reagan administration; President Reagan was repeatedly frustrated by Congress's refusal to vote aid, military or otherwise, to the contras. When Nicaragua's president Ortega visited the Soviet Union in late April 1985, Reagan urged an economic embargo against Nicaragua, which met with virtually no international support other than from Honduras.

Issues and Events

By the beginning of 1984, the contra forces claimed fifteen thousand men among their four groups—the Nicaraguan Democratic Front (FDN) in Honduras, the Democratic Revolutionary Alliance (ARDE) in Costa Rica, and two Indian organizations on Nicaragua's remote Atlantic coast. Their strategy consisted of attacks upon economic targets—schools, hospitals, grain-storage facilities, and petroleum reserves—upon government officials, and upon civilians seen as furthering the aims of the Sandinistas, such as teachers, doctors, members of peasant cooperatives, and progovernment business people. By the end of 1984, approximately ten thousand Nicaraguans had died as a result of the four-year-old war.

United States aid to the contras became open in 1984 as operatives of the CIA mined Nicaragua's harbors, acts that caused the Nicaraguan government to sue the United States in the World Court. (The United States, for the first time in history, announced that it would disregard any decision of that court.)

Tensions between the Sandinistas and the Reagan administration in 1984 also arose over the Nicaraguan elections in November. The elections, which gave Sandinista leader Daniel Ortega Saavedra the presidency with 63 percent of the vote, were denounced by President Reagan as a "sham." Immediately afterward, the United States president claimed that advanced Soviet MIG fighter planes had arrived in Nicaragua along with a shipment of Eastern-bloc civilian and military equipment. The Nicaraguans continued to insist that the United States was planning a military invasion aimed at overthrowing the Sandinista government. The United States public experienced renewed fears of such a possibility upon the publication by *The New York Times* of information from a secret report that allegedly contained a contingency plan for armed intervention by the United States.

Background

United States involvement in Nicaragua's affairs goes back more than a century, to William Walker's ill-fated attempt to set up a proslavery colony on the eve of the Civil War. Later, the United States helped engineer the fall of the Liberal party government of José Santos Zelaya, and United States marines were sent in 1912 to ensure control over a region that was at that time considered a possible route for a canal between the Atlantic and Pacific oceans. Widespread rural poverty, coupled with the concentration of wealth in the hands of foreigners and their Nicaraguan agents, led to Augusto César Sandino's peasant revolt in 1926. Despite modern weaponry and superior forces, the marines were unable to dislodge Sandino and his supporters. In 1933 the marines withdrew, after the signing of a treaty that made concessions to the peasants and gave Sandino a voice in the government. Yet one year later, Sandino was assassinated in a plot directed by Anastasio Somoza García, the head of the National Guard, who was widely regarded as being backed by the United States.

Somoza took power soon afterward. He exterminated Sandino's supporters, occupied their land, and silenced the middle-class opposition. For almost fifty years the Somoza dynasty, with United States backing, ruled Nicaragua in a corrupt and brutal manner. Peaceful protests in 1959 and 1967 were met with gunfire and mass arrests. After a 1972 earthquake, which leveled the center of Managua and took fifteen thousand lives, Somoza's son, Anastasio Somoza Debayle, diverted millions of dollars in relief money into his own companies. As discontent with his regime grew, he turned the National Guard on the people of his country. Claiming that children and teenagers, who make up half of Nicaragua's population, were the lifeblood of the Sandinistas, Somoza reserved his most savage attacks for the country's youngsters.

The Sandinista National Liberation Front (named in honor of the murdered Sandino) was founded in 1961 and within the decade began to gain support from the desperately poor landless peasants in the interior of the country. As opposition to the Somoza dictatorship grew, students, women, and, ultimately, many members of the middle and upper classes joined the revolutionaries, making possible the July 1979 victory. The Sandinistas embarked almost immediately upon an ambitious program of social change. The 1980 literacy crusade reduced the illiteracy rate from 54 percent to 34 percent, and a health campaign that began the following year has dramatically reduced the infant mortality rate. Lands belonging to Somoza and to those of his supporters who fled the country were confiscated and parceled out as part of an agrarian-reform program.

These measures improved the lives of ordinary Nicaraguans, but they also alienated the more conservative supporters of the revolution, who felt they had been denied a significant voice in the new government. As Sandinista opponents turned to the United States and the contras for help, the Sandinistas alternately hardened and relaxed their positions on such issues as press censorship, provoking criticisms from the Roman Catholic church and from Latin American and Western European nations that have generally been supportive of the government.

International efforts to end the Sandinista-contra war have been fruitless. Nicaragua accepted the terms of a draft peace pact proposed by other Central American nations. However, the pact was effectively blocked by the United States, apparently in the belief that Nicaragua's neighbors would be far more sympathetic to the Sandinista government than the Reagan administration could countenance.

South America

Despite their relative economic stability and social conservatism, the South American republics have often been characterized by political instability. The military plays an important part in the political life of many of the republics, and civilian governments frequently rule only with the approval of the military. Popularly elected democratic governments are frequently overthrown and replaced by military juntas. The imprisonment or exile of political leaders fallen from power is commonplace, as is assassination by political opponents, and the civil liberties of the citizens are often violated. Amnesty International, an organization that aims at protecting civil and political rights around the world, is often critical of nations in South America.

In many South American countries there is dramatic economic polarity: a political elite who enjoys luxury and privilege, contrasted with oppressed masses who survive in the most dire poverty. This large underprivileged majority has often been systematically exploited by a succession of rulers interested only in personal wealth and power; ironically, many of the poor are nearly apolitical; their main concern is day-to-day survival for themselves and their families, rather than political organization.

The patterns of inequity in South America's wealth distribution were set down hundreds of years ago, during the region's colonial period, and the situation in modern South America is partly a result of European colonial influences

upon an indigenous population. In this sense, South America has much in common with other Third World regions that saw European colonization.

The dominant colonial power in South America was Spain, although Portugal, the Netherlands, and France also acquired possessions in the area. The influence of Portugal is evidenced in Brazil, where Portuguese is the predominant language. French Guiana is yet under French rule, having the status of an overseas department of France.

Prior to the arrival of the Europeans around the sixteenth century, various Indian peoples inhabited the region. Among these were the Incas, whose sophisticated civilization flourished in the areas of present-day Ecuador, Peru, and Bolivia.

The first major wave of European settlement occurred in the 1500s with the arrival of the Spanish conquistadores. The resistance offered by most Indian groups was ineffectual, and for the most part, Indian lands quickly fell to the invaders. However, the Araucanian Indians, who inhabited the region of modern Chile, long fought against Spanish dominance.

Many of the early settlers were drawn to South America by the promise of wealth. As word of the continent's natural riches spread back to Europe, fortune-seeking colonists flocked to the region. Oftentimes the promise of gold and silver remained unfulfilled, but most settlers stayed on, establishing large plantations that laid the basis for much of South America's present economy. The colonists took the conquered Indians as slaves to work their farmlands, and soon a thriving agriculture was established.

Much of the indigenous population disappeared during the colonial period. Wars with the settlers, labor-intensive plantations, and exposure to European diseases claimed thousands of Indian lives. In addition, many Indians who managed to survive intermarried with the Europeans. Modern South America's large mestizo population, of mixed Spanish and Indian blood, is a result of these liaisons.

As the Indians died out, blacks were brought from Africa to continue slave labor on the plantations. Development increased, and the descendants of the early settlers soon established a uniquely South American culture, combining influences of both their Spanish ancestors and the indigenous peoples into a life-style evolved from the plantation economy. Many of the Indians continued their traditional way of life, however, and remained far from the centers of development, unaffected by the waves of change.

Prosperity continued, and in time the large-estate holders, many of them mestizos, found themselves wielding economic influence but enjoying few of the benefits of their profits. Native-born South Americans of Spanish descent were equally dissatisfied with colonial status. Political power remained in the hands of the mother country, whose people and government now had little in common with South American life. Resentment toward the ruling powers grew, along with the colonies' demands for a voice in a government that did not always consider their welfare.

The struggle for independence began in the late eighteenth century. Two prominent men emerged as leaders of the fight for freedom: the Venezuelan Simón Bolívar and the Argentine José de San Martín. The colonists were aided in achieving their goal by wars on the European continent during the nineteenth century; both Spain and Portugal were economically and politically weakened as a result of these conflicts. The Spanish and Portuguese holdings in South America gained independence in the 1800s.

Politically, the region was unstable following independence. The fight for self-rule had been led and won by a class already possessed of a certain amount of influence, and in general the change in government only shifted power from the European rulers to South Americans of economic dominance. Thus the change in leadership did not result in reforms beneficial to the many people outside the small circle of those

with economic influence. Dissent and upheaval often resulted; civilian governments alternated with military rule, power shifted from party to party and group to group, yet many remained ensconced in poverty.

Economically, however, the newly independent nations continued to develop, concentrating the wealth more solidly in the hands of the few. Foreign investment increased as well, and immigration brought people from Europe and other parts of the world. In the face of this, it became increasingly difficult to institute significant reform and dismantle an oligarchic system rooted in the past.

Today agriculture continues its important role in South America's economy, with large commercial plantations producing crops for export and domestic consumption. Mining is a major contributor in some countries, and manufacturing is growing. Yet many South Americans are isolated from twentieth-century development, living much as their ancestors did and practicing subsistence agriculture according to ancient methods.

Political stability remains an important goal of the South American nations. Argentina has been governed by a series of military dictatorships over the years, the most stable of which was that of Juan Perón. Unlike most such governments, the influence of the Perón regime continued after the death of Perón himself. His widow, Isabel Perón, succeeded him to the presidency; and even after she was ousted, the strength of the Peronists was such that their opponents thought it necessary to force her into exile. It was one of the series of post-Perón juntas that instigated, in 1982, the Falklands War. Argentina's defeat in that confrontation with Great Britain resulted in the fall of the junta and the eventual installation of a democratically elected government in Argentina.

Colombia, the South American country with perhaps the strongest tradition of democracy, found itself in a new kind of war in the 1980s: a war against international drug traffickers. Cocaine—made from the coca plant, which thrives in Colombia—has become the nation's most profitable agricultural product. Pressure from the United States in particular has forced the Colombian government to use a strong hand against the producers of the coca plant and especially against the international traffickers who buy the processed cocaine in Colombia to sell all over the world, primarily the United States. The cocaine trade generates such huge profits, however, that corruption of government officials and law-enforcement personnel remains a serious problem.

Colombia: Drug Wars in the Jungle

Perspective

1899–1902	*Bloody civil war casts Colombia into series of bitter class struggles.*
1948–1968	*Era of terrorism and widespread street violence known as La Violencia rages for two decades, sustained by further class dissension following assassination of the popular Jorge Eliécer Gaitán.*
1970s	*Marijuana becomes Colombia's first big illicit drug product.*
1982	**August 7.** *President Betancur is sworn into office.*
1984	**March 10.** *Colombian narcotics squads raid huge drug operation of Tranquilandia.*
	April 30. *Assassination of Minister of Justice Lara leads to antidrug campaign by Betancur government.*
	May 1. *National state of emergency is declared by Betancur; all-out war is declared against cocaine mafia. Arrests without warrant are legalized and extradition of traffickers to United States is sanctioned.*
	May 28. *First of series of guerrilla truces is arranged by President Betancur in hope of establishing peace with political dissidents and rebels.*
	July. *Aerial spraying programs to destroy coca crops are begun.*
	September 24. *Betancur admits that possible military coup threatens his regime; jungle drug wars face uncertain future.*

Colombia is one of the poorest of the Latin American countries. Still, it is one of the greatest producers of coffee, accounts for most of the world's precious emeralds, and has lately been involved in exploring and developing its coal and oil reserves. But few exports have brought such wealth to this land of little as the enormous trade in illicit drugs—marijuana and, especially, cocaine—that has mushroomed over the last decade.

Issues and Events

The Colombian government in 1984 began a crackdown on the drug trafficking that has been transforming the thick Colombian jungle into an international drug capital. In March, Colombian forces raided a major Yari River drug operation called Tranquilandia ("land of tranquility"), 400 miles (650 kilometers) south of the capital city, Bogotá. Over a billion dollars' worth of cocaine was seized: The bust revealed a band of *narcotraficantes* ("drug dealers") operating behind a small protective force composed of the Armed Forces of the Colombian Revolution (FARC) guerrillas.

The government has also fought to clean house within its own chambers as well as in those of the law enforcement. Over three hundred air force and police personnel have been discharged for their involvement in the drug trade, while some four hundred court judges have been placed under investigation. Yet, the chore seems almost unbearably treacherous. In February 1985, the president's personal secretary was arrested on drug smuggling charges. The attorney general was soundly scolded by President Belisario Betancur Cuartes for having met in Panama with exiled bosses of Colombian organized crime.

Meanwhile, Betancur and his aides have taken the fight to the jungles and the countryside where coca is grown, where processing plants operate around the clock, and where the skyways are filled with small craft searching for clandestine private runways. Having touched down and loaded up with marijuana and cocaine, the airplanes lift off in an attempt to make their final connection.

It is in these remote forest lands that the government has embarked on its most ardent mission to cut the illicit drug trafficking. And indeed, it has met with a string of successes that have the narcotraficantes reeling for the moment. The government has scored heavily in the jungle that harbors a full three-quarters of the United States cocaine supply and nearly two-thirds of its marijuana supply. It is not surprising that the United States—urged on by President Reagan—has poured in millions of dollars (over $9 million in 1985) to bolster these raids.

In December 1984, a processing plant at Villa Julia, just outside of Medellín, yielded over 1,200 pounds (550 kilograms) of high-grade cocaine to Colombia's narcotics squad. Within a week, almost twice that amount was rounded up in La Guajira and was promptly tossed into the Caribbean. Before another month had passed, over thirty more processing plants had been put out of business. Aerial spraying and ground programs that had been started in July 1984 destroyed vast crops of the coca plant.

The 1984 to 1985 period in Colombia has seen the greatest crackdown ever on the "Cocaine Mafia." While Colombia's narcotraficantes had been bringing in some $1 billion annually to their homeland's economy, that figure promises to be cut at least in half.

The war against cocaine production is slowed by the reluctant cooperation of the Colombians who grow the coca plant. They are loath to give up what in many cases is their only cash crop. Furthermore, as a people they have long indulged in the narcotic effects of the chewed coca leaf. Thus, they see no moral issue involved in their production of coca leaves for cocaine.

In 1984 the exiled drug dealers attempted to make a deal with Betancur. They promised to pour $2 billion into building up the poverty pockets of their country and would even dismantle their illicit drug operation and political designs forever. They asked in return that Betancur give them amnesty. But Betancur was not swayed by the promises of these crime bosses, who have ordered the cold-blooded murders and assassinations of countless foes.

Background

Ever since the constitutions of 1853 and 1858 were instituted, Colombia has been held up as a model republic—one of Latin America's few enduring democracies. But this has not prevented it from having a turbulent and violent history. While it has suffered through relatively few dictatorships or bloody coups, it has had more than its share of civil unrest and violent reactionism. Between 1899 and 1902 it underwent a horrendous civil war during which nearly a hundred thousand people were killed. Two more decades of unabated violence terrorized the country between 1948 and 1968, following the assassination of Jorge Eliécer Gaitán—hero of the underprivileged classes. During this era known as La Violencia, a quarter of a million people were murdered as city streets became battlegrounds and the countryside was drowned in anarchy.

The greatest cause of so much unrest in Colombia's history has been the gross inequities of land and wealth distribution. Class conflict has been virtually ingrained in Colombian politics and culture. Amid all this confusion, the economy typically has had to rely on bonanza crops of one sort or another, rather than on a steady growth reflecting diversified interests and sound policymaking. This sort of economic scenario has proved to be detrimental to the country as a whole, but especially to the lower classes, who never share in the real wealth of the bonanza crops and their short-lived exploitation.

The latest bonanza crop has not only increased the class rift between the very rich few and the very poor masses, but it has also attracted international scorn while increasing the violence on Colombia's streets. This crop is the illicit drug crop: first marijuana in the mid-1970s, and then the coca plant of the cocaine processors from the late 1970s to the present.

It was Pablo Escobar Gavira who had first recognized the economic potential of cocaine processing and smuggling. In the late 1970s, he built a powerful organization aided by an army of "cocaine cowboys" who muscled their way into the lucrative United States marketplace with overt extortion and violence. Escobar went on to become a prominent Colombian politician and head of a cartel of drug dons known as the Medellín Mafia—the most powerful organization in the world of drug smuggling.

Drug trafficking was scorned publicly by Colombian officials, but tolerated and even indulged in privately. After all, by 1980—the height of the cocaine bonanza—drug trafficking was clearly the number-one income producer in Colombia, accounting for revenue in the neighborhood of $3 billion. President Julio César Turbay Ayala had made some apparently honest though soft attempts to limit the illegal trade of drugs in the late 1970s, but his successor, President López, was embarrassingly tolerant of such activities. Even the highly esteemed national bank—the Banco de la República—handled the finances of prominent drug dealers without question.

Despite the success of Betancur in his jungle wars against Colombia's cocaine bosses, observers question the prospects of his government's ability to make the victories stick and to embark on true economic recovery. Unemployment nearly doubled from 7 percent to 13.5 percent between 1981 and 1984. National revenues dropped sharply, forcing cuts in government spending, job and wage-hike freezes, income-tax increases, and highly inflationary new *emisiones*, or "monetary issues," from the Banco de la República. Meanwhile, Betancur initiated in 1984 a series of guerrilla truces with groups such as the Marxist group known as FARC. While they have served his purpose of giving Colombians some break from relentless wars and guerrilla raids, the truces have not helped his national popularity overall. On September 24, 1984, he acknowledged the existence of plans to oust him from power.

Whether or not Colombia can win its jungle drug wars, the greatest question for outsiders is whether or not such a victory would help to slow down international drug trafficking. The drug traffickers might simply pick up stakes and restart their operations elsewhere, as they have already done to a considerable extent in Panama.

Argentina: A Fragile Democracy

Perspective

1816	*Argentina declares independence from Spain.*
1943	*Revolution ushers in era of bloody revolt and suppression.*
1946	*Juan Perón comes to power, aided by his wife Eva Duarte. Labor reforms ensue at expense of political freedoms and human rights.*
1955	*Perón is ousted from power.*
1973	*Perón returns from exile and is reelected president.*
1974	*Perón dies; his second wife, Isabel, assumes presidency.*
1976– -1983	*Violent struggles for leadership ensue among Peronists; bloody campaigns of terror are waged against Marxist guerrillas and political dissidents.*
1982	**April 3.** *Argentine junta announces takeover of South Georgia Island in Falklands.*
	April 12. *British blockade island.*
	May 2. *Open warfare begins in Falklands.*
	June 15. *Argentine forces surrender in Stanley to end Falklands War.*
1983	**October.** *Raúl Alfonsín and Radical Civic Union come to power; they vow to establish constitutional democracy.*
1984	**September 25.** *Argentina accepts International Monetary Fund assistance in return for initiating austerity programs.*

Although Argentina is one of the most modern and industrialized, most culturally and educationally advanced nations in South America, it has been plagued by political and economic upheavals for a good part of the twentieth century. The elections of October 1983 represented a major turnaround, when the Radical Civic Union, headed by Raúl Alfonsín, won a startling upset victory over Italo Luder and the Peronists. For the first time in many years, it seemed that a constitutional democracy might deliver the democratic reforms so desperately desired in a country worn-out by militarism, repression, and strong-arm leadership. But it was only a matter of months before the initial enthusiasm was tempered by the reality that Argentina's new democracy was—as it still is—very fragile indeed.

Issues and Events

The Peronists are the chief political rival of Alfonsín's Radical Civic Union. As the traditional champions of the masses, the Peronists are quick to accuse the Radicals of bourgeoisie favoritism and of a weakness of character and resolution that will, they charge, undermine Argentina's strength in the world community and its struggle to achieve national unity.

Ironically, many features of the current government that the Peronists perceive as weaknesses are what the Radicals seem to be counting on to provide their sustaining strength. For example, it may be true that Alfonsín, a longtime advocate of human rights, has been dragging his feet on prosecuting and punishing those in charge of the Peronist reign of terror, still deeply etched in the Argentines' memories. This delay is not for a lack of resolution or authority, however, but for an insistence on dealing with such matters within the constraints of the law and for the pragmatic purpose of maintaining a working relationship with the military.

Cunningly, Alfonsín turned the matter of punishing the military leaders of his country's recent dark past to the military courts themselves, although their decisions would be subject to the review of the civil courts. While this has displeased many liberals, Alfonsín has thereby averted a showdown with a military leadership still trying to recover from its humiliation in the 1982 war with Great Britain over the Falkland Islands, a British colony.

The Radicals have been trying desperately to live not only with the Peronists but also with the Peronist-supported labor bosses of the General Confederation of Labor (CGT). Here again, Alfonsín has shown his ability to seek a positive, pragmatic course of action when he found it necessary to compromise his loftier ideals. Initially he had decided to take on the corrupt leadership of the CGT directly. Alfonsín proposed legislation early in 1984 by which the labor bosses would have had to submit to free elections by member laborers. But when the Peronists effectively blocked the legislation, he accepted his defeat. Rather than press on with a headstrong mission to clean up the abuses of the CGT leadership, he embarked on a stated policy of *concertación,* or "unity."

While the Peronists and the labor bosses of Buenos Aires pose serious threats to the success of Argentina's toddling democracy, the greatest threat of all comes from the economic malaise that has plagued the nation for the last three decades. The national inflation rate has been one of the most perplexing problems. It has been over 100 percent in all but one of the last ten years and had reached 400 percent by the 1983 elections. To attack this staggering inflation and an equally troublesome national debt, the government dedicated 1984 to combining price controls to curb inflation with graduated wage indexes to maintain the support of labor.

By September 1984, though, that program had to be scrapped when the International Monetary Fund (IMF) insisted that Argentina carry out specific austerity measures in order to have its $40 billion national debt, past due since 1982, refinanced. Atop the list of such austerity measures were a slowdown of wage increases and a reduction of Argentina's gross national product. Alfonsín refused to accept these terms, which he had asserted would in effect satisfy international creditors "with the hunger of our people." But his program had not solved the problem of inflation, and $1.6 billion in national debt came due. On September 25 the IMF guidelines were accepted, and by December, the central bank had agreed to refinance $25 billion of Argentina's foreign debt. The national economy was still far from safe, however. As 1985 began, the national inflation rate had soared to over 1,000 percent.

The fragility of Argentina's new constitutional democracy remains apparent. Yet, it has met with some startling successes. Basic freedoms—such as those of speech, the press, and religion—have been granted to people who only a few years ago would not have dreamed of such privileges. Masses of people exiled during the Peronist years of rule have been welcomed back to their homeland.

Background

Argentina has never had a true democracy. The years following its attainment of independence from Spain in 1816 were filled with power struggles between the leaders of Buenos Aires and those of the outlying provinces. The era between 1835 and 1852 was marked by dictatorship, terror, and reactionism. The country received its first constitution in 1853 and finally became a united republic in 1862. Beginning in the 1880s Argentina underwent enormous economic growth. During the first decades of the twentieth century, it gained cultural and educational prominence.

General Uriburu, a military tyrant, staged a successful coup d'état in 1930, and various military regimes ruled ineptly until the 1943 revolution ushered in a period of absolute oppression, violence, and censorship. Meanwhile, Juan Perón had emerged as an outspoken champion of the working class. In 1946 he ascended to the presidency with strong support from the CGT. While his nine-year rule introduced widespread labor reform, he and his popular wife Eva Duarte proved to be brutal tyrants who completely curtailed personal freedoms, initiated strict censorship of the press, and suppressed political dissidence. Perón was finally ousted in 1955 by a military coup.

Following nearly twenty years of revolving-door military regimes, Perón returned from exile to become president in 1973. A year later, following his death, his second wife, Isabel, took over the presidency until she was deposed in 1976. From that time until 1983, Argentina suffered through years of bloody power struggles, censorship, and political terror. In 1980 a human-rights commission criticized the government for its exile, torture, and execution of political dissidents. The government excused itself on the grounds of self-defense against the intended intervention of Marxist guerrillas.

The rise to power of the Radicals in 1983 came on the heels of a great military blunder in 1982. In a bold move to take possession of the Falkland Islands, called Malvinas by the Argentines, whose British administration and claim Argentina had long disputed, Argentine troops seized control of South Georgia Island in the Falklands on April 3, 1982. The issue was settled in a matter of about three months, as the British swept to an overwhelming victory.

During the next twelve months more than half the generals and two-thirds of the admirals were forced into retirement. Former president General Leopoldo Galtieri, commander of the armed forces, became something of a scapegoat for the military regime at large. He, along with Admiral Jorge Isaac Anaya, was recommended for court-martial and held accountable for alleged war crimes. Galtieri accepted much of the blame for the humiliating defeat, while Admiral Horacio Zaratiegui was incarcerated for his criticisms of the government's handling of the war. Meanwhile, President Reynaldo Bignone promised that the defeat was only temporary and that Argentina would fight on for the Falklands.

When the smoke had cleared away, though, military purges and politically motivated clean-ups were not enough to overcome the great embarrassment. Elections were forced, ushering the Radicals into power. Unwilling to humiliate the military any further, the new president has been slow to progress with war-crime hearings. He has sought instead to redirect Argentina and improve his country's international reputation.

Europe and the Soviet Union

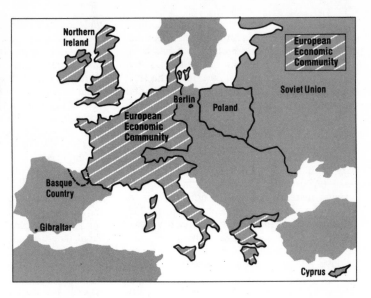

The European countries and the Soviet Union share problems common to industrialized nations around the world, yet they are marked by differences of national direction. While Europe is attempting to bridge centuries of national and economic rivalries to restore a common prosperity, the Soviet Union is just beginning to tap the almost limitless potential of its largely undeveloped natural wealth.

The European continent has always been divided by intense rivalries nearly as old as the land itself. With a large population confined to a relatively small land area, each group was fiercely protective of its territory, and strong national identities emerged. As the age of exploration dawned in the fourteenth and fifteenth centuries, each nation sought preeminence through the acquisition of territories rich in precious natural resources.

Spain and Portugal were the first to reap the benefits of exploration when they opened the African subcontinent to trade. Later, Asia was to prove another rich source of exotic goods to European merchants anxious to provide products for an increasingly discriminating public. England and France were quick to enter the arena, and by the seventeenth century there were European trading outposts and colonies in India, Africa, China, and North and South America. However, many of the settlers and indigenous peoples of these territories began to demand self-determination and a share in the prosperity arising from their resources. Thus over the next three hundred years Europe lost the tremendous wealth of its colonial empire, becoming at last dependent upon its own resources.

The European Economic Community (EEC) was organized to aid coordination and development of potential markets. Its efforts to coordinate production have not met with total success, however, partly because of traditional competition among the member nations and varied internal needs. To achieve cooperation in production, the community will need to consider the capabilities of each nation; because of the countries' geographic proximity, there is also a certain amount of overlap in output. Greece, Italy, and France are all major wine producers, for example, and in 1986 Spain and Portugal, both with strong wine industries, will become members of the EEC.

The Soviet Union, on the other hand, has barely begun to exploit the natural riches of its interior. That country possesses untold mineral wealth, but development has been hindered by the remoteness of the resources and other economic factors. The country is the world's largest oil producer and has the largest oil reserves outside the Persian Gulf region. Soviet gas reserves are also enormous, and energy exports are the principal sources of Soviet hard currency earnings. These revenues permit acquisition of equipment and technology for a variety of activities. Much of this natural wealth, however, is found in relatively distant regions, necessitating a costly relocation of the labor force and causing attendant transportation and refining costs. Nonetheless, the Soviet Union has entered international energy projects to tap the oil, gas, and coal deposits of its interior. The 2,766-mile (4,451 kilometer) natural-gas pipeline from central Siberia to Czechoslovakia is the most widely publicized. Another major factor, in addition to remoteness, that limits development of the interior mineral and forest riches is the tenuous agricultural base in relation to the population. The Soviet Union has a triangle of rich agricultural land tapering to the east, but the cold of the north and desertic conditions of the south meet to limit agricultural productivity. Each year the Soviet Union is forced to import wheat and other agricultural goods, diverting funds that might otherwise be used for mineral development.

The Soviet Union has alleviated their resource problem somewhat with control and coordination of the economies of the Soviet-bloc countries. Russia imports raw materials such as farm goods from Czechoslovakia and Bulgaria and bauxite from Hungary and, in return, exports manufactured goods and processed petroleum for their industries. This attempt to create a self-sustaining economic cycle by combining the resources of this enormous region continues to generate political tension and has so far been only partially successful.

Although the Soviet Union's plans to expand and explore its potential contrast markedly with the general European trend of retrenching economies no longer rich in raw minerals, both economic systems suffer maladies endemic to industrialized nations. All highly developed economies are plagued by the vicious circle of inflation, recession, and unemployment. Each country is in its own way trying to stimulate purchasing power for individuals while minimizing balance of trade deficits on the national scale. Both the Soviet Union and Europe depend on the rich oil fields of the Middle East for much of their petroleum needs, and both were hit hard by the sharp increase in oil prices in the early seventies and the worldwide recession which followed. Both economies must deal with an aging industrial base and face costly retooling. Some European countries such as Britain and France are attempting to diversify into high-technology industries; because of political and strategic decisions made by the West, the Soviet Union has found its access to advanced microchip technology limited. In addition, Soviet production has been impeded by morale problems among the work force, including absenteeism and drunkenness, and by unprecedented changes in leadership occasioned by the closely timed deaths of three premiers. Though neither the Soviet Union nor any European nation is in danger of imminent economic collapse, nearly all are at a turning point, balanced between geographic limitations and the demands of the marketplace.

In the first half of the 1980s the Soviet Union seemed to have solved its worst food-production problems and was turning out more consumer goods—in addition to its high-technology arms production. With one exception, Soviet relations with its Eastern European satellites had become relatively serene. The one exception was Poland, where a trade union, Solidarity, continued to oppose many of the policies of the Soviet-backed government. Soviet relations with Poland's Roman Catholic church, whose leaders displayed unmistakable sympathy with the Solidarity movement, were in delicate balance.

Two members of the Common Market, France and Greece, were experimenting with new socialist policies, while Great Britain under Prime Minister Margaret Thatcher was resolutely conservative. Thatcher's government, in an attempt to reverse Britain's lagging economy, was involved in a long-term plan to dismantle much of the socialist economic organization that had been in place for more than a generation. Her government was less enthusiastic about dismantling the social programs (such as socialized medicine) that have become an integral part of British life. Northern Ireland remains the primary domestic problem of the British government. It is a problem that has defied solution; no modern British government has been able to make any effective headway there.

In France the Socialist government of François Mitterrand has encountered economic and political difficulties in carrying out its policies. It came into office with a program to nationalize key French industries such as banking but by 1985 was proceeding with great caution, amid signs that the Socialists were reversing their policies in key areas.

In Greece, Socialist Andreas Papandreou received a resounding vote of confidence at the polls in 1985, and he reiterated his pledge to loosen Greece's ties with the West, especially with the United States. The status of Cyprus is another major concern of the Greek government.

The democratic monarchy of Spain continued to solidify its position. Two problems remain: the Basque separatist movement and the status of Gibraltar. The Basques of the provinces in northern Spain (and to a lesser degree, the Catalans in the south) have persistently pressured the Spanish government for greater autonomy and even independence, and Basque terrorist groups have been the source of much bloodshed in Spain. Gibraltar has been a British military base for centuries, and one that Britain shows no inclination to cede back to Spain; the presence of a British crown colony on what was once Spanish soil is a continuing affront to Spanish pride.

Northern Ireland:
Religion and Violence

Perspective

1609	Plantation of Ulster is established.
1690	Battle of the Boyne finally confirms Protestant community.
1801	Union with Great Britain is proclaimed.
1886	First Home Rule bill is defeated.
1893	Second Home Rule bill is defeated.
1900	Sinn Fein is founded.
1912	Third Home Rule bill is defeated.
1916	Easter Rebellion is quelled by British troops.
1919	Irish Republican Army (IRA) is formed; War of Independence begins.
1920	Government of Ireland Act is passed, providing for separate parliaments in Belfast and Dublin.
1922	Irish Free State is created, excluding six counties of Ulster.
1923	IRA calls off hostilities with Irish Free State.
1931	In Irish Free State, IRA is outlawed.
1949	Ireland withdraws from Commonwealth of Nations.
1962	End of unification campaign is announced by IRA.
1968	Civil-rights movements are organized by Catholics in Northern Ireland.
1969	Disagreement leads to IRA split into provisional and official factions; violence escalates.
1972	Direct British rule is imposed in Northern Ireland.
1979	Lord Mountbatten is murdered.
1981	Hunger strike kills ten imprisoned IRA members.
1984	Brighton, England, hotel accommodating British prime minister Thatcher and cabinet is bombed by IRA.

R oman Catholics in the northern counties of Ireland—and the Irish in the nation of Ireland, for that matter—have never accepted the British solution to the religious problem in Ireland: the separation of the island into two parts.

Ireland was divided into the predominantly Catholic south, which eventually became the nation of Ireland, and the predominantly Protestant north, which as Northern Ireland was retained as an integral part of the United Kingdom. British firms have large investments in the industrial sector of Northern Ireland, and there is strong popular support in England for the Protestants in Northern Ireland, who claim that their lives and property will be in jeopardy if Ulster, as Northern Ireland is also called, ever becomes part of the nation of Ireland.

The explosion that ripped through the Grand Hotel in Brighton, England, early on October 12, 1984, was a perfect symbol of the violent, fanatical passions that characterize Anglo-Irish relations. The bomb, planted by members (Provos) of the provisional arm of the Irish Republican Army (IRA), killed four people and injured more than thirty others. But it was aimed at Prime Minister Margaret Thatcher and her cabinet members, nearly all of whom were staying at the hotel. The IRA, which is a clandestine terrorist organization and is not associated with the army of Ireland, regretted that it had missed that time but stated, "Remember, we only have to be lucky once." It was recalled that only five years earlier the IRA had killed Earl Mountbatten of Burma, a member of the royal family.

Issues and Events

When the Civil Rights Association in Northern Ireland was organized in the late 1960s, it was, like the civil-rights movement in the United States that so obviously had inspired it, a nonviolent group, composed mainly of Roman Catholics using the methods of civil disobedience. It organized peaceful rallies and marches to protest discrimination against Catholics, who represent the poorest sector of the population in Northern Ireland, by the Protestant majority, as well as to demand jobs for the unemployed and equality in housing. As it moved along, however, it was taken over by political extremists willing to use violence to achieve the total removal of Great Britain from Northern Ireland.

The killings began in 1969. After several relatively minor clashes between the sectarian groups, in July of that year a rampage of Protestant thugs through the main Catholic district of Londonderry prompted the IRA to come to the residents' aid. When the Royal Ulster constabulary in turn moved in to "maintain law and order," a head-on collision resulted. The fighting quickly spread to other cities, especially Belfast, the streets becoming a war zone, the violence escalating. This again compelled the British government to intervene, and by 1970 thousands of

British troops were trying to prevent a full-scale civil war. In so doing, however, the army instituted its own oppression, with raids and searches, roundups of suspects, and curfews—and mounting casualties.

Through 1971 the violence grew, and in 1972 the British abolished the Northern Ireland Parliament, imposing direct rule from London. After two years of that—and hundreds more dead—a promising new start was made when an executive body composed of both Protestants and Catholics took office. But the cosectarian government foundered on the obduracy of Protestant unionists, who organized a general strike. The resulting disruption prompted a renewed imposition of direct British rule.

Other tacks were also tried. In 1975, a women's peace movement attracted a good deal of support, and a hope was born that some reconciliation between the religious communities could be effected. For their initiative, the two leaders of the movement, Mairead Corrigan and Betty Williams, were awarded the Nobel Peace Prize in 1976. But theirs was a vain effort.

Britain has maintained its direct rule at a high cost. Hundreds of British soldiers have been killed and thousands wounded, as up to twenty thousand regular troops, in addition to the regular and auxiliary police forces of Northern Ireland, have been required to keep a semblance of order and engage in countermeasures against IRA attacks and individual violence. The IRA on its part has kept up the pressure with bombings, ambushes, and other kinds of terrorist attacks not only in Ireland but in England as well.

Through all this, the Protestants have remained equally adamant against any kind of power sharing with the Catholics. The British have resorted to ever more stringent measures, such as internment without trial for IRA suspects. The IRA members and suspects in custody have in turn engaged in protests, strikes, and jailbreaks. From 1969 to the end of 1984, more than 2,400 people died in the continuing struggle.

Background

The first seeds of the present conflict were sown by the English in the early seventeenth century when, trying to consolidate their control over Ireland, they adopted the policy of implanting loyal English communities on the island. The most successful of these settlements was the plantation of Ulster, established in 1609. During the succeeding reigns the Protestant community was greatly enlarged. Catholic Irish landowners were thrown out and transplanted elsewhere, and their land was awarded to Protestants.

But the Irish were never acquiescent under British rule. Repeated rebellions finally induced British prime minister William Pitt the Younger to engineer the union of England and Ireland in the belief that it would solve the Irish problem. The union was formally proclaimed in 1801.

The British secretary and undersecretary for Ireland were murdered in 1882, an indication of the levels to which terrorism had risen. Alert to the Irish problem, British prime minister William Gladstone advocated home rule for Ireland and twice introduced bills to that effect—in 1886 and 1893—but both failed to pass.

In 1900 the Sinn Fein organization was founded to promote the complete independence of Ireland. At the same time, Ulster Protestant unionists redoubled their efforts against home rule, and they managed to defeat the third home rule bill in 1912. After the Easter Rebellion of 1916, however, Sinn Fein became the strongest political force in Ireland, and in the elections of 1918 it won 73 out of 106 Irish seats in the British Parliament. But rather than take their seats in London, the elected members, calling themselves the Dail Eireann, "national assembly," convened in Dublin and proclaimed the independence of their country. Insurgents at the same time commenced guerrilla attacks on British forces in Ireland, particularly the hated Black and Tans, a British auxiliary police force sent to Ireland. This was the beginning of the IRA.

In 1920 the British Parliament passed the Government of Ireland Act, providing for two legislatures, one in Belfast for Northern Ireland and another in Dublin for the rest of the country. Dublin refused to recognize the provision regarding Northern Ireland, and warfare continued until 1921, when a truce was arranged. In 1922 a treaty with Britain established the Irish Free State with its capital at Dublin, while Northern Ireland was separated with its seat of government in Belfast. The boundary between the states was permanently fixed in 1925.

The 1921 treaty split the Sinn Fein, and the IRA fought the Free State until 1923, when hostilities were supposedly called off. The IRA was outlawed in the Free State in 1931, but it never disbanded. When Ireland left the Commonwealth of Nations and became a republic in 1949, the underground IRA turned its energy toward the unification of Northern Ireland with the republic. But sympathy with the organization dwindled, and in 1962 it announced an end to its campaign. It began to pick up support again in the late 1960s, but disagreement over tactics led to a split in the ranks in 1969 into the so-called Provisional IRA and the official one. It is the provisional arm that has carried out the terrorist acts.

European Economic Community: Family Squabbles

Perspective

1950	French foreign minister Robert Schuman proposes creation of common Franco-German coal and steel authority.
1951	Belgium, France, Italy, Luxembourg, Netherlands, and West Germany sign treaty in Paris, establishing European Coal and Steel Community (ECSC).
1952	ECSC begins operations.
1957	ECSC countries sign treaties in Rome, creating European Economic Community (EEC), or Common Market, and European Atomic Energy Community (EURATOM).
1958	EEC and EURATOM begin operations.
1961	Denmark, Ireland, and United Kingdom begin negotiations for admittance to EEC.
1962	Norway joins negotiations.
1963	Negotiations break off, vetoed by French president Charles de Gaulle.
1967	Three European communities merge into one. President de Gaulle again vetoes enlargement of EEC.
1970	Negotiations are successfully renewed between EEC and Denmark, Ireland, Norway, and United Kingdom, following de Gaulle's resignation.
1972	Four would-be members sign treaty of accession, but Norway backs out after negative national referendum.
1973	Denmark, Ireland, and United Kingdom become active members of EEC.
1975	Summit meetings are regularized on thrice-yearly basis.
1979	Greece signs treaty of accession. Direct elections to European Parliament are adopted.
1981	Greece becomes active member of EEC.
1985	Members agree to admit Spain and Portugal to EEC in 1986.

If France's president Charles de Gaulle were still alive, he might well be saying "I told you so" to the European Economic Community (EEC), or Common Market. De Gaulle twice vetoed the enlargement of the EEC—a move directed primarily against the United Kingdom, which he considered too submissive to United States leadership—but since the United Kingdom, along with Denmark and Ireland, was embraced by the family of six in 1973, the arguments in the community household have become ever louder and more persistent. Nor did things improve with the entrance of Greece in 1981; it only added one more voice to the cacophony. As the members of the family continued to bicker over wine, fruit, fish, and rebates, de Gaulle's judgment seemed to be confirmed.

Issues and Events

At the heart of recent disputes was the problem of reconciling ideology with economic self-interest. For political reasons, all the community members declared themselves in favor of admitting Spain and Portugal, the argument being that membership would bring them closer to their Western European neighbors and thereby strengthen the new democratic forces in both nations, which until a decade ago were ruled by dictators. Thus, while the community leaders at a summit meeting in March 1984 agreed in principle to admit the two Iberian countries, thorny budgetary issues kept them arguing. Greece, specifically, threatened to block the entry of Spain and Portugal, fearing competition from these two countries with Greece's wine and other agricultural products. Greece withdrew its objection after the EEC had passed a Mediterranean farm-aid package, and in 1985 the community officially agreed that Spain and Portugal would enter as of January 1986. Because the community works by consensus, national or regional interests such as those displayed by Greece make it enormously hard, even with the best of intentions, to come to any kind of agreement—and the more so as the membership increases.

Many EEC quarrels have revolved around budgetary payments by the member countries. Because a large part of the EEC budget is spent to support agriculture in the member countries with payments from the industrial sector, the United Kingdom, soon after its accession, found itself, as a primarily industrial nation, making huge contributions that in effect went to subsidize inefficient agricultural producers. Under the EEC's common agricultural policy (CAP), all farmers were guaranteed the same price for their products, which kept prices high and encouraged overproduction. And the more the agricultural sector produced, the more the industrial countries would have to lay out in subsidies. As a consequence, Britain, one of the poorer of the member nations, became the major contributor to the communal budget.

In 1979 the United Kingdom's prime minister Margaret Thatcher began a determined effort to have this imbalance corrected. Despite opposition from the eight other heads of government, she finally won a concession in the form of a temporary rearrangement of the members' contributions. West Germany, which had inherited the United Kingdom's place as the largest contributor, then began balking, too. At the same time, it became clear that negotiations with Spain and Portugal on their membership applications—submitted some years earlier—would have to be delayed by the protracted discussions on reform.

Reform, however, came neither quickly nor easily. Europe was in the middle of a recession, and budget strains within each of the member nations also contributed to the slowness of new policy negotiations. What was up for review was nothing less than the whole system of EEC expenditures, and any change would affect the budget of every member nation. The United Kingdom, which had won only an interim agreement on a ceiling for its budget payments, reiterated its demand for a long-term policy change and a freeze in agricultural prices in 1982. Neither was granted. Instead, the ceiling on its contributions was merely extended—another temporary solution—and in the meantime the council of agricultural ministers awarded large price increases to the community's farmers as it had done the previous year.

It soon became evident that surplus stocks of dairy products were increasing at an alarming pace. Yet any drastic revision of the CAP costs, insisted upon both by the United Kingdom and by West Germany, were once more put aside. All tampering with the basic CAP structure was simply considered too risky in countries where the farmers' organizations were politically strong. At the summit meeting in Athens in December 1983, the quarreling members were so far apart that they could not even agree on a joint communiqué at the end of their session.

In March 1984 agricultural ministers finally agreed on a plan that called for a ceiling on milk production and the gradual abolition of the complex tangle of monetary compensations. Production quotas would be set and distributed on a national basis. All extra output would be subject to fines.

The sigh of relief was almost audible before it was stifled in midbreath. At the summit meeting in Brussels a week later, Irish prime minister Garret FitzGerald stalked out when the other leaders would not exempt Ireland from the cut in milk production. In addition, there was still no agreement on the size of the budgetary rebate to the United Kingdom, although the principle of such a payment was generally accepted.

It was again left to the agricultural ministers to fight over the CAP proposals, and they soon afterward gave in to the Irish, as well as doling out some other concessions to Luxembourg, Northern Ireland, and Italy. But the essential fact of the plan remained intact: the end of a system that guaranteed European farmers inordinately high prices for a virtually unlimited production.

The ten family members again turned to the negotiations with Spain and Portugal over their terms of accession, letting it be known that the conditions offered for admission would be exceptionally tough. One of the thorniest issues was what to do with the surplus table wine with which the community was inundated and which threatened to increase once Spain and Portugal, both major wine producers, were admitted.

The Common Market

The European Economic Community (EEC), or Common Market, began in 1958, with Belgium, France, Italy, Luxembourg, the Netherlands, and West Germany as the original members. Great Britain, Ireland, and Denmark joined in 1973, and Greece joined in 1981. Its purpose was to integrate the economies of Western Europe by gradually eliminating tariff barriers and by establishing common price levels and monetary union. Despite the at times acrimonious disputes in which the member nations have indulged, the Common Market is generally considered to have been a resounding success, and much of the economic growth of Western Europe in the 1960s and 1970s can be attributed to the union.

In 1967 the EEC was formally consolidated with the European Coal and Steel Community (ECSC) and the European Atomic Energy Community (EURATOM); the collective name for the three supranational groups is the European Community.

The ruling body of the European Community is the European Council, consisting of the heads of government of the member nations. It meets on a regular basis, usually three times a year. The European Parliament is the legislative branch. Its members are popularly elected by the voters of the member nations, but it has little actual power. The European Court of Justice renders judgments of disputes that arise among member nations.

To resolve all this, the EEC government leaders met in Dublin in December 1984, and the meeting seemed to be going well. But no sooner had the family reached an accord on the wine question than Premier Andreas Papandreou of Greece threatened to veto the accession plans unless the community adopted a five-year plan, costing some $5 billion, for special aid to Mediterranean (Greek, Italian, southern French) farmers. The demand temporarily created a cloud of doubt about the whole enlargement issue. As the EEC adopted a version of Papandreou's plan, and the accession of Spain and Portugal was assured at the summit meeting in March 1985, one more seemingly insurmountable obstacle was overcome.

Background

In the years following World War II, many European statesmen expressed their apprehension that the pattern of acrimony and ill feelings that had persisted on the Continent after World War I might repeat itself. Consequently, there developed in Western Europe a federalist movement of considerable strength, the members of which dreamed not only of economic cooperation but of a political union—a kind of United States of Europe.

It was in this atmosphere that visionaries such as Jean Monnet and Robert Schuman began to grope for ways to bring their ideas of supranational bonds to fruition. Schuman, then the foreign minister of France, in a speech on May 9, 1950, outlined a plan for the integration, or pooling, of French and German resources in coal and steel. Far from being a closed proposition, however, the Schuman Plan envisioned a community open to other Western European nations. Less than a year later, on April 18, 1951, six nations—Belgium, France, Italy, Luxembourg, the Netherlands, and West Germany—signed a treaty in Paris establishing the European Coal and Steel Community (ECSC), which became operative on August 10, 1952. The United Kingdom chose not to join because of the proposed supranational character of the organization.

The success of the ECSC under the direction (until 1955) of Jean Monnet was such that further integration was soon considered desirable. On March 25, 1957, the six nations—the United Kingdom again declined—signed two treaties in Rome, one of them establishing the European Economic Community (EEC, also known as the Common Market), and the other, the European Atomic Energy Community (EURATOM). Both of these organizations began operations on January 1, 1958.

As the benefits of the Common Market to the six nations became increasingly apparent, other European nations began to have second thoughts. Even the United Kingdom changed its mind and applied for membership in the EEC. As negotiations on the terms of entry were under way in January 1963, however, President Charles de Gaulle of France abruptly terminated the process by his veto. Although de Gaulle's action was directly aimed at the United Kingdom, which he saw as too servile to the United States, his veto effectively postponed any enlargement of the community since it also blocked the entrance of Denmark, Ireland, and Norway. De Gaulle again used his veto in 1967.

When President de Gaulle resigned in May 1969, his successor, Georges Pompidou, was much more receptive to new initiatives within the organization. On January 22, 1972, after nearly two years of bargaining, a treaty of accession was signed; pending ratification, the four applicants were scheduled to become full members of the community on January 1, 1973. Denmark, Ireland, and the United Kingdom joined as planned, but Norway backed out after the government's recommendation for membership was narrowly defeated in a national referendum in the summer of 1972.

Greece had long been associated with the community (as had several other nations), although relations with the country had been frozen from 1967 to 1974, during the Colonels' Rule. When democracy was reestablished in the country, its application for regular membership was favorably considered, and Greece joined the community as a full member in 1981.

According to the original Treaty of Rome—that is, the one establishing the EEC (EURATOM has proved to be of little consequence)—the member nations would, over a period of twelve years, eliminate tariffs and trade barriers among themselves, allowing free flow of goods and manpower from one nation to another; instead, common tariffs would be established against nonmember nations. Furthermore, community-wide price supports were envisioned for agricultural products, as well as an economic union bound together by common policies in the fields of taxation, labor supply, transportation antitrust laws, capital movement, and new enterprises.

On the whole, the cooperation has worked out well. The hopes of the founders for continuing progress toward the political unification of Western Europe have not come true, however. On the contrary, the trend during the past decade or so has been toward ever larger injections of narrow national interest and concomitant opposition to supranational authority.

Basque Country: Spanish Separatists and Terrorism

Perspective

400s   *Basques are driven into mountains by invading Visigoths.*

920   *Basque territories are included in kingdom of Navarre, coming under rule of Spain.*

1936   *Basques organize autonomous government at Guernica.*

1937   *Separatists are crushed by Franco.*

1974   *Basque Homeland and Liberty (ETA) group splits into two factions after General Franco's death.*

1977   **December 31.** *Spanish government approves statute of limited home rule for Basque provinces.*

1979   **October 25.** *Basques and Catalans approve government-proposed home-rule bill. Spanish government is given last word on most divisive issues.*

1980   **March 9.** *Local Basque parties win forty-two of sixty seats in first-ever election for local Basque parliament. Both moderate and separatist wings of ETA demand phased withdrawal of all police troops and amnesty for political prisoners.*

1981   **March 23.** *Violence and murders increase; Spanish government gives armed forces greater power in fight against Basque terrorists.*

1983   **December.** *Antiterrorist Liberation Group (GAL) emerges, vowing to avenge ETA killings one for one.*

1984   **February 23.** *Enrique Casas Vila, socialist and senator, is assassinated; ETA denies complicity.*

February 26. *Second regional elections since Basques won home rule are held; Madrid's controlling Socialist party consolidates as second party in Basque country.*

The Basques are a culturally distinct people numbering about two million who live in northern Spain. (A small group lives across the border in France.) Their language bears no kinship with either Spanish or French, and they are culturally and racially a distinct people. Their culture, based mostly on sheepherding, is often in conflict with that of their Spanish and French neighbors. In Spain, the issue of Basque separatism has plagued the central government in Madrid at least since the civil war of the 1930s.

Issues and Events

Not surprisingly, the Basque separatist movement is divided into factions. The largest group is the Basque Nationalist party (PNV). The Basque Homeland and Liberty organization (ETA) and the Herri Batasuna coalition are more radical and are generally held responsible for the various acts of terrorism that Basque separatists periodically commit as a way of calling attention to their demands.

In 1979 the Basques (along with the Catalans, another ethnic group in Spain) won a measure of home rule. That victory fell far short of the ambitions of the Basques, who have traditionally been willing to settle for nothing less than complete independence from Spain.

In 1984 regional elections were held in the Basque provinces. They were preceded by violence and murder, but the results solidified the position of the moderate PNV.

Background

With the formation of the Spanish republic in 1931, the Basque provinces of Vizcaya, Guipúzcoa, and Alava were willing to work for autonomy within the republic, while the province of Navarre rebelled. The attempt to organize an autonomous government at Guernica was crushed by General Franco in 1937.

On July 17, 1979, against a backdrop of strikes, demonstrations, and murders, the Basque Nationalist party and the Spanish government agreed on a bill supporting home rule in the Basque region. The bill was approved by Basques and Catalans on October 25, 1979, even though the government in Madrid retained the right to decide the most divisive issues. With autonomy, the violence continued, culminating in a Basque ambush and killing of six civil guardsmen in San Sebastián, the bloodiest attack in the 140 years of the national police. On March 9, 1980, the local Basque parties won forty-two of sixty seats in the first-ever election for a local Basque parliament. Both the moderate and separatist wings of ETA demanded a phased withdrawal of all police troops, as well as amnesty for political prisoners. Enhancing the tensions was the emergence, in December 1983, of the Antiterrorist Liberation Group (GAL), which vowed to avenge ETA killings one for one. As the Basques' struggle for independence continues, the only promise the future seems to hold is one of continued violence and instability.

Gibraltar: A Thorn in Spain's Toe

Perspective

1704	Gibraltar is captured from Spain by combined Dutch and English forces.
1713	Peace of Utrecht, signed by Spain, recognizes British possession of Gibraltar.
1830	Gibraltar is made British crown colony.
1964	British grant internal autonomy to colony. Spain claims right under terms of Peace of Utrecht.
1967	Referendum overwhelmingly favors continued British rule.
1969	New constitution is introduced by British. Spain closes border.
1983	Border is reopened to limited foot traffic.
1985	Border is opened to all traffic.

Local tradition has it that as long as the Barbary apes that inhabit the Rock of Gibraltar remain there, the British will also stay. The primates have not shown much inclination to leave, and neither have the British, who have claimed sovereignty over the colony since 1713 and who maintain a naval and air-force base there. The British presence has long been a humiliation to Spain, which has sought the transfer of sovereignty over the rocky fortress.

Issues and Events

When Spain, in 1713, ceded Gibraltar to Britain by the Peace of Utrecht, which ended the War of the Spanish Succession, the treaty included a stipulation: should Britain ever contemplate selling or otherwise alienating the territory, Spain would be guaranteed first right of refusal.

In 1964, when the United Kingdom granted Gibraltar virtually complete self-government, the Spanish contended that this was, in fact, alienation of the colony and that they should, accordingly, be given sovereignty over the Rock. The British refused.

From that time on—although Spain had often before claimed its right to what it regards as a natural part of its territory—the festering spot began throbbing as seldom before. Nor did it relieve the Spanish hurt when a referendum was held in Gibraltar on September 10, 1967, on the question of whether the inhabitants preferred to retain their ties to the United Kingdom or pass under Spanish sovereignty. Out of 12,762 voters who cast their ballots, only 44 chose Spanish rule. In 1969 Spain closed its border to practically all traffic, including that of some five thousand Spanish workers employed in Gibraltar.

Finally, in 1980, both parties agreed in principle on reopening the border, but the implementation was twice delayed because the British, clumsily, kept irritating the Spanish. In 1981 the newly wed Prince and Princess of Wales announced that they would make the Rock the first stop on their honeymoon—a decision the Spanish could only take as a direct taunt. Again in 1983, after some relaxation of the border controls had been effected, the British sent several ships to Gibraltar, including HMS *Invincible*, which had served prominently in Britain's 1982 war with Argentina over the Falkland Islands, another British colony. The parallel between the Falklands and Gibraltar was not lost on the Spanish, who strongly protested this latest indignity. Sensing, however, that a reasonable attitude of negotiation might be a better response, Spain remained calm and reopened its border in February 1985.

Background

Given its strategic location at the entrance of the Mediterranean, it is little wonder that Gibraltar has long been a coveted spot. The Moorish general Tariq captured it in 711 and turned it into a formidable citadel. The Spanish gained possession of it in 1462.

Dutch and British forces seized Gibraltar in 1704 during the War of the Spanish Succession, a European-wide conflict lasting from 1701 to 1714. The Peace of Utrecht, a series of treaties that ended the war, formally put the area under British control in 1713.

Spain, however, was obviously not happy to harbor a foreign garrison on its doorstep and later in the same century tried to wrest Gibraltar back from the British. This was during the American Revolution, when Spain, assisted by France, imposed a strict blockade on the fortress for more than three years. Gibraltar, however, withstood the test, which ended in 1783 when the American hostilities ceased. In 1830 the British sealed Gibraltar's status by making it a crown colony.

Gibraltar was an important base during the two world wars of this century, but with the advent of nuclear weapons and ballistic missiles, its military importance has diminished somewhat. But naval control of the western entrance to the Mediterranean is still an important strategic advantage.

Berlin: Divided Outpost of the West

Perspective

1200	*Berlin and its partner city of Kölln are first mentioned in official records.*
1432	*Berlin and Kölln are united, eventually becoming royal seat.*
1701	*Frederick I becomes first king of Prussia in Berlin.*
1918	***November 9.*** *After World War I, Berlin becomes capital of first German republic.*
1933	*Hitler becomes chancellor of Germany.*
1945	***April.*** *Hitler commits suicide. Allies subsequently divide country and city.*
1948	***June 24.*** *Soviets withdraw from Allied Control Council. Communist blockade of city begins.*
1948– 1949	*Berlin Airlift is carried out by Allies in response to blockade.*
1961	*Construction begins on Berlin Wall.*
1971	*Quadripartite Agreement is signed, implicitly formalizing division of Berlin.*

A wall roughly twenty-six miles (forty-two kilometers) long snakes across this city located within East Germany, separating East from West Berlin. East Germany officially calls it the antifascist protective barrier. In the West, it is known as the Berlin Wall.

Issues and Events

Escape attempts from East Germany to West Berlin have dwindled; an estimated 1.5 million people succeeded in escaping between 1945 and 1961, but now there are only about twelve attempts per month, with very few successes. The Wall was the original reason for the decline, but today the urgent desire to escape has quieted in East Germany as economic conditions there have improved; the differences in the standards of living in East Germany and West Germany have narrowed considerably. East Germany is now on top of the Eastern European economic ladder. Its standard of living is one of the highest in the Eastern bloc, and East Berlin is its showplace. West Germany, on the other hand, is plagued by increasing unemployment.

Politically, East Berlin's citizens are kept on a tight rein. Protests are banned, and approximately a half million Russian and East German troops are garrisoned in the city. While West Ber-

lin has a history of demonstrations and unrest, the routine expressions of dissatisfaction today come largely from the student and foreign guest-worker populations and generally have little to do with the division of the city or the presence of the Wall. The majority of protests come from environmentalists, antinuclear activists, and the homeless protesting a critical housing shortage. The twelve thousand United States, French, and British troops maintain a presence more symbolic and formal than active.

In early 1985, however, the placidity was broken when Soviet guards shot and killed a United States officer they claimed had trespassed into the Soviet territory taking photographs. Despite protestations, it was clear that the United States had no desire to escalate the incident into a major confrontation.

Background

Ironically, Berlin began as a divided city in the thirteenth century, being settled on opposite banks of the Spree River as Berlin and Kölln. In 1432 the two towns were united, and Berlin grew into a major European city. After the various German states were unified in the late nineteenth century, Berlin became the capital of the German Empire.

With the defeat of Germany at the end of World War II, Berlin was divided by the victorious Allies. Britain, France, and the United States each administered a section of what is now West Berlin, and the Soviet Union was placed in charge of what is now East Berlin. The Western powers united their zones in 1948, but no agreement was reached with the Soviet Union, and the city was split into East and West Berlin.

In an attempt to secure control over the entire city, the Soviets began a blockade of access routes to West Berlin in June 1948 but were forced to withdraw after the Western allies, led by President Harry S Truman, instituted the famous Berlin Airlift. For more than a year, the Allies flew supplies into West Berlin, thereby circumventing the Soviet blockade.

In 1953 there was serious unrest among East German workers, resulting in a mass exodus of almost three million East Germans to West Germany. These defectors tended to be the youngest and most productive of East Germany's work force, and in 1961 the East Germans and the Soviet Union retaliated by erecting the Berlin Wall. The exodus was effectively halted. In 1971 the Quadripartite Agreement guaranteed the Western powers unimpeded access to West Berlin and allowed limited access to East Berlin by West Berliners. It also had the implicit effect of formalizing the division of Berlin.

Poland:
Solidarity Goes Underground

Perspective

1386–1572	Poland reaches height of its power.
1772	First partition of Poland is agreed to by Russia, Prussia, and Austria.
1793	Two-thirds of Poland's remaining territory is divided between Russia and Prussia.
1795	Austria annexes what land remains; Poland ceases to exist as independent country.
1830	Armed insurrection is crushed by Russia.
1863	After series of rebellions, Russification is greatly increased.
1918	Poland regains its independence.
1926	Józef Pilsudski establishes dictatorship by coup d'état.
1939	Germans invade Poland, starting World War II.
1944	Soviet forces drive out Germans.
1949	Stalinist regime is installed after purges in Polish United Workers' party.
1956	Demonstrations lead to liberalized government under Wladyslaw Gomulka.
1970	Rioting topples Gomulka; Edward Gierek succeeds him as Poland's leader.
1980	Strikes lead to formation of Solidarity.
1981	Martial law is declared.
1983	**July.** Martial law is officially lifted. **October.** Lech Walesa is awarded Nobel Peace Prize.
1984	Father Jerzy Popieluszko is murdered.

The formation of the workers' trade union federation, Solidarity, in Poland in 1980 was a momentous development: for the first time within the Soviet bloc, a labor federation was formed outside the official Polish United Workers' (Communist) party hierarchy. Its quick success perhaps caught the government unaware. Within a year, the movement had attracted ten million members (out of a nation then of about thirty-six million) and, unheard of in a Commu-nist country, actually exercised the right of its workers to strike.

Pressure was placed on the Polish government to end the independence of Solidarity, and in De-cember 1981, a military government took over. Solidarity was banned and its leader, Lech Wa-lesa, was placed under house arrest. Solidarity refused to die, however, and went underground. Prominent among those who continued to cham-pion the outlawed labor federation were individ-ual priests of the Polish Roman Catholic church.

One of those priests was Jerzy Popieluszko. To all appearances, he was just an ordinary Polish priest. But for some time, the thirty-seven-year-old priest had been preaching monthly sermons at a Warsaw parish church in which, couched in double meanings and symbolic rhetoric, he would deliver the message of faith in freedom and Solidarity.

Then, on the night of October 19, 1984, his car was stopped by three state security policemen. They beat the priest, bound and gagged him, threw him into the trunk of their unmarked ve-hicle, and drove off. A search was made for the priest, and a week and a half later his body was fished out of a nearby reservoir. The three police-men were apprehended, confessed to the crime, and implicated their immediate superior. In an open trial, remarkable in itself in a Soviet-bloc country, the four men were convicted and sen-tenced in 1985 to long prison terms. However, nothing was revealed in the trial about whether the military government was involved in the murder.

Issues and Events

Postwar Poland has experienced several up-heavals but none so prolonged or serious as what happened after the birth of Solidarity. The troubles began in protests over rising food prices, which are set by the government. The protests were spearheaded by workers of the Lenin Shipyard in Gdańsk under the leadership of electrician Lech Walesa. Striking and taking over the yard in the middle of August 1980, the workers of Gdańsk were soon emulated by their comrades in other cities. Surprisingly, the gov-ernment granted concessions in the form of wage increases and recognition of an indepen-dent Solidarity. Included among the concessions was Solidarity's right to strike—an unprece-dented allowance in a Communist-bloc country.

The birth of Solidarity soon brought down the government. Party leader Edward Gierek re-signed in humiliation, and the party hierarchy floundered about in confusion and indecision. The Soviet Union leaned hard on the Polish United Workers' party to bring the situation under control. In 1981 leadership of the party as well as the government was given to a career military man, General Wojcieck Jaruzelski. When some impatient Solidarity leaders suggested a national referendum on the continued retention of communism itself, Jaruzelski immediately responded with a military crackdown in December 1981. Tanks rolled through the streets, military officers moved into administrative positions, even civilian newscasters had to yield to uniformed army personnel. Thousands of Solidarity members and supporters were arrested, and the organization itself was banned, its office shut. Lech Walesa was arrested. After some eleven months of internment, Walesa was released and given back his job at the Lenin Shipyard in Gdańsk.

The Roman Catholic church in Poland has long kept an uneasy truce with the Communist regime, while the party has considered the church to be a government adversary. Some clergymen, such as Father Popieluszko, were more outspoken than others; but generally the church authorities showed their sympathies in a more unobtrusive way. The church hierarchy also saw its role as one of keeping Solidarity members to a moderate, nonconfrontational stance.

Martial law was suspended in December 1982, when most of the detainees still interned were released; in July 1983, martial law was formally lifted. The government tried with limited success to build its own trade unions instead of those it had dissolved, but mass demonstrations continued on significant commemorative dates, and Solidarity lived underground. In October 1983, to the government's chagrin, Lech Walesa was awarded the Nobel Peace Prize.

Background
After its great period of power and glory in the Middle Ages, Poland was forced over the centuries to withstand the encroachment of Russia in the east and Prussia and Austria in the west. In 1772 these three powers partitioned Poland, each taking a portion of its territory that together amounted to a quarter of its total area. Russia and Prussia again carved up between them some two-thirds of the remaining territory in 1793. In 1795 Austria annexed the rest.

Frequent rebellions, however, kept the national spirit alive. In 1794, even before the third partition, Thaddeus Kosciusko, who had fought in the American Revolution, led an unsuccessful rebellion for independence, and many more followed. Napoleon Bonaparte of France created the duchy of Warsaw in 1807, but after Napoleon's defeat in 1815 this became a Polish kingdom with the Russian czar on the throne. The

Lech Walesa—leader of the Polish Solidarity movement (1980–   ). Born in 1943(?) in Popowo during World War II . . . was fired from his job as an electrician in the Gdańsk Shipyard after protesting rising food prices . . . founded Solidarity (1980), an independent union to represent Polish workers, the only such organization in a Communist-bloc country . . . received international acclaim as Solidarity gained power but was frequently imprisoned or under house arrest . . . was arrested along with other union supporters when Solidarity was banned (1981) . . . received the Nobel Peace Prize (1983).

Poles rose in a powerful rebellion against this state in 1830 and were defeated only after six months of hard fighting. The harsh measures taken after this revolt again spurred other insurgencies.

After World War I, Poland was granted independence once again. Political life was turbulent in the new state, and financial crises added to the instability. Finally, in 1926, General Józef Pilsudski staged a coup d'état and established a dictatorship, which he led until his death in 1935. After the Nazis came to power in Germany, Poland became one of Hitler's targets, and German demands on Polish territory, when refused, led to the invasion of the country in 1939, touching off World War II.

Soviet troops liberated Poland in 1944, and the country again regained its independence. But under Soviet occupation, the government was Communist-dominated from the beginning, even though the party secretary, Wladyslaw Gomulka, advocated a ''Polish road to socialism.'' For that, in fact, he was purged from the party in 1949, and Poland then became strictly Stalinist.

Following the death of Stalin in 1953, the easing of various strictures led to greater demands from the populace. Massive demonstrations in 1956 led to a change in the government. Gomulka was recalled to the helm, and he remained in charge for the next fourteen years. For most of that time things were relatively calm. In 1970, as the economy slumped and the government imposed major price increases, workers in several cities took to the streets. There followed demonstrations that turned into rioting and led to a state of emergency. The disturbances were quelled, Gomulka was removed, and Edward Gierek became the party leader. The economy remained a problem. Foreign debts, especially to the West, piled up until the country was in danger of defaulting.

Soviet Union:
The Leadership Crisis

Perspective

1934–1938	*Stalin purges old revolutionary leadership.*
1953	*Stalin dies.*
1956	*Andropov serves as ambassador to Hungary during Hungarian Revolution.*
1964	*Brezhnev is appointed general secretary of Communist party.*
1982	**November.** *Brezhnev dies; Andropov is appointed general secretary.*
1983	**February.** *Andropov introduces his economic reform.*
	September. *Russian fighter planes shoot down South Korean airliner.*
1984	**Feburary 9.** *Andropov dies; Chernenko is appointed general secretary.*
1985	**March 10.** *Chernenko dies; within hours Mikhail Gorbachev is named his successor.*

In 1984, after the deaths of several of the aging members of the ruling elite of the Communist party, Soviet society began moving fitfully from the last direct links with the static programs of the Stalin era toward a new future. Changes in the complex, varied facets of Soviet political and economic life began during Yuri Andropov's fifteen-month rule. With the death of Konstantin Chernenko and the quick accession of Mikhail Gorbachev the full impact of these changes can be expected to be felt.

Issues and Events

When Leonid Brezhnev died on November 20, 1982, he left behind a stagnating society. The party leaders promoted under Brezhnev's patronage gave the appearance of being more interested in maintaining their political influence and ensuring their special privileges than in confronting the nation's more difficult economic and political problems. Brezhnev's leadership did nothing to correct this attitude among the elite, so these became the qualities he imparted to his era. The Brezhnev rule—unable to direct agricultural growth, expand worker production, discipline industrial management, control military spending, or organize a moral identity for society—allowed the country to flounder.

During the spring of 1982, when it became apparent that Brezhnev's health was failing rapidly, Yuri Andropov began to organize his bid for power. The former secret service (KGB) head, ambassador to Hungary, and senior Communist party official knew that the Brezhnev clique would not relinquish power willingly; therefore, he developed a Western-style public relations campaign to portray himself as the intelligent, cultured, but tough man dedicated to revitalizing the country. This campaign succeeded and gained him the support of the military and the KGB. In the days following Brezhnev's death these two agencies, through their representatives on the Politburo, the Soviet Union's ruling and decision-making body, successfully directed their support to Andropov. On November 12, 1982, Andropov was named general secretary of the Communist party, making him the most important member of the Politburo and in effect the head of government of the Soviet Union.

During his first hundred days in office, Andropov began a process of political and economic reform. Within weeks, he had removed two Brezhnev cronies for incompetent management of their important ministerial posts. Consumer goods that had long been denied to the public and had been available only to the party elite and used for bribes and payoffs began appearing on store shelves. The elite social groups—bureaucrats, sport stars, and artists—used Western currency stores and big cars less. In a nod toward a more egalitarian society, courts were given broad powers to define and prosecute abuses of privilege.

Andropov used similar tactics in his economic reforms. In an economy where everyone has to be employed, workers' laziness, absenteeism, and drunkenness are continuing problems. Management success depends not on keeping cost down while producing quality goods but on meeting production goals established by a central planning agency and on extending political connections. Andropov's reform effort was aimed at motivating the workers and manage-

Recent Leaders of the Soviet Union

Name	Date In Office	Reason Rule Ended
Joseph Stalin	1927–1953	Died in office
Georgi Malenkov	1953–1955	Forced to resign
Nikita S. Khrushchev	1955–1964	Dismissed
Leonid I. Brezhnev	1964–1982	Died in office
Yuri I. Andropov	1982–1984	Died in office
Konstantin Chernenko	1984–1985	Died in office
Mikhail Gorbachev	1985–	

ment to produce good products. He did this by requiring mandatory attendance policies, by instituting police sweeps of public places to round up absent workers, and by making managers directly accountable for the quality and quantity of their products.

The mechanisms for these reforms were instituted by the end of February 1983. However, before the reform measures could be fully implemented, Andropov dropped from public view. This absence marked the beginning of the long decline in his health and energy; despite major political incidents, such as the Soviet attack on a South Korean airliner, Andropov remained secluded. On February 9, 1984, he succumbed to his illnesses. He was succeeded by Konstantin Chernenko, a Brezhnev protégé.

Old, ailing, and unimaginative, Chernenko was dedicated to the status quo and stopped the momentum of Andropov's reforms. Chernenko's rule was viewed by the Politburo leadership as a holding action during which the younger members' credentials could be assessed and evaluated. So, when Chernenko died on March 10, 1985, it was only a few hours before Mikhail Gorbachev was named his successor. Gorbachev, born in 1931, became the youngest general secretary since Stalin. He is regarded as the party's expert on ideology and agriculture. A lawyer from the generation of leaders who began their careers when the Soviet Union was already an established power, he has a reputation as a civil, intelligent, and self-assured man eager to continue and enlarge the scope of Andropov's reforms. Gorbachev's program—as gleaned from his public speeches—would expand the consumer economy and limit military spending.

Western leaders who came in contact with Gorbachev were uniformly impressed with his diplomatic talents and with his seeming mastery of those public relations skills that are more associated with politicians in the democratic nations of the West than with leaders of the Communist-bloc countries.

Background

What Joseph Stalin accomplished as general secretary still greatly affects Soviet life. A ruthless and cynical man, he took the early revolutionary ideas of Russian communism and molded these concepts to justify his arbitrary, personal rule. Because his regime was not based on any clearly articulated doctrines and seemingly lacked popular support, he maintained power by strict control of Soviet society. By 1934, five years after he was appointed general secretary, Stalin had created a personal state within existing government operations. The members of this personal state, approximately one-half million secret police and bureaucrats, were responsible only to Stalin or his elite.

Mikhail Sergeyevich Gorbachev—president of the Politburo and Communist party general secretary (1985–   ). Born in 1931 in Stavropol province, son of a southern Russian peasant farmer . . . attended Moscow University law school (1950–1955) . . . worked in local politics (from 1955) before becoming first secretary of the Communist party in Stavropol (1970–1978) . . . was admitted to full Central Committee membership (1971) . . . was made secretary of agriculture (1978) by Leonid Brezhnev . . . became a full member of the Politburo (1980) . . . served as aide to Yuri Andropov (1982–1983) . . . became the first of the new, younger generation to lead the Soviet Union.

Andropov, Brezhnev, and Chernenko were members of this personal state and part of the post-Stalin leadership. All three were born into poor, rural families before the 1917 Russian Revolution. They received technical educations, joined the Communist party in the late 1920s, and in a few years had been promoted into party positions on a regional level. After Stalin's purges of the late 1930s, which eliminated all of the old revolutionary leadership, these young men were given responsible bureaucratic positions in the personal state. This sudden rise into the party hierarchy gave them access to the privileges of power and a vested interest in preserving the system. They would maintain their authority through the 1940s and early 1950s by subordinating their personalities and developing an unquestioning loyalty to Stalin's constantly changing ideology and policy pronouncements and by stifling any initiative that would change the operation of their bureaus. When the three future general secretaries were put into government positions after 1953, they had become members of the conservative ruling elite dedicated to preserving the status quo.

The recent Soviet leadership had learned its ruling skills in a particular historical period and under harsh circumstances. Soviet society, when Stalin's terror subsided, moved in different directions from its leaders. The abilities of the "old guard" were clearly inadequate to govern a changing society with many problems. It remains to be seen whether the younger generation, which is not bound to memories of Stalin, can or will institute new techniques to run a vast nation.

Cyprus:
An Island Divided

Perspective

1571	Ottoman Empire captures Cyprus from Venetians.
1878	Sultan Abd el-Hamid II invites British to administer island.
1882	Legislative council is established.
1914	British annex Cyprus.
1923	Turkey formally recognizes British possession in Treaty of Lausanne.
1925	Cyprus is made British crown colony.
1931	Greek Cypriots riot for enosis, or union with Greece. Legislative council is abolished.
1943	Municipal government is introduced, based on adult suffrage.
1955	National Organization of Cypriot Fighters, favoring enosis, initiates campaign of terror against British.
1956	Archbishop Makarios III is exiled to Seychelles.
1959	Agreement is reached among Greece, Turkey, and United Kingdom on constitution for independent Cyprus. Archbishop Makarios is elected president.
1960	**August.** Cyprus is declared independent republic.
1963	Greek and Turkish Cypriots clash over proposals by President Makarios for changes in constitution.
1964	Turkish vice-president resigns; Greek-Turkish corule suffers de facto breakdown. United Nations peacekeeping force is introduced.
1968	Makarios is reelected president.
1973	Makarios is elected for third time.
1974	Greek-led National Guard stages coup d'état; Makarios flees to United States. Turkey invades Cyprus and occupies northern third of island.
1975	Turkish Cypriot state is proclaimed in Turkish-held territory.
1977	Makarios dies and is succeeded by Spyros Kyprianou.
1983	Kyprianou is reelected president. Turkish Republic of Northern Cyprus issues unilateral declaration of independence.
1984	Greek and Turkish Cypriot leaders agree to meet under United Nations auspices to discuss federation of their states.
1985	**January.** Leaders hold abortive talks in New York City.

W hen the former British crown colony of Cyprus became an independent republic in 1960, it came equipped with a constitution that took into account the ethnic makeup of the island: 78 percent Greek and 18 percent Turkish. The Turkish population, for example, was guaranteed the office of vice-president, three out of ten cabinet posts, and the power to veto acts of the legislature. That constitution failed to ameliorate the long-festering enmity between the Greeks and Turks; in fact, relations deteriorated rather than improved. The Greek majority, led by Archbishop Makarios III, was intent on enosis, or union with Greece. The Turkish minority, on the other hand, was determined to form a separate federated Turkish republic in the northern part of the island, where most of the Turkish population lived.

For twenty-five years, the situation worsened: British troops had to intervene, the United Nations sent in a peacekeeping force, the Greek government in Athens engineered a coup, and a force from Turkey invaded the island and set up what was in effect a separate government in the Turkish enclave. Thus when the leader of the Turkish Cypriots and the president of the Greek part of Cyprus met in January 1985, the international community hoped that an agreement could be reached that would finally bring peace to the island republic. After three days the talks broke down with no agreement of any kind but plenty of recriminations.

Issues and Events

The unilateral declaration of independence by Turkish Cypriots on November 15, 1983, established in the Turkish-occupied part of the island the Turkish Republic of Northern Cyprus. This step was only a logical culmination of developments there during the nine years since Turkey invaded the country, although it seemed to make the prospects of unification under a central government so much more distant.

Most Greek Cypriots had always considered their ultimate destiny to be enosis with the Greek motherland. So no sooner was Archbishop Makarios III installed as the republic's first president than he began to prepare the ground for modifications of the constitutional agreements that took into account the Turkish population, and on which the establishment of the state of Cyprus was based.

When Makarios, therefore, in 1963 proposed changes in the constitution that quite decisively would diminish the power of the Turkish minority, serious clashes occurred between the two ethnic groups. With the hostilities spreading over the island, the Turkish contingent of the legislature ceased to attend, the Turkish ministers withdrew from the cabinet, and in January 1964 the Turkish vice-president resigned. Full-scale civil war was averted only by the intervention of British troops. The United Nations later arranged for a peacekeeping force, which has remained there ever since.

Increased tensions on the island in the early 1970s, partly created by the colonels' junta then in power in Athens, culminated in July 1974 in a junta-backed coup d'état by the Greek Cypriot National Guard that temporarily ousted Makarios. The coup brought on an invasion by Turkish forces, which quickly occupied the northern third of the island, effectively dividing it along ethnic lines. Some 200,000 Greek Cypriots fled the Turkish-held territory, while Turkish Cypriots from other parts of the island sought refuge there. In February 1975 a Turkish Cypriot state was proclaimed.

Makarios died in 1977 and was succeeded by Spyros Kyprianou, his former foreign minister. While sporadic talks between the factions have been attempted under United Nations auspices—generally centering on the idea of a federated republic of a Turkish and a Greek state—all progress has foundered on mutual distrust and bitterness. The unilateral declaration of independence by the Turkish Cypriots in 1983 did not really change the status quo, although the action, sounding as it did of finality, sent shock waves through the diplomatic community.

Background

Greeks began to colonize the island in the 1600s B.C., and during the following millennia, while ruled successively by the Assyrians, Persians, Macedonians, Egyptians, Romans, and Byzantines, its character remained predominantly Greek.

Nor did it change much when King Richard the Lionhearted of England, in 1191, captured the island on his way to fight the Saracens and promptly sold it to Guy of Lusignan, the deposed Crusader king of Jerusalem.

In the late Middle Ages, the Italian city-states Genoa and Venice vied for control of Cyprus as a strategic command post to protect their trade routes to the Middle East—the same reason that had made the island valuable to the ancient empires. Through family alliance, the Venetians won out, gaining hold of Cyprus in 1489. But the growing power of the Ottoman Empire on the Anatolian mainland only fifty or sixty miles (eighty to ninety-five kilometers) to the north made it costly for the Venetians to maintain their garrisons. They taxed the islanders so heavily that when Sultan Selim II and his Ottoman Turks finally captured Cyprus in 1571, they were greeted as liberators rather than as foes.

Under Turkish rule, much of the pattern that up to this day has characterized Cypriot life was established. The Turks allowed the islanders to restore their own church and hierarchy, which previously had been subjugated to Roman Catholicism, but they also introduced, by immigration from Anatolia, the problem of a second ethnic community, which today divides the island into antagonistic camps.

After his 1878 defeat by Russia in the Russo-Turkish War, Sultan Abd el-Hamid II, in an attempt to check further Russian advances into the area, persuaded the British to assume the administration of Cyprus while retaining nominal title to it. Petitions by the populace for enosis with Greece were ignored. And when the Turks sided with the Central Powers in World War I, the administrators annexed the island to the British crown. Turkey consented to this arrangement by the Treaty of Lausanne in 1923, and two years later Cyprus was made a crown colony.

In 1931, serious riots broke out on the island as a consequence of continued agitation for enosis. The British answered by abolishing the legislative council they had introduced in 1882. In 1943, however, they established municipal government based on adult suffrage in preparation for self-government after World War II. But the postwar plans they proposed were resisted by Greek and Turkish Cypriots alike, and in 1955 the National Organization of Cypriot Fighters, known by its Greek acronym EOKA, initiated a campaign of terror in its fight for enosis. The following year, believing he was linked to EOKA, the British deported Archbishop Makarios, exiling him to the Seychelles in the Indian Ocean. The violent reaction to this move forced them to declare an island-wide state of emergency.

International attempts to find a solution to the crisis finally resulted in an accord among Greece, Turkey, and the United Kingdom for the establishment of an independent republic whose constitution would be jointly guaranteed by all three countries. As the history of that republic demonstrates, however, the search for solutions must continue.

The Middle East and North Africa

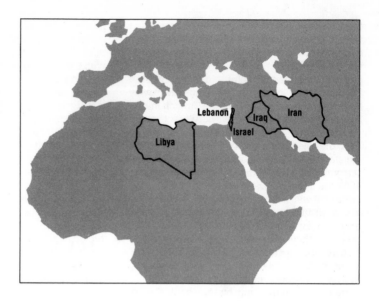

The description of the Middle East as a "powder keg" was already a cliché in the nineteenth century, and the twentieth century has seen nothing render that description less meaningful. Much of the modern-day explosiveness of the area has resulted from the founding of a Jewish state, Israel, in 1948. The end of World War II also saw the termination of the artificial peace that had been imposed by the great powers since the nineteenth century. Great Britain and France in particular had carved out their individual spheres of influence, and each had respected and supported the other in maintaining a truce among the various religious and racial groups that were forced to live together in the Middle East. Britain and France pulled out of the Middle East at the end of World War II, leaving the newly independent nations to fend for themselves. The United States became increasingly interested in the area, while the Soviet Union, the other great power after World War II, was involved to a lesser degree.

The creation and protection of Israel was the focus of United States activity in the Middle East in the years immediately following World War II. Later, in the 1970s, the protection of American petroleum interests in Arab nations became an objective of the American government. These two interests, a free Israel and a free-flowing oil supply, tend to pull American diplomacy in two directions. Policies aimed at bolstering Israel are opposed by the Arab oil-producing nations, and pro-Arab policies are deemed unacceptable by Israel.

The area known as the Middle East generally includes the countries of the Arabian peninsula and Iraq, Iran, Israel, Jordan, Lebanon, and Syria, and its influence extends to encompass the countries of North Africa in the same general region. The nations of this area have a common history, and the majority of the people are Islamic Arabs, sharing religion, culture, and language. These similarities are the basis of the concept of Arab unity.

Because of the region's mineral riches and strategic value, internal conflicts quickly take on international significance. The Middle East and North Africa contain vast oil deposits, upon which the industrialized world depends. In addition the area's waterways, including the Strait of Hormuz and the Suez Canal, are of both commercial and military importance. In a less influential part of the world, a border war such as that between Iraq and Iran would most likely remain a regional concern. But when the flow of oil to the West is threatened, a conflict such as this quickly gains international attention.

Many of the historic troubles of the Middle East, however, are indigenous. It is the birthplace of three of the world's great religions: Judaism, Christianity, and Islam. All three religions have become intertwined with the political and economic problems of the region. Islam, the religion of the overwhelming majority, is mainly composed of two sects: the majority Sunnis and the minority Shiites. A third Muslim group, especially prominent in Lebanon, is the Druze, who regard their religion as a branch of Islam, but whom other Muslim sects look upon as heretical. Much of the unrest and violence of the Middle East is the result of the long-standing enmity that each of these groups feels toward the other two. The Christians of the Middle East are also in schism: the Maronites have long been the majority Christian group (often allied with the Israelis), but in recent years the Greek Orthodox Christians have increased in numbers and may soon be the largest Christian group in the area. In Israel there is considerable tension as well between the Orthodox and the other branches of Judaism.

The site of some of the world's most ancient civilizations, the Middle East was the logical place for these religions to evolve. The great civilization of ancient Egypt developed on the banks of the Nile, and the area of the Tigris and Euphrates rivers saw the society of Mesopotamia flourish. Invaders and immigrants were diverse, and the many peoples coming to the region included Assyrians, Hebrews, Phoenicians, Chaldeans, Medes, and Persians. Islam was founded in the seventh century A.D., and as the Arabs expanded their empire, their religion and culture spread throughout the Middle East and North Africa.

The Arab Empire came to an end about the tenth century and was followed some centuries later by the empire of the Ottoman Turks, who were also Muslim. The Ottoman Empire dominated until Turkey was defeated in World War I. Many of the Arab states remained under foreign rule, however, as British or French mandates of the League of Nations.

The area of Palestine, comprising present-day Israel, was mandated to the British at this time. As Jewish immigration to the region increased, so did Arab-Jewish hostility. In an attempt to quell the growing discontent, Britain placed restrictions on Jewish immigration.

Following World War II, many Jews directed their energies to establishing the nation of Israel, and at the same time postwar sentiment for the Jews was widespread. Although immigration restrictions had not been rescinded, Jewish immigration to Palestine increased, and with it Arab-Jewish hostility. In 1947 Britain turned to the United Nations for help in solving the problem.

The result was the division of Palestine into a state with specified Arab and Jewish zones, plus the neutral city of Jerusalem. Fighting soon broke out between Arabs and Jews, and in 1948 the independent State of Israel was proclaimed.

Hostilities between Israel and the surrounding Arab states have continued. Major conflicts included a 1956 war focused on the Suez Canal, the Six-Day War of 1967, and a war in October of 1973. A milestone in Arab-Israeli relations came in 1979 with the signing of a peace treaty between Egypt and Israel.

Finally, the Arabs as an ethnic group are not nearly so united as their combined opposition to Israel would imply. The Palestinians, who were displaced from their homeland by the Israelis, have created dissension in the lands to which they fled, principally Jordan and Lebanon.

Although part of the African continent, North Africa is linked by religion and culture to the Middle East. The region of North Africa generally includes Algeria, Morocco, Tunisia, and Libya. Three of these nations, Algeria, Morocco, and Tunisia, are former French colonies. In the past Libya was governed by Italy.

Despite North Africa's cultural link with the Middle East, its colonial past ties it to the rest of the African continent. The period of European expansion in Africa saw colonists drawn by the profits of slave and other trades, and they settled in enclaves that had little regard for the natural boundaries that had arisen from ethnicity or tribal allegiance. The colonies thus came to be demarcated by artificial borders created by treaties and agreements among the colonial powers. The land of the region had fostered a nomadic life-style, and the foreign-imposed boundaries prevented the people from following their traditional way of life. When independence was finally achieved, the artificial boundaries remained, sometimes uniting diverse peoples into a single nation, and sometimes separating a single people by an international border. Dissension was often the result; many borders were finalized only recently, and many remain in dispute. Libya's Bedouin tribes, for example, long presented a unified resistance to the imposition of what they viewed as artificial borders.

Libya is also an example of the nationalistic determination that sometimes arose as a result of foreign intervention and control. Colonel Mu'ammar al-Qadhafi, the head of the Libyan state, is of Bedouin descent, not part of the traditional Libyan elite and thus well acquainted with the widespread poverty often resulting from minority rule and foreign influence. Motivated by antiimperialistic beliefs, Qadhafi came to power in 1969, promoting the removal of foreign interests from his country and establishing a government based on Islam. Although most of Libya is desert, the country benefits from its large oil deposits, and in this oil Qadhafi has found a weapon of international significance. A goal of the Qadhafi government is unification of the Arab world, and strategies have included terrorism and revolving alliances.

Lebanon:
The Fuse Still Burns

Perspective

1860	*Druze-Maronite fighting brings French intervention.*
1943	*Independent Lebanese state is established.*
1948	*Israel is founded. Palestinians settle in neighboring Arab countries.*
1958	*United States sends marines to Beirut.*
1967	*In Six-Day War Israel annexes Golan Heights, Sinai, and West Bank; many more Palestinians seek refuge in Lebanon.*
1969	*Cairo Agreement recognizes Palestinian autonomy within Lebanon.*
1970	*"Black September" rout of Palestinians is conducted by Jordan. Palestine Liberation Organization (PLO) headquarters moves to Beirut.*
1975	**May.** *Fighting erupts in Beirut.*
1976	**June.** *Syrian troops enter Lebanon.*
1978	**March.** *Israel invades Lebanon.*
1982	**June.** *Israel invades Lebanon, stopping outside Beirut four days later.*
	August. *Evacuation of PLO from Beirut is carried out by multinational force.*
	September 10. *Multinational forces are withdrawn.*
	September 14. *Recently elected president Bashir Gemayel is murdered.*
	September 15. *Israel enters West Beirut.*
	September 16–17. *Civilians in Palestinian refugee camps are massacred by Phalangist militiamen.*
	September 21. *Amin Gemayel, brother of Bashir, is elected president.*
1983	**May.** *Lebanon, Israel, and United States sign accord.*
	October. *United States marine headquarters is bombed.*
1984	**February.** *Marines evacuate Beirut; Muslims in Lebanese army rebel.*
1985	*Israelis withdraw from Lebanon.*

T oday, with Lebanon in physical, economic, and political ruin, it is difficult to believe that for most of the period following World War II, that country was looked upon as the one area of the Middle East that seemed to be meeting and solving its political and religious problems. Its capital, Beirut, was the financial center of the Middle East, with a cultural and educational life that was the envy of other cities in the area. The peace in Lebanon during those years was frequently broken by coups and attempted coups and by the intervention of outside powers to restore the peace. Nevertheless, the country's government seemed to be working, based as it was on a delicate balance of its various factions.

Religion and politics have long been inextricably intertwined in Lebanon, with political groupings based on religious affiliations. Religion, and thus politics, are sensitive issues here, and official figures on religious affiliation were last obtained in 1932, when the country was almost equally divided into Christian and Muslim groups. It is now assumed that Muslims outnumber Christians. The Christians are primarily Maronite; their religion is associated with Roman Catholicism. Politically, the Maronites usually belong to the Phalange party, and the Phalangists support independent militia groups; Christians also have traditionally controlled the Lebanese army. Among the Christians there are also considerable numbers of Greek Orthodox, Greek Catholic, and Armenian Orthodox adherents. The Muslim community is almost equally divided between Sunni and Shiite factions. There is also a significant minority of Druzes, whose religion is separate from Islam but based on its tenets.

To deal with this religious, and thus political, multiplicity, the Lebanese constitution in effect during the postwar years took formal notice of the religious divisions and called for proportional representation of the various religious groups in the civil service, the cabinet, and the legislature. But in the late 1970s, political rivalries, fueled by religious animosity, upset the delicate balance in Lebanon.

Issues and Events

Sectarian tensions erupted into civil war in 1975, when the PLO clashed with the Maronite Christians. Syria entered the civil war in 1976, when President Hafez Assad, at the request of the Lebanese government, sent Syrian army regulars into Lebanon as part of the Arab Deterrent Force, hoping to prevent a partitioned Lebanon and possible Israeli intervention.

The Phalangists bridled under Syrian occupation and grew more and more dependent on Israel, who saw in them a means of creating a pro-Israeli buffer zone. Encouraged and armed by the Israelis, the Phalangists stepped up their resistance to the Syrians and Palestinians, as well as those Christians who opposed them. Unable to control the Phalangists, Syria shelled the Christian enclave of East Beirut, only deepening the Christians' resolve.

The PLO stepped up its attacks on Israel, shelling and rocketing from miles within the Lebanese border. Israel in retaliation invaded Lebanon in March 1978.

The Israeli government invaded Lebanon a second time, after numerous Lebanese-based PLO attacks on Israel in 1981 and 1982. The June 6 operation, named Peace for Galilee, was to create a twenty-five-mile (forty kilometer) zone, leaving Israel out of the reach of the PLO long-range artillery. Syrian reaction was costly and ineffective.

Against a background of Israeli air raids, Phalangist strongman Bashir Gemayel was elected president of Lebanon in August 1982. The PLO, routed from the Lebanese countryside, was evacuated by a multinational force sent to oversee the operation, as well as to protect the residents of West Beirut from the Israelis and their triumphant Phalangist allies. Consisting of United States marines and Italian and French combat troops, the multinational force withdrew on September 10, almost immediately after the last PLO guerrillas were removed. On September 14, a bomb in Phalange party headquarters killed president-elect Gemayel. The next day, in contravention of their agreement with American envoy Philip Habib, Israeli troops entered West Beirut.

On September 16 and 17, Palestinian civilians in the Sabra and Shatila camps were massacred by Phalangist militiamen, ostensibly to avenge their slain leader, demonstrating that those Palestinians who remained in Lebanon did so at their own peril. The multinational force returned to West Beirut. On September 28, West Beirut was handed over to the Lebanese army by the Israelis.

Amin Gemayel, brother of the assassinated Bashir Gemayel, was elected president, and in 1983 he presided over a largely Christian government. He generated resentment and disenchantment among the Muslims and Druzes for his heavy-handedness in appointing Maronites to positions Muslims or Druzes had traditionally held and for his unwillingness to restrain the marauding Phalangist militiamen, who now occupied areas designated by Israel.

The Shuf Mountains, the homeland of the Druzes, were threatened by Israeli-led Phalangists patrolling the area. The Israelis left in early September, the Lebanese army relieving them and assisting the Phalangists. Druze militiamen,

assisted by Syrian artillery, drove the Lebanese army from its positions, often after savage hand-to-hand combat.

The protector of the Lebanese army, the United States, was already unpopular after it signed a May 17 accord, permitting the Israelis to stay in Lebanon for as long as the Syrians remained. Naval and marine shelling of the Druzes, who were besieging the Lebanese army in Suk el Gharb, put the United States firmly in the role of the aggressor. Snipings and ambushes of United States marines in Beirut stepped up, culminating in the bombing of marine headquarters at Beirut airport. Over two hundred marines were killed. Confused and unsure, the marines stayed in Beirut until February 1984. Control of West Beirut was in the hands of rival Muslim militias. In 1984 there was mass desertion from the Lebanese army, especially after the resignation of many Muslim government ministers. The influence of the various Shiite groups widened.

Israeli weariness with its longest military campaign was instrumental in its decision to withdraw from Lebanon, in planned phases. That withdrawal, begun in early 1985, was accompanied by further violence as the Israeli army passed through Muslim settlements in southern Lebanon.

Background

The delicate sectarian balance that had prevailed in Lebanon was upset in 1970, when hundreds of thousands of Palestinian refugees fled Jordan for Lebanon. Acting as a "state within a state" according to the Cairo Agreement of 1969, the heavily armed Palestinian guerrillas had threatened King Hussein's reign in Jordan with their depredations. Hussein unleashed his British-trained Bedouins against them, in a purge Palestinians called Black September. With its ineffective military, Lebanon was not able either to expel the Palestinians or to police them.

Syria, the primary sponsor of the Palestinian guerrillas, arms most factions and has incorporated Palestinian units into the Syrian army. Syria has always had a dominant influence on Lebanese affairs; Lebanon had been part of Syria until a 1920 League of Nations created the state of Lebanon under French mandate.

Moderating elements in Lebanon are on the wane. Among the disaffected Lebanese, the Shiites, largely poor and uneducated, have emerged as a volatile and increasingly radical element. Iran's Islamic revolution has attracted many followers, with its call to a *jihad*, or "holy war," against the Israelis, their Christian allies, and the United States.

Israel:
The Money Crisis

Perspective

1948	*State of Israel is proclaimed at Tel Aviv–Yafo.*
1949	*Truce agreements are achieved between Israel and its Arab neighbors. Elections for Knesset (Israeli parliament) are held. Chaim Weizman is elected president and David Ben-Gurion is chosen as prime minister.*
1956	*Israel is joined by France and Great Britain in successful attempt to seize Suez Canal from Egypt.*
1957	*Israel returns Egyptian territory in exchange for Egyptian president Nasser's promise of peace.*
1967	*June 2. Egypt's Nasser blockades Gulf of Aqaba and vows to "drive the Jews into the sea."*
	June 5. Israel launches preemptive strike against Egypt, Syria, and Jordan; Six-Day War ends with Israel victorious and possessing huge parcels of its enemies' land.
	October. The UN adopts Resolution 242, guaranteeing Israel "secure and defensible" boundaries.
1973	*September. Egypt leads Syria and Jordan in surprise attack on Israel.*
	October. Arab states raise oil prices.
1977	*Egyptian president Sadat travels to Israel at invitation of Israeli prime minister Begin.*
1979	*Egypt-Israel peace treaty is signed.*
1980	*Partial fiscal restraint program, imposed on government by Finance Minister Hurwitz, fails.*
1982	*Israel invades southern Lebanon to aid Lebanese government troops in repelling Palestine Liberation Organization and Muslim guerrilla attacks. Israel's economy begins to fall apart; inflation zooms to triple-digit level.*
1984	*With its economy in chaos, Israel votes out Begin; Labor party leader Peres forms coalition government.*
1985	*With inflation at 400 percent, Israel initiates withdrawal from Lebanon and appeals to United States for almost $4 billion in foreign aid.*

It has become a truism that Israel is in trouble. Involved in several strenuous and costly wars, Israel has been under military pressure from Arab states since its inception in 1948. Now, however, economic chaos, precipitated by a defense obligation that accounts for a phenomenal 60 percent of the government budget, has plunged the little country into a situation where unemployment is up, the trade deficit is intolerable, and annual inflation has soared into the triple-digit stratosphere: an annual rate of over 400 percent in early 1985.

Supporters of Israel, both in Israel and in the United States, point to the economic stresses that have been aggravated by Israel's political and military achievements. Israel, they say, has gotten into this situation because in thirty-seven years it has absorbed new people, amounting to five times its original population, and has done so in spite of the wars it repeatedly had to fight against its neighbors. It has attempted successfully to absorb Jewish émigrés from all over, most recently seven thousand Ethiopian Jewish refugees, while simultaneously maintaining the only democratic society in the Middle East.

Issues and Events

The Israeli economy is now feeling the impact of built-in structural problems that have plagued it since 1948. Currently, inadequate monetary controls, huge budget demands for military security, and the absorption of émigrés have taxed the nation, blessed with little in the way of natural resources, to the breaking point. The impact of the Arab-Israeli wars of 1967 and 1973, the oil price shocks of 1973 and 1974, and 1979 and 1980, and the cost of the Egyptian peace treaty signed in 1979 have added new burdens to the Israeli economy.

Much of the needed military funding—especially crucial after the 1973 war—was in the form of loans, and this substantially increased Israel's foreign debt. Indeed, one-third of that debt, now $23 billion, is owed to the United States on loans for weapons purchased since 1973. Defense spending, which in the early 1960s was a relatively modest 10 percent of Israel's gross national product (GNP), increased by almost 10 percent of GNP after each of the two most recent wars. The 1973 war caused Israel's military costs to rise sharply and, consequently, caused economic growth rates to decline from 10 percent per year to between 2 percent and 3 percent per year. Between 1968 and 1973, defense expenditures and defense imports averaged 22 percent of Israel's GNP; by 1975 defense expenditures had soared to 34 percent.

The drain of the 1973 war, which cost Israel

$12 billion, was worsened by the quadrupling of oil prices, especially burdensome to Israel, which has no indigenous oil supply.

This situation, to a considerable degree, was brought on by the Israeli-Egyptian peace treaty, the Camp David accords signed in 1979. The costs of the removal of Israeli forces and air bases from the Sinai were staggering and only partially overcome by United States assistance provided by President Carter. The loss of the Egyptian oil fields (acquired in the Six-Day War of 1967) as a result of the treaty once again made Israel totally dependent on foreign sources of oil.

As if all this were not enough, Israel in 1985 began a phased withdrawal of its forces from southern Lebanon and, since the first phase of withdrawal on February 6, 1985, Palestine Liberation Organization (PLO) guerrillas have stepped up their attacks on both Israeli and Christian Lebanese positions. Thus, the withdrawal was slower than predicted, with a daily cost of maintaining the troops of $1.2 million.

The significance of the war in Lebanon is that it divided public opinion in Israel, forced the government to accept a coalition cabinet led by Labor party leader Shimon Peres, and tore the social fabric of Israel. Since the 1982 invasion, over 140 Israeli citizens have been convicted of draft evasion; before 1982 conscientious objection was unknown.

If Israel is to turn its economy around by reducing its budget, enforcing austerity programs, and curtailing its extensive welfare benefits, it will need an undivided and loyal populace to share the requisite sacrifices. And these sacrifices will have to be made if Israel is to get anything close to its requested military and economic aid from the United States. This is due to the free-market orientation of the Reagan administration, which leads it to be less sensitive to the welfare state that has historically prevailed in Israel. The Reagan administration prefers that nations receiving American dollars act in accord with classic conservative doctrines and accept a diminished government role in the economy. United States secretary of state George Shultz said that aid was contingent on reform; certain Israeli policy changes had to be made at once if United States aid is expected. The most important action is a real budget cut of $2 million for the Israeli fiscal year that began on April 1, 1985. If the United States gives the requested aid, and budget cuts are made, Israel's deficit might be more manageable. The restraints imposed, however, would lead to significant unemployment (especially in Israel's bloated public sector), and, at least temporarily, to a real drop in the standard of living.

What remains to be seen is not only the acceptance of restraints by the Israeli government but, even more critical in the long run, the willingness of the Israeli people to pull together, make sacrifices, and, finally, wean themselves away from the welfare state concept to which they have been committed since 1948.

Background

When the nation of Israel was created by a United Nations mandate in 1948, the political-economic structure chosen was democratic socialism. Israeli president Chaim Weizman and premier David Ben-Gurion immediately set themselves the tasks of rendering arable the Israeli desert, exploiting what mineral resources the country possessed, and, above all, catching up with the industrially developed nations of the world.

No examination of Israel's economic system can be attempted without considering the full impact of the defense requirements upon the state. After the Six-Day War in 1967, Israel became determined to produce more defense equipment at home. While ultimately this led to the production of several superb fighter planes and, in 1984, the *Merkava*, a sophisticated ground tank, this effort fueled inflation because the goal of partial military self-sufficiency could be attained only through massive government spending. From 1967 through 1973 this seemed to work for the Israelis, but after the Yom Kippur War in 1973, government expenditures and inflation began to accelerate. With both foreign and domestic debts skyrocketing in the 1970s, Prime Minister Begin began a departure from quasi-socialist economics and attempted a more conservative fiscal approach. In 1980 Finance Minister Yigal Hurwitz attempted to apply some classic free-market nostrums to Israel's sagging economy. He cut subsidies and reduced government employment but in the opinion of many did not go far enough. The results were disastrous; unemployment more than doubled, the GNP fell, and real wages dipped sharply, while inflation remained high. In 1981 Hurwitz and his partial "austerity program" were replaced with a more traditional welfare-oriented program. The results were even worse.

United States insistence that Israel adhere to a more conservative fiscal policy may or may not lead to a solution. Whether it will be a new economic order imposed because of pressure from the United States, or the obvious benefit of a $4-billion foreign-aid transfusion, it is clear today that Israel is looking to the West for the source of its economic deliverance as well as that of its national security.

Legacies of the Six-Day War: Jerusalem, Gaza Strip, Golan Heights, West Bank

Israel's most spectacular victory in the series of Arab-Israeli wars that began with Israel's independence in 1948 was the Six-Day War of 1967. On June 5, 1967, Israel responded to Egyptian provocations by launching an air attack that effectively destroyed Arab air capabilities. With its domination of the air assured, Israel quickly moved its ground troops into Arab territory on several fronts. By the time the war ended on June 10, Israel had occupied the Sinai Peninsula, the Gaza Strip, the Arab section of Jerusalem, the Golan Heights bordering Syria, and that part of Jordan located on the west bank of the Jordan River. Israel announced that, except for Jerusalem, it would give back the occupied territories only after substantial progress had been made in Arab-Israeli relations. Jerusalem, according to the Israelis, would never be returned and would become the capital of the Jewish state.

Although the Six-Day War is the most significant of recent clashes, the first full-scale war between the Jews and the Arabs was triggered by Israeli independence on May 14, 1948, and conflict had erupted spasmodically since Great Britain received the League of Nations mandate for Palestine in 1920. The withdrawal of the British left Israel facing the armies of Egypt, Iraq, Lebanon, Syria, and Transjordan (modern Jordan), all of which considered Israel to be on Arab land. Early gains by the Arabs were halted by a cease-fire in January 1949. A United Nations–enforced truce lasted until the Israeli attack into the Sinai Peninsula in October 1956, which resulted in territorial gains that Israel traded a month later for the promise of access to the Gulf of Aqaba. The 1967 war was triggered when Egypt shut off this access. In 1973, Egypt, Syria, and Jordan attacked Israel but they were repulsed by 1974.

The Camp David accords of 1979 (in which Egypt and Israel agreed to a peace treaty) stipulated that Israel would return the Sinai Peninsula to Egypt, a transfer that was completed in 1982. In the accords, Egypt and Israel also agreed to begin negotiations for the rights of the native Palestinians in the Gaza Strip and the West Bank. Virtually no progress had been made in those negotiations at the time of the assassination of Anwar el-Sadat, the president of Egypt, in 1981.

A hardening of attitude in Israel occurring about the same time effectively ended any tendency to negotiate the return of occupied territories. Furthermore, the reluctance of Syria and Jordan—which claim sovereignty over the Golan Heights and the West Bank, respectively—even to admit the legitimacy of Israel and open negotiations has meant that those two areas remain in Israeli hands. Thus, as the twentieth anniversary of the Six-Day War approached, the Israelis had given up only the Sinai; the rest of their conquests remained firmly in their hands.

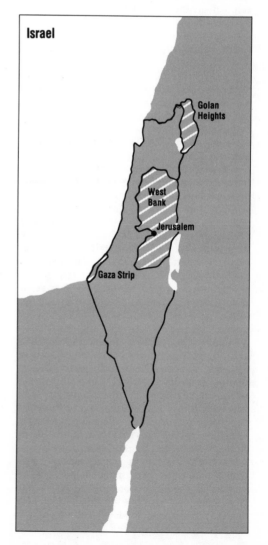

Jerusalem

Perspective

1244	*Jerusalem is held by Turks.*
1920	*Jerusalem becomes part of British mandate for Palestine.*
1947	*United Nations votes to partition mandated territory into Jewish and Arab states with autonomous Jerusalem under international supervision.*
1948	*Jerusalem is divided between Jordan and Israel during Arab-Israeli War.*
1950	*Israel designates Jerusalem its capital.*
1967	*Following Six-Day War, East Jerusalem is overrun by Israel and annexed. Partition of Jerusalem ends.*
1969	*Jewish families begin to move into formerly Arabian East Jerusalem.*
1980	*Prime Minister Menachem Begin, backed by Knesset, Israeli legislature, proclaims reunited Jerusalem eternal capital of Israel, incurring UN disapproval.*

Of all the Israeli conquests of the Six-Day War, probably none struck a more responsive chord in the hearts of Jews everywhere than the occupation of Jerusalem. The ancient city, while also sacred to Christians and Muslims, occupies a special place in the tradition of Judaism and the Jewish people. As Rome is the focus of the Roman Catholic church and Mecca is that of Islam, so Jerusalem occupies a central position in Judaism. Therefore, it was inevitable that the Israeli occupation of Jerusalem would take on a significance far in excess of its political and military significance.

In 1947 as British influence in the Holy Land was being dissipated, the United Nations evolved a plan to make Jerusalem an autonomous city under international supervision. Instead, Jordan seized Jerusalem's Old City during the Arab-Israeli conflict of 1948 and divided the city. The Wailing Wall, one of the most sacred sites in the Jewish faith, was closed to Jewish worship. The city's sections were separated by concrete barriers, barbed wire, and land mines. It remained a divided city until the Six-Day War, when the Israelis triumphantly captured the Old City. The army blew up the walls that separated Israeli and Jordanian sectors of the city. In 1980 the Israeli government announced that henceforth Jerusalem would be the permanent capital

city of Israel. Most foreign countries continued to maintain their embassies in Tel Aviv–Yafo, however, as a way of staying out of the conflict between Israel and Jordan over sovereignty of the Old City.

Issues and Events

Before 1967, Jerusalem had suffered considerable decline in importance. However, under the administration of Mayor Teddy Kollek, it has rebounded into a richly diverse city vibrant with prosperity and change. Within fifteen years of its reunification, the population has grown from 275,000 to 415,000 (1981). More than a million visitors pour in every year. Huge strides have been made in improving the roads, the sewage system, and many other amenities.

The changes have been made with great attention to preserving the beauty and historic appearance of the city. To maintain its historical character, Kollek organized the Jerusalem Committee, an international group of persons of note. With the committee's help all superhighways were banned from the city. There was a limit set of eight stories for new buildings, which had to be faced with the distinctively colored Jerusalem stone. Flower gardens were planted all over, particularly in the Old City.

Such innovations are expensive. Local taxes in Jerusalem are the highest in the country but provide only one-third of the municipal budget. The rest comes from the national government. The Jerusalem Foundation, with funds raised in Europe and America, has also dispensed many millions of dollars.

The Israeli dominance over Jerusalem has created a potential problem with its large Arab population. Before 1967 there were no Jews in the twenty-eight square mile (seventy-three square kilometer) area of East Jerusalem. The Israeli government decided to establish Jewish settlements there. In 1969 the new suburb of Ramat Eshkol was founded, and by the 1980s, there were more than seventy thousand Jews in East Jerusalem.

There has been little actual violence in the city, but the potential is great. Arabs for the most part are concentrated in the lower economic classes; they are the menial workers, domestic workers, waiters, and construction workers. Integration has proved difficult to accomplish. Arab and Israeli children attend separate schools.

Arab residents of Jerusalem have been given the choice of becoming Israeli citizens, but more than 99 percent have opted to retain their Jordanian citizenship. Arabs may vote in Israeli elections, but only about 10 percent exercise the right.

Arab resentment has been fanned by the actions of Jewish extremists, whose target has been Temple Mount, where three religions intersect and clash. Muslims believe Temple Mount is where Muhammad ascended through the seven heavens into the presence of God. It is administered by a Muslim political-religious trust; members of the Christian and Jewish religions are allowed only limited access to the area. But Temple Mount is also the site of Solomon's Temple; it is where Abraham came to sacrifice his son, Isaac, and it is where Jesus taught and threw the moneychangers out of the temple.

In 1983 about forty Jewish activists were arrested, and arms and explosives were confiscated. They were suspected of planning to invade the Temple Mount and remove the Muslim administrators. The government was able to contain the problem, but it is not so optimistic as to believe that the problem will not continue to plague the authorities.

Gaza Strip

Perspective

1920	Gaza becomes part of British mandate for Palestine.
1948– 1949	Fleeing from Arab-Israeli War, Palestinian refugees stream into Gaza from other parts of Palestine. Gaza becomes Egyptian possession.
1967	During Six-Day War, Gaza is occupied by Israeli troops.
1982	Menachem Begin, prime minister of Israel, swears Israel will never leave Gaza Strip.

A small strip of land, 140 square miles (360 square kilometers) in area, along the Mediterranean Sea, the Gaza Strip has been the site of Jewish-Arab problems since 1947. Originally part of the British mandate for Palestine, it became the sanctuary of many thousands of Palestinians as Jews occupied the areas that now make up Israel. Refugee camps under UN auspices were set up, and the region came under Egyptian rule.

In the Six-Day War of 1967, Israel occupied the Gaza Strip and set up administrative control over the area. It announced that the area, along with the other Arab territories it conquered in that war, would be returned only after substantive progress was made in Israeli-Arab relations. In the Camp David accords of 1979, Israel agreed to negotiate with Egypt over the eventual conver-

sion of Gaza to "autonomous control." Little progress has been made in that direction, however, and Gaza remains under Israeli administration.

Issues and Events

Gaza has continued to be a site of violence on both sides. For example, on April 13, 1984, Israeli troops stormed a bus that had been hijacked by four armed Arabs. A passenger was killed, but the other thirty-four Israeli hostages were released. Two of the Arab terrorists were killed in the gunfire, but the fate of the other two caused a storm of controversy. An Israeli army spokesman said that they had died on their way to the hospital. A few hours later, their bodies were turned over to relatives for burial. Yet a photograph surfaced showing the Israeli security men leading one of the men away from the scene, apparently uninjured. Several weeks later, a commission of inquiry concluded that the Israeli security men had taken the offenders into a field and beaten them to death. The case illustrates the volatile nature of the Gaza Strip.

The growth of Israeli settler vigilante groups committed to carrying out violent reprisals against Arabs and their counterparts—Arab terrorists committed to violence against Jews—has disturbed many Israelis, who see it as a sign of deterioration in the quality of Israeli society and morality. There is growing concern about the price Israel must pay for the continued occupation and administration of Gaza. Israel has been forced to spend great amounts of money on developing the infrastructure of the Gaza Strip, money that is increasingly seen as being better spent elsewhere.

Under the leadership of Menachem Begin, Israel was rigidly committed to retaining all of the land within its biblical borders, including the Gaza Strip. Under his successor, Prime Minister Shimon Peres, Israel is much more likely to recognize the principle of negotiating the status of the Gaza Strip in accordance with UN Security Council resolutions. Peres's more flexible attitude toward negotiations with the Arabs is in line with the traditional Labor Alignment party position of reaching accords with the Arab populations in the area.

In early 1985, Jordan's King Hussein and Yasir Arafat, head of the largest branch of the Palestine Liberation Organization (PLO), announced that they were working on a formula for beginning a bargaining process with Israel. They hoped to reach some kind of peaceful settlement in the Gaza Strip and the other territories occupied by Israel.

Golan Heights

Perspective

1946	*Syria becomes fully independent from French League of Nations mandate. Historically Golan Heights is part of Syria.*
1948– 1967	*With establishment of state of Israel, Syrian gunmen use Golan Heights to harass Israeli settlements.*
1966	*Coup d'état brings extremist regime into power. Attacks on Israel from Golan Heights escalate.*
1967	*During Six-Day War, Israelis capture Golan Heights.*
1974	*Following another conflict, Syria and Israel agree to "area of separation" between their forces patrolled by UN.*
1981	*Menachem Begin announces that Israel has annexed Golan Heights.*
1985	*United States State Department holds that peace-for-territory bargain in Middle East applies to all Israeli fronts, including Golan Heights.*

T he Golan Heights is a strategic hilly region on the border separating Syria and Israel. Traditionally a part of Syria, the region remained a part of the new nation in 1946, when Syria gained its independence from France. The hills were fortified by Arab forces during the 1947-to-1948 Arab-Israeli war. After the Jewish state of Israel was founded in 1948, Arab artillery embedded in the heights heavily damaged new Israeli settlements across the border.

In the Six-Day War of 1967, Israel attacked and occupied the Golan Heights. Israel announced that, along with other Arab-conquered lands, the Golan Heights would be returned to Syria only after substantive progress was made in improving Israeli-Arab relations.

After the 1973 Arab-Israeli war, Israel and Syria agreed to an "area of separation" between their forces; this demilitarized zone ranges from about one thousand yards to three miles (one to five kilometers) in width and stretches for forty-eight miles (seventy-seven kilometers). An international force under the auspices of the UN patrols the buffer zone; it is regarded as one of the more successful of UN peacekeeping missions. United States and Soviet officers work together in truce-supervision offices in Cairo and Damascus. The truce held even during Israel's invasion of Lebanon in 1982.

Issues and Events

A near crisis occurred in 1981 when Israeli prime minister Menachem Begin announced that Israel was annexing the Golan Heights. The Israeli legislature, or Knesset, promptly approved the annexation by a wide margin.

It was a highly popular move in Israeli quarters, particularly among the seven thousand Israeli settlers in the Golan Heights. It was less popular among the Syrian population there.

The Israeli action was denounced in most of the rest of the world. The UN Security Council voted unanimously to declare the annexation null and void. The United States protested the action by suspending $300 million in special aid to Israel. Syria led the denunciations that came from the Arab world; but Syrian president Hafez Assad, with large numbers of troops bogged down in Lebanon, was unable to counter the action. Begin was adamant on the action; it was an important step in the fulfillment of a cherished dream: an Israel that encompassed all its biblical territories.

Meanwhile, the ruggedly beautiful plateau has become a tourist attraction. Vacationers take photographs of the wrecks of tanks and trucks destroyed in the Israeli-Syrian clashes of 1967 and 1973.

The Arabs and Druzes who live on the Golan Heights are divided on the subject of Israeli annexation. The Druzes, an important minority sect in Syria and Lebanon, who number about 12,500 in the Golan, are generally more friendly toward Israel than the traditional Muslims. A small minority have accepted Israeli citizenship. Most of the Muslims are opposed to the annexation and support the Syrians, who consider recovery of the Golan a sacred cause.

The Syrians, not being in any position to reopen hostilities with Israel, have been forced to rely on diplomacy and international public opinion. Syria has claimed itself to be the victim of unprovoked Israeli aggression and has used the Israeli occupation and annexation of the Golan as a further reason for refusing to recognize the existence of the state of Israel.

While achieving some propaganda successes, Syria seems unable to alter the status quo in the Golan Heights. However, Syrian power appears to be growing in other areas—and that growth may eventually affect the Golan.

In general, President Assad seems to be concentrating on efforts to increase the discontent of the fundamentalist Shiite Muslims living in the Israeli-occupied West Bank, giving a lower priority to the Syrian ambitions to regain its sovereignty over the Golan Heights.

West Bank

Perspective

1922	*Palestine west of Jordan River becomes part to which term "British mandate for Palestine" is restricted; eastern part becomes Transjordan and later Jordan.*
1948– 1949	*During Arab-Israeli War, Jordan seizes and occupies West Bank.*
1950	*Jordan annexes West Bank.*
1967	*In Six-Day War, Israel seizes and occupies West Bank. Israeli settlement begins.*
1977	*Under Prime Minister Menachem Begin, Israel increases settlements.*
1981	*Begin declares that Israel will never leave Judea or Samaria, ancient names for West Bank.*
1984	*Jewish settlers in West Bank are accused of anti-Arab terrorism.*

O f all the issues that separate Israel from its Arab neighbors, nothing so inflames emotions as Israel's occupation and settlement of the West Bank. International criticism of Israel's settlement policy of the territory notwithstanding, Israel has consistently carried out a policy of planting such a large Jewish population in the West Bank that its return to Jordan would never be feasible.

The seeds of the modern dilemma go back to the years following World War I, when the British mandate for Palestine was established. That mandate included land west of the Jordan River. The land immediately east of the river became known as Transjordan, later Jordan. During the first Arab-Israeli war, from 1948 to 1949, the Hashemite Kingdom of Jordan seized and occupied a portion of the former mandate on the west bank of the river. Known as the West Bank, it was annexed by Jordan in 1950 and continued to be governed by that nation until the Six-Day War of 1967. At that time, Israel quickly overran the West Bank, forced out the Jordanian army, and occupied the territory. Jewish settlement of the West Bank began almost immediately, and in 1981 Israel announced that it had no intention of giving up the territory, that it in fact represented the biblical Judea and Samaria, and that it traditionally belonged to the Jewish people.

Issues and Events

By the mid-1980s, the total number of Jewish settlers, exclusive of East Jerusalem, in the West Bank was more than 40,000; there were about 9,000 Jewish families living in more than one hundred settlements. It was expected that the number of settlers would total 100,000 by 1990. Over half the Jewish settlers live in large communities that are in effect suburbs of Tel Aviv–Yafo and Jerusalem. Most of the new building being carried out by the Israeli government is concentrated in these large urban centers.

Since 1981 the West Bank has been governed by regional councils. They have changed the West Bank's status from a frontier zone into a normal part of the Israeli administrative system, receiving funds from the different ministries just like any other municipality. Although this continuing process of integration has achieved a momentum of its own, it could be slowed considerably by Israel's massive unsolved economic woes. There have been complaints that individual builders and major contractors have been hit by a slowdown because the government has had to make severe budget cuts on such basic West Bank projects as roads, sewers, and electrical lines.

But probably the most serious problem of Israel's annexation of the West Bank is its large Arab population: over 600,000 and growing, due to a high birth rate. The presence of such a large non-Jewish population within Israel would in time drastically alter the character of what was originally devised as a Jewish state.

The immediate problem of the large Arab population is its opposition to Jewish occupation of the territory. Despite a tough military program to root out all support for the Palestine Liberation Organization (PLO), there is no question of the PLO's popularity there. Violence has been the inevitable result. By the 1980s, Arab violence was endangering travel in the West Bank; and Jewish vigilante groups sprang up to impose law and order in the territory. In 1984 about twenty-five settlers were accused of organized terrorist activities. Among them were leaders of the West Bank Jewish settlements and Israeli army officers. They were suspected of several notorious attacks, including the attempted murder of Arab mayors in towns in the West Bank.

Terrorism—both Arab and Jewish—in the West Bank has had a polarizing effect on Israel's population. Most politicians condemned acts of Jewish terrorism; and both of the nation's major political parties, Labor Alignment and Likud, called for prosecution of the Jewish underground responsible for the acts. But a few right-wing groups, including the militant settlers' organization Gush Emunim, "bloc of the faithful," blamed the government for failing to protect Jewish settlers in the West Bank, forcing the settlers to take the law into their own hands.

Iran and Iraq: Gulf War

Perspective

1935   *International body awards Iraq control
over Shatt-al-Arab, important
waterway emptying into Persian Gulf.*

1980   *Iran revives its claim to sovereignty
over Shatt-al-Arab.*

September 22. *Iraq bombs Tehrān
airport and three other Iranian airfields,
thereby starting war.*

September 23. *Iraq attacks Iran's huge
oil refineries at Ābādān.*

October. *Jordan declares its support of
Iraq. Libya declares its support of Iran.*

November. *Fighting centers in Iran's
Khūzestān province. Kuwait accuses
Iran of rocket attack; Saudi Arabia
announces its intention of aiding in
defense of Kuwait.*

December. *War is extended to entire
border between Iran and Iraq.*

1981   **April.** *Islamic Commission fails to
achieve cease-fire.*

September. *Iran claims to have broken
Iraqi siege of Ābādān.*

1982   **April 18.** *Syria closes pipeline through
its territory, thereby denying Iraqi oil
access to Mediterranean.*

June. *Iraq offers to withdraw from
Iranian territory and institutes
unilateral cease-fire; Iran vows to
continue war.*

1983   **February 7.** *Iran launches offensive that
recovers some land lost to Iraq.*

1984   **February.** *War escalates as Iraq
attempts blockade of Kharg Island.*

May. *Both sides begin attacking foreign
ships in Persian Gulf.*

June. *Secretary-general of UN works
out agreement whereby both sides
agree not to attack residential areas.*

December. *Lull in war ends with
attacks on foreign oil tankers.*

1985   **March 5.** *Iranian forces shell Basra; Iraq
claims attack violated June 1984
agreement.*

T he 1980s, like the decades that preceded
them, witnessed turmoil in virtually every
part of the Middle East: Israel still faced hostile
Arab neighbors, and Lebanon was disintegra-
ting as a nation as Muslim and Christian factions

battled for control. For the first time, however, a
major conflict between two Muslim nations—
Iran and Iraq—played a significant role in the
turmoil. At times fierce, the war has had long
periods of relatively inactive stalemate since it
began in 1980.

In ordinary circumstances the border war between Iran and Iraq would have been regarded
as a purely local war. It quickly assumed worldwide importance because it threatened international access to the Persian Gulf, through which
passes 60 percent of the world's petroleum—petroleum that is the lifeblood of the industry of
much of the world. The causes of the war were
rooted in historical conflicts between the two nations over control of the Shatt-al-Arab waterway
that forms part of their mutual border and in rivalry between the Sunni and the Shiite Muslims,
the two major factions of Islam. Iraq, while governed by the Sunnis, has a Shiite majority; revolutionary Shiite Iran wanted to export its
ideology to Iraq. As always in the Middle East,
the economic importance of oil, of which Iran and
Iraq are both major producers, heightened
tensions.

At the beginning of the Persian Gulf war in
1980, the economies of the world's nations were
still suffering from the dislocations brought on
by the oil boycotts of the 1970s and by the resultant rise in oil prices.

The Muslim world had an additional concern.
After the fall of the shah, Iran had become an
Islamic republic—in fact a theocracy—under the
control of the most militant wing of the Shiite
branch of Islam. The leader of the Iranian Shiites,
Ayatollah Ruhollah Khomeini, became the absolute ruler of Iran, and his regime began eliminating political opposition in the nation. In addition,
he began calling for revolution throughout the
Muslim world, revolution that would replace the
existing governments with fundamentalist Islamic theocracies based on the Iranian model.
Since most of the nations of the Middle East had
large Shiite Muslim communities within their
borders, those nations took the threat of uprisings quite seriously.

Khomeini was especially aiming his revolutionary rhetoric at the Shiites in Iraq, where they
constitute a majority, but his words were carefully listened to—and feared—by the conservative rulers of the oil-producing states of the
Persian Gulf region, especially the conservative
ruling family of Saudi Arabia. The Saudis became
the major backer of Iraq in the war.

Issues and Events

In February 1985, the Iraqis went on the offensive. After about two years of hoping for peace

negotiations, they again began putting pressure on the Iranians. In the south, the offensive centered on the Majnoon islands. Iraq claimed to have retaken virtually all the territory seized by Iran. The Iraquis also made an attack along Iran's northern border. On March 5, the Iranians retaliated by shelling Basra. The Iraquis claimed that the attack on Basra violated a UN agreement of the previous year. Shellings of cities on both sides of the border followed, rekindling fears in the civilian populations in the south.

With no sign of peace negotiations in the immediate future, the war dragged on. For a "small border war," the losses have been severe: an estimated 250,000 dead plus 500,000 wounded on each side.

International fears about the effects of the war have not, for the most part, been realized. Despite threats and sporadic attacks by both sides, the Strait of Hormuz remains open. The movement of crude oil out of the Persian Gulf has not been so severely restricted as to have an adverse effect on the economies of the nations that depend on that oil.

The economic consequences of the war have turned out to be less than anyone would have predicted five years earlier. The worldwide economic recession of the early 1980s, coupled with oil conservation programs in most countries of the world, caused a significant drop in the demand for oil. Members of the Organization of Petroleum Exporting Countries (OPEC) for the first time found themselves unable to agree on voluntary limitations on the production of crude oil and on the worldwide price structure. As production exceeded demand, prices fell. All of this meant that the reduced production of oil in Iran and Iraq had no deleterious effects on the world economy.

The fear of Islamic fundamentalism remains a real one among some in the conservative Persian Gulf states, but after more than six years, the Khomeini regime in Iran is no longer looked upon with the former dread. During that period, not one Muslim country had seen its government fall to the fundamentalists. Despite the rhetoric of Iran's Islamic republic, most Persian Gulf nations are in fact working to normalize relations with Iran.

Background

The Shatt-al-Arab is a tidal river formed by the confluence of the Tigris and Euphrates rivers. It flows south for 120 miles (195 kilometers) and empties into the Persian Gulf. The Tigris and Euphrates—and the Shatt-al-Arab—form the major waterway for a large part of that section of the Middle East and are of crucial importance to both Iran and Iraq. Sovereignty over the Shatt-al-Arab has long been claimed by both countries. In 1935 an international commission awarded sovereignty to Iraq. Iran had no choice then but to accept the commission's findings, but its loss of the waterway continued to be a matter of national shame. The highly nationalistic Khomeini government regarded the recovery of the Shatt-al-Arab as a matter of national pride.

Relations between Iran and Iraq had generally worsened since the overthrow of Iran's monarchy. Iraq's president, Saddam Hussein, was convinced that the Iranian radical Muslims were deliberately fostering discontent among Iraq's Shiite Muslims, a matter of great concern to the rulers in Iraq; the Sunni Muslims, who controlled the government, were in fact outnumbered in Iraq by members of the Shiite sect.

Although it was the Iranians who wished to regain control of the Shatt-al-Arab, the Iraqis actually began the war as a preventive measure. Obviously believing that Iran was badly weakened by the revolutionary activities in the country, Iraq opened hostilities on September 22, 1980, by attacking Tehrān airport and three other Iranian airfields. Iran quickly retaliated by attacking Iraqi bases.

From the beginning, it was a difficult war to interpret. Both sides for the most part did not allow reporters in the area of the war, and the world media were forced to rely on official reports from the two sides and on carefully selected television films. Both sides made extravagant claims about their own victories.

Despite the shortage of hard news from the war front, it was clear that Iraq was winning in the early days of the war. Iraq attacked in Iran's oil-rich Khūzestān province. Iraqi troops penetrated fifty miles (eighty kilometers) into Iran but encountered stiff resistance and were forced to halt their advance. The war became stalemated on that front; but in late October Iraq took Khorramshahr, the Iranian port city adjacent to Ābādān. Iran, for its part, bombed Baghdād and several oil centers in northern Iraq.

Most foreign nations were reluctant to take sides in the war and hoped that the hostilities would end before petroleum shipping was curtailed. Nevertheless, it was inevitable that nations could not remain neutral. Iraq's armed forces had been largely supplied by the Soviet Union, and Iraq had long had close political and economic ties with France. In October 1980 Jordan declared its support of Iraq. Kuwait accused Iran of a rocket attack on its territory near the war zone, and Saudi Arabia declared itself ready to come to the defense of Kuwait if called upon. The United States was in something of a quandary. Its relations with Iran were at an all-time low—the American hostages were still being held in the American Embassy in Tehrān; but the United States was reluctant to come to the aid of Iraq, which was widely regarded as a tool of the Soviet Union. The United States government, which has important oil interests in the area, confined itself to announcing its intention of maintaining access to the Strait of Hormuz by the world's oil tankers. (Virtually all Persian Gulf oil must pass through the strait on its way to world markets.) In a further indication of United States sentiments, President Carter, despite considerable pro-Israeli pressure from the Congress, sold several AWAC spy planes to Saudi Arabia in order to boost its defenses against a possible Iranian attack. Only Libya announced support for Iran.

On the face of it, Iran seemed to have most of the advantages in its confrontation with Iraq. It is a much larger country, both in area (about 636,000 square miles, or 1,648,000 square kilometers, to about 168,000 square miles, or 435,000 square kilometers, for Iraq) and in population (44.5 million to 15.3 million). Iran is believed to have a much larger army: about 550,000 men, plus up to 250,000 paramilitary forces. Iraq is estimated to have about 640,000 men in uniform. Only in its air force was Iraq superior. Its more than five hundred planes were both more sophisticated and more numerous than the approximately 100 warplanes of Iran. Most of Iran's planes were, in fact, aging United States aircraft that had originally been sold to Iran during the shah's regime; whether they remained airworthy was a large question.

Iraq was not able to maintain its early chain of victories, and in 1981 the war became increasingly stalemated. In April the Islamic Commission, a body comprising most of the Arab powers, tried and failed to achieve a cease-fire. In September, Iran claimed to have broken the Iraqi siege of Ābādān, which had been under daily bombardment for a year.

Iran continued to improve its position in 1982. In early June it announced that it had retaken Khorramshahr from the Iraqis—along with thirty thousand Iraqi prisoners of war. Later that month, Iraq offered to withdraw from all Iranian territory in exchange for a cease-fire. When Iran did not respond, Iraq began a unilateral cease-fire. Iran became increasingly belligerent, stating that it would not honor a cease-fire even if Iraq evacuated all Iranian territory.

In October 1982 the war escalated once again, with each side claiming gains. In fact, there was little change in the two positions, although eighty thousand men had been killed, two hundred thousand wounded, and forty thousand taken prisoner.

In 1984 the war heated up once again. In February and March, the fighting centered on the man-made islands of Majnoon, located in the marshland north of Basra. It was during this campaign that the Iranian use of its "human waves" of troops was first reported. These human waves were made up of tens of thousands of untrained teenagers, some believed to be as young as twelve, who were members of the Islamic Revolutionary Guard and the Mobilization Corps. It was also during this campaign that the Iranians accused the Iraqis of using chemical warfare against those human waves.

In the spring of 1984, Iranian troops estimated at 350,000 were massed for a major offensive; but the summer came and went with no Iranian attack forthcoming. This puzzling lack of action is perhaps explained by Iraq's threat that it would destroy the Iranian oil facilities on Kharg Island in retaliation for any attack by Iran. Iran moves 80 percent of its oil through Kharg Island and perhaps was not willing to test the air strength of Iraq.

In May the war took a suddenly ominous turn. Both sides, each hoping to damage the other, began attacking foreign ships in the Persian Gulf. President Hussein called on foreign nations, including "Arab brothers," to stop using the Iranian facilities on Kharg Island and attacked two Saudi Arabian tankers in the vicinity. The United States reiterated its intention of seeing that the Strait of Hormuz remained open to international shipping. The attacks continued; in the ensuing months Indian, Greek, Cypriot, and Spanish ships were attacked. In June 1984, Javier Pérez de Cuéllar, secretary-general of the United Nations, succeeded for the first time in arranging a partial cease-fire: both sides agreed not to attack areas with large civilian populations.

Khomeini, Ayatollah Ruhollah—Iranian head of government (1979–   ) and spiritual leader of Iran's Shiite Muslims. Born in Khumain in northeast Iran in 1900 . . . became prominent Islamic scholar and teacher. . . . was exiled to France (1964–1978) because of his severe criticism of Shah Mohammed Reza Pahlavi. . . . returned to Iran to lead a revolution that ousted the shah and placed Khomeini in control of the government (1979) . . . instituted an Islamic fundamentalist regime that faced civil war, conflict with Iraq, and international isolation.

Libya:
The Enigmatic Qadhafi

Perspective

1942– 1943	Britain expels Germans and Italians.
1949	**June.** Britain recognizes Mohammed Idris al-Senussi as emir.
1951	**December 24.** Idris is named king of United Kingdom of Libya.
1963	Qadhafi graduates from University of Libya.
1965	Qadhafi graduates from Libyan Military College with associates from Secret Unionist Free Officers Movement; enters Libyan army.
1969	**September 1.** King Idris is overthrown. Revolutionary Command Council proclaims republic.
1973	**August.** Qadhafi successfully takes control of foreign-held oil interests.
1977	Short war is fought with Egypt. Association with Palestine Liberation Organization (PLO) is evident. Relations with West begin to cool.
1979	Qadhafi resigns as secretary-general of General People's Congress.
1979– 1983	Libya steps up incursions into Chad to prop up pro-Qadhafi regime.
1981	**May.** United States expels all Libyan diplomats.
	August. United States and Libyan planes engage in dogfight over Khalij Surt (Gulf of Sidra); one Libyan jet is shot down.
1984	**May.** Qadhafi survives assassination attempt in Tripoli.
1985	**February 24.** Qadhafi urges black United States servicemen to create separate army.

Colonel Mu'ammar al-Qadhafi, the head of state of the Socialist People's Libyan Arab Jamahiriya, or Libya, is a favorite villain in the Western press and is even at times characterized as a "madman." Relations between Libya and the West, notably the United States, have been especially bitter. The United States, and most of the other Western powers, have objected in particular to Qadhafi's support, financial and otherwise, of international terrorist organizations. He has been the chief supporter of the Palestine Lib-eration Organization (PLO), and his denunciations of Israel have been particularly virulent. He has also angered other African leaders by his territorial ambitions, notably in Chad and the Sudan, which have had a disruptive influence on African political affairs. Qadhafi's power is a direct result of the petroleum revenues that have been at his disposal since the mid-1970s, when the Arab oil boycotts caused the world price of oil to escalate dramatically.

Issues and Events

The form of socialism that Qadhafi's regime has introduced into Libya undermines the traditional power of tribal leaders and restricts private ownership of business and real estate. Qadhafi characterizes this socialism as the *jamahiriya*, or "state of the masses." He draws inspiration from a personal interpretation of Islam not always congruent with the views held by Muslim clergy, emphasizing a direct relationship between believers and God.

Previously many of Libya's assets have been used to strengthen its military forces. The Libyan navy is an important presence in the Mediterranean, a large fraction of its personnel having been trained by the Soviet Union. The country's army and air force are also well equipped. However, Libya, like the other members of the Organization of Petroleum Exporting Countries (OPEC), found its revenues declining in the 1980s as world oil prices fell. Budget cutbacks have resulted, and several important military projects have been cancelled. It is clear that Qadhafi is aware of the importance of Libya's oil revenues to his country's influence in the world. His policies reflect his determination to see that his country will survive even when the oil runs out.

Background

Following Libya's independence from Italian colonial rule after World War II, the country was ruled by Emir Mohammed Idris al-Senussi. Idris became king in 1951, with British and French interests transferring their powers to the federal government in accordance with UN decisions handed down in 1949 and 1950.

The government granted access to the United States, Great Britain, and France to construct military bases in the country. Many segments of the Libyan population viewed these bases with hostility, regarding them as staging areas for the West's support of Israel, to which Libya's Arab population was totally opposed.

Libya's officialdom, doling out limited concessions to foreign interests, became corrupt. The resources of Libya were funneled into the pockets of foreigners and the elite Libyan minority, while the general population became increasingly poor.

During the years of his schooling, Qadhafi became increasingly convinced that his country was being exploited by imperialists. He became an earnest and dedicated revolutionary, enlisting the aid of like-minded schoolmates, who followed him into the Libyan army. In the army he gathered about himself a cadre of young revolutionaries convinced that a military context was the only means through which Libya could be changed. Axiomatic was the belief that the ruling elite would resist any form of social or political reform; and Qadhafi had seen early on that the vital resource of oil was finite—its use as an economic tool to force political change was clearly imperative.

The Free Officers' Union of the Libyan army staged a military coup on September 1, 1969, under Lieutenant Mu'ammar al-Qadhafi. Within four hours the country was under the control of the Revolutionary Command Council (RCC).

As chairman of the council, Qadhafi quickly moved to institute massive economic and religious reforms. He promoted public works, granted major wage increases, and laid the foundations for a working welfare system. Strict adherence to Koranic law was imposed. Qadhafi launched a cultural revolution to free Libya from foreign influences. He threatened to nationalize the oil industry unless the companies agreed to increase Libya's share of the profits. When the oil companies acquiesced, Qadhafi was spurred to try for wider Arab unity, using oil as a political weapon.

During this period his regime was being actively wooed by foreign interests. The United States Central Intelligence Agency (CIA) warned him of at least two attempts to overthrow him. Qadhafi learned quickly that in the complex Middle Eastern world of fluid alliances and intelligence leaks and rumors he needed to give priority to the buildup of Libyan intelligence. He became the primary PLO sponsor and offered financial support and political asylum to international terrorist groups.

Other Arab leaders were suspicious of Qadhafi's motives, unsure of his methods, and otherwise occupied with their own internal problems. Relations deteriorated to the point where Libya and Egypt fought a brief war in 1977. His territorial ambitions in Chad and the Sudan have particularly alarmed his fellow African leaders.

In 1979 Qadhafi resigned as secretary-general of the General People's Congress, the governing organization that succeeded the RCC in 1977, to work to "further the revolution." He remained the ideological voice and leader of the Revolutionary Committees. These committees originated the liquidation orders aimed at several "enemies of the revolution" in the late 1970s and early 1980s.

Other African leaders have viewed Qadhafi as too radical and uncompromising. As a result, Libya has been shunned by its neighbors. This isolation, and the views of the Western media, make it all but impossible to know what is going on in Libya.

It is important to remember that Qadhafi is of Bedouin stock. The Bedouin life-style is alien to Westerners, embodying sparse, puritanical principles. Courage, dignity, vengeance, honor, and independence mean far more to the Bedouin than does luxury or "civilized" concerns. To the Bedouin, dangerous men are to be respected—and shame, as to the Oriental, is the biggest threat of all. The Bedouin world is one of constantly shifting allegiances, swings of power and influence, and continuous mergers and feuds. This is one reason that Middle Eastern alliances are always changing—the purpose of the moment is served, rather than any enduring agreement.

The cutbacks in Libyan economic planning caused by decreased oil revenues have had impact not only on the military but also on large-scale industrial and agricultural projects. The vast amounts of money spent on arms, while necessary in the early years of Qadhafi's regime, are now seen by some Libyan scholars as indicative of a lack of realistic long-range planning. Libyans are increasingly aware that the country's domestic policies need to become more practical, that foreign ventures such as the support of terrorism need to be reevaluated. It is too soon to say whether Qadhafi is willing to spend as much effort on agricultural and industrial activity as on antiimperialistic campaigning.

Mu'ammar Muhammad al-Qadhafi—Libyan leader and head of government. Born in the desert near Tripoli in 1942 . . . graduated from the University of Libya (1963) and Libyan Military College (1965) . . . led a military coup overthrowing King Idris (1969) . . . became president of the Revolutionary Command Council (1969–1977) and secretary of the General People's Congress (1977–1979) then continued rule with no formal title . . . was known as a fundamentalist Muslim and Arab nationalist . . . was influential in the world oil market and encouraged international terrorism.

Sub-Saharan Africa

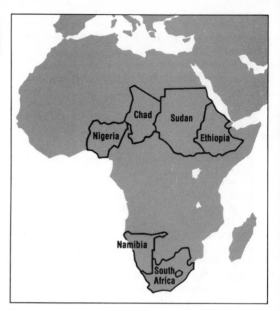

As the twentieth century nears its final decade, Africa—especially that part south of the Sahara—is beset by problems that most of the rest of the world has solved or at least alleviated to a large degree. Widespread famine is the most serious issue, and it is accompanied by the related problem of an out-of-control population explosion. Southern Africa is still torn by conflicts arising from colonial policies of the past, including land distribution, racial and ethnic rivalries, and religious divisions. Nigeria, with its enormous oil deposits, made what appeared to be great economic strides in the 1970s. But the collapse of the world market for oil in the 1980s made it especially vulnerable; it suffered from the same kinds of problems faced by industrial nations in economic recession while still trying to cope with the strains present in a developing nation.

During the early 1980s a widespread and long-lasting drought struck the middle of Africa. Its effects were felt most by the already poverty-stricken nomadic and seminomadic peoples of the area. Accustomed to living just above the starvation level in even the best years, these peoples died by the hundreds of thousands. Worldwide efforts to rush relief to the famine victims resulted in vast amounts of food finding its way to mid-Africa, but it is believed that inefficient government agencies have slowed food distribution. Despite those relief efforts, experts agreed that the real cure for the famine would come only when the drought ended.

In southern Africa, especially in the Republic of South Africa, racial tensions are getting worse. The black, Colored (people of mixed racial heritage), and Asian populations are dissatisfied with the apartheid (racial separation) policies of the white-minority government. Despite efforts of the government to set up black "homelands," and constitutional reforms that allow a minimum political role for nonblack minorities, the large black majority is becoming increasingly restive. Strikes, job actions, demonstrations, and other forms of civil disobedience are widespread, and despite the state of emergency declared in the summer of 1985, disturbances continue and the death toll of blacks is growing amid increasing international scrutiny.

Namibia and Angola also continue to suffer from problems left over from colonial days. Angola, long a Portuguese colony, is finding it difficult to achieve and maintain its status as an independent republic, while Namibia has been trying to free itself of imperialism since World War I. A former German colony, it found itself after that war in the unique position of being in effect the colony of another colony, the Union (now Republic) of South Africa. Since World War II, South Africa has consistently refused to relinquish its control over Namibia, despite orders to do so by the United Nations, in part because it serves as a buffer state between South Africa and its black-ruled neighbors.

Sudan: Refugees, Civil War, and Military Coup

Perspective

1896–1898	*British and Egyptian forces conquer Sudan.*
1952	*British and Egyptians begin preparations for Sudanese independence.*
1956	*British leave Sudan.*
1969	*Military coup removes democratic government. Al-Jaafar Nimeiry comes to power.*
1972	*Nimeiry's government and rebels in southern Sudan sign Addis Ababa accord.*
1985	**January.** *Two million to four million Sudanese are affected by drought. Sudan is unable to make interest payments on loans.*
	February. *United States freezes $114 million in economic aid. Libya offers to fill aid gap.*
	March. *United States vice-president Bush visits Sudan.*
	April 6. *Nimeiry is overthrown by General Dahab following food riots and general strike.*

United States vice-president George Bush's trip to Sudan in early March 1985, focused attention on a country enmeshed in turbulent activity: Sudan was the site of overflowing relief camps for Ethiopian drought and famine victims. The Sudanese themselves are now being affected by the rain and food shortages that all Africa suffers. Economic instability, an ongoing civil war with rebels in the south, and the repressive regime of Al-Jaafar Nimeiry led in early April 1985 to a revolution in which Nimeiry was overthrown and General Siwar el-Dahab (Swareddahab) assumed power.

Issues and Events

From April through June 1985, Dahab set up a military council and then appointed an interim civilian cabinet. He reaffirmed Sudan's allegiance to the United States but also made overtures to pro-Soviet Ethiopia and Libya, possibly with a view toward ending their support of the southern Sudan rebels. Overtures to the rebels, including offers of a cease-fire and a general amnesty; the reunion of the three southern subregions created by Nimeiry; and an agreement to

abide by the 1972 Addis Ababa accord, which granted limited self-rule to the south, have so far failed to gain acceptance from the rebels, who demand a civilian government and an end to Islamic law, which Dahab has offered to amend but not to end.

The new government still faces the overwhelming problems of a $9 billion foreign debt, the civil war, and the estimated one million Ethiopian refugees and four million or more Sudanese affected by the African drought and famine. With numerous relief agencies concentrating on Sudan's overflowing medical and relief camps, it is hoped that Sudan will be able to compensate for the loss, due to drought, of half the country's normal harvest of two million metric tons of sorghum.

Background

Between 1896 and 1898, British and Egyptian forces under the future Lord Kitchener conquered Sudan. In 1952 the two countries began planning to relinquish power in the Sudan in 1956. The southern Sudanese, mostly Christians and animists, were afraid that northern Muslims would be too dominant a political power in the independent government, and started a revolt that still continues. Despite this, Sudan attained its independence in 1956.

In 1969 Colonel Nimeiry seized control of the government in a military coup. He established a leftist government, abolishing political parties and nationalizing most industries and banks. In 1972 he signed the Addis Ababa pact with the southern Sudanese, granting them some autonomy and temporarily halting the civil war.

President Nimeiry imposed a national state of Islamic law in 1984, despite opposition from Christians and animists in the south (approximately one-fifth of the population), giving rise to insurgency throughout the country. In early 1985, Nimeiry's government faced the serious problem of not being able to make the interest payments on the country's $9 billion debt to the International Monetary Fund, and in February 1985 the United States cut off aid until the government could make arrangements for payment of the interest due. In an austerity move, Nimeiry lifted government subsidies on such essentials as bread and gasoline, which resulted in skyrocketing prices and food riots.

While Nimeiry was in the United States and Egypt in early April, there was a general strike, with the workers calling for the ouster of Nimeiry. On the day of his arrival in Egypt, April 6, Nimeiry's government was overthrown by General Siwar el-Dahab, whom Nimeiry had appointed defense minister.

Ethiopia: Famine's Impact

Perspective

1930   *Haile Selassie becomes emperor of Ethiopia and shortly thereafter gives Ethiopia its first constitution.*

1955   *Constitution is revised to provide for appointed Senate and elected lower house.*

1962   *Ethiopia absorbs former Italian colony of Eritrea. Eritrean guerrillas begin fight to regain control of their homeland, a civil war that continues.*

1971   *Drought begins in northern provinces of Wollo and Tigre; Selassie endeavors to cover up seriousness of situation.*

1974   *September. Haile Selassie is overthrown in military coup. Eventually Mengistu Haile Mariam takes over as leader of government.*

1982   *Serious drought arises when rain does not fall in most of country.*

1984   *August. World attention begins to focus on relief-agency reports stating that famine in Africa has grown to overwhelming proportions.*

        September. Government celebrates ten-year anniversary of military takeover. Formation of Communist party led by Mengistu is announced. Mengistu calls for world assistance in famine relief.

        December. Death estimates range from 400,000 to more than a million.

1985   *February. Mengistu announces seven-point austerity plan, outlining steps to end famine crisis.*

        Spring. International relief efforts continue.

S ince 1984, world attention has focused on Ethiopia, where continued drought has created a famine. According to a report made public by the UN in August 1984, more than seven million Ethiopians then faced the threat of starvation. A large part of Ethiopia's population lives on the edge of poverty even in the best years and is especially vulnerable to drought. Parts of the northern region of the country have not received rain or harvested food in ten years. In the south as well, effects of the rain shortage are being felt. As bad as 1984 was, most predictions saw 1985 as even worse. The refugees, returning to Ethiopia from adjoining countries such as Somalia or Sudan, where shortages are now equally serious, are adding two million individuals to the five million already suffering in the country.

In addition, foreign relief-agency officials say that relief efforts are complicated by lack of roads, guerrilla warfare in some provinces, and the remoteness of affected areas. Some of these officials charge that the Ethiopian government could have predicted the famine as early as two years before it struck and taken precautions to ameliorate its worst effects. It has also been accused of failing to use the equipment and funds provided for aiding victims, spending aid money on elaborate and expensive celebrations of the tenth anniversary of the overthrow of Emperor Haile Selassie and on the formation of a Communist party in Ethiopia. Other criticisms revolve around the large amounts spent by Ethiopia on its armed forces—to the detriment of its famine victims. Relief-agency officials have also charged that promised food has been withheld from the areas of Eritrea and Tigre, where secessionist guerrillas are based.

Issues and Events

By February 1985 some relief officials estimated that as many as a half-million people had died in Ethiopia alone, at least seven million people were believed to be starving, and perhaps twenty million in total were thought to be affected on the entire African continent. Ethiopia, like many African nations, is highly susceptible to drought, although its economy and people remain dependent on agriculture. The effects of previous droughts, soil erosion, and deforestation already plagued commercial and subsistence farming when planting-season rains failed to fall in thirteen of the fourteen provinces in 1982. Severe famine was the result. Exacerbating the problem was an ethnically diverse populace marked by disunity, political instability, and ongoing guerrilla warfare.

Difficult access into and around Ethiopia has increased the problems of getting food to famine victims. Less than 15 percent of the populace lives in urban areas; most inhabit mountain villages that are inaccessible to vehicles of any variety. In addition, the country's port system is too antiquated to accept more than 50,000 tons of food a month. The Ethiopian government estimated that 1.2 million metric tons were needed for 1985 but received pledges for less than one-third that amount.

On February 10, 1985, Mengistu Haile Mariam, Ethiopia's head of state, implemented a seven-point austerity program designed to improve the desperate situation. Measures included tightening import controls on nonessential items, rationing petroleum, and encouraging contributions of time and money to the relief effort by Ethiopians. Reactions to Mengistu's announcement were mixed: some Western officials felt that Mengistu was stating his commitment to a Soviet-style economic system, while others felt that Mengistu's plan was the first sign that Ethiopia would commit its own resources to ending the crisis and hailed the plan as a step in the right direction.

Also in February 1985, UN officials announced that nineteen ships carrying one-tenth of Ethiopia's anticipated needs for 1985 could be expected by the end of the month. Italy, West Germany, and the Soviet Union promised to donate trucks to move food from ports to warehouses and relief centers. Early spring saw the beginning of rain in parts of Ethiopia, but a cautious optimism was tempered by fears that the farmers lacked the seed, tools, and oxen needed for planting.

Background

Haile Selassie gave Ethiopia its first constitution shortly after taking the throne in 1930. A descendant of Ethiopia's ruling family, Selassie could trace his ancestry back over 2,400 years, legend has it, to a ruler who was the son of King Solomon and the Queen of Sheba. Selassie's 44-year reign was notable for its enduring and autocratic nature: the constitution stated that "the person of the Emperor is sacred, his dignity is inviolable, and his power indisputable."

Selassie revised the constitution in 1955 and offered to reform Ethiopia's system of government completely in 1974, largely because his powerful image was being tarnished by an inability to control increasing poverty. Growing popular awareness of the weakness of the feudalistic landholding system led to conflict over the need for land reform and modern agricultural methods. Haile Selassie's government was overthrown by a group composed of the country's own military in September 1974. Speculation at the time was that Selassie's failure to control food shortages, soaring prices, and poor living conditions had brought on the revolution. Even with a per capita income of about eighty-five dollars a year, a population that was 90 percent illiterate, and drought conditions from 1971 to 1974 that killed a hundred thousand people, Selassie had refused to ask for international aid, preferring to keep the country's troubled condition a secret.

The military junta, known as the Dergue, initially moved with irresolution and a lack of clear planning. It installed two prime ministers and then ousted them before appointing General Aman Michael Andom as head of government. A radical faction came to the fore and its members in the Dergue shot Aman. Ultimately a leader of the radical faction emerged: Mengistu Haile Mariam, who was only thirty-two years of age at the time he became Ethiopia's head of state.

Rains again failed to arrive in 1982, and on August 20, 1984, the UN Children's Fund made public its projections of large-scale starvation and famine-related illness, predicting that seven million would suffer in Ethiopia. Two weeks after the UN announcement, the Ethiopian government moved formally toward establishing a single legal political party, which would be the country's first Communist party. Mengistu Haile Mariam would be named head of the party, which was formed to reflect the government's desire to institutionalize communism.

The Workers' party was formally established on September 10, ostensibly marking Ethiopia's move from military to civilian rule. Less than two weeks later, Mengistu officially requested international famine aid. The delay in turning attention to famine conditions could be ascribed to the fears of the junta that, because of the disunity among the diverse population, its position of power was unstable and could be jeopardized by bad news of such magnitude.

Relief workers argued that Ethiopia's Marxist government had made it a far less attractive recipient for aid than other drought-stricken African nations. Other experts cited the logistical problems of transporting food in Ethiopia as the main reason for the extent of the disaster.

In addition, the government refused to distribute aid in "unsafe" regions, that is, areas occupied by antigovernment insurgents. The most active secessionist group is the Marxist Eritrean People's Liberation Front, which is fighting for autonomy for Eritrea, a onetime Italian colony incorporated into Ethiopia in 1962. Guerrilla activity continues in Tigre province and among Somali separatists as well. The Eritrean guerrillas have accused the Ethiopian government of attempting to starve the secessionists into concluding the long civil war.

According to reports in September 1984, the Ethiopian government had warned in March of the need for food aid. Ethiopia can produce only 6.2 million tons of grain a year, 1 million less than it normally needs. Over the summer, drought and pest infestations exacerbated the situation, raising the numbers of the population at risk. By August 1984, international focus was on Ethiopia's crisis, and experts all over the world were considering how best to deal with the tragic situation.

Chad:
Everyone's Pawn

Perspective

700s	*Arab tribes penetrate area.*
700s–1200s	*Kingdom of Kanem flourishes.*
1200s–1800s	*Kingdom of Bornu flourishes.*
1900	*French establish protectorate.*
1960	*Chad achieves independence from France.*
1966	*Libya begins active support of northern Muslim rebels.*
1975	*President is assassinated; government is taken over by military junta.*
1979	*Junta is overthrown; coalition government is formed.*
1980	*Libyan troops enter country.*
1981	***January.*** *Chad and Libya announce plans to unite.*
	November. *Libya is forced to withdraw troops.*
1982	*Hissène Habré overthrows pro-Libyan government.*

The Republic of Chad is a landlocked nation in north-central Africa, large in size and small in population. Even in the best of times, most of its inhabitants live on the edge of poverty, and for a decade much of the country has suffered from severe drought. As a nation, it exists largely because of boundaries imposed by France around the turn of the century. Like many modern African nations, it has little natural unity either in geography or in the ethnic makeup of its population. In the northern part of the country are Muslim herdsmen of Arab descent. In the south are found mostly black agriculturists. They have existed in uneasy peace for many years, but relations between them have become increasingly tense.

Issues and Events

Chad has been besieged by political problems since its independence in 1960. Chadians in the south, the most prosperous region, have fought Chadians in the north; Libya, its oil-rich neighbor to the north, has tried to absorb it; and France, looking back to the days of a French empire in Africa, has flexed its muscles there.

After independence, Chad was ruled by an un-easy coalition of north and south. In 1966 Libya began supporting Muslim rebels in the north, who opposed the increasing political influence of the more prosperous south. The government called on France that same year to aid in the battle against the northern guerrillas. The rebellion was effectively put down in 1973, but in 1975 President Ngarta Tombalbaye was assassinated, and a military junta took control. In 1979 a new coalition took over the government; it was headed by Goukouni Oueddei, a former rebel from the north. New fighting between the north and south broke out in 1980, and Goukouni asked the Libyans to come to the government's aid.

In January 1981 Libya and the Chadian government announced plans to unite the countries, which meant, in effect, that Chad would be absorbed into Libya and cease to exist as a political entity. This development also alarmed the Organization of African Unity (OAU), which dispatched a body of troops to aid the anti-Goukouni forces. A contingent of French troops also entered the war. Later that year, Libya and the government were forced to renounce plans to unite, and Libya withdrew its troops. In 1982 Goukouni's pro-Libyan government was overthrown, and Hissène Habré, a pro-French southerner, became president.

Both France and Libya agreed to withdraw their troops, but in late 1984 France claimed that Libya still had troops in northern Chad. By 1985 France and Libya were still arguing about the future of Chad. And Chadians, as always, were seeking to make a living in a harsh, dry land.

Background

In the eighth century, a tribe of nomadic herdsmen, probably related to the Berber nomads of North Africa, arrived and established the Kanem kingdom. It flourished until the thirteenth century, when it was replaced by the Sefawa, or Saifi, dynasty, probably from the Sudan. The Sefawa subjugated the So people, a black agriculturist group, and later intermarried with them and established the Bornu kingdom. It became the great center of Muslim culture in central Africa. Its economy was based on the slave trade; slaves were captured in southern Africa and sold at the port cities of North Africa.

The French began establishing their control over the area in the 1890s and created a protectorate in 1900. In 1910 French Equatorial Africa was established, incorporating modern Chad, Gabon, Congo, and Central African Republic. France relinquished sovereignty in 1960, but Chad remained within the French sphere of influence, in large part dependent on French aid and also military support.

Nigeria: Democracy in Africa's Oil-Rich Giant

Perspective

1000s	*Hausa city-states are founded; leaders are converted to Islam.*
1300s	*Yoruba states of Oyo and Benin are founded in southern Nigeria.*
1500s	*Slave trade flourishes under Portuguese, French, British, and Dutch.*
1861	*Britain begins its consolidation of power over all of Nigeria.*
1956	*Oil is discovered in Port Harcourt area.*
1960	*Nigeria becomes independent republic.*
1967	*Ibo secede and form Republic of Biafra.*
1970	*Biafran civil war is brought to an end.*
1983	*President Shehu Shagari is ousted from office by military coup.*
1984	*New regime institutes widespread economic and political reforms.*
1985	*Illegal aliens are forced to leave Nigeria.*

L ike most African nations whose boundaries are based on artificial borders imposed by European colonial powers, Nigeria has been beset by economic and ethnic problems since it became independent in 1960. Despite these difficulties, Nigeria has met with more success than most new nations. In large part, the income from mineral deposits is responsible.

Issues and Events

The 1970s were heady times for Nigeria. The most populous country in Africa, it had become one of the richest nations in black Africa. Petroleum had been discovered along the coast of Nigeria in the 1950s, and it turned out to be one of the world's richest deposits. By 1979 Nigeria was a major producer of crude oil and a member of the Organization of Petroleum Exporting Countries (OPEC).

Politically, the country remained relatively stable. The attempt by the Ibo to set up the separate republic of Biafra collapsed in 1970, thereby putting an end to civil war. The military regime headed by Lieutenant Colonel Yakuba Gowon was overthrown by civilians in 1975. A new constitutional government headed by President Shehu Shagari took office. The change in government caused scarcely a ripple in the nation's economic boom.

By the late 1970s, however, a hesitation was beginning to be felt in the Nigerian surge. A worldwide economic recession and energy conservation lessened the demand for oil. Nigeria cut the price of its oil in the hope that a lower price would stimulate demand. This move had little effect, however. By 1984, Nigeria's income from oil sold abroad had dropped from $24 billion per year in 1980 to $10 billion.

In the early 1980s, the Nigerian government seemed to be surviving its austerities surprisingly well. In January 1983 President Shagari ordered the deportation of all foreign workers. More than two million were forced out of the country. Confident that his measures were meeting with success, President Shagari called for national elections in August 1983.

Although the election was a great personal victory for Shagari, he was suddenly ousted by the military, who cited economic and corruption problems, on December 31, 1983. The new Federal Military Government (FMG) took power, meeting with great popular support. Major General Muhammad Buhari became the head of state and commander in chief of the armed forces.

General Buhari charged that the previous government had been riddled with corruption, and hundreds of public officials were removed. The government quickly attacked inflation, drastically reducing public expenditures, imposing a pay freeze and instituting new taxes. The currency was reformed to check speculation. All political activity was banned, and severe press restrictions were imposed.

Background

European penetration began in the 1400s, and in the next centuries, the slave trade flourished. In 1807, Great Britain attempted, with little success, to abolish it. In 1861, Great Britain annexed Lagos, subsequently consolidating its hold inland. In 1914, Britain amalgamated Lagos and the northern provinces, thereby creating the unified colony of Nigeria.

Beginning in 1947, Britain put forward various independence schemes, but there was considerable intergroup rivalry, mainly among the Hausa-Fulani, the Yoruba, and the Ibo. Each group was intent on protecting its rights and privileges as much as possible, and it was not until 1960 that an acceptable constitution could be devised.

After violence against them, the minority Ibo seceded in 1967 and formed the Republic of Biafra. The Nigerian government gradually reduced the area being held by the Biafrans, and on January 15, 1970, Biafra surrendered.

Namibia:
Independence or War?

Perspective

1884	*Germany extends its protection over South West Africa.*
1915	*South African troops conquer German South West Africa.*
1920	*League of Nations mandates South West Africa to South Africa.*
1960s	*South West Africa People's Organization (SWAPO) is formed.*
1966	*UN General Assembly adopts resolution declaring mandate terminated and takes on direct responsibility until independence.*
1973	*United Nations recognizes SWAPO as "authentic" representative of Namibia.*
1970s	*Guerrilla action and South African incursions into Angola increase.*
1978	*South African–sponsored elections are held.*
1981	*United States suggests concept of "linkage."*
1984	*Tentative agreement is reached on military disengagement in southern Angola; some progress is made toward linkage.*

T he status of Namibia, formerly South West Africa, has been unsettled since the end of World War I, when the League of Nations gave the onetime German colony the status of mandate and placed it under the protection of the Union (now Republic) of South Africa. Instead of administering South West Africa as a mandate under its protection, South Africa in effect annexed the vast area and governed it as an integral part of its territory. After World War II, when the United Nations replaced the League of Nations, all holders of League mandates surrendered their protection to the UN—except for South Africa, which refused and continued to claim its sovereignty over South West Africa.

In 1966 a UN General Assembly resolution terminated the mandate and in 1968 resolved that the country should be called Namibia, after the Nama, one of the historic tribes of the area. In 1971 the International Court of Justice ordered South Africa to end its administration of the country. South Africa refused to recognize the jurisdiction of the court, however, and continued

its rule over what it insisted on calling South West Africa, known as Namibia to most of the rest of the world.

The status of Namibia has become an especially emotional issue, as the black African republics object to the area's being governed by the white-supremacist government of South Africa. One reason South Africa is unwilling to surrender sovereignty over the country is that it views Namibia as a strategic buffer state between it and these black African nations surrounding it. Angola, immediately to the north of Namibia, has had a Marxist government since 1976, and this has only increased South Africa's intransigence. In addition, South Africa wishes to retain control of Namibia's mineral resources, particularly diamonds.

Within Namibia itself, most of the pressure for independence has been exerted by the South West Africa People's Organization (SWAPO). The SWAPO guerrillas—who are backed by the Soviet Union, Cuba, and Angola and are recognized by the UN as Namibia's representatives—have not generally been successful in their clashes with the far more powerful South African military force. Although South Africa is winning the military battle against SWAPO, and by economic, military, and diplomatic pressures, South Africa's diplomats are increasingly successful in forcing neighboring countries to deny sanctuary to the guerrillas, eventually the government will have to decide if the price of the war is worthwhile.

Issues and Events

In 1984, after two decades of increasing military conflict, the likelihood of real progress toward Namibian independence seemed possible. In the spring South Africa and Angola reached a tentative agreement on a military disengagement in southern Angola, where most of the SWAPO forces are based. In return for the Angolan denial of bases in the area to SWAPO and the Cubans, South Africa pledged to withdraw its direct aid to the National Union for the Total Independence of Angola (UNITA) guerrillas, who continued to aggravate Angola's political instability by attacks against its Marxist government.

Some regarded this disengagement as the first step in a number of linked events that could eventually lead to the independence of Namibia. The process of linkage, introduced by the United States in 1981, seeks to link South African moves toward allowing UN-supervised elections and granting independence for Namibia with dismissal of the Cuban troops that have been aiding Angola's Marxist government. The assumption is that South Africa will never agree to Namibian elections (in which it is conceded that SWAPO will win) so long as there is a leftist government, antagonistic toward South Africa, in neighboring Angola. Both Angola and South Africa have given tentative indications that they are willing to consider the linkage plan. However, these steps guarantee little in this volatile situation.

Background

The earliest known inhabitants of southern and central Namibia were Bushmen and nomadic Hottentots who periodically crossed the Orange River, which constitutes the territory's southern border. Sometime before the eighteenth century, the Herero, a Bantu-speaking, cattle-raising people, occupied much of central Namibia and reduced the Bushmen to serfdom. Later the Ovambo, another Bantu group, crossed the Nunene River from the north and occupied the more fertile areas of northern Namibia. Major conflicts over grazing lands arose in the mid-1800s between white-influenced Nama (largely descendants of white and Hottentot liaisons) and the Herero. These battles were extremely fierce and continued sporadically until 1892.

The British government of the Cape Colony in what is now South Africa first took advantage of the native wars and calls for help by annexing about 385 square miles (1,000 square kilometers) around Walvis Bay in 1878. In 1884 Adolph Luderitz established a trading post at Angra Pequena on the southern coast, and Germany soon extended its protection to almost all of what is now Namibia. The Germans brutally imposed their rule on South West Africa. They first routed the Nama and, in response to a native revolt, virtually annihilated the Herero.

The revolt profoundly changed Namibian life. As a result the remaining Herero and Nama were forced to carry passes and to labor for whites. Their cattle were confiscated. Most importantly for future events, the majority of people in Namibia were now Ovambo rather than Herero.

During World War I, South African troops conquered German South West Africa and became the rulers of the eighty thousand native inhabitants. South Africa wished to incorporate South West Africa into the Union, but the League of Nations declared it a mandate. In contravention of the intent of the 1920 mandate, South Africa began to administer the area as if it had been annexed. It also seized land from the majority blacks and gave it to minority whites and instituted a strict policy of apartheid, or separation of the races. Many blacks were dispossessed and turned into contract laborers. Revolts by blacks in 1922 and 1925 were brutally suppressed.

During the 1930s the South African government continued along a path that would have led to the gradual incorporation of Namibia into the Union. This path was interrupted by World War II and the creation of the United Nations, which took over the administration of the old mandates. In 1946 South Africa called upon the UN to allow the formal incorporation of South West Africa into South Africa. The UN, committed to a policy of turning mandates into self-governing countries, denied the request. Nevertheless, South Africa continued its policy of gradual incorporation. In 1961 the UN General Assembly upheld the right of the Namibian people to independence, and in 1966 it officially terminated South Africa's mandate over Namibia. The South Africans countered by passing the South West Africa Affairs Act of 1969. It abolished the autonomy of the South West African legislative assembly and transferred its power to Pretoria, South Africa's capital. They also began to carry out a "homelands" policy in South West Africa. That policy, modeled on the one inaugurated in South Africa itself, forced people into racially segregated black communities that were puppet creations of Pretoria.

The 1960s also saw the emergence and growth of SWAPO, a liberation organization made up primarily of Ovambo dissidents who had decided that the preparations for independence were taking too long. In 1966 they began guerrilla raids into Namibia from Zambia. In 1973 the UN recognized SWAPO as the "authentic" representatives of the Namibian people.

In the mid-1970s, when Angola, Namibia's northern neighbor, gained its independence from Portugal, a power struggle developed there between the Popular Movement for the Liberation of Angola (MPLA) and the UNITA forces. South Africa, anxious to ensure a non-Communist and friendly government so close to its borders, gave logistical support to UNITA. When the MPLA, with Cuban help, triumphed in 1976, SWAPO was allowed to move its bases from Zambia to Angola. The South Africans continued to support the UNITA guerillas who remained in the field, and the South African army made repeated incursions into Angolan territory to destroy SWAPO bases.

In the early 1980s international pressures on South Africa to grant independence increased along with South African pressures on both SWAPO and the government of Angola. South African military incursions grew both in number and in size. The United States introduced the concept of linking South African concessions on elections and aid to UNITA with Angolan moves to get rid of Cuban troops, deny bases to SWAPO, and share power with UNITA.

South Africa: Apartheid and the Homelands

Perspective

1650s	First Dutch settlement of cape is established.
1803	British occupy Cape Colony.
1834	Slavery is abolished in South Africa.
1835	Great Trek begins.
1899– 1902	Boer War is fought between British and Boers.
1910	Union of South Africa is created.
1913	Native Lands Act is passed.
1926	Color bar is established.
1936	Native Representation Act is passed.
1950s	National party institutes apartheid policies.
1951	Black homelands are created.
1960	Uprising at Sharpesville occurs.
1961	**May 10.** Republic of South Africa is established.
1976	Riots occur at Soweto.
1984	New constitution with limited political rights for Coloreds and Asians is put into force.
1985	Crossroads riots end in killings. **July.** Government declares state of emergency, detaining blacks without charges.

The practice of the South African government has been to take one step forward and then one step back on the easing of apartheid, its policy of strict racial segregation. Although the white minority, which makes up less than 20 percent of the population, continues to maintain its complete political, economic, and social domination of the majority black Africans, pressure to change has escalated in recent years. Once sheltered from black-majority African governments by the Portuguese colonies of Mozambique and Angola and by white-supremacist Rhodesia (now Zimbabwe), South Africa has seen these states come under black rule. These states support the aspirations of blacks in South Africa and are seen by the South African government as a threat to the status quo.

Apartheid, which is Afrikaans for "apartness,"

has been used to separate the races in all aspects of life and thereby maintain white supremacy. An important part of apartheid has been the creation of "homelands" for the native black population, known collectively as the Bantu. The Bantustans, or "Bantu nations," were scheduled to encompass almost 15 percent of South Africa's land area but none of its more productive land; they were to be organized along ethnic lines and given what the South African government called "full independence." Black African leaders, and most foreign observers, denied that they would have true independence, since their governments would be creatures of the South African government.

The first of these homelands, Bophuthatswana, was granted "full independence" in 1976. Transkei became independent the same year. Venda was given independence in 1979, and Ciskei was created in 1981. Neither the UN nor any foreign nation has recognized these as sovereign countries.

Black leaders in South Africa have opposed the creation of these homelands and the forcible removal of the black population to them. In Bophuthatswana, for example, 65 percent of its population of more than two million was forcibly moved there from white areas of South Africa. The South African government has agreed in principle to halt the forced resettlements.

Issues and Events

Pressures from within and without to abolish apartheid are becoming increasingly undeniable even to the leaders of South Africa's ruling and normally intransigent National party. This reassessment of total apartheid has a number of causes, including the termination of Portugal's African empire in the 1970s, uprisings in Soweto (a black-inhabited section of Johannesburg) in 1976, the demography of a nation whose black population is growing faster than that of its ruling white minority, the increasing need for black labor, and increasing pressure from the international community.

The new constitution that came into force in 1984 and the events that followed its passage provide an example of the ruling party's attempt to adapt to realities and at the same time maintain racial dominance. The new constitution is extremely complicated. It provides for a system in which whites (18 percent of the population), Coloreds (9 percent; persons of mixed racial parentage), and Asians (3 percent; Indians) hold parliamentary sessions on separate "affairs" in three different languages in three different chambers. The proportion of power is roughly four whites to two Coloreds to one Asian. Blacks, who make up 70 percent of the population, continue to be excluded from any national power.

The National attempt to defuse pressures with the new constitution and reforms has been unsuccessful. Less than one-third of the eligible nonwhite voters went to the polls in the August 1984 election, an indication of a lack of trust in the good intentions of the Nationals. The election was followed by the arrest and detention of a number of United Democratic Front (UDF) leaders who had spoken out against it. The UDF represents all racial groups in a broad-based alliance of community organizations and has, up to this time, been considered the moderate alternative to the outlawed African National Congress (ANC), which is committed to armed struggle. The international community has found little to praise in the new constitution, and pressures in the UN and elsewhere for true reform of the South African political system have not abated. In 1985 dissatisfaction among blacks led to numerous demonstrations and protests. In response to continued protest, the government declared a state of emergency in July, thus assuming the right to arrest blacks and hold them without charges or explanation.

Background

Race has been the central cause of problems in South Africa since the arrival of the first Dutch settlers in the 1650s. When the British took over the Cape Colony in 1803, the territory was inhabited by four major groups of people: the Boers, or Afrikaners; slaves of African-Malay descent who would be the basis of the country's "Colored" population; the nomadic Hottentots, who were badly treated by the Boers; and the black Bantu peoples, who lived beyond the frontiers and were in constant conflict with the expanding settlements. Under the influence of reform movements originating in Britain, Hottentots were put on an equal racial footing with whites in 1828, and slavery was abolished in the Cape Colony in 1834.

These acts, combined with British restriction on settlement, the establishment of English as the sole official language, and the abolition of the old Dutch administrative system, led to the Great Trek, which began in 1835. Over fourteen thousand Boers left the colony for Natal and the Transvaal to the northeast, where they created their own states and laws. In the Boer states laws were passed whose object was to prevent vagrancy and establish the "proper relation between master and servant," and strict lines of demarcation between Boer and Bantu areas were established.

After the discovery of diamonds and gold in the Transvaal, the assertion of British rule in the area led to the Boer War from 1899 to 1902. By 1910, under British auspices, the Union of South Africa had been created from the thirteen states that had existed in the area. The status of blacks did not improve under the Act of Union.

In 1913 the Native Lands Act was passed, in which Bantu areas were established and black ownership of land within the Union was forbidden. An act in 1926 laid down the principle of the color bar, in which blacks were excluded from skilled jobs. In 1936 the Native Representation Act put blacks, who in some areas had the right to vote, on separate voting rolls from whites and circumscribed other political rights. When the predominantly Afrikaner National party came to power in 1948, the concept of "separate development," or apartheid, came to fruition.

In 1951 the black homelands were officially established. In the later 1950s many laws established "petty apartheid." The petty apartheid laws closely resemble the segregation laws of the American South before the 1950s. In 1958 Hendrik Verwoerd became prime minister, and it was under his leadership that the republic was proclaimed on May 10, 1961, and that the apartheid and homelands policies were extended and fully implemented.

After Soweto there was a sharp upsurge in black political and union activities on one hand and a commitment to armed struggle on the other. The 1976 riots at Soweto and their brutal repression in which 575 blacks died led to the first substantial exodus of blacks to Swaziland and Tanzania for guerrilla training. The outlawed African National Congress continues to lead the armed struggle from military bases in neighboring states. The ANC has United Nations recognition and observer status.

More moderate forces operating within South Africa come under the umbrella of the United Democratic Front and are led by prominent figures such as the Nobel Peace Prize winner Bishop Desmond Tutu. A third force on the black political scene is Inkatha, a Zulu-based national movement led by Chief Gatsha Buthelezi.

In recent years the thrust of South African policy has been simultaneously to destroy armed opposition and to put into place sufficient minor reforms to defuse growing black militancy without threatening white rule. Efforts have also been made to induce neighboring black states to deny bases to guerrillas. Tensions within South Africa and international condemnation of the government's policies are likely to increase, unless the black majority can make real progress toward equality.

South Asia

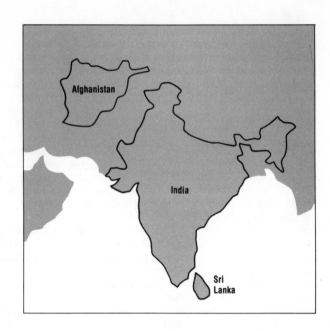

The major sources of conflict in South Asia are modern examples of ancient problems. In India the Sikhs have been fighting the majority Hindus since Sikhism was founded in the fifteenth century. In Sri Lanka, the tribal wars between the majority Sinhalese and the minority Tamils can be traced as far back as the sixth century B.C., when the ancestors of the modern Tamils began migrating south from India. Afghanistan, strategically located between such great powers as the Soviet Union, Iran, and India, has historically been seen as a buffer state by its powerful neighbors and fought over on that account. The modern-day invasion of Afghanistan by the Soviet Union in order to aid the local Communist party is only the modern equivalent of the traditional desire of Russia to extend its power to the south—the goal being Russian access to the Indian Ocean.

The situation in Afghanistan is compounded by the fiercely independent tribalism of the Pushtuns, who occupy much of the mountainous countryside. Their opposition to the Soviet-backed central government is steeped in history and tradition: the Afghan tribes have always resisted any central government, whatever the nominal leadership.

Religious and tribal antagonisms and rivalries continue to abound throughout South Asia. The seemingly irreconcilable differences between the Hindus and Muslims in India have cost the lives of millions of Indians in the twentieth century. The separation of the former British colony of India into three nations (India, Pakistan, and Bangladesh) is the most dramatic illustration of the religious strife there.

Another religious minority, the Sikhs, is now urging the formation of an independent state in India's Punjab. The violence between the Sikhs and the Indian government, which led to Indira Gandhi's assassination, continues, as Rajiv Gandhi and the Indian government attempt to meet some of the Sikh demands.

The desire of the minority Tamils for independence from the majority Sinhalese on Sri Lanka has led to violence on that island. The Tamils complain of increasingly harsh government reprisals, while the government charges that the Tamils are being aided by the large minority of Tamils in India, who are suspected of mounting guerrilla attacks. The situation has led to strain between normally friendly India and Sri Lanka.

India is plagued by boundary disputes with many of the nations of South Asia. India has argued—and occasionally fought—with Pakistan over the Kashmir region ever since Indian independence.

Armed conflict between India and Pakistan or even between India and China, which also have a long-standing border dispute, is always a possibility in the Indian subcontinent, a possibility that becomes even more serious upon consideration of India's and China's nuclear capabilities.

Sri Lanka:
Tamil Separatists Rebel

Perspective

500 B.C. *Indo-Aryan tribes migrate to Ceylon from northern India.*

200 B.C. *Sinhalese kingdoms begin.*

1796 *British seize control of Ceylon.*

1948 **February 4.** *Ceylon becomes independent dominion.*

1972 **May 22.** *Ceylon adopts new constitution, becomes Republic of Sri Lanka.*

1977 **October 20.** *Constitution is amended to provide for president with strong powers.*

1978 **January.** *Junius Jayawardene assumes office.*

1982 **July 30.** *Government declares emergency following riots between Sinhalese and Muslims.*

1983 **July 20.** *Government orders censorship of all stories concerning Tamil unrest.*

July 23–27. *Intense violence erupts between majority Sinhalese and minority Tamils.*

September 23. *Tamil separatists storm prison in Batticaloa, freeing 217 prisoners.*

1984 **December.** *Talks between Tamils and Jayawardene break off; violence escalates.*

1985 **January 11.** *Sri Lankan naval vessels open fire on Indian fishing boats suspected of aiding insurgents. India seizes Sri Lankan boat in return.*

February 5. *President Jayawardene announces plans to settle 200,000 Sinhalese in northern Tamil territories.*

S ri Lanka, formerly Ceylon, a teardrop-shaped island off the southern tip of India, has, in recent months, been plagued by a rapidly escalating climate of violence between the majority Sinhalese and the minority Tamil separatists. The Sinhalese, who comprise three-quarters of the population, are primarily Buddhist, while the Tamils are primarily Hindu and speak the language of the fifty million Tamils in India. The Tamils live mainly in northern Sri Lanka, which is generally less prosperous than the south.

Issues and Events
While these two groups have a centuries-old history of disputes, the last few years have seen the level of violence increase dramatically. A cycle has been established in which each new attack provokes a retaliatory response from the other side, pushing both camps into increasingly irreconcilable positions. Negotiations between moderate Tamil leaders and President J. R. Jayawardene broke down in December 1984 when the Tamils rejected a proposal that would give them limited autonomy while still leaving them subject to control by government police. Jayawardene has vowed never again to negotiate with anyone who continues to advocate a separate Tamil state. He also began beefing up the Sri Lankan armed forces.

India, which officially opposes a separate Tamil state, has nonetheless been reluctant to prevent Tamils of southern India from helping their counterparts on Sri Lanka. Tensions between these two countries took a turn for the worse in January 1985 when a Sri Lankan naval vessel was seized by the Indians.

Background
The Sinhalese have been established on Sri Lanka since the sixth century B.C. They first came into contact with the Tamils of southern India soon thereafter, although the Tamils did not appear in substantial numbers in Ceylon until the tenth century. Controlled first by India, then by the Portuguese, the Dutch, and, finally, the British, Ceylon achieved independence on February 4, 1948. A new constitution was adopted on May 22, 1972, changing the island's name from Ceylon to the Republic of Sri Lanka.

During 1983 violence between the Sinhalese and Tamils escalated sharply, with major clashes in July and August. Since then, the unrest between the two groups has grown geometrically. It was estimated that in 1984 some 2,500 people died as a result of the conflict; and the killing of Tamil insurgents, government troops, and civilians continued in 1985. With the increase in hostilities there have been charges of indiscriminate killings and brutalities on the part of government troops. Further exacerbating tensions was the announcement on February 5, 1985, by President Jayawardene that 200,000 armed Sinhalese would be settled in northern Tamil territories. This threat enraged even moderate Tamil leaders, indicating that the violence and unrest may continue and perhaps grow.

India: Conflict over Sikh Nationalism

Perspective

1469	*Nanak, founder of Sikhism, is born.*
1574	*Amritsar, holy city of Sikhs, is founded.*
1699	*Military brotherhood of Khalsa is established.*
1849	*British conquer Punjab, ending Sikh independence.*
1857	*Sikh troops support British suppression of Indian mutiny.*
1947	*Partition of India and Pakistan creates independent nations with Hindu and Muslim majorities but no independent Sikh state.*
1966	*Indian government creates new Punjab State with Sikh majority.*
1983	***October.** Emergency rule is invoked in Punjab to suppress terrorist violence by Sikh militants.*
1984	***May 31.** Sikh extremists vow to stop exports from Punjab to rest of India.* ***June 2–3.** Golden Temple, Sikhdom's holiest shrine, is cordoned off; federal government declares Punjab "restricted," "shoot-at-sight" curfew is imposed.* ***June 6.** Indian troops storm Golden Temple.* ***October 31.** Indian prime minister Indira Gandhi is assassinated by two Sikh members of her security guard; in ensuing violence, Hindu mobs kill almost two thousand Sikhs.*

T he assassination on October 31, 1984, of Indian prime minister Indira Gandhi by two Sikh members of her personal bodyguard focused world attention on the problems and demands of India's Sikh minority. Indira Gandhi's son and successor, Rajiv Gandhi, stated that the Sikh problem had the highest priority of his new administration. Concentrated in the strategically important and economically prosperous state of Punjab, the Sikhs have had increasingly tense relations with India's central government during the 1980s. The Sikhs' holy city of Amritsar and their shrine there—the Golden Temple—were the center of conflict.

Issues and Events

Violence escalated from late 1983 in the Sikhs' northwestern border state of Punjab, which sep-arates the predominantly Hindu sections of India from Muslim Pakistan and therefore is militarily important to the Indian government. The violence had its roots with several radical nationalist factions that developed in the early 1980s. Some advocated an independent Sikh nation, to be called Khalistan, while others supported the transformation of the Punjab into an autonomous Sikh homeland. Growing violence in 1983 caused hundreds of deaths and led to the imposition in October of direct rule in the Punjab by India's central government.

By the spring of 1984, Sikh militants, led by Jarnail Singh Bhindranwale, were stockpiling arms and supplies in the Golden Temple. Jarnail, a charismatic leader who rose to prominence by charging that the rest of India was exploiting the Punjab, promised to oppose any attempt by the military to enter the temple. Terrorist attacks on prominent Hindus and on Sikh leaders who disagreed with extremist tactics were followed by increased government security measures, including curfews in major Sikh cities in May. On May 31, Sikh extremists declared that they would block the transfer of grain, water, and power from the Punjab to other areas of India. The next day eleven died in a police-Sikh clash at the Golden Temple.

On June 2 the federal government declared the Punjab "restricted," which put it off limits to journalists and foreigners. About fifty thousand police and federal militia were put under the control of the army, which had a growing presence in the state. This was followed on June 3 with a curfew, a halt in transportation, and a military presence at other Sikh shrines.

The assault on the Golden Temple by Indian army troops on June 6 was supported by machine guns, mortars, and antitank rockets. The Sikh militants were finally defeated with almost one thousand dead, including Jarnail and other leading extremists.

The assassination of Prime Minister Gandhi in her residential compound in New Delhi was interpreted in India as a reprisal for the storming of the Golden Temple. Despite initial assurances by Rajiv Gandhi that the assassination was an act by individuals, not a conspiracy, violence against Sikhs and their property erupted throughout the country, resulting in almost two thousand Sikh deaths by mid-November. Reactions to the assassination in overseas Sikh communities ranged from joy over the death of Gandhi—seen as an oppressor—to sorrow that the extremist faction had precipitated a crisis.

As violence continued, Prime Minister Gandhi made several gestures toward resolving the conflict. In March 1985 eight prominent Sikh leaders were released from prison; however, Sikhs continued to demand the release of thousands more. In April the government announced that it would meet three of the Sikh demands: to lift the ban on the militant All-India Sikh Students Federation, to release some of the Sikhs who had been detained after the government-Sikh confrontation at the Golden Temple in 1984, and to instigate a judicial inquiry into the anti-Sikh riots that followed Indira Gandhi's assassination. Speculation exists that the riots were planned in retribution by political leaders from the Gandhis' own party.

However, the Sikhs continue to press their other demands: that the government dissolve the special courts that were formed to try purported terrorists; that Sikh army deserters no longer be court-martialed; that the Indian army be withdrawn from the Punjab; that all detainees held without charge be released; and that the government make restitution for losses suffered in the November riots. Meanwhile, four Sikhs (one of whom was already dead) were charged with conspiracy in the assassination of Indira Gandhi.

Violence continued in May 1985 as three Hindu politicians were assassinated within ten days and a series of bombs was set off in New Delhi and three northern states. The bombings, in which eighty people were killed and one hundred fifty wounded, were attributed to Sikh extremists. Approximately fifteen hundred people were arrested, and peace between the Sikhs and the Indian government remains doubtful.

Background

The Sikh religion is a relative newcomer, and the development of the Sikhs as a distinct people is even more recent. Sikhism took form during the fifteenth and sixteenth centuries in the Punjab, the northwestern region of the Indian subcontinent, spanning the present Punjab states in India and Pakistan.

The first guru, or spiritual leader, of Sikhism was Nanak, born in 1469 about forty miles (sixty-five kilometers) from Lahore (in present-day Pakistan). Unsuccessful in his marriage and career, Nanak became a spiritual seeker, wandering across the countryside. One day he had a vision in which God appeared before him, and shortly thereafter, Nanak proclaimed that he was neither a Hindu nor a Muslim but instead was the bearer of a new teaching that superseded both Hinduism and Islam.

Nanak drew on both religions in framing his beliefs. From Islam Nanak took the idea of the unity of God and an absolute prohibition of images and idols. From the Hindus came the belief in an eternal cycle of death and rebirth, and the word *sikh* derives from the Hindi word for *disciple*.

Early in the seventeenth century, the teachings of Nanak and others were gathered together in the *Adi Granth*, "First Book," the sacred scripture of the Sikhs. The bound volume of scripture, housed in the Golden Temple at Amritsar, remains an object of daily veneration.

After Nanak died in 1539, he was followed by nine gurus. During this period, the Sikhs were forced to take up arms against Muslim persecution. In 1699 the last of the gurus, Gobind Rai, established the brotherhood of the Khalsa, "Pure Ones"; to each of the five brothers of the Khalsa he gave the surname Singh, meaning "lion." When the succession of gurus came to an end with the assassination of Gobind Rai, in 1708, military and spiritual leadership of the Sikhs fell to the members of the Khalsa brotherhood. During the eighteenth century the Khalsa successfully harassed the Muslim rulers of the Punjab. By the beginning of the nineteenth century, the Khalsa leader Ranjit Singh had taken possession of the Punjab's capital city of Lahore and had proclaimed himself maharaja of the Punjab.

Inevitably, the Sikhs clashed with the British in India. By 1849, the Sikhs were defeated, and the Punjab was annexed to British India. Thereafter, the Sikhs served the British loyally. Sikh troops played an important part in suppressing the Indian mutiny of 1857 and made up more than 20 percent of the British Indian Army in World War I. After the war relations between British and Sikhs deteriorated.

In the sectarian upheaval that preceded the partition of India and Pakistan in August 1947, no riots were more violent than those in the Punjab between the Sikhs and their traditional foes, the Muslims. Thus, when Pakistan and India became independent, more than two million Sikhs fled into India from Islamic Pakistan.

Bitterly disappointed that they had failed to secure their own independence and to reestablish a Sikh nation, the Sikhs of the Indian Punjab began agitating for greater political autonomy and a new era of Sikh nationalism began. In 1966, in an effort to mollify the Sikhs, the Indian government redrew the boundaries of Punjab State so that it contained a majority of Punjabi-speaking Sikhs.

Minority communities of Sikhs can be found throughout much of India. Sikhs still have an important role in India's security forces, and there are Sikhs in civilian occupations from cab driver to cabinet minister. In 1982, at the urging of Prime Minister Indira Gandhi, Zail Singh was elected by the Indian parliament as president of India—the first Sikh ever to hold that office.

Afghanistan: The Russian Vietnam?

Perspective

328 B.C.	*Alexander the Great conquers territory.*
A.D. 652	*Arabs bring Islam to region.*
1300s	*Genghis Khan sacks countryside.*
1600s	*Babar incorporates territory into Mogul dynasty.*
1747	*Ahmad Shah Durrani consolidates tribes to form independent kingdom of Afghanistan.*
1838– 1919	*British control over Afghan foreign policy results in three wars.*
1919	**May 27.** *Total independence is achieved.*
1964	*Parliamentary constitution is put into effect.*
1973	**July 17.** *Mohammad Daoud abolishes constitution. Afghanistan is made a republic under Daoud.*
1978	**April.** *People's Democratic party of Afghanistan (PDPA) stages Marxist coup.*
1979	**September.** *Internal rivalry splits PDPA; half the party is exiled, and a leader killed.*
	December. *Soviet Union invades. Babrak Karmal is installed as head of new government.*
1984	**November 23.** *Once again UN General Assembly calls for withdrawal of foreign troops from Afghanistan.*

When more than fifty thousand Soviet troops invaded Afghanistan in December 1979 and early 1980, Moscow claimed that the soldiers were being sent in response to the request of a friendly government there. Six years later, with three times that number of troops involved in Afghanistan's civil war, the Soviet Union seemed to be settling into involvement in a long frustrating civil war—with no conclusive ending in sight.

The Russians and their Afghan supporters are trying to create a Soviet-style political and economic system out of a traditional, primarily agricultural society. But the political-economic aspects of the war cannot be separated from its religious overtones, and perhaps religion is what gives the guerrillas—known as *mujaheddin*, or

"holy warriors"—their strength. Like many others in the region, the mujaheddin are Muslim and thus part of a religious group experiencing a resurgence of political unity and visibility. Their opposition to communism and foreign influence is supported by religious beliefs that influence virtually every aspect of life. The fighting has been bitter and extremely costly to both sides.

Issues and Events

On November 23, 1984, the UN General Assembly called for "immediate withdrawal of foreign troops from Afghanistan" and asked for all parties concerned to work for urgent achievement of a political solution that would allow the four million Afghan refugees, most of them in Pakistan, to return home in safety and honor. With the exception of the refugee clause, it was the same plea, virtually word for word, made every year since the invasion took place. The UN Security Council has been unable to take action, due to the veto power possessed by permanent members and used by the Soviet Union, Afghanistan, and Soviet allies.

Observers believe that the Afghan government is not strong enough to allow the Soviets to withdraw. Nevertheless, it appears that the Soviets and the Soviet-controlled Afghan army may have found a way to combat the mujaheddin. Instead of carefully staged maneuvers using long convoys, which are comparatively easy to ambush and paralyze, the Soviets are now using helicopters for lightning raids. In addition, for the first time high-level saturation bombing to destroy villages and crops has been used in Afghanistan, and some charge the Soviets with chemical warfare as well.

The Soviet strategy is apparently not to win over the rebels but to subdue them. Camouflaged land mines, intended to injure rather than kill, cover roads. The intent is to cause added burdens for the guerrillas, who must care for the injured that will probably die anyway due to lack of proper medical facilities. In addition, fields, animals, and villages are destroyed in an attempt to cut off the vital supply chain that connects with the mujaheddin.

The Soviet offensive in the spring of 1984, in which twenty thousand new troops and five hundred new tanks were deployed against an estimated ten thousand poorly equipped guerrillas in the Panjshir Valley, led to severe losses on both sides. A major gain for the mujaheddin, however, was a pact among several established chieftains to put past tribal differences behind them, for the first time uniting the faction-ridden country. In the 1985 spring offensive, however, the Soviets were more successful in moving against their Afghan opponents.

The mujaheddin enjoy overwhelming national and international support for their cause. Substantial amounts of money and arms from the United States, for example, are funneled to the mujaheddin through Pakistan. They say they will fight to the death to protect their Islamic way of life. The Soviets, meanwhile, continue to fight a strategic battle. The Soviet Union obviously considers it important to secure a Communist regime in a border country of significant strategic value. The Soviets have manpower, money, and weapons and appear determined to persevere in their efforts to realize their goals.

The mujaheddin, together with international support, may yet be influential. Crop-burning tactics have had less effect than the Soviets anticipated, because fully one-third of the population has fled, leaving fewer mouths to feed. The mujaheddin fight on, capturing almost 80 percent of their weapons from the other side. Neither side appears close to victory, although the Soviets have retained the upper hand.

Background

The people of modern Afghanistan are extremely poor, and as in many Islamic nations, only their religion binds them together. Ethnically, there is great diversity and rivalry. About half the population is Pushtun, who are sometimes considered the true Afghans. They are related to a Pakistani people and speak Pushtu. The Tajiks, who are of Iranian origin, are the next largest group. They are closely related to the people of the Tadzhik republic of the Soviet Union. Other groups include the Uzbeks, Turkomans, and Kirghiz, who are of Turkish origin, and the Hazara, who speak an archaic Persian. The Nuri speak a Dardic language and are related to the people of Kashmir.

Turbulence is the only constant in the region now called Afghanistan, located in the path of major trade and invasion routes from central Asia into the Middle East and India. Starting in 328 B.C., a succession of conquerors, from Alexander the Great to Genghis Khan, swept across Afghanistan, mostly through the legendary Khyber Pass in nearby Pakistan.

Afghanistan as an independent kingdom was not founded until 1747, when Ahmad Shah Durrani consolidated the many chieftainships and provinces under one ruler, convincing neighboring countries to respect the borders. In 1838 the British sought to counter Russian influence in Persia, present-day Iran, and protect British interests in India by establishing a presence in Afghanistan, and the first of three wars between Britain and Afghanistan was ignited. The third

came in 1919, and a war-weary Britain, which had maintained control over Afghanistan's foreign affairs, gave in to King Amanullah's demands for total independence.

Attempts at modernization succeeded only in the assassination of rulers responsible for countering tribal rituals. The throne continued to change hands until 1964, when parliamentary rule was put into effect with a new constitution. Extremists on both sides, however, grew increasingly vocal, and amid charges of corruption and the problems of a drought-ridden economy, former prime minister Mohammad Daoud staged a bloodless coup on July 17, 1973. Daoud declared Afghanistan a republic, which it remained until the People's Democratic party of Afghanistan (PDPA), a newly formed coalition of two rival Marxist parties, overthrew Daoud, killing him and his family in 1978. Noor Mohammad Taraki took control of the new government.

Effective recruitment of young military officers by the Marxist parties had made the coup possible, in spite of support from only 2 percent of the population, mostly radicals and students. The Marxists attempted rapid social change by enacting radical decrees. While most were ignored, the land-reform decree caused national revolt. The state attempted to redistribute land to heads of families, with a five-acre (two hectare) limit for choice parcels, and a thirty-acre (twelve hectare) limit for arid land. Many families were told to move hundreds of miles to their new holdings.

Violent opposition, mostly based on Islamic beliefs conflicting with the PDPA's policies, developed immediately and grew into countrywide insurgency. After the original Marxist coup in April 1978, the Soviet Union had signed the Treaty of Friendship and Cooperation with the new regime. As the insurgency movement grew, Russian advisers and equipment became critical to the survival of the government and Marxism in Afghanistan.

In 1979 rivalry within the PDPA ended in the death of Taraki. Members of his Parcham, "Flag," faction were exiled, and former prime minister Hafizullah Amin seized power for the Khalq, "People," faction. Three months later, a bloody coup engineered by the Soviet Union overthrew Amin, who was executed along with his family. The exiled leader of the Parcham, Babrak Karmal, was installed as head of the new puppet government for the Soviets.

The Afghan government that developed is a mix of the two rival parties, with Karmal the leader of the Revolutionary Council, the Council of Ministers, and the Politburo of the PDPA. Soviet authority, however, reigns supreme.

East Asia and the Pacific

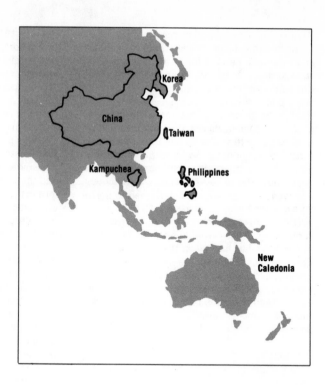

The overwhelming presence of the People's Republic of China is the dominant factor in the political and economic life of the Far East. Although Japan is the largest international power in the area, the influence of the "sleeping giant" of China pervades all planning in the Orient. Japan itself has for a decade been involved in a carefully thought-out program to increase its trade and financial relations with mainland China. Modernization of China's industry, technology, defense, and agriculture is the primary goal of the government, and in order to achieve such a modernization, government leaders have expressed a willingness to embrace many of the capitalistic business practices that were once shunned. Japan has been quick to accept the invitation to develop close financial ties with China. The United States, although somewhat more reticent where high-technology sales are concerned, has also entered into numerous trade agreements with the Chinese. Not only has the United States government begun active trade negotiations with China, but private American corporations are encouraged to seek out business deals with the Chinese.

Hong Kong and Taiwan, both historically part of China and both scenes of vigorous capitalist economies, have found their futures inextricably tied to mainland China. Taiwan was a province of China until the Nationalists fled the mainland in 1949 and set up the Republic of China there, and Taiwan traditionally depended on the United States to protect it from Communist China. However, increasing friendliness between the United States and China has Taiwanese leaders concerned about the future of their island republic. Hong Kong, a British colony leased from China, will revert to Chinese sovereignty by the end of the twentieth century. The addition of this successful, aggressively capitalistic island will represent another step away from China's traditional economic practices.

Kampuchea (Cambodia), Korea, and the Philippines are Asian nations with different problems. Kampuchea, devastated by the Vietnam War, is being fought over by competing Communist factions, one supported by China and the other by the Soviet Union. Koreans, who have lived in a divided country since the end of World War II, fear a new outbreak of hostilities between the Communist government of North Korea and the capitalist government of South Korea. In the Philippines, President Ferdinand Marcos's controversial regime has forced the nation to face the inevitable problems that will confront his successors.

Taiwan: Adrift in the China Sea

Perspective

1590	*Portuguese explorers name island Formosa, or "beautiful."*
1624	*Dutch and Spanish build rival forts.*
1641	*Dutch defeat Spanish.*
1661	*Koxinga (Cheng Ch'eng-kung) ousts Dutch and sets up independent Chinese kingdom.*
1683	*Manchus (Qing dynasty) seize control and decree Taiwan province of China.*
1895	*Taiwan is ceded to Japan following first Sino-Japanese War.*
1945	*Taiwan is returned to China after World War II defeat of Japan.*
1949	*Chiang Kai-shek and his remnant Kuomintang (Nationalist) forces retreat to Taiwan as Mao Zedong's Communists take over mainland.*
1954	*United States and Taiwan sign mutual defense treaty.*
1971	*Republic of China (Taiwan) loses UN's "China seat" to People's Republic of China.*
1972	*Shanghai communiqué pledges United States to gradual withdrawal of American forces from Taiwan.*
1979	*Diplomatic relations between Washington and Peking (Beijing) normalized; mutual defense treaty with Taiwan is ended; Congress enacts Taiwan Relations Act.*

Taiwan is trying hard these days to shed the name Taiwan, one more stratagem in the island nation's uphill battle for survival. This new stress on the use of Republic of China, the official name of the Kuomintang (Nationalist) government on Taiwan, is to counter Communist China's claim to Taiwan province in an escalating propaganda war. The precarious existence of the Nationalists on Taiwan has been brought into sharp focus by the recent agreement between the People's Republic of China and Great Britain for the transfer of sovereignty over Hong Kong in 1997. Seeing ominous implications for the future independence of Taiwan, officials are busy marshaling every political, economic, and military defense for the inevitable confrontation.

Issues and Events

Their trump card is the economic miracle of an industrialization even more rapid than Japan's. The booming capitalist economy of tiny Taiwan (a large trading partner of the United States) was the product of a relatively restrictive system of government domination or monopolistic control of basic industries. As their political security continues to erode, however, Taiwanese officials plan to internationalize and liberalize their trade policies for a better image in the international community.

But overhanging the economic future of Taiwan is concern for the autonomy of the Republic of China if the People's Republic decides to accelerate the unification of capitalist Taiwan with the Communist mainland. Hence the Taiwan government is pursuing every political or military option for defensive action.

Background

Ever since Chiang Kai-shek, the leader of Republican China, was defeated by the Communists and retreated to Taiwan in 1949, the Republic of China (ROC) has been a problem for the People's Republic of China (PRC). Another source of tension for the Communist Chinese has been United States support of the Nationalist government on Taiwan, which began as support for China as an ally in World War II. At first economic only, aid to Taiwan grew to include military equipment.

In 1971, however, Taiwan lost the "China seat" in the United Nations to the PRC government. This was followed in 1972 by the Shanghai communiqué, which capped President Richard Nixon's historic visit to the PRC and which pledged the United States to reduce its military presence on Taiwan and work toward full diplomatic relations with the PRC.

Chiang Kai-shek died in 1975 and was soon succeeded as president by his son Chiang Ching-kuo, who was elected just before the severest blow to Nationalist aspirations: the 1979 normalization of diplomatic relations between Washington and Peking (Beijing). Within months, responding to a conservative uproar over the abandonment of an important ally in Asia, Congress passed the Taiwan Relations Act (TRA), an awkward but effective substitute for official diplomatic exchanges.

As for other political resources, ROC strategists must contend with the general alignment of Western countries with United States policy priorities. This leaves the ROC's best leverage in its economic power. Under sufficient pressure from Communist China, the ROC would almost certainly resort to arms, with the possibility of triggering a superpower war.

China:
Four Modernizations

Perspective

1949	People's Republic of China is founded.
1950	Land-reform law is adopted.
1951	Collectivization of agricultural production begins.
1958	Mao Zedong inaugurates Great Leap Forward.
1966	Cultural Revolution begins.
1967	Deng Xiaoping, disgraced, is sent into exile in Hebei province.
1971	People's Republic of China takes seat at United Nations; United States table tennis team visits Canton.
1972	President Nixon goes to China and signs Shanghai communiqué.
1975	Deng Xiaoping is appointed vice-chairman of Communist party and first vice-premier.
1976	Zhou Enlai dies; Mao Zedong dies; Deng Xiaoping announces Four Modernizations at Fifth National People's Congress.
1979	Peking (Beijing) and Washington normalize diplomatic relations; China authorizes "special economic zones."
1984	Deng Xiaoping concludes agreement for return of Hong Kong, long a British colony, to China in 1997.

The Chinese are obsessive numerologists who have over the centuries attributed symbolic qualities to every number. The number four is fundamental as are the four cardinal points of the compass or the "four treasures" (ink, paper, brush, inkstone) of the traditional Chinese scholar. So the ambitious plans announced by the People's Republic of China in 1976 for developing a "modern" socialist economy, a fundamental policy shift from pure socialism to some capitalist borrowings, were perhaps fittingly structured as the Four Modernizations—of agriculture, industry, defense, and technology.

By the end of the century, Communist party vice-chairman Deng Xiaoping proclaimed, "China will have a new look" and be an economic power "in the front ranks of the world."

In agriculture, which occupies about 80 per-cent of the population, incentives of a capitalist tinge, such as the "responsibility system," which offers bonuses to peasants for producing more than their quotas, have dramatically increased rice production.

In the more urban areas thousands of projects for building new industrial capacity are in progress, some fully financed by the Chinese, some representing joint ventures with foreign companies. Foreign capital and technologies being essential to the rapid industrialization of their country, the Chinese have made numerous concessions to foreign business practice. In 1979, Guangdong and Fujian provinces were authorized to set up "special economic zones" where foreign trade and investment could be conducted more freely than was possible elsewhere in China. There are now four of these: Shenzhen, Zhuhai, and Shantou in Guangdong adjacent to Hong Kong and Xiamen, and the former Amoy in Fujian.

Modernization of the industrial sector is linked to bringing Chinese defenses up to world standards, a cornerstone of Deng Xiaoping's economic liberalization program. China, which detonated its first atomic bomb in 1964, put on line in 1980 its first advanced nuclear reactor, every one of its fifty thousand parts made in China. Massive improvements in transport, communications, and other elements of the infrastructure have been pushed, including the massive Gezhou dam project to control the Yangtze River while generating hydroelectric power.

The Chinese have had to do a lot of catching up in technology, and this is the sector of the economy where foreign participation is the most welcome. American companies have concluded countless deals with the Chinese since normalization of diplomatic relations in 1979, but the Japanese, with proximity to their advantage, have been far more successful. Furthermore, the United States government prohibits export licenses for many high-technology products as a security measure, which has resulted in a troublesome amount of licensing evasion as well as smuggling. The smugglers are Chinese, usually with good connections in Hong Kong, looking for quick money.

Issues and Events

In Peking (Beijing) aging veterans of the Communist revolution see a betrayal of socialism in the policies for modernizing the economy. The people see a better life as economic liberalization proceeds. Deng Xiaoping, in the *Little Yellow Book* of his sayings, calls the Four Modernizations' goal "socialism with a Chinese face."

The ideological issue centers on how much

capitalism the Chinese economy can countenance without jeopardizing the socialist structure for which the revolution was fought. Each side cites Marxism to support its position. Maoists (supporters of former Chairman Mao Zedong) dismiss as premature the argument that public ownership of the means of production, rigid central planning, the exclusion of market mechanisms, and the other Marxist economic directives have failed in China.

The pragmatists, economic and political, dismiss the Maoists as overly fearful of change and in torrents of rhetoric press the virtues of a little capitalism. A rigidly planned economy is a "typical example of oversimplification and dogmatization of Marxism" read a recent article in the *People's Daily* of Peking. The article continued: "The policy of encouraging some people to take the lead in becoming rich is an important Marxist policy because it gives a free hand to and encourages the advanced and spurs on the backward."

Violent policy swings have been the common experience in the People's Republic, and some wariness about the future can be found. But for the moment one thing is sure: the modernization program will continue full force as long as Deng Xiaoping lives.

Deng rose steadily in party rank alongside his lifelong friend and mentor, Zhou Enlai. But his relationship with Mao Zedong was always somewhat stormy, although tempered by mutual respect. Deng, a loyal admirer of Mao as revolutionary, remained an irrepressible critic of his dogmatic economic policies. It was while arguing in 1962 for less theory and more production that Deng made his famous comment that "white cat, black cat, as long as it catches mice it's a good cat."

In the ongoing rivalries of Peking politics, Deng was accumulating enemies, including Mao's powerful wife Jiang Qing and her radical supporters, whose leaders and she were known as the Gang of Four. With the launching in 1966 of the Cultural Revolution that these radicals supported, Deng was sent off to ten years of exile. Brought back to office by Zhou Enlai in 1975, Deng was accused of causing the riots in Peking following Zhou's death in 1976 and was again stripped of power. When Mao died in September 1976, however, the Gang of Four was ousted, and Deng moved dexterously into the power vacuum.

Background

When the Communists took over China in 1949, the economy was in a shambles. Wars, floods, and famines had brought agriculture and indus-

> **Deng Xiaoping**—Chinese political leader and first vice-premier, vice-chairman of the Chinese Communist party (1975–   ). Born in 1904 in Kuang-en in Sichuan province . . . was a close associate of Zhou Enlai from student days in Paris . . . joined the Chinese Communist party . . . held high positions after the founding of the People's Republic of China (1949) . . . was purged during Cultural Revolution (1960s) . . . reappeared in ruling hierarchy (1973–1976) but soon lost favor again . . . gradually emerged as China's foremost leader after death of Chairman Mao Zedong.

try to a virtual standstill. Mao Zedong first tackled the problems of the agricultural sector through land reform and the establishment of communes. Then in 1958, before any real progress had been made in the rural areas, Mao instituted his Great Leap Forward, the "iron smelter in every backyard" campaign arising from his conviction that ideological incentives could produce economic results. It was a disaster that came close to toppling Mao from power.

Other ventures in pure socialism followed with equally dismal economic impact, even as more pragmatic party leaders—notably Liu Shaoqi, Zhou Enlai, and Deng Xiaoping—tried to redirect party policy. After Mao purged Liu and Deng as "capitalist roaders" in the Cultural Revolution, Zhou Enlai, the urbane party peacemaker, quietly continued his elaboration of a plan for modernization.

To some extent Zhou Enlai is the architect of the Four Modernizations. Yet Deng Xiaoping is the one who, if China emerges with a strong and uniquely Chinese socialist economy, will get most of the credit, perhaps taking his place in history beside Mao Zedong himself.

Several developments could sidetrack China's progress toward the goal, the most devastating being a power struggle and reversal of policies after Deng Xiaoping's death. His greatest contribution to a continuation of China's new economic direction lies in his long and shrewd revamping of the central government. Aging revolutionaries have been persuaded to make way for a younger generation of party leaders, and thousands of Deng loyalists have been retrieved from their Cultural Revolution vilification to fill key posts. Two of these, Zhao Ziyang and Hu Yaobang, head the government and the party respectively and are already carrying out Deng's program on a daily basis.

Kampuchea: Vietnam's New Battleground

Perspective

A.D. **100**	*Funan Empire is established.*
700s	*Cambodia is united under god-king Jayavaraman II.*
1400s	*Cambodia falls to Thai invasion.*
1590	*Spanish influence helps reestablish Cambodian state; series of weak kings allow expansion of Vietnam.*
1860	*French colonize Indochina; King Norodom signs treaty establishing Cambodia as French protectorate.*
1953	**January.** *Sihanouk dissolves parliament.*
	November. *French grant independence.*
1965	**May.** *Sihanouk breaks relations with United States.*
1970	**March.** *United States–backed Lon Nol overthrows Sihanouk; Khmer Republic is established.*
1975	**April.** *Capital city of Phnom Penh falls to Khmer Rouge.*
1976	**January.** *Democratic Kampuchea is established under Pol Pot.*
1979	**January.** *After invasion, Vietnam installs Heng Samrin and People's Republic of Kampuchea.*

K ampuchea may have been the worst casualty of the Vietnam war. Caught geographically and politically between more powerful neighbors and their superpower supporters, Kampuchea eventually collapsed. Civil strife soon proved even more devastating than the Vietnam War. Geographically, Kampuchea, then called Cambodia, was advantageous to the neighboring Vietnamese Communists, called the Viet Cong, who supposedly used neutral Cambodian territory as a protected route between North and South Vietnam and as a sanctuary when pursued by hostile enemy troops. Politically, Cambodia was first squeezed between the opposing aims of the United States, which supported South Vietnam, and the Soviet Union, which backed North Vietnam. After the United States left the Vietnam arena in 1975, China, the other great Communist power, exerted more influence in the region. China's opposition to the united Vietnam allowed China to confront the Soviet Union, its rival for leadership of the Communist forces, and the Vietnamese, for whom the Chinese and the Cambodians shared a historical animosity.

Cambodia's hereditary ruler, Prince Norodom Sihanouk, distrusted all parties in the Vietnam War, but he was unable to prevent the United States from bombing the jungles of Cambodia in its efforts to flush out Viet Cong they suspected were based there.

Sihanouk's government fell in 1970 to one of his generals, Lon Nol, who established the Khmer Republic. Lon Nol, who had United States support, was unable to unite the country. In fact, the Communist forces, known as the Khmer Rouge and led by Pol Pot, grew from a small force of four thousand to about seventy thousand in the five years Lon Nol was in office. In 1975, as the Vietnam War was drawing to a close and the United States began withdrawing from Indochina, the Khmer Rouge became strong enough to overthrow the Khmer Republic.

The new government, known as Democratic Kampuchea, was formally led by the National United Front of Kampuchea and headed by Sihanouk, who was brought back from exile in China. The real ruler, however, was Pol Pot, who began a genocidal reign of terror. Determined to make Kampuchea self-supporting in food production, the Pol Pot regime emptied the cities. Former urban residents, young and old, were placed in work camps whose purpose was to create farmland out of the jungle. Determined to rid the country of its middle class, the regime systematically set about exterminating all those with college educations. Between the political exterminations and those who succumbed to the rigors of the work camps, it has been estimated that at least one million of Kampuchea's six million people died.

The Pol Pot regime was forced out of power in 1979—but not as a result of its barbarisms against the Kampuchean people. Rather, it lost on the larger stage of the international competition between the two great Communist nations, the Soviet Union and China. Pol Pot had the support of China, while the newly unified Vietnam had become a close ally of the Soviet Union. After a series of bitter border battles, an invasion by Vietnamese troops succeeded in installing a former lieutenant of Pol Pot, Heng Samrin, in power. Pol Pot and many of his Khmer Rouge supporters escaped to the hills.

Issues and Events

On October 31, 1984, the UN General Assembly voted, for the sixth time since the invasion of 1978, to call on Vietnam to withdraw its forces and influence from Kampuchea and let the Kampuchean people work out their own form of government. Vietnam has expressed a readiness to compromise, but fear of China's close relationship with the Khmer Rouge and the consequent possibility of a Chinese-influenced government in proximity to Vietnam prevents compliance. In addition, most Kampucheans fear that without Vietnamese support, the rule of their country would again pass into the hands of the dreaded Pol Pot. Experts say diplomatic negotiations could go on for years.

Neither the United States nor a majority of members of the UN General Assembly has as yet formally recognized the People's Republic of Kampuchea. Instead, the officially recognized government of Kampuchea remains the Khmer Rouge of Pol Pot, now guerrilla soldiers hiding in western Kampuchean jungles. The rationale is not support for a regime internationally known for the genocidal terrorism of its own people but refusal to reward the aggression of Vietnam.

The Khmer Rouge fights on. Intellectual moderate Khiew Samphan recently became the new leader of the party, but Pol Pot retains control of the army, which causes many to suspect the change to be merely propaganda. Despite the support of China, the Khmer Rouge's strength has lessened in the past two years as the numbers of a rival revolutionary group have grown.

A former premier under Sihanouk, Son Sann, leads the Khmer People's National Liberation Front (KPNLF), a moderate-to-right-wing guerrilla organization of approximately fifteen thousand and growing. In spite of increased popularity among Kampucheans and a small number of foreign governments, the KPNLF would be drastically outnumbered and outfinanced by the Soviet-backed Vietnamese army even if they merged with the hated Khmer Rouge, a development rejected by both sides.

One international tactic being implemented to force Vietnam out of Kampuchea is the discontinuation of economic aid to either country by major foreign powers. Most funds now come from international relief agencies and nations such as the Netherlands, Australia, and Sweden.

While diplomacy founders, guerrillas wage war, and international superpowers match wits and weapons, the People's Republic of Kampuchea struggles to reverse the destruction of a country. Kampuchea's educational and economic systems were virtually destroyed by wars and the Pol Pot regime. While one-half of the nation's children remain moderately to severely malnourished, many at least can now receive an education. Attempts are being made to revive the rubber industry and agriculture. The Communist regime continues slowly to rebuild the capital city. And rebel groups, consisting largely of underfed teenagers, continue the war to regain their country.

Background

Kampuchea broke away from French rule in 1953, when Prince Norodom Sihanouk, then king, who had ruled under French auspices since 1941, dissolved the parliamentary system and declared martial law, forcing the French to grant independence later that year. Sihanouk's reign was moderate, although he was largely ineffective at industrializing a country populated by subsistence farmers living in isolated villages. However, the growth of several small cities as well as the emergence of rubber as a major export were indications of Kampuchea's economic improvement. Sihanouk's alignment with China was primarily a move to maintain neutrality in the Vietnam War. His efforts were doomed to failure, and in 1970 he was forced into exile in China.

Under Lon Nol, who staged the coup in March 1970 that established Cambodia as the Khmer Republic, the nation slid into involvement in the war. Meanwhile Pol Pot waged guerrilla warfare against Lon Nol from the jungle. In the five years of Lon Nol's regime, hatred of the United States, due to the relentless bombing by the United States military, caused the Khmer Rouge forces to swell from four thousand to seventy thousand. By 1975, after a bloody civil war, the Khmer Rouge was strong enough to overthrow the Khmer Republic. While the new constitution for Democratic Kampuchea, which was allied with Communist China, did not come about until January 5, 1976, the terror and torture for the Kampuchean people began immediately. The ensuing reign of terror was supervised by Pol Pot and implemented by his secret police, the Nokorbal.

Traditional hostilities between Vietnam and Kampuchea came to a head in December 1977, when relations were broken off. Some outsiders suspected that the Vietnamese used the atrocities of the Khmer Rouge merely as a public excuse masking an ancient desire to control all of Indochina.

Total guerrilla forces now number around forty thousand and the critically starving around two million. While Vietnam apparently feels it cannot achieve total domination of Indochina, rebel forces remain divided. For the immediate future, Kampuchea appears likely to remain a battleground unless the Kampucheans can assemble a national government that can achieve world recognition and can avoid Vietnamese domination.

Korea: Uncertainty in North and South

Perspective

1392	*Yi dynasty, which ruled Korea up to annexation by Japan in 1910, is founded.*
1876	*Japan forces Korea to sign commercial treaty.*
1894	*Japan assumes control of Korea at beginning of Sino-Japanese War.*
1910	**August 22.** *Japan annexes Korea.*
1945	*Following Japanese surrender in World War II, Korea is divided into Soviet and United States occupation zones north and south of thirty-eighth parallel.*
1948	*Democratic People's Republic of Korea is established in north under Kim Il-sung; Republic of Korea is founded in south under Syngman Rhee.*
1950	**June 25.** *North Korea invades South Korea; United States sends combat troops as part of United Nations multinational force.*
1953	**July 27.** *Armistice agreement is reached; United States and South Korea sign mutual defense treaty.*
1960	*Syngman Rhee's victory in rigged election is followed by riots, proclamation of martial law, and his resignation.*
1961	*Park Chung Hee takes control of South Korea in military coup.*
1968	*North Koreans seize United States intelligence ship Pueblo.*
1979	*Park Chung Hee is assassinated.*
1980	*Chun Doo Hwan stages military coup in South Korea, bans opposition leaders from political activity.*
1985	*Kim Dae Jung returns to South Korea from exile, galvanizing opposition to Chun Doo Hwan government.*

Like the faraway rumble of thunder before a storm, reverberations of the belligerency in Korea are frequently heard—the massacre by North Koreans of a group of top South Korean officials on a state visit to Burma, gunfire at the truce talks site of Panmunjŏm, the roughing up and house arrest of opposition leader Kim Dae Jung upon his return to South Korea from exile in the United States. The two Koreas facing each other across the thirty-eighth parallel, the Democratic People's Republic of Korea, or North Korea, and the Republic of Korea, or South Korea, have the same objective—reunification—but on their own seemingly irreconcilable terms.

Since the division of the country at the thirty-eighth parallel following World War II, the contrast between the two Koreas has become ever sharper. Today, after some forty years, the North Korean regime set up by Kim Il-sung in Pyŏngyang wields dictatorial control over a solidly socialist system. South Korea, reflecting American influence, has a capitalist economy and a semblance of democracy.

Issues and Events

Both above and below the thirty-eighth parallel Korea is ruled by former soldiers. Kim Il-sung, founder and still head of the North Korean regime, was an anti-Japanese guerrilla leader based in Manchuria who returned to Korea after the Communist victory in China as a Red Army captain. At the end of the Korean War, Kim assumed the title of marshal of the Korean People's Army and established dictatorial power.

The politics in South Korea are far more volatile. A fragile democracy supports a presidential system, but real power is maintained by factional alliances and military authority. Chun Doo Hwan, who seized control in a military coup in 1980 following President Park Chung Hee's assassination in 1979, gave the world a glimpse of the actual process of government in South Korea on the return from exile of a prominent dissident.

Kim Dae Jung, Chun's chief political rival, arrived at Seoul's Kimpo International Airport on February 8, 1985, with an escort of more than thirty American and Korean supporters, including two United States congressmen and a former United States ambassador. While some seventeen thousand riot police kept an estimated fifty thousand sympathizers in check, Kim was forcibly separated from the rest of his party by security agents and rushed off to house arrest. Several of the Americans reported being knocked to the ground during the dispute.

The glare of publicity, assured by the United States State Department's extraction of a promise from the Koreans to keep the arrival "trouble free," exposed the repressive nature of Chun's regime to the detriment of South Korea's international image. But Chun Doo Hwan was fighting for his political life. Kim Dae Jung, who narrowly lost a 1971 presidential election, was the most formidable of the opposition leaders Chun banned from public activity in 1980 on sedition charges. Kim's return four days before a legislative election galvanized the fragmented and intimidated opposition, which led to a small victory in the elections.

Opposition to Chun's rule will almost certainly become better organized and more vocal as the 1988 presidential election approaches. Chun is relying on the people to acknowledge his accomplishments in halting the rampant corruption of the Park Chung Hee era, in setting the economy on a strong growth path, and in keeping North Korea at bay (a hefty 6 percent of South Korea's gross national product goes for defense). Kim Dae Jung and the other opposition leaders speak for a silent constituency that has seen economic progress and political stability bought at the price of limiting democracy.

Background

Most Koreans, north or south, perceive the territorial division of their country as foreign intervention, a consequence of international rivalries. There is a long history of foreign interest in the peninsula, for the area by fate of geography forms a buffer region where China, Japan, and Russia have over the centuries met and clashed. The Koreans preserved their cultural identity by keeping a low profile, choosing seclusion and political conservatism as camouflage. Also, from 108 B.C. during the Han dynasty in China up to Korea's annexation by Japan in 1910, Korea derived a measure of security from its status as a cultural and economic appendage of China, first as an integral part of the empire and thereafter as China's most valuable tributary state.

Thus, with the World War II defeat of Japan in 1945, the Koreans fully expected restoration of their independence, but their hopes were dashed as the "transitional" occupation of their country by Soviet and American forces dragged on. The territorial division began to look forever set with the establishment in 1948 of separate governments in the two occupation zones. In the north the Soviets, refusing to comply with a UN call for a national election, installed the Russian-trained Kim Il-sung. In the south the Americans, complying with the UN resolution, supervised the election, which resulted in the victory of the United States–educated Syngman Rhee.

Then on June 25, 1950, the Soviet-supported North Koreans invaded the south in a surprise attack that aimed at taking the entire peninsula. Within three days they had pushed the South Korean and American defenders south of Seoul to a small area in the extreme southeast. President Truman's quick action brought a UN force of mostly United States troops into the war, and by September General Douglas MacArthur had turned back the invaders by his successful amphibious landing on the west coast at Inchon. A stalemate might have ensued except for MacArthur's decision to drive the belligerents northward across the Yalu River border with China and so to unite all of Korea under the elected government in the south. But this was to overlook Chinese security interests. Chinese Communist troops came to the assistance of the North Koreans, prolonging the war even after truce talks began at Panmunjŏm in July 1951.

An armistice was signed on July 27, 1953, but the war goes on in other guises. The initial United States policy of helping Korea to its feet through economic aid, technical advice, and limited military assistance evolved into a commitment to the defense of South Korea by full military support. The North Koreans, backed by the Soviet Union and China, are waging a propaganda war while exploiting any and every opportunity to demoralize their potential foes to the south.

North Korean tactics include both terrorism and conciliation. One terrorist target is the American presence in South Korea, and among many incidents in this offensive have been the seizure of the United States intelligence ship *Pueblo* and its crew in 1968, the shooting down of a United States helicopter that had strayed across the thirty-eighth parallel in 1977, and several outbursts of gunfire in the demilitarized zone. The massacre by North Korean agents of South Korean officials visiting Burma in 1983 was a tragically visible aspect of ongoing efforts to disrupt the government in the south. More recently the campaign shifted to a posture of conciliation. North Korea sent $12 million in flood aid to South Korea in October 1984 and a month later agreed to trade talks at Panmunjŏm.

As long as an artificial and essentially indefensible boundary is the only protection China, the Soviet Union, and the United States—all of which provide money and other support to the local governments—see for their international security interests, the sparring will continue. Reunification of Korea as an independent state capable of serving as a neutral buffer would resolve much of the present crisis. But the refusal of both Koreas to accede to any formula proposed by the other and the powerlessness of the UN to intervene because of veto privileges dim the prospect of reunification by negotiation. Trying to settle the issue by military force could quickly involve the superpowers and trigger a calamity without winners. Patience has helped to solve many problems, and the East is stronger in this virtue than the West. As the Koreans say, "After ten years, even the mountains and rivers change."

Philippines: The Marcos Regime

Perspective

1521	*Ferdinand Magellan claims Philippines for Spain.*
1892	*Filipinos declare independence from Spain.*
1898	*Spain cedes Philippines to United States.*
1946	*Philippines gains independence from United States.*
1965	**November.** *Ferdinand E. Marcos is elected president.*
1969	*Marcos becomes first president of Philippines to win reelection.*
1972	**September 22–23.** *Marcos declares martial law and arrests Benigno S. Aquino along with several hundred other opposition members.*
1980	**May.** *Aquino is allowed to leave for United States.*
1981	**January.** *Martial law is lifted.*
1983	**August 21.** *Aquino is assassinated at Manila International Airport while attempting to return to Philippines.*
1984	**October.** *Citizens' panel investigating Aquino's death unanimously rejects government contention that he was killed by Communist gunman, recommends indictments.*
1985	**February.** *General Fabian C. Ver, army chief of staff, and twenty-five others go on trial for Aquino murder.*

On August 21, 1983, Benigno S. Aquino, popular and outspoken critic of President Ferdinand E. Marcos, attempted to return to the Philippines after a three-year American exile. Within moments of being escorted from his plane by military security guards, Aquino had been shot dead. His assassination galvanized a mass public outcry in a country that had been until recently under martial law and focused world attention on the character of the Marcos government. It also focused attention on the Philippines itself, a country with a small, very rich ruling class and a large, undereducated population living in great poverty.

Issues and Events

Initially elected president in 1965 and reelected in 1969, Marcos was barred by the Philippines constitution from holding office for more than two successive terms. But by 1970 he was seeking to consolidate his political power by forcing the adoption of a new constitution creating a parliamentary government that would enable him to remain in office. Political resistance led to violent clashes between the government and the opposition, and when Marcos declared martial law in September 1972, he claimed that the action was necessary to maintain law and order. He immediately ordered the arrests of several hundred opposition leaders, the most prominent of whom was Benigno S. Aquino, then a senator. In 1973 Marcos proclaimed the ratification of the new constitution, pronouncing himself both prime minister and president.

Aquino was held in prison until May 1980. During that time he was accused of murder and subversion, tried by a military court whose legitimacy he refused to acknowledge, and found guilty. He almost died during a forty-day fast to protest the trial. He was given a death sentence, but public outrage both within the Philippines and from the United States forced Marcos to grant him a reprieve. In 1980 Marcos allowed him to go to the United States for heart bypass surgery.

Remaining in America for three years, Aquino continued to speak out against Marcos. Yet, he believed that the only hope for restoring democratic freedoms to the Philippines lay in persuading Marcos gradually to restore them, rather than in ousting Marcos, and it was with this mission in mind that he decided to return in 1983.

Immediately following the assassination, the government insisted that Aquino had been shot by a Communist gunman, Rolando Galman, who in turn was shot and killed by security guards. But public protests (two million people marched in Aquino's funeral procession, and a million showed up to commemorate the first anniversary of his death) forced Marcos to appoint an independent commission to investigate the military's involvement in the shooting. In October 1984, the five-member commission released two reports, both rejecting the government's assertion that Galman had shot Aquino. The minority report named one general and six soldiers as participants in the shooting, while the report of the four-member majority implicated twenty-six conspirators. Among the twenty-six was General Fabian C. Ver, the army chief of staff, who is Marcos's third cousin and his close friend. Many Filipino opposition leaders maintain that Ver would not have authorized such an action without Marcos's knowledge and consent. The accused, including Ver, went on trial early in 1985.

Problems of missing witnesses and conflicting testimony marred the proceedings.

Background

A southeastern Asian archipelago comprising more than seven thousand islands (many uninhabited), the Philippines gained its independence in 1946 after more than four hundred years of Western domination. The Spanish, represented by Ferdinand Magellan, arrived in 1521, when the majority of Filipinos still lived in extended kinship groups without any broad political unity. Settlers under Philip II, for whom the islands are named, brought Roman Catholicism, and the country is still 83 percent Roman Catholic. The Spanish controlled international trade and internal politics until the end of the nineteenth century, when nationalist revolutionary forces began agitating for independence. These groups met with little success until the time of the Spanish-American War, when the United States began supporting them.

Independence was declared on June 12, 1892, and although the date is still celebrated, independence proved illusory. The peace treaty the United States signed with Spain in 1898 specified cession of the Philippines to the United States, and in the end, it was America that put down the nationalist revolution in an extremely bloody campaign. That campaign ended costing more lives and money than had the Spanish-American War.

Democratic self-rule was recognized as the ultimate goal of American involvement. To this end, American policy placed emphasis on improving education in the Philippines, with great success. But America kept tight control over defense and foreign policy, and little attempt was made to expand economic opportunity. Businesses remained in the hands of Americans and of a small, wealthy, Filipino elite. In addition, United States army and naval bases in the Philippines were regarded as crucial to America's growing position as a Pacific power.

Independence was mandated within ten years by the Tydings-McDuffie Act of 1934, but the Japanese invasion and occupation during World War II upset the schedule and wreaked havoc with the economy. As a condition of providing reconstruction aid, the United States extracted generous trade and military concessions. The economic troubles, exacerbated by the widespread corruption in business dealings by the Filipino elite, became a problem that was handed down from president to president until 1965, when Marcos was elected. By that time, ties to the United States had become a highly sensitive political issue, with a large part of the

> **Ferdinand (Edralin) Marcos**—president of the Republic of the Philippines. Born in 1917 in Sarrat, Ilocos Norte province . . . graduated from the University of the Philippines (1935) . . . was admitted to the bar after being acquitted of murder . . . was his country's most decorated soldier in World War II . . . served in the Philippine Congress (1949–1959) and the Senate (1959–1965) . . . became president of the Philippines (1965–   ) . . . declared martial law (1972–1981) and instituted a new constitution (1973).

population especially opposed to United States military bases in the Philippines. Marcos ran for reelection in 1969 on a platform that included the renegotiation of treaties with the United States and trade with Communist countries.

Marcos's political and economic policies have all been aimed at consolidating wealth and power for himself, his wife Imelda, and an elite group of associates. Since lifting martial law in 1981, Marcos has continued to run a one-man government by decree. Observers within the country and in the U.S. State Department, however, believe that he is losing his grip on power because of the deteriorating economic situation and because of the extent to which the Aquino assassination has intensified pressure for reform from inside and outside the country.

The aftermath of Aquino's death saw an unprecedented degree of activism among the people. Demonstrations in the streets became common; often they were led by Aquino's brother Agapito (Butz) Aquino. The police have met them sometimes with restraint, more often with tear gas and water cannons, but even violent confrontation does not appear to deter the demonstrators from organizing again.

Presidential elections are scheduled for 1987. While some Filipino opposition leaders and U.S. State Department skeptics doubt that Marcos, in view of rising public resistance and his own uncertain health, can hold on that long, Marcos himself insists that he will remain in power.

Politically, the opposition is gaining strength; in the May 1984 Assembly elections, opposition candidates won almost a third of the Assembly's two hundred seats. But within the opposition there is broad disagreement over specific policy issues as well as over the tactical question of whether reform can be accomplished through Marcos or whether he should be ousted. If he is ousted, if he dies, or if he is forced by ill health to resign, a power vacuum will exist that could further destabilize the country.

New Caledonia: Rocky Road to Independence

Perspective

1774	*Captain James Cook lands at New Caledonia.*
1853	*New Caledonia is annexed by France.*
1946	*New Caledonia becomes French overseas territory.*
1957	*July 22. General Council is replaced by Territorial Assembly.*
1958	*December 17. Territorial Assembly decides New Caledonia will remain overseas territory of France.*
1984	*November 18. French candidates opposed to independence come to power in elections.*
	November 24. Amid widespread violence, France announces it will speed up process of self-determination.
	December 4. Special envoy from France attempts to mediate dispute between Kanak separatists and white minority favoring continued ties with France.
1985	*January 15. French envoy Edgard Pisani proposes that New Caledonia be given partial independence, in association with France.*
	January 19. French president François Mitterrand travels to New Caledonia in attempt to ease hostilities.

French president François Mitterrand's long journey to New Caledonia in January 1985 underscored the growing concern about this strife-torn French territory's internal struggle over the issue of independence. Hoping to calm escalating hostilities, as well as to sell a plan that would grant the island partial independence, President Mitterrand found himself in the center of a controversy that threatened to divide forever the allegiances of New Caledonia's residents.

Of the population of more than 140,000, about 42 percent are indigenous Melanesians, or Kanaks; about 40 percent are French; and the remainder are Vietnamese, Indonesians, Chinese, and Polynesians. The Europeans, who are concentrated in and around the capital city of Nouméa, favor retaining close ties with France. This arrangement would permit them to maintain economic control and perhaps political dominance. Represented by the Kanak Socialist National Liberation Front (FLNKS), the Kanaks,

who find France's government sympathetic, demand independence and control of their native land. The European settlers feel that such a course would discriminate against them.

Issues and Events

A crisis began to develop in November 1984 when Kanak separatists began setting up roadblocks, raiding homes, and burning cars in order to disrupt the November 18 elections for a semi-autonomous territorial government. The separatists urged a boycott of the elections, saying that they would not lead to independence soon enough. New Caledonia's French police fired tear gas and stun grenades as militants tore up ballots, terrorized voters, and burned down a town hall. In the election itself, French settlers opposed to independence won thirty-four seats in the new forty-two-seat assembly. As violence continued, France, on November 24, 1984, announced that it would speed up the process of self-determination, saying that this could lead the way to eventual independence. The Kanak militants demanded a referendum on independence in which only Kanaks could take part.

On December 4, 1984, special French envoy Edgard Pisani arrived in Nouméa with the mission of finding a solution acceptable to both sides of the dispute. In mid-January 1985, Pisani recommended a form of partial independence for New Caledonia and proposed elections to establish a semiautonomous nation. This proposal at first did nothing to quell the violence. Finally, in a determined effort to bring peace, President Mitterrand himself visited the island in January 1985. Violence continued into the spring, with the death toll reaching twenty, but in May the FLNKS agreed to participate in polls to establish regional councils. A referendum on independence was scheduled for 1987.

Background

New Caledonia became a French overseas territory in 1946, its population receiving French citizenship. In 1958 its Territorial Assembly voted to retain the status of overseas territory, reflecting the wishes of most of the island's French. At issue ever since, and especially today, is whether or not a country so divided can continue along its present course. In effect, New Caledonia has been partitioned, and many of the New Caledonians that remain loyal to France are questioning that government's desire and ability to protect them. With the recent, although less violent, unrest in the French overseas department of Guadeloupe, action taken in New Caledonia could set precedents in the French government's handling of its possessions.

World Scoreboard: People, Power, and Politics

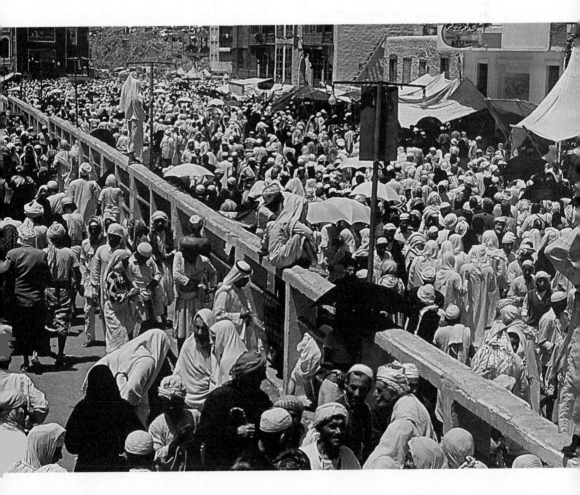

Introduction

The independent nations of the world are tied together through a network of political, economic, and social contacts. This section uses contrasts such as largest and smallest, richest and poorest, most developed and least developed, and others to present a general overview and interpretation of world conditions.

Less Developed Nations

Africa, a continent of developing nations, typifies the quandary in which most Third World countries find themselves. Many of these nations, having recently gained independence from colonial powers, are basically agrarian in nature; subsistence farming engages most of the population. Due to high birth rates (which have led to huge population increases), drought conditions, and general poverty, food shortages occur and slow starvation results. To compete economically with the world's more developed countries, less developed countries must industrialize.

Developed Nations

Highly developed, or industrialized, nations share many similar characteristics. In most of these countries, for example, the population is marked by a declining or zero population growth rate and a low death rate. People are mainly urban, and attempts have been made to establish equal rights for women. Industry is supported by the capacity to create energy, an efficient and modern transportation system, and a balance of trade; and a highly organized military establishment is generally present.

An industrialized society also has the means to educate its population, and scientific and technological research combats disease, hunger, exploding population growth, and high death rates while maintaining the industrial system. The life-style in these nations, however, often results in a high incidence of heart disease, cancer, alcoholism, and mental illness. Much research is devoted to solving the health problems that typify a developed society.

World Overview

Country	Population (In 1,000s)	Area (In mi²)	Area (In km²)	Density (Per mi²)	Density (Per km²)	GNP/GDP (In $US millions)
Africa						
Algeria	21,695	919,595	2,381,741	24.0	9.1	42,900*
Angola	7,875	481,353	1,246,700	16.0	6.3	3,900*
Benin	3,970	43,484	112,622	91.0	35.0	1,100
Botswana	1,055	231,805	600,372	4.6	1.8	722*
Burkina Faso	6,820	105,869	274,200	64.0	25.0	1,100
Burundi	4,760	10,747	27,834	443.0	171.0	1,200*
Cameroon	9,640	183,569	475,442	53.0	20.0	7,000
Cape Verde	300	1,557	4,033	193.0	74.0	142
Central African Republic	2,620	240,535	622,984	11.0	4.2	658*
Chad	5,180	495,755	1,284,000	10.0	4.0	500*
Comoros	460	838	2,171	549.0	212.0	90
Congo	1,770	132,047	342,000	13.0	5.2	1,800*
Djibouti	360	8,880	23,000	41.0	16.0	116*
Egypt	47,755	386,643	1,001,400	124.0	48.0	30,800
Equatorial Guinea	280	10,831	28,051	26.0	10.0	100
Ethiopia	34,050	472,434	1,223,600	72.0	28.0	4,800*
Gabon	975	103,347	267,667	9.4	3.6	3,500*
Gambia, The	715	4,361	11,295	164.0	63.0	240
Ghana	14,030	92,100	238,537	152.0	59.0	10,500

*Figure reflects gross domestic product (GDP). All other figures indicate gross national product (GNP).

Country	Population (In 1,000s)	Area (In mi²)	Area (In km²)	Density (Per mi²)	Density (Per km²)	GNP/GDP (In $US millions)
Guinea	5,655	94,926	245,857	60.0	23.0	1,710
Guinea-Bissau	850	13,948	36,125	61.0	24.0	177*
Ivory Coast	9,325	123,847	320,763	75.0	29.0	7,700*
Kenya	18,970	224,961	582,646	84.0	33.0	6,300*
Lesotho	1,495	11,720	30,355	128.0	49.0	569
Liberia	2,195	43,000	111,369	51.0	20.0	800*
Libya	3,785	679,362	1,759,540	5.6	2.2	26,500*
Madagascar	9,775	226,658	587,041	43.0	17.0	3,200*
Malawi	6,940	45,747	118,484	152.0	59.0	1,340*
Mali	7,650	478,766	1,240,000	16.0	6.2	1,000*
Mauritania	1,640	397,955	1,030,700	4.1	1.6	720
Mauritius	1,025	790	2,045	1,297.0	501.0	960*
Morocco	21,750	172,414	446,550	126.0	49.0	15,200
Mozambique	13,700	302,329	783,030	45.0	17.0	1,500
Niger	6,390	489,191	1,267,000	13.0	5.0	2,000
Nigeria	85,219	356,699	923,768	239.0	92.0	74,000*
Rwanda	5,935	10,169	26,338	584.0	225.0	1,388*
São Tomé and Principe	89	372	964	239.0	92.0	30*
Senegal	6,650	75,955	196,722	88.0	34.0	2,500*
Seychelles	66	171	443	386.0	149.0	128*
Sierra Leone	3,855	27,925	72,325	138.0	53.0	1,200*
Somalia	6,465	246,200	637,657	26.0	10.0	1,875*
South Africa	26,855	433,680	1,123,226	62.0	24.0	73,600*
Sudan	21,390	967,500	2,505,813	22.0	8.5	7,100*
Swaziland	660	6,704	17,364	98.0	38.0	500*
Tanzania	21,525	364,900	945,087	59.0	23.0	5,200*
Togo	2,965	21,925	56,785	135.0	52.0	950
Tunisia	7,295	63,170	163,610	115.0	45.0	8,700
Uganda	14,505	91,134	236,036	159.0	61.0	4,800*
Zaire	32,625	905,567	2,345,409	36.0	14.0	3,400*
Zambia	6,660	290,586	752,614	23.0	8.8	2,900*
Zimbabwe	8,190	150,804	390,580	54.0	21.0	7,100*
North America						
Antigua and Barbuda	78	170	440	459.0	177.0	126*
Bahamas	230	5,382	13,939	43.0	17.0	1,400
Barbados	250	166	430	1,506.0	581.0	998*
Belize	160	8,866	22,963	18.0	7.0	169*
Canada	25,270	3,831,033	9,922,330	6.6	2.5	288,800
Costa Rica	2,725	19,730	51,100	138.0	53.0	3,300*
Cuba	9,770	44,218	114,524	221.0	85.0	14,900
Dominica	74	290	752	290.0	98.0	56
Dominican Republic	6,205	18,704	48,442	332.0	128.0	7,600
El Salvador	4,905	8,124	21,041	604.0	233.0	3,600*
Grenada	114	133	344	857.0	331.0	119
Guatemala	8,080	42,042	108,889	192.0	74.0	8,600*
Haiti	5,305	10,714	27,750	495.0	191.0	1,500
Honduras	4,500	43,277	112,088	104.0	40.0	2,620
Jamaica	2,170	4,244	10,991	511.0	197.0	3,000
Mexico	78,670	761,604	1,972,547	103.0	40.0	168,000*
Nicaragua	2,970	50,193	130,000	59.0	23.0	2,500*
Panama	2,155	29,762	77,082	72.0	28.0	3,945
St. Christopher and Nevis	45	104	269	433.0	167.0	42
Saint Lucia	120	238	616	504.0	195.0	122*
Saint Vincent and the Grenadines	140	150	389	933.0	360.0	69
Trinidad and Tobago	1,240	1,980	5,128	626.0	242.0	7,316

*Figure reflects gross domestic product (GDP). All other figures indicate gross national product (GNP).

Country	Population (In 1,000s)	Area (In mi²)	Area (In km²)	Density (Per mi²)	Density (Per km²)	GNP/GDP (In $US millions)
United States	237,640	3,679,245	9,529,200	65.0	25.0	3,363,300
South America						
Argentina	30,340	1,068,301	2,766,889	28.0	11.0	130,000
Bolivia	6,115	464,164	1,098,581	14.0	5.6	5,600
Brazil	134,340	3,265,075	8,456,508	41.0	16.0	295,000
Chile	11,740	292,135	756,626	40.0	16.0	23,600*
Colombia	28,545	439,737	1,138,914	65.0	25.0	40,000
Ecuador	9,235	109,483	283,561	84.0	33.0	13,300
Guyana	840	83,000	214,469	10.0	3.9	430
Paraguay	3,230	157,048	406,752	21.0	7.9	5,800*
Peru	19,520	496,224	1,285,216	39.0	15.0	19,200
Suriname	375	63,037	163,265	5.9	2.3	1,044*
Uruguay	2,930	68,037	176,215	43.0	17.0	9,400*
Venezuela	16,040	352,144	912,050	46.0	18.0	69,300*
Asia						
Afghanistan	14,650	250,000	647,000	65.0	25.0	2,800
Bahrain	415	256	662	1,621.0	627.0	4,000*
Bangladesh	101,130	55,598	143,998	1,819.0	702.0	11,000
Bhutan	1,435	18,147	47,000	79.0	31.0	131*
Brunei	220	2,226	5,765	99.0	38.0	19,800*
Burma	36,795	261,228	676,577	141.0	54.0	5,900*
China	1,080,980	3,718,783	9,631,600	291.0	112.0	313,000
Cyprus	675	3,572	9,251	189.0	73.0	2,172*
India	754,600	1,237,061	3,203,975	610.0	236.0	146,000
Indonesia	166,070	741,101	1,919,443	224.0	87.0	70,000
Iran	44,500	636,296	1,648,000	70.0	27.0	66,500
Iraq	15,255	167,925	434,924	91.0	35.0	30,000
Israel	4,189	8,302	21,501	505.0	195.0	22,200
Japan	120,200	145,834	377,708	824.0	318.0	1,060,000
Jordan	2,475	35,135	91,000	70.0	27.0	4,900
Kampuchea	6,180	69,898	181,035	88.0	34.0	n.a.
Korea, North	19,855	46,540	120,538	427.0	165.0	16,200
Korea, South	42,315	38,025	98,484	1,113.0	430.0	70,800
Kuwait	1,815	6,880	17,818	264.0	102.0	27,600
Laos	3,775	91,429	236,800	41.0	16.0	320
Lebanon	2,610	4,015	10,400	650.0	251.0	4,100*
Malaysia	15,500	128,430	332,632	121.0	47.0	25,100
Maldives	175	115	298	1,522.0	587.0	74*
Mongolia	1,885	604,250	1,565,000	3.1	1.2	1,200*
Nepal	16,785	56,135	145,391	299.0	115.0	2,300
Oman	1,025	82,030	212,457	12.0	4.8	6,300
Pakistan	101,300	339,732	879,902	298.0	115.0	33,020
Philippines	55,140	115,831	300,000	476.0	184.0	39,000
Qatar	280	4,247	11,000	65.0	25.0	7,900*
Saudi Arabia	10,970	830,000	2,149,690	13.0	5.1	120,000*
Singapore	2,545	224	581	11,361.0	4,380.0	14,200*
Sri Lanka	16,070	24,962	64,652	644.0	249.0	4,400*
Syria	10,485	71,498	185,180	147.0	57.0	18,400*
Taiwan	19,090	13,900	36,002	1,373.0	530.0	49,800
Thailand	52,200	198,115	513,115	264.0	102.0	38,400
Turkey	50,730	300,948	779,452	169.0	65.0	53,800
United Arab Emirates	1,600	32,278	83,600	50.0	19.0	30,000*
Vietnam	58,930	127,242	329,556	463.0	179.0	10,700
Yemen PDR (Aden)	2,180	128,560	332,968	17.0	6.5	792
Yemen AR (Sana)	5,985	75,290	195,000	79.0	31.0	3,800

*Figure reflects gross domestic product (GDP). All other figures indicate gross national product (GNP).

Country	Population (In 1,000s)	Area (In mi²)	Area (In km²)	Density (Per mi²)	Density (Per km²)	GNP/GDP (In $US millions)
Europe						
Albania	2,935	11,100	28,748	264.0	102.0	2,150
Andorra	39	175	453	223.0	86.0	n.a.
Austria	7,580	32,377	83,855	234.0	90.0	66,890
Belgium	9,875	11,783	30,518	838.0	324.0	85,420
Bulgaria	8,980	42,823	110,912	210.0	81.0	35,300
Czechoslovakia	15,490	49,381	127,896	314.0	121.0	147,100
Denmark	5,010	16,633	43,080	301.0	116.0	56,400
Finland	4,885	130,558	338,145	37.0	14.0	49,100
France	55,020	211,208	547,026	261.0	101.0	542,000*
Germany, East	16,600	41,768	108,179	397.0	153.0	165,600
Germany, West	61,390	96,019	248,687	639.0	247.0	658,400
Greece	10,030	50,944	131,944	197.0	76.0	38,600
Hungary	10,675	35,921	93,036	297.0	115.0	65,200
Iceland	240	39,769	103,000	6.0	2.3	2,200
Ireland	3,595	27,136	70,283	132.0	51.0	17,000
Italy	56,940	116,319	301,266	490.0	189.0	347,000
Liechtenstein	27	62	160	435.0	169.0	439*
Luxembourg	365	998	2,586	366.0	141.0	3,400
Malta	360	122	316	2,951.0	1,139.0	1,140
Monaco	28	.6	1.5	46,667.0	18,667.0	n.a.
Netherlands	14,465	15,892	41,160	910.0	351.0	137,300
Norway	4,150	149,158	386,317	28.0	11.0	56,200
Poland	37,055	120,728	312,683	307.0	119.0	186,800
Portugal	10,065	35,516	91,985	283.0	109.0	23,400
Romania	22,860	91,699	237,500	249.0	96.0	104,800
San Marino	23	24	61	958.0	377.0	n.a.
Spain	38,515	194,882	504,741	198.0	76.0	179,700
Sweden	8,335	173,780	450,089	48.0	19.0	81,000*
Switzerland	6,485	15,943	41,293	408.0	157.0	95,600
U.S.S.R.	275,590	8,600,383	22,274,900	32.0	12.0	1,715,000
United Kingdom	56,040	94,092	243,694	596.0	230.0	482,700
Vatican City	.7	.2	.4	3,500.0	1,750.0	n.a.
Yugoslavia	23,075	98,766	255,804	234.0	90.0	53,900
Oceania						
Australia	15,565	2,967,909	7,686,850	52.0	20.0	153,000
Fiji	695	7,055	18,272	99.0	38.0	1,850*
Kiribati	62	275	712	225.0	87.0	36*
Nauru	8	8.2	21	951.0	371.0	155,400
New Zealand	3,155	103,515	268,103	30.0	12.0	25,390
Papua New Guinea	3,400	178,703	462,840	19.0	7.3	2,000
Solomon Islands	270	11,506	29,800	23.0	9.1	110
Tonga	107	270	699	396.0	153.0	50
Tuvalu	8	10	26	820.0	315.0	4
Vanuatu	130	5,714	14,800	23.0	8.8	n.a.
Western Samoa	160	1,097	2,842	146.0	56.0	130

*Figure reflects gross domestic product (GDP). All other figures indicate gross national product (GNP).

n.a. = not available

A Changing World: New Nations and New Names

The geographical knowledge of anyone out of school for even a few years has been rendered obsolete in recent years by the emergence of dozens of new countries and assumptions of new names by "old" countries. Adding to the confusion is the emergence in South Africa of "self-governing" units under that country's apartheid policy. The list below summarizes some of the major changes made since the early 1970s.

Antigua and Barbuda   Nation of three small islands in the West Indies in the Caribbean. Gained independence from Britain in 1981.

Bahamas   Nation comprising more than seven hundred small islands off the coast of Florida. Gained independence from Britain in 1973.

Bangladesh   Populous Asian country bordering India. Seceded from Pakistan in 1971. Formerly East Pakistan, a province of Pakistan.

Belize   Small country in Central America. Gained independence from Britain in 1981. As colony, called British Honduras until 1973.

Benin   New name (1975) for small country in western Africa. Formerly called Dahomey; renamed for ancient African kingdom.

Bophuthatswana—*See* **South Africa.**

Brunei   Small oil-rich sultanate on the island of Borneo in southeastern Asia. Gained independence from Britain in 1984.

Burkina Faso   New name (1984) for sparsely populated country in interior of western Africa. Formerly called Upper Volta. Name changed to reflect African heritage.

Cape Verde   Small nation occupying an archipelago in the eastern Atlantic Ocean off the "bulge" of western Africa. Gained independence from Portugal in 1975.

Central African Republic   Landlocked country in central Africa. Pre-1976 name restored in 1979 after brief period as Central African Empire.

Ciskei—*See* **South Africa.**

Comoros   Small nation occupying three volcanic islands in the Indian Ocean off Mozambique in southeastern Africa. Gained independence from France in 1975. Island of Mayotte voted to remain under French control.

Djibouti   Small country on the "horn" of eastern Africa near southern approach to Red Sea. Gained independence from France in 1977. As colony called French Somaliland and then French Territory of Afars and Issas before assuming new name at independence.

Dominica   Small island of the West Indies in the Caribbean. Gained independence from Britain in 1978.

Grenada   Small island of the West Indies in the Caribbean. Gained independence from Britain in 1974.

Guinea-Bissau   Small country on the "bulge" of western Africa. Gained independence from Portugal and took present name in 1974. Formerly called Portuguese Guinea.

Kampuchea   Small country bordering Thailand and Vietnam in southeastern Asia. Formerly called Cambodia.

Kiribati   Far-flung group of small islands in the Pacific Ocean. Gained independence from Britain in 1979. Formerly called the Gilbert Islands Colony, which was separated in 1975 from the former Gilbert and Ellice Islands Colony.

Libya   Official name changed in 1977 to Socialist People's Libyan Arab Jamahiriya.

Madagascar   New name (1975) for island nation in the Indian Ocean off the east coast of Africa. Formerly called Malagasy Republic.

Mozambique   Large country in southern Africa. Gained independence from Portugal in 1975 after long civil war.

Pakistan   Remnant of pre-1971 Pakistan after its Eastern Province of Pakistan seceded in 1971 to form modern **Bangladesh**. What is now Pakistan was known before 1971 as West Pakistan.

Papua New Guinea   The eastern half of the island of New Guinea and adjacent islands bordering Australia and Indonesia. Gained independence in 1975 from Australia, which had administered Papua since 1906 and New Guinea (formerly a German colony) since 1920 under mandate from the League of Nations and, later, as a trusteeship for the United Nations.

Saint Christopher and Nevis Nation of two small islands in the West Indies of the Caribbean. Gained independence from Britain in 1983. Also called St. Kitts-Nevis. Anguilla, once part of larger St. Kitts-Nevis-Anguilla, opted to revert to colonial status in 1967.

Saint Lucia Small island nation in the West Indies of the Caribbean. Gained independence from Britain in 1979.

Saint Vincent and the Grenadines Small nation occupying St. Vincent and adjacent islands of the northern Grenadines in the West Indies of the Caribbean. Gained independence from Britain in 1979.

São Tomé and Príncipe Small nation occupying two small volcanic islands in the Gulf of Guinea to the south of the "bulge" of western Africa. Gained independence from Portugal in 1975.

Seychelles Small nation occupying an archipelago of more than one hundred small islands in the Indian Ocean off the east coast of Africa. Gained independence from Britain in 1976. Formerly called Seychelles Islands.

Solomon Islands Nation in the South Pacific occupying Guadalcanal and adjacent islands. Gained independence from Britain in 1978. Formerly called the British Solomon Islands Protectorate.

South Africa White-ruled South Africa has established ten controversial black (Bantu) "homelands" within South Africa's traditional boundaries as part of its apartheid policy of separation of the races. All black South Africans are ultimately to be classified on the basis of ethnic considerations as residents of one of the homelands, which are to be granted "independence." To date, four of the ten homelands have been declared "independent" by South Africa and are regarded as separate "nations" by South Africa and each other. All other countries, including the United States, refuse to recognize the four "new nations," which are:

Bophuthatswana A territory consisting of seven discontinuous areas assigned to the Tswana people. Declared "independent" by South Africa in 1977.

Ciskei A territory consolidated in 1982 that originally consisted of nineteen discontinuous areas. Declared "independent" by South Africa in 1981.

Transkei A territory of three discontinuous areas. Declared "independent" by South Africa in 1976.

Venda A territory of two discontinuous areas for the Vhavenda people. Declared "independent" by South Africa in 1979.

Suriname New spelling since 1980 for country in northern South America that gained independence from the Netherlands in 1975 as Surinam. Formerly called Dutch Guiana.

Transkei—*See* **South Africa.**

Tuvalu Small nation occupying several small islands in the western Pacific Ocean. Gained independence from Britain in 1978. Formerly called the Ellice Islands Colony, which was separated from the former Gilbert and Ellice Islands Colony in 1975.

Vanuatu Small nation occupying an archipelago of some eighty small islands in the South Pacific between Fiji and New Caledonia. Gained independence in 1980 from joint rulers Britain and France. Formerly called the New Hebrides.

Venda—*See* **South Africa.**

Vietnam New nation formed in 1975 following reunification of the former nations of North Vietnam and South Vietnam under Communist rule after the Vietnam War.

People's Democratic Republic of Yemen New name since 1970 for country formerly called Southern Yemen or South Yemen.

Yemen Arab Republic Commonly called North Yemen or Yemen since 1970 to distinguish it from the People's Democratic Republic of Yemen. The national capital is San'ā'.

Zimbabwe Large country in southern Africa, named for powerful ancient city. Formerly known as Rhodesia. Gained independence from Britain under black rule in 1980 following a long civil war with a white minority government that had unilaterally declared independence for Britain's Southern Rhodesia colony as independent Rhodesia.

Population

For Americans the size of the planet seems to decrease as the world's population increases and communications improve, bringing the reality of life in other countries—most of them with few of the advantages of the United States—into our homes. And, although it is true that the world's population is steadily increasing, the annual rate of growth is slowing slightly (see Table A). The actual rate of population growth is dependent not only on the number of live births, but also on the death rate—generally falling in recent decades because of increased longevity and, more especially, a decrease in infant mortality. Thus, a comparatively high rate of population growth does not necessarily mean women are having more children, but often that more children are surviving infancy.

The decline in the population growth rate has been most dramatic in Asia since it reached a high point of 2.3 percent a year in 1970. Much of this recent decline in the Asian rate is attributable to official policies in China, which has nearly a quarter of the world's population. From a peak growth of 2.9 percent from 1965 to 1970, China's rate of increase fell to a rate of 1.5 percent in 1980. The Chinese government has vigorously supported family planning, encouraging couples to have only one child. The government not only offers financial incentives and better housing to one-child families, it penalizes families with more than two children by special taxes. In some areas, sterilization quotas have been set. Still, because of its huge population of more than one billion, one of each six births in the world occurs in China.

Africa's Population Explosion

Africa, in which almost all countries are underdeveloped, has both the highest birth rates and the highest death rates in the world, and it is the only region where the annual growth rate is accelerating. All regions showed an increasing growth rate from 1955 to 1985. One of the primary reasons for the continuing population explosion in Africa is the high fertility rate among women, who have an average of slightly over six children. The eastern and western African subregions have the highest birth rates in the world, led by Kenya, where there are fifty-four births per thousand people annually and where women give birth to an average of just over eight children. As health standards have improved

and life expectancy has risen since 1955, the continent's population has soared because fertility and birth rates have also increased.

Latin America's Slower Growth

Latin America appears to be a continent in transition. Although the region had the fastest-growing population between 1950 and 1970 and is still second (after Africa), the growth rate has declined since the early 1970s.

The decline in growth rates and birth rates in developing countries tends to be tied to a variety of factors, the most important of which may be economic. As parents see that limiting their family size can make a difference in the quality of life for themselves and the children they already have, they are more likely to do so willingly. Other factors include increased availability of birth control, along with wider dissemination of family-planning information, and, as societies become more modernized, increased opportunities for women's education and employment.

Table A / Population and Growth

Area	Population (In Millions)	% Annual Growth Rate	Area	Population (In Millions)	% Annual Growth Rate
World			Latin America		
1950	2,536	1.8	1950	166	2.6
1970	3,722	2.0	1970	286	2.5
1980	4,478	1.8	1980	385	2.3
1985	4,889	1.7	1985	409	2.3
Africa			North America, Europe, Soviet Union		
1950	222	2.2			
1970	359	2.7	1950	738	1.2
1980	472	2.8	1970	929	0.8
1985	548	3.0	1980	1,001	0.6
Asia			1985	1,033	0.6
1950	1,397	2.0	Oceania		
1970	2,129	2.3	1950	12	2.3
1980	2,618	1.9	1970	19	1.9
1985	2,875	1.8	1980	23	1.6
			1985	24	1.4

Since 1950, Africa's population has increased about 150 percent, while the world's has less than doubled and that of the developed countries of North America, Europe, and the Soviet Union has grown about 40 percent. The trends in annual growth rates—still increasing only in Africa—indicate that the most developed countries of the world will continue to have slow rates of increase while the populations of less developed nations will continue to increase more rapidly.

Brazil and Columbia, where fertility rates have dropped, contributed most significantly to the slowing growth. Mexico, which faced a population explosion in the 1960s and early 1970s, when growth rates exceeded 3 percent, by 1985 had a population increase of about 2.5 percent annually. Although Mexico loses population through migration to the United States, it also gains through refugees from the war-torn countries to its south. In the island nations of the Caribbean, trends vary widely, representing the considerable differences in prosperity, health care, and culture. In Puerto Rico the life expectancy at birth is seventy-four years, while in Haiti it is only forty-eight; Cuba's population is growing at less than 1 percent annually, while that of St. Vincent and the Grenadines increases at more than 3 percent. Significant drops in infant mortality rates have led to overall population growth, even though fertility has declined.

Table B / Life Statistics

Country	Births (Per 1,000)	Deaths (Per 1,000)
Africa	43–47	15–17
Asia	28–31	10–11
Latin America	30–32	8
North America, Europe, Soviet Union	15–16	10
Oceania	20–21	8

Current rates of birth and death for the world's population regions show clearly that Africa is growing faster than the other regions. Although death rates are somewhat higher, the birth rates are much greater in these less developed regions.

Table C / Life Statistics: Selected Countries

Country	Births (Per 1,000)	Deaths (Per 1,000)	Life Expectancy Male	Life Expectancy Female
Africa				
Kenya	54	14	54	58
Tunisia	34	8	59	63
Asia				
Bangladesh	49	19	47	48
India	35	15	51	50
Japan	13	6	75	79
Latin America				
Argentina	24	9	69	73
Brazil	32	9	62	66
Mexico	33	7	64	68
North America, Europe				
Soviet Union	19	10	70	75
United States	16	9	73	78
United Kingdom	13	12	72	76
Oceania				
Australia	16	7	72	77
Kiribati	35	14	50	54

Birth and death rates and life expectancy vary substantially not only among the population regions but also within the regions themselves. Highly developed Japan has rates closer to those of North America than Asia's India. In the United Kingdom birth and death rates are nearly the same, resulting in a negative growth rate when factors such as emigration are included. As life expectancy improves in Asia and Africa, where people die an average of twenty years sooner than in the United States, population pressure may force a decrease in the birth rate.

Developed Nations' Low Growth Rate

The most developed population region in the world—North America, Europe, and the Soviet Union—has the lowest growth rate. Most nations in this highly developed region have population growth rates below 1 percent per year. Some countries actually have negative growth rates, with fertility rates falling to below the replacement level. Decreases in birth rates in developed countries, a fairly recent phenomenon, cannot be attributed to any one factor. Various explanations offered include the suggestion that, as societies become more consumer oriented, the choice to have children becomes an economic decision. As women enter universities and the work force in greater numbers, they may delay marriage and childbearing, or they may feel that having more than one or two children is incompatible with a career. Additionally, the emphasis on careers for women has made childbearing a less attractive choice for many women, as has the fragmenting of families by divorce. Whatever the causes, incentives to bear children, such as cash bonuses or penalties for failure to produce offspring, have been markedly unsuccessful in raising declining birth rates. Although the Soviet Union has a higher birth rate than other nations in the region, its death rate compensates.

Oceania, consisting of the developed countries of Australia and New Zealand plus the thousands of islands of Melanesia, Micronesia, and Polynesia, contains only 0.5 percent of the world's population. In Australia both the rate of natural increase and the rate of immigration fell substantially; New Zealand's fertility rate fell 50 percent and the flow of immigration became emigration. The less developed island nations of the Pacific had considerably higher growth rates. High fertility rates and improved life expectancy were somewhat balanced by significant emigration to other parts of the world.

Urbanization

Throughout history, civilization and the growth of cities have been linked. (The word *civilization* in fact comes from the Latin *civis*, meaning "citizen" or, more precisely, "resident of a city.") Athens and Sparta define the civilization of the Greek city-states, as Rome did that of the Roman Empire. Medieval Paris, Renaissance Florence and London, and nineteenth-century New York were not only the shining symbols of the civilizations of which they were the product but were in a real sense the distillations of those civilizations.

The second half of the twentieth century (beginning for convenience's sake in 1945 at the end of World War II) has been no exception to the rule that in developing countries there is a one-way movement from the countryside to the city. In modern Greece, for example, whole areas of the countryside have been virtually depopulated as thousands flock into Athens. The same trend of migration to urban areas is visible in India, Nigeria, China, and Brazil.

Table A / Urban Population

| Country | % of Population (Estimated) in Urban Areas | | |
	1970	1980	1985
Africa			
Egypt	43.2	48.6	51.4
Nigeria	22.8	28.5	31.7
Asia			
China	25.5	33.5	37.9
India	19.6	22.9	24.6
Japan	53.3	63.5	68.3
Europe			
Soviet Union	57.1	64.2	67.5
Spain	49.2	55.5	58.5
United Kingdom	80.7	83.0	84.0
North America			
Canada	76.2	82.0	84.4
United States	74.1	78.0	79.8
South America			
Brazil	56.5	66.4	70.9
Colombia	59.6	69.6	74.0
Oceania			
Australia	84.3	87.3	88.6
New Zealand	79.0	82.8	84.5

As farming becomes more mechanized throughout the world, fewer people are required to grow the food necessary for survival. Other occupations center around towns and cities, and the movement of a large segment of the population from the country to the city is a usual effect of the industrialization of a country. Conversely, the more rural a country is, the more its urban areas can grow. Likewise, the longer a country has been settled, the less change is likely in its ratio of urban to rural populations. The long-urbanized United Kingdom, for example, became only slightly more urban. However, relatively undeveloped countries such as Nigeria and China experienced a rapid growth in their urban populations between 1970 and 1985.

Table B / Growth of Large Cities

Country	City Population 1970s	City Population 1980s
Africa		
Cairo, Egypt	4,961,000	5,650,000
Kinshasa, Zaire	1,323,039	3,000,000
Asia		
Beijing (Peking), China	2,768,000*	5,597,972
Jakarta, Indonesia	4,750,000	6,503,449
Seoul, S. Korea	5,509,993	8,366,756
Shanghai, China	7,900,000	6,320,872
Tōkyō, Japan	8,875,103	8,351,893
Europe		
London, England	7,353,810	6,765,100
Madrid, Spain	3,146,071	3,188,297
Moscow, USSR	7,151,000	8,111,000
Rome, Italy	2,781,993	2,830,569
North America		
Los Angeles, USA	2,811,801	2,966,850
Mexico City, Mexico	2,902,969	9,373,400
New York City, USA	7,895,563	7,071,639
South America		
Bogota, Colombia	2,512,000	4,486,200
São Paulo, Brazil	5,921,796	8,493,598
Oceania		
None		

*1953

The population of the city proper must be differentiated from that including the surrounding metropolitan area (see Table C). From the 1970s to the 1980s there was a trend of flight from the inner city, especially in older cities. Notable exceptions, probably due to increasing poverty in rural areas and rapid development of the cities, are Seoul, South Korea; São Paulo, Brazil; and Mexico City, Mexico, which gained an astonishing number of residents in one decade. The growth of Chinese cities, while substantial, is more difficult to measure because of statistical unreliability.

On the other hand, in the more "mature" cities of the industrialized nations, generally known as the older cities, the trend has been toward either very limited growth or, more usual, a loss of population. After World War II there was a mass movement from these older cities into the suburbs surrounding them. This was partly caused by the simple fact that the cities were filled up, leaving no room for expansion. More important perhaps was the growing desire of city dwellers to move out of rented apartments into single-family houses that they were able to own. This created a new kind of urban mix: an inner city composed of mainly the very rich and the very poor, surrounded by the suburbs, in which the middle classes (blue collar, white collar, professional, and executive level) lived. Daily commuting over long distances became standard in the world's urban areas. As more and more residents moved from the inner city into the suburbs, the metropolitan area, which includes the city itself as well as its suburbs, has become more impor-

tant than the city proper (that is, the area within the city's borders) as a measurement of population and economics.

The United States has examples of both kinds of city growth. The Sun Belt area of the South and West has seen the growth of essentially new cities (or metropolitan areas): Jacksonville and Tampa–St. Petersburg in Florida; Houston and Dallas–Fort Worth in Texas; Tucson and Phoenix in Arizona; and Los Angeles and San Diego in California.

The older cities of the Northeast and Middle West, on the other hand, either have remained stable in population or have lost both people and sources of employment. Efforts to revitalize these cities have met with only spotty success. In general, however, the larger older cities have been more successful in holding onto their economic bases (that is, factories, corporate headquarters, transportation facilities) than have the smaller cities of the region that tend to rely on single industries.

Table C / Largest Metropolitan Areas

Country	Rank, 1975	Population Estimate, 1975	Rank, 1985	Population Estimate, 1985
Africa				
Cairo, Egypt	14	7,850,000	13	10,200,000
Asia				
Bombay, India	15	7,700,000	10	11,250,000
Calcutta, India	7	9,750,000	8	12,000,000
Osaka, Japan	3	14,400,000	4	16,400,000
Seoul, S. Korea	16	7,600,000	6	13,100,000
Shanghai, China	12	8,100,000	16	9,350,000
Tōkyō, Japan	1	23,900,000	1	27,400,000
Europe				
London, England	6	10,425,000	11	11,050,000
Moscow, USSR	5	10,650,000	7	12,700,000
Paris, France	10	9,150,000	15	9,550,000
North America				
Los Angeles, USA	11	8,960,000	12	10,500,000
Mexico City, Mexico	4	11,500,000	2	17,300,000
New York, USA	2	17,150,000	2	16,700,000
South America				
Buenos Aires, Argentina	9	9,400,000	9	11,350,000
Rio de Janeiro, Brazil	13	7,950,000	14	9,800,000
São Paulo, Brazil	8	9,600,000	5	14,600,000
Oceania				
No cities in top 25				

A metropolitan area is a region that includes a central city, neighboring communities linked to the city by continuous built-up areas, and more distant communities if the bulk of their population is supported by commuters to the central city. Some metropolitan areas have more than one central city—Tōkyō-Yokohama or San Francisco-Oakland-San Jose, for example. In 1985 there were more than thirty metropolitan areas in the world with populations over five million. Half of these are located in Asia; the rest are divided about equally among the United States and Canada, Latin America, and Europe and the Soviet Union. One metropolitan area, Cairo, is in Africa.

While many inner cities found their inhabitants fleeing in the last ten years, searching for their preferred housing and living conditions, their surrounding metropolitan areas continued to grow. However, exceptions exist on both sides, with New York shrinking slightly and Seoul, São Paulo, and Mexico City mirroring their enormous growth in the city proper by almost doubling their metropolitan-area populations. Tōkyō and Osaka also grew significantly, giving Japan the two most populous metropolitan areas in Asia.

Health

Most people in the industrialized part of the world look upon good health and proper medical treatment as a human right. In the Scandinavian countries, for example, a national health service takes care of all citizens regardless of ability to pay.

Throughout history, our ancestors looked upon good health as something one had only if one's luck was good. Malnutrition, undoubtedly the most common and pervasive cause of bad health, still exists in many parts of the world. In recent years, due to media attention to the

Table A / Public Health Expenditures
(In Dollars Per Capita)

Rank	Country	Expenditure
1	Sweden	$924
2	Denmark	823
3	Norway	721
4	Netherlands	691
5	West Germany	676
6	France	654
7	Switzerland	625
8	Iceland	602
9	Canada	460
10	Belgium	454
11	Austria	453
12	United States	383
13	Japan	378
14	New Zealand	372
15	Australia	350
16	United Kingdom	343
17	Finland	341
18	United Arab Emirates	327
19	Kuwait	289
20	Ireland	263

The Scandinavian nations, with their tradition of totally socialized medicine, spend the most per citizen for health care. The United States, with publicly subsidized health care only for the indigent and the elderly, falls about halfway in the list of the top twenty nations. The Soviet Union spends ninety-one dollars per person per year; in the Communist nations, all medical personnel, including physicians, are part of the civil service, which reduces medical costs appreciably. The underdeveloped nations spend far less for health; in Mexico it is thirteen dollars per person; in South Africa, eight dollars; in India, two dollars; and in Pakistan, one dollar.

Table B / Life Expectancy at Birth in the United States, 1920–1983 (In Years)

Year	Male	Female	Total
1920	53.6	54.6	54.1
1930	58.1	61.6	59.7
1940	60.8	65.2	62.9
1950	65.6	71.1	68.2
1960	66.6	73.1	69.7
1970	67.1	74.8	70.9
1975	68.8	76.6	72.6
1980	70.0	77.5	73.7
1983	71.0	78.3	74.7

Statistics on life expectancy in the United States present two dramatic facts: women live longer than men, and life expectancy for both sexes has increased dramatically since the twenties. One reason women are living longer is that great progress has been made in reducing deaths related to childbirth, formerly a leading cause of death among women.

No such progress has been made in the leading killers of men, cancer and heart disease, for example. As the figures for life expectancy show, the trend has been consistently toward longer lives for all Americans, and there is no indication that the trend is changing.

chronic droughts of Africa, the world has been made painfully aware that starvation and hunger remain major problems.

Communicable diseases historically have been a major cause of death. The great plagues that spread across Europe in the Middle Ages (and later) were only the most dramatic of death-causing diseases. It is in this area that modern medical science has made the most dramatic progress. Smallpox has officially been eradicated all over the world, and most of the other communicable diseases are relatively rare today. Only in those underdeveloped parts of the world with virtually no medical services are these diseases still a significant cause of human suffering. The World Health Organization (WHO), a UN organization, has concentrated much of its energies on the eradication of such diseases and has met with considerable success.

Other diseases, unfortunately, have not been so easily disposed of. Heart disease and cancer are the most dramatic examples of illnesses that continue to plague human beings in the industrialized nations. Mental illnesses, alcoholism, and drug abuse continue to take their toll of modern men and women. Only moderate success has been attained in the battle against these threats.

Table C / Birth Rates (Per 1,000 Inhabitants)

Rank	Country	Rate	Rank	Country	Rate
1	Kenya	53.8	6	Rwanda	49.6
2	Niger	51.4	7	Malawi	49.4
3	Botswana	50.7	8	Zambia	49.2
4	Mauritania	50.2	9	Liberia	48.7
5	Nigeria	49.8			
	Selected Nations				
	Bolivia	44.8		Greece	15.7
	Iran	44.4		Canada	15.5
	Bangladesh	42.7		United States	15.5
	Mexico	38.3		Japan	14.2
	India	33.6		France	14.1
	Ethiopia	31.2		East Germany	14.0
	Israel	24.7		United Kingdom	13.1
	China	19.6		Italy	11.8
	Soviet Union	18.2		West Germany	9.5
	Spain	15.9			

The most arresting fact in a comparison of the birth rates of the various countries of the world is that the nine nations with the highest birth rates are in Africa. Latin American countries, India, and Pakistan, all of which formerly were believed to have the highest birth rates, lag behind. Another interesting fact is that the more industrialized and prosperous a nation becomes, the lower its birth rate becomes. The modern Western custom of the small family seems to be spreading. It is also interesting to note that countries that are predominantly Roman Catholic—a religion that prohibits abortion and most forms of birth control—do not have higher birth rates than non-Catholic countries.

Table D / Death Rates (Per 1,000 Inhabitants, Excluding Fetal Deaths)

Rank	Country	Rate	Rank	Country	Rate
1	Yemen Arab Republic	24.0	6	Ethiopia	21.3
2	Guinea-Bissau	23.0	7	Gabon	21.3
3	Niger	22.4	8	Malawi	19.1
4	Mauritania	22.3	9	Angola	19.1
5	Mali	22.3	10	Madagascar	19.0
	Selected Nations				
	Saudi Arabia	14.4		Italy	9.5
	East Germany	13.9		Bolivia	9.1
	United Kingdom	12.9		Greece	8.7
	India	12.8		United States	8.5
	West Germany	11.6		Spain	7.8
	Sweden	11.0		China	7.4
	Denmark	10.7		Australia	7.3
	South Africa	10.3		Canada	7.1
	France	10.1		Israel	6.8
	Mexico	10.1		Japan	6.0
	Soviet Union	10.1			

The countries with the highest death rate are also among the poorest nations in the world. Malnutrition, even in the best years, is ever present; there are virtually no medical services available; and the education level is exceedingly low. All except one are in Africa, and that one (the Yemen Arab Republic) is a poor country surrounded by oil-rich neighbors.

Deaths from cancer, heart disease, and automobile accidents are peculiar to the industrial world and tend to balance the lower death rates in those countries from communicable diseases, infant mortality, and childbirth fatalities among mothers. The death rates in the developed world can be expected to drop as scientific advances are made in the prevention and treatment of cancer and heart disease. Some progress has been made in cutting down the incidence of automobile fatalities by improving the safety of cars and by imposing lower speed limits. In the United States, it will be interesting to see if the nationwide campaign against drunken driving—a significant cause of automobile fatalities—results in fewer deaths caused by cars.

Table E / Worldwide Life Expectancy at Birth
(In Years)

Years	Total	Male	Female
1965–70	52.6	51.3	53.9
1970–75	55.4	54.0	56.8
1975–80	57.3	55.9	58.8
1980–85	58.2	57.5	60.3

The same patterns are evident in life expectancy on a worldwide basis as are apparent in the life expectancy tables of Americans (see Table B): women live longer than men, and there has been a steady rise in the life expectancy of both sexes.

Education

For countries enduring long-standing military conflicts or physical hardships such as drought or famine, it would seem on the surface that lack of education is the least of their problems. However, research has shown that the education of a people is the surest way to counteract permanently such problems as malnutrition, widespread disease due to bad sanitation habits, and other physical hardships.

A statistical correlation clearly exists between poverty and illiteracy. When comparing the literacy rates of industrial nations to developing countries, a drastic disparity can be seen (see Table A). Even countries in the same region may have widely varied rates.

Increased Emphasis on Education

Governmental recognition of the importance of education can be seen in the universal increase in public funding for schools (see Table B). While Africa has shown the most marked change, other regions are not far behind. The resulting increase in enrollment extends all the way to college-level education, now recognized as essential for the progress of a nation by worldwide standards. Without exception, the rest of the world has followed the American trend of aiming toward three levels of education.

Mandatory school attendance varies from country to country, with many developed nations requiring children to attend school for twelve years and some more agrarian societies requiring them to attend for only about six. Egypt has compulsory school for ages six to twelve, while the Soviet Union requires ten years of schooling. West Germany also has nearly 100 percent attendance for ten years, but enrollment at the tertiary (college) level is much less than that in the United States. West Germany is in the process of implementing a comprehensive secondary school program to replace one in which students choose among technical, vocational, and academic secondary schools. Thus, tertiary schooling will not be ruled out for some students before they reach the secondary school level.

Developing nations, such as Indonesia, which reports 86 percent attendance at the primary level but only 15 percent at the secondary, allow their children to go to work much sooner. Usually this is because children are expected to contribute to the family's welfare by working, which is common in agricultural economies.

Table A / Literacy Rates

Country	% of Population	Country	% of Population
Africa		*North America*	
Algeria	46	Canada	99
Chad	20	Cuba	96
Egypt	40	Haiti	23
Liberia	24	Mexico	74
South Africa	70	United States	100
Sudan	20	*Oceania*	
Asia		Kiribati	90
Afghanistan	12	New Zealand	98
China	76	Papua New Guinea	32
India	36	Solomon Islands	60
Japan	99		
Syria	50	*South America*	
Vietnam	78	Argentina	94
		Brazil	75
Europe		El Salvador	65
Belgium	98	Peru	72
Hungary	98	Venezuela	86
Norway	100		
Spain	97		
United Kingdom	99		

An examination of the literacy rates of various countries shows clearly that those nations with high levels of education, of which literacy is a key indicator, are also those nations that are most developed. The heavily industrialized European countries, with a tradition of educational excellence, are near 100 percent literacy, while the emerging African states, whose education systems are weak, are generally well below 50 percent in literacy. Even within a continent the disparities in literacy achievement illustrate the differences between countries. In Africa the poor countries of Chad and Sudan are well behind Algeria, which has benefited from petroleum revenues, and mineral-rich South Africa, which has an education system developed during its long rule by white settlers. In North America, the poverty of Haiti is reflected in its low literacy rate, while prosperous Canada and the United States are near 100 percent literacy. As the education systems develop, literacy rates become higher, as in the generally good literacy levels in South America.

Education and Infant Mortality

One aspect of education that has an important bearing on the future of developing countries is whether they allow women the benefit of learning. In countries with a high literacy rate for women, infant mortality is almost universally low (see Table C). Countries with a substantial proportion of women who cannot read have tragically high infant death rates. Improvement of the standard of education of mothers and potential mothers is widely believed to result in improved levels of nutrition, health, and education for their children, as well as in smaller families.

Table B / Public Expenditure on Education and Distribution of Enrollment

Major Region	Year	% Distribution of Total Enrollment Primary Level	Secondary Level	Tertiary Level	% of GNP Spent on Education
Africa	1960	91.0	8.1	0.8	2.7
	1976	82.0	16.3	1.7	5.0
Asia*	1960	75.4	22.3	2.3	2.9
	1976	69.6	26.9	3.6	5.6
Europe and Soviet Union	1960	73.5	21.9	4.6	4.2
	1976	57.8	32.6	9.6	5.9
North America	1960	62.4	29.6	8.0	3.8
	1976	44.0	35.7	20.3	6.2
Latin America	1960	85.1	13.1	1.8	2.2
	1976	77.1	17.6	5.3	3.4
Oceania	1960	69.8	26.6	3.6	3.0
	1976	56.8	35.1	8.1	6.3

*Not including China and Korea

While Africa exhibits the most dramatic increase in public expenditures on education, all areas show marked increases. As more money is spent, students stay in school longer, as the distribution changes illustrate. Larger percentages in all areas are enrolled in college-level schooling, with the greatest increase by far occurring in North America.

Table C / Relationship Between Female Literacy and Infant Mortality in Developing Countries

Infant Mortality Rate 1975–1980 (Per 1,000 Live Births)	Female Literacy (1980) Very Low (15% and Less)	Low (16%–30%)	Middle (31%–50%)	High (51%–80%)	Very High (Over 80%)
Very High (150 +)	13 countries, including Afghanistan and Ethiopia	7 countries	1 country	0	0
High (100–149)	3 countries	15 countries, including Nigeria, Bangladesh, Papua New Guinea, and Haiti	11 countries, including Turkey, Libya, and Zaire	3 African countries	0
Middle (50–99)	0	1	6 African countries	13 countries, including Mexico, Brazil, and Indonesia	4 countries, including Colombia and Thailand
Low (Less Than 50)	0	0	2 countries	9 countries, including Fiji	14 countries, including Argentina, Korea, and Cuba

The statistical correlation between increased female literacy and decreased infant mortality can be seen clearly in developing nations. No countries with high literacy rates among women had high death rates for infants, and, conversely, no countries with low female literacy rates had low infant mortality rates. The conclusion is obvious: the more knowledge women possess, the longer lives their children will have.

As citizens of industrial countries increase their education at all levels, but especially the tertiary, in order to compete in a more educated, technically advanced world, the people of developing nations must increase their basic education in order to keep pace.

Science and Technology

At no period in history have the scientist and technologist been held in higher regard than they have been in the twentieth century. Today, virtually every nation, whether capitalistic or communistic, rich or poor, looks to technology to provide the way to raise the standard of living of its people and to improve the national economy. Countries in which the economy has been based on subsistence agriculture for thousands of years struggle to catch up with nations in which only a small percentage of the population is required to operate agribusinesses producing food surpluses.

In India, it is to the agricultural sciences that the government turns to improve the output of the land so that its millions of citizens can be provided with an adequate food supply. In a highly industrialized nation like Japan, the scientists and technologists are expected to perform the miracles that will keep that nation's products at least abreast in a competitive world. In both Israel and Saudi Arabia, scientific water desalinization techniques are looked to as a way of turning the arid desert into productive farmland. The dream of making the desert flower goes far back in human history, but only in this century has it been within the realm of possibility.

Perhaps in no other field of endeavor is formal training so important, even necessary, as in science and technology. In former centuries, most of that training was attained by the age-old apprentice method: the young learned by watching the old do the job and following their lead. Only in the nineteenth century did scientific education become a formal discipline studied in the schoolroom and the academic laboratory. Prior to that, such science as was studied in the university was chiefly what was known as natural philosophy. It emphasized the theoretical rather than the practical and was in fact as well as in name a branch of philosophy.

Table A / Scientists and Engineers

Rank	Country	Total Number	% in R and D*
1	Soviet Union	12,073,000	11.4
2	Japan	4,127,200	†
3	United States	2,120,000	23.4
4	West Germany	1,981,000	6.2
5	France	1,981,000	†
6	Philippines	1,083,742	†
7	Poland	1,075,000	†
8	India	697,000	4.0
9	Italy	557,879	†
10	Brazil	541,328	†
11	Canada	537,925	†
12	East Germany	500,700	22.5

*Research and development
†Not available

Statistics that purport to give the number of scientists and engineers can be used only as a broad indication of the relative standings of the nations reporting them. The relatively large numbers reported by the Soviet Union and Japan may indicate that they include categories that in the United States and Western Europe would be called "technicians." Countries make a commitment to research and development in the expectation that the investment in time and money will result in technological and scientific benefits. Statistics are not available for China.

Table B / Expenditures on Research and Development

Rank	Country	% of GNP
1	Soviet Union	4.6
2	East Germany	4.4
3	Bulgaria	2.7
4	Israel	2.5
5	United States	2.4
6	West Germany	2.4
7	Switzerland	2.3
8	United Kingdom	2.2
9	Japan	2.1
10	Netherlands	1.9

Unlike most comparisons of the industrialized nations of the world, those that indicate the relative amount spent on scientific research and development of the different countries show these amounts to be more or less even. Research and development may cover a broad spectrum of activity, from nonprofit cancer research to private sector product development. Although the Soviet Union's expenditure percentage of its gross national product (GNP) is roughly twice that of the United States, the GNP of the United States is so large that the amounts are not so different as the percentages would seem to indicate. The amount spent by China is not available.

Modern Technical Education

The United States Military Academy at West Point, New York, with its strong curriculum in military engineering, is generally considered the nation's first engineering school and was a forerunner of the many engineering schools that followed later in the century. The single greatest impetus to technological education was the passage by Congress of the Morrill Act in 1862. For the first time, federal funds were used to found state scientific schools. In this case, they were the land-grant colleges. Most of these became known as agricultural and mechanical colleges (later universities), and they were the real beginnings of public higher education in the fields of science and engineering.

American Preeminence

American technology came into its own in the twentieth century. The automobile, the airplane, radio and television, and the motion picture all made their greatest advances in the United States. During World War II the preeminence of American technology became indisputable. Just as United States technology was largely responsible for the success of the Allies in World War II, it was United States technology that contributed greatly to the rebuilding of industry in much of Europe and Asia.

United States complacence in the field of science and technology received a rude jolt in 1957 when the Soviet Union placed the first artificial satellite, called Sputnik, in orbit around the earth. This accomplishment showed that the Soviet Union, at least in space technology, had caught up with the United States. The launching of Sputnik propelled the United States into a full-scale space race with the Soviet Union.

The Computer Age

The proliferation of computers that began at the end of World War II has further increased dependence on science and technology. The invention of the transistor and the development of the microchip have revolutionized the ways in which records are kept, research of all types is conducted, goods are manufactured, and people communicate with one another. The demand for all kinds of trained technicians to administer this revolution has continued to rise. That fact dramatizes the importance of education today as never before. It has been especially apparent that minorities and women must be educated to enter this new field if the current earnings differentials between these groups and white males are to be equalized. Similarly, the underdeveloped nations have acknowledged that they must improve their technology.

Table C / College and University Students Studying Science and Technology

Rank	Country	%	Rank	Country	%
1	Romania	78	33	West Germany	47
2	Guinea	73	43	Argentina	44
3	Bolivia	69	48	East Germany	43
4	Haiti	67	53	Spain	42
5	Czechoslovakia	62	54	United Kingdom	42
6	Singapore	60	61	France	39
7	Burma	59	76	Israel	33
8	Cyprus	59	78	China	32
9	Bulgaria	58	81	India	32
10	Iraq	57	83	Australia	31
Selected Nations			94	Japan	27
16	Poland	54	100	New Zealand	26
18	Iran	53	102	Canada	25
19	Mexico	53	104	United States	25
26	Italy	50	111	Saudi Arabia	21

The developing countries, in an attempt to catch up with the industrialized nations, tend to spend to their limit on research and development and that includes emphasizing scientific education. A chronic problem, however, has been the loss to the industrialized countries, where pay and living standards are higher, of their trained scientists and technicians—the so-called brain drain. The large number of Indian and Pakistani physicians on the staffs of United States hospitals is a good example of the brain drain.

Table D / U.S. College Enrollment in Various Scientific and Technological Categories

Field of Study	Number of Students
Agriculture and forestry	144,000
Biological sciences	303,000
Health and medical professions	872,000
Engineering	565,000
Mathematics and statistics*	142,000
Physical sciences	193,000

*Includes computer sciences

Probably the fastest growing category of technological education is that of computer sciences, which is not adequately represented in college enrollment statistics. A large percentage of computer training—especially at the hands-on practical level—is done at specialized institutions rather than at colleges and universities.

Industry, and especially the computer industry, also recognizes the need for specialized training in the new technology. Many employers provide extensive training programs for education in the computer sciences, thus augmenting the education acquired in the formal setting of colleges, universities, and specialized institutions.

Modern Women

The age of the modern woman began in the nineteenth century with the emergence of the suffragist movement. Women in the United States and England, in particular, mounted campaigns aimed at forcing the male voters and politicians to open the political ranks to women. Finally, in 1920, the Nineteenth Amendment to the Constitution gave United States women full voting rights. In Great Britain, full voting rights came in 1928. On the European continent, Finland in 1906 and Norway in 1913 were pioneers in women's suffrage. France did not grant women suffrage until 1945.

Other Issues

Securing the right to vote was only one of the issues raised by feminists of the late nineteenth and early twentieth centuries. The most controversial issue was that of the right to practice birth control. Its advocates were regularly jailed in both England and America. Until 1936, it was illegal to disseminate birth control information through the United States mail, and various states banned all contraceptive devices. The last such law, in Connecticut, was declared unconstitutional by the United States Supreme Court in 1965. Abortion was illegal in most jurisdictions under most circumstances until 1973, when the Supreme Court struck down such laws.

> ### The Equal Rights Amendment
> On March 22, 1972, the United States Congress passed the Equal Rights Amendment, which provided that "equality of rights under the law shall not be denied or abridged by the United States or by any state on account of sex." As its deadline for ratification neared and it had been ratified by only thirty-five states (thirty-eight were needed), Congress voted to extend its deadline to June 30, 1982. The women's movement, especially the National Organization for Women (NOW), lobbied vigorously for its passage, and polls indicated that a large majority of Americans favored it. Nevertheless, when the deadline came, the amendment was still three states short, and the amendment died. Advocates of the ERA announced plans to reactivate it, but by 1985 Congress had not passed a new amendment.

Abortion was made legal in Great Britain in 1967 and is authorized in many other nations.

The right to an education was also long denied women. In the nineteenth century women were seldom allowed into universities and almost never granted degrees. Today, however, they are seeking higher education in record numbers.

Economic Equality

Despite the dramatic increase of women in the United States labor force (see Table C), women still suffer economically there. Statistics abound proving that women doing the same jobs as men make less money, that categories of jobs that are customarily done by women pay less than jobs

Table A / Women Enrolled in Universities

Rank	Country	% of Total Enrollment	Rank	Country	% of Total Enrollment
1	Seychelles	89	14	Norway	47
2	Bulgaria	57	15	Cuba	46
3	East Germany	57	16	France	46
4	Poland	56	17	Sweden	46
5	United States	51	18	Australia	45
6	Argentina	50	19	Belgium	44
7	Canada	50	20	Austria	42
8	Finland	50	21	Czechoslovakia	41
9	Hungary	50	22	West Germany	41
10	Soviet Union	50	23	Spain	40
11	Denmark	48	24	Greece	39
12	Portugal	48	25	Brazil	38
13	Israel	47			

The percentage of women to men in colleges and universities in the industrialized countries is nearer equal than in almost any other statistical category in which men and women are compared. This does not, of course, mean that men and women are receiving the same education. Scientific and technical education is still, in most countries, primarily a man's bastion. Nursing and teaching tend to be areas in which women are studying. Nevertheless, the percentage of women in previously male-dominated occupations has been increasing dramatically. Graduate business schools, law schools, and medical colleges are seeing far more women now than only a decade ago.

The 1970s and 1980s

In 1980 the Republican National Convention for the first time did not endorse the Equal Rights Amendment (ERA), and in 1982, ERA officially died when the required thirty-eight states failed to ratify it. To many feminists, these two actions illustrated the fact that the more conservative 1980s would be a difficult time for reforms aimed at aiding women. Those two events were in marked contrast to the milestones of the 1970s, which was one of the most fruitful periods in the history of feminism. Following are some of the recent achievements in women's quest for equal status with men:

1970 The United States Senate holds its first hearings on Equal Rights Amendment (ERA).

1971 Billie Jean King becomes first woman athlete to make more than $100,000 in a year.

1972 Congress passes ERA and sends it to states for ratification.

1972 Shirley Chisholm, a black congresswoman, runs for Democratic nomination for president.

1973 Supreme Court strikes down anti-abortion statutes, essentially legalizing abortion under most conditions.

1974 Ella Grasso becomes first woman to be elected governor of a state (Connecticut) in her own right. (Other women governors had succeeded their husbands.)

1975 United States service academies open their ranks to women.

1977 Rosalyn Yalow wins Nobel Prize for medicine.

1978 Congress extends deadline for passage of ERA.

1979 Margaret Thatcher becomes prime minister of Great Britain, first woman in nation's history to hold that office.

1984 Geraldine Ferraro, a Democrat, becomes first female major-party candidate for vice-president of the United States.

done by men, that women are promoted more slowly than men, and that certain categories of jobs are virtually closed to women. Some of these inequities have been lessened in recent years by a series of court decisions in which employers were ordered to stop discriminating against women.

Table B / Literacy Rates: Women

Country	Female Literacy %	Male Literacy %
United States	99.5	99.5
Australia	99.0	99.0
France	99.0	99.0
Panama	84.0	86.0
Iran	35.0	59.0
Libya	30.0	67.0
India	25.0	47.0
Pakistan	19.0	29.0
Ghana	18.0	43.0
Bangladesh	13.0	37.0
Iraq	13.0	36.0
Yemen Arab Republic	2.0	26.0

In countries where the literacy rate approaches 100 percent, there is virtually no difference between percentages of literate males and literate females. As overall literacy drops off, however, the gap between males and females widens. Thus in some of the more traditional societies of Africa and Asia, the number of women who can read and write are hardly enough to create a statistic in the literacy tables. Illiteracy among women can have a devastating effect on efforts to improve the living conditions of a people, for example, a mother who is unable to read cannot understand labels on food or medicine.

Table C / Women in the U.S. Labor Force

Year	Total Work Force (In Millions)	Total Women (In Millions)	% of Women in Total Work Force
1950	58.9	17.3	31.9
1960	65.8	21.9	35.5
1970	78.7	29.7	40.8
1975	85.8	34.0	42.0
1980	99.3	42.1	47.6
1983	100.8	44.0	48.0

In 1983, out of a total civilian force of 100.8 million, there were 44 million women, making up 48 percent of the work force. Thus, the traditional picture of the American family showing a husband coming home from work to be greeted by his wife, who has been home all day doing housework, is no longer applicable. Today, more than half the mothers with children of school age work outside the home. In more and more families, the family budget is predicated on two paychecks. In the economic recession of the late 1970s and early 1980s—when unemployment reached higher figures than any time since the Great Depression of the 1930s—economists pointed out that the effects of it were felt far less than would have been expected because in many households one worker remained employed while the other was laid off, and this trend is expected to continue.

Background to Peace

The twentieth century has hardly been a peaceful one. People living in the modern age have suffered through two world wars, civil wars, and countless smaller wars, border clashes, and coups d'état. All these hostilities were conducted in the face of the largest collection of international organizations for keeping the peace in the history of the world.

Twentieth-Century Peace Organizations

The Hague Conferences of 1899 and 1907

The purpose of both conferences, attended by the world powers at the invitation of Russia, was to reduce armaments. Twenty-six governments participated in the first conference, forty-four in the second. The conferences' main purpose was never achieved, but a number of conventions were adopted and ratified by the participating nations; these were attempts to codify the rules of war and to reduce the human suffering caused by modern technology.

The Hague Tribunal

Founded in 1899 by the first Hague Conference as the Permanent Court of Arbitration, its purpose was to arbitrate disputes between two or more nations, with the disputing nations voluntarily submitting their arguments to the court for settlement. World War I effectively ended whatever power the court exercised, and most of its activities were taken over by the World Court. More than seventy nations are currently members.

The League of Nations

Founded in 1919 at the end of World War I, the League of Nations was championed especially by President Woodrow Wilson. His idealistic dream was of an international organization that would intervene in all future disputes between nations and settle arguments before the countries went to war. Most of the world's nations (sixty-three in all) joined the organization, but the United States did not. An isolationist United States Senate refused to ratify the agreement.

The League of Nations was in existence in the 1920s and 1930s but was never able to fulfill the hopes of its creators. Its most spectacular failure was its members' inability to agree on a way to stop Italy's invasion of Ethiopia in the 1930s. The advent of World War II effectively ended the League of Nations, although much of its machinery and some of its agencies were incorporated into the United Nations.

The World Court

The Permanent Court of International Justice, popularly known as the World Court, was founded by the League of Nations in 1920. Fifty-nine nations were members. The United States was never a member of the court, but an American judge always sat on the court. The court's principal accomplishment was its help in creating a body of international law. It replaced the Hague Tribunal and was itself replaced in 1945 by the International Court of Justice, an agency of the UN.

The United Nations

The United Nations was founded in 1945 by the victorious Allies at the end of World War II. It was the successor to the League of Nations and its general purpose, world peace, was the same. It inherited much of the administrative apparatus and some of the subsidiary agencies of the League of Nations. Its two major bodies are the General Assembly, in which all members sit, and the Security Council on which sit representatives of the major powers (China, France, Great Britain, the Soviet Union, and the United States) and ten members chosen from the other nations in the

---

Camp David

Camp David, a hideaway retreat in the Catoctin Mountains of Maryland in the United States, has been used by every United States president since President Franklin D. Roosevelt (when it was known as Shangri-La; Dwight D. Eisenhower renamed it for his grandson). Camp David has been the site of two important summit conferences.

In 1959 President Eisenhower met there with Soviet premier Nikita Khrushchev. That meeting was widely regarded as an important milestone in Soviet-American détente and ushered in the spirit of Camp David.

In 1979 President Jimmy Carter was host there to President Anwar Sadat of Egypt and Prime Minister Menachem Begin of Israel. Under President Carter's encouragement, the two men came to the first important agreement that Israel had ever made with one of its Arab neighbors. In the Camp David accords, signed in Washington, D.C., on March 26, 1979, Israel agreed to return the Sinai to Egypt, and Israel and Egypt agreed to negotiate the question of Palestinian autonomy.

Table A / Nuclear Disarmament Efforts

The 1963 Nuclear Test Ban Treaty (Moscow Agreement)	The United States, Great Britain, and the Soviet Union agreed to halt the testing of nuclear weapons in space, above ground, and underwater. Underground testing was not banned.
The 1966 Outer Space Treaty	The major nuclear powers agreed not to introduce nuclear-weapons testing in outer space.
The 1968 Nonproliferation Treaty	Approved by the UN General Assembly, it enjoined the nuclear powers from aiding other nations to build nuclear weapons.
The 1972 Strategic Arms Limitation Treaty (SALT I)	The United States and the Soviet Union agreed to limit their arsenal of defensive nuclear weapons. Antiballistic missiles were limited to two silos of 100 missiles for each country. The nations also agreed on a five-year moratorium on the testing and deployment of intercontinental ballistic missiles (ICBMs) and submarine-launched ballistic missiles (SLBMs). SALT I officially came to an end in 1977, but both countries voluntarily and informally indicated that they would continue to abide by its terms while SALT II talks continued.
The 1974 Protocol on Antiballistic Missiles and Underground Testing	The United States and the Soviet Union agreed to limit antiballistic-missile testing and the underground testing of nuclear weapons in general.
The 1974 Vladivostok Agreement	The United States and the Soviet Union agreed on the framework for a comprehensive agreement on offensive nuclear arms, thereby setting the guidelines for SALT II.
The 1979 SALT II Agreement	The United States and the Soviet Union agreed to limit offensive nuclear weapons. Each side was to be limited to 2,400 missile launchers and heavy bombers. Each side also agreed to a ceiling of 1,320 ICBMs and SLBMs with multiple warheads. The treaty was unpopular among more conservative members of the United States Senate, and President Carter later withdrew it from Senate consideration. His successor, Ronald Reagan, never resubmitted it to the Senate for ratification. Both nations voluntarily agreed to honor most of the terms of the treaty, and in June 1985, President Reagan announced that the United States would continue to abide by the treaty for an indefinite period.
The 1985 Geneva Disarmament Talks	Representatives of the United States and the Soviet Union resumed negotiations early in 1985 on the Strategic Arms Reduction Talks (START); they had begun in 1982 and were subsequently halted.

When the United States exploded two atomic bombs over Japan in 1945, thereby ending World War II, it was the only nation in the world with the ability to build such a weapon. Four years later, in 1949, the Soviet Union exploded its first bomb. Other nations later joined the "nuclear club": Great Britain in 1952, France in 1960, China in 1964, and India in 1974. Furthermore, it is widely believed that other nations (particularly Israel, South Africa, and Pakistan) *could easily build such a bomb whenever they choose to. The proliferation of countries capable of waging an atomic war underlined the need for international control over the use and testing of nuclear armaments. The earliest attempts by the UN to control atomic weaponry were frustrated by the animosities of the cold war, but later attempts have met with some success as various limited disarmament treaties have been put forth.*

General Assembly. Eventually virtually every nation in the world joined, including all the former colonial territories that became independent republics in the years after the establishment of the UN. The ability of the UN to intercede in international disputes has to a large extent been undermined by the right of the major powers to veto any action voted by the Security Council.

Each of the 159 (as of 1984) members of the UN has one vote in the General Assembly. Critics of the UN have pointed to this extreme exercise of democracy as ignoring the realities of the political world and thereby vitiating the influence of the UN. For example, the vote of Nauru, with a population of about eight thousand, carries the same weight as that of China, with a population of more than one billion. Nevertheless, despite all its drawbacks, the UN has achieved some degree of success.

The International Court of Justice The International Court of Justice was founded in 1945 as an agency of the UN and as successor to the World Court. It is made up of fifteen judges (each from a different country) chosen by the UN General Assembly. Its jurisdiction has been kept narrow and, realistically speaking, can adjudicate only in cases where the parties agree to let it do so. The United States, for example, has refused the court jurisdiction over whatever the federal government declares to be a "domestic matter." Furthermore, the court has no way of enforcing its decisions.

Military Preparedness

The costs of military preparedness, usually called defense expenditures, have risen rapidly during the 1980s. In the United States the defense budgets have more than doubled since 1980. One of the major factors in the cost of military preparedness is the high-priced technology that has come to be a part of all modern armed forces. Intercontinental ballistic missiles, nuclear submarines and aircraft carriers, supersonic airplanes that virtually fly themselves, and tanks outfitted with sophisticated electronic gear are all extremely expensive. Salaries of military personnel, at least in the armed forces of the industrialized nations, are far higher than they ever have been before.

NATO and the Warsaw Pact

In the decade following the end of World War II, when the cold war was at its height, both the Western allies, under the leadership of the United States, and the Communist bloc, under the leadership of the Soviet Union, formed military alliances. The primary purpose of both alliances is the unification of the military forces of the member nations for use in case of war in Europe.

The treaty alliance known as the North Atlantic Treaty Organization (NATO) was founded in 1949. Its original members were Belgium, Canada, Denmark, France, Great Britain, Iceland, Italy, Luxembourg, the Netherlands, Norway, Portugal, and the United States. Greece and Turkey joined in 1952, West Germany in 1955, and Spain in 1982. Its coordinating body, the North Atlantic Council, has its headquarters in Brussels, Belgium.

The Warsaw Treaty Organization, known informally as the Warsaw Pact, was founded in 1955 in reaction to the forming of NATO. Its military headquarters is in Moscow. The original members were Albania, Bulgaria, Czechoslovakia, East Germany, Hungary, Poland, Romania, and the Soviet Union. Albania withdrew from the alliance in 1968 because of its then-alliance with China. The Warsaw Pact's major military excursion was the suppression in 1968 of a reform Communist government in Czechoslovakia.

Table A / Men and Women Under Arms

Rank	Country	Size of Armed Forces
1	China	4,750,000
2	Soviet Union	3,673,000
3	United States	2,049,100
4	India	1,104,000
5	Vietnam	1,029,000
6	North Korea	782,000
7	South Korea	601,600
8	Turkey	569,000
9	France	504,630
10	West Germany	495,000
11	Taiwan	451,000
12	Pakistan	450,600
13	Egypt	367,000
14	Italy	366,000
15	United Kingdom	343,646
16	Spain	342,000
17	Poland	319,500
18	Indonesia	273,000
19	Brazil	272,550
20	Iraq	252,250
21	Yugoslavia	252,000
22	Japan	243,000
23	Thailand	238,100
24	Ethiopia	230,000
25	Cuba	227,000

Since ancient times, the size of a nation's armed forces has been the main criterion by which its military strength was judged. Size has never been the sole indicator of strength, however; large forces have often been defeated by smaller ones. And in modern times, perhaps more than in the past, it is the kind of armaments, equipment, and transportation that will determine which side will triumph. Furthermore, the elusive criteria of leadership of a nation's officer corps and noncommissioned cadre, the training and morale of its forces, and the military supply facilities all play their part. Despite these other criteria, however, the size of a country's military forces remains an important factor.

Yet today's nations, large and small, rich and poor, have almost all opted to pay the price. There is scarcely a nation in the world—even traditionally neutral countries like Switzerland and Sweden—that does not have modernized armed forces to protect it from outside inva-

Table B / Military Expenditures by Country, 1980

Rank	Country	Annual Expenditures (In Billions of U.S. Dollars)	Rank	Country	Annual Expenditures (In Billions of U.S. Dollars)
1	United States	136.0	14	East Germany	3.9
2	Soviet Union	114.0	15	Poland	3.9
3	China	32.0	16	India	3.8
4	West Germany	24.0	17	Belgium	3.6
5	France	22.0	18	Spain	3.5
6	United Kingdom	19.0	19	Sweden	3.3
7	Saudi Arabia	17.0	20	South Korea	3.3
8	Japan	9.0	21	Australia	3.0
9	Italy	7.0	22	Iraq	2.6
10	Israel	5.0	23	Turkey	2.5
11	Netherlands	5.0	24	Greece	2.4
12	Iran	4.4	25	South Africa	2.3
13	Canada	4.1			

The United States and the Soviet Union, by far the most powerful nations in the world, spend approximately the same amount for their military establishments. China, which is sometimes looked upon as the third great world power, spends far less. Many critics believe that the military preparedness of the two nations has passed the bounds of defense and presents a clear danger not just to the United States and the Soviet Union but to the whole world.

Table C / Defense Expenditures Per Capita

Rank	Country	Amount Spent (In U.S. Dollars)
1	Qatar	4,762
2	Saudi Arabia	1,837
3	Israel	1,461
4	United Arab Emirates	1,321
5	Oman	902
6	Brunei	808
7	Kuwait	705
8	United States	543
9	Soviet Union	433
10	France	424

Israel and Arab nations rich with the income from petroleum lead the nations of the world in the relative amount they spend on a military establishment. The Arab oil nations, confronting internal dissension, Middle East rivals, and the Jewish state of Israel, spend a large part of their defense money on sophisticated air forces. Since its founding, Israel has been forced to devote an uncommonly large part of its resources to maintaining a military establishment to defend itself from its hostile neighbors.

Table D / Arms Exporting Nations

Country	Amount (In U.S. Dollars)	% of World Arms Exports
Soviet Union	8.8 billion	33.0
United States	6.5 billion	25.0
France	2.9 billion	11.0
United Kingdom	1.8 billion	7.0
Czechoslovakia	700.0 million	3.0
Italy	650.0 million	2.5
Yugoslavia	340.0 million	1.3
Poland	320.0 million	1.2
Switzerland	290.0 million	1.1

In addition to building up their own strength, the two major powers—the Soviet Union and the United States—are also by far the largest supplier of arms to other nations. Between them, they supply more than half of the armaments bought by smaller nations.

The major importers of arms are the underindustrialized nations of the Third World, some of which spend a sizable part of their national budget on arms. The ten largest importers are Syria, Libya, Saudi Arabia, India, Egypt, Iraq, Israel, South Korea, Iran, and Vietnam.

sion or from interior revolution or terrorism. The size of these armed forces is often large (see Table A).

The United States and the Soviet Union, of course, are the two nations that spend the most on military matters (see Table B). They do not, however, spend the most per capita (see Table C). Both the United States and the Soviet Union are the leaders of regional organizations set up for mutual defense; the Soviet Union has organized its satellites in Eastern Europe into the Warsaw Pact, which corresponds to the North Atlantic Treaty Organization (NATO) of Western Europe, Canada, and the United States (see box). A large part of the defense budgets of both the United States and the Soviet Union is spent on maintaining the capabilities of the two organizations. Both the superpowers maintain navies that constantly cruise virtually all the world's oceans and each maintains a weapons system having many times over the ability to destroy the other. It is these arsenals of nuclear weapons—and the means to deliver them—that frighten so much of the world.

Nuclear Powers

Early in World War II, the United States government established the top-secret Manhattan Project—first at Columbia University in New York City on Manhattan Island (hence its name) and later at the University of Chicago. Its mission was to achieve atomic fission, that is, to split the atom, releasing great amounts of energy. Instantaneous, uncontrolled release of this energy would result in an explosion—an atomic bomb. That bomb was to become the secret weapon that would tip the balance of the war toward the Allies. A reactor was built in Chicago in 1942, and on June 16, 1945, the first atomic bomb was exploded in great secrecy at Alamogordo, New Mexico.

By that time, the war in Europe was over, and the Allies were preparing for what everyone expected to be a bloody invasion of Japan—a military campaign that was believed to be necessary if Japan was to be forced to surrender and bring the Pacific war to a successful close. Therefore, when President Harry S Truman was presented with the option of forcing Japan to surrender by exploding atomic bombs over Japanese cities, he accepted their use. On July 26, 1945, the Allies issued an ultimatum demanding Japan's surrender but did not mention the atomic bomb. Japan refused to consider any terms of surrender that did not ensure the future of the emperor. Therefore, on August 6, an atomic bomb was exploded over Hiroshima, and on August 9, another was detonated over Nagasaki. The emperor quickly offered unconditional surrender, and by August 14 the war was officially over.

Nuclear Power

Scientists had long known that atomic fission was capable of doing more than creating a weapon of destruction. It was widely believed that fission, when controlled by a nuclear reactor, could generate electricity far more cheaply than could be done in conventional plants powered by coal, water, or petroleum. Generating plants fired by nuclear energy were expected to be the particular salvation of those poorer nations with no hydropower available and those lacking in coal and petroleum.

In 1947 the facilities of the Manhattan Project, including the research laboratories and plants at Oak Ridge, Tennessee, were turned over to the newly created Atomic Energy Commission (AEC—now the Nuclear Regulatory Commission, or NRC). The AEC was given the responsibility for the research and development of both military and civilian uses of nuclear energy. As part of the Atoms for Peace program, the AEC was also given the responsibility for supplying equipment to foreign nations so that they could carry on their own research into the peaceful uses of nuclear power and for making sure that none of that material would be used for creating weaponry.

In 1956 the British put into operation a full-scale nuclear reactor for the production of electrical power. In 1957 the first such reactor went into operation in the United States, at Shippingport, Pennsylvania.

Numerous other uses of nuclear energy were being developed. The *Nautilus*, a nuclear-powered submarine, was launched by the United States in 1955. It was the first of many nuclear-powered submarines and aircraft carriers.

Table A / Countries Producing Nuclear Energy

Rank	Country	Capacity (In Billions of Kilowatt Hours)	Rank	Country	Capacity (In Billions of Kilowatt Hours)
1	United States	251.0	12	East Germany	11.0
2	Japan	83.0	13	Bulgaria	6.0
3	Finland	60.9	14	Spain	5.4
4	France	60.9	15	Czechoslovakia	4.5
5	Soviet Union	60.0	16	Netherlands	4.2
6	West Germany	41.5	17	South Korea	3.5
7	Canada	35.9	18	India	2.9
8	United Kingdom	33.5	19	Argentina	2.3
9	Sweden	21.5	20	Italy	2.3
10	Switzerland	13.6	21	Pakistan	0.2
11	Belgium	12.5			

Only twenty-one nations generate electricity by the use of nuclear energy, and most of those are in the industrialized world. The United States alone produces about 41 percent of the total capacity. The developing world, despite its urgent need for increased energy production, has for the most part been unable to afford the expensive technology involved in nuclear power. In Asia, only India, Japan, and Pakistan have nuclear energy plants, and there are none in Africa or Latin America.

Nuclear Weapons

Meanwhile, the military uses of nuclear energy were being developed at a fast pace. America's arsenal of atomic bombs was being constantly enlarged, and in 1950 President Truman approved the development of the hydrogen bomb; it made use of the technique of thermonuclear fusion and was to be far more powerful than the atomic bomb. The first hydrogen bomb was detonated by the United States at Eniwetok in the Marshall Islands on November 1, 1952. The Soviet Union was not far behind. Great Britain built its first atomic bomb in 1952, France in 1960, China in 1964, and India in 1974.

It was realized from the beginning that atomic weapons represented more than merely a sophisticated kind of weaponry. For the first time, it became obvious that human beings were capable of destroying the world. The fear of nuclear war has been one of the nightmares with which the world has had to live since 1945.

The first breakthrough in controlling atomic weaponry came in 1963 with the Nuclear Test Ban Treaty (Moscow Agreement). The United States, Great Britain, and the Soviet Union agreed to halt all testing of nuclear weapons in space, above ground, and under water. In 1966 the major powers agreed not to introduce nuclear weapons into outer space. Testing continues, however, underground.

The SALT Talks

By the late 1960s, both the United States and the Soviet Union possessed gigantic nuclear arsenals. Mutual fear and pressure from the rest of the world caused the two nations to begin what came to be known as the Strategic Arms Limitation Talks (SALT). In 1972 a SALT Treaty was signed. For the first time, the superpowers agreed to limit their stockpiles of deadly weapons. Antiballistic missiles carrying nuclear warheads were limited to two silos of one hundred missiles for each country. Furthermore, the two nations agreed on a five-year moratorium on the testing and deployment of intercontinental ballistic missiles (ICBMs) and submarine-launched ballistic missiles (SLBMs). The treaty became known as SALT I because the two powers immediately entered new talks that were expected to result in a more comprehensive treaty.

In 1979 the negotiators arrived at an agreement and SALT II was signed. Under its terms each side was limited to 2,400 missile launchers and heavy bombers. Each side also agreed to a ceiling of 1,320 ICBMs and SLBMs. Opposition to the treaty quickly solidified in the United States. Critics claimed that it did not offer proper safeguards against violations by the Soviet Union

Table B / Nuclear Powers

Country	Year of First Detonation
United States	1945
Soviet Union	1949
Great Britain	1952
France	1960
China	1964
India	1974

Although only six nations have actually detonated nuclear and thermonuclear weapons, it is known that a number of other nations possess both the knowledge and the facilities to produce at least a rudimentary atomic bomb. Israel, Pakistan, and South Africa are believed to have the capabilities at hand. The Nonproliferation of Nuclear Weapons Treaty, signed in 1968 by the United States, Great Britain, and the Soviet Union, was aimed at keeping the "nuclear club" small. It did not succeed at keeping India from developing the bomb, and it cannot be counted on to be a major deterrent to any other nation that wishes to build a bomb.

and that it in general overly favored the Soviet Union. President Carter recalled it from consideration by the Senate. He gave as his reason the Soviet invasion of Afghanistan. His successor, Ronald Reagan, never resubmitted it for ratification.

In 1982 the United States and the Soviet Union began a new series of negotiations. After several fits and starts, they were reconvened in Geneva, Switzerland, in 1985.

Current Attitudes

During the 1960s and early 1970s, the peaceful development of nuclear energy was concentrated in the production of electrical power. The early expectation that nuclear power would be significantly less expensive than conventionally generated power proved to be illusory. The cost of building nuclear power plants turned out to be far more than had been anticipated. Fear of nuclear accidents, such as the partial meltdown at Three-Mile Island nuclear plant in Pennsylvania, forced the power companies to build elaborate and expensive safeguards into their generating plants. There was great popular opposition to nuclear plants in the United States, regardless of how safe the power companies claimed they were. As a result, by the 1980s most power companies were not planning any nuclear plants beyond those already in the works. Despite this, the United States now receives approximately one-eighth of its electricity from nuclear plants and that percentage may reach one-fourth by the end of the century.

The Richest and the Poorest Nations

In the late twentieth century, the gap between the richest nations and the poorest nations is widening. This trend would come as a surprise to earlier economists who liked to predict that as technology became more universally available, the poorer nations would draw nearer the wealthier ones. Instead, the traditional economic factors that determine the relative prosperity of a nation tend to remain unchanged. Among these are political and social stability, access to natural resources, a sophisticated financial system, a skilled labor force, excess financial resources that can be converted into

Table A / Total and Per Capita GNP/GDP in Selected Developed Countries

Country	GNP/GDP Per Capita (In $ U.S.)	GNP/GDP (In $ U.S. Millions)
1 United Arab Emirates*	30,000	30,000
2 Kuwait*	25,850	27,600
3 Switzerland	14,270	95,600
4 Saudi Arabia*	14,117	120,000
5 Norway	13,600	56,200
6 United States	12,530	3,363,300
7 Canada	11,725	288,800
8 Denmark	11,016	56,400
9 Austria	10,995	66,890
10 West Germany	10,682	658,400
11 Sweden*	10,285	81,000
12 Finland	10,124	49,100
13 Australia	10,087	153,000
14 France*	9,996	542,000
15 East Germany	9,903	165,600
16 Netherlands	9,807	137,300
17 Japan	8,947	1,060,000
18 Belgium	8,628	85,420
19 United Kingdom	8,620	482,700
20 New Zealand	7,947	25,390
21 Libya*	7,600	26,500
22 Trinidad and Tobago	6,651	7,316
23 Soviet Union	6,352	1,715,000
24 Ireland	5,667	17,000
25 Israel	5,612	22,200

*Figures for these countries reflect gross domestic product (GDP). All other figures indicate gross national product (GNP).

Productivity per person is represented by GNP per capita and is probably a more accurate measurement of standard of living. The disparity between the highest GNP per capita in the world and the twenty-fifth highest exemplifies the concentration of the world's wealth in only a few countries.

Table B / GNP/GDP Per Capita and Distribution of Labor in Developed Countries, by Region

Region Country	GNP/GDP Per Capita, 1980 (In $ U.S.)	Distribution of Labor— Agriculture/Industry and Commerce/Services (Unless Otherwise Indicated)
Africa	760	
South Africa*	2,500	30% / 29% / 34% / 7% mining
Asia (Excluding Japan and Middle East)	330	
Singapore*	5,745	2% / 52% / 33%
Japan	8,947	11% / 34% / 48%
Middle East	5,790	
United Arab Emirates*	30,000	5% / 85% / 5% / 5% government
Europe (Excluding USSR)	7,540	
Switzerland	14,270	7% / 39% / 50%
Central America	1,746	
Panama	1,934	29% / 24.4%
North America	11,460	
United States	12,530	3.5% / 62% / 29.3% / 5.2% government
South America	2,070	
Venezuela*	4,716	15% / 42% / 41%
Oceania	7,810	
Australia	10,087	7% / 30% / 32.6%

*Figures for these countries reflect gross domestic product (GDP). All other figures indicate gross national product (GNP).

The concentration of the world's wealth and the world's productivity is in highly industrialized and in oil-rich areas. The disparities between North America and Central and South America, between Japan and the Middle East and the rest of Asia, between Europe and Africa, all show the differences created by geographical advantages, location, and industrial history.

Table C / Total and Per Capita GNP/GDP in Selected Less Developed Countries

Country	GNP/GDP Per Capita (In $ U.S.)	GNP/GDP (In $ U.S. Millions)
1 Laos	90	320
2 Bhutan*	109	131
3 Chad*	110	500
4 Bangladesh	117	11,000
5 Mali	138	1,000
6 Ethiopia*	141	4,800
7 Nepal*	149	2,300
8 Burkina Faso	169	1,100
9 Burma*	180	5,900
10 India	209	146,000
11 Malawi*	213	1,340
12 Rwanda	270	1,388
13 Burundi*	272	1,200
14 Central African Republic*	273	658
15 Tanzania*	281	5,200
16 Sri Lanka*	286	4,400
17 Sierra Leone*	291	1,200
18 Benin	294	1,100
19 Haiti	300	1,500
20 China	308	313,000
21 Guinea	329	1,710
22 Uganda*	357	4,800
23 Madagascar*	360	3,200
24 Somalia*	375	1,875
25 Niger	425	2,000

*Figures for these countries reflect gross domestic product (GDP). All other figures indicate gross national product (GNP).

Perhaps a better barometer of standard of living, gross national product per capita reflects a country's total production divided by its population. Therefore, enormous countries such as China and India, which may have high GNPs, can be shown to have a low standard of living because their GNP per capita is low.

venture capital, and a well-developed trading network.

National Wealth

A nation's wealth is generally rated by its productivity and that in turn is measured by the gross national product (GNP). The GNP is based on the value of the total amount of goods and services produced by a country in a year. But a high GNP is not necessarily an indication of a high standard of living, although it often determines international influence. The GNP per capita is a more accurate indication of a nation's standard of living.

National Poverty

The truly poor nations of the world are not nations well known to the West. While undeniably related, national productivity and individual wealth are not always found in the same countries. The pressure of enormous ever-growing populations in many countries outweighs high

Table D / GNP/GDP Per Capita and Distribution of Labor in Less Developed Countries, by Region

Region Country	GNP/GDP Per Capita (In $ U.S.)	Distribution of Labor
Africa	760	
Chad	110*	85% agriculture
Mali	138	85% agriculture
Asia (Excluding Japan and Middle East)	330	
Laos	90	76% agriculture
Bhutan	109*	95% agriculture
Japan	8,947	11% agriculture 34% manufacturing 48% services
Middle East	5,790	
People's Democratic Republic of Yemen	430	43.8% agriculture 28% industry and commerce 28% services
Yemen Arab Republic	740	55% agriculture 4% industry and commerce 16% services
Europe (Excluding U.S.S.R.)	7,540	
Turkey	1,096	61% agriculture 12% industry and commerce 27% services
Oceania	7,810	
Papua New Guinea	650	53% agriculture 17% industry and commerce 10% services
Central America	1,746	
Honduras	675	59% agriculture 20% industry and commerce 15% services
North America	11,460	
Haiti	300	79% agriculture
South America	2,070	
Bolivia	933	47% agriculture 34% services

*Figures reflect gross domestic product (GDP). All other figures indicate gross national product (GNP).

While Africa and Asia exhibit the most widespread poverty, the poorest nations in every region of the world, except perhaps Europe, have similarly low GNPs or GDPs per capita. The difference lies in the relative frequency of such poverty in a region. Africa's alarming predominance of poverty can also be linked to its distribution of labor, which, like all of the poorest countries, is largely agricultural.

GNPs to create poverty for individuals.

In all cases, the statistic that recurs consistently is that these poor nations are overwhelmingly agricultural. Whether this is a manifestation of poverty's constraints or a quagmire from which industrialization cannot extract a country cannot be determined.

International Trade in the Modern World

It is generally conceded today that any nation looking to improve its economic standing, especially as judged by the standard of living of its citizens, must maintain a large and varied trade with other nations (see Table A). Ideally, one supposes, every nation would like to be as sovereign economically as it professes to be politically. Practically, no nation even nearly attains such a goal. To begin with, natural resources are not evenly distributed over the earth, and the climate and soil conditions vary so greatly that no nation can hope to produce the raw materials needed for a high standard of living (or even for survival in many cases) for its people. For example, coffee cannot be raised in the United States

GATT General Agreement on Tariffs and Trade
The GATT is a specialized agency of the United Nations created in 1948 for the purpose of helping to settle international trade problems. Its general aim is to promote world trade, principally through the lowering and elimination of tariffs. It also seeks to eliminate the practice of "dumping," whereby a nation creates an unfair competitive advantage by selling large quantities of its products abroad at artificially low prices. Nations who become members of GATT automatically extend to other members the status of "most favored nation." This assures each nation that it will receive the same tariff advantages as all other GATT members (except for those members that belong to a regional trade association, such as the Common Market, and for certain advantages given to developing nations). The agency has 89 member nations, with another 29 nations in effect abiding by GATT regulations. Those 118 nations represent about 80 percent of world trade. Except for Czechoslovakia, the Communist bloc has generally avoided membership in GATT.

and thus must be purchased from South American nations, just as tea has to be imported into the United Kingdom from the Orient.

The ability to produce manufactured goods is as spotty as is the presence of minerals and raw materials. Japan has emerged as the world's most efficient producer of automobiles; the United States is miles ahead of its nearest rivals in the production of sophisticated computer equipment and other high-technology products. South Korea and Hong Kong can produce men's shirts and women's dresses less expensively than can Japan or any of the Western industrial nations. So theoretically, Japan will buy its oil from the Middle East, its computer machinery from the United States, its shirts and dresses from South Korea and Hong Kong—and sell its automobiles to all of them. And somehow or other the accounts will all balance out.

Such a perfect balance of trade almost never occurs, of course. The United States imports much more than it exports, thereby creating both a balance of trade and a balance of payments deficit (see Table B). Japan, on the other hand, year after year, enjoys a balance of trade surplus, as do the oil-producing nations of the Middle East (except for Iraq, which spends vast sums to maintain its military forces in order to keep up its war with Iran). The developing nations, which must buy expensive manufactured goods with their much cheaper raw materials, find themselves more often than not with dangerous levels of foreign debts.

At least since the end of World War II, it has generally been accepted by the world's economists that the economic health of the world depends on free trade and that world prosperity would be seriously jeopardized by a system of high tariff walls that would impede the natural trading between nations. In 1948 the United Nations established the General Agreement on Tariffs and Trade (GATT, see box), aimed at reducing the artificial barriers to trade that protective tariffs raise.

Nevertheless, trade barriers still exist; the

Table A / World Trade: The Twenty-Five Top Traders
(In Billions of U.S. Dollars)

Rank	Country	Exports	Imports
1	United States	233.6	273.3
2	West Germany	176.0	164.0
3	Japan	151.5	124.1
4	United Kingdom	103.0	104.1
5	France	101.0	120.0
6	Soviet Union	79.3	73.1
7	Italy	75.5	91.2
8	Saudi Arabia	74.0	40.0
9	Canada	72.2	65.5
10	Netherlands	68.5	65.9
11	Belgium and Luxembourg	55.5	61.9
12	Sweden	28.4	28.8
13	Switzerland	27.0	30.6
14	Indonesia	23.2	20.0
15	Brazil	23.0	22.0
16	Taiwan	22.6	21.2
17	Hong Kong	21.8	24.7
18	China	21.6	17.0
19	Australia	21.2	23.2
20	East Germany	21.2	21.5
21	South Korea	20.9	26.1
22	Mexico	20.8	24.4
23	South Africa	20.5	20.6
24	Singapore	19.5	25.8
25	Iran	18.4	10.6

Neither wealth nor population determines which nations lead in international trade; some national economies, such as those of the Commonwealth of Nations members, are based on trade. Other economies, particularly those of Eastern Europe, are more insular and self-contained.

The United States is the world's richest country, so it would seem to follow that it also heads the list of the world's top leaders in world trade. However, the two do not necessarily go together—as a quick analysis of the list will show. The Soviet Union, certainly the second-richest nation, ranks behind West Germany, Japan, France, and the United Kingdom. China, the world's most populous nation, ranks only eighteenth on the list—with imports hardly more than that of Hong Kong, the British-leased city on Chinese soil. India, another of the world's most populous nations, is not on the list at all.

Table B / United States Balance of Payments, 1955–1983

(Plus sign [+] indicates a surplus; minus sign [−] indicates a deficit)

1955	− $345.0 million
1960	+ 52.8 billion
1965	+ 5.4 billion
1970	+ 2.3 billion
1975	+ 18.0 billion
1980	+ 3.7 billion
1983	− 41.6 billion

By the mid-1980s, the United States for the first time was experiencing a serious balance of payments deficit. To a large extent, this deficit was caused by the imbalance of exports and imports, or the balance of trade. Several reasons account for the deficit in the United States balance of trade: the high cost of the oil it must import and the heavy inroads made by foreign manufacturers, especially the Japanese, into United States' markets—particularly the automobile, electronics, steel, and textile industries. The strong United States dollar is another factor; it makes American goods uncompetitively expensive in the world market, thereby cutting back on United States exports. Conversely, the relative cheapness of foreign currencies makes imports more attractive to American consumers.

Japanese economy—probably the most spectacular success story of the postwar world—is based on a rigid system of protecting its domestic industry (and agriculture) by virtually forbidding the importation of a wide variety of foreign products. This policy has led to pressure on the United States government to retaliate. The American automobile, steel, and textile industries have been especially hurt by Japanese imports, and those industries—and the labor unions representing their workers—have led the attack on Japanese trade restrictions. Despite some minor voluntary concessions by the Japanese, United States negotiators have not been noticeably successful in breaking down those Japanese restrictions.

The inability of Third World nations (at least those without large petroleum reserves) to compete in world markets continues to be the most serious roadblock to the efforts of those nations to upgrade their economies. It also largely accounts for the continuing gap between the rich nations and the poor nations. Most of the poorer nations have large populations that desire the goods produced by the industrial nations, goods that the industrial nations would like to sell to them, but the developing nations have no products of equivalent worth to sell to the industrial world.

The people of the Third World must therefore do without those imports or their governments must pay for them with borrowed money, usually from international lending organizations. Often this borrowed money is earmarked for capital improvements that will enhance the developing nation's economic position so that it can take part in international trade on an equal footing with more industrially advanced nations. Such efforts typically have left the borrowing nations saddled with debts.

World's Food Supply

It is a sobering experience to look outside the United States and see that the more than 100 million inhabitants of Bangladesh have an estimated individual daily intake of only 1,837 calories; similarly, the more than 754 million people of India consume an average of only 2,056 calories a day. Other countries in Asia with food supply levels equivalent to or below those of India include Kampuchea (Cambodia), Laos, Vietnam, Nepal, and Maldives.

In Ethiopia, drought and political factors exacerbate a growing food deficit. Other drought-induced food shortages are appearing in many of the countries of sub-Saharan Africa.

Food shortages also afflict some Western Hemisphere nations. Haitians have a daily calorie supply of only 1,904. Inhabitants of newly independent St. Christopher and Nevis have 2,037 calories a day, Bolivians 2,082, and Nicaraguans 2,188.

Americans, by contrast, consume an average of 3,641 calories a day, with more than a third of them derived from animal sources. But hunger in the United States—especially among the very young and the very old—has been widely attested to by social agencies and religious groups.

In Europe, Australia, Canada, parts of South America, and other Western industrial nations, food levels are roughly equivalent to those of the United States. Belgium-Luxembourg tops the world's daily calorie intake list at 3,774 a day. Others with food intakes higher than the United States include East Germany (3,689), Greece (3,668), Ireland (3,699), and Italy (3,688). Japan has a total calorie level of 2,852 a day.

Ghost of Thomas Robert Malthus

In 1798 Thomas Malthus issued his pronouncement that poverty and famine are an unavoidable consequence of humanity's capacity to reproduce faster than its capacity to increase food supplies. Modern Africa, hit by a series of droughts and widening desertification of the land, is clearly losing the classical Malthusian human versus food race. Since 1960, high birth rates of between 2.5 percent and 4.5 percent have far outstripped increases in food produc-

Table A / Per Capita Daily Food Supply, World's Ten Most Populous Countries

Country	Total Calories	Vegetable	Animal
World Average	2624	2195	429
China	2426	2180	246
India	2056	1952	104
Soviet Union	3360	2489	871
United States	3641	2325	1316
Indonesia	2373	2320	53
Brazil	2580	2196	383
Japan	2852	2263	590
Bangladesh	1837	1771	66
Pakistan	2180	1949	231
Nigeria	2378	2271	107

Table B / Growth in Food Production
(Average Annual Percentage Change)

	Total 1960–1970	Total 1970–1980	Per Capita 1960–1970	Per Capita 1970–1980
Developing countries*	2.9	2.8	0.4	0.4
Africa	2.6	1.6	0.1	− 1.1
Middle East	2.6	2.9	0.1	0.2
Latin America	3.6	3.3	0.1	0.6
Southeast Asia	2.8	3.8	0.3	1.4
South Asia	2.6	2.2	0.1	0.0
Southern Europe	3.2	3.5	1.8	1.9
Industrial economies (market oriented)	2.3	2.0	1.3	1.1
Other	3.2	1.7	2.2	0.9
World	2.7	2.3	0.8	0.5

*Excludes China

tion, resulting in declining per capita food levels.

Industrialization, birth control, emigration to new lands, and improved agricultural techniques long ago made Malthus's views inapplicable to economically developed nations. Instead, shortages are now seen not as inevitable but as regional and developmental problems arising from a lack of the social, educational, and political institutions essential for implementing technological change.

Green Revolution

Some countries of Southeast Asia are particularly noted for combining strategies to limit births with adoption of modern scientific food production and storage methods popularly known as the Green Revolution.

High costs are a principal deterrent to wider

Table C / Top Ten in Rice

Producers Country	Metric Tons	Exporters Country	Metric Tons	Importers Country	Metric Tons
China	172,184	Thailand	3,620	Soviet Union	750
India	90,000	United States	2,487	Nigeria	649
Indonesia	34,300	Pakistan	794	Iran	600
Bangladesh	21,700	Burma	713	Saudi Arabia	500
Thailand	18,535	India	602	Senegal	430
Burma	14,500	Australia	530	Bangladesh	415
Vietnam	14,500	China	500	Mauritania	388
Japan	12,958	Japan	318	Iraq	386
Philippines	8,150	Italy	314	Madagascar	360
South Korea	7,608	Taiwan	275	Hong Kong	353

Table D / Top Ten in Wheat

Producers Country	Metric Tons	Exporters Country	Metric Tons	Importers Country	Metric Tons
Soviet Union	82,000	United States	41,500	Soviet Union	19,500
China	81,392	Canada	21,000	China	13,200
United States	66,010	France	14,000	Egypt	5,800
India	42,502	Argentina	8,500	Japan	5,577
Canada	26,914	Australia	7,500	Brazil	4,470
France	24,781	United Kingdom	2,600	Italy	3,500
Australia	21,780	Italy	1,800	Algeria	2,592
Turkey	16,400	West Germany	1,400	India	2,265
Pakistan	12,414	Belgium-Luxembourg	1,100	Morocco	2,228
Argentina	11,700	Netherlands	950	South Korea	1,979

Table E / Top Ten in Meat

Producers Country	Beef/Veal Slaughters	Exporters Country	All Meats Metric Tons	Importers Country	All Meats Metric Tons
United States	40,147	Australia	1,182	United States	1,175
Soviet Union	39,600	Denmark	882	United Kingdom	1,105
Brazil	11,500	Netherlands	861	Italy	814
Argentina	11,100	New Zealand	802	Soviet Union	739
Australia	9,109	Argentina	546	West Germany	680
France	7,555	France	409	France	626
West Germany	5,414	West Germany	406	Japan	555
Italy	4,900	Belgium-Luxembourg	351	Netherlands	112
Canada	4,350	Brazil	348	Canada	107
Poland	4,058	Canada	277	Belgium-Luxembourg	99

acceptance of the modern agricultural technology by the world's food-deficient, less developed countries. Scientific research is costly. So, too, is the creation of needed support facilities. Political factors also slow acceptance of the new methods. Some leaders, for political reasons, keep food prices artificially low to win elections and promote industrialization as part of their modernization program. Such policies usually deter investment in farming and accelerate migration of experienced farmers to urban areas in search of a better life.

The World's Oil Supply

Table A / World Crude Oil Production, 1973–1984 (In Thousands of Barrels Per Day)

Region and Country	1973	1974	1975	1976	1977	1978	1979	1980	1981	1982	1983	1984
Western Hemisphere												
Canada	1,800	1,684	1,439	1,295	1,320	1,313	1,496	1,435	1,285	1,372	1,346	1,430
Mexico	465	571	705	831	981	1,209	1,461	1,936	2,313	2,478	2,702	2,743
United States	9,208	8,774	8,375	8,132	8,245	8,707	8,552	8,597	8,572	8,649	8,669	8,750
Argentina	420	414	395	398	431	453	473	491	496	491	481	467
Brazil	169	176	177	167	161	160	166	182	213	260	315	437
Venezuela*	3,366	2,976	2,346	2,294	2,238	2,165	2,356	2,168	2,102	1,895	1,791	1,724
Total†	**16,141**	**15,281**	**14,100**	**13,821**	**14,092**	**14,779**	**15,311**	**15,615**	**15,826**	**16,225**	**16,143**	**16,405**
Western Europe												
Norway	32	35	189	279	280	356	403	528	501	520	600	688
United Kingdom	2	2	12	245	768	1,082	1,568	1,622	1,811	2,065	2,260	2,452
Total†	**450**	**453**	**598**	**916**	**1,419**	**1,817**	**2,355**	**2,530**	**2,704**	**3,025**	**3,206**	**3,541**
U.S.S.R.	8,465	9,000	9,625	10,143	10,682	11,185	11,460	11,773	11,909	12,080	12,388	12,230
Middle East												
Iran*	5,861	6,022	5,350	5,883	5,663	5,242	3,168	1,662	1,380	2,214	2,606	2,166
Iraq*	2,018	1,971	2,262	2,415	2,348	2,563	3,477	2,514	1,000	1,012	905	1,218
Kuwait*	3,020	2,546	2,084	2,145	1,969	2,131	2,500	1,656	1,125	823	912	925
Qatar*	570	518	438	497	445	487	508	472	405	330	270	404
Saudi Arabia*	7,596	8,480	7,075	8,577	9,245	8,301	9,532	9,900	9,815	6,483	4,872	4,545
United Arab Emirates*	1,533	1,679	1,664	1,936	1,999	1,831	1,831	1,709	1,474	1,250	1,119	1,142
Total†	**21,066**	**21,796**	**19,522**	**22,056**	**22,255**	**21,101**	**21,558**	**18,408**	**15,731**	**12,641**	**11,711**	**11,416**
Africa												
Algeria*	1,097	1,009	983	1,075	1,152	1,161	1,154	1,012	805	710	687	608
Egypt	165	150	235	330	415	485	525	595	598	670	690	790
Libya*	2,175	1,521	1,480	1,933	2,063	1,983	2,092	1,787	1,140	1,150	1,020	1,090
Nigeria*	2,054	2,255	1,783	2,067	2,085	1,897	2,302	2,055	1,433	1,295	1,232	1,414
Total†	**5,887**	**5,393**	**4,965**	**5,809**	**6,228**	**5,966**	**6,524**	**6,031**	**4,575**	**4,456**	**4,548**	**4,672**
Far East and Oceania												
Australia	369	388	409	426	431	432	441	380	394	370	405	481
Brunei	216	193	181	203	210	205	234	235	163	154	155	160
China	1,090	1,315	1,490	1,670	1,874	2,082	2,122	2,114	2,012	2,045	2,107	2,250
India	147	156	165	175	199	226	245	182	325	390	390	543
Indonesia*	1,339	1,375	1,307	1,504	1,686	1,635	1,591	1,577	1,605	1,339	1,292	1,332
Malaysia	91	81	98	165	184	217	283	283	264	306	370	462
Total†	**3,276**	**3,532**	**3,672**	**4,167**	**4,609**	**4,823**	**4,974**	**4,848**	**4,822**	**4,681**	**4,812**	**5,334**
World Total†	**55,674**	**55,852**	**52,880**	**57,312**	**59,685**	**60,057**	**62,535**	**59,538**	**55,903**	**53,458**	**53,259**	**54,090**

*Major OPEC member (smaller OPEC producers, not listed, are Ecuador and Gabon)
†Includes smaller producers not listed

Table A reveals the trend over the last decade for the oil production of OPEC nations to decrease, as they attempted to limit supply and hold oil prices at the high level reached during the 1970s embargo. Inversely, oil production in other nations has risen sharply to counteract OPEC's tactics.

The world's industrial nations will long remember the decade of 1973 to 1983 for cutoffs and unprecedented price increases in their oil supplies. These cutoffs, or "oil shocks," slowed or halted economic growth, severely disrupted world trade, and exposed the extreme vulnerability of an industrial world grown dependent on overseas energy sources.

The impetus for the disruption in the world's oil trade came from the Organization of Petroleum Exporting Countries (OPEC). Members of OPEC include Iran, Iraq, Kuwait, Qatar, Saudi Arabia, and the United Arab Emirates in the Middle East, as well as Venezuela and Ecuador in South America, Indonesia in the Far East, and Algeria, Libya, Gabon, and Nigeria in Africa.

World oil production continues to be determined by OPEC nations, even though their combined output was reduced from 31 million barrels a day in 1977 to 16 million barrels daily in 1984. Production quotas were imposed on members in 1983 in an effort to maintain prices. As a result, OPEC's share of world production fell from 49 percent in 1979 to less than 33 percent in 1984.

The Soviet Union now ranks as the world's second-largest oil producer after the combined members of OPEC with an estimated 1984 output of 12.2 million barrels daily. The Middle East, where most producers are also members of OPEC, now ranks third among world producers with 1984 output estimated at 11.4 million barrels daily, down from over 22 million barrels daily in 1977. Saudi Arabia remains the largest Middle East producer.

Largest producers in the Far East are China, with 1984 output up to an estimated 2.3 million barrels daily, and OPEC member Indonesia. Japan, with negligible domestic oil supplies, is by far that region's largest oil importer.

The United States, with 1984 production of 8.8 million barrels daily, remains the largest oil producer in the Western Hemisphere. In Mexico, which replaced Saudi Arabia as the chief source of United States oil imports in the 1970s, 1984 output was 2.7 million barrels a day, up from only 465,000 barrels a day eleven years earlier. On the other hand, Venezuela, a member of OPEC, now holds third place in Western Hemisphere oil production. Canada, Brazil, and Argentina are other significant Western Hemisphere producers.

In Western Europe, the United Kingdom, chief developer of the North Sea's oil resources, emerged as a major new oil exporter in 1984. Norway produces an estimated 688,000 barrels daily from the same source.

Table B / Official Prices of Selected Foreign Crude Oils, January 1 (In U.S. Dollars Per Barrel)

Area Country Crude Type (API Gravity)	1973	1974	1975	1976	1977	1978	1979	1980	1981	1982	1983	1984
North America												
Canada	*	*	*	*	*	*	14.25	26.60	34.09	28.86	26.61	24.83
Mexico	*	*	*	12.10	13.35	13.40	14.10	32.00	38.50	35.00	32.50	29.00
Western Europe												
Norway	*	*	*	*	14.33	14.20	15.10	32.50	40.00	37.25	34.25	30.25
United Kingdom	*	*	*	*	14.10	13.65	15.50	29.75	39.25	36.50	33.50	29.90
Middle East												
Iran	2.40	11.04	10.67	11.62	12.81	12.81	13.45	30.37	37.00	34.20	31.20	28.00
Saudi Arabia	2.41	10.84	10.46	11.51	12.09	12.70	13.34	26.00	32.00	34.00	34.00	29.00
Africa												
Algeria	3.30	14.00	12.00	12.85	14.30	14.25	14.81	30.00	40.00	37.00	35.50	30.50
Libya	2.87	11.98	11.10	12.21	13.74	13.80	14.52	34.50	40.78	36.50	35.15	30.15
Nigeria	3.31	13.66	10.85	12.70	14.31	14.31	14.80	29.97	40.00	36.50	35.50	30.00
Far East and Oceania												
Indonesia	3.73	10.80	12.60	12.80	13.55	13.55	13.90	27.50	35.00	35.00	34.53	29.53

*No significant volume of exports

Oil prices skyrocketed from 1973 levels to more than thirteen times as much by 1981. Conservation efforts coupled with discovery of new fields have led to the slight drop in prices experienced since 1981.

Energy

Since before the dawn of history, human beings have used outside sources of energy to assist them in performing jobs that human strength alone could not accomplish. In fact, the ingenuity with which humans have harnessed animals, water, wind, and such natural resources as wood and coal to make life easier has been one of the characteristics of human culture—other forms of life have relied on their own strength and dexterity to supply their needs. From the time of the ancient Greeks until the eighteenth century, many great empires were based to a large extent on wind power—their merchant marines and navies composed of sailing ships. The introduction of steam power in the eighteenth century reinforced the importance of great maritime powers. Similarly on land, the invention of the steam engine—powered by wood and coal energy—ushered in the industrial revolution. In the late nineteenth and early twentieth centuries, steam power was largely replaced by electric power, also created by the burning of coal. Later, petroleum, water power, and, finally, nuclear power also produced electricity.

In the modern world, a nation's capacity to create energy is a major factor in its economic status and therefore in the standard of living of its people. Only nations with substantial energy resources, or the ability to purchase energy, can develop the industrial capacity necessary for an advanced economy. Thus the industrialized nations (see Table A) with their vast energy resources are able to maintain a high standard of living for their populations, while the less developed nations struggle to create the sources of energy that will lift them economically and help reduce the vast chasm between the rich nations and the poor ones.

Energy became a serious world issue in the 1970s, when the Organization of Petroleum Exporting Countries (OPEC) was able to organize a cartel that drove the price of crude oil to more than thirty dollars per barrel. This sudden rise in the price of oil created severe economic problems, both to the industrial powers, which relied on imported oil to meet their energy needs, and to the developing countries, which found their efforts to increase industrialization suddenly much more expensive because of the increased cost of oil.

The crisis created by OPEC had several ramifications: it caused a worldwide search for new

Table A / Electric Power Production

Country	Kilowatt Hours Per Annum (In Billions)	Kilowatt Hours Per Capita
Argentina	275.0	4,900
Australia	115.0	3,840
Austria	41.5	5,525
Belgium	51.0	5,160
Brazil	148.0	1,160
Canada	390.0	15,900
China	318.0	300
Czechoslovakia	76.9	4,993
Denmark	21.4	4,175
Finland	41.0	8,500
France	282.0	5,200
East Germany	105.0	6,273
West Germany	370.0	6,000
India	130.0	180
Iran	23.9	580
Israel	14.5	3,705
Italy	184.5	3,220
Japan	520.0	4,435
Mexico	14.6	870
Netherlands	18.5	4,340
New Zealand	6.5	9,270
Norway	100.0	24,300
Pakistan	2.0	990
Poland	11.5	3,175
Portugal	19.2	1,910
Saudi Arabia	33.0	1,667
South Africa	115.0	3,840
Soviet Union	1,359.0	5,018
Spain	145.6	3,840
Sweden	94.0	11,280
Switzerland	48.5	7,630
Taiwan	40.6	2,202
United Kingdom	275.0	4,900
United States	2,244.0	10,277

Although Norway and Sweden have recently outstripped it, the United States for many years was by far the largest user, per capita, of electricity. Conservationists look upon this as wasteful of natural resources and, in the case of coal-burning facilities, polluting to the atmosphere. Despite such warnings, the world tendency has been for other nations to bring their electricity-producing capacities up toward that of the United States rather than the reverse.

sources of petroleum; nations began serious efforts to reduce energy consumption; coal once again became a favored source of energy as industry looked to alternatives to oil; industry began to develop vast oil-shale deposits; modern science and technology for the first time took a serious look at the possibility of using wind as a source of energy, experimenting with electricity-producing windmills; and solar energy was explored as a potential source of heat.

Table B / Nuclear Energy

% of Electrical Power Generated by Nuclear Energy
(In Selected Countries)

Belgium	25.3%
Finland	35.8%
Germany, West	14.6%
Italy	1.5%
Netherlands	5.7%
Spain	8.6%
Sweden	35.3%
Switzerland	28.1%
United Kingdom	12.7%
United States	12.6%

When the atom was split in the 1940s, creating the atomic bomb for Allied use in World War II, the harnessing of nuclear reaction as a source of energy was immediately apparent. The United States government set up the Atomic Energy Commission (now the Nuclear Regulatory Commission) to sponsor development of nuclear energy as an alternate to fossil fuel–based energy. The early expectations that nuclear energy would be incredibly cheap were not borne out. Principally because of the elaborate safety precautions necessary in nuclear energy plants, the cost of electricity produced in them often cost more than that from coal-fired or oil-fired plants. Chiefly for that reason, by the 1980s most nations had cut back dramatically their plans for nuclear energy plants.

By the 1980s the economies of most nations had adjusted to the new energy costs. A worldwide recession in the early 1980s, augmented by conservation measures coming into practice, lowered the demand for crude oil, and its price dropped.

In 1985 OPEC found itself unable to cut the flow of oil to meet this reduced demand, and thus the world continued to witness energy costs lower than expected. Such a situation aids not only the industrialized nations but, perhaps more importantly, the oil-deficient and economically disadvantaged nations in meeting their energy needs. The reduced prices have also meant lowered incentives for developing alternate sources of energy, as witnessed by the stopping of oil-shale development in the western United States.

The supply-and-demand situation is at best temporary, and OPEC or any number of economic-political factors can cause the situation to change as quickly as it did in the 1970s. The long-term reality is that the future demand for more and more energy will continue, and the search for fossil fuels and alternative energy sources must continue as well. The methods selected to accomplish the acquisition of additional energy

Table C / Coal Production

Average Annual Production (In Millions of Metric Tons)

Soviet Union	704	United Kingdom	128
United States	686	India	123
China	618	Australia	101
Poland	163	West Germany	88
South Africa	131	North Korea	35

Coal is the most widely available of the world's energy-producing natural resources. It was the fuel that made possible the industrial revolution. Although it was largely replaced by petroleum in the early twentieth century, its importance revived in the 1970s as the price of crude oil increased alarmingly. Despite its extensive availability and its relative cheapness, coal as an energy producer has two serious disadvantages: its recovery, chiefly by strip mining, leaves great scars on the landscape, and its burning creates serious pollution of the atmosphere unless expensive precautions are used.

Table D / Natural Gas Production
(In Teracalories)

United States	4.8 billion
Soviet Union	3.1 billion
Canada	687.0 million
Netherlands	670.0 million
United Kingdom	362.0 million
Romania	352.0 million
Iran	182.0 million
West Germany	172.0 million
Norway	152.0 million
Mexico	145.0 million

New natural-gas reserves are being discovered at a faster rate than any other of the world's energy sources. Some reserves have been located in countries that never had proven reserves before, including Cameroon, Ivory Coast, Spain, and Tanzania. Most new reserves, however, are being found in countries already rich in natural gas. These include the Soviet Union, Iran, the United States, Saudi Arabia, and Algeria. The demand for natural gas rose throughout the 1970s but fell during the 1980s as the price of oil dropped. A relatively new process for creating liquefied natural gas (LNP) has made possible the transport of natural gas without the necessity of building expensive and vulnerable gas pipelines.

sources will have considerable impact on the political, economic, and natural environment of the world. Solutions to the ever-increasing global need for energy must take into account the less developed, agricultural nations as well as the industrial, resource rich countries. Only in this way can a stable and balanced world economy be ensured.

Transportation

World transportation networks are most heavily concentrated in the urban and industrial areas of Europe and North America. The communication system provided by such a network contributes to the rapid dissemination of ideas, methods, and tools and thus to the cultural evolution of these areas. In sharp contrast, the lack of transportation and communication systems in less developed countries is as much a barrier to progress as overpopulation or lack of resources. Nigeria recognized this and in the late 1970s, when it was reaping the rewards of its oil fields, embarked on an ambitious program of building roads, air fields, and ports. Most of the emerging nations have only a rudimentary transportation network, and that lack is a severe hindrance to their efforts to bring their economies up to the standards of the late twentieth century.

Historical Background

The Roman Empire was famous for its efficient road system. Its armies could move easily from one part of the empire to another, and goods could be traded overland with an ease that had been unknown in previous civilizations.

The nineteenth century saw great improve-

Table A / Highway Systems of the World

Country	Total System (In Kilometers)	Paved (In Kilometers)
Argentina	5 million	800,000
Australia	208,000	47,500
Brazil	1.4 million	84,000
Canada	830,000	190,000
China	900,000	262,000
France	1.5 million	800,000
Germany, East	120,000	47,000
Germany, West	460,000	170,000
India	1.3 million	515,000
Iran	85,000	19,000
Italy	294,000	260,000
Japan	1.1 million	474,000
Mexico	213,000	96,000
New Zealand	92,000	47,000
Nigeria	108,000	30,000
Pakistan	80,500	23,500
Poland	306,000	65,000
Portugal	58,000	49,500
Saudi Arabia	30,000	16,500
South Africa	229,000	80,000
Soviet Union	1.4 million	386,000
Spain	149,000	*
Sweden	97,500	52,000
Turkey	60,000	36,500
United Kingdom	363,000	339,000
United States	See Table B.	

*Not available

Since the time of the Roman Empire, one of the marks by which a civilization has been judged is its system of roads. All-weather roads are important in developing the economy of a nation and have always been considered a crucial part of a nation's military defenses.

Table B / U.S. Highway System

Total miles of public roads and streets: 3.85 million
Total miles of rural roads: 3.22 million
Total miles of urban streets: 632,000
Total miles of paved roads: 3.4 million (88% of total)
Total miles of state-controlled roads: 876,250
Total miles of locally controlled roads: 2,720,335
Total miles of federal roads: 256,112*

Expenditures

State highway systems:	$23.8 billion
County and local systems:	6.2 billion
City streets:	7.8 billion
Federal roads:	1.0 billion*
Total:	$38.8 billion

Disbursement of Expenditures

50% capital outlay
30% maintenance
20% administration, police and safety, interest on bonds
*National parks, reservations, etc.

The United States, in a reflection of its federal system of government, has a multilayered highway, road, and street system. At the local level, streets are usually the responsibility of the municipal government. In many areas, especially in rural parts of the country, there is a county system of roads. Next comes the state system, by far the largest and most important of the highway systems. Finally, there is the transcontinental Interstate Highway System. Although this is largely paid for by the federal government (as indeed are many of the lesser state roads), it is administered by the state highway systems. For example, each portion of Interstate Highway 95, which roughly follows the Atlantic coastline from Maine to Florida, is administered, maintained, and policed by the states through which it runs.

ment in world transportation. The industrial revolution in Europe and America had created unprecedented demands for moving raw materials from their source to the factory, and finished products to their marketplace. To accommodate steamships, American and European rivers were dredged and elaborate canal systems were dug.

The steam locomotive was the other great transportation advance of the nineteenth century. By midcentury all major cities in Europe and America were connected by railroads. By the end of the century, railroads served virtually the entire population in Europe and the United States.

The automobile and the airplane revolution-ized transportation in the twentieth century just as the steamship and the locomotive had done in the nineteenth. The United States, in particular, created a national highway system that literally covered the nation. By the 1980s, there was scarcely a community or business in the country that was not connected with its neighbors by an all-weather, usually paved, road.

The use of airplanes for the movement of passengers, mail, and freight began in the 1920s, greatly increased in the 1930s, but saw its greatest growth in the decades following World War II. Railroad passenger service and much commercial service were almost completely replaced by air travel, especially for medium- and long-distance travel and shipment.

Table C / Passenger Cars and Commercial Vehicles

The Ten Countries with the Most Passenger Cars		The Ten Countries with the Most Commercial Vehicles	
Country	Number of Vehicles	Country	Number of Vehicles
United States	121,723,650	United States	34,166,042
Japan	24,612,277	Japan	15,020,133
West Germany	23,680,911	Canada	2,955,299
France	19,750,000	France	2,716,000
Italy	17,900,000	United Kingdom	1,854,000
United Kingdom	15,267,000	West Germany	1,548,357
Brazil	9,565,914	Spain	1,466,257
Spain	7,943,325	Italy	1,450,000
Soviet Union	7,500,000	Mexico	1,277,425
Australia	6,977,000	Argentina	1,260,250

The United States, Japan, and Western Europe account for most of the world's automobiles, trucks, and buses. It is interesting to note that the Communist bloc of nations, even a superpower like the Soviet Union, manages its highly industrialized economies with far fewer vehicles than do the West and Japan. Statistics for China are not available.

Table D / Railroad Systems

Country	Length of System (In Kilometers)	Country	Length of System (In Kilometers)
Argentina	39,738	Israel	767
Australia	42,855	Italy	20,085
Austria	6,497	Japan	29,711
Belgium	4,130	Kenya	2,040
Bolivia	3,651	Mexico	14,210
Brazil	24,600	New Zealand	4,716
Canada	67,067	Nigeria	3,505
China	52,500	Pakistan	8,815
Czechoslovakia	13,131	Poland	27,236
France	36,500	Saudi Arabia	575
Germany, East	14,248	South Africa	35,434
Germany, West	33,555	Soviet Union	142,000
Greece	2,476	Spain	16,282
Hungary	7,864	Taiwan	4,550
India	60,693	Turkey	8,138
Iran	4,601	United Kingdom	17,664
Iraq	1,700	United States	262,323
Ireland	2,190		

The United States has almost twice as many kilometers of railroad track as the nearest competitor, the Soviet Union. However, Western Europe, in terms of land mass, has the best developed rail system; many more small towns and villages in Europe are served by the railroad than is the case in the United States. The British were great builders of railroads in their far-flung empire; most of the railroads in India, Pakistan, Australia, Kenya, and Nigeria were built by the British.

Drowning in Debt

During the 1970s, the external debts (that is, the debts owed to foreign banks or organizations) increased sharply among nations of the Third World, also known as the developing nations. This rise in debt resulted from the industrialization projects sponsored as a result of the general feeling that if these nations were to improve their economic standing and increase the standard of living of their people, they would have to create new industry. In addition, the reformation of agricultural practices as a way of producing more food required vast sums of money, most of which had to be borrowed from foreign sources.

Even a modest industrialization program is extremely expensive. It usually entails, in addition to the building of the actual factories or processing plants, a considerable outlay of capital for what is generally called infrastructure. This category includes highways and streets; railroads; port facilities; airfields; electric power plants; water, irrigation, and sewage systems; and in many cases housing developments for workers. In the industrialized nations, such facilities are to a large extent already in place, but the developing nations often must in effect start from scratch. Added to the cost of actually building the production facilities, the cost of this infrastructure adds an imposing burden to a country that already is strained to increase its economic production.

The industrial nations have long been concerned with the tremendous gap between the haves and have-nots, that is between the rich nations and the poor nations. In addition to the general humanitarian wish to raise the living standards of peoples who are living at best on the verge of starvation, there is the recognition that a volatile political and economic situation exists in a world where more than half the people are living in what Westerners would describe as poverty.

To help alleviate this situation, governments of the rich nations, along with such international organizations as the UN and the International Monetary Fund (IMF), actively encouraged the governments of developing nations to embark on ambitious capital projects (agricultural as well as industrial) that would, it was hoped, pull them out of poverty. Private banks in the West were encouraged to lend great sums of money to these nations, and the IMF and the World Bank also transferred funds to them. During the 1970s, the debts for the Third World increased on the average of 21 percent a year.

Not all of this money was spent wisely. Ill-thought-out schemes ate away vast sums, corruption in high places transferred millions of dollars into private accounts in European banks, and rising interest rates all over the world made

Table A / Debts of Developing Countries

Country	Amount (In U.S. Dollars)	Country	Amount (In U.S. Dollars)
Brazil	93 billion	Chile	18 billion
Mexico	89 billion	Turkey	17 billion
Argentina	44 billion	Algeria	15 billion
Venezuela	34 billion	Malaysia	12 billion
Indonesia	25 billion	Nigeria	12 billion
Philippines	24 billion		

The four nations with the highest debts are in Latin America, as is the seventh ranked country, Chile. The other debt leaders are either strategically important to the West, such as Turkey and the Philippines; have significant mineral resources, as in Algeria and Nigeria; or have a combination of these attributes. The Latin American nations, with large populations and economic potential, have long been favored for lending, which has led to their astronomical debts.

Table B / External Debts of Selected Nations
(As Percentage of Gross National Product [GNP])

Country	%	Country	%
Mauritania	139.7	Philippines	18.2
Israel	62.2	Venezuela	18.0
Egypt	51.7	Chile	18.0
Algeria	38.7	Brazil	16.4
Bolivia	36.4	Malaysia	13.7
Indonesia	22.5	India	10.0
Turkey	22.4	Argentina	7.2
Mexico	20.6	Nigeria	5.5

Although Mexico and Brazil are the two nations whose external debts have created the most fear in international banking circles, their debts as compared with their gross national product are in fact in the middle range. Israel, for example, after years of spending vast sums on defense, has an abnormally high debt. The chronic inflation rates suffered by that country are one result of that high debt.

Table C / U.S. Public Debt, 1791–1983

Year	Amount (In Dollars)	Year	Amount (In Dollars)
1791	75.4 million	1950	256.1 billion
1800	82.9 million	1955	272.8 billion
1825	83.8 million	1960	284.1 billion
1850	63.4 million	1965	313.8 billion
1875	2.1 billion	1970	370.1 billion
1900	1.2 billion	1975	533.2 billion
1910	1.1 billion	1977	698.8 billion
1920	24.3 billion	1979	826.5 billion
1930	16.1 billion	1980	907.7 billion
1935	28.7 billion	1981	997.9 billion
1940	43.0 billion	1982	1,142.0 billion
1945	258.7 billion	1983	1,377.2 billion

Prior to World War II, the federal debt was mainly a result of United States involvement in war. Some economists today feel that as long as the United States economy, measured by the gross national product, is strong and growing, the nation is able to support a rising debt. While the argument continues over exactly what is a safe debt limit, the debt itself continues to increase.

it difficult at times for the borrowers even to make their interest payments.

In the late 1970s, a worldwide economic recession greatly exacerbated the problems of the debt-ridden countries. Even in countries that had created new industrial capacities, economic competition decreased the amount of income that could be realized from them. Interest rates, particularly in the United States, reached unprecedented heights, making it ever more difficult for the borrowers to meet their obligations to the lending agencies. For the first time, it became a possibility that some nations would default on their debts, thereby in effect going into bankruptcy. Alarm spread through Western banking circles as the possibility loomed that some of the world's largest banks could themselves go under if such nations as Brazil and Mexico (see Table A) defaulted on their loans.

Starting in about 1980, the banking centers began greatly reducing the flow of capital to the Third World. Under pressure from international organizations and governments—and from their own wishes not to see the debtor nations default on their loans—the lending agencies created new schemes that would stretch out the repayment of the debts, thereby relieving some of the pressure on the debtors. The debtor nations themselves called on the lending agencies to reduce the interest they were charging, their argument being that they were not responsible for

the international economic situation that resulted in abnormally high interest rates. In particular, they called attention to the high interest rates in the United States, which were the result of the constantly rising United States public debt (see Table C). That debt, in turn, was largely the result of the huge federal deficits under which the government was operating year after year.

The United States Debt

Until after World War II, the federal debt was largely the result of the expenses of war. In the 1930s, for the first time, the government adopted a deliberate policy of operating at a deficit as a way of creating more money that would get the economy moving and bring the nation out of the Great Depression.

During World War II, the government sold billions of dollars' worth of war bonds, both to finance the costs of the war and as a way of taking money out of the economy. This policy decreased the demand for consumer goods and kept inflation within bounds.

It was expected that after the war, unless another depression occurred, the government would retire its great public debt. In the ensuing peacetime, the federal government as a general rule operated well within its budget. However, the new position of world leadership in which the United States found itself called for budgets almost as large as those of wartime. At first, aid to its former allies, in particular through the Marshall Plan, sent billions of dollars out of the country. Then with the coming of the cold war, the cost of rearming and of supplying much of the armaments for the North Atlantic Treaty Organization (NATO) added new burdens to the national debt.

In the 1960s, President Lyndon B. Johnson greatly added to the federal budget with his ambitious Great Society social-welfare programs; then the costs of the Vietnam War caused budget deficits, and the public debt, to reach astronomical heights. Ronald Reagan was elected president in 1980 with the promise of reducing the national debt and balancing the federal budget. His plan, known as supply-side economics, or Reaganomics, was predicated on the idea that a massive tax cut would so activate the economy that the additional tax revenues would pour enough new money into the Treasury so as to balance the budget. His policies were successful in creating a prosperous economy, but the great inpouring of taxes into the Treasury did not occur. Thus in 1982, for the first time, the United States national debt went over the $1 trillion ($1,000 billion) mark.

United States Money Woes

Economists, politicians, and commentators cannot agree on what exactly is wrong with the fi-

nancial condition of the United States and what should be done to correct it. In 1982 the public debt (that is, the amount of money owed by the federal government to the people of the United States) went above a trillion dollars for the first time (see Table B).

It is difficult for most people even to visualize how much money a trillion dollars is. If the debt is broken down into the amount owed to each citizen in the nation, however, it becomes much more understandable. In 1940 each citizen's share of the national debt was $325; in 1972 it was $2,037; and in 1983 it was $5,870. When looked at from that point of view, the public debt does not seem so formidable.

Nevertheless, most people would agree that the national debt is too high, that the federal government in a period of prosperity and when there is no war going on should not operate at a deficit. The federal budget should in fact offer a surplus that would reduce the debt. A large public debt absorbs much of the capital of the nation, money that could be put to more constructive uses in the private sector. It also attracts investment money from abroad, which in turn creates a dollar that is stronger than the currencies of the trading partners of the United States. A strong dollar is a threat to American farmers and manufacturers who need to export their products—because foreign consumers find it more expensive to buy American products if their currency is weak in relation to the dollar.

Table A / United States Budget Surpluses and Deficits Since World War II
(In Billions of Dollars)

Fiscal Year	Surplus	Deficit	Fiscal Year	Surplus	Deficit
1946		15.9	1966		3.8
1947	3.9		1967		8.7
1948	15.0		1968		25.2
1949	0.6		1969	3.2	
1950		3.1	1970		2.8
1951	6.1		1971		23.0
1952		1.5	1972		23.4
1953		6.5	1973		14.8
1954		1.2	1974		4.7
1955		3.0	1975		45.2
1956	4.1		1976		79.4
1957	3.2		1977		44.9
1958		2.9	1978		48.8
1959		12.9	1979		27.7
1960	0.3		1980		59.6
1961		3.4	1981		57.9
1962		7.1	1982		110.6
1963		4.8	1983		195.4
1964		5.9	1984		183.7*
1965		1.6	1985		180.4*

*Estimate

The federal government has spent less than it took in only eight years since World War II. Until the late 1960s, however, the federal deficit was so low as to be inconsequential (by today's standards). The first great deficits came during the Vietnam War, when the Johnson administration was not willing either to raise taxes or to cut back on its social programs after the costs of the Vietnam War rose dramatically. The deficit rose again dramatically during the Reagan administration, largely because of massive tax cuts.

Table B / Public Debt: 1940–1983
(In Dollars)

Year	Total (In billions)	Per Capita	Year	Total (In billions)	Per Capita
1940	43.0	325	1975	533.2	2,475
1945	258.7	1,849	1976	620.4	2,852
1950	256.1	1,688	1977	698.8	3,170
1955	272.8	1,651	1978	771.5	3,463
1960	284.1	1,572	1979	826.5	3,669
1970	370.1	1,814	1980	907.7	3,985
1971	397.3	1,921	1981	997.9	4,338
1972	426.4	2,037	1982	1,142.0	4,913
1973	457.3	2,164	1983	1,377.2	5,870
1974	474.2	2,223			

Traditionally, the United States federal government has borrowed large sums of money only during times of war. The first break with that tradition came during the 1930s, when it was the policy of the New Deal to "prime the pump" by using the government's borrowing power to put more money in circulation in the hope that the extra money would stimulate the economy. That policy has generally been followed in recessionary periods since World War II.

World Gazetteer: Profiles of Nations and Places

The following World Gazetteer presents an up-to-date overview of the world's independent countries and their possessions. Geographic, political, and population-related information is derived from the most current Rand McNally data available. Ethnic groups, religions, trade partners, exports, and imports are listed in order of decreasing size and/or importance. Languages are similarly organized, with official language(s) listed first. Political parties are cited alphabetically, as are membership entries, which represent member nations of the following organizations:

Arab League (AL)
Commonwealth of Nations (CW)
Council for Mutual Economic
  Assistance (COMECON)
North Atlantic Treaty
  Organization (NATO)
Organization for Economic
  Cooperation and Development
  (OECD)

Organization of
  African Unity (OAU)
Organization of
  American States (OAS)
Organization of
  Petroleum Exporting
  Countries (OPEC)
United Nations (UN)
Warsaw Pact

AFGHANISTAN

Official name Democratic Republic of
Afghanistan
PEOPLE
Population 14,650,000. **Density** 59/mi² (23/km²). **Urban**
16%. **Capital** Kābul, 913,164. **Ethnic groups** Pushtun
50%, Tajik 25%, Uzbek 9%, Hazara 9%. **Languages**
Dari, Pushtu. **Religions** Sunni Muslim 87%, Shiite
Muslim 12%. **Life expectancy** 40 female, 41 male.
Literacy 12%.
POLITICS
Government Socialist republic. **Parties** People's
Democratic. **Suffrage** Universal, over 18. **Memberships**
UN. **Subdivisions** 29 provinces.
ECONOMY
GNP $2,800,000,000. **Per capita** $200. **Monetary unit**
Afgháni. **Trade partners** U.S.S.R., Eastern European
countries. **Exports** Fruits, nuts, natural gas, carpets.
Imports Food, petroleum.
LAND
Description Southern Asia, landlocked. **Area** 250,000
mi² (647,497 km²). **Highest point** Nowshāk, 24,557 ft
(7,485 m). **Lowest point** Amu Darya River valley, 837 ft
(255 m).

People. Afghanistan shares borders with the Soviet
Union, China, India, Pakistan, and Iran, and this
crossroads position has resulted in a population that
is both ethnically and linguistically diverse. Religion,
however, plays a strong unifying role. Most Afghans
are Muslim, and Islamic laws and customs determine life-styles and beliefs both religious and secular. The population is mainly rural, most are
farmers, and there is a small nomad population.

Economy and the Land. The main force of Afghanistan's underdeveloped economy is agriculture,
with subsistence farming and animal husbandry accounting for much activity. Crop production has been
greatly aided by irrigation systems. A terrain of
mountains and valleys, including the Hindu Kush,
separates the desert region of the southwest from
the more fertile north, an area of higher population
density and the site of natural-gas deposits. Increased development has made natural gas an im-

portant export. Winters are generally cold, and
summers hot and dry.

History and Politics. Once part of the Persian Empire, the area of present-day Afghanistan saw invasions by Persians, Macedonians and Greeks,
Turks, Arabs, Mongols, and other peoples. An Arab
invasion in 652 introduced Islam. In 1747 Afghan
tribes led by Ahmad Shah Durrani united the area
and established today's Afghanistan. Power remained with the Durrani tribe for more than two centuries. In the nineteenth and early twentieth
centuries, Britain controlled Afghanistan's foreign
affairs. A Durrani tribe member and former prime
minister led a military coup in 1973 and set up a
republic, ending the country's monarchical tradition.
This new government's failure to improve economic
and social conditions led to a 1978 revolution that
established a Marxist government and brought Soviet aid. Intraparty differences and citizenry dissent
resulted in a Soviet invasion in 1979. Fighting between government forces and the *mujaheddin,* "holy
warrior," guerrillas continues, and the government
has failed to gain complete control. In foreign affairs,
the country's policy has been nonalignment and
neutrality.   ■

ALBANIA

Official name People's Socialist Republic of
Albania
PEOPLE
Population 2,935,000. **Density** 264/mi² (102/km²).
Urban 33%. **Capital** Tiranë, 198,000. **Ethnic groups**
Albanian 96%. **Languages** Albanian, Greek.
Religions Muslim 70%, Albanian Orthodox 20%, Roman
Catholic 10%. **Life expectancy** 72 female, 68 male.
Literacy 75%.
POLITICS
Government Socialist republic. **Parties** Workers'.
Suffrage Universal, over 18. **Memberships** UN.
Subdivisions 26 districts.

ECONOMY

GNP $2,150,000,000. **Per capita** $820. **Monetary unit** Lek. **Trade partners** Yugoslavia, Czechoslovakia, Italy. **Exports** Asphalt, bitumen, petroleum products. **Imports** Machinery, machine tools, iron and steel products.

LAND

Description Southeastern Europe. **Area** 11,100 mi² (28,748 km²). **Highest point** Korabit 9,026 ft (2,751 m). **Lowest point** Sea level.

People. A homogeneous native population characterizes Albania, with Greeks the main minority. Five centuries of Turkish rule shaped much of the culture and led many Albanians to adopt Islam. Since 1944, when the current Communist regime was established, an increased emphasis on education has more than tripled the literacy rate. In 1967 religious institutions were banned, and Albania claims to be the world's first atheist state.

Economy and the Land. Reputedly one of the poorest countries in Europe, Albania has tried to shift its economy from agriculture to industry. Farms employed about 60 percent of the work force in 1970, a significant decrease from more than 80 percent before 1944. Mineral resources make mining the chief industrial activity. The terrain consists of forested hills and mountains, and the climate is mild.

History and Politics. Early invaders and rulers included Greeks, Romans, Goths, and others. In 1468 the Ottoman Turks conquered the area, and it remained part of their empire until the First Balkan War in 1912. Invaded by Italy and occupied by Germany during World War II, Albania set up a Communist government in 1944, following the German retreat. A strict approach to communism caused the country to sever ties with its onetime allies—Yugoslavia, the Soviet Union, and most recently China—and today the country remains unallied. Relations with some nations have improved. ∎

ALGERIA

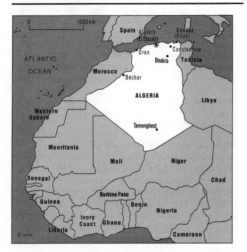

Official name Democratic and Popular Republic of Algeria

PEOPLE

Population 21,695,000. **Density** 24/mi² (9.1/km²). **Urban** 52%. **Capital** Algiers, 1,523,000. **Ethnic groups** Arab-Berber. **Languages** Arabic, Berber, French. **Religions** Sunni Muslim 99%. **Life expectancy** 58 female, 55 male. **Literacy** 46%.

POLITICS

Government Socialist republic. **Parties** National Liberation Front. **Suffrage** Universal, over 19. **Memberships** OAU, UN. **Subdivisions** 31 departments.

ECONOMY

GDP $42,900,000,000. **Per capita** $2,142. **Monetary unit** Dinar. **Trade partners** U.S., West Germany, France. **Exports** Petroleum, natural gas. **Imports** Capital equipment, semifinished goods, food.

LAND

Description Northern Africa. **Area** 919,595 mi² (2,381,741 km²). **Highest point** Tahat, 9,541 ft (2,908 m). **Lowest point** Chott Melrhir, 131 ft (40 m) below sea level.

People. Indigenous Berbers and invading Arabs shaped modern Algeria's culture, and today most of the population is Muslim, of Arab-Berber, Arab, or Berber descent. European cultural influences, evidence of over a century of French control, exist in urban areas, however. Since independence in 1962, free medical care has been instituted and the educational system has been greatly improved.

Economy and the Land. A member of the Organization of Petroleum Exporting Countries (OPEC), Algeria produces oil and natural gas. Agriculture is divided between state and privately owned farms. The government continues to emphasize gas production and exportation while it maintains a socialistic economy and promotes development of private business. Algeria's terrain is varied. The Tell, Arabic for "hill," is a narrow Mediterranean coastal region that contains the country's most fertile land and highest population. South of this lie high plateaus and the Atlas Mountains, which give way to the Sahara Desert. The climate is temperate along the coast and dry and cool in the plateau region.

History and Politics. In the eighth and eleventh centuries invading Arabs brought their language and religion to the native Berbers. The Berbers and Arabs together became known as Moors, and conflicts between Moors, Turks, and Spaniards erupted periodically over several centuries. France began conquering Algeria in 1830, and by 1902 the entire country was under French control. The revolution against French rule began in 1954, but it was not until 1962 that the country was declared independent. Since a bloodless coup in 1965, the political situation has been relatively stable. The centralized government follows a policy of independence and nonalignment, but it is influenced by other Third World countries. ∎

AMERICAN SAMOA

See UNITED STATES.

ANDORRA

Official name Principality of Andorra
PEOPLE
Population 39,000. **Density** 223/mi² (86/km²). **Capital** Andorra, 14,928. **Ethnic groups** Spanish 61%, Andorran 30%, French 6%. **Languages** Catalan, Spanish, French. **Religions** Roman Catholic. **Literacy** 100%.
POLITICS
Government Coprincipality (France, Spain). **Parties** None. **Suffrage** Third-generation Andorrans, over 21. **Memberships** None. **Subdivisions** 7 districts.
ECONOMY
Monetary unit Spanish peseta, French franc. **Trade partners** Spain, France.
LAND
Description Southwestern Europe, landlocked. **Area** 175 mi² (453 km²). **Highest point** Coma Pedrosa, 9,665 ft (2,946 m). **Lowest point** Valira River valley, 2,756 ft (840 m).

People. Much of Andorran life and culture has been shaped by its mountainous terrain and governing countries, France and Spain. Population is concentrated in the valleys, and despite a tourism boom in the past decades, the peaks and valleys of the Pyrenees have isolated the small country from many twentieth-century changes. Catalan is the official language, and cultural and historic ties exist with the Catalonian region of northern Spain. The majority of the population is Spanish; Andorran citizens are a minority.

Economy and the Land. The terrain has established Andorra's economy as well as its life-style. Improved transportation routes together with other factors have resulted in a thriving tourist industry— a dramatic shift from traditional sheepherding and tobacco growing. In addition, duty-free status has made the country a European shopping mecca. Tobacco is still the main agricultural product, though only about 4 percent of the land is arable. Climate varies with altitude; winters are cold, and summers cool and pleasant.

History and Politics. Tradition indicates that Char-

lemagne freed the area from the Moors in A.D. 806. A French count and the Spanish bishop of Seo de Urgel signed an agreement in the 1200s to act as coprinces of the country, establishing the political status and boundaries that exist today. The coprincipality is governed by the president of France and the bishop of Seo de Urgel. The country has no formal constitution, no armed forces other than a small police force, and no political parties.   ∎

ANGOLA

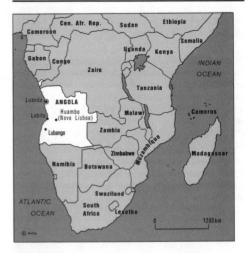

Official name People's Republic of Angola
PEOPLE
Population 7,875,000. **Density** 16/mi² (6.3./km²). **Urban** 21%. **Capital** Luanda, 475,328. **Ethnic groups** Ovimbundu 38%, Kimbundu 23%, Kongo 13%. **Languages** Portuguese, indigenous. **Religions** Animist, Roman Catholic, Protestant. **Life expectancy** 43 female, 41 male. **Literacy** 20%.
POLITICS
Government Socialist republic. **Parties** Popular Movement for Liberation–Labor. **Suffrage** Undetermined. **Memberships** OAU, UN. **Subdivisions** 18 provinces.
ECONOMY
GDP $3,900,000,000. **Per capita** $591. **Monetary unit** Kwanza. **Trade partners** Cuba, U.S.S.R., Portugal, U.S. **Exports** Petroleum, coffee, diamonds. **Imports** Capital equipment, wines, iron and steel.
LAND
Description Southern Africa. **Area** 481,353 mi² (1,246,700 km²). **Highest point** Serra do Môco, 8,596 ft (2,620 m). **Lowest point** Sea level.

People. Angola today is made up mostly of various Bantu peoples—mainly Ovimbundu, Kimbundu, Kongo, and Chokwe. Despite influences resulting from a half-century of Portuguese rule, Angolan traditions remain strong, especially in rural areas. Each group has its own language, and although Portuguese is the official language, it is spoken by a minority. Many Angolans, retaining traditional animist beliefs, worship ancestral spirits.

Economy and the Land. A 1975 civil war, the resultant departure of skilled European labor, and continuing guerrilla activity have taken their toll on Angola's economy. The country has been working toward recovery, however, encouraging development of private industries and foreign trade. Although not a member of the Organization of Petroleum Exporting Countries (OPEC), Angola is a large oil producer. Cabinda, an enclave separated from the rest of the country by Zaire and the Zaire River, is the main site of oil production. Diamond mining remains an important activity, as does agriculture. Much of the land is forested, however, and is therefore not suited for commercial farming. The flat coastal area gives way to inland plateaus and uplands. The climate varies from tropical to subtropical.

History and Politics. Bantu groups settled in the area prior to the first century A.D. In 1483 a Portuguese explorer became the first European to arrive in Angola, and slave trade soon became a major activity. Portuguese control expanded and continued almost uninterrupted for several centuries. In the 1960s ignored demands led to two wars for independence. Three nationalist groups emerged, each with its own ideology and supporters. In 1974 a coup in Portugal resulted in independence for all Portuguese territories in Africa, and Angola became independent in 1975. A civil war ensued, with the three liberation groups fighting for power. By 1976, with the assistance of Cuban military personnel, the Popular Movement for the Liberation of Angola had established control. Unrest continues, with occasional guerrilla activity, an independence movement in Cabinda, and controversy over South African influence. Nonalignment is a government policy, and the country is attempting to expand its Western relationships, having already established ties with Cuba and the Soviet Union. ∎

ANGUILLA

See UNITED KINGDOM.

ANTARCTICA

PEOPLE
Population No permanent population. **Capital** None.
LAND
Description Continent in Southern Hemisphere. **Area** 5,400,000 mi² (14,000,000 km²). **Highest point** Vinson Massif, 16,864 ft (5,140 m). **Lowest point** Sea level.

People. Antarctica, which surrounds the South Pole, is the southernmost continent, the coldest place on earth, and one of the last frontiers. There are no native inhabitants, and its temporary population is made up mainly of scientists from various countries operating research stations.

Economy and the Land. Harsh climate and terrain inhibit both resource exploration and exploitation.

Antarctica's natural resources include coal, various ores, iron, and offshore oil and natural gas. Fishing for krill, a marine protein source, is currently being conducted. Crossed by several ranges collectively known as the Transantarctic Mountains, Antarctica can be roughly divided into a mountainous western region and a larger eastern sector consisting of an icy plain rimmed by mountains. With its tip about 700 miles (1,127 kilometers) from southern South America, the mountainous Antarctic Peninsula and its offshore islands jut northward. Nearly all Antarctica is ice covered; precipitation is minimal, and the continent is actually a desert.

History and Politics. In the 1770s Captain James Cook of Britain set out in search of the southernmost continent and sailed completely around Antarctica without sighting land. Explorations beginning in 1820 resulted in sightings of the mainland or offshore islands by the British, Russians, and Americans. British explorer Sir James C. Ross conducted the first extensive explorations. After a lull of several decades, interest in Antarctica was renewed in the late nineteenth and early twentieth centuries. The main figures were Captain Robert F. Scott and Ernest Shackleton of Britain and Roald Amundsen of Norway. The race to the South Pole was won by Amundsen in 1911. According to the Antarctic Treaty of 1959, only peaceful scientific research can be conducted in the region. The treaty also delays the settlement of overlapping territorial claims for thirty years. Claims to Antarctica are held by Norway, Australia, France, New Zealand, Chile, Britain, and Argentina. ∎

ANTIGUA AND BARBUDA

Official name Antigua and Barbuda

PEOPLE
Population 78,000. **Density** 459/mi² (177/km²). **Urban** 34%. **Capital** St. John's, Antigua I., 24,359. **Ethnic groups** Black. **Languages** English. **Religions** Anglican. **Life expectancy** 64 female, 60 male. **Literacy** 88%.
POLITICS
Government Parliamentary state. **Parties** Labor, Progressive Labor Movement, United People's Movement. **Suffrage** Universal, over 18. **Memberships** CW, OAS, UN.
ECONOMY
GDP $125,600,000. **Per capita** $1,650. **Monetary unit** East Caribbean dollar. **Trade partners** U.K., U.S., Caribbean countries. **Exports** Clothing, rum, lobsters. **Imports** Fuels, food, machinery.

LAND

Description Caribbean islands. **Area** 170 mi² (440 km²). **Highest point** Boggy Pk., Antigua I., 1,319 ft (402 m). **Lowest point** Sea level.

People. Most Antiguans are descendants of black African slaves brought by the British to work sugarcane plantations. The largest urban area is St. John's, but most Antiguans live in rural areas. British rule for about three centuries resulted in a population that is mostly Protestant.

Economy and the Land. The dry, tropical climate and white-sand beaches attract many visitors, making tourism the economic mainstay. Farmers grow sugarcane, which is refined into sugar locally. The country is made up of three islands: Antigua, the largest island; Barbuda; and uninhabited Redondo. Formed by volcanoes, the low-lying islands are flat.

History and Politics. The original inhabitants of Antigua and Barbuda were the Carib Indians. Columbus arrived at Antigua in 1493, and after unsuccessful Spanish and French attempts at colonization, the British began settlement in the 1600s. The country remained a British colony until 1967, when it became an associated state of the United Kingdom. Antigua gained independence in 1981. ∎

ARGENTINA

Official name Argentine Republic

PEOPLE
Population 30,340,000. **Density** 28/mi² (11/km²). **Urban** 82%. **Capital** Buenos Aires, 2,908,001. **Ethnic groups** White 85%; mestizo, Indian, and others 15%. **Languages** Spanish. **Religions** Roman Catholic 90%, Jewish 2%, Protestant 2%. **Life expectancy** 73 female, 69 male. **Literacy** 94%.

POLITICS
Government Republic. **Parties** Justicialist, Movement for Industrial Development, Radical Civic Union. **Suffrage** Universal, over 18. **Memberships** OAS, UN. **Subdivisions** 22 provinces, 1 district, 1 territory.

ECONOMY
GNP $130,000,000,000. **Per capita** $4,610. **Monetary unit** Peso. **Trade partners** Western European countries, U.S., Brazil, U.S.S.R. **Exports** Meat, corn, wheat. **Imports** Machinery, lubricating oils, iron and steel.

LAND
Description Southern South America. **Area** 1,068,301 mi² (2,766,889 km²). **Highest point** Cerro Aconcagua, 22,831 ft (6,959 m). **Lowest point** Salinas Chicas, 138 ft (42 m) below sea level.

People. An indigenous Indian population, Spanish settlement, and a turn-of-the-century influx of immigrants have made Argentina an ethnically diverse nation. Today, most Argentines are descendants of Spanish and Italian immigrants. Other Europeans, mestizos of mixed Indian-Spanish blood, Indians, Middle Easterners, and Latin American immigrants diversify the population further. Spanish influence is evidenced by the major religion, Roman Catholicism; the official language, Spanish; and many aspects of cultural life.

Economy and the Land. Political difficulties beginning in the 1930s have resulted in economic problems and have kept this onetime economic giant from realizing its potential. The most valuable natural resource is the rich soil of the pampas, fertile plains in the east-central region. The greatest contributors to the economy, however, are manufacturing and services. The second largest country in South America, Argentina has a varied terrain, with northern lowlands, the east-central pampas, the Andes Mountains in the west, and the southern Patagonian steppe. The climate likewise varies, from subtropical in the north to subarctic in the south.

History and Politics. The earliest inhabitants of the area were Indians. In the 1500s silver-seeking Spaniards arrived, and by 1580 they had established a colony on the site of present-day Buenos Aires. In 1816 Argentina officially announced its independence from Spain, a successful struggle for independence ensued, and in 1853 a constitution was adopted and a president elected. Prosperity continued through the 1920s, and immigration and foreign investment increased. Unsatisfactory power distribution and concern over foreign investment resulted in a military coup in 1930. Thus began a series of civil and military governments; coups; the election, overthrow, and reelection of Juan Perón; and controversial human-rights violations. In 1982 Argentina lost a war with Britain over the Falkland Islands. Elections in 1983 resulted in a new government that is trying to resolve continued economic problems, deal with human-rights transgressions, and institute other reforms. ∎

See also FALKLAND ISLANDS.

ARUBA

See NETHERLANDS.

ASCENSION ISLAND

See UNITED KINGDOM.

AUSTRALIA

Official name Commonwealth of Australia

PEOPLE

Population 15,565,000. **Density** 5.2/mi² (2/km²). **Urban** 86%. **Capital** Canberra, 219,323. **Ethnic groups** White 99%, Asian and aborigine 1%. **Languages** English. **Religions** Anglican 28%, Roman Catholic 26%, other Protestant 25%. **Life expectancy** 77 female, 72 male. **Literacy** 99%.

POLITICS

Government Parliamentary state. **Parties** Democratic, Labor, Liberal, National. **Suffrage** Universal, over 18. **Memberships** CW, OECD, UN. **Subdivisions** 6 states, 2 territories.

ECONOMY

GNP $153,000,000,000. **Per capita** $10,087. **Monetary unit** Dollar. **Trade partners** Japan, U.S., Western European countries. **Exports** Coal, wool, wheat. **Imports** Capital equipment, consumer goods, transportation equipment.

LAND

Description Continent between South Pacific and Indian oceans. **Area** 2,967,909 mi² (7,686,850 km²). **Highest point** Mt. Kosciusko, 7,310 ft (2,228 m). **Lowest point** Lake Eyre (north), 52 ft (16 m) below sea level.

People. Australia's culture reflects a unique combination of British, other European, and aboriginal influences. Settlement and rule by the United Kingdom gave the country a distinctly British flavor, and many Australians trace their roots to early British settlers. Planned immigration also played a major role in Australia's development, bringing more than three million Europeans since World War II. Refugees, most recently from Indochina, make up another group of incoming peoples. The country is also home to a small number of aborigines. The nation's size and a relatively dry terrain have resulted in uneven settlement patterns, with people concentrated in the rainier southeastern coastal area. Because of this, the population is mainly urban, though overall population density remains low.

Economy and the Land. Australia's economy is similar to economies in other developed nations, characterized by a postwar shift from agriculture to industry and services, and problems of inflation and unemployment. Wool is a major export, and livestock raising takes place on relatively flat, wide grazing lands surrounding an arid central region. Commercial crop raising is concentrated on a fertile southeastern plain. Plentiful mineral resources provide for a strong mining industry. Australia is the world's smallest continent but one of its largest countries. The climate is varied, and part of the country lies within the tropics. Because it is south of the equator, Australia has seasons the reverse of those in the Northern Hemisphere.

History and Politics. Aboriginal peoples probably arrived about forty thousand years ago and established a hunter-gatherer society. The Dutch explored the area in the seventeenth century, but no claims were made until the eighteenth century, when British captain James Cook found his way to the fertile east and annexed the land to Britain. The first colony, New South Wales, was founded in 1788, and many of the early settlers were British convicts. During the 1800s a squatter movement spread the population to other parts of the island, and the discovery of gold led to a population boom. Demands for self-government soon began, and by the 1890s all the colonies were self-governing, with Britain maintaining control of foreign affairs and defense. Nationalism continued to increase, and a new nation, the Commonwealth of Australia, was created in 1901. During both world wars, Australia fought on the side of the British, and postwar years saw increased attention to the rights of the much-declined aboriginal population. Since World War II, participation in international affairs has expanded, with attention being turned to Asian countries. ∎

Places and Possessions of Australia

Entity	Status	Area	Population	Capital / Population
Ashmore and Cartier Islands (north of Australia)	External territory	1.9 mi² (5 km²)	*None*	None
Christmas Island (Indian Ocean)	External territory	52 mi² (135 km²)	*3,300*	None
Cocos (Keeling) Islands (Indian Ocean)	Part of Australia	5.4 mi² (14 km²)	*600*	None
Coral Sea Islands (South Pacific)	External territory	1 mi² (2.6 km²)	*No permanent population*	None
Heard and McDonald islands (Indian Ocean)	External territory	113 mi² (293 km²)	*No permanent population*	None
Norfolk Island (South Pacific)	Part of Australia	14 mi² (36 km²)	*1,700*	Kingston
Tasmania (island south of Australia)	State	26,383 mi² (68,332 km²)	*440,000*	Hobart, *47,920*

AUSTRIA

Official name Republic of Austria
PEOPLE
Population 7,580,000. **Density** 234/mi² (90/km²). **Urban** 55%. **Capital** Vienna, 1,515,666. **Ethnic groups** German 98%. **Languages** German. **Religions** Roman Catholic 85%, Protestant 7%. **Life expectancy** 76 female, 71 male. **Literacy** 98%.
POLITICS
Government Republic. **Parties** Communist, Liberal, People's, Socialist. **Suffrage** Universal, over 19. **Memberships** OECD, UN. **Subdivisions** 9 states.
ECONOMY
GNP $66,890,000,000. **Per capita** $10,995. **Monetary unit** Schilling. **Trade partners** West Germany, Italy, Eastern European countries. **Exports** Iron and steel products, machinery, wood. **Imports** Machinery, chemicals, textiles, clothing.
LAND
Description Central Europe, landlocked. **Area** 32,377 mi² (83,855 km²). **Highest point** Grossglockner, 12,457 ft (3,797 m). **Lowest point** Neusiedler See, 377 ft (115 m).

People. Nearly all Austrians are native born, German speaking, and most are Roman Catholic, a homogeneity belying a history of invasions by diverse peoples. With a long cultural tradition, the country has contributed greatly to music and the arts; and Vienna, the capital, is one of the great cultural centers of Europe.

Economy and the Land. Austria's economy is a blend of state and privately owned industry. After World War II the government began nationalizing industries, returning many to the private sector as the economy stabilized. Unemployment is low, and the economy remains relatively strong. The economic mainstays are services and manufacturing. Agriculture is limited because of the overall mountainous terrain, with the Danube River basin in the east containing the most productive soils. The alpine landscape also attracts many tourists, as does the country's cultural heritage. The climate is generally moderate.

History and Politics. Early in its history, Austria was settled by Celts, ruled by Romans, and invaded by Germans, Slavs, Magyars, and others. Long rule by the Hapsburg family began in the thirteenth century, and in time Austria became the center of a vast empire. In 1867 Hungarian pressure resulted in the formation of the dual monarchy of Austria-Hungary. Nationalist movements against Austria culminated in the 1914 assassination of the heir to the throne, Archduke Francis Ferdinand, and set off the conflict that became World War I. In 1918 the war ended, the Hapsburg emperor was overthrown, Austria became a republic, and present-day boundaries were established. Political unrest and instability followed. In 1938 Adolf Hitler incorporated Austria into the German Reich. A period of occupation after World War II was followed by Austria's declaration of neutrality and ongoing political stability. Austria today frequently serves as a bridge for exchanges between Communist and non-Communist countries. ∎

AZORES

See PORTUGAL.

BAHAMAS

Official name The Commonwealth of the Bahamas
PEOPLE
Population 230,000. **Density** 43/mi² (17/km²). **Urban** 65%. **Capital** Nassau, New Providence I., 135,000. **Ethnic groups** Black 85%, white 15%. **Languages** English. **Religions** Baptist 29%, Anglican 23%, Roman Catholic 22%. **Life expectancy** 67 female, 64 male. **Literacy** 89%.
POLITICS
Government Parliamentary state. **Parties** Free National Movement, Progressive Liberal. **Suffrage** Universal, over 18. **Memberships** CW, OAS, UN. **Subdivisions** None.

ECONOMY
GNP $1,400,000,000. **Per capita** $6,000. **Monetary unit** Dollar. **Trade partners** U.S., U.K. **Exports** Pharmaceuticals, rum, cement. **Imports** Food, manufactured goods, fuels.

LAND
Description Caribbean islands. **Area** 5,382 mi^2 (13,939 km^2). **Highest point** Mt. Alvernia, Cat I., 206 ft (63 m). **Lowest point** Sea level.

People. Only about twenty-nine of the seven hundred Bahamian islands are inhabited, and most of the people live on Grand Bahama and New Providence. Blacks are a majority, mainly descendants of slaves routed through the area or brought by British Loyalists fleeing the American colonies during the revolutionary war.

Economy and the Land. The thin soils of these flat coral islands are not suited for agriculture, and for years the country struggled to develop a strong economic base. The solution was tourism, which capitalizes on the islands' most valuable resource— a semitropical climate. Because it is a tax haven, the country is also an international finance center.

History and Politics. Christopher Columbus's first stop on his way to America in 1492, the Bahamas were originally the home of the Lucayo Indians, whom the Spaniards took for slave trade. The British arrived in the 1600s, and the islands became a British colony in 1717. Independence was achieved in 1973. ∎

BAHRAIN

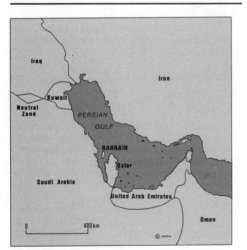

Official name State of Bahrain
PEOPLE
Population 415,000. **Density** 1,621/mi^2 (627/km^2). **Urban** 81%. **Capital** Manama, Bahrain I., 108,684. **Ethnic groups** Bahraini 63%, Asian 13%, other Arab 10%, Iranian 8%. **Languages** Arabic, English. **Religions** Shiite Muslim 60%, Sunni Muslim 40%. **Life expectancy** 69 female, 65 male. **Literacy** 47%.

POLITICS
Government Constitutional monarchy. **Parties** None. **Suffrage** None. **Memberships** AL, UN. **Subdivisions** None.

ECONOMY
GDP $4,000,000,000. **Per capita** $10,000. **Monetary unit** Dinar. **Trade partners** Japan, U.K., U.S., Saudi Arabia. **Exports** Petroleum, aluminum, fish. **Imports** Machinery, motor vehicles, manufactured goods, food.

LAND
Description Persian Gulf islands. **Area** 256 mi^2 (662 km^2). **Highest point** Mt. Dukhān, Bahrain I., 440 ft (134 m). **Lowest point** Sea level.

People. Most residents of Bahrain are native-born Muslims, with the Sunni sect predominating in urban areas and Shiites in the countryside. Many of the country's thirty-three islands are barren, and population is concentrated in the capital city—Manama, on Bahrain Island—and on the smaller island of Muharraq. The oil economy has resulted in an influx of foreign workers and considerable westernization, and Bahrain is a Persian Gulf leader in free health care and education.

Economy and the Land. The onetime pearl-and-fish economy was reshaped by exploitation of oil and natural gas, careful management, and diversification. A major refinery processes crude oil piped from Saudi Arabia as well as the country's own oil, and Bahrain's aluminum industry is the Gulf's largest nonoil activity. Because of its location, Bahrain is able to provide Gulf countries with services such as dry docking, and the country has also become a Middle Eastern banking center. Agriculture exists on northern Bahrain Island, where natural springs provide an irrigation source. But much of the state is desert; summers are hot and dry, and winters mild.

History and Politics. From around 2000 to 1800 B.C. the area of Bahrain flourished as a center for trade. After early periods of Portuguese and Iranian rule, the al-Khalifa family came to power in the eighteenth century, and it has governed ever since. Bahrain became a British protectorate in the nineteenth century, and independence was gained in 1971. Friendly international relations and political allegiance to the Arab League characterize the current government. ∎

BALEARIC ISLANDS

See SPAIN.

BANGLADESH

Official name People's Republic of Bangladesh
PEOPLE
Population 101,130,000. **Density** 1,819/mi^2 (702/km^2). **Urban** 11%. **Capital** Dacca, 1,850,000. **Ethnic groups** Bengali 98%. **Languages** Bangla, English. **Religions**

Muslim 83%, Hindu 16%. **Life expectancy** 48 female, 47 male. **Literacy** 25%.

POLITICS
Government Republic. **Parties** None (banned). **Suffrage** Universal, over 18. **Memberships** CW, UN. **Subdivisions** 21 districts.

ECONOMY
GNP $11,000,000,000. **Per capita** $117. **Monetary unit** Taka. **Trade partners** Western European countries, Japan, U.S. **Exports** Jute, leather, tea. **Imports** Grain, fuels, cotton, fertilizer.

LAND
Description Southern Asia. **Area** 55,598 mi² (143,998 km²). **Highest point** Reng Mtn., 3,141 ft (957 m). **Lowest point** Sea level.

People. Bangladesh's population is characterized by extremes. The people, mostly peasant farmers, are among Asia's poorest and most rural. With a relatively small area and a high birthrate, the country is also one of the world's most densely populated. Many Bangladeshis are victims of disease, floods, and ongoing medical and food shortages. Islam, the major religion, has influenced almost every aspect of life—from culture to politics.

Economy and the Land. Fertile floodplain soil is the chief resource of this mostly flat, river-crossed country, and farming is the main activity. Farm output fluctuates greatly, however, subject to the frequent monsoons, floods, and droughts of a semitropical climate. Because of this and other factors, foreign aid, imports, and an emphasis on agriculture have not assuaged the continuing food shortage. The country has yet to recover from damage sustained in a 1971 civil war and a 1985 tidal wave, but efforts to eliminate poverty and achieve self-sufficiency continue.

History and Politics. Most of Bangladesh lies in eastern Bengal, an Asian region whose western sector encompasses India's Bengal province. Early religious influences in Bengal included Buddhist rulers in the eighth century and Hindus in the eleventh. In 1200 Muslim rule introduced the religion to which the majority of eastern Bengalis eventually con-

verted, while most western Bengalis retained their Hindu beliefs. British control in India, beginning in the seventeenth century, expanded until all Bengal was part of British India by the 1850s. When British India gained independence in 1947, Muslim population centers were united into the single nation of Pakistan in an attempt to end Hindu-Muslim hostilities. More than 1,000 miles (1,600 km) separated West Pakistan, formed from northwest India, from East Pakistan, composed mostly of eastern Bengal. The bulk of Pakistan's population resided in the eastern province and felt the west wielded political and economic power at its expense. A civil war began in 1971, and the eastern province declared itself an independent nation called Bangladesh, or "Bengal nation." That same year West Pakistan surrendered to eastern guerrillas joined with Indian troops. The state has seen political crises since independence, including two leader assassinations and several coups. In 1982 a martial-law government was established. Protests continued, however, with occasional outbreaks of violence. A moderate, nonaligned foreign policy is maintained. ∎

BARBADOS

Official name Barbados

PEOPLE
Population 250,000. **Density** 1,506/mi² (581/km²). **Urban** 41%. **Capital** Bridgetown, 7,552. **Ethnic groups** Black 80%, mixed 16%, European 4%. **Languages** English. **Religions** Anglican 70%, Methodist 9%, Roman Catholic 4%. **Life expectancy** 72 female, 67 male. **Literacy** 99%.

POLITICS
Government Parliamentary state. **Parties** Democratic Labor, Labor. **Suffrage** Universal, over 18. **Memberships** CW, OAS, UN. **Subdivisions** 11 parishes, 1 independent city.

ECONOMY
GDP $997,500,000. **Per capita** $3,977. **Monetary unit** Dollar. **Trade partners** U.S., Caribbean countries, U.K. **Exports** Sugar and sugarcane by-products, clothing, electrical equipment. **Imports** Food, machinery, consumer goods, fuels.

LAND
Description Caribbean island. **Area** 166 mi² (430 km²). **Highest point** Mt. Hillaby, 1,115 ft (340 m). **Lowest point** Sea level.

People. A history of British rule is reflected in the Anglican religion and English language of this easternmost West Indian island. It is one of the world's most densely populated countries, and most citizens are black descendants of African slaves.

Economy and the Land. Barbados's pleasant tropical climate and its land have determined its economic mainstays: tourism and sugar. Sunshine and year-round warmth attract thousands of visitors and, in conjunction with the soil, provide an excellent environment for sugarcane cultivation. Manufacturing consists mainly of sugar processing. The coral island's terrain is mostly flat, rising to a central ridge.

History and Politics. Originally settled by South American Arawak Indians, followed by Carib Indians, Barbados was uninhabited when the first British settlers arrived in the 1600s. More colonists followed, developing sugar plantations and bringing slaves from Africa to work them. The country remained under British control until it became independent in 1966. ∎

BELGIUM

Official name Kingdom of Belgium
PEOPLE
Population 9,875,000. **Density** 838/mi² (324/km²).
Urban 95%. **Capital** Brussels, 137,738. **Ethnic groups**
Fleming 55%, Walloon 33%, mixed and others 12%.
Languages Dutch (Flemish), French, German. **Religions**
Roman Catholic 75%. **Life expectancy** 75 female, 69
male. **Literacy** 98%.
POLITICS
Government Constitutional monarchy. **Parties** Flemish:
Liberal, Social Christian, Socialist. Walloon: Liberal,
Socialist. **Suffrage** Universal, over 18. **Memberships**
NATO, OECD, UN. **Subdivisions** 9 provinces.
ECONOMY
GNP $85,420,000,000. **Per capita** $8,628. **Monetary
unit** Franc. **Trade partners** West Germany, France,
Netherlands. **Exports** Machinery, chemicals, food,
livestock. **Imports** Machinery, fuels, food, motor vehicles.
LAND
Description Western Europe. **Area** 11,783 mi² (30,518
km²). **Highest point** Botrange, 2,277 ft (694 m). **Lowest
point** Sea level.

People. Language separates Belgium into two main regions. Northern Belgium, known as Flanders, is dominated by Flemings, Flemish-speaking descendants of Germanic Franks. French-speaking Walloons, descendants of the Celts, inhabit southern Belgium, or Wallonia. Both groups are found in centrally located Brussels. In addition, a small German-speaking population is concentrated in the east. Flemish and French divisions often result in discord, but diversity has also been a source of cultural richness. Belgium has often been at the hub of European cultural movements.

Economy and the Land. The economy as well as the population was affected by Belgium's location at the center of European activity. Industry was early established as the economic base, and today the country is heavily industrialized. Although agriculture plays a minor economic role, Belgium is nearly self-sufficient in food production. The north and west are dominated by a flat fertile plain, the central region by rolling hills, and the south by the Ardennes Forest, often a tourist destination. The climate is cool and temperate.

History and Politics. Belgium's history began with the settlement of the Belgae tribe in the second century B.C. The Romans invaded the area around 50 B.C. and were overthrown by Germanic Franks in the A.D. 400s. Trade, manufacturing, and art prospered as various peoples invaded, passed through, and ruled the area. In 1794 Napoleon annexed Belgium to France. He was defeated at Waterloo in Belgium in 1815, and the country passed into Dutch hands. Dissatisfaction under Netherland rule led to revolt and, in 1830, the formation of the independent country of Belgium. The country was overrun by Germans during both world wars. Linguistic divisions mark nearly all political activity, from parties split by language to government decisions based on linguistic rivalries. ∎

BELIZE

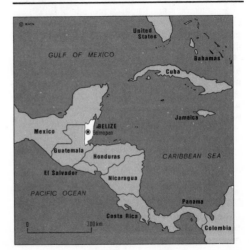

Official name Belize
PEOPLE
Population 160,000. **Density** 18/mi^2 (7/km^2). **Urban** 52%. **Capital** Belmopan, 4,500. **Ethnic groups** Black 51%, mestizo 22%, Amerindian 19%. **Languages** English, Spanish, indigenous. **Religions** Roman Catholic 50%, Anglican, other Protestant. **Literacy** 90%.
POLITICS
Government Parliamentary state. **Parties** People's United, United Democratic. **Suffrage** Universal adult. **Memberships** CW, UN. **Subdivisions** 6 districts.
ECONOMY
GDP $169,000,000. **Per capita** $1,120. **Monetary unit** Dollar. **Trade partners** U.S., U.K. **Exports** Sugar, clothing, fish, citrus fruits. **Imports** Food, machinery, consumer goods, transportation equipment.
LAND
Description Central America. **Area** 8,866 mi^2 (22,963 km^2). **Highest point** Victoria Pk., 3,680 ft (1,122 m). **Lowest point** Sea level.

People. With the lowest population of any Central American country, Belize has a mixed populace, including descendants of black Africans; mestizos of Spanish-Indian ancestry; and Indians. Population is concentrated in six urban areas along the coast. Most people are poor, but participation in the educational system has led to a high literacy rate.

Economy and the Land. An abundance of timberland resulted in an economy based on forestry until woodlands began to be depleted in the twentieth century. Today the economy focuses on agriculture, with sugar the major crop and export. Arable land is the primary resource, but only a small portion has been cultivated. Industrial activity is limited. The recipient of much foreign aid, Belize hopes to expand export of agricultural surpluses and to develop a tourist industry based on its climate and sandy beaches. The coastal region consists of swampy lowlands rising to the Maya Mountains inland. The hot, humid climate is offset by sea breezes.

History and Politics. Between 1500 B.C. and A.D. 300 Belize was the site of a flourishing Mayan civilization. In the 1500s Spain claimed the region. A British shipwreck in 1638 resulted in the first European settlement and began a process of British colonization, accompanied by extensive logging, piracy, and occasional Spanish and Indian attacks. In 1862 the area officially became the crown colony of British Honduras. Its name was changed to Belize in 1973, and independence was achieved in 1981. To assist economic and political development, Belize seeks closer relations with Spanish-speaking Central American countries and English-speaking Caribbean states. ∎

BENIN

Official name People's Republic of Benin
PEOPLE
Population 3,970,000. **Density** 91/mi^2 (35/km^2). **Urban**

26%. **Capital** Porto-Novo, 123,000. **Ethnic groups** Fon, Adja, Yoruba, Bariba, others. **Languages** French, Fon, Adja, indigenous. **Religions** Animist 70%, Christian 15%, Muslim 15%. **Life expectancy** 52 female, 48 male. **Literacy** 20%.
POLITICS
Government Socialist republic. **Parties** People's Revolutionary. **Suffrage** Universal adult. **Memberships** OAU, UN. **Subdivisions** 6 provinces.
ECONOMY
GNP $1,100,000,000. **Per capita** $294. **Monetary unit** CFA franc. **Trade partners** France, other Western European countries. **Exports** Palm products, cotton. **Imports** Clothing, consumer goods, construction materials.
LAND
Description Western Africa. **Area** 43,484 mi^2 (112,622 km^2). **Highest point** 2,103 ft (641 m). **Lowest point** Sea level.

People. The mostly black population of Benin is composed of numerous peoples. The main groups are the Fon, the Adja, the Yoruba, and the Bariba. The nation's linguistic diversity reflects its ethnic variety; French is the official language, a result of former French rule. Most Beninese are rural farmers, although urban migration is increasing. Animist beliefs predominate, but there are also Christians, especially in the south, and Muslims in the north.

Economy and the Land. Political instability has been both the cause and effect of Benin's economic problems. The agricultural economy is largely undeveloped, and palm trees and their by-products provide the chief source of income and activity for both farming and industry. Some economic relief may be found in the exploitation of offshore oil. The predominately flat terrain features coastal lagoons and dense forests, with mountains in the northwest. Heat and humidity characterize the coast, with less humidity and varied temperatures in the north.

History and Politics. In the 1500s, Dahomey, a Fon kingdom, became the power center of the Benin area. European slave traders came to the coast in the seventeenth and eighteenth centuries, establishing posts and bartering with Dahomey royalty for slaves. As the slave trade prospered, the area became known as the Slave Coast. In the 1890s France defeated Dahomey's army and subsequently made the area a territory of French West Africa. Independence was gained in 1960. P-˙˙ical turmoil followed, with various coups and ru, and in 1972 a military overthrow installed the current socialist government. In 1975 the nation's name was changed from Dahomey to Benin. A nonaligned country, Benin models its politics, economy, and society after Eastern European and Third World nations. ∎

BERMUDA

Official name Bermuda
PEOPLE
Population 70,000. **Density** 3,333/mi² (1,321/km²).
Urban 100%. **Capital** Hamilton, Bermuda I., 1,600.
Ethnic groups Black 61%, white and others 39%.
Languages English. **Religions** Anglican 37%, other Protestant 21%, Roman Catholic 14%, Black Muslim and others 28%. **Life expectancy** 72 female, 66 male.
Literacy 98%.
POLITICS
Government Colony (U.K.). **Parties** Progressive Labor, United. **Suffrage** Universal, over 21. **Memberships** None.
Subdivisions 9 parishes.
ECONOMY
GDP $598,000,000. **Per capita** $16,150. **Monetary unit** Dollar. **Trade partners** U.S., Caribbean countries, U.K.
Exports Semitropical produce, light manufactures.
Imports Fuels, food, machinery.
LAND
Description North Atlantic islands (east of North Carolina). **Area** 21 mi² (53 km²). **Highest point** Town Hill, Bermuda I., 259 ft (79 m). **Lowest point** Sea level.

People. The people of this British colony are mainly black descendants of African slaves, but the population also includes Portuguese, British, Canadian, and Caribbean peoples. Situated about 650 miles (1,046 km) east of North Carolina in the United States, the archipelago consists of many small islands and islets. About twenty are inhabited, several of which are connected by bridges and collectively known as the Island of Bermuda.

Economy and the Land. A mild climate, beautiful beaches, and a scenic, hilly terrain make tourism Bermuda's economic mainstay. Foreign businesses, attracted by tax exemptions, provide additional economic contributions. There is limited light manufacturing, agriculture, and fishing and no heavy industry.

History and Politics. The colony received its name from Juan de Bermudez, a Spanish explorer who sailed past the islands in 1503, not landing because of the dangerous coral reefs. Colonization began following a British shipwreck in 1609. Racial inequality resulted in unrest in the late 1960s and 1970s. As a British colony, Bermuda recognizes Great Britain's queen as the head of state. ∎

BHUTAN

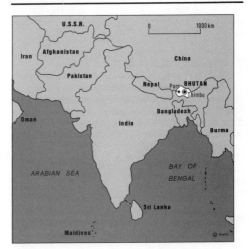

Official name Kingdom of Bhutan
PEOPLE
Population 1,435,000. **Density** 79/mi² (31/km²). **Urban** 4%. **Capital** Thimbu, 8,982. **Ethnic groups** Bhote 60%, Nepalese 25%, others 15%. **Languages** Dzongkha, English, Nepalese dialects. **Religions** Buddhist 75%, Hindu 25%. **Life expectancy** 43 female, 44 male.
Literacy 5%.
POLITICS
Government Monarchy (Indian protection). **Parties** None. **Suffrage** One vote per family. **Memberships** UN.
Subdivisions 4 regions.
ECONOMY
GDP $131,000,000. **Per capita** $109. **Monetary unit** Ngultrum, Indian rupee. **Trade partners** India. **Exports** Agricultural products, wood, coal. **Imports** Textiles, grain, vehicles, fuels.
LAND
Description Southern Asia, landlocked. **Area** 18,147 mi² (47,000 km²). **Highest point** Kula Kangri Mtn., 24,784 ft (7,554 m). **Lowest point** Manãs River valley, 318 ft (97 m).

People. A mountainous terrain long isolated Bhutan from the outside world and limited internal mingling of peoples. The population is ethnically divided into the Bhotes, Nepalese, and various tribes. Of Tibetan ancestry, the Bhotes are a majority and as such have determined the major religion, Buddhism, and language, Dzongkha, a Tibetan dialect. The Nepalese are mostly Hindu and speak Nepalese; tribal dialects diversify language further. The population is largely rural, and many villages grew up around *dzongs,* monastery fortresses built in strategic valley locations during Bhutan's past. Literacy is low, and skilled labor scarce. Training programs have been instituted to remedy this.

Economy and the Land. Partially due to physical isolation, Bhutan has one of the world's least developed economies and remains dependent on foreign aid. There is potential for success, however. Forests cover much of the land, limiting agricultural area but offering opportunity for the expansion of forestry.

Farming is concentrated in the more densely populated, fertile valleys of the Himalayas, and the country is self-sufficient in food production. The climate
varies with altitude; the icy Himalayas in the north
give way to temperate central valleys and a subtropical south.

History and Politics. Bhutan's early history remains mostly unknown, but it is thought that by the
early sixteenth century descendants of Tibetan invaders were ruling their lands from strategically located dzongs. In the 1600s a Tibetan lama
consolidated the area and became political and religious leader. Proximity to and interaction with British
India resulted in British control of Bhutan's foreign
affairs in the nineteenth and early twentieth centuries. In 1907 the current hereditary monarchy was
established. India gained independence from Britain
in 1947 and soon assumed the role of adviser in
Bhutan's foreign affairs. Indian ties were strengthened in the late fifties to counter Chinese influence.
At the same time, modernization programs were instituted, improving primitive transportation and communication systems and bringing Bhutan further into
the twentieth-century mainstream. ■

BOLIVIA

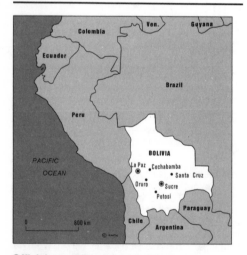

Official name Republic of Bolivia
PEOPLE
Population 6,115,000. **Density** 14/mi² (5.6/km²). **Urban**
45%. **Capital** La Paz (seat of government), 719,780;
Sucre (seat of judiciary), 68,426. **Ethnic groups**
Quechua 30%, Aymara 25%, mixed, European.
Languages Spanish, Quechua, Aymara. **Religions**
Roman Catholic 95%. **Life expectancy** 53 female, 49
male. **Literacy** 68%.
POLITICS
Government Republic. **Parties** Movement of the
Revolutionary Left, Nationalist Democratic Action,
Nationalist Revolutionary Movement of the People,
National Revolutionary Movement of the Left. **Suffrage**

Universal adult (married, 18; single, 21). **Memberships**
OAS, UN. **Subdivisions** 9 departments.
ECONOMY
GNP $5,600,000,000. **Per capita** $933. **Monetary unit**
Peso. **Trade partners** Argentina, U.S., Brazil, Western
European countries. **Exports** Tin, natural gas, silver.
Imports Machinery, consumer goods, food.
LAND
Description Central South America, landlocked. **Area**
464,164 mi² (1,098,581 km²). **Highest point** Nevado
Illimani, 22,579 ft (6,882 m). **Lowest point** Paraguay
River valley, 325 ft (100 m).

People. Indians compose the majority of Bolivia's
population. Minorities include mestizos, of Spanish-
Indian descent, and Europeans. Although most people are poor, Bolivia has a rich cultural heritage, evidenced by early Aymaran and Quechuan artifacts;
Spanish-influenced Indian and mestizo art; and
twentieth-century achievements. Roman Catholicism
is the major religion, frequently combined with Indian
beliefs. Sucre is the judicial seat and constitutional
capital, while La Paz is the center of government.

Economy and the Land. Bolivia is underdeveloped
and among South America's poorest nations. It is
rich in natural resources, however. Farming is the
main activity, although mining makes the largest
contribution to the gross national product. Population, industry, and major cities are concentrated on
the western altiplano, an Andean high plateau,
where many continue to practice agriculture according to ancestral methods. The eastern llano, or lowland plain, contains fuel deposits and is the site of
commercial farming. The yungas, hills and valleys
between the altiplano and the llano, form the most
developed agricultural region. Successful development of Bolivia's rich resources is partially dependent upon political stability. The climate varies from
tropical to semiarid and cool, depending on altitude.

History and Politics. The Aymara Indian culture
flourished in the area that is now Bolivia between
the seventh and tenth centuries. In the mid-1400s
the area was absorbed into the expanding empire
of the Incas, who controlled the region until ousted
by the Spanish in 1535. Simón Bolívar, the Venezuelan organizer of the South American movement
to free Spanish colonies, helped lead the way to independence, which was gained in 1825. As Bolivia
developed economically, the Indian population remained ensconced in poverty and enjoyed few
rights. After years of turmoil, a 1952 revolution installed a government that introduced suffrage, land,
and education reforms. Since the regime was
ousted in a 1964 coup, instability and social unrest
have continued. ■

BOTSWANA

Official name Republic of Botswana
PEOPLE
Population 1,055,000. **Density** 4.6/mi² (1.8/km²). **Urban**
16%. **Capital** Gaborone, 59,700. **Ethnic groups** Tswana

Intertribal wars in the early nineteenth century were followed by conflicts with the Boers, settlers of Dutch or Huguenot descent. These conflicts led the Tswana to seek British assistance, and the area of present-day Botswana became part of the British protectorate of Bechuanaland. When the Union of South Africa was created in 1910, those living in Bechuanaland, later Botswana; Basutoland, later Lesotho; and Swaziland requested exclusion from the Union and were granted it. British rule continued until 1966, when the protectorate of Bechuanaland became the Republic of Botswana. The country maintains a policy of nonalignment in foreign affairs and is seeking to expand relations with other nations and reduce economic dependence on South Africa, whose apartheid policy it opposes. ∎

BRAZIL

94%, Bushmen 5%, European 1%. **Languages** English, Setswana. **Religions** Indigenous 40%, Christian 15%. **Life expectancy** 58 female, 52 male. **Literacy** 35%.

POLITICS
Government Republic. **Parties** Democratic, Independence, National Front. **Suffrage** Universal, over 21. **Memberships** CW, OAU, UN. **Subdivisions** 12 districts.

ECONOMY
GDP $721,600,000. **Per capita** $830. **Monetary unit** Pula. **Trade partners** Switzerland, U.S., U.K., Southern African countries. **Exports** Diamonds, cattle, animal products, copper. **Imports** Food, machinery, vehicles, petroleum, textiles.

LAND
Description Southern Africa, landlocked. **Area** 231,805 mi² (600,372 km²). **Highest point** Ootse Mtn., 4,886 ft (1,489 m). **Lowest point** Confluence of Shashi and Limpopo rivers, 1,684 ft (513 m).

People. The population of this sparsely populated country is composed mostly of Tswana, Bantu peoples of various groups. Following settlement patterns laid down centuries ago, Tswana predominate in the more fertile eastern region, and Bushmen, a minority group, are concentrated in the Kalahari Desert. English is the official language, resulting from years of British rule, but the majority speak Setswana. Religion follows a similar pattern, with most people following traditional beliefs, and Christianity a minority practice.

Economy and the Land. Agriculture is the primary activity, although limited by the southwestern Kalahari Desert. The most productive farmland lies in the east and north, where rainfall is higher and grazing lands plentiful. Since the early seventies, when increased exploitation of natural resources began, the economy has developed rapidly. Diamond mining is the main focus of this growth, together with development of copper, nickel, and coal. The climate is mostly subtropical.

History and Politics. In Botswana's early history, Bushmen, the original inhabitants, retreated into the Kalahari region when the Tswana invaded and established their settlements in the more fertile east.

Official name Federative Republic of Brazil

PEOPLE
Population 134,340,000. **Density** 41/mi² (16/km²). **Urban** 68%. **Capital** Brasília, 1,177,393. **Ethnic groups** White 55%, mixed 38%, black 6%. **Languages** Portuguese. **Religions** Roman Catholic 89%. **Life expectancy** 66 female, 62 male. **Literacy** 75%.

POLITICS
Government Republic. **Parties** Democratic Movement, Social Democratic. **Suffrage** Universal, over 18 (excluding illiterates). **Memberships** OAS, UN. **Subdivisions** 23 states, 3 territories, 1 federal district.

ECONOMY
GNP $295,000,000,000. **Per capita** $2,360. **Monetary unit** Cruzeiro. **Trade partners** U.S., Saudi Arabia, Japan, West Germany. **Exports** Soybeans, coffee, transportation equipment, iron ore. **Imports** Petroleum, machinery, chemicals, pharmaceuticals.

LAND
Description Eastern South America. **Area** 3,265,075 mi² (8,456,508 km²). **Highest point** Pico da Neblina, 9,888 ft (3,014 m). **Lowest point** Sea level.

People. The largest South American nation, Brazil is also the most populous. The mixed population was shaped by indigenous Indians, Portuguese colonists, black African slaves, and European and Japanese immigrants. Today, native Indians compose less than 1 percent of the population, and the group is disappearing rapidly due to contact with modern cultures and other factors. Brazil is the only Portuguese-speaking nation in the Americas, and Roman Catholicism is the major religion.

Economy and the Land. Brazil's prosperous economy stems from a diversified base of agriculture, mining, and industry. Most commercial farms and ranches lie in the southern plateau region, and coffee, cocoa, soybeans, and beef are important products. Mineral resources include iron-ore deposits, many found in the central and southern plateau regions. Additional mineral deposits have recently been discovered in the Amazon area. Industrial expansion during and after World War II was focused in the southeast, and the capital was moved from Rio de Janeiro to Brasília in 1960 to redistribute activity. Undeveloped states have been targeted for development, but programs may require displacement of the Indian population. Forests cover about half the country, and the Amazon River basin is the site of the world's largest rain forest. The northeast consists of semiarid grasslands, and the central-west and south are marked by hills, mountains, and rolling plains. Overall the climate is semitropical to tropical, with heavy rains.

History and Politics. Portugal obtained rights to the region in a 1494 treaty with Spain and claimed Brazil in 1500. As the native Indian population died out, blacks were brought from Africa to work the plantations. In the 1800s, during the Napoleonic Wars, the Portuguese royal family fled to Rio de Janeiro, and in 1815 the colony became a kingdom. In 1821 the Portuguese king departed for Portugal, leaving Brazil's rule to his son, who declared Brazil an independent country and himself emperor in 1822. Economic development in the mid-1800s brought an influx of Europeans. Following a military takeover in 1889, Brazil became a republic. Economic problems resulted in a 1930 military coup and a dictatorship lasting until 1945, plus military takeovers in 1954 and 1964. In 1985 Brazil's electoral college voted civilian Tancredo de Almeida Neves to the presidency, ending twenty-one years of military rule. He died, however, before taking office. Brazil's economic importance has led to greater involvement in global affairs. ∎

BRITISH INDIAN OCEAN TERRITORY

See UNITED KINGDOM.

BRUNEI

Official name State of Brunei Darussalam

PEOPLE
Population 220,000. **Density** 99/mi² (38/km²). **Urban** 76%. **Capital** Bandar Seri Begawan, 63,868. **Ethnic groups** Malay 75%, Chinese 20%. **Languages** Malay, English, Chinese. **Religions** Muslim 60%, Christian 8%, Buddhist and others 32%. **Life expectancy** 62 female, 62 male. **Literacy** 45%.

POLITICS
Government Constitutional monarchy. **Parties** People's Independence Front. **Suffrage** Universal, over 21. **Memberships** ASEAN, CW, UN. **Subdivisions** 4 districts.

ECONOMY
GDP $19,800,000,000. **Per capita** $27,000. **Monetary unit** Dollar. **Trade partners** Japan, U.S., Singapore, U.K. **Exports** Petroleum, natural gas. **Imports** Machinery, transportation equipment, manufactured goods, food.

LAND
Description Southeastern Asia (island of Borneo). **Area** 2,226 mi² (5,765 km²). **Highest point** Mt. Pagon, 6,070 ft (1,850 m). **Lowest point** Sea level.

People. The majority of Brunei's population is Malay, with minorities of Chinese and indigenous peoples. Most Malays are Muslim, and the Chinese are mainly Christian or Buddhist. Many Chinese, although wealthy, are unable to become citizens due to language-proficiency exams and strict residency requirements. The standard of living is high because of Brunei's oil-based economy, yet wealth is not equally distributed.

Economy and the Land. Oil and natural gas are the economic mainstays, giving Brunei a high per capita gross domestic product. Much food is imported, however, and a current goal is diversification. Situated on northeastern Borneo, Brunei is generally flat and covered with dense rain forests. The climate is tropical.

History and Politics. Historical records of Brunei date back to the seventh century. The country was an important trading center, and by the sixteenth century the sultan of Brunei ruled Borneo and parts of nearby islands. In 1888 Brunei became a British protectorate. Independence from Great Britain was gained in 1984. ∎

BULGARIA

Official name People's Republic of Bulgaria
PEOPLE
Population 8,980,000. **Density** 210/mi² (81/km²). **Urban** 64%. **Capital** Sofia, 1,056,945. **Ethnic groups** Bulgarian 85%, Turkish 9%, Gypsy 3%, Macedonian 3%.
Languages Bulgarian. **Religions** Bulgarian Orthodox 85%, Muslim 13%. **Life expectancy** 75 female, 71 male. **Literacy** 95%.
POLITICS
Government Socialist republic. **Parties** Communist. **Suffrage** Universal, over 18. **Memberships** COMECON, UN, Warsaw Pact. **Subdivisions** 28 provinces.
ECONOMY
GNP $35,300,000,000. **Per capita** $3,963. **Monetary unit** Lev. **Trade partners** U.S.S.R., Eastern European countries, West Germany. **Exports** Machinery, agricultural products, fuels. **Imports** Fuels, machinery, transportation equipment.
LAND
Description Southeastern Europe. **Area** 42,823 mi² (110,912 km²). **Highest point** Musala, 9,596 ft (2,925 m). **Lowest point** Sea level.

People. Bulgaria's ethnic composition was determined early in its history when Bulgar tribes conquered the area's Slavic inhabitants. Bulgarians, descendants of these peoples, are a majority today, and Turks, Gypsies, and Macedonians compose the main minority groups. Postwar development is reflected in an agriculture-to-industry shift in employment and a resultant rural-to-urban population movement.

Economy and the Land. Following World War II, the Bulgarian government began a program of expansion, turning the undeveloped agricultural nation into an industrial state modeled after the Soviet Union. Today the industrial sector is the greatest economic contributor and employer. Farming, however, continues to play an economic role. A climate similar to that of the American Midwest and rich soils in river valleys are suited for raising livestock and growing grain and other crops. The overall terrain is mountainous.

History and Politics. The area of modern Bulgaria had been absorbed by the Roman Empire by A.D. 15 and was subsequently invaded by the Slavs. In the seventh century Bulgars conquered the region and settled alongside Slavic inhabitants. Rule by the Ottoman Turks began in the late fourteenth century and lasted until 1878, when the Bulgarians defeated the Turks with the aid of Russia and Romania. The Principality of Bulgaria emerged in 1885, with boundaries approximating those of today, and in 1908 Bulgaria was declared an independent kingdom. A desire for access to the Aegean Sea and increased territory was partially responsible for Bulgaria's involvement in the Balkan Wars of 1912 and 1913 and alliances with Germany during both world wars. Following Bulgaria's declaration of war on the United States and Britain in World War II, the Soviet Union declared war on Bulgaria. Defeat came in 1944, the monarchy was overthrown, and a Communist government established shortly thereafter. Foreign policy is guided by alliance with the Soviet Union and other Communist nations, but lately more attention has been given to relations with Western European countries and developing nations in Africa and the Middle East. ∎

BURKINA FASO

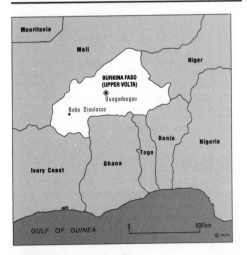

Official name Burkina Faso
PEOPLE
Population 6,820,000. **Density** 64/mi² (25/km²). **Urban** 9%. **Capital** Ouagadougou, 235,000. **Ethnic groups** Mossi, Bobo, Mande, Fulani, others. **Languages** French, indigenous. **Religions** Animist 65%, Muslim 25%, Christian 10%. **Life expectancy** 45 female, 43 male. **Literacy** 10%.
POLITICS
Government Provisional military government. **Parties** None (banned). **Suffrage** Universal adult. **Memberships** OAU, UN. **Subdivisions** 10 departments.
ECONOMY
GNP $1,100,000,000. **Per capita** $169. **Monetary** unit CFA franc. **Trade partners** Ivory Coast, Western

European countries, Ghana. **Exports** Livestock, peanuts, shea-nut products. **Imports** Food, fuels, transportation equipment, consumer goods.

LAND

Description Western Africa, landlocked. **Area** 105,869 mi² (274,200 km²). **Highest point** Téna Kourou, 2,451 ft (747 m). **Lowest point** Volta Noire River valley, 650 ft (200 m).

People. The agricultural Mossi, descendants of warrior migrants, are Burkina Faso's majority population. Other groups include the Bobo, Mande, and Fulani. Languages vary from group to group, although French is the official language.

Economy and the Land. Burkina Faso's agricultural economy suffers from frequent droughts and an underdeveloped transportation system. Most people engage in subsistence farming or livestock raising, and industrialization is minimal. Resources are limited but include gold and manganese. The country remains dependent on foreign aid, much of it from France. The land is marked by northern desert, central savanna, and southern forests. The climate is generally tropical.

History and Politics. The Mossi arrived from central or eastern Africa during the eleventh century and established their kingdom in the area of Burkina Faso. The French came in the late nineteenth century. In 1919 France united various provinces and created the colony of Upper Volta. The colony was divided among other French colonies in 1932, reinstituted in 1937 as an administrative unit called the Upper Coast, and returned to territorial status as Upper Volta in 1947. Independence was gained in 1960. Economic problems and accusations of government corruption led to leadership changes and military rule, including coups in 1966, 1980, 1982, and 1983. The country's name was changed from Upper Volta to Burkina Faso in 1984. ∎

BURMA

Official name Socialist Republic of the Union of Burma

PEOPLE

Population 36,795,000. **Density** 141/mi² (54/km²). **Urban** 29%. **Capital** Rangoon, 2,276,000. **Ethnic groups** Burman 72%, Karen 7%, Indian 6%, Shan 6%, Chinese 3%. **Languages** Burmese, indigenous. **Religions** Buddhist 85%; animist, Christian, and others 15%. **Life expectancy** 56 female, 53 male. **Literacy** 78%.

POLITICS

Government Socialist republic. **Parties** Socialist Program. **Suffrage** Universal, over 18. **Memberships** UN. **Subdivisions** 7 divisions, 7 states.

ECONOMY

GDP $5,900,000,000. **Per capita** $180. **Monetary unit** Kyat. **Trade partners** Singapore, Japan, Western European countries. **Exports** Rice, teak, hardwoods, base metals. **Imports** Machinery, transportation equipment, construction materials.

LAND

Description Southeastern Asia. **Area** 261,228 mi² (676,577 km²). **Highest point** Hkakabo Razi, 19,296 ft (5,881 m). **Lowest point** Sea level.

People. The population of Burma is characterized by variety. The many ethnic groups include Tibetan-related Burmans, who compose the majority; Karen, who inhabit mainly the south and east; and Thai-related Shan, found on the eastern plateaus. Diversity results in many languages, although Burmese predominates. Buddhist monasteries and pagodas dot the landscape, and minority religions include Christianity; animism, a traditional belief; and Islam. The primarily rural population is concentrated in the fertile valleys and on the delta of the Irrawaddy River.

Economy and the Land. Fertile soils, dense woodlands, and mineral deposits provide a resource base for agriculture, forestry, and mining. Burma has been beset with economic problems, however, caused mainly by the destruction of World War II and postindependence instability. Today agriculture continues as the economic mainstay, and the hot, wet climate is ideal for rice production. In addition, dense forests provide for a timber industry, and resource deposits include petroleum and various minerals. Burma's economic future most likely depends on exploitation of natural resources and political stability. The terrain is marked by mountains, rivers, and forests, and the climate is tropical.

History and Politics. Burma's Chinese and Tibetan settlers were first united in the eleventh century. Independence ended with the invasion of Mongols led by Kublai Khan, followed by national unification in the fifteenth and eighteenth centuries. Annexation to British India in the nineteenth century ended Burma's monarchy. During World War II, Japanese occupation and subsequent Allied-Japanese conflicts caused much economic and physical damage. Burma officially became independent in 1948. After initial stability, the government was unable to withstand separatist and political revolts, and military rule alternated with civilian governments. In 1974, a new government was installed and a new constitution adopted. A strongly nationalistic country, Burma maintains a policy of neutrality. Sporadic uprisings continue, often carried out by ethnic minorities. ∎

BURUNDI

Official name Republic of Burundi
PEOPLE
Population 4,760,000. **Density** 443/mi² (171/km²).
Urban 4%. **Capital** Bujumbura, 160,000. **Ethnic groups** Hutu 85%, Tutsi 14%, Twa 1%. **Languages** Kirundi, French, Swahili. **Religions** Roman Catholic 62%, Protestant 5%, indigenous 32%, Muslim 1%. **Life expectancy** 46 female, 42 male. **Literacy** 25%.
POLITICS
Government Republic. **Parties** Unity and Progress. **Suffrage** Universal adult. **Memberships** OAU, UN. **Subdivisions** 15 provinces.
ECONOMY
GDP $1,200,000,000. **Per capita** $272. **Monetary unit** Franc. **Trade partners** U.S., Western European countries. **Exports** Coffee, tea, cotton. **Imports** Textiles, food, transportation equipment.
LAND
Description Eastern Africa, landlocked. **Area** 10,747 mi² (27,834 km²). **Highest point** 9,055 ft (2,760 m). **Lowest point** Lake Tanganyika, 2,534 ft (772 m).

People. One of Africa's most densely populated nations, Burundi has a populace composed mainly of three Bantu groups. The Hutu are a majority; the Tutsi, descendants of invaders from Ethiopia, wield most of the power; and the Twa are Pygmy hunters, probably the area's inhabitants prior to the influx of the Hutu. Most Burundians are subsistence farmers, and most are Roman Catholic, evidence of foreign influence and rule.

Economy and the Land. An undeveloped country, Burundi relies mainly on agriculture, although undependable rainfall, depleted soil, and erosion occasionally combine for famine. Exploitation of nickel deposits, industrial development through foreign investment, and expansion of tourism offer potential for growth. Although the country is situated near the equator, its high altitude and hilly terrain result in a pleasant climate.

History and Politics. In the fourteenth century invading pastoral Tutsi warriors conquered the peasant Hutu and established themselves as the region's power base. The areas of modern Burundi and Rwanda were absorbed into German East Africa in the 1890s. Following Belgian occupation during World War I, in 1919 the League of Nations placed present-day Burundi and Rwanda under Belgian rule as part of Ruanda-Urundi. After World War II Ruanda-Urundi was made a United Nations trust territory under Belgian administration. Urundi became Burundi, an independent monarchy in 1962, and political turmoil soon followed. A Tutsi-dominated government replaced the monarchy in 1966. An unsuccessful Hutu coup attempt in 1972 was followed by the massacre of thousands of Hutu and the flight of thousands more to other countries. A 1976 coup installed a government that seeks a redistribution of power. ∎

CAMBODIA

See KAMPUCHEA.

CAMEROON

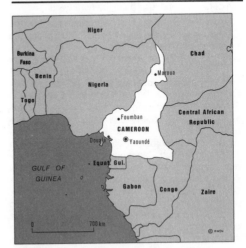

Official name United Republic of Cameroon
PEOPLE
Population 9,640,000. **Density** 53/mi² (20/km²). **Urban** 36%. **Capital** Yaoundé, 313,706. **Ethnic groups** Cameroon Highlander 31%, Equatorial Bantu 19%, Kirdi 11%, Fulani 10%, others. **Languages** English, French, indigenous. **Religions** Animist 50%, Christian 34%, Muslim 16%. **Life expectancy** 51 female, 48 male. **Literacy** 65%.

POLITICS
Government Republic. **Parties** National Union. **Suffrage** Universal, over 21. **Memberships** OAU, UN. **Subdivisions** 10 provinces.

ECONOMY
GNP $7,000,000,000. **Per capita** $845. **Monetary unit** CFA franc. **Trade partners** France, other Western European countries, U.S. **Exports** Petroleum, cocoa, coffee, wood. **Imports** Machinery, transportation equipment, petroleum products, consumer goods.

LAND
Description Central Africa. **Area** 183,569 mi² (475,442 km²). **Highest point** Mt. Cameroon, 13,451 ft (4,100 m). **Lowest point** Sea level.

People. Immigration and foreign rule shaped Cameroon's diverse population, composed of some two hundred groups speaking twenty-four major African languages. Both English and French are official languages, resulting from the merging of former French-ruled eastern and British-ruled western territories. Population is concentrated in the French-speaking eastern region. The majority of people practice animism, a traditional belief often influencing Islamic and Christian practices as well.

Economy and the Land. Recent economic plans have focused on agriculture, industry, and the development of oil deposits. Agriculture is the primary employer and economic contributor, and farm output is diverse. A varied terrain features southern coastal plains and rain forests, central plateaus, mountainous western forests, and northern savanna and marshes. This has hindered transportation development and thus certain aspects of the economy. Improvements are underway, however. Climate varies from a hot, humid coastal region to fluctuating temperatures and less humidity northward.

History and Politics. The Sao people reached the Cameroon area in the tenth century. The Portuguese arrived in the 1500s, and the following three centuries saw an influx of European and African peoples and an active slave trade along the coast. In 1884 Germany set up a protectorate that included modern Cameroon by 1914. During World War I British and French troops occupied the area, and in 1919, following the war, the League of Nations divided Cameroon into eastern French and western British mandates. The Cameroons became trust territories in 1946, and French Cameroon became an independent republic in 1960. In 1961 the northern region of British Cameroon elected to join Nigeria, and the southern area chose to unite with the eastern Republic of Cameroon. The resulting Federal Republic of Cameroon consisted of two states with separate governments. A 1972 referendum combined the states into the United Republic of Cameroon. The government maintains a foreign policy of nonalignment. ∎

CANADA

Official name Canada

PEOPLE
Population 25,270,000. **Density** 6.6/mi² (2.5/km²). **Urban** 76%. **Capital** Ottawa, 295,163. **Ethnic groups** British Isles origin 45%, French 29%, other European 23%, Indian and Inuit 2%. **Languages** English, French. **Religions** Roman Catholic 46%, United Church 18%, Anglican 12%. **Life expectancy** 77 female, 73 male. **Literacy** 99%.

POLITICS
Government Parliamentary state. **Parties** Liberal, New Democratic, Progressive Conservative. **Suffrage** Universal, over 18. **Memberships** CW, NATO, OECD, UN. **Subdivisions** 10 provinces, 2 territories.

ECONOMY
GNP $288,800,000,000. **Per capita** $11,725. **Monetary unit** Dollar. **Trade partners** U.S., Western European countries, Japan. **Exports** Transportation equipment, wood and paper, petroleum, food, natural gas. **Imports** Transportation equipment, machinery, petroleum, communication equipment.

LAND
Description Northern North America. **Area** 3,831,033 mi² (9,922,330 km²). **Highest point** Mt. Logan, 19,524 ft (5,951 m). **Lowest point** Sea level.

People. Canada was greatly influenced by its years under French and British rule, and its culture reflects this dual nature. Descendants of British and French settlers compose the two main population groups, and languages include both English and French. French-speaking inhabitants, called Québecois, are concentrated in the Province of Québec. Minorities include descendants of various European groups, indigenous Indians, and Inuit. Because of the rugged terrain and harsh climate of northern Canada, population is concentrated near the United States border.

Economy and the Land. Rich natural resources—including extensive mineral deposits, fertile land, forests, and lakes—helped shape Canada's diversified economy, which ranks among the world's most prosperous. Economic problems are those common to most modern industrial nations. Agriculture, mining, and industry are highly developed: Canada is a major wheat producer; mineral output includes asbestos, zinc, silver, and nickel; and crude petroleum is an important export. The service sector is also active. Second only to the U.S.S.R. in land area, Canada has a terrain that varies from eastern rolling hills and plains to mountains in the west. The Canadian Shield consists of ancient rock and extends from Labrador to the Arctic Islands. It is covered by thick forests in the south and tundra in the north. Overall, summers are moderate and winters long and cold.

History and Politics. Canada's first inhabitants were Asian Indians and Inuit, an Arctic people. Around the year 1000 Vikings became the first Europeans to reach North America, and in 1497 John Cabot claimed the Newfoundland coastal area for Britain. Jacques Cartier established French claim when he landed at the Gaspé Peninsula in the 1500s. Subsequent French and British rivalry culminated in several wars during the late seventeenth and eighteenth centuries. The wars ended with the 1763 Treaty of Paris, by which France lost Canada and other North American territory to Britain. To aid in resolving the continued conflict between French and English residents, the British North America Act of 1867 united the colonies into the Dominion of Canada. During World War I Canada fought on the side of the British. In 1926, along with other dominions, Canada declared itself an independent member of the British Commonwealth, and in 1931 Britain recognized the declaration through the Statute of Westminster. Canada once more allied with Britain during World War II, and postwar years saw an improved economy and the domination of two parties: Liberal and Progressive Conservative. The Québec separatist movement is striving for independent status for French-speaking Québec.   ∎

CANARY ISLANDS

See SPAIN.

CAPE VERDE

Official name Republic of Cape Verde

PEOPLE
Population 300,000.
Density 193/mi² (74/km²).
Urban 20%. **Capital**
Praia, São Tiago I.,
37,480. **Ethnic groups**
Mulatto 71%, African 28%,
European 1%. **Languages**
Portuguese, Crioulo.
Religions Roman
Catholic. **Life expectancy**
64 female, 60 male.
Literacy 37%.
POLITICS
Government Republic.
Parties African Party for
the Independence of Cape
Verde. **Suffrage** Universal,
over 15. **Memberships**
OAU, UN. **Subdivisions**
10 islands.

ECONOMY
GNP $142,000,000. **Per capita** $473. **Monetary unit** Escudo. **Trade partners** Portugal, U.K., Japan. **Exports** Fish, bananas, salt. **Imports** Petroleum products, corn, rice, machinery.
LAND
Description Western African islands. **Area** 1,557 mi² (4,033 km²). **Highest point** Pico, Fogo I., 9,281 ft (2,829 m). **Lowest point** Sea level.

People. The Portuguese-African heritage of Cape Verde's population is a result of Portuguese rule and the forced transmigration of Africans for slavery. Although Portuguese is the official language, the majority speaks Crioulo, a creole dialect. Most people are Roman Catholic, but animist practices exist, sometimes in combination with Catholicism. The mainly poor population is largely undernourished and plagued by unemployment. The country consists of five islets and ten main islands, and all but one are inhabited.

Economy and the Land. The volcanic, mountainous islands have few natural resources and low rainfall; thus the country's economy remains underdeveloped. Fishing and agriculture are important for both subsistence and commercial purposes. Much of the land is too dry for farming, and drought is a frequent problem. Cape Verde's location on air and sea routes and its tropical climate offer potential for expansion into services and tourism. However, Cape Verde will most likely continue to rely on foreign aid for some time.

History and Politics. The islands that make up Cape Verde were uninhabited when the Portuguese arrived around 1460. Settlement began in 1462, and by the sixteenth century Cape Verde had become a shipping center for the African slave trade. Until 1879 Portugal ruled Cape Verde and present-day Guinea-Bissau as a single colony. A movement for the independence of Cape Verde and Guinea-Bissau began in the 1950s, and a 1974 coup in Portugal ultimately resulted in autonomy for both countries, with Cape Verde proclaiming independence in 1975. Plans to unify Cape Verde and Guinea-Bissau were abandoned following a 1980 coup in Guinea-Bissau. Cape Verde follows a foreign policy of nonalignment and takes a special interest in African affairs.   ∎

CAYMAN ISLANDS

See UNITED KINGDOM.

CENTRAL AFRICAN REPUBLIC

Official name Central African Republic
PEOPLE
Population 2,620,000. **Density** 11/mi² (4.2/km²). **Urban** 35%. **Capital** Bangui, 387,143. **Ethnic groups** Baya 34%,

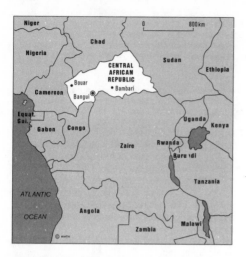

Banda 28%, Sara 10%, others. **Languages** French, Sangho. **Religions** Protestant 25%, Roman Catholic 25%, indigenous 24%, Muslim 10%. **Life expectancy** 48 female, 44 male. **Literacy** 33%.

POLITICS
Government Republic. **Parties** None (banned). **Suffrage** Universal, over 21. **Memberships** OAU, UN.
Subdivisions 14 prefectures.

ECONOMY
GDP $658,000,000. **Per capita** $273. **Monetary unit** CFA franc. **Trade partners** France, Belgium, Japan, other Western European countries. **Exports** Cotton, coffee, diamonds, wood. **Imports** Petroleum products, machinery, textiles, motor vehicles.

LAND
Description Central Africa, landlocked. **Area** 240,535 mi² (622,984 km²). **Highest point** Mont Ngaoui, 4,626 ft (1,410 m). **Lowest point** Ubangi River, 1,100 ft (335 m).

People. Lying near Africa's geographical center, the Central African Republic was the stopping point for many precolonial nomadic groups. The resultant multiethnic populace was further diversified by migrations during the slave-trade era. Of the country's many languages, Sangho is most widely used. Overall, the population is rural and suffers from poverty and a low literacy rate.

Economy and the Land. Fertile land, extensive forests, and mineral deposits provide adequate bases for agriculture, forestry, and mining. Economic development remains minimal, however, impeded by poor transportation routes, a landlocked location, lack of skilled labor, and political instability. Subsistence farming continues as the major activity, and agriculture is the chief contributor to the economy. The country consists of a plateau region with southern rain forests and a northeastern semidesert. The climate is temperate, and ample rainfall sometimes results in impassable roads.

History and Politics. Little is known of the area's early history except that it was the site of many migrations. European slave trade in the nineteenth century led to the 1894 creation of a French territory called Ubangi-Chari. This in turn combined with the areas of the present-day Congo, Chad, and Gabon

in 1910 to form French Equatorial Africa. The Central African Republic gained independence in 1960. A 1966 military coup installed military chief Jean-Bedel Bokassa, who in 1976 assumed the title of emperor, changed the republic to a monarchy, and renamed the nation the Central African Empire. A 1979 coup ended the monarchy and reinstated the name Central African Republic. Another coup in 1981 deposed this government, proposing to solve the state's economic problems. ∎

CHAD

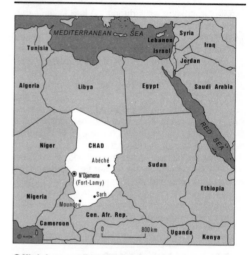

Official name Republic of Chad
PEOPLE
Population 5,180,000. **Density** 10/mi² (4/km²). **Urban** 18%. **Capital** N'Djamena, 224,000. **Ethnic groups** 200 distinct groups. **Languages** French, Arabic, indigenous. **Religions** Muslim 52%, indigenous 43%, Christian 5%. **Life expectancy** 45 female, 42 male. **Literacy** 20%.
POLITICS
Government Republic. **Parties** None (banned). **Suffrage** Universal, over 18. **Memberships** OAU, UN.
Subdivisions 14 prefectures.
ECONOMY
GDP $500,000,000. **Per capita** $110. **Monetary unit** CFA franc. **Trade partners** Nigeria, France, other Western European countries. **Exports** Cotton, meat, fish. **Imports** Food, petroleum, machinery, motor vehicles, textiles.
LAND
Description North-central Africa, landlocked. **Area** 495,755 mi² (1,284,000 km²). **Highest point** Emi Koussi, 11,204 ft (3,415 m). **Lowest point** Bodélé Depression, 525 ft (160 m).

People. Centuries ago Islamic Arabs intermixed with indigenous black Africans and established Chad's diverse population. This variety has led to a rich and often divisive culture. Descendants of Arab invaders mainly inhabit the north, where Islam is the major religion and nomadic farming the major activity. In the south—traditionally the economic and political center—the black Sara predominate, operating small farms and practicing animist or Christian faiths. Chad's many languages also reflect its ethnic variety.

Economy and the Land. Natural features and instability arising from ethnic and regional conflict have combined to prevent Chad from prospering. Agriculture and fishing are economic mainstays and are often conducted at subsistence levels. The Sahara extends into Chad's northern region, and the southern grasslands with their heavy rains compose the primary agricultural area. The relative prosperity of the region, in conjunction with its predominantly Sara population, has fueled much of the political conflict. Future growth is greatly dependent on political equilibrium. Climate varies from the hot, dry northern desert to the semiarid central region and rainier south.

History and Politics. African and Arab societies began prospering in the Lake Chad region as early as the eighth century. Subsequent centuries saw the landlocked area become an ethnic crossroads for Muslim nomads and African groups. European traders made their way to the region in the late 1800s, and by 1900 France had gained control. French Equatorial Africa was created in 1910, its boundaries including modern Chad, Gabon, the Congo, and the Central African Republic. Following Chad's independence in 1960, the southern Sara gained dominance over the government. A northern rebel group emerged, and government-rebel conflict has continued, resulting in shifting governments. ∎

CHANNEL ISLANDS

See UNITED KINGDOM.

CHILE

Official name Republic of Chile

PEOPLE
Population 11,740,000. **Density** 40/mi² (16/km²). **Urban** 81%. **Capital** Santiago, 425,924. **Ethnic groups** White and mestizo 91%, Indian 3%. **Language** Spanish. **Religions** Roman Catholic 89%, Protestant 11%. **Life expectancy** 65 male, 70 female. **Literacy** 90%.

POLITICS
Government Republic. **Parties** None (recessed). **Suffrage** None. **Memberships** OAS, UN. **Subdivisions** 13 regions.

ECONOMY
GDP $23,600,000,000. **Per capita** $2,178. **Monetary unit** Peso.

Trade partners U.S., Japan, West Germany, Brazil. **Exports** Copper, molybdenum, iron ore, paper products. **Imports** Petroleum, sugar, wheat, capital equipment, vehicles.

LAND
Description Southern South America. **Area** 292,135 mi² (756,626 km²). **Highest point** Nevado Ojos del Salado, 22,572 ft (6,880 m). **Lowest point** Sea level.

People. Chile's land barriers—the eastern Andes, western coastal range, and northern desert—have resulted in a mostly urban population concentrated in a central valley. Mestizos, of Spanish-Indian heritage, and descendants of Spanish immigrants predominate. In addition to an Indian minority, the population includes those who trace their roots to Irish and English colonists or nineteenth-century German immigrants. The country enjoys a relatively high literacy rate, but poverty remains a problem.

Economy and the Land. Chile's land provides the natural resources necessary for a successful economy, but longtime instability has taken its toll. The northern desert region is the site of mineral deposits, and mining is a major component of trade, making Chile vulnerable to outside market forces. An agricultural zone lies in the central valley, and the south contains forests, grazing land, and some petroleum deposits. The climate varies from region to region but is generally mild.

History and Politics. Upon their arrival in the 1500s, the Spanish defeated the northern Inca Indians, but many years were spent in conflict with Araucanian Indians of the central and south. From the sixteenth through nineteenth centuries, Chile received little attention from ruling Spain, and colonists established a successful agriculture. In 1818 Bernardo O'Higgins led the way to victory over the Spanish and became ruler of independent Chile. By the 1920s dissent arising from unequal power and land distribution united the middle and working classes, but social-welfare, education, and economic programs were unable to eliminate inequalities rooted in the past. A 1960 earthquake and tidal wave added to the country's problems. Leftist Salvador Allende Gossens was elected to power in 1970, but a 1973 military coup resulted in his death and began a reign marked by human-rights violations. Military rule continues, but Chile's foreign relations, damaged by the government's human-rights abuses, have improved somewhat. ∎

CHINA

Official name People's Republic of China
PEOPLE
Population 1,080,980,000. **Density** 291/mi² (112/km²). **Urban** 21%. **Capital** Peking (Beijing), 5,597,972. **Ethnic groups** Han Chinese 93%. **Languages** Chinese dialects. **Religions** Confucian, Taoist, Buddhist. **Literacy** 76%.
POLITICS
Government Socialist republic. **Parties** Communist. **Suffrage** Universal, over 18. **Memberships** UN.

Subdivisions 21 provinces, 3 municipalities, 5 autonomous regions.
ECONOMY
GNP $313,000,000,000. **Per capita** $308. **Monetary unit** Yuan. **Trade partners** Japan, Hong Kong, U.S. **Exports** Manufactured goods, agricultural products, petroleum. **Imports** Grain, chemical fertilizer, raw materials.
LAND
Description Eastern Asia. **Area** 3,718,783 mi² (9,631,600 km²). **Highest point** Mt. Everest, 29,028 ft (8,848 m). **Lowest point** Turfan Depression, 505 ft (154 m) below sea level.
The above information excludes Taiwan.

People. Population is concentrated in the east, and Han Chinese are the majority group. Uighur, Hui, Mongol, Korean, Manchu, Zhuang, Yi, Miao, and Tibetan peoples compose minorities. Many Chinese languages are spoken, but the national language is Putonghua—Standard Chinese, or Mandarin—based on a northern dialect. Following a Communist revolution in 1949, religious activity was discouraged. It is now on the increase, and religions include Confucianism, Taoism, and Buddhism, plus Islam and Christianity. China ranks first in the world in population, and family-planning programs have been implemented to aid population control. With a recorded civilization going back about 3,500 years, China has contributed much to world culture.

Economy and the Land. Most economic progress dates from 1949, when the new People's Republic of China was faced with a starving, war-torn, and unemployed population. Industry is expanding, but agriculture continues as the major activity. Natural resources include coal, oil, natural gas, and minerals, many of which remain to be explored. An economic plan begun in the seventies focuses on growth in agriculture, industry, science and technology, and national defense. China's terrain is varied: two-thirds consists of mountainous or semiarid land, with fertile plains and deltas in the east. The climate is marked by hot, humid summers, and the dry winters are often cold.

History and Politics. China's civilization ranks among the world's oldest. The first dynasty, the Shang, began sometime during the second millennium B.C. Kublai Khan's thirteenth-century invasion brought China the first of its various foreign rulers. In the nineteenth century, despite government efforts to the contrary, foreign influence and intervention grew. The government was weakened by the Opium War with Britain in the 1840s; the Taiping Rebellion, a civil war; and a war with Japan from 1894 to 1895. Opposition to foreign influences erupted in the antiforeign and anti-Christian Boxer Rebellion of 1900. After China became a republic in 1912, the death of the president in 1916 triggered the warlord period, in which conflicts were widespread and power concentrated among military leaders. Attempts to unite the nation began in the 1920s with Sun Yat-sen's Nationalist party, initially allied with the Communist party. Under the leadership of Chiang Kai-shek, the Nationalist party overcame the warlords, captured Peking, and executed many Communists. Remaining Communists reorganized under Mao Zedong, and the Communist-Nationalist conflict continued, along with Japanese invasion and occupation. By 1949 the Communists controlled most of the country, and the People's Republic of China was proclaimed. Chiang Kai-shek fled to Taiwan, proclaiming Taipei China's provisional capital. Since Mao's death in 1976 foreign trade and contact have expanded. In 1979 the United States recognized Peking (Beijing), rather than Taipei, as China's capital. Five autonomous regions are included within China's boundaries—Inner Mongolia, Xinjiang Uygur, Guangxi Zhuangzu, Ningxia Huizu, and Tibet. ∎

See also TAIWAN.

CHRISTMAS ISLAND

See AUSTRALIA.

COCOS ISLANDS

See AUSTRALIA.

COLOMBIA

Official name Republic of Colombia
PEOPLE
Population 28,545,000. **Density** 65/mi² (25/km²). **Urban** 64%. **Capital** Bogotá, 4,067,000. **Ethnic groups** Mestizo 58%, white 20%, mulatto 14%, black 4%. **Languages** Spanish. **Religions** Roman Catholic 95%. **Life expectancy** 64 female, 61 male. **Literacy** 81%.
POLITICS
Government Republic. **Parties** Conservative, Liberal. **Suffrage** Universal, over 18. **Memberships** OAS, UN. **Subdivisions** 22 departments, 3 *intendencias*, 5 *comisarías*, 1 special district.

and Ecuador had seceded from the republic, and Panama did the same in 1903. The Conservative and Liberal parties, dominating forces in Colombia's political history, arose from differences between supporters of Bolívar and Santander. Conservative-Liberal conflict led to a violent civil war from 1899 to 1902 and to La Violencia, "The Violence," a civil disorder that continued from the 1940s to the 1960s and resulted in about 200,000 deaths. From the late fifties through the midseventies, a government program alternated Conservative and Liberal rule every four years. Political unrest led to a 1980 embassy siege by a group demanding freedom for political prisoners. A pursuit of diplomatic relations with all nations defines Colombian foreign policy. ∎

ECONOMY

GNP $40,000,000,000. **Per capita** $1,435. **Monetary unit** Peso. **Trade partners** U.S., West Germany, Venezuela, Japan. **Exports** Coffee, cotton, fuels, bananas. **Imports** Transportation equipment, machinery, metals, chemicals.

LAND

Description Northwestern South America. **Area** 439,737 mi² (1,138,914 km²). **Highest point** Pico Cristóbal Colón, 19,029 ft (5,800 m). **Lowest point** Sea level.

People. Colombia's mixed population traces its roots to indigenous Indians, Spanish colonists, and black African slaves. Most numerous today are mestizos, those of Spanish-Indian descent. Roman Catholicism, the Spanish language, and Colombia's overall culture evidence the long-lasting effect of Spanish rule. Over the past decades the population has shifted from mainly rural to urban as the economy has expanded into industry.

Economy and the Land. Industry now keeps pace with traditional agriculture in economic contributions, and mining is also important. Natural resources include oil, coal, natural gas, most of the world's emeralds, plus fertile soils. The traditional coffee crop also remains important, and Colombia is a leading coffee producer. The terrain is characterized by a flat coastal region, central highlands, and wide eastern llanos, or plains. The climate is tropical on the coast and in the east, with cooler temperatures in the highlands.

History and Politics. In the 1500s Spaniards conquered the native Indian groups and established the area as a Spanish colony. In the early 1700s Bogotá became the capital of the viceroyalty of New Granada, which included modern Colombia, Venezuela, Ecuador, and Panama. Rebellion in Venezuela in 1796 initiated revolt elsewhere in New Granada, including Colombia, and in 1813 independence was declared. In 1819 the Republic of Greater Colombia was formed, which came to include all the former members of the Spanish viceroyalty. Independence leader Simón Bolívar became president, and Francisco de Paula Santander vice-president. By 1830 Venezuela

COMOROS

Official name Federal Islamic Republic of the Comoros

PEOPLE

Population 460,000. **Density** 549/mi² (212/km²). **Urban** 19%. **Capital** Moroni, Grande Comore I., 20,112. **Ethnic groups** Antalote, Cafre, Makua, Oimatsaha, Sakalava. **Languages** Arabic, French, Swahili. **Religions** Shirazi Muslim 86%, Roman Catholic 14%. **Literacy** 15%.

POLITICS

Government Republic. **Parties** Union for Progress. **Suffrage** Universal adult. **Memberships** OAU, UN. **Subdivisions** 7 regions.

ECONOMY

GNP $90,000,000. **Per capita** $230. **Monetary unit** CFA franc. **Trade partners** France, Madagascar, Kenya. **Exports** Perfume oils, vanilla, copra, cloves. **Imports** Rice, fuels, textiles, machinery.

LAND

Description Southeastern African islands. **Area** 838 mi² (2,171 km²). **Highest point** Kartala, Grand Comore I., 7,746 ft (2,361 m). **Lowest point** Sea level.
The above information includes Mayotte.

People. The ethnic groups of Comoros' Grande Comore, Anjouan, and Moheli islands are mainly of

Arab-African descent, practice the Muslim religion, and speak a Swahili dialect. Roman Catholic descendants of Malagasy immigrants compose the majority on French-ruled Mayotte Island. Arab culture, however, predominates throughout the island group. Poverty, disease, a shortage of medical care, and low literacy continue to plague the nation.

Economy and the Land. The economic mainstay of Comoros is agriculture, and most Comorans practice subsistence farming and fishing. Plantations employ workers to produce the main cash crops. Of volcanic origin, the islands have soils of varying quality, and some are unsuited for farming. Terrain varies from the mountains of Grande Comore to the hills and valleys of Mayotte. The climate is cool and dry, with a winter rainy season.

History and Politics. The Comoro Islands saw invasions by coastal African, Persian Gulf, Indonesian, and Malagasy peoples. Portuguese explorers landed in the 1500s, around the same time Arab Shirazis, most likely from Persia, introduced Islam. The French took Mayotte in 1843 and had established colonial rule over the four main islands by 1912. Comoros declared unilateral independence in 1975. Mayotte, however, voted to remain under French administration. ■

CONGO

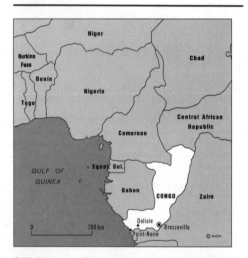

Official name People's Republic of the Congo
PEOPLE
Population 1,770,000. **Density** 13/mi² (5.2/km²). **Urban** 48%. **Capital** Brazzaville, 442,400. **Ethnic groups** Kongo 48%, Sangha 20%, M'Bochi 12%, Teke 17%. **Languages** French, indigenous. **Religions** Animist 48%, Christian 47%, Muslim 2%. **Life expectancy** 61 female, 57 male. **Literacy** 50%.
POLITICS
Government Republic. **Parties** Workers'. **Suffrage** Universal, over 18. **Memberships** OAU, UN. **Subdivisions** 9 regions.

ECONOMY
GDP $1,800,000,000. **Per capita** $1,140. **Monetary unit** CFA franc. **Trade partners** France, other Western European countries, U.S. **Exports** Petroleum, wood, coffee, cocoa. **Imports** Machinery, transportation equipment, consumer goods, food.
LAND
Description Central Africa. **Area** 132,047 mi² (342,000 km²). **Highest point** 2,963 ft (903 m). **Lowest point** Sea level.

People. The Congo's four main groups, the Kongo, Sangha, M'Bochi, and Teke, create an ethnically and linguistically diverse populace. The official language, French, is a result of former colonial rule. Population is concentrated in the south, away from the dense forests, heavy rainfall, and hot climate of the north. Educational programs, and thus literacy, have improved, although rural inhabitants remain relatively isolated.

Economy and the Land. Brazzaville was the commercial center of the former colony called French Equatorial Africa, and the Congo now benefits from the early groundwork laid for service and transport industries. Subsistence farming occupies most Congolese, however, as well as most cultivated land. Low productivity and a growing populace create a need for foreign aid, much of it from France. Offshore petroleum is the most valuable mineral resource and a major economic contributor. The land is marked by coastal plains, a south-central valley, a central plateau, and the Congo River basin in the north. The climate is tropical, with high temperatures and humidity.

History and Politics. Several tribal kingdoms existed in the area during its early history. The Portuguese arrived on the coast in the 1400s, and slave trade flourished until it was banned in the 1800s. Shortly thereafter a Teke king signed a treaty placing the area, then known as Middle Congo, under French protection. In 1910 Middle Congo, the present-day Central African Republic, Gabon, and Chad were joined to form French Equatorial Africa. The Republic of the Congo became independent in 1960. Subsequent years saw unrest, including coups, a presidential assassination, and accusations of corruption and human-rights violations. In 1979 a newly elected president granted amnesty to political prisoners, and the country has remained relatively stable. The nation maintains a policy of nonalignment and diplomatic relations with both Communist and Western countries. ■

COOK ISLANDS

See NEW ZEALAND.

CORSICA

See FRANCE.

COSTA RICA

Official name Republic of Costa Rica
PEOPLE
Population 2,725,000. **Density** 138/mi² (53/km²). **Urban** 48%. **Capital** San José, 259,126. **Ethnic groups** White and mestizo 96%, black 3%, Indian 1%. **Languages** Spanish. **Religions** Roman Catholic 95%. **Life expectancy** 74 female, 70 male. **Literacy** 90%.
POLITICS
Government Republic. **Parties** Christian Democratic, National Liberation, Popular Union, Republican Calderonista, Unity Coalition of Democratic Renovation. **Suffrage** Universal, over 18. **Memberships** OAS, UN. **Subdivisions** 7 provinces.
ECONOMY
GDP $3,300,000,000. **Per capita** $1,390. **Monetary unit** Colón. **Trade partners** U.S., Central American countries, West Germany. **Exports** Coffee, bananas, beef, sugar. **Imports** Manufactured goods, machinery, transportation equipment.
LAND
Description Central America. **Area** 19,730 mi² (51,100 km²). **Highest point** Cerro Chirripó, 12,530 ft (3,819 m). **Lowest point** Sea level.

People. Compared with most other Central American countries, Costa Rica has a relatively large population of European descent, mostly Spanish with minorities of German, Dutch, and Swiss ancestry. Together with mestizos, people of Spanish-Indian heritage, they compose the bulk of the population. Descendants of black Jamaican immigrants inhabit mainly the Caribbean coastal region. Indigenous Indians in scattered enclaves continue traditional lifestyles; some, however, have been assimilated into the country's majority culture.

Economy and the Land. Costa Rica's economy has long been one of the most prosperous in Central America, but it has not been without problems, some resulting from falling coffee prices and rising oil costs. Agriculture remains important, producing traditional coffee and banana crops, while the country attempts to expand industry. Population and agriculture are concentrated in the central highlands.

Much of the country is forested, and the mountainous central area is bordered by coastal plains on the east and west. The climate is semitropical to tropical.

History and Politics. In 1502 Christopher Columbus arrived and claimed the area for Spain. Spaniards named the region Rich Coast, and settlers soon flocked to the new land to seek their fortune. Rather than riches, they found an Indian population unwilling to surrender its land. But many Spaniards remained, establishing farms in the central area. In 1821 the Central American provinces of Costa Rica, Guatemala, El Salvador, Honduras, and Nicaragua declared themselves independent from Spain, and by 1823 they had formed the Federation of Central America. Despite efforts to sustain it, the federation was in a state of virtual collapse by 1838, and Costa Rica became an independent republic. Since the first free elections in 1889, Costa Rica has experienced a presidential overthrow in 1919 and a civil war in 1948, arising over a disputed election. ∎

CUBA

Official name Republic of Cuba
PEOPLE
Population 9,770,000. **Density** 221/mi² (85/km²). **Urban** 69%. **Capital** Havana, 1,924,886. **Ethnic groups** Mulatto 51%, white 37%, black 11%, Chinese 1%. **Languages** Spanish. **Religions** Roman Catholic 85%. **Life expectancy** 75 female, 71 male. **Literacy** 96%.
POLITICS
Government Socialist republic. **Parties** Communist. **Suffrage** Universal, over 16. **Memberships** COMECON, UN. **Subdivisions** 14 provinces.
ECONOMY
GNP $14,900,000,000. **Per capita** $1,534. **Monetary unit** Peso. **Trade partners** U.S.S.R., Eastern European countries. **Exports** Sugar, nickel, shellfish, tobacco. **Imports** Capital equipment, raw materials, petroleum, food.

LAND

Description Caribbean island. **Area** 44,218 mi² (114,524 km²). **Highest point** Pico Turquino, 6,476 ft (1,974 m). **Lowest point** Sea level.

People. Most Cubans are descendants of Spanish colonists, African slaves, or a blend of the two. The government provides free education and health care, and although religious practices are discouraged, most people belong to the Roman Catholic church. Despite improvements in personal income, health, education, and housing since the 1959 revolution, food shortages remain a problem, and rationing is an ongoing activity.

Economy and the Land. Cuba's economy is largely dependent on sugar. Other forms of agriculture are important as well, and the most fertile soils lie in the central region between mountain ranges. The island is also the site of mineral deposits, and nickel is found in the northeast. In addition to agriculture and mining, industry is an economic contributor. Most economic activity is nationalized, and Cuba remains dependent on aid from the Soviet Union. Mountains, plains, and a scenic coastline make Cuba one of the most beautiful islands in the West Indies. The climate is tropical.

History and Politics. Christopher Columbus claimed Cuba for Spain in 1492, and Spanish settlement began in 1511. Soon the native Indian population died out, and African slaves were brought to work plantations. The United States joined with Cuba against Spain in the Spanish-American War in 1898. Spain surrendered that same year, and full independence was gained in 1902. Unrest continued, however, and the United States again intervened from 1906 to 1909 and in 1917. A 1933 coup ousted a nine-year dictatorship, and a subsequent government overthrow in 1934 ushered in an era dominated by Sergeant Fulgencio Batista. After ruling through other presidents and serving an elected term himself, Batista seized power in a 1952 coup that established an unpopular and oppressive regime. Led by lawyer Fidel Castro, a revolutionary group opposed to Batista gained quick support, and Batista fled the country on January 1, 1959, leaving the government to Castro. Early United States support of Castro soured when nationalization of American businesses began. American aid soon ceased, and Cuba looked to the Soviet Union for assistance. The United States ended diplomatic relations with Cuba in 1961. In 1962 the United States and the Soviet Union became embroiled in a dispute over Soviet missile bases in Cuba that nearly led to nuclear war. The nation maintains ties with the Soviet Union and has sent aid to several Third World countries. ■

CURAÇAO

See NETHERLANDS.

CYPRUS

Official name Republic of Cyprus

PEOPLE

Population 675,000. **Density** 189/mi² (73/km²). **Urban** 53%. **Capital** Nicosia, 48,222. **Ethnic groups** Greek 78%, Turkish 18%. **Languages** Greek, Turkish. **Religions** Greek Orthodox 78%, Muslim 18%. **Life expectancy** 76 female, 72 male. **Literacy** 90%.

POLITICS

Government Republic. **Parties** Greek: Democratic, Democratic Rally, Progressive Party of the Working People. Turkish: Communal Liberation, National Unity. **Suffrage** Universal, over 21. **Memberships** CW, UN. **Subdivisions** 6 districts.

ECONOMY

GNP $2,172,000,000. **Per capita** $3,342. **Monetary unit** Pound. **Trade partners** U.K., other Western European countries, Iraq, Greece, Turkey. **Exports** Food and beverages, clothing, cement. **Imports** Petroleum, machinery, transportation equipment, manufactured goods, food.

LAND

Description Eastern Mediterranean island. **Area** 3,572 mi² (9,251 km²). **Highest point** Ólimbos, 6,401 ft (1,951 m). **Lowest point** Sea level.

People. Most Cypriots are of Greek ancestry, and the island's religion, language, and general culture reflect this heritage. Muslim, Turkish-speaking descendants of Turks are a minority. Although the two groups have some common customs, ethnicity usually supersedes national allegiance, and a 1974 Turkish invasion resulted in formal segregation. Greek Cypriots now inhabit the island's southern two-thirds, and Turkish Cypriots the northern third. Other minorities include Armenians and Maronites.

Economy and the Land. Relocation of Greek Cypriots in the south and Turkish Cypriots in the north has severely disrupted the economy. With foreign assistance, Greek Cypriots have made progress, expanding traditional southern agriculture to light manufacturing and tourism. Northern Turkish Cypriots lack capital, experience, foreign aid, and official recognition, and they remain agriculturally based and dependent on Turkey for tourism, trade, and assistance. Known for its scenic beauty and tourist appeal, Cyprus is marked by a fertile central plain bordered by mountains in the southwest and north. Sandy beaches dot the coastline. The Mediterranean climate results in hot, dry summers and damp, cool winters.

History and Politics. In the Late Bronze Age—from 1600 to 1050 B.C.—a Greek culture flourished in Cyprus. Rule by various peoples followed, including Assyrians, Egyptians, Persians, Romans, Byzantines, French, and Venetians. The Ottoman Turks invaded in 1571. In the nineteenth century Turkey ceded the island to the British as security for a loan. Although many Turks remained on Cyprus, the British declared it a crown colony in 1925. A growing desire for enosis, or union with Greece, led to rioting and guerrilla activity by Greek Cypriots. The Turkish government, opposed to absorption by Greece, desired separation into Greek and Turkish sectors. Cyprus became independent in 1960, with treaties forbidding either enosis or partition, but Greek-Turkish conflicts continued. A 1974 coup by pro-enosis forces led to an invasion by Turkey and the current partition. In foreign affairs, the Republic of Cyprus follows a policy of nonalignment. The Turkish Republic of Northern Cyprus, which is not recognized internationally, maintains a separate government with a prime minister and a president.　■

CZECHOSLOVAKIA

Official name Czechoslovak Socialist Republic
PEOPLE
Population 15,490,000. **Density** 314/mi² (121/km²). **Urban** 67%. **Capital** Prague, 1,185,693. **Ethnic groups** Czech 65%, Slovak 30%, Hungarian 3%. **Languages** Czech, Slovak, Hungarian. **Religions** Roman Catholic 77%, Protestant 20%, Greek Orthodox 2%. **Life expectancy** 74 female, 67 male. **Literacy** 99%.
POLITICS
Government Socialist republic. **Parties** Communist. **Suffrage** Universal, over 18. **Memberships** COMECON, UN, Warsaw Pact. **Subdivisions** 2 semiautonomous republics.
ECONOMY
GNP $147,100,000,000. **Per capita** $9,550. **Monetary unit** Koruna. **Trade partners** U.S.S.R., East Germany, Poland, Hungary, West Germany. **Exports** Machinery, transportation equipment, iron and steel, consumer goods. **Imports** Fuels, machinery, raw materials, transportation equipment.

LAND
Description Eastern Europe, landlocked. **Area** 49,381 mi² (127,896 km²). **Highest point** Gerlachovka, 8,737 ft (2,655 m). **Lowest point** Bodrog River, 308 ft (94 m).

People. Czechs and Slovaks, descendants of Slavic tribes, predominate in Czechoslovakia. Characterized by a German-influenced culture, Czechs are concentrated in the regions of Bohemia and Moravia. Slovaks, whose culture was influenced by Hungarian Magyars, reside mainly in Slovakia. Both Czech and Slovak are official languages. Minorities include Hungarians, or Magyars; Ukrainians; Germans; Poles; and Gypsies, a rapidly growing group concentrated in Slovakia. Most people are Roman Catholic, and the government licenses and pays clergy.

Economy and the Land. An industrial nation, Czechoslovakia has a centralized economy and one of the highest standards of living among Communist countries. Coal deposits in Bohemia and Moravia provided a base for industrial development, and Bohemia remains an economically important region. Nearly all agriculture is collectivized, and farm output includes grains, potatoes, sugar beets, and livestock. Farming areas are found in the river valleys of north-central Bohemia and central Moravia, and Slovakia remains largely agricultural. Czechoslovakia's terrain is characterized by a rolling western area, low mountains in the north and south, central hills, and the Carpathian Mountains in the east. The climate is temperate.

History and Politics. Slavic tribes were established in the region by the sixth century. By the tenth century Hungarian Magyars had conquered the Slovaks in the region of Slovakia. Bohemia and Moravia became part of the Holy Roman Empire, and by the twelfth century Bohemia had become a strong kingdom that included Moravia and parts of Austria and Poland. Austria gained control of the area in 1620, and it later became part of Austria-Hungary. With the collapse of Austria-Hungary at the end of World War I, an independent Czechoslovakia consisting of Bohemia, Moravia, and Slovakia was formed. Nazi Germany invaded Czechoslovakia in 1939, and the Soviet Union liberated the nation from German occupation in the winter and spring of 1944 to 1945. By 1948 Communists controlled the government, and political purges continued from 1949 to 1952. A 1968 invasion by the Soviet Union and Bulgaria, Hungary, Poland, and East Germany resulted when the Czechoslovakian Communist party leader introduced liberal reforms. Efforts to eliminate dissent continued into the seventies. Foreign policy closely follows that of the Soviet Union.　■

DENMARK

Official name Kingdom of Denmark
PEOPLE
Population 5,010,000. **Density** 301/mi² (116/km²). **Urban** 83%. **Capital** Copenhagen, 498,850. **Ethnic**

groups Scandinavian. **Languages** Danish. **Religions**
Lutheran 97%. **Life expectancy** 77 female, 73 male.
Literacy 99%.

POLITICS
Government Constitutional monarchy. **Parties**
Conservative, Liberal, Social Democratic, Socialist
People's. **Suffrage** Universal, over 21. **Memberships**
NATO, OECD, UN. **Subdivisions** 14 counties.

ECONOMY
GNP $56,400,000,000. **Per capita** $11,016. **Monetary
unit** Krone. **Trade partners** West Germany, U.K.,
Sweden, U.S., Norway. **Exports** Meat and dairy products,
machinery, transportation equipment, textiles. **Imports**
Raw materials, fuels, machinery, transportation equipment.

LAND
Description Northern Europe. **Area** 16,633 mi² (43,080
km²). **Highest point** Yding Skovhøj, 568 ft (173 m).
Lowest point Lammefjord, 23 ft (7 m) below sea level.
The above information excludes the Faeroe Islands.

People. Denmark is made up of the Jutland Peninsula and more than four hundred islands, about
one hundred of which are inhabited. In addition to
nearby islands, Greenland, situated northeast of
Canada, and the Faeroe Islands, between Scotland
and Iceland in the North Atlantic, are part of Denmark. Lutheran, Danish-speaking Scandinavians
constitute the homogeneous population of the peninsula and surrounding islands, although a German
minority is concentrated near the West German border. Faeroese-speaking people inhabit the Faeroe
Islands. The literacy rate is high, and Denmark has
made significant contributions to science, literature,
and the arts.

Economy and the Land. Despite limited natural
resources, Denmark has a diversified economy. Agriculture contributes to trade, and pork and bacon
are important products. Postwar expansion focused
on industry, and the country now imports the raw
materials it lacks and exports finished products. The
North Sea is the site of oil and natural-gas deposits.
On the Faeroe Islands, traditional fishing continues
as the economic mainstay. Most of Denmark's terrain is rolling, with hills covering much of the peninsula and the nearby islands. Coastal regions are
marked by fjords and sandy beaches, especially in

the west. The climate is temperate, with North Sea
winds moderating temperatures. The rugged Faeroe
Islands are damp, cloudy, and windy.

History and Politics. By the first century access to
the sea had brought contact with other civilizations
and led to the Viking era, lasting from the ninth to
eleventh centuries and resulting in temporary Danish
rule of England. In the fourteenth century, Sweden,
Norway, Finland, Iceland, the Faeroe Islands, and
Greenland were united under Danish rule. Sweden
and Finland withdrew from the union in the 1500s,
and Denmark lost Norway to Sweden in 1814. A constitutional monarchy was instituted in 1849. Late
nineteenth-century social reform, reflected in a new
constitution in 1915, laid the groundwork for Denmark's current welfare state. The country remained
neutral during World War I. Iceland gained independence following the war but maintained its union
with Denmark until 1944. Despite declared neutrality
during World War II, Denmark was invaded by Germany in 1940 and occupied until 1945. Compromise
and gradual change characterize Danish politics,
and foreign policy emphasizes relations with developing nations and peaceful solutions to international
problems. ∎

DJIBOUTI

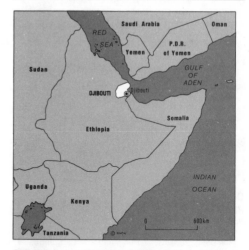

Official name Republic of Djibouti
PEOPLE
Population 360,000. **Density** 41/mi² (16/km²). **Urban**
74%. **Capital** Djibouti, 120,000. **Ethnic groups** Somali
Issa 60%, Afar 35%. **Languages** French, Somali,
Afar, Arabic. **Religions** Muslim 94%, Christian 6%.
Literacy 20%.
POLITICS
Government Republic. **Parties** People's Progress
Assembly. **Suffrage** Universal adult. **Memberships** OAU,
UN. **Subdivisions** 5 districts.
ECONOMY
GDP $116,000,000. **Per capita** $400. **Monetary unit**
Franc. **Trade partners** France, U.K., Japan, Ethiopia.
Exports Hides and skins, coffee. **Imports** Machinery,
food, transportation equipment, textiles.

LAND

Description Eastern Africa. **Area** 8,880 mi² (23,000 km²). **Highest point** Mousâ'alli, 6,768 ft (2,063 m). **Lowest point** Lake 'Asal, 509 ft (155 m) below sea level.

People. Characterized by strong cultural unity, Islam, and ethnic ties to Somalia, Somali Issas compose Djibouti's majority. Afars, who make up the other main group, are also mostly Muslim and are linked ethnically with Ethiopia. Rivalry between the two groups has marked the nation's history. Because of unproductive land, much of the population is concentrated in the city of Djibouti. Poverty is an ongoing problem.

Economy and the Land. A dry land, poor in soils and mineral resources, Djibouti remains economically undeveloped. Traditional nomadic herding continues as a way of life for many Djiboutians, despite heat, aridity, and limited grazing area. Several assets promote Djibouti as a port and trade center: a strategic position on the Gulf of Aden, an improved harbor, and a railway linking the city of Djibouti with Addis Ababa in Ethiopia. Marked by mountains that divide a coastal plain from a plateau region, the terrain is mostly desert. The climate is extremely hot and dry.

History and Politics. In the ninth century Arab missionaries introduced Islam to the population, and by the 1800s a pattern of conflict between the Issas and Afars had developed. The French purchased the port of Obcock from Afar sultans in 1862, and their territorial control expanded until the region became French Somaliland. The goal of the proindependence Issas was defeated in elections in 1958 and 1967 when the majority voted for continued French control. The name was changed to the French Territory of Afars and Issas in 1967, and as the Issa population grew, so did demands for independence. A 1977 referendum resulted in the independent Republic of Djibouti. ∎

DOMINICA

Official name Commonwealth of Dominica

PEOPLE
Population 74,000. **Density** 255/mi² (98/km²). **Urban** 27%. **Capital** Roseau, 8,346. **Ethnic groups** Black, Carib Indian. **Languages** English, French. **Religions** Roman Catholic 80%, Anglican, Methodist. **Life expectancy** 59 female, 57 male. **Literacy** 94%.

POLITICS
Government Republic. **Parties** Freedom, Labor, United Labor. **Suffrage** Universal, over 18. **Memberships** CW, OAS, UN. **Subdivisions** 10 parishes.

ECONOMY
GNP $56,400,000. **Per** capita $883. **Monetary unit** East Caribbean dollar. **Trade partners** U.S., U.K., other Western European countries, Caribbean countries. **Exports** Bananas, coconuts, lime juice and oil. **Imports** Machinery, food, manufactured goods, fuels.

LAND
Description Caribbean island. **Area** 290 mi² (752 km²). **Highest point** Morne Diablotin, 4,747 ft (1,447 m). **Lowest point** Sea level.

People. Dominica's population consists of descendants of black Africans brought to the island as slaves and Carib Indians descended from early inhabitants. English is widely spoken in urban areas, but villagers, who compose a majority, speak mainly a French-African blend, resulting from French rule and the importation of Africans.

Economy and the Land. Of volcanic origin, the island has soils suitable for farming, but a mountainous and densely forested terrain limits land accessible to cultivation. Agriculture is the economic mainstay; hurricanes, however, have hindered production. Forestry and fishing offer potential for expansion, and a tropical climate and scenic landscape create a basis for tourism.

History and Politics. In the fourteenth century Carib Indians conquered the Arawak who originally inhabited the island. Although Christopher Columbus arrived at Dominica in 1493, Spanish settlement was discouraged by Carib hostilities. French and British rivalry for control of the island followed, and British possession was recognized in 1783. Independence was gained in 1978. ∎

DOMINICAN REPUBLIC

Official name Dominican Republic

PEOPLE
Population 6,205,000. **Density** 332/mi² (128/km²). **Urban** 52%. **Capital** Santo Domingo, 1,313,172. **Ethnic groups** Mixed 73%, white 16%, black 11%. **Languages**

Spanish. **Religions** Roman Catholic 95%. **Life expectancy** 64 female, 60 male. **Literacy** 68%.

POLITICS

Government Republic. **Parties** Liberation, Reformist, Revolutionary. **Suffrage** Universal, over 18 or married. **Memberships** OAS, UN. **Subdivisions** 26 provinces, 1 national district.

ECONOMY

GNP $7,600,000,000. **Per capita** $1,400. **Monetary unit** Peso. **Trade partners** U.S., Puerto Rico, Venezuela. **Exports** Sugar, nickel, coffee, tobacco. **Imports** Food, petroleum, raw materials, machinery.

LAND

Description Caribbean island (eastern Hispaniola Island). **Area** 18,704 mi² (48,442 km²). **Highest point** Pico Duarte, 10,417 ft (3,175 m). **Lowest point** Lago Enriquillo, 131 ft (40 m) below sea level.

People. Occupying eastern Hispaniola Island, the Dominican Republic borders Haiti and has a population of mixed ancestry. Haitians, other blacks, Spaniards, and European Jews compose minority groups. Population growth has resulted in unemployment and made it difficult for the government to meet food and service needs.

Economy and the Land. Agriculture remains important, with sugar a main component of trade, and sugar refining a major manufacturing activity. Farmland is limited, however, by a northwest-to-southeast mountain range and an arid region west of the range. Mineral exploitation, especially of nickel, contributes to trade, and a number of American firms have subsidiaries here. Tourism is growing, aided by the warm, tropical climate.

History and Politics. In 1492 Christopher Columbus arrived at Hispaniola Island. Spanish colonists followed, and the Indian population was virtually wiped out, although some intermingling with the Spanish probably occurred. In 1697 the western region of the island, which would become Haiti, was ceded to France. The entire island came under Haitian control as the Republic of Haiti in 1822, and an 1844 revolution established the independent Dominican Republic. Since independence the country has experienced periods of instability, evidenced by military coups and rule, U.S. military intervention and occupation, and human-rights abuses. United States troops were last sent in 1965. Various presidents have been installed since 1966. ■

ECUADOR

Official name Republic of Ecuador

PEOPLE

Population 9,235,000. **Density** 84/mi² (33/km²). **Urban** 44%. **Capital** Quito, 918,884. **Ethnic groups** Mestizo 55%, Indian 25%, Spanish 10%, African 10%. **Languages** Spanish, Quechua. **Religions** Roman Catholic 95%. **Life expectancy** 64 female, 60 male. **Literacy** 84%.

POLITICS

Government Republic. **Parties** Concentration of Popular Forces, Democratic Left, Popular Democracy, Social

Christian. **Suffrage** Universal, over 18. **Memberships** OAS, OPEC, UN. **Subdivisions** 20 provinces.

ECONOMY

GNP $13,300,000,000. **Per capita** $1,507. **Monetary unit** Sucre. **Trade partners** U.S., Western European countries, Japan. **Exports** Petroleum, bananas, coffee, cocoa, fish products. **Imports** Machinery, raw materials, transportation equipment, chemical products.

LAND

Description Western South America. **Area** 109,483 mi² (283,561 km²). **Highest point** Chimborazo, 20,702 ft (6,310 m). **Lowest point** Sea level.

People. Ecuador's ethnicity was established by an indigenous Indian population and Spanish colonists. Minority whites, of Spanish or other European descent, live mainly in urban areas or operate large farms called haciendas. Of mixed Spanish-Indian blood, mestizos compose about half the population, although economic and political power is concentrated among whites. Minority Indians speak Quechua or other Indian languages and maintain traditional customs in Andean villages or nomadic jungle tribes. Blacks are concentrated on the northern coastal plain. Recent trends show a movement from the interior highlands to the fertile coastal plain and a rural-to-urban shift. A history of economic inequality has produced a literary and artistic tradition that has focused on social reform.

Economy and the Land. Despite an oil boom in the 1970s, Ecuador remains underdeveloped. Minor oil production began in 1911, but since a 1967 petroleum discovery in the *oriente,* a jungle region east of the Andes, Ecuador has become an oil exporter and a member of the Organization of Petroleum Exporting Countries (OPEC). Agriculture remains important for much of the population, although primitive, thus inefficient, practices continue among the poor. Rich soils of the *costa,* extending from the Pacific to the Andes, support most of the export crops. Forestry and fishing have growth potential, and the waters around the Galápagos Islands are rich in tuna. Manufacturing is mainly devoted to meeting domestic needs. The oriente and costa lie

on either side of the sierra, a region of highland plateaus between the two Andean chains. Varied alti-
tudes result in a climate ranging from tropical in the
lowlands to temperate in the plateaus and cold in the
high mountains. A variety of wildlife inhabits the Galápagos Islands, five large and nine small islands
about 600 miles (966 kilometers) off Ecuador's
coast in the Pacific Ocean.

History and Politics. In the fifteenth century Incas
conquered and subsequently united the area's various tribes. In the 1500s the Spanish gained control,
using Indians and African slaves to work the plantations. Weakened by the Napoleonic Wars, Spain
lost control of Ecuador in 1822, and Simón Bolívar
united the independent state with the Republic of
Greater Colombia. Ecuador left the union as a separate republic in 1830, and subsequent years saw
instability and rule by presidents, dictators, and juntas. From 1925 to 1948 no leader was able to complete a full term in office. A new constitution was
established in 1978, and a 1979 election installed a
president who died in a plane crash in 1981. Power
rivalries continue, complicated by numerous parties
and economic problems. ∎

EGYPT

Official name Arab Republic of Egypt
PEOPLE
Population 47,755,000. **Density** 124/mi² (48/km²). **Urban**
44%. **Capital** Cairo, 5,278,000. **Ethnic groups** Egyptian,
Bedouin, Nubian. **Languages** Arabic. **Religions** Muslim
94%, Coptic Christian and others 6%. **Life expectancy**
59 female, 55 male. **Literacy** 40%.
POLITICS
Government Socialist republic. **Parties** National
Democratic, Socialist Labor, Socialist Liberal. **Suffrage**
Universal, over 18. **Memberships** OAU, UN.
Subdivisions 26 governorates.
ECONOMY
GNP $30,800,000,000. **Per capita** $690. **Monetary unit**
Pound. **Trade partners** U.S., Western European

countries, Japan. **Exports** Petroleum, cotton, cotton yarn
and fabric. **Imports** Food, machinery, transportation
equipment, fertilizer.
LAND
Description Northeastern Africa. **Area** 386,643 mi²
(1,001,400 km²). **Highest point** Jabal Kātrīna, 8,668 ft
(2,642 m). **Lowest point** Qattara Depression,
436 ft (133 m) below sea level.

People. Egypt's population is relatively homogeneous, and Egyptians compose the largest group.
Descended from ancient Nile Valley inhabitants,
Egyptians have intermixed somewhat with Mediterranean and Asiatic peoples in the north and with
black Africans in the south. Minorities include Bedouins, Arabic-speaking desert nomads; Nubians,
black descendants of migrants from the Sudan; and
Copts, a Christian group. Islam, the major religion,
is also a cultural force, and many Christians as well
as Muslims follow Islamic life-styles. A desert terrain
confines about 99 percent of the population to less
than 4 percent of the land, in the fertile Nile River
valley and along the Suez Canal.

Economy and the Land. Egypt's economy has
suffered from wars, shifting alliances, and limited
natural resources. Government-sponsored expansion and reform in the 1950s concentrated on manufacturing, and most industry was nationalized
during the 1960s. Agriculture, centered in the Nile
Valley, remains an economic mainstay, and cotton,
a principal crop, is both exported and processed.
Petroleum, found mainly in the Gulf of Suez, will
most likely continue its economic role, and tourism
is a contributor as well. Much of Egypt is desert, with
hills and mountains in the east and along the Nile
River. The climate is warm and dry.

History and Politics. Egypt's recorded history began when King Menes united the region in about
3100 B.C., beginning a series of Egyptian dynasties.
Art and architecture flourished during the Age of the
Pyramids, from 2700 to 2200 B.C. In time native
dynasties gave way to foreign conquerors, including
Alexander the Great in the fourth century B.C. The
Coptic Christian church emerged between the fourth
and sixth centuries A.D., but in the 600s Arabs conquered the area and established Islam as the main
religion. Ruling parties changed frequently, and in
1517 the Ottoman Turks added Egypt to their empire.
Upon completion of the strategically important Suez
Canal in 1869, foreign interest in Egypt increased.
In 1875 Egypt sold its share of the canal to Britain,
and a rebellion against foreign intervention ended
with British occupation in 1882. Turkey sided with
Germany in World War I, and the United Kingdom
made Egypt a British protectorate in 1914. The country became an independent monarchy in 1922, but
the British presence remained. In 1945 Egypt and
six other nations formed the Arab League, and the
founding of Israel in 1948 initiated an era of Arab-
Israeli hostilities, including periodic warfare in which
Egypt often had a major role. Dissatisfaction over
dealings with Israel and continued British occupation
of the Suez Canal led to the overthrow of the king,
and Egypt became a republic in 1953. Following a

power struggle, Gamal Abdel Nasser was elected president in 1956, and the British agreed to remove their troops. Upon the death of Nasser in 1970, Vice-President Anwar Sadat came to power. Negotiations between Egyptian president Sadat and Israeli prime minister Menachem Begin began in 1977, and in 1979 the leaders signed a peace treaty ending conflicts between Egypt and Israel. As a result, Egypt was suspended from the Arab League. In 1981 President Sadat was assassinated. The current government continues to follow the policies of Sadat.   ∎

EL SALVADOR

Official name Republic of El Salvador
PEOPLE
Population 4,905,000. **Density** 604/mi² (233/km²).
Urban 39%. **Capital** San Salvador, 397,100. **Ethnic groups** Mestizo 89%, Indian 10%, white 1%. **Languages** Spanish. **Religions** Roman Catholic 97%. **Life expectancy** 65 female, 62 male. **Literacy** 65%.
POLITICS
Government Republic. **Parties** Authentic Institutional, Christian Democratic, National Republican Alliance.
Suffrage Universal, over 18. **Memberships** OAS, UN.
Subdivisions 14 departments.
ECONOMY
GDP $3,600,000,000. **Per capita** $700. **Monetary unit** Colón. **Trade partners** U.S., Central American countries, Western European countries. **Exports** Coffee, cotton, sugar. **Imports** Machinery, petroleum, fertilizer, motor vehicles, food.
LAND
Description Central America. **Area** 8,124 mi² (21,041 km²). **Highest point** Cerro Monte Cristo, 7,933 ft (2,418 m). **Lowest point** Sea level.

People. Most Salvadorans are Spanish-speaking mestizos, people of Spanish-Indian descent. An Indian minority is mainly descended from the Pipil, a Nahuatl group related to the Aztecs. The Nahuatl dialect is still spoken among some Indians. El Salvador, the smallest Central American country in area, has the highest population density in mainland Latin America, with inhabitants concentrated in a central valley-and-plateau region.

Economy and the Land. El Salvador's economy has been plagued by political instability, a low literacy rate, rapid population growth, and resulting unemployment. Agriculture remains the economic mainstay, and nearly all arable land has been cultivated. Coffee, cotton, and sugar are produced on large commercial plantations, while subsistence farmers rely on corn, bean, and sorghum crops. East-to-west mountain ranges divide El Salvador into a southern coastal region, central valleys and plateaus, and northern mountains. The climate is subtropical.

History and Politics. Maya and Pipil predominated in the area of El Salvador prior to Spanish arrival. In the 1500s Pipil defeated invading Spaniards but were conquered in a subsequent invasion. In 1821 the Spanish-controlled Central American colonies declared independence, and in 1823 they united as the Federation of Central America. By 1838 the problem-ridden federation was in a state of collapse, and as the union dissolved, El Salvador became independent. Instability and revolution soon followed, and the expansion of the coffee economy in the late 1800s exacerbated problems by further concentrating wealth and power among large-estate holders. A dictatorship from 1931 to 1944 was followed by instability under various military rulers, and in 1969 a brief war with Honduras arose from resentment toward land-ownership laws, border disputes, and nationalistic feelings following a series of soccer games between the two countries. Discontent increased throughout the seventies until a civil war erupted, accompanied by right-wing death squads and human-rights abuses by the government. A new president, who is trying to deal with these problems, was elected in 1984, and guerrilla activity continues. The United States has played a major role in furnishing military and economic aid to the government. ∎

EQUATORIAL GUINEA

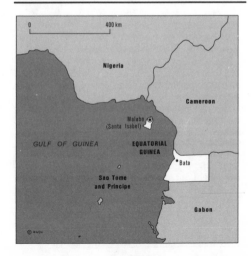

Official name Republic of Equatorial Guinea
PEOPLE
Population 280,000. **Density** 26/mi² (10/km²). **Urban** 54%. **Capital** Malabo, Bioko I., 17,500. **Ethnic groups** Fang 80%, Bubi 15%. **Languages** Spanish, indigenous, English. **Religions** Roman Catholic 83%, Protestant, animist. **Life expectancy** 48 female, 44 male. **Literacy** 20%.

POLITICS
Government Republic. **Parties** None (suspended). **Suffrage** Universal adult. **Memberships** OAU, UN. **Subdivisions** 3 regions.

ECONOMY
GNP $100,000,000. **Per capita** $417. **Monetary unit** Ekuele. **Trade partners** Spain. **Exports** Cocoa, wood, coffee. **Imports** Food, petroleum, machinery, textiles.

LAND
Description Central Africa. **Area** 10,831 mi² (28,051 km²). **Highest point** Pico de Santa Isabel, Bioko I., 9,868 ft (3,008 m). **Lowest point** Sea level.

People. Several ethnic groups inhabit Equatorial Guinea's five islands and the mainland region of Río Muni. The majority Fang, a Bantu people, are concentrated in Río Muni, but they also inhabit Bioko, the largest island. Found mainly on Bioko Island are the minority Bubi, also a Bantu people. Coastal groups known as *playeros,* or "those who live on the beach," live on both the mainland and the small islands. The Fernandino, of mixed African heritage, are concentrated on Bioko. Equatorial Guinea is the only black African state with Spanish as its official language.

Economy and the Land. Equatorial Guinea's economy is based on agriculture and forestry, and cocoa, wood, and coffee are the main products. Cocoa production is centered on fertile Bioko Island, and coffee in Río Muni. The mainland's rain forests also provide for forestry. Mineral exploration has revealed petroleum and natural gas in the waters north of Bioko, and petroleum, iron ore, and radioactive materials exist in Río Muni. Bioko is of volcanic origin, and Río Muni consists of a coastal plain and interior hills. The climate is tropical, with high temperatures and humidity.

History and Politics. Pygmies most likely inhabited the Río Muni area prior to the thirteenth century, when mainland Bubi came to Bioko. From the seventeenth to the nineteenth centuries Bantu migrations brought the coastal tribes and, lastly, the Fang. Portugal claimed Bioko and part of the mainland in the 1400s, then ceded them to Spain in 1778. From 1827 to 1843 British antislavery activities were based on Bioko, which became the home of many former slaves, the ancestors of the Fernandino population. In 1959 the area became the Spanish Territory of the Gulf of Guinea, and the name was changed to Equatorial Guinea in 1963. Independence was achieved in 1968, and a subsequent dictatorship resulted in human-rights violations, the flight of many residents, and a general deterioration of the economy. A 1979 military coup ended the regime, but ethnic power rivalries continue. The official foreign policy is nonalignment. ∎

ETHIOPIA

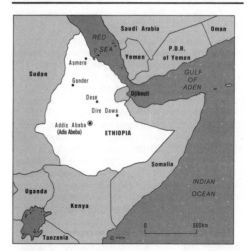

Official name Ethiopia
PEOPLE
Population 34,050,000. **Density** 72/mi² (28/km²). **Urban** 14%. **Capital** Addis Ababa, 1,408,068. **Ethnic groups** Galla 40%, Amhara and Tigrai 32%, Sidamo 9%, Shankella 6%, Somali 6%. **Languages** Amharic, Arabic, indigenous. **Religions** Muslim 40–45%, Coptic Christian 35–40%, animist 15–20%. **Life expectancy** 48 female, 45 male. **Literacy** 15%.

POLITICS
Government Provisional military government. **Parties** Workers'. **Suffrage** Universal, over 21. **Memberships** OAU, UN. **Subdivisions** 14 provinces.

ECONOMY
GDP $4,800,000,000. **Per capita** $141. **Monetary unit** Birr. **Trade partners** U.S.S.R., Italy, West Germany, Japan, U.S. **Exports** Coffee, hides and skins. **Imports** Petroleum, machinery, motor vehicles, chemicals.

LAND
Description Eastern Africa. **Area** 472,434 mi² (1,223,600 km²). **Highest point** Ras Dashen, 15,158 ft (4,620 m). **Lowest point** Lake Asālē, 381 ft (116 m) below sea level.

People. Ethiopia is ethnically, linguistically, and religiously diverse, but the Galla and the Amhara predominate. The Galla include agricultural Muslims, Christians, and nomadic practitioners of traditional religions. Mainly Christian and also agricultural, the Amhara have dominated the country politically, as evidenced by the official language of Amharic, and are closely related to the Tigrai. In all, Ethiopia's boundaries encompass more than forty ethnic groups.

Economy and the Land. In addition to problems caused by political instability, drought has plagued Ethiopia's agricultural economy. Existing problems of soil erosion and deforestation resulted in disaster in 1982 when planting-season rains failed to fall in much of the country. The consequences of drought are especially severe in the north and west. Subsistence farming remains a major activity, and much arable land is uncultivated. Mines produce gold, copper, and platinum, and there is potential for expansion. A central plateau is split diagonally by the Great Rift Valley, with lowlands on the west and plains in the southeast. The climate is temperate on the plateau and hot in the lowlands.

History and Politics. Ethiopia's history is one of the oldest in the world. Its ethnic patterns were established by indigenous Cushites and Semite settlers, who probably arrived from Arabia about three thousand years ago. Christianity was introduced in the early fourth century. During the 1800s modern Ethiopia began to develop under Emperor Menelik II. Ras Tafari Makonnen became emperor 1930, taking the name Haile Selassie. Italians invaded in the 1930s and occupied the country until 1941, when Haile Selassie returned to the throne. Discontent with the feudal society increased until Haile Selassie was ousted by the military in 1974. Reform programs and the change in leadership have done little to ease political tensions, which have sometimes erupted in governmental and civilian violence. Government troops continue their battle with separatists in Eritrea, a former Italian colony and autonomous province incorporated into Ethiopia in 1962, and Somali separatists are active as well. In foreign relations Ethiopia remains unaligned but maintains friendly relations with the Soviet Union and Cuba. ∎

FAEROE ISLANDS

See DENMARK.

FALKLAND ISLANDS

Official name Colony of the Falkland Islands
PEOPLE
Population 2,000. **Density** 0.4/mi² (0.2/km²). **Urban** 53%. **Capital** Stanley, East Falkland I., 1,050. **Ethnic groups** British. **Languages** English. **Religions** Anglican.
POLITICS
Government Colony (U.K.). **Parties** None. **Suffrage** Universal, over 18. **Memberships** None. **Subdivisions** None.
ECONOMY
Monetary unit Pound. **Trade partners** U.K. **Exports** Wool, hides and skins. **Imports** Food, clothing, fuels, machinery.
LAND
Description South Atlantic islands (east of Argentina). **Area** 4,700 mi² (12,173 km²). **Highest point** Mt. Usborne, East Falkland I., 2,312 ft (705 m). **Lowest point** Sea level.

The above information excludes dependencies.

People. Most Falkland Island inhabitants are of British descent, an ancestry reflected in their official language, English, and majority Anglican religion.

Economy and the Land. Sheep raising is the main activity, supplemented by fishing. Situated about 300 miles (482 kilometers) east of southern Argentina,

East and West Falkland compose the main and largest islands. About two hundred islands are classified as dependencies, including South Georgia and the South Sandwich Islands, lying to the southeast. The climate is cool, damp, and windy.

History and Politics. The British sighted the islands in 1592. In 1764 the French established the first settlement, on East Falkland, followed by British settlement on West Falkland the next year. Spain, who ruled the Argentine territories to the west, purchased the French area and drove out the British in 1770. When Argentina gained independence from Spain in 1816, it claimed Spain's right to the islands. Britain reasserted its sovereignty over the islands in the 1830s, and the Falklands became a British colony in 1892, with dependencies annexed in 1908. Continued Argentine claim resulted in an April 1982 Argentine invasion and occupation. The British won the subsequent battle and continue to govern the Falklands. ∎

FIJI

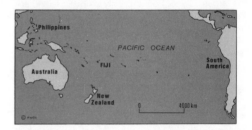

Official name Fiji
PEOPLE
Population 695,000. **Density** 99/mi² (38/km²). **Urban** 37%. **Capital** Suva, Viti Levu I., 68,178. **Ethnic groups** Indian 50%, Fijian 45%. **Languages** English, Fijian, Hindustani. **Religions** Christian, Hindu, Muslim. **Life expectancy** 63 female, 60 male. **Literacy** 80%.
POLITICS
Government Parliamentary state. **Parties** Alliance, National Federation, Western United Front. **Suffrage** Universal adult. **Memberships** CW, UN. **Subdivisions** 14 provinces.
ECONOMY
GDP $1,850,000,000. **Per capita** $1,852. **Monetary unit** Dollar. **Trade partners** Australia, New Zealand, Japan, U.K. **Exports** Sugar, copra. **Imports** Machinery, food, fuels.
LAND
Description South Pacific islands. **Area** 7,055 mi² (18,272 km²). **Highest point** Tomanivi, Viti Levu I., 4,341 ft (1,323 m). **Lowest point** Sea level.

People. Fiji's majority population is descended from laborers brought from British India between 1879 and 1916. Most Indians are Hindu, but a Muslim minority exists. Native Fijians are of Melanesian and Polynesian heritage, and most are Christian. English is the official language, a result of British rule, but Indians speak Hindustani, and the main Fijian dialect is Bauan. Tensions between the two groups occasionally arise because plantation owners, who are mainly Indian, must often lease their land from Fijians, the major landowners. About one hundred of the several hundred islands are inhabited.

Economy and the Land. The traditional sugarcane crop continues as the basis of Fiji's economy, and agricultural diversification is a current goal. Tourism is another economic contributor, and expansion of forestry is planned. Terrain varies from island to island and is characterized by mountains, valleys, rain forests, and fertile plains. The tropical islands are cooled by ocean breezes.

History and Politics. Little is known of Fiji's history prior to the arrival of Europeans. Melanesians probably migrated from Indonesia, followed by Polynesian settlers in the second century. After a Dutch navigator sighted Fiji in 1643, Captain James Cook of Britain visited the island in the eighteenth century. The nineteenth century saw the arrival of European missionaries, traders, and whalers, and several native wars. In 1874 tribal chiefs ceded Fiji to the British, who established sugar plantations and brought indentured Indian laborers. The country became independent in 1970. Foreign policy is based on regional cooperation. ∎

FINLAND

Official name Republic of Finland
PEOPLE
Population 4,885,000. **Density** 37/mi² (14/km²). **Urban** 60%. **Capital** Helsinki, 483,051. **Ethnic groups** Finnish, Swedish, Lappish. **Languages** Finnish, Swedish. **Religions** Lutheran 97%, Greek Orthodox 1%. **Life expectancy** 78 female, 69 male. **Literacy** 100%.
POLITICS
Government Republic. **Parties** Center, National Coalition, People's Democratic League, Social Democratic. **Suffrage** Universal, over 18. **Memberships** OECD, UN. **Subdivisions** 12 provinces.
ECONOMY
GNP $49,100,000,000. **Per capita** $10,124. **Monetary**

unit Markka. **Trade partners** U.S.S.R., Sweden, West Germany, U.K. **Exports** Wood, paper and wood pulp, machinery. **Imports** Fuels, chemicals, machinery, food.
LAND
Description Northern Europe. **Area** 130,558 mi² (338,145 km²). **Highest point** Haltiatunturi, 4,357 ft (1,328 m). **Lowest point** Sea level.

People. As a result of past Swedish rule, the mainly Finnish population includes minorities of Swedes, in addition to indigenous Lapps. Because part of northern Finland lies in the Arctic Circle, population is concentrated in the south. Finland's rich cultural tradition has contributed much to the arts, and its highly developed social-welfare programs provide free education through the university level and nationalized health insurance.

Economy and the Land. Much of Finland's economy is based on its rich forests, which support trade and manufacturing activities. The steel industry is also important. Agriculture focuses on dairy farming and livestock raising; hence many fruits and vegetables must be imported. Coastal islands and lowlands, a central lake region, and northern hills mark Finland's scenic terrain. Summers in the south and central regions are warm, and winters long and cold. Northern Finland—located in the Land of the Midnight Sun—has periods of uninterrupted daylight in summer and darkness in winter.

History and Politics. The indigenous nomadic Lapps migrated north in the first century when the Finns arrived, probably from west-central Russia. A Russian-Swedish struggle for control of the area ended with Swedish rule in the 1100s. Finland was united with Denmark from the fourteenth through the sixteenth centuries, and from the sixteenth through the eighteenth centuries Russia and Sweden fought several wars for control of the country. In 1809 Finland became an autonomous grand duchy within the Russian Empire. The Russian czar was overthrown in the 1917 Bolshevik Revolution, and Finland's declaration of independence was recognized by the new Russian government. During World War II Finland fought against the Soviets and, by the peace treaty signed in 1947, lost a portion of its land to the Soviet Union. During the postwar years Finland and Russia renewed their economic and cultural ties and signed an agreement of friendship and cooperation. Foreign policy emphasizes friendly relations with the U.S.S.R. and Scandinavia. ∎

FRANCE

Official name French Republic
PEOPLE
Population 55,020,000. **Density** 261/mi² (101/km²). **Urban** 73%. **Capital** Paris, 2,176,243. **Ethnic groups** Celtic, Latin. **Languages** French. **Religions** Roman Catholic 90%, Protestant 2%. **Life expectancy** 78 female, 70 male. **Literacy** 99%.
POLITICS
Government Republic. **Parties** Communist, Rally for the

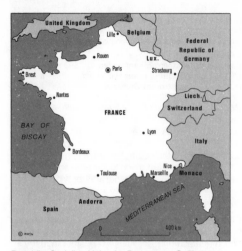

Republic, Socialist, Union for Democracy. **Suffrage** Universal, over 18. **Memberships** NATO, OECD, UN. **Subdivisions** 96 departments.

ECONOMY
GDP $542,000,000,000. **Per capita** $9,996. **Monetary unit** Franc. **Trade partners** West Germany, Italy, Belgium, Luxembourg, U.S., U.K. **Exports** Machinery, transportation equipment, food. **Imports** Petroleum, machinery, chemicals.

LAND
Description Western Europe. **Area** 211,208 mi² (547,026 km²). **Highest point** Mt. Blanc, 15,771 ft (4,807 m). **Lowest point** Étang de Cazaux et de Sanguinet, 10 ft (3 m) below sea level.

The above information excludes French overseas departments.

People. Many centuries ago Celtic tribes, Germanic tribes, and Latins established France's current ethnic patterns. The French language developed from the Latin of invading Romans but includes Celtic and Germanic influences as well. Language and customs vary somewhat from region to region, but most people who speak dialects also speak French. France has long contributed to learning and the arts, and Paris is a world cultural center. In addition to mainland divisions, the country has overseas departments and territories.

Economy and the Land. The French economy is highly developed. The nation is a leader in agriculture and industry, and its problems of inflation and unemployment are common to other modern countries. Soils in the north and northeast are especially productive, and grapes are grown in the south. Minerals include iron ore and bauxite. Industry is diversified, centered in the Paris manufacturing area, and tourism is also important. About two-thirds of the country is flat to rolling, and about one-third is mountainous, including the Pyrenees in the south and the Alps in the east. In the west and north winters are cool and summers mild. Climate varies with altitude in the mountains. The southern coast has a Mediterranean climate with hot summers and mild winters.

History and Politics. In ancient times Celtic tribes inhabited the area that encompasses present-day France. The Romans, who called the region Gaul, began to invade about 200 B.C. , and by the 50s B.C. the entire region had come under Roman rule. Northern Germanic tribes—including the Franks, Visigoths, and Burgundians—spread throughout the region as Roman control weakened, and the Franks defeated the Romans in A.D. 486. In the 800s Charlemagne greatly expanded Frankish-controlled territory, which was subsequently divided into three kingdoms. The western kingdom and part of the central kingdom included modern France. In 987 the Capetian dynasty began when Hugh Capet came to the throne, an event which is often considered the start of the French nation. During subsequent centuries the power of the kings increased, and France became a leading world power. Ambitious projects, such as the palace built by Louis XIV at Versailles, and several military campaigns resulted in financial

Places and Possessions of France

Entity	Status	Area	Population	Capital / Population
Corsica (Mediterranean island)	Part of France	3,352 mi² (8,681 km²)	220,000	None
Guadeloupe and dependencies (Caribbean islands)	Overseas department	687 mi² (1,779 km²)	320,000	Basse-Terre, 13,656
Kerguelen Islands (Indian Ocean)	Part of French Southern and Antarctic territories	2,700 mi² (6,993 km²)	76	None
Martinique (Caribbean island)	Overseas department	425 mi² (1,100 km²)	320,000	Fort-de-France, 97,814
Mayotte *See* COMOROS *entry.*				
St. Pierre and Miquelon (North Atlantic islands)	Overseas department	93 mi² (242 km²)	6,200	Saint-Pierre, 5,646
Wallis and Futuna (South Pacific islands)	Overseas territory	98 mi² (255 km²)	12,000	Mata-Utu, 558

difficulties. The failing economy and divisions between rich and poor led to the French Revolution in 1789 and the First French Republic in 1792. Napoleon Bonaparte, who had gained prominence during the revolution, overthrew the government in 1799 and established the First Empire, which ended in 1815 with his defeat at Waterloo in Belgium. The subsequent monarchy resulted in discontent, and a 1848 revolution established the Second French Republic with an elected president, who in turn proclaimed himself emperor and set up the Second Empire in 1852. Following a war with Prussia in 1870, the emperor was ousted, and the Third Republic began. This republic endured Germany's invasion in World War I but ended in 1940 when invading Germans defeated the French. By 1942 the Nazis had control of the entire country. The Allies liberated France in 1944, and General Charles de Gaulle headed a provisional government until 1946, when the Fourth Republic was established. Colonial revolts in Africa and French Indochina took their toll on the economy during the fifties, and controversy over a continuing Algerian war for independence brought de Gaulle to power once more and resulted in the Fifth Republic in 1958. Dissension and national strikes erupted during the 1960s, a result of dissatisfaction with the government, and de Gaulle resigned in 1969. In 1981 the country elected a Socialist president. France is active in European foreign relations and continues to play a role in its former African colonies. ∎

FRENCH GUIANA

Official name Department of French Guiana
PEOPLE
Population 81,000. **Density** 2.3/mi² (0.9/km²). **Urban** 61%. **Capital** Cayenne, 38,091. **Ethnic groups** African and Afro-European 66%; European 12%; East Indian, Chinese, and Amerindian 12%. **Languages** French. **Religions** Roman Catholic. **Life expectancy** 65. **Literacy** 74%.
POLITICS
Government Overseas department (France). **Parties** Rally for the Republic, Socialist, Union of the People. **Suffrage** Universal, over 18. **Memberships** None. **Subdivisions** 2 arrondissements, 19 communes.

ECONOMY
GNP $120,000,000. **Per capita** $1,935. **Monetary unit** French franc. **Trade partners** France, U.S., Trinidad and Tobago. **Exports** Shrimp, wood, rum. **Imports** Food, manufactured goods, petroleum.
LAND
Description Northeastern South America. **Area** 35,135 mi² (91,000 km²). **Highest point** 2,723 ft (830 m). **Lowest point** Sea level.

People. French Guiana has a majority population of black descendants of African slaves and people of mixed African-European ancestry. Population is concentrated in the more accessible coastal area, but the interior wilderness is home to minority Indians and descendants of slaves who fled to pursue traditional African life-styles. French is the predominant language, but a French-English creole is also spoken. Two Indo-Chinese refugee settlements were established in 1977 and 1979.

Economy and the Land. Shrimp production and a growing timber industry are French Guiana's economic mainstays. The land remains largely undeveloped, however, and reliance on French aid continues. Agriculture is limited by wilderness, but mineral deposits offer potential for mining. The fertile coastal plains of the north give way to hills and finally mountains along the Brazilian border. Rain forests cover much of the landscape. The climate is tropical.

History and Politics. Indigenous Indians and a hot climate defeated France's attempt at settlement in the early 1600s. The first permanent French settlement was established in 1634, and the area became a French colony in 1667. For almost one hundred years, beginning in the 1850s, penal colonies such as Devil's Island brought an influx of European prisoners. The region became a French overseas department in 1946. A minority nationalist group exists, striving for greater autonomy and eventual independence. ∎

FRENCH POLYNESIA

Official name Territory of French Polynesia
PEOPLE
Population 160,000. **Density** 103/mi² (40/km²). **Urban** 57%. **Capital** Papeete, Tahiti I., 23,453. **Ethnic groups** Polynesian 78%, Chinese 12%, French 6%. **Languages** French, Tahitian. **Religions** Protestant 55%, Catholic 32%, Mormon 6%. **Life expectancy** 63 female, 60 male. **Literacy** 98%.
POLITICS
Government Overseas territory (France). **Parties** Here Ai'a, Tahoeraa Huiraatira. **Suffrage** Universal adult. **Memberships** None. **Subdivisions** 5 districts.
ECONOMY
GDP $1,052,400,000. **Per capita** $6,400. **Monetary unit** CFP franc. **Trade partners** France, U.S. **Exports** Coconut products, mother-of-pearl. **Imports** Fuels, food.
LAND
Description Central South Pacific islands. **Area** 1,544 mi² (4,000 km²). **Highest point** Mont Orohena, Tahiti I., 7,352 ft (2,241 m). **Lowest point** Sea level.

People. Most inhabitants are Polynesian, with minorities including Chinese and French. More than one hundred islands compose the five archipelagoes, and population and commercial activity is concentrated in Papeete on Tahiti. Although per capita income is relatively high, wealth is not equally distributed. Emigration from the poorer islands to Tahiti is common. Polynesia's reputation as a tropical paradise has attracted European and American writers and artists, including French painter Paul Gauguin.

Economy and the Land. The islands' economy is based on natural resources, and coconut, mother-of-pearl, and tourism are economic contributors. This South Pacific territory, located south of the equator and midway between South America and Australia, is spread over roughly 1.5 million square miles (3.9 million square kilometers) and is made up of the Marquesas Islands, the Society Islands, the Tuamotu Archipelago, the Gambier Islands, and the Austral Islands. The Marquesas, known for their beauty, form the northernmost group. The Society Islands, southwest of the Marquesas, include Tahiti and Bora-Bora, both popular tourist spots. The Tuamotu Archipelago lies south of the Marquesas and east of the Society Islands, the Gambier Islands are situated at the southern tip of the Tuamotu group, and the Austral Islands lie to the southwest. The region includes both volcanic and coral islands, and the climate is tropical, with a rainy season extending from November to April.

History and Politics. The original settlers probably came from Micronesia and Melanesia in the east. Europeans began arriving around the sixteenth century. By the late 1700s they had reached the five major island groups, and visitors to the area included mutineers from the British vessel *Bounty*. By the 1880s the islands had come under French rule, although they did not become an overseas territory until 1946. During European settlement, many Polynesians died as a result of exposure to foreign diseases. The French use several of the islands for nuclear testing. ∎

GABON

Official name Gabonese Republic
PEOPLE
Population 975,000. **Density** 9.4/mi² (3.6/km²). **Urban** 36%. **Capital** Libreville, 340,000. **Ethnic groups** Fang, Eshira, Bapounou, Teke. **Languages** French, indigenous. **Religions** Christian 80%, Muslim, animist. **Life expectancy** 45 female, 42 male. **Literacy** 65%.
POLITICS
Government Republic. **Parties** Democratic. **Suffrage** Universal, over 18. **Memberships** OAU, OPEC, UN. **Subdivisions** 9 provinces.
ECONOMY
GDP $3,500,000,000. **Per capita** $2,742. **Monetary unit** CFA franc. **Trade partners** France, U.S., West Germany. **Exports** Petroleum, wood and wood products, minerals. **Imports** Machinery, electrical equipment, transportation equipment, food.

LAND
Description Central Africa. **Area** 103,347 mi² (267,667 km²). **Highest point** 3,346 ft (1,020 m). **Lowest point** Sea level.

People. Of Gabon's more than forty ethnic groups, the Fang are a majority and inhabit the area north of the Ogooué River. Other major groups include the Eshira, Bapounou, and Teke. The French, who colonized the area, compose a larger group today than during colonial times. Each of the groups has its own distinct language as well as culture, but French remains the official language.

Economy and the Land. Gabon is located astride the equator, and its many resources include petroleum, manganese, uranium, and dense rain forests. The most important activities are oil production, forestry, and mining. The economy depends greatly on foreign investment and imported labor, however, and many native Gabonese continue as subsistence farmers. The terrain is marked by a coastal plain, inland forested hills, and savanna in the east and south. The climate is hot and humid.

History and Politics. First inhabited by Pygmies, Gabon was the site of migrations by numerous Bantu peoples during its early history. The thick rain forests isolated the migrant groups from one another and thus preserved their individual cultures. The Portuguese arrived in the fifteenth century, followed by the Dutch, British, and French in the 1700s. The slave and ivory trades flourished, and the Fang, drawn by the prosperity, migrated to the coast in the 1800s. By 1885 France had gained control of the area, and in 1910 it was united with present-day Chad, the Congo, and the Central African Republic as French Equatorial Africa. Gabon became independent in 1960, and in 1964 French assistance thwarted a military takeover. Because Gabon's economy relies on foreign investment, foreign policy is often influenced by economic interests. ∎

GALAPAGOS ISLANDS

See ECUADOR.

THE GAMBIA

Official name Republic of The Gambia
PEOPLE
Population 715,000. **Density** 164/mi² (63/km²). **Urban** 18%. **Capital** Banjul, 49,181. **Ethnic groups** Mandingo 38%, Fulani 16%, Wolof 14%, Jola 8%, Serahuli 5%. **Languages** English, indigenous. **Religions** Muslim 85%, Christian 14%. **Life expectancy** 36 female, 32 male. **Literacy** 15%.
POLITICS
Government Republic. **Parties** National Convention, People's Progressive. **Suffrage** Universal, over 21. **Memberships** CW, OAU, UN. **Subdivisions** 6 districts.
ECONOMY
GNP $240,000,000. **Per capita** $370. **Monetary unit** Dalasi. **Trade partners** U.K., China, Netherlands. **Exports** Peanuts and peanut products, fish. **Imports** Manufactured goods, machinery, food.
LAND
Description Western Africa. **Area** 4,361 mi² (11,295 km²). **Highest point** 150 ft (50 m). **Lowest point** Sea level.

People. The Gambia's population includes the Mandingo, or Malinke; Fulani; Wolofs; Jola; and Serahuli. Most people are Muslim, and language differs from group to group, although the official language is English. Gambians are mainly rural farmers, and literacy is low, with educational opportunities focused in the Banjul area. The population's size varies with the arrival and departure of seasonal Senegalese farm laborers.

Economy and the Land. The Gambia's economy relies on peanut production, and crop diversification is a current goal. Subsistence crops include rice, and the government hopes increased rice production will decrease dependence on imports and foreign aid. Fishing and tourism have expanded in the past years. In addition, the Gambia River, which provides a route to the African interior, offers potential for an increased role in trade. The low-lying Gambia is virtually an enclave within Senegal. Bordering the Gambia River are dense mangrove swamps, giving way to flat ground that floods in the rainy season.

Behind this lie sand hills and plateaus. The climate is subtropical.

History and Politics. From the thirteenth to the fifteenth centuries the flourishing Mali Empire included the Gambia area. The Portuguese arrived in the fifteenth century, established slave trading posts, and in 1588 sold trade rights to Britain. During the seventeenth and eighteenth centuries France and Britain competed for control of the river trade. By the late 1800s the Banjul area had become a British colony and the interior a British protectorate. In 1965 the Gambia achieved independence as a monarchy, and the country became a republic in 1970. In 1982 the Gambia and Senegal formed the Confederation of Senegambia, which combined the countries' security and armed forces and strengthened economic ties. The official foreign policy is nonalignment. ∎

GERMANY, EAST

Official name German Democratic Republic
PEOPLE
Population 16,600,000. **Density** 397/mi² (153/km²). **Urban** 76%. **Capital** East Berlin, 1,152,529. **Ethnic groups** German. **Languages** German. **Religions** Protestant 47%, Roman Catholic 7%. **Life expectancy** 75 female, 69 male. **Literacy** 99%.
POLITICS
Government Socialist republic. **Parties** Socialist Unity. **Suffrage** Universal, over 18. **Memberships** UN, Warsaw Pact. **Subdivisions** 14 districts, 1 independent city.
ECONOMY
GNP $165,600,000,000. **Per capita** $9,903. **Monetary unit** Mark. **Trade partners** U.S.S.R., Eastern European countries, West Germany. **Exports** Machinery, chemical products, textiles. **Imports** Raw materials, machinery, fuels.
LAND
Description Eastern Europe. **Area** 41,768 mi² (108,179 km²). **Highest point** Fichtelberg, 3,983 ft (1,214 m). **Lowest point** Sea level.

People. The population of East Germany is mainly German and German speaking. A small minority of

Slavs exists. East Germans are mostly Protestant, especially Lutheran, although many people remain religiously unaffiliated. The standard of living is relatively high, and citizens benefit from extensive educational and social-insurance systems. The arts also receive much government and public support. The people of East and West Germany are divided by a guarded border but share a cultural heritage of achievements in music, literature, philosophy, and science.

Economy and the Land. Postwar economic expansion emphasized industry, and today East Germany is one of the world's largest industrial producers. The economy is centralized: industry is state owned and most agriculture is collectivized. Mineral resources are limited. The terrain is marked by northern lakes and low hills; central mountains, productive plains, and sandy stretches; and southern uplands. The climate is temperate.

History and Politics. History of East and West Germany follows WEST GERMANY.

GERMANY, WEST

Official name Federal Republic of Germany
PEOPLE
Population 61,390,000. **Density** 639/mi² (247/km²). **Urban** 94%. **Capital** Bonn, 293,852. **Ethnic groups** German. **Languages** German. **Religions** Roman Catholic 45%, Protestant 44%. **Life expectancy** 76 female, 70 male. **Literacy** 99%.
POLITICS
Government Republic. **Parties** Christian Democratic Union, Christian Social Union, Free Democratic, Social Democratic. **Suffrage** Universal, over 18. **Memberships** NATO, OECD, UN. **Subdivisions** 11 states.
ECONOMY
GNP $658,400,000,000. **Per capita** $10,682. **Monetary unit** Deutsche mark. **Trade partners** Western European countries, U.S. **Exports** Machinery, motor vehicles, chemicals, iron and steel products. **Imports** Manufactured goods, fuels, raw materials.

LAND
Description Western Europe. **Area** 96,019 mi² (248,687 km²). **Highest point** Zugspitze, 9,721 ft (2,963 m). **Lowest point** Freepsum Lake, 7 ft (2 m) below sea level.

People. West Germany, like East Germany, is homogeneous, with a Germanic, German-speaking population. Religious groups include Roman Catholics and mostly Lutheran Protestants. The populace is generally well educated. The country is about twice as large as East Germany and has about four times the population.

Economy and the Land. Despite destruction incurred in World War II and Germany's division into two countries, West Germany has one of the world's strongest economies. Industry provides the basis for prosperity, with mining, manufacturing, construction, and utilities important contributors. The Ruhr district is the nation's most important industrial region, situated near the Ruhr River in northwest-central Germany and including cities such as Essen and Dortmund. The Rhine River, the most important commercial waterway in Europe, is found in the west. Agriculture remains important in the south. Germany's terrain varies from northern plains to western and central uplands and hills that extend to the southern Bavarian Alps. The dark green firs of the Black Forest lie in the southwest. The mild climate is tempered by the sea in the north, and in the south the winters are colder because of proximity to the Alps.

History and Politics. In ancient times Germanic tribes overcame Celtic inhabitants in the area of Germany and established a northern stronghold against Roman expansion of Gaul. As the Roman Empire weakened, the Germanic peoples invaded, deposing the Roman governor of Gaul in the fifth century A.D. The Franks composed the strongest tribe, and in the ninth century Frankish-controlled territory was expanded and united under Charlemagne. The 843 Treaty of Verdun divided Charlemagne's lands into three kingdoms, with the eastern territory encompassing modern Germany. Unity did not follow, however, and Germany remained a disjointed territory of feudal states, duchies, and independent cities. The Reformation, a movement led by German monk Martin Luther, began in 1517 and evolved into the Protestant branch of Christianity. In the eighteenth century the state of Prussia became the foremost rival of the powerful Austrian state. The rise of Prussian power and growing nationalism eventually united the German states into the German Empire in 1871, and Prussian chancellor Otto von Bismarck installed Prussian king Wilhelm I as emperor. Reconciliation with Austria-Hungary came in 1879, and Germany allied with Austria in World War I in 1914. The empire collapsed as a result of the war, and the Weimar Republic was established in 1919. Instability and disunity arose in the face of economic problems. Promising prosperity and encouraging nationalism, Adolf Hitler of the National Socialist, or Nazi, party became chancellor in 1933. Hitler did away with the freedoms of speech and assembly and began a genocidal program to eliminate Jews and other peoples. Hitler's ambitions led to World War II; and in April 1945 Hitler committed suicide, and in May Germany unconditionally surrendered to the Allies. The United States, Britain, the Soviet Union, and France divided Germany into four zones of occupation.

East Germany. After World War II, eastern Germany was designated the Soviet-occupied zone. The Communist party combined with the Social Democrats and, following the formation of the western Federal Republic of Germany in 1949, the eastern region proclaimed itself the German Democratic Republic. In 1955 the country became fully independent. Berlin, not included in the occupation zones, was a separate entity under the four Allied nations. When the Soviet Union ceased to participate in Allied negotiations in 1948, the city was divided. The Berlin Wall, constructed in 1961, separates East from West Berlin.

West Germany. The Federal Republic of Germany was established in 1949, composed of the American-, French-, and British-occupied zones. The republic became fully independent in 1955. Military forces of the United States, France, and Britain continue to occupy West Berlin. West German politics have been marked by stability under various chancellors. The Green party, formed in the 1970s by environmentalists, has grown in importance in the 1980s. ■

GHANA

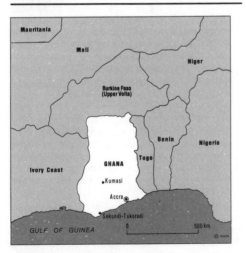

Official name Republic of Ghana
PEOPLE
Population 14,030,000. **Density** 152/mi² (59/km²).
Urban 36%. **Capital** Accra, 1,045,381. **Ethnic groups** Akan, Ewe, Ga. **Languages** English, Akan, indigenous. **Religions** Christian 42%, indigenous 38%, Muslim 12%. **Life expectancy** 56 female, 53 male. **Literacy** 30%.
POLITICS
Government Provisional military government. **Parties** None. **Suffrage** Universal, over 18. **Memberships** CW, OAU, UN. **Subdivisions** 9 regions.

ECONOMY
GNP $10,500,000,000. **Per capita** $895. **Monetary unit** Cedi. **Trade partners** U.K., U.S., West Germany, Netherlands. **Exports** Cocoa, wood, gold. **Imports** Manufactured goods, fuels, food, transportation equipment.
LAND
Description Western Africa. **Area** 92,100 mi² (238,537 km²). **Highest point** Afadjoto, 2,905 ft (885 m). **Lowest point** Sea level.

People. Nearly all Ghanaians are black Africans. The Akan, the majority group, are further divided into the Fanti, who live mainly along the coast, and the Ashanti, who inhabit the forests north of the coast. The Ewe and Ga live in the south and southeast. Other groups include the Guan, living on the Volta River plains, and the Moshi-Dagomba in the north. Ghana's more than fifty languages and dialects reflect this ethnic diversity, and English, the official language, is spoken by a minority. Christianity and traditional African religions predominate, but a Muslim minority also exists. Most people live in rural areas, and the literacy rate is low.

Economy and the Land. Agriculture is the economic mainstay, but Ghana's natural resources are diverse. Production of cocoa, the most important export, is concentrated in the Ashanti region, a belt of tropical rain forest extending north from the coastal plain. Resources include forests and mineral deposits, and exploitation of gold, diamonds, manganese ore, and bauxite is currently underway. Ghana's coastal plain gives way to the Ashanti rain forest and northern savanna. The climate is tropical.

History and Politics. The ancestors of today's Ghanaians probably migrated from the northern areas of Mauritania and Mali in the thirteenth century. The Portuguese reached the shore around 1470 and called the area the Gold Coast. Many countries competed for the region, but in 1874 the Gold Coast was made a British colony. By 1901 Britain had extended its control to the inland Ashanti area, which became a colony, and the northern territories, which became a protectorate. The three regions were merged with British Togoland, a onetime German colony under British administration since 1922, and in 1957 the four regions united as independent Ghana. Instability resulted, arising from a history of disunity and economic problems. The parliamentary state became a republic in 1960, and civilian rule has alternated with military governments. Ghana follows a foreign policy of nonalignment, and although Ghanaians' loyalties are based on community rather than national allegiance, they are in general agreement on foreign affairs. ■

GIBRALTAR

Official name Gibraltar
PEOPLE
Population 30,000. **Density** 13,043/mi² (5,000/km²).
Urban 100%. **Capital** Gibraltar, 30,000. **Ethnic groups** Italian, English, Maltese. **Languages** English, Spanish.

Religions Roman Catholic 75%, Anglican 8%, Jewish 2%. **Literacy** 100%.

POLITICS

Government Colony (U.K.). **Parties** Democratic, Labor/Association for the Advancement of Civil Rights, Socialist Labor. **Suffrage** Universal adult Gibraltarians (other U.K. subjects in residence six months or more). **Memberships** None. **Subdivisions** None.

ECONOMY

Monetary unit Pound. **Trade partners** U.K., Morocco, Portugal. **Exports** Reexport of tobacco, petroleum, wine. **Imports** Manufactured goods, fuels, food.

LAND

Description Southwestern Europe (peninsula on Spain's southern coast). **Area** 2.3 mi² (6 km²). **Highest point** 1,398 ft (426 m). **Lowest point** Sea level.

People. Occupying a narrow peninsula on Spain's southern coast, the British colony of Gibraltar has a mixed population of Italian, Maltese, Portuguese, and Spanish descent. A large number of British residents are also present, many of them military personnel. Most are bilingual in English and Spanish.

Economy and the Land. With land unsuited for agriculture and a lack of mineral resources, Gibraltar depends mainly on the British military presence and tourism. Shipping-related activities also provide jobs and income. Connected to Spain by an isthmus, Gibraltar consists mainly of the limestone-and-shale ridge known as the Rock of Gibraltar. The climate is mild.

History and Politics. Drawn by Gibraltar's strategic location at the Atlantic entrance to the Mediterranean, Phoenicians, Carthaginians, Romans, Vandals, Visigoths, and Moors all played a role in the land's history. After nearly three hundred years under Spanish control, Gibraltar was captured by Britain in 1704, during the War of the Spanish Succession. It was officially ceded to the British in the 1713 Peace of Utrecht. In a 1967 referendum, residents voted to remain under British control. British-Spanish competition for the colony has continued, however, and the border between Spain and Gibraltar was closed by the Spanish government in 1969 and did not reopen until 1985. ∎

GREECE

Official name Hellenic Republic

PEOPLE

Population 10,030,000. **Density** 197/mi² (76/km²). **Urban** 65%. **Capital** Athens, 885,737. **Ethnic groups** Greek 98%, Turkish 1%. **Languages** Greek. **Religions** Greek Orthodox 98%, Muslim 1%. **Life expectancy** 76 female, 72 male. **Literacy** 95%.

POLITICS

Government Republic. **Parties** Communist, New Democracy, Panhellenic Socialist Movement. **Suffrage** Universal, over 18. **Memberships** NATO, OECD, UN. **Subdivisions** 51 prefectures.

ECONOMY

GNP $38,600,000 000. **Per capita** $3,959. **Monetary unit** Drachma. **Trade partners** West Germany, Italy,

France, U.S. **Exports** Textiles, fruits, minerals. **Imports** Machinery, transportation equipment, petroleum, chemicals, consumer goods.

LAND

Description Southeastern Europe. **Area** 50,944 mi² (131,944 km²). **Highest point** Mt. Olympus, 9,570 ft (2,917 m). **Lowest point** Sea level.

People. Greece has played a central role in European, African, and Asian cultures for thousands of years, but today its population is almost homogeneous. Native Greek inhabitants are united by a language that dates back three thousand years and a religion that influences many aspects of everyday life. Athens, the capital, was the cultural center of an ancient civilization that produced masterpieces of art and literature and broke ground in philosophy, political thought, and science.

Economy and the Land. The economy of Greece takes its shape from terrain and location. Dominated by the sea and long a maritime trading power, Greece has one of the largest merchant fleets in the world and depends greatly on commerce. The mountainous terrain and poor soil limit agriculture, although Greece is a leading producer of lemons and olives. The service sector, including tourism, provides most of Greece's national income. Inhabitants enjoy a temperate climate, with mild, wet winters, and hot, dry summers.

History and Politics. Greece's history begins with the early Bronze Age cultures of the Minoans and the Mycenaeans. The city-state, or polis, began to develop around the tenth century B.C., and Athens, a democracy, and Sparta, an oligarchy, gradually emerged as Greece's leaders. The Persian Wars, in which the city-states united to repel a vastly superior army, ushered in the Golden Age of Athens, a cultural explosion in the fifth century B.C. The Parthenon, perhaps Greece's most famous building, was built at this time. Athens was defeated by Sparta in the Peloponnesian War, and by 338 B.C. Philip II of Macedon had conquered all of Greece. His son, Alexander the Great, defeated the Persians and spread Greek civilization and language all over the known world. Greece became a Roman province in 146 B.C. and part of the Byzantine Empire in A.D. 395, but its traditions had a marked influence on these empires. Absorbed into the Ottoman Empire in the 1450s, Greece had gained independence by 1830 and became a constitutional monarchy about fifteen years later. For much of the twentieth century the nation was divided between republicans and monarchists. During World War II Germany occupied Greece, and postwar instability led to a civil war, with Communist rebels eventually losing. Greece was ruled by a repressive military junta from 1967 until 1974, when the regime relinquished power to a civilian government. The Greeks then voted for a republic over a monarchy. A Socialist government was elected in 1981. ∎

GREENLAND

Official name Greenland
PEOPLE
Population 53,000. **Density** 0.06/mi² (0.02/km²). **Urban** 75%. **Capital** Godthåb, 9,717. **Ethnic groups** Greenlander (Inuit and native-born whites) 86%, Danish 14%. **Languages** Danish, indigenous. **Religions** Lutheran. **Life expectancy** 67 female, 60 male. **Literacy** 99%.
POLITICS
Government Part of Denmark. **Parties** Atassut, Inuit Atagatigik, Siumut. **Suffrage** Universal, over 21. **Memberships** None. **Subdivisions** 3 counties, 19 communes.
ECONOMY
Monetary unit Danish krone. **Trade partners** Denmark, Finland, West Germany, U.S. **Exports** Fish and fish products, metallic ores and concentrates. **Imports** Petroleum, machinery, transportation equipment, food.
LAND
Description North Atlantic island. **Area** 840,004 mi² (2,175,600 km²). **Highest point** Gunnbjørn Mtn., 12,139 ft (3,700 m). **Lowest point** Sea level.

People. Most Greenlanders are native-born descendants of mixed Inuit-Danish ancestry, and Lutheranism, the predominant religion, reflects Danish

ties. Descended from an indigenous Arctic people, pure Inuit are a minority and usually follow traditional life-styles. Most of the island lies within the Arctic Circle, and population is concentrated along the southern coast.

Economy and the Land. Fishing is the state's economic mainstay. Despite difficulties presented by the arctic environment, mining of zinc and lead continues, but iron, coal, uranium, and molybdenum deposits remain undeveloped. The largest island in the world, Greenland is comprised of an inland plateau, coastal mountains and fjords, and offshore islands. More than 80 percent of the island lies under permanent ice cap. Greenland is situated in the Land of the Midnight Sun, and certain areas have twenty-four consecutive hours of daylight in summer and darkness in winter. The climate is cold, with warmer temperatures and more precipitation in the southwest.

History and Politics. Following early in-migration of Arctic Inuit, Norwegian Vikings sighted Greenland in the ninth century, and in the tenth century Erik the Red brought the first settlers from Iceland. Greenland united with Norway in the 1200s, and the two regions, along with several others, came under Danish rule in the 1300s. Denmark retained control of Greenland when Norway left the union in 1814. American troops defended the island during World War II. In 1953 the colony became a province of Denmark, and in 1979 the island gained home rule. ∎

GRENADA

Official name Grenada

PEOPLE
Population 114,000. **Density** 857/mi² (331/km²). **Urban** 75%. **Capital** St. George's, 7,500. **Ethnic groups** Black. **Languages** English. **Religions** Roman Catholic, Anglican, other Protestant. **Life expectancy** 67 female, 60 male. **Literacy** 98%.
POLITICS
Government Parliamentary state. **Parties** Democratic Movement, National Democratic. **Suffrage** Universal adult. **Memberships** CW, UN. **Subdivisions** 6 parishes.
ECONOMY
GNP $119,000,000. **Per capita** $870. **Monetary unit** East Caribbean dollar. **Trade partners** U.K., Benelux countries, U.S., Trinidad and Tobago. **Exports** Cocoa, nutmeg, bananas. **Imports** Food, machinery, construction materials.
LAND
Description Caribbean island. **Area** 133 mi² (344 km²). **Highest point** Mt. St. Catherine, 2,756 ft (840 m). **Lowest point** Sea level.

People. Grenada's culture bears the influences of former British and French rule. The most widely spoken language is English, although a French patois is also spoken, and the majority of the population is Roman Catholic. Most Grenadians are black, descended from African slaves brought to the island by the British, but there are small East Indian and European populations.

Economy and the Land. Rich volcanic soils and heavy rainfall have made agriculture the chief economic activity. Also known as the Isle of Spice, Grenada is one of the world's leading producers of nutmeg and mace. Many tropical fruits are also raised, and the small plots of peasant farmers dot the hilly terrain. Another mainstay of the economy is tourism, with visitors drawn by the beaches and tropical climate. There is little industry on Grenada, and high unemployment has plagued the nation in recent years.

History and Politics. European attempts to colonize Grenada were resisted by the Carib Indians for more than one hundred years after the island's discovery by Christopher Columbus in 1498. The French established the first settlement in 1650 and slaughtered the Caribs, but the British finally gained control in 1783. In 1974 Grenada achieved full independence under Prime Minister Eric Gairy, despite widespread opposition to his policies. In 1979 foes of the regime staged a coup and installed a Marxist government headed by Maurice Bishop. Power struggles resulted, and a military branch of the government seized power in 1983 and executed Bishop, along with several of his ministers. The United States led a subsequent invasion that deposed the Marxists. A new government was installed in 1984 elections. ∎

GUADELOUPE

See FRANCE.

GUAM

See UNITED STATES.

GUATEMALA

Official name Republic of Guatemala
PEOPLE
Population 8,080,000. **Density** 192/mi² (74/km²).
Urban 44%. **Capital** Guatemala, 749,784. **Ethnic groups** Ladino (mestizo and westernized Indian) 59%, Indian 41%. **Languages** Spanish, indigenous. **Religions** Roman Catholic, Protestant, indigenous. **Life expectancy** 56 female, 54 male. **Literacy** 50%.
POLITICS
Government Republic. **Parties** Democratic Institutional, National Liberation Movement, National United Front, Revolutionary. **Suffrage** Universal, over 18. **Memberships** OAS, UN. **Subdivisions** 22 departments.

ECONOMY
GDP $8,600,000,000. **Per capita** $1,114. **Monetary unit** Quetzal. **Trade partners** U.S., Central American countries, Japan, West Germany. **Exports** Coffee, cotton, sugar. **Imports** Manufactured goods, machinery, transportation equipment, chemicals, fuels.
LAND
Description Central America. **Area** 42,042 mi² (108,889 km²). **Highest point** Volcán Tajumulco, 13,845 ft (4,220 m). **Lowest point** Sea level.

People. Guatemala's population is made up of majority ladinos and minority Indians. Ladinos include both mestizos, those of Spanish-Indian origin, and westernized Indians of Mayan descent. Classified on the basis of culture rather than race, ladinos follow a Spanish-American life-style and speak Spanish. Nonladino Indians are also of Mayan descent; they generally speak Mayan dialects, and many are poor, uneducated, and isolated from the mainstream of Guatemalan life. Roman Catholicism often combines with traditional Indian religious practice. Population is concentrated in the central highland region.

Economy and the Land. Most Guatemalans practice agriculture in some form. Indians generally operate small, unproductive subsistence farms, and export crops are mainly produced on large plantations on the fertile southern plain that borders the Pacific. Although light industry is growing, it is unable to absorb rural immigrants seeking employment in the cities. Much of the landscape is mountainous, with the Pacific plain and Caribbean lowlands bordering central highlands. Northern rain forests and grasslands are sparsely populated and largely undeveloped. The climate is tropical in low areas and temperate in the highlands.

History and Politics. Indians in the region were absorbed into the Mayan civilization that was flourishing in Central America by the fourth century. In 1523 the Spanish defeated the indigenous Indians and went on to establish one of the most influential colonies in Central America. Guatemala joined

Costa Rica, El Salvador, Nicaragua, and Honduras in 1821 to declare independence from Spain, and the former Spanish colonies formed the Federation of Central America in 1823. Almost from the start, the federation was marked by dissension, and by 1838 it had, in effect, been dissolved. Following a series of dictatorships, social and economic reform began in 1944 and continued under two successive presidents. The government was ousted in a 1954 revolution, and military rule established. A presidential assassination, accusations of government corruption and human-rights violations, guerrilla activities, and violence followed. A 1976 earthquake resulted in thousands of deaths, and physical and economic damage. Military rule continued following a 1983 coup. ∎

GUERNSEY

See UNITED KINGDOM.

GUINEA

Official name People's Revolutionary Republic of Guinea
PEOPLE
Population 5,655,000. **Density** 60/mi² (23/km²). **Urban** 19%. **Capital** Conakry, 600,000. **Ethnic groups** Fulani, Mandingo, Soussou, others. **Languages** French, indigenous. **Religions** Muslim 75%, indigenous 24%, Christian 1%. **Life expectancy** 45 female, 42 male. **Literacy** 48% in indigenous languages, 20% in French.
POLITICS
Government Republic. **Parties** None. **Suffrage** Universal, over 18. **Memberships** OAU, UN. **Subdivisions** 35 regions.
ECONOMY
GNP $1,710,000,000. **Per capita** $329. **Monetary unit** Syli. **Trade partners** Western European countries, U.S., U.S.S.R., China. **Exports** Bauxite, alumina, pineapples, coffee. **Imports** Petroleum, metals, machinery, transportation equipment, food.

LAND
Description Western Africa. **Area** 94,926 mi² (245,857 km²). **Highest point** Mont Nimba, 5,748 ft (1,752 m). **Lowest point** Sea level.

People. Guinea's population is composed of several ethnic groups, with three—the Fulani, Mandingo, and Soussou—forming nearly half the total. Most Guineans are rural farmers, living in hamlets, and the only true urban center is Conakry. Mortality as well as emigration rates are high. Eight official languages besides French, the language of the colonial power, are taught in schools.

Economy and the Land. Rich soil and a varied terrain suited for diverse crop production have made agriculture an important economic activity. Guinea also has vast mineral reserves, including one of the world's largest bauxite deposits. Centralized economic planning and state enterprise have characterized the republic, but Guinea now encourages private and foreign investments. The terrain is mostly flat along the coast and mountainous in the interior. The climate is tropical on the coast, hot and dry in the north and northeast, and cooler with less humidity in the highlands.

History and Politics. As part of the Ghana, Mali, and Songhai empires that flourished in West Africa between the fourth and fifteenth centuries, Guinea was a trading center for gold and slaves. The Portuguese arrived on the coast in the 1400s, and European competition for Guinean trade soon began. In the 1890s France declared the area a colony and named it French Guinea. A movement for autonomy began after World War II with a series of reforms by the French and the growth of a labor movement headed by Sékou Touré, later the nation's first president. The first of the French colonies in West Africa to attain independence, in 1958, Guinea was also the only colony to reject membership in the French Community. Under Touré, a one-party state dedicated to nonalignment was created. ∎

GUINEA-BISSAU

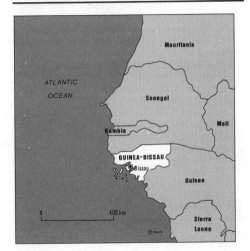

Official name Republic of Guinea-Bissau
PEOPLE
Population 850,000. **Density** 61/mi² (24/km²). **Urban**
24%. **Capital** Bissau, 109,486. **Ethnic groups** Balanta
30%, Fulani 20%, Manjaca 14%, Mandingo 13%.
Languages Portuguese, indigenous. **Religions**
Indigenous 65%, Muslim 30%, Christian 5%.
Life expectancy 42. **Literacy** 9%.
POLITICS
Government Republic. **Parties** African Party for the
Independence of Guinea-Bissau and Cape Verde.
Suffrage Universal, over 15. **Memberships** OAU, UN.
Subdivisions 9 regions.
ECONOMY
GDP $177,000,000. **Per capita** $198. **Monetary unit**
Peso. **Trade partners** Portugal, other Western European
countries. **Exports** Peanuts, palm kernels, shrimp.
Imports Food, machinery, transportation equipment, fuels.
LAND
Description Western Africa. **Area** 13,948 mi²
(36,125 km²). **Highest point** 1,017 ft (310 m). **Lowest
point** Sea level.

People. Guinea-Bissau's largest ethnic group, the
Balanta, mainly inhabit the coastal area. Most prac-
tice traditional beliefs, although some are Christian.
Predominately Muslim peoples, the Fulani and Man-
dingo are concentrated in the northwest. The Man-
jaca inhabit the northern and central coastal regions.
The official language is Portuguese, but many speak
Crioulo, a creole dialect also spoken in Cape Verde.

Economy and the Land. Guinea-Bissau's economy is underdeveloped and dependent upon agriculture, and its soils are relatively productive.
Peanuts, cotton, corn, and sorghum are grown in
the north, and palm-oil production is concentrated
along the coast. Timber is produced primarily in the
south. Fishing, especially shrimp production, has increased since 1976. Bauxite deposits have been located, and exploration for additional resources
continues. Mineral exploitation is hindered by a lack
of transportation routes, however. A swamp-covered
coastal plain rises to an eastern savanna. The climate is tropical. The country includes the Bijagos
Archipelago, lying just off the coast.

History and Politics. The area of Guinea-Bissau
was inhabited by diverse peoples prior to the arrival
of the Portuguese in 1446. Ruled as a single colony
with Cape Verde, the region soon developed into a
base for the Portuguese slave trade. In 1879 it was
separated from Cape Verde as Portuguese Guinea,
and its status changed to overseas province in 1951.
A movement for the independence of Guinea-Bissau
and Cape Verde developed in the 1950s, and a coup
in Portugal in 1974 resulted in independence the
same year. Attempts to unite Guinea-Bissau and
Cape Verde were unsuccessful, and a 1980 coup
installed an antiunification government.   ∎

GUYANA

Official name Cooperative Republic of Guyana

PEOPLE
Population 840,000. **Density** 10/mi² (3.9/km²). **Urban**
30%. **Capital** Georgetown, 72,049. **Ethnic groups** East
Indian 51%, African and mixed 43%, Amerindian 4%.
Languages English. **Religions** Christian 57%, Hindu
33%, Muslim 9%. **Life expectancy** 72 female, 67 male.
Literacy 92%.
POLITICS
Government Republic. **Parties** People's National
Congress, People's Progressive, United Force. **Suffrage**
Universal, over 18. **Memberships** CW, UN. **Subdivisions**
10 districts.
ECONOMY
GNP $430,000,000. **Per capita** $539. **Monetary unit**
Dollar. **Trade partners** Caribbean countries, U.K., U.S.
Exports Bauxite, sugar, rice. **Imports** Manufactured
goods, petroleum, food.
LAND
Description Northeastern South America. **Area** 83,000
mi² (214,969 km²). **Highest point** Mt. Roraima, 9,094 ft
(2,772 m). **Lowest point** Sea level.

People. Guyana's population is composed of descendants of black African slaves and East Indian,
Chinese, and Portuguese laborers brought to work
sugar plantations. Amerindians, the indigenous peoples of Guyana, are a minority. Ninety percent of the
people live along the fertile coastal plain, where
farming and manufacturing are concentrated.

Economy and the Land. Agriculture and mining
compose the backbone of the Guyanese economy.
Sugar and rice continue to be important crops, and
in addition to bauxite, mines produce manganese,
diamonds, and gold. Guyana's inland forests give
way to savanna and a coastal plain. The climate is
tropical.

History and Politics. First gaining European notice
in 1498 with the voyages of Christopher Columbus,
Guyana was the stage for competing colonial interests—British, French, and Dutch—until it officially
became British Guiana in 1831. Slavery was abolished several years later, causing the British to import indentured laborers, the ancestors of today's
majority group. In the early 1960s racial tensions
erupted into riots between East Indians and blacks.

Independence was gained in 1966, and the name Guyana adopted. Guyana became a republic in 1970 and has pursued socialist policies. The two main political parties continue to reflect Guyana's ethnic divisions: the People's National Congress is supported by blacks, and the People's Progressive party by East Indians. ∎

HAITI

Official name Republic of Haiti
PEOPLE
Population 5,305,000. **Density** 495/mi² (191/km²). **Urban** 26%. **Capital** Port-au-Prince, 745,700. **Ethnic groups** Black 95%, mulatto and European 5%. **Languages** French. **Religions** Roman Catholic, Protestant, Voodoo. **Life expectancy** 52 female, 49 male. **Literacy** 23%.
POLITICS
Government Republic. **Parties** Inactive. **Suffrage** Universal, over 18. **Memberships** OAS, UN. **Subdivisions** 5 departments.
ECONOMY
GNP $1,500,000,000. **Per capita** $300. **Monetary unit** Gourde. **Trade partners** U.S., France. **Exports** Coffee, light manufactures, bauxite. **Imports** Consumer goods, food, industrial equipment, petroleum products.
LAND
Description Carribean island (western Hispaniola Island). **Area** 10,714 mi² (27,750 km²). **Highest point** Pic La Selle, 8,773 ft (2,674 m). **Lowest point** Sea level.

People. The world's oldest black republic, Haiti has a population composed mainly of descendants of African slaves. Most people are poor and rural. Although French is the official language, Haitian Creole, a combination of French and West African languages, is more widely spoken. Religions include Roman Catholicism, Protestantism, and Voodooism, which blends Christian and African beliefs.

Economy and the Land. Haiti's economy remains underdeveloped. Most people rely on subsistence farming, though productivity is hampered by high population density in productive regions. Coffee is the main commercial crop and export. Recent growth of light industry is partially attributable to tax exemptions and low labor costs. Occupying the western third of Hispaniola Island, Haiti has an overall mountainous terrain and a tropical climate.

History and Politics. Christopher Columbus reached Hispaniola in 1492, and the indigenous Arawak Indians almost completely died out during subsequent Spanish settlement. Most Spanish settlers had gone to seek their fortunes in other colonies by the 1600s, and western Hispaniola came under French control in 1697. Slave importation increased rapidly, and in less than a hundred years black Africans far outnumbered the French. In a 1791 revolution led by Toussaint L'Ouverture, Jean Jacques Dessalines, and Henri Christophe, the slaves rose against the French. By 1804 independence from France had been achieved, and the area renamed Haiti. The eastern region of the island, now the Dominican Republic, was conquered by Haitians in the 1820s, and it remained part of Haiti until 1844. Instability increased under various dictatorships from 1843 to 1915, and United States marines occupied the country from 1915 to 1934. After a time of alternating military and civilian rule, François Duvalier came to office in 1957, declaring himself president-for-life in 1964. His rule was marked by repression, corruption, and human-rights abuses. His son, Jean-Claude, succeeded him as president-for-life in 1971. Political dissension is not allowed, and since the seventies many Haitians have fled to other Caribbean nations and the United States. ∎

HONDURAS

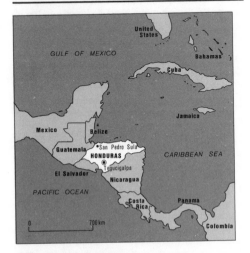

Official name Republic of Honduras
PEOPLE
Population 4,500,000. **Density** 104/mi² (40/km²). **Urban** 26%. **Capital** Tegucigalpa, 444,749. **Ethnic groups** Mestizo 90%, Indian 7%. **Languages** Spanish. **Religions** Roman Catholic 97%. **Life expectancy** 59 female, 55 male. **Literacy** 60%.

POLITICS
Government Republic. **Parties** Liberal, National, National Innovation and Unity. **Suffrage** Universal, over 21. **Memberships** OAS, UN. **Subdivisions** 18 departments.

ECONOMY
GNP $2,620,000,000. **Per capita** $675. **Monetary unit** Lempira. **Trade partners** U.S., Central American countries, West Germany, Japan. **Exports** Bananas, coffee, wood, meat. **Imports** Manufactured goods, machinery, transportation equipment, chemicals, petroleum.

LAND
Description Central America. **Area** 43,277 mi² (112,088 km²). **Highest point** Cerro Las Minas, 9,347 ft (2,849 m). **Lowest point** Sea level.

People. Most Hondurans are mestizos, of Spanish-Indian descent. Other groups include Indians and descendants of black Africans and Europeans. Most Indians have been assimilated into the majority culture, but a minority continues to practice a traditional Indian life-style. The Spanish language predominates, and English is spoken by a small population of British descent on the northern coast and Bay Islands. Poverty is an ongoing problem for the mainly rural population, and economic and educational improvements mostly affect urban inhabitants.

Economy and the Land. Honduras has an underdeveloped economy based on banana cultivation. Other activities include livestock raising, coffee production, forestry, and some mining. Lowlands along both the northern Caribbean and southern Pacific coasts border a mountainous interior. The climate varies from tropical in the lowlands to temperate in the mountains.

History and Politics. Early in its history Honduras was part of the Mayan Empire. By 1502, when Christopher Columbus arrived to claim the region for Spain, the decline of the Maya had rendered the Indians weakened and unable to stave off Spanish settlement. The Spanish colonial period introduced gold and silver mines, cattle ranches, and African slaves. In 1821 Honduras, El Salvador, Nicaragua, Costa Rica, and Guatemala declared independence from Spain and, in 1823, formed the Federation of Central America. The unstable union had virtually collapsed by 1838, and the member states became independent as the federation dissolved. Instability, Guatemalan political influence, and the development of a banana economy based on United States–owned plantations marked the 1800s and early 1900s. Frequent revolutions have characterized the twentieth century, and a dictator governed from 1933 to 1948. Since the 1950s civilian governments have alternated with military coups and rule. Controversies focus on issues of poverty, land distribution, and a border dispute with El Salvador. The country has become an important base for United States activities in Central America, evidenced by ongoing American military maneuvers. ∎

HONG KONG

Official name Hong Kong

PEOPLE
Population 5,435,000. **Density** 13,256/mi² (5,123/km²). **Urban** 92%. **Capital** Hong Kong, 1,183,621. **Ethnic groups** Chinese 98%. **Languages** Cantonese, English. **Religions** Indigenous 90%, Christian 10%. **Life expectancy** 76 female, 70 male. **Literacy** 75%.

POLITICS
Government Colony (U.K.). **Parties** None. **Suffrage** Limited to 200,000–300,000 professional or skilled persons. **Memberships** None. **Subdivisions** 3 divisions.

ECONOMY
GDP $25,900,000,000. **Per capita** $4,900. **Monetary unit** Dollar. **Trade partners** U.S., China, U.K., Japan, West Germany. **Exports** Clothing, plastic articles, textiles, electrical equipment. **Imports** Raw materials, consumer goods, capital equipment, food.

LAND
Description Eastern Asia (islands and mainland area on China's coast). **Area** 410 mi² (1,061 km²). **Highest point** Tai Mo Shan, 3,140 ft (957 m). **Lowest point** Sea level.

People. Hong Kong has a mainly Chinese population. Cantonese, a Chinese dialect, is spoken by most of the people, although English is an official language. Hong Kong is one of the world's most densely populated areas.

Economy and the Land. Low taxes, duty-free status, an accessible location, and an excellent natural harbor have helped make Hong Kong an Asian center of trade, finance, manufacturing, and transportation. Situated on the coast of China, Hong Kong borders Guangdong province. The colony consists of the islands of Hong Kong and Lan Tao, the Kowloon Peninsula, and the New Territories, which include a mainland area and many islands. In addition to mountains, the New Territories contain some level areas suitable for agriculture, and the islands are hilly. The climate is tropical, with hot, rainy summers and cool, humid winters.

History and Politics. Inhabited since ancient times, Hong Kong came under Chinese rule around the third century B.C. In 1839 British opium smuggling led to the Opium War between Britain and China, and a victorious Britain received the island of Hong Kong in an 1842 treaty. In 1860 the British gained control of the Kowloon Peninsula, and in 1898 the New Territories came under British rule through a ninety-nine-year lease with China. British-Chinese discussions are underway concerning the expiration of the New Territories' lease in 1997 and the transfer of the area to China. ∎

HUNGARY

Official name Hungarian People's Republic
PEOPLE
Population 10,675,000. **Density** 297/mi² (115/km²). **Urban** 54%. **Capital** Budapest, 2,064,000. **Ethnic groups** Hungarian 92%, Gypsy 3%, German 3%. **Languages** Hungarian. **Religions** Roman Catholic 68%, Calvinist 20%, Lutheran 5%. **Life expectancy** 73 female, 66 male. **Literacy** 98%.
POLITICS
Government Socialist republic. **Parties** Socialist

Hungary succeeded in obtaining equal status with Austria, and the dual monarchy of Austria-Hungary emerged. Discontent and nationalistic demands increased until 1914, when a Bosnian Serb killed the heir to the Austro-Hungarian throne. Austria-Hungary declared war on Serbia, and World War I began, resulting in a loss of territory and population for Hungary. At the end of the war, in 1918, Hungary became a republic, only to revert to monarchical rule in 1919. Hungary entered World War II on the side of Germany, and Adolf Hitler set up a pro-Nazi government in Hungary in 1944. The Soviet Union invaded that same year, and a Hungarian-Allied peace treaty was signed in 1947. Coalition rule evolved into a Communist government in 1949. Discontent erupted into rebellion in 1956, a new premier declared Hungary neutral, and Soviet forces entered Budapest to quell the uprising. Since the early sixties, the standard of living has improved and economic and cultural liberties have increased. The country remains allied with the Soviet Union, and Western ties are expanding. ∎

Workers'. **Suffrage** Universal, over 18. **Memberships** COMECON, UN, Warsaw Pact. **Subdivisions** 19 counties, 6 autonomous cities.

ECONOMY
GNP $65,200,000,000. **Per capita** $6,901. **Monetary unit** Forint. **Trade partners** U.S.S.R., West Germany, East Germany. **Exports** Machinery, transportation equipment, agricultural products. **Imports** Machinery, transportation equipment, fuels, chemicals.

LAND
Description Eastern Europe, landlocked. **Area** 35,921 mi² (93,036 km²). **Highest point** Kékes, 3,330 ft (1,015 m). **Lowest point** Tisza River valley, 259 ft (79 m).

People. Hungary's major ethnic group and language evolved from Magyar tribes who settled the region in the ninth century. Gypsies, Germans, and other peoples compose minorities. Most people are Roman Catholic, and the government supervises religious activities through a state office. The government also controls educational programs, and the literacy rate is high. Growth of industry since the 1940s has caused a rural-to-urban population shift.

Economy and the Land. Following World War II, Hungary pursued a program of industrialization, and the onetime agricultural nation now looks to industry as its main economic contributor. Agriculture is almost completely socialized, and farming remains important, with productivity aided by fertile soils and a mild climate. Economic planning was decentralized in 1968, thus Hungary's economy differs from that of other Soviet-bloc nations. A flat plain dominates the landscape, and the lack of varying physical features results in a temperate climate throughout the country.

History and Politics. In the late 800s Magyar tribes from the east overcame Slavic and Germanic residents and settled the area. In the thirteenth century invading Mongols caused much destruction, and in the early 1500s, after repeated attacks, the Ottoman Turks gained domination of central Hungary. By the late seventeenth century the entire region had come under the rule of Austria's Hapsburgs. In 1867

ICELAND

Official name Republic of Iceland
PEOPLE
Population 240,000. **Density** 6/mi² (2.3/km²). **Urban** 89%. **Capital** Reykjavík, 84,593. **Ethnic groups** Mixed Norwegian and Celtic. **Languages** Icelandic. **Religions** Lutheran 95%. **Life expectancy** 80 female, 74 male. **Literacy** 100%.
POLITICS
Government Republic. **Parties** Independence, People's Alliance, Progressive, Social Democratic. **Suffrage** Universal, over 20. **Memberships** NATO, OECD, UN. **Subdivisions** 7 districts.
ECONOMY
GNP $2,200,000,000. **Per capita** $9,322. **Monetary unit** Króna. **Trade partners** U.S., Scandinavian countries, U.K., West Germany. **Exports** Fish and fish products, animal products, aluminum. **Imports** Machinery, transportation equipment, petroleum, food, textiles.

LAND
Description North Atlantic island. **Area** 39,769 mi² (103,000 km²). **Highest point** Hvannadalshnúkur, 6,952 ft (2,119 m). **Lowest point** Sea level.

People. Most Icelanders are of Norwegian or Celtic ancestry, live in coastal cities, and belong to the Lutheran church. Icelandic, the predominant language, has changed little from the Old Norse of the original settlers and still resembles the language of twelfth-century Nordic sagas.

Economy and the Land. Fish, found in the island's rich coastal waters, are the main natural resource and export. Iceland has a long tradition based on fishing, but the industry has recently suffered from decreasing markets and catches. Glaciers, lakes, hot springs, volcanoes, and a lava desert limit agricultural land but provide a scenic terrain. Although the island lies just south of the Arctic Circle, the climate is moderated by the Gulf Stream. Summers are damp and cool, and winters relatively mild but windy. Proximity to the Arctic Circle puts Iceland in the Land of the Midnight Sun, resulting in periods of twenty-four-hour daylight in June.

History and Politics. Norwegians began settlement of Iceland around the ninth century. The world's oldest parliament, the Althing, was established in Iceland in A.D. 930. Civil wars and instability during the thirteenth century led to the end of independence in 1262, when Iceland came under Norwegian rule. In the fourteenth century Norway was joined to Denmark's realm, and rule of Iceland passed to the Danes. The Althing was abolished in 1800 but reestablished in 1843. In the 1918 Act of Union, Iceland became a sovereign state but retained its union with Denmark under a common king. Germany occupied Denmark in 1940, during World War II; and British troops, replaced by Americans in 1941, protected Iceland from invasion. Following a 1944 plebiscite, Iceland left its union with Denmark and became an independent republic. The country has no military.■

INDIA

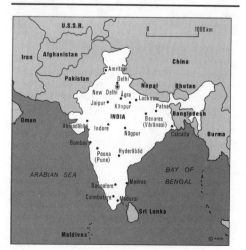

Official name Republic of India
PEOPLE
Population 754,600,000. **Density** 610/mi² (236/km²). **Urban** 23%. **Capital** New Delhi, 271,990. **Ethnic groups** Indo-Aryan 72%, Dravidian 25%, Mongoloid 3%. **Languages** Hindi, English, indigenous. **Religions** Hindu 83%, Muslim 11%, Christian 3%, Sikh 2%. **Life expectancy** 50 female, 51 male. **Literacy** 36%.

POLITICS
Government Republic. **Parties** Congress (I), Congress (S), Lok Dal. **Suffrage** Universal, over 21. **Memberships** CW, UN. **Subdivisions** 22 states, 9 union territories.

ECONOMY
GNP $146,000,000,000. **Per capita** $209. **Monetary unit** Rupee. **Trade partners** U.S., U.K., U.S.S.R., Japan. **Exports** Engineering goods, textiles, clothing, tea. **Imports** Machinery, transportation equipment, petroleum, fertilizer.

LAND
Description Southern Asia. **Area** 1,237,061 mi² (3,203,975 km²). **Highest point** Kānchenjunga, 28,208 ft (8,598 m). **Lowest point** Sea level.
The above information includes part of Jammu and Kashmir.

People. India's population is composed of two main ethnic groups: the Indo-Aryan and the Dravidian. Found mostly in the north are the Indo-Aryans, a central Asian people who arrived in India around 1500 B.C., pushing the Dravidians to the south, where they remain concentrated today. A Mongoloid minority inhabits the mountains of the far north, and aboriginal groups live in the central forests and mountains. Hindi is the official language, English is spoken by a minority of educated persons, and more than fourteen indigenous languages are in use as well. India is second only to China in population, and although Hindus are the religious majority, the country also has one of the world's largest Muslim populations. Christians, Sikhs, Jains, and Buddhists comprise additional religious minorities.

Economy and the Land. Economic conditions have improved since India became independent from Britain in 1947. Agriculture, upon which most Indians depend, is now more efficient, a result of modernization programs. Industry has expanded as well, and the country ranks high in its number of scientists and skilled laborers. Poverty, unemployment, and underemployment continue to plague the nation, however, partly due to rapid population growth and improved life expectancy. Many natural resources, including coal, iron ore, bauxite, and manganese, remain undeveloped. India is made up of three land regions: the Himalayas along the northern border; the Gangetic plain, a fertile northern region; and the peninsula, made up mostly of the Deccan, a plateau region. The climate ranges from temperate to tropical monsoon.

History and Politics. India's civilization dates back to 2500 B.C., when the Dravidians flourished in the region. Aryan tribes invaded about one thousand years later, bringing the indigenous beliefs that evolved into Hinduism, and various empires followed. In the sixth or fifth century B.C., Siddhārtha Gautama, who came to be called Buddha, founded

Buddhism, a major influence on Indian life until about A.D. 800. Invasions beginning around A.D. 450 brought the Huns, and during the seventh and eighth centuries Arab conquerors introduced Islam. The Mogul Empire, under a series of Muslim rulers, began in the 1500s, and the British East India Company established trading posts in the 1600s. By 1757 the East India Company had become India's major power, and by the 1850s the company controlled nearly all present-day India, Pakistan, and Bangladesh. An Indian rebellion in 1857 caused Britain to take over the East India Company's rule. Demands for independence increased after a controversial massacre of Indians by British troops in 1919, and by 1920 Mohandas Gandhi had emerged as the leader of an independence campaign based on nonviolent disobedience and noncooperation. The nation gained independence in 1947, establishing Pakistan as a separate Muslim state because of Muslim-Hindu hostilities. Recent disputes included a border conflict with China that erupted into fighting in 1959 and 1962 and a disagreement with Pakistan over the mainly Muslim region of Kashmir. In 1984 Sikhs demanding an independent state assassinated Prime Minister Indira Gandhi. India's foreign policy is based on nonalignment. ∎

INDONESIA

Official name Republic of Indonesia
PEOPLE
Population 166,070,000. **Density** 224/mi² (87/km²). **Urban** 22%. **Capital** Jakarta, Java I., 6,503,449. **Ethnic groups** Javanese 45%, Sundanese 14%, Madurese 8%, coastal Malay 8%. **Languages** Bahasa Indonesia, Malay-Polynesian languages, English, Dutch. **Religions** Muslim 90%, Christian 5%, Hindu 3%. **Life expectancy** 55 female, 52 male. **Literacy** 64%.

POLITICS
Government Republic. **Parties** Democratic, Golkar, Unity Development. **Suffrage** Universal, over 17 (no age requirement if married). **Memberships** OPEC, UN. **Subdivisions** 27 provinces.

ECONOMY
GNP $70,000,000,000. **Per capita** $440. **Monetary unit** Rupiah. **Trade partners** Japan, U.S., Singapore. **Exports** Petroleum, natural gas, wood, natural rubber. **Imports** Food, machinery, transportation equipment, chemicals, petroleum products.
LAND
Description Southeastern Asian islands. **Area** 741,101 mi² (1,919,443 km²). **Highest point** Jaya Pk., New Guinea I., 16,503 ft (5,030 m). **Lowest point** Sea level.

People. Indonesia is the fifth most populous nation in the world. The majority of the people are of Malay stock, which includes several subgroups, such as Javanese, Sundanese, Madurese, and coastal Malay. More than two hundred indigenous languages are spoken, but the official, unifying language is Bahasa Indonesia. Most people live in small farm villages and follow ancient customs stressing cooperation. Muslim traders brought Islam to Indonesia, and most of the population is Muslim. Many Indonesians combine spirit worship with Islam or Christianity. Indonesia's rich cultural heritage includes many ancient temples.

Economy and the Land. Indonesia is a leading producer of petroleum in the Far East. The area also has large deposits of minerals and natural gas. Agriculture is still a major economic activity, and rice remains an important crop. Overpopulation threatens the economy and food supply. The nation's more than 13,600 islands form a natural barrier between the Indian and Pacific oceans, making the straits between the islands important for world trade and military strategy. Java, the most industrial and heavily populated island, is characterized by volcanic mountains and narrow fertile plains along the northern coast. Indonesia includes most of Borneo, the third largest island in the world. Other major Indonesian islands are Celebes, Sumatra, and the western half of New Guinea, which also feature inland mountains and limited coastal plains. The climate is tropical, with seasonal monsoons.

History and Politics. Indonesian civilization is more than 2,500 years old and has produced two major empires with influence throughout Southeast Asia. The Portuguese arrived in the sixteenth century but were outnumbered by the Dutch, who eventually gained control of most of the islands and established a plantation colony. An independence movement began early in the twentieth century and slowly gained momentum. Japan encouraged Indonesian nationalism during World War II, and shortly after the Japanese surrender in 1945, Indonesia proclaimed itself an independent republic. Economic and political instability led to an attempted Communist coup in 1965, after which the government outlawed communism, cut its ties with China, and strengthened relations with Western powers. ∎

IRAN

Official name Islamic Republic of Iran

PEOPLE
Population 44,500,000. **Density** 70/mi² (27/km²). **Urban** 49%. **Capital** Tehrān, 4,496,159. **Ethnic groups** Persian 63%, Turkish 18%, other Iranian 13%, Kurdish 3%, Arab 3%. **Languages** Farsi, Turkish, Kurdish, Arabic. **Religions** Shiite Muslim 93%, Sunni Muslim 5%, Zoroastrian, Jewish, Christian, Baha'i. **Life expectancy** 59 female, 57 male. **Literacy** 48%.

POLITICS
Government Republic. **Parties** Islamic Republican. **Suffrage** Universal, over 15. **Memberships** OPEC, UN. **Subdivisions** 23 provinces.

ECONOMY
GNP $66,500,000,000. **Per capita** $1,621. **Monetary unit** Rial. **Trade partners** Japan, West Germany, Italy. **Exports** Petroleum, carpets, fruits, nuts. **Imports** Machinery, military equipment, food.

LAND
Description Southwestern Asia. **Area** 636,296 mi² (1,648,000 km²). **Highest point** Mt. Demavand, 18,386 ft (5,604 m). **Lowest point** Caspian Sea, 92 ft (28 m) below sea level.

People. Most Iranians are of Aryan ancestry, descended from an Asiatic people who migrated to the area in ancient times. The Aryan groups include majority Persians and minority Gilani, Mazanderani, Kurds, Lur, Bakhtiari, and Baluchi. Arabs and Turks are among the non-Aryan minorities. Until 1935, when the shah officially changed its name, Iran was known to the rest of the world as Persia; Farsi, or Persian, remains the main language. Nearly all Iranians are Muslim, mainly of the Shiite sect, and the country is an Islamic republic, with law based on Islamic teachings. Minority religious groups, especially Baha'is, have been victims of persecution. Aridity and a harsh mountain-and-desert terrain result in a population concentrated in the west and north.

Economy and the Land. Iran's previously rapid economic development has slowed as a result of a 1979 revolution and an ongoing war with Iraq. Small-scale farming, manufacturing, and trading appear to be current economic trends. Oil remains the most important export, although output has decreased due to changes in economic policy and other factors.

Persian carpets also continue as elements of trade. Iran's terrain consists mainly of a central plateau marked by desert and surrounded by mountains; thus agriculture is limited, and the country remains dependent on imported food. The central region is one of the most arid areas on earth, and summers throughout most of the country are long, hot, and dry, with higher humidity along the Persian Gulf and Caspian coast. Winters are cold in the mountains of the northwest, but mild on the plain. The Caspian coastal region is generally subtropical.

History and Politics. Iran's history is one of the world's oldest, with a civilization dating back several thousand years. Around 1500 B.C. Aryan immigrants began arriving from central Asia, calling the region Iran, or land of the Aryans, and splitting into two groups: the Medes and the Persians. In the sixth century B.C. Cyrus the Great founded the Persian, or Achaemenian, Empire, which came to encompass Babylonia, Palestine, Syria, and Asia Minor. Alexander the Great conquered the region in the fourth century B.C. Various dynasties followed, and Muslim Arabs invaded in the A.D. 600s and established Islam as the major religion. The following centuries saw Iran's boundaries expand and recede under various rulers, and increasing political awareness resulted in a 1906 constitution and parliament. In 1908 oil was discovered in the region, and modernization programs began during the reign of Reza Shah Pahlavi, who came to power in 1925. Despite Iran's declared neutrality in World War II, the Allies invaded, obtaining rights to use the country as a supply route to the Soviet Union. The presence of foreign influences caused nationalism to increase sharply after the war. Mohammad Reza Pahlavi—who succeeded his father, Reza Shah Pahlavi, as shah—instituted social and economic reforms during the sixties, although many Muslims felt the reforms violated religious law and resented the increasing Western orientation of the country and the absolute power of the shah. Led by Muslim leader Ayatollah Ruholla Khomeini, revolutionaries seized the government in 1979, declaring Iran an Islamic republic, based upon fundamental Islamic principles. Khomeini remained the religious leader of Iran, and in 1980 the first president of the republic was elected. Since 1980 the country has been involved in a war with Iraq over territorial and other disputes, and internal unrest continues as well. ∎

IRAQ

Official name Republic of Iraq
PEOPLE
Population 15,255,000. **Density** 91/mi² (35/km²). **Urban** 68%. **Capital** Baghdād, 1,300,000. **Ethnic groups** Arab 75%; Kurdish 15%; Turkish, Assyrian, and others 10%. **Languages** Arabic, Kurdish. **Religions** Shiite Muslim 55%, Sunni Muslim 40%, Christian 5%. **Life expectancy** 58 female, 55 male. **Literacy** 70%.
POLITICS
Government Republic. **Parties** None (banned). **Suffrage** Universal adult. **Memberships** AL, OPEC, UN. **Subdivisions** 18 provinces.

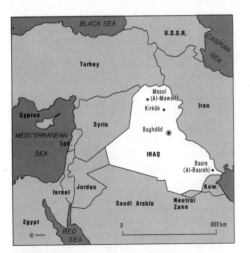

ECONOMY
GNP $30,000,000,000. **Per capita** $2,150. **Monetary unit** Dinar. **Trade partners** Japan, West Germany, other Western European countries, U.S. **Exports** Petroleum, dates. **Imports** Construction equipment, machinery, motor vehicles.

LAND
Description Southwestern Asia. **Area** 167,925 mi² (434,924 km²). **Highest point** 11,835 ft (3,607 m). **Lowest point** Sea level.

People. Descendants of the founders of one of the world's oldest civilizations inhabit Iraq. Most Iraqis are Muslim Arabs and Arabic speaking. The minority Kurds, also mainly Muslim, are concentrated in the northwest; speak their own language, Kurdish; and follow a non-Arab life-style. Kurdish demands for self-rule have led to occasional rebellion.

Economy and the Land. Oil is the mainstay of Iraq's economy, and nearly all economic development has focused on the petroleum industry, nationalized in the 1970s. Despite its oil wealth, the Iraqi economy, like the Iranian, has been drained by the continuing Iran-Iraq war. Most farmland lies near the Tigris and Euphrates rivers; dates are the most important export crop. The terrain is marked by northeastern mountains, southern and western deserts, and the plains of upper and lower Iraq, which lie between the Tigris and Euphrates rivers. The climate is generally hot and dry.

History and Politics. Civilizations such as the Sumerian, Babylonian, and Parthian flourished in the area of the Tigris and Euphrates in ancient times. Once known as Mesopotamia, the region was the setting for many biblical events. After coming under Persian rule in the sixth century B.C., Mesopotamia fell to Alexander the Great in the fourth century B.C. Invading Arabs brought the Muslim religion in the seventh century A.D., and for a time Baghdād was the capital and cultural center of the Arab empire. Thirteenth-century Mongol invaders were followed by Ottoman Turks in the sixteenth century. Ottoman rule continued, and following a British invasion during World War I, Mesopotamia became a British mandate at the end of the war. In 1921 the monarchy of Iraq was established, and independence was gained in 1932. Iraq and other nations formed the Arab League in 1945 and participated in a war against Israel in 1948. Opposition to monarchical rule increased during the 1950s; following a 1958 military coup, the country was declared a republic. Instability, evidenced by coups, continued into the seventies, and the political climate was further complicated by occasional uprisings by Kurds demanding autonomy. In 1980 a border dispute and other disagreements with Iran resulted in a continuing war. Foreign policy is often influenced by the Arab-Israeli conflict. ■

IRELAND

Official name Ireland
PEOPLE
Population 3,595,000. **Density** 132/mi² (51/km²). **Urban** 56%. **Capital** Dublin, 525,882. **Ethnic groups** Celtic, English. **Languages** Irish Gaelic, English. **Religions** Roman Catholic 94%, Anglican 4%. **Life expectancy** 75 female, 71 male. **Literacy** 99%.

POLITICS
Government Republic. **Parties** Fianna Fail, Fine Gael, Labor. **Suffrage** Universal, over 18. **Memberships** OECD, UN. **Subdivisions** 26 counties.

ECONOMY
GNP $17,000,000,000. **Per capita** $5,667. **Monetary unit** Pound. **Trade partners** U.K., other Western European countries, U.S. **Exports** Meat and dairy products, textiles, machinery. **Imports** Petroleum, petroleum products, machinery, chemicals, manufactured goods.

LAND
Description Northwestern Europe (five-sixths of island of Ireland). **Area** 27,136 mi² (70,283 km²). **Highest point** Carrantuohill, 3,414 ft (1,041 m). **Lowest point** Sea level.

People. Most of Ireland's population is descended from the Celts, a people who flourished in Europe and Great Britain in ancient times. Irish Gaelic, a form of ancient Celtic, and English are official languages. Most people are Roman Catholic, and Protestants mainly belong to the Church of Ireland, a member of the Anglican Communion. The country has a long literary tradition and has contributed greatly to world literature.

Economy and the Land. Ireland's economy was agricultural until the 1950s, when a program of rapid industrialization began. This expansion has resulted in significant foreign investment, especially by the United States. Most of the Irish labor force is unionized. Agriculture continues to play an important role, however, and food is produced for both domestic consumption and trade. The country of Ireland occupies most of the island of Ireland but excludes Northern Ireland, which is part of the United Kingdom. The fertile central region features green, rolling hills, suitable for farming and pastureland, and is surrounded by coastal highlands. The climate is temperate maritime, with mild summers and winters and plentiful rainfall.

History and Politics. Around the fourth century B.C. Ireland's indigenous population was conquered by Gaels, a Celtic tribe, from continental Europe and Great Britain. Christianity was introduced by St. Patrick in A.D. 432, and periodic Viking raids began near the end of the eighth century. In the twelfth century the pope made the Norman king of England, Henry II, overlord of the island; the English intervened in a dispute between Irish kings; and centuries of British influence began. As British control grew, so did Irish Catholic hostility, arising from seizure of land by English settlers, the Protestant Reformation, and the elimination of political and religious freedoms. The Protestant majority of present-day Northern Ireland was established in the 1600s, when land taken from the Irish was distributed to English and Scottish Protestants. In 1801 the British Act of Union established the United Kingdom of Great Britain and Ireland. Religious freedom was regained in 1829, but the struggle for independence continued. Most of the Irish depended upon potatoes as a staple food, and hundreds of thousands died or emigrated in the 1840s when the crop failed because of a plant disease. Following an armed rebellion, the Irish Free State, a dominion of Great Britain, was created in 1921, with the predominantly Protestant counties in the north remaining under British rule. The nation became a republic in 1948. Many Irish citizens and Catholics in Northern Ireland continue to demand unification of the country, and the struggle occasionally erupts into violence. Neutrality remains the basis of foreign policy, and the nation is a strong supporter of European unity. ∎

ISLE OF MAN

See UNITED KINGDOM.

ISRAEL

Official name State of Israel

PEOPLE
Population 4,189,000. **Density** 505/mi² (195 km²). **Urban** 87%. **Capital** Jerusalem, 415,000. **Ethnic groups** Jewish 85%, Arab 15%. **Languages** Hebrew, Arabic, English. **Religions** Jewish 85%, Muslim 11%. **Life expectancy** 76 female, 73 male. **Literacy** 88%.

POLITICS
Government Republic. **Parties** Labor Alignment, Likud. **Suffrage** Universal, over 18. **Memberships** UN. **Subdivisions** 6 districts.

ECONOMY
GNP $22,200,000,000.
Per capita $5,612. **Monetary unit** Shekel. **Trade partners** U.S., U.K., West Germany, other Western European countries. **Exports** Polished diamonds, fruits, textiles, clothing, machinery, fertilizer. **Imports** Military equipment, rough diamonds, petroleum, machinery, chemicals.

LAND
Description Southwestern Asia. **Area** 8,302 mi² (21,501 km²). **Highest point** Mt. Meron, 3,963 ft (1,208 m). **Lowest point** Dead Sea, 1,312 ft (400 m) below sea level.

People. Most Israelis are Jewish immigrants or descendants of Jews who settled in the region in the late 1800s. The two main ethnic groups are the Ashkenazim of central and eastern European origin and the Sephardim of the Mediterranean and Middle East. The non-Jewish population is predominantly Arab and Muslim. Hebrew and Arabic are the official languages, and both are used on documents and currency. Most farmers belong either to a cooperative community called a moshav or a collective community called a kibbutz.

Economy and the Land. Despite drastic levels of inflation and a constant trade deficit, Israel has experienced continuous economic growth. Skilled labor supports the market economy based on services, manufacturing, and commerce. Taxes are a major source of revenue, as are grants and loans from other countries and income from tourism. The country is poor in natural resources, but through improved irrigation and soil conservation, Israel now produces much of its own food. Because of its limited natural resources, Israel must import most of the raw materials it needs for industry. The region's varied terrain includes coastal plains, central mountains, the Jordan Rift Valley, and the desert region of the Negev. Except in the Negev, the climate is temperate.

History and Politics. Israel comprises much of the historic region of Palestine, known in ancient times as Canaan and the site of most biblical history. The region saw the arrival of the Hebrews around 1900 B.C. and subsequent immigration and invasion by diverse peoples, including Assyrians, Babylonians, and Persians. In 63 B.C. it became part of the Roman Empire and was renamed Judaea and finally, Palestine. In the A.D. 600s invading Arabs brought Islam to the area, and by the early 1500s, when Ottoman Turks conquered the region, Muslims comprised a majority. During the late 1800s, as a result of oppression in eastern Europe, many Jews immigrated to Palestine, hoping to establish a Jewish state. This movement, called Zionism, and the increasing Jewish population, led to Arab-Jewish tensions. Turkey sided with Germany in World War I, and after the war the Ottoman Empire collapsed. Palestine became a mandated territory of Britain in 1920. Jewish immigration, and thus Arab-Jewish hostility, increased during the years of Nazi Germany. Additional unrest arose from conflicting interpretations of British promises and the terms of the mandate. In 1947 Britain turned to the United Nations for help in resolving the problem, and in 1948 the nation of Israel was established. Neighboring Arab countries invaded immediately, and war ensued, during which Israel gained some land. A truce was signed in 1949, but violence continued along the borders, and hostilities broke out periodically throughout the fifties, sixties, and seventies. Israel's relations with Egypt have improved since the two countries signed a peace treaty in 1979, but tensions remain between Israel and other Arab nations. ∎

ITALY

Official name Italian Republic
PEOPLE
Population 56,940,000. **Density** 490/mi² (189/km²). **Urban** 69%. **Capital** Rome, 2,830,569. **Ethnic groups** Italian, others. **Languages** Italian. **Religions** Roman Catholic. **Life expectancy** 76 female, 72 male. **Literacy** 93%.
POLITICS
Government Republic. **Parties** Christian Democratic, Communist, Socialist, Social Movement. **Suffrage** Universal, over 18. **Memberships** NATO, OECD, UN. **Subdivisions** 20 regions.

ECONOMY
GNP $347,000,000,000. **Per capita** $5,314. **Monetary unit** Lira. **Trade partners** West Germany, France, Benelux countries, U.S., U.K. **Exports** Machinery, transportation equipment, textiles, food. **Imports** Machinery, transportation equipment, food, petroleum.
LAND
Description Southern Europe. **Area** 116,319 mi² (301,266 km²). **Highest point** Mt. Blanc (Monte Bianco), 15,771 ft (4,807 m). **Lowest point** Sea level.

People. Italy is populated mainly by Italian Roman Catholics. Most speak Italian; however, dialects often differ from region to region. Despite an ethnic homogeneity, the people exhibit diversity in terms of politics and culture. The country has about twelve political parties, and northern inhabitants are relatively prosperous, employed primarily in industry, whereas southerners are generally farmers and often poor. The birthplace of the Renaissance, Italy has made substantial contributions to world culture.

Economy and the Land. The Italian economy is based on private enterprise, although the government is involved in some industrial and commercial activities. Industry is centered in the north, producing steel, textiles, and chemicals. Much commercial agriculture is also based in the north, taking place on the rich soils of the Po Valley. A hilly terrain makes parts of the south unsuited for crop raising, and livestock grazing is a main activity. Tourism is also an important contributor, with visitors drawn by the northern Alps, the sunny south, and the Italian cultural tradition. The island of Sicily, lying off the southwest coast, produces fruits, olives, and grapes. Sardinia, a western island, engages in some sheep and wheat raising. Except for the northern Po Valley, narrow areas along the coast, and a small section of the southern peninsula, Italy's terrain is mainly rugged and mountainous. The climate varies from cold in the Alps to mild and Mediterranean in other parts of the country.

History and Politics. Early influences in Italy included Greeks, Etruscans, and Celts. From the fifth century B.C. to the fifth century A.D., the dominant people were Romans descended from Sabines and neighboring Latins, who inhabited the Latium coast. Following the demise of the Roman Empire, rulers and influences included Byzantines; Lombards, an invading Germanic tribe; and the Frankish king Charlemagne, whom the pope crowned emperor of the Romans in 800. During the eleventh century, Italy became a region of city-states, and their cultural life led to the Renaissance, which started in the 1300s. As the city-states weakened, Italy fell victim to invasion and rule by France, Spain, and Austria, with these countries controlling various regions at different times. In 1861 Victor Emmanuel II, the king of Sardinia, proclaimed Italy a kingdom, and by 1871 the nation included the entire peninsula, with Rome as the capital and Victor Emmanuel as king. In 1922 Benito Mussolini, the leader of Italy's Fascist movement, came to power. By 1925 Mussolini was ruling as dictator, and an almost continuous period of warfare followed. In World War II the country allied with Germany, and a popular resistance movement evolved. The monarchy was ended by plebiscite in 1946, and the country became a republic. There are now many political parties, but the Christian Democratic, Communist, and Socialist parties are dominant. Italy's Communist party is the world's largest nonruling Communist party.   ∎

IVORY COAST

Official name Republic of the Ivory Coast
PEOPLE
Population 9,325,000. **Density** 75/mi² (29/km²). **Urban** 38%. **Capital** Abidjan (de facto), 1,500,000; Yamoussoukro (designated), 35,585. **Ethnic groups** Agni, Baule, Krou, Senoufou, Mandingo, others. **Languages** French, indigenous. **Religions** Indigenous 63%, Muslim 25%, Christian 12%. **Life expectancy** 48 female, 46 male. **Literacy** 24%.
POLITICS
Government Republic. **Parties** Democratic. **Suffrage** Universal, over 21. **Memberships** OAU, UN. **Subdivisions** 24 departments.
ECONOMY
GDP $7,700,000,000. **Per capita** $871. **Monetary unit** CFA franc. **Trade partners** France, other Western European countries, U.S. **Exports** Cocoa, coffee, wood. **Imports** Machinery, petroleum, motor vehicles, consumer goods.
LAND
Description Western Africa. **Area** 123,847 mi² (320,763 km²). **Highest point** Mont Nimba, 5,748 ft (1,752 m). **Lowest point** Sea level.

People. Ivory Coast is composed almost entirely of black Africans from more than sixty ethnic groups. French is the nation's official language, a result of former French rule, but many indigenous languages are spoken as well. Traditional religions predominate, though a significant number of Ivorians are Muslim or Christian. Most Ivorians live in huts in small villages, but increased numbers have moved to the cities to find work. Overcrowding is a major problem in the cities.

Economy and the Land. Once solely dependent upon the export of cocoa and coffee, Ivory Coast now produces and exports a variety of agricultural goods. Forestland, when cleared, provides rich soil for agriculture—still the country's main activity. Petroleum, textile, and apparel industries also contribute to the strong economy. Ivory Coast pursues a policy of economic liberalism in which foreign investment is encouraged. As a result, foreigners hold high-level positions in most Ivory Coast industries. The hot, humid coastal region gives way to inland tropical forest. Beyond the forest lies savanna, and to the northwest are highlands.

History and Politics. Ivory Coast once consisted of many African kingdoms. French sailors gave the region its present name when they began trading for ivory and other goods in 1483. Missionaries arrived in 1637, but European settlement was hindered by the rugged coastline and intertribal conflicts. Ivory Coast became a French colony in 1893. Movements toward autonomy began after World War II, and in 1960 Ivory Coast declared itself an independent republic. The nation has enjoyed political stability since independence and has maintained close economic ties with France. Ivory Coast has one political party, which controls the government. Foreign policy stresses favorable relations with the West.   ∎

JAMAICA

Official name Jamaica
PEOPLE
Population 2,170,000. **Density** 511/mi² (197/km²). **Urban** 50%. **Capital** Kingston, 671,000. **Ethnic groups** African 76%, Afro-European 15%, East Indian and Afro–East Indian 4%, white 3%. **Languages** English. **Religions** Anglican, Baptist, other Protestant, Roman Catholic. **Life expectancy** 73 female, 69 male. **Literacy** 76%.
POLITICS
Government Parliamentary state. **Parties** Labor, People's National. **Suffrage** Universal, over 18. **Memberships** CW, OAS, UN. **Subdivisions** 12 parishes, 1 corporate area.

ECONOMY

GNP $3,000,000,000. **Per capita** $1,360. **Monetary unit** Dollar. **Trade partners** U.S., Venezuela, Caribbean countries. **Exports** Alumina, bauxite, sugar, bananas. **Imports** Fuels, machinery, transportation equipment, electrical equipment, food.

LAND

Description Caribbean island. **Area** 4,244 mi^2 (10,991 km^2). **Highest point** Blue Mountain Pk., 7,402 ft (2,256 m). **Lowest point** Sea level.

People. Most Jamaicans are of African or Afro-European descent, and the majority are Christian. English is the official language, but many Jamaicans also speak a local dialect of English. Population is concentrated on the coastal plains, where the main commercial crops are also grown.

Economy and the Land. Agriculture is the traditional mainstay, and more than a third of the population is engaged in farming. Sugarcane and bananas are principal crops. Mining is also important, and Jamaica is a leading producer of bauxite. The tropical climate, tempered by ocean breezes, makes the island a popular tourist destination. A mountainous inland region is surrounded by coastal plains and beaches.

History and Politics. Christopher Columbus claimed the island for Spain in 1494. As the enslaved native population died out, blacks were brought from Africa to work plantations. Britain invaded and gained control of Jamaica in the seventeenth century, and for a time the island was one of the most important sugar and slave centers of the New World. In 1838 the British abolished slavery, the plantation economy broke down, and most slaves became independent farmers. Local political control began in the 1930s, and the nation became fully independent in 1962. Since independence the nation has faced unemployment, inflation, and poverty, with periodic social unrest. Jamaica maintains a foreign policy of nonalignment. ∎

JAPAN

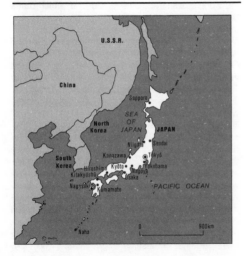

Official name Japan

PEOPLE

Population 120,200,000. **Density** 824/mi^2 (318/km^2). **Urban** 76%. **Capital** Tōkyō, Honshū I., 8,351,893. **Ethnic groups** Japanese. **Languages** Japanese. **Religions** Shinto and Buddhist 84%, others 16%. **Life expectancy** 79 female, 75 male. **Literacy** 99%.

POLITICS

Government Constitutional monarchy. **Parties** Clean Government, Communist, Liberal Democratic, Socialist. **Suffrage** Universal, over 20. **Memberships** OECD, UN. **Subdivisions** 47 prefectures.

ECONOMY

GNP $1,060,000,000,000. **Per capita** $8,947. **Monetary unit** Yen. **Trade partners** U.S., southeastern Asian countries, Western European countries, Saudi Arabia. **Exports** Machinery, motor vehicles, textiles, manufactured goods. **Imports** Petroleum, raw materials, food, machinery.

LAND

Description Eastern Asian islands. **Area** 145,834 mi^2 (377,708 km^2). **Highest point** Mt. Fuji, Honshū I., 12,388 ft (3,776 m). **Lowest point** Hachiro-gata reclamation area, Honshū I., 13 ft (4 m) below sea level.

People. The Japanese constitute Japan's major ethnic group; minority enclaves include Koreans and Chinese. Shintoism and Buddhism are the principal religions, and most Japanese observe both. Almost all the population lives on the coastal plains. Japan's culture blends East and West, with karate, tea ceremonies, and kimonos balanced by baseball, fast food, and business suits. Although its arts have been greatly influenced by China, Japan has developed distinctive music, literature, and painting.

Economy and the Land. One of the world's leading industrial powers, Japan is remarkable for its economic growth rate since World War II, considering it has few natural resources. It has also become famous for its innovative technology and continues to be a major user of robots in industry. Manufacturing is the basis of the economy, and Japan is a leading shipbuilder and produces machinery, cars, and electronic equipment. Its chemical and iron and steel industries are extremely profitable. Agriculture's part in the economy is small, since little of the rugged island terrain is arable. Fishing still plays a significant role in Japan's economy, though exports in this area have not been as high in recent years. Overseas trade has expanded rapidly since the 1960s, as Japan requires raw materials for its many industries. Trade barriers and the competitiveness of Japanese products overseas have led to trade deficits among Western nations. Japan's mountainous terrain includes both active and dormant volcanoes; earthquakes occasionally occur. The climate ranges from subtropical to temperate.

History and Politics. Legend states that Japan's first emperor was descended from the sun goddess and came to power around 600 B.C. The arrival of Buddhism, Confucianism, and new technologies from China in the fifth and sixth centuries A.D. revolutionized society. Feuding nobles controlled Japan between 1192 and 1867 and ruled as shoguns, or generals, in the name of the emperor. The warrior class, or samurai, developed early in this period. The arrival of Europeans in the sixteenth century caused fear of an invasion among the shoguns, and in the 1630s they dissolved all foreign contacts. Japan's isolation lasted until 1853, when Commodore Matthew Perry of the United States opened the nation to the West with a show of force. The subsequent Meiji Restoration modernized Japan by adopting Western technologies and legal systems and by stressing industrialization and education. Japan embarked on military expansion in the late nineteenth century, annexing Korea in 1910 and adding to its holdings after participating in World War I as a British ally. It occupied Manchuria in 1931 and invaded China in 1937. As part of the Axis powers in World War II, Japan attacked United States military bases in Pearl Harbor, Hawaii, in 1941. After the United States dropped atomic bombs on Hiroshima and Nagasaki in 1945, Japan surrendered. Allied forces occupied the nation until 1947. At that time the Japanese approved a constitution that shifted political power from the emperor to the people and that abolished the military. To uphold its own security, Japan maintains several branches of a self-defense force. Since the war, Japan has been ruled by conservative governments that seek close relations with the West. ∎

JERSEY

See UNITED KINGDOM.

JORDAN

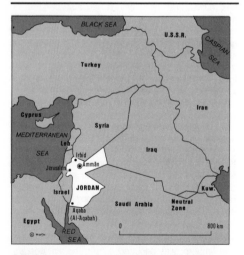

Official name Hashemite Kingdom of Jordan
PEOPLE
Population 2,475,000. **Density** 70/mi² (27/km²). **Urban** 60%. **Capital** Ammān, 648,587. **Ethnic groups** Arab 98%, Circassian 1%, Armenian 1%. **Languages** Arabic, English. **Religions** Sunni Muslim 92%, Christian 8%. **Life expectancy** 64 female, 60 male. **Literacy** 70%.

POLITICS
Government Constitutional monarchy. **Parties** None (illegal). **Suffrage** Universal, over 20. **Memberships** AL, UN. **Subdivisions** 5 governorates.
ECONOMY
GNP $4,900,000,000. **Per capita** $1,875. **Monetary unit** Dinar. **Trade partners** Saudi Arabia, U.S., West Germany, Japan, Iraq, Italy. **Exports** Phosphates, fruits, vegetables. **Imports** Machinery, transportation equipment, petroleum, food.
LAND
Description Southwestern Asia. **Area** 35,135 mi² (91,000 km²). **Highest point** Mt. Ramm, 5,755 ft (1,754 m). **Lowest point** Dead Sea, 1,312 ft (400 m) below sea level.

People. Most Jordanians are Arabs, but there are Circassian, Armenian, and Kurdish minorities, as well as a small nomadic population, the Bedouins, in desert areas. Many Palestinians live on the Jordan River's West Bank, once part of Palestine and now occupied by Israel. The Palestinians are refugees displaced by the Arab-Israeli wars; some have resettled and others live in refugee camps. Arabic is the official language, and most people are Sunni Muslim, legacies of the Muslim conquest of the seventh century A.D.

Economy and the Land. A nation with few natural resources, limited rainfall, and little arable land, Jordan has suffered further economic damage from an influx of refugees and the chronic political instability of the Middle East. In a 1967 war with Israel, Jordan lost the economically active West Bank, which made up about half the country's farmland. Agriculture remains the most important activity, and tourism has helped boost a weak economy that relies heavily on foreign aid and investment from the United States and Arab nations. There is some light industry and mining. The Jordan River divides Jordan into the West Bank and the East Bank, and the terrain is marked by deserts, mountains, and rolling plains. The climate ranges from Mediterranean in the west to desert in the east.

History and Politics. Jordan is the site of one of the world's oldest settlements, Jericho, which dates back to about 8000 B.C. The area later came under the rule of the Hebrews, Assyrians, Egyptians, Persians, Greeks, and Romans, and around A.D. 636 Arab Muslims conquered the region. Rule by the Ottoman Turks began in the sixteenth century, and in World War I Arab armies helped the British defeat Turkey. At the end of the war present-day Israel and Jordan became the British mandate of Palestine, which in 1922 was divided into the mandates of Transjordan, lying east of the Jordan River, and Palestine, lying to the west. Transjordan gained full independence in 1946. In 1948 Israel was created from the Palestine mandate, and Arab-Israeli fighting ensued. After capturing the West Bank, Transjordan was renamed Jordan in 1949. During the Arab-Israeli Six-Day War in 1967, this region and the Jordanian section of Jerusalem fell to Israel. As a result of these conflicts, Jordan's Palestinian-refugee population grew, and a 1970 civil war pitted the government against Palestinian guerrillas, who, like

Jordan, desired control of the West Bank. The guerrillas were expelled following the war, but subsequent Arab-Israeli hostilities led to Jordan's recognition of the Palestine Liberation Organization and support for the creation of an independent Palestinian state that would include the West Bank. Recent Israeli settlement of the area has led to violence between Arabs and Jews. ∎

KAMPUCHEA

Official name People's Republic of Kampuchea
PEOPLE
Population 6,180,000. **Density** 88/mi² (34/km²). **Urban** 15%. **Capital** Phnom Penh, 400,000. **Ethnic groups** Khmer 90%, Chinese 5%. **Languages** Khmer. **Religions** Theravada Buddhist 95%. **Life expectancy** 31 female, 29 male. **Literacy** 48%.
POLITICS
Government Socialist republic. **Parties** People's Revolutionary, United Front for National Construction and Defense. **Suffrage** Universal, over 18. **Memberships** UN. **Subdivisions** 19 provinces.
ECONOMY
Monetary unit Riel. **Trade partners** Vietnam, U.S.S.R. **Exports** Natural rubber. **Imports** Food, machinery, petroleum.
LAND
Description Southeastern Asia. **Area** 69,898 mi² (181,035 km²). **Highest point** Aoral, 5,810 ft (1,771 m). **Lowest point** Sea level.

People. The Khmer, one of the oldest peoples in Southeast Asia, constitute the major ethnic group in Kampuchea, formerly known as Cambodia. The population has declined significantly since the mid-1970s due to war, famine, human-rights abuses, and emigration. Because of an urban-evacuation campaign initiated by the Khmer Rouge, Kampuchea's previous regime, most Kampucheans live in rural areas, working as farmers or laborers. Although the new government does not encourage religious activity, it was often punished by death during the Khmer Rouge era, and the practice of Buddhism, the main religion, is on the rise.

Economy and the Land. Kampuchea's flat central region and wet climate make it well suited for rice production. Along with rubber, rice was the mainstay of the economy before the seventies, but the Vietnam and civil wars all but destroyed agriculture. This sector of the economy has begun to recover recently. A shortage of skilled labor, combined with the effects of war, have held back industry. The terrain is marked by the central plain, forests, and mountains in the south, west, and along the Thai border. The climate is tropical, with high rainfall and humidity.

History and Politics. Kampuchea traces its roots to the Hindu kingdoms of Funan and Chenla, which reigned in the early centuries A.D. The Angkor Empire dominated until the fifteenth century, incorporating much of present-day Laos, Thailand, and Vietnam and constructing the stone temples of Angkor Wat, considered one of Southeast Asia's greatest architectural achievements. By 1431 the Siamese had overrun the region, and subsequent years saw the rise of the Siamese, Vietnamese, and Lao. By the mid-1700s Cambodia's boundaries approximated those of today, and during the 1800s, as French control in Indochina expanded, the area became a French protectorate. Cambodia gained independence in 1953 under King Sihanouk, who, after changing his title to "prince," became prime minister in 1955 and head of state in 1960. In 1970, after Sihanouk was ousted, Lon Nol was installed as prime minister, and the monarchy of Cambodia changed to the Khmer Republic. During this time the Vietnam War spilled over the Khmer Republic's borders as United States forces made bombing raids against what they claimed were North Vietnamese bases. Resulting anti-American sentiment gave rise to discontent with Lon Nol's pro–United States regime. The Khmer Communists, or Khmer Rouge, seized power in 1975 and, led by Pol Pot, exiled most Kampucheans to the countryside. An estimated one million died under the Khmer Rouge, many executed because they were educated or had links to the former government. Vietnamese troops supported by some Kampuchean Communists invaded Kampuchea in late 1978, and by early 1979 they had overthrown the Khmer Rouge and established the People's Republic of Kampuchea. Several insurgent groups, including the Khmer Rouge, have continued guerrilla warfare against the Vietnamese-installed government. ∎

KENYA

Official name Republic of Kenya
PEOPLE
Population 18,970,000. **Density** 84/mi² (33/km²). **Urban** 13%. **Capital** Nairobi, 827,775. **Ethnic groups** Kikuyu 21%, Luhya 14%, Luo 13%, Kalenjin 11%, Kamba 11%, Kisii 6%, Meru 5%. **Languages** English, Swahili, indigenous. **Religions** Protestant 38%, Catholic 28%, indigenous 26%, Muslim 6%. **Life expectancy** 58 female, 54 male. **Literacy** 47%.

POLITICS
Government Republic. **Parties** Africa National Union.
Suffrage Universal, over 21. **Memberships** CW, OAU,
UN. **Subdivisions** 7 provinces, 1 capital district.
ECONOMY
GDP $6,300,000,000. **Per capita** $316. **Monetary unit**
Shilling. **Trade partners** Western European countries,
Japan, Iran, U.S. **Exports** Petroleum products, coffee,
tea, livestock products. **Imports** Petroleum, machinery,
motor vehicles, iron and steel.
LAND
Description Eastern Africa. **Area** 224,961 mi² (582,646
km²). **Highest point** Mt. Kenya, 17,058 ft (5,199 m).
Lowest point Sea level.

People. Nearly all Kenyans are black Africans belonging to one of more than forty different groups,
each with its own language and culture. Some
groups are nomadic, like the Masai. Arab and European minorities—found mostly along the coast—
reflect Kenya's history of foreign rule. Most Kenyans
live in the southwestern highlands, raising crops or
livestock. Over half of the citizens practice a form of
Christianity, while the rest pursue indigenous beliefs
or Islam. Swahili, a blend of Bantu and Arabic, is
the official language; it serves as a communication
link among Kenya's many ethnic groups. English is
also spoken. The national slogan of *harambee,* or
"pull together," illustrates the need for cooperation
among Kenya's diverse groups, and the government
promotes national unity.

Economy and the Land. Scenic terrain, tropical
beaches, and abundant wildlife have given Kenya a
thriving tourist industry, and land has been set aside
for national parks and game preserves. Agriculture
is the primary activity, even though the northern
three-fifths of the country is semidesert. The most
productive soils are found in the southwestern highlands, and coffee is the main export crop. Much of
the land is also used for raising livestock, another
leading economic contributor. Oil from other nations
is refined in Kenya, and food processing and cement
production are also significant activities. Kenya's climate varies from arid in the north, temperate in the
highlands, and tropical along the coast.

History and Politics. Remains of early humans
dating back more than two million years have been
found in Kenya. Settlers from other parts of Africa
arrived about 1000 B.C. A thousand years later Arab
traders reached the coast; they controlled the area
by the eighth century A.D. The Portuguese ruled the
coast between 1498 and the late 1600s. Kenya came
under British control in 1895 and was known as the
East African Protectorate. Opposition to British rule
began to mount in the 1940s as Kenyans demanded
a voice in government. The Mau Mau rebellion of the
fifties, an armed revolt, was an outgrowth of this
discontent. Kenya gained independence from Britain
in 1963 and became a republic in 1964. Its first president was Jomo Kenyatta, a Kikuyu who had been
an active leader in the previous revolt. Recent admin-
istrations have pursued a policy of Africanization,
under which land and other holdings have been
transferred from European to African hands. ∎

KERGUELEN ISLANDS

See FRANCE.

KIRIBATI

Official name Republic of Kiribati
PEOPLE
Population 62,000. **Density** 225/mi² (87/km²). **Urban**
32%. **Capital** Bairiki, Tarawa I., 1,800. **Ethnic groups**
Micronesian. **Languages** English, Gilbertese. **Religions**
Roman Catholic, Protestant. **Life expectancy** 54 female,
50 male. **Literacy** 90%.
POLITICS
Government Republic. **Parties** Christian Democratic,
Gilbertese National. **Memberships** CW.
ECONOMY
GDP $36,000,000. **Per capita** $630. **Monetary unit**
Australian dollar. **Trade partners** Australia, New Zealand.
Exports Copra, fish. **Imports** Food, fuels, transportation
equipment.
LAND
Description Central Pacific islands. **Area** 275 mi²
(712 km²). **Highest point** 265 ft (81 m). **Lowest point**
Sea level.

People. The people of Kiribati, a nation of thirty-
three islands in the central Pacific, are mostly Micronesian. Almost all the population lives on the Gilbert Islands in small villages and practices Roman
Catholicism or Protestantism. English, the official
language, and Gilbertese are spoken.

Economy and the Land. A small, unskilled work
force combined with small land area and few natural
resources have given Kiribati a subsistence economy. Phosphate deposits have been depleted, and
copra is now the main export. Kiribati depends on
economic aid from Australia, New Zealand, and
Great Britain. The islands of Kiribati are almost all
coral reefs, composed of hard sand and little soil;
many surround a lagoon. The climate is tropical.

History and Politics. Kiribati was invaded by Samoa in the 1400s. From 1916 the islands were part of the British Gilbert and Ellice Islands Colony. Fighting between the United States and Japan took place during World War II on Tarawa Island. The Ellice Islands became independent in 1978 as the nation of Tuvalu, and the Republic of Kiribati came into existence a year later. ∎

KOREA, NORTH

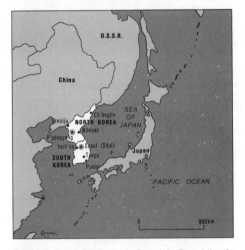

Official name Democratic People's Republic of Korea
PEOPLE
Population 19,855,000. **Density** 427/mi² (165/km²). **Urban** 33%. **Capital** P'yŏngyang, 1,700,000. **Ethnic groups** Korean. **Languages** Korean. **Religions** Buddhist, Confucian. **Life expectancy** 65 female, 61 male. **Literacy** 95%.
POLITICS
Government Socialist republic. **Parties** Workers'. **Suffrage** Universal, over 17. **Memberships** None. **Subdivisions** 11 provinces.
ECONOMY
GNP $16,200,000,000. **Per capita** $786. **Monetary unit** Won. **Trade partners** U.S.S.R., Japan, West Germany. **Exports** Minerals, machinery, textile fibers. **Imports** Petroleum, machinery, food, coal.
LAND
Description Eastern Asia. **Area** 46,540 mi² (120,538 km²). **Highest point** Mt. Paeku, 9,003 ft (2,744 m). **Lowest point** Sea level.

People. Despite a history of invasions, North Korea has a homogeneous population with virtually no minorities. Several dialects of Korean are spoken, and North Koreans use the Hankul, or Korean, alphabet exclusively. Traditionally, Korean religions included Buddhism and Confucianism, although religious activity has been discouraged by the government. Urban population has grown rapidly since 1953 as the result of an emphasis on manufacturing. The nation remains more sparsely populated than South Korea.

Economy and the Land. The division of the Korean peninsula after World War II left North Korea with most of the industry and natural resources but little agricultural land and few skilled workers. The country has succeeded in becoming one of the most industrialized nations in Asia and has overcome its agricultural problems as well. Most industry is government owned, and mines produce a variety of minerals. Farming is collectivized, and output has been aided by irrigation and other modern practices. The Soviet Union and China aided North Korea's development, but the theory of self-reliance was the government's guiding principle. A central mountainous region is bounded by coastal plains, and the climate is temperate.

History and Politics. History of North and South Korea follows SOUTH KOREA. ∎

KOREA, SOUTH

Official name Republic of Korea
PEOPLE
Population 42,315,000. **Density** 1,113/mi² (430/km²). **Urban** 57%. **Capital** Seoul, 8,366,756. **Ethnic groups** Korean. **Languages** Korean. **Religions** Buddhist, Christian, Shamanic, Confucian. **Life expectancy** 69 female, 64 male. **Literacy** 90%.
POLITICS
Government Republic. **Parties** Democratic, Democratic Justice, National. **Suffrage** Universal, over 20. **Memberships** None. **Subdivisions** 9 provinces, 4 independent cities.
ECONOMY
GNP $70,800,000,000. **Per capita** $1,800. **Monetary unit** Won. **Trade partners** U.S., Japan, Middle Eastern countries, West Germany. **Exports** Textiles, transportation equipment, footwear, electrical machinery. **Imports** Petroleum, machinery, transportation equipment, chemicals.
LAND
Description Eastern Asia. **Area** 38,025 mi² (98,484 km²). **Highest point** Mt. Halla, 6,398 ft (1,950 m). **Lowest point** Sea level.

People. The homogeneous quality of South Korea's population is similar to that of North Korea. Population density, however, is much greater in South Korea: about two million Koreans migrated to the south following World War II. The major language, Korean, is written predominantly in the Hankul, or Korean, alphabet, with some Chinese characters. Buddhism is practiced by most South Koreans, although Confucianism has influenced much of life.

Economy and the Land. South Korea was traditionally the peninsula's agricultural zone, and following the 1945 partition of the country, the south was left with little industry and few resources but abundant manpower. The economy has advanced rapidly since 1953, and today agriculture and industry are of almost equal importance. Rice, barley, and beans are principal crops; machinery and textiles are significant manufactured products. Central mountains give way to plains in the south and west, and the climate is temperate.

History and Politics. Korea's strategic location between Russia, China, and Japan has made it prey to foreign powers. China conquered the northern part of the peninsula in 108 B.C., influencing culture, religion, and government, and Mongols controlled Korea for most of the thirteenth and fourteenth centuries. The rule of the Yi dynasty began in 1392 and endured until 1910, when Japan annexed Korea. In 1945, following Japan's defeat in World War II, Soviet troops occupied northern Korea while the United States military occupied the south. The Soviet Union, the United States, and Great Britain tried to aid unification of the country but failed, and a subsequent plan for United Nations–supervised elections was opposed by the Soviets. In 1948 two separate governments were formed: the northern Democratic People's Republic of Korea and the southern Republic of Korea. Both governments claimed the peninsula, and relations became strained. After several border clashes, North Korea invaded South Korea in 1950. Chinese Communists fought on the side of North Korea, and United States forces aided the south. The war ended in 1953 with an armistice, but a permanent peace treaty has never been signed. Both countries continue to claim the entire peninsula. Sporadic fighting has broken out between the north and south in recent years, and tense relations have stalled steps toward reunification.

North Korea. The Democratic People's Republic of Korea was established in 1948, several months after the formation of South Korea. The country incurred about 2.5 million casualties during the war with South Korea. Following the war, the government moved quickly to modernize industry and the military; North Korea maintains one of the world's largest armies. Despite its ties to the Soviet Union and China, North Korea strives for an independent foreign policy based on the country's emphasis on self-reliance.

South Korea. The Republic of Korea came into being on August 15, 1948. Since the war, the country has experienced a presidential overthrow, military rule, and a presidential assassination. Continued claims by students and others of government civil-rights abuses erupted in violence in 1979, when civilians and military personnel clashed. The fifth constitution since 1948, initiating the Fifth Republic, was adopted in 1980. ∎

KUWAIT

Official name State of Kuwait
PEOPLE
Population 1,815,000. **Density** 264/mi² (102/km²). **Urban** 90%. **Capital** Kuwait, 60,365. **Ethnic groups** Kuwaiti 39%, other Arab 39%, Southern Asian 9%, Iranian 4%. **Languages** Arabic, English. **Religions** Muslim 95%. **Life expectancy** 73 female, 68 male. **Literacy** 71%.
POLITICS
Government Constitutional monarchy. **Parties** None (prohibited). **Suffrage** Native-born and naturalized males, over 21 (20-year residency required after naturalization).

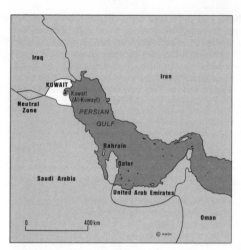

Memberships AL, OPEC, UN. **Subdivisions** 3 governorates.
ECONOMY
GNP $27,600,000,000. **Per capita** $25,850. **Monetary unit** Dinar. **Trade partners** Japan, Western European countries, U.S. **Exports** Petroleum, petroleum products. **Imports** Machinery, transportation equipment, manufactured goods, food.
LAND
Description Southwestern Asia. **Area** 6,880 mi² (17,818 km²). **Highest point** 951 ft (290 m). **Lowest point** Sea level.

People. Kuwait's recent prosperity has drawn emigrants from the Persian Gulf and beyond, giving it a diverse population; there are Palestinian, Iranian, and Pakistani minorities. The population has risen dramatically since the thirties, when the oil industry began. Arabic is the official language; English is also taught and widely spoken. Almost all residents of Kuwait observe Islam, the state religion. Most belong to the Sunni branch, but there is a sizable Shiite community.

Economy and the Land. The economy centers on the largely government-controlled petroleum industry. Kuwait is one of the world's largest oil producers, and its oil reserves are among the world's most extensive. However, oil production and refining require a limited work force, and Kuwait has recently tried to diversify to create more jobs. Commercial fishing and shrimp exporting are gaining importance in Kuwait's economy. Because of the desert terrain, agriculture is marginal. Kuwait's climate is subtropical.

History and Politics. Arab nomads settled Kuwait Bay around A.D. 1700. The Al Sabah dynasty has ruled the nation since the mid-1700s. Alarmed by the designs of the Turks and Arabs, Kuwait in 1899 signed an agreement with Britain in which Britain guaranteed Kuwait's defense. Drilling for oil began in 1936, and by 1945 Kuwait had become a major exporter. Independence came in 1961. Iraq immediately made a claim to the state but was discouraged from attacking by the arrival of British troops. Official border agreements have never been made between Kuwait and Iraq. Kuwait briefly cut off oil shipments to Western nations in retaliation for their support of Israel in the 1967 and 1973 Arab-Israeli wars. Kuwait's remarkable oil wealth, which transformed it from a poor nation into an affluent one, has enabled it to offer its citizens a wide range of benefits and to aid other Arab states. Poised at the tip of the Persian Gulf, Kuwait must always be sensitive to the interests of its many neighbors. The ongoing Iran-Iraq war has presented a problem, as have tensions among various religious and ethnic groups. Despite the conflicts, Kuwait strives to remain neutral. ∎

LAOS

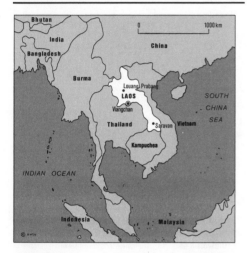

Official name Lao People's Democratic Republic
PEOPLE
Population 3,775,000. **Density** 41/mi² (16/km²). **Urban** 13%. **Capital** Viangchan, 174,229. **Ethnic groups** Lao 48%; Phoutheung 25%; Tai 14%; Miao, Yao, and others 13%. **Languages** Lao, French. **Religions** Buddhist 50%, animist and others 50%. **Life expectancy** 45 female, 42 male. **Literacy** 28%.
POLITICS
Government Socialist republic. **Parties** People's Revolutionary. **Suffrage** Universal, over 18. **Memberships** UN. **Subdivisions** 13 provinces.
ECONOMY
GNP $320,000,000. **Per capita** $90. **Monetary unit** Kip. **Trade partners** Thailand, U.S.S.R., Eastern European countries, Singapore. **Exports** Hydroelectric power, wood, coffee, tin. **Imports** Food, petroleum, machinery, transportation equipment.
LAND
Description Southeastern Asia, landlocked. **Area** 91,429 mi² (236,800 km²). **Highest point** Phu Bia, 9,252 ft (2,820 m). **Lowest point** 230 ft (70 m).

People. Laos is peopled by many ethnic groups, each with its own customs, religion, and language. Its history of culturally diverse communities is mirrored in the political divisions of recent years. The Lao are numerically and politically dominant, and Lao is the official language. Small Vietnamese and Chinese minorities exist. Most of Laos's residents are farmers engaged in rice production.

Economy and the Land. Years of warfare, a landlocked position, and a poor transportation system have hindered the development of Laos's economy. Although agriculture is the basis of the economy, very little of the fertile land is cultivated. Substantial mineral deposits and large timber reserves also have not been exploited to their potential. Manufacturing is limited, partly because of an unskilled work force. Situated in a mountainous, densely forested region, Laos has a tropical climate and experiences seasonal monsoons.

History and Politics. By A.D. 900 the forerunners of the Lao had arrived from southern China. The first united Lao kingdom was founded in 1353 and included much of modern Thailand. It dissolved into three rival states by the early 1700s, setting the stage for interference by Burma, Vietnam, and Siam, present-day Thailand. In 1899 France made Laos part of French Indochina. Laos gained some autonomy in 1949, but this period saw the growth of Communist and anti-Communist factions whose rivalry would prevent any unified government until 1975. Although Geneva peace agreements declared Laos's neutrality in 1954 and 1962, the nation became increasingly embroiled in the Vietnam War as belligerents in that conflict entered Laos. A protracted civil war began in 1960 between the Pathet Lao, a Communist faction aided by the North Vietnamese, and government forces backed by the Thai and South Vietnamese. A cease-fire was signed in 1973 and a new coalition government was formed a year later. Following Communist victories in Vietnam and Kampuchea, the Pathet Lao gained control in 1975 and established the Lao People's Democratic Republic. Opposed to Communist rule, many Lao abandoned their country to seek refuge in Thailand and the United States. Laos retains close ties with Vietnam. ∎

LEBANON

Official name Republic of Lebanon
PEOPLE
Population 2,610,000. **Density** 650/mi² (251/km²). **Urban** 78%. **Capital** Beirut, 474,870. **Ethnic groups** Arab 93%, Armenian 6%. **Languages** Arabic, French, English. **Religions** Christian 50%, Muslim and Druze 50%. **Life expectancy** 68 female, 65 male. **Literacy** 75%.
POLITICS
Government Republic. **Parties** Political activity organized along sectarian lines, with numerous groups. **Suffrage** Females, over 21 (with elementary education); males, over 21. **Memberships** AL, UN. **Subdivisions** 5 provinces.

ECONOMY

GDP $4,100,000,000. **Per capita** $1,316. **Monetary unit** Pound. **Trade partners** Middle Eastern countries, Western European countries, U.S. **Exports** Fruits, vegetables, textiles. **Imports** Metals, machinery, food.

LAND

Description Southwestern Asia. **Area** 4,015 mi² (10,400 km²). **Highest point** Mt. Sauda, 10,115 ft (3,083 m). **Lowest point** Sea level.

People. Traditionally home to many diverse groups, Lebanon has recently been shaken by the conflicting demands of its population. Almost all Lebanese are of Arab stock, and Arabic is the official language. Palestinian refugees have settled here since the creation of Israel in 1948, many of them living in refugee camps. Lebanon's religious makeup is notable for its variety, encompassing seventeen recognized sects. There has been no official census since 1932, and although those figures show almost an equal division between Islam and Christianity, recent estimates indicate that Muslims are now a majority. Among Muslims there are members of the majority Shiite, minority Sunni, and Druze sects, while most Christians are Maronites.

Economy and the Land. Situated strategically between the West and the Middle East, Lebanon has long been a center of commerce. Its economy is fueled by the service sector, particularly banking. Prolonged fighting, beginning with the 1975 civil war, has greatly damaged all economic activity. Much of the work force is engaged in agriculture, and a variety of crops is grown. The coastal area consists of a plain, behind which lie mountain ranges separated by a fertile valley. The climate is Mediterranean.

History and Politics. The Phoenicians settled parts of Lebanon about 3000 B.C. and were followed by Egyptian, Assyrian, Persian, Greek, and Roman rulers. Christianity came to the area during the Byzantine Empire, around A.D. 325, and Islam followed in the seventh century, brought by Arab Muslims. In 1516 Lebanon was incorporated into the Ottoman Empire. Between the end of World War I, when the Ottoman Empire collapsed, and 1943, when Lebanon became independent, it was a French mandate. A government in which Muslims and Christians shared power was set up after independence. Opposition to Lebanon's close ties to the West led to a 1958 insurrection, which United States marines put down at the government's request. The Palestine Liberation Organization (PLO), a group working to establish a Palestinian state, began operating from bases in Lebanon and in the late sixties clashed with Israel in southern Lebanon. The presence of the PLO in Lebanon divided Muslims, who generally supported it, from Christians, who opposed it. The increasing Muslim population also demanded a greater voice in the government. Civil war between Muslims and Christians broke out in 1975, and fighting ended the next year with the requested aid of Syrian deterrent forces. Internal instability continued, however, along with Israeli-Palestinian hostilities; in June 1982 Israel invaded Lebanon, driving the PLO from Beirut and the south. Hundreds of Palestinian refugees were killed by Christian militiamen in September. A multinational peacekeeping force arrived shortly afterward but left after falling victim to terrorist attacks. Israel began a gradual withdrawal from Lebanon in 1985, and Syrian troops yet occupy parts of the country. Attempts to reconcile warring factions have been unsuccessful, and fighting in Lebanon has continued. ∎

LESOTHO

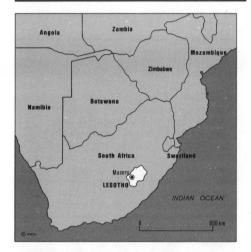

Official name Kingdom of Lesotho

PEOPLE

Population 1,495,000. **Density** 128/mi² (49/km²). **Urban** 5%. **Capital** Maseru, 14,686. **Ethnic groups** Sotho. **Languages** English, Sesotho. **Religions** Christian 80%, indigenous 20%. **Life expectancy** 54 female, 51 male. **Literacy** 55%.

POLITICS

Government Monarchy. **Parties** Basotho National, Basutoland Congress. **Suffrage** Universal adult. **Memberships** CW, OAU, UN. **Subdivisions** 10 districts.

ECONOMY

GNP $569,000,000. **Per capita** $424. **Monetary unit** Loti. **Trade partners** South Africa. **Exports** Wool, mohair, food. **Imports** Food, construction materials, clothing, vehicles.

LAND

Description Southern Africa, landlocked. **Area** 11,720 mi² (30,355 km²). **Highest point** Mt. Ntlenyana, 11,424 ft (3,482 m).

People. The Sotho, a black African group, comprise Lesotho's majority population. Most Sotho live in the lowlands and raise livestock and crops. The official languages are Sesotho, a Bantu tongue, and English. The traditional religion is based on ancestor worship, but many Sotho are Christian. A system of tribal chieftaincy is followed locally.

Economy and the Land. Surrounded by South Africa and having few resources, Lesotho is almost entirely dependent on South Africa for economic survival. Much of the male population must seek employment there, usually spending several months a year in South African mines or industries. Agriculture remains at the subsistence level, and soil erosion threatens production. Livestock raising represents a significant part of Lesotho's economy. Wool and mohair are among the chief exports. Diamond mining, one of the few industries, employs a small portion of the population. Most of the terrain is mountainous; the fairly high elevations give Lesotho a temperate climate.

History and Politics. Refugees from tribal wars in southern Africa arrived in what is now Lesotho between the sixteenth and nineteenth centuries A.D. Chief Moshoeshoe united the Sotho tribes in 1818 and led them in war against the Boers, settlers of Dutch or Huguenot descent. At Moshoeshoe's request, Basutoland came under British protection in 1868. It resisted attempts at absorption by the Union of South Africa and became the independent Kingdom of Lesotho in 1966. The government of Prime Minister Leabua Jonathan, threatened by an apparent defeat at the polls, suspended the constitution in 1970 and set up a provisional assembly in 1973. Opposition to the Jonathan administration has erupted in periodic violence. Lesotho, although unforgiving of South Africa's racial policies, is forced by its geographic and economic situation to cooperate with its powerful neighbor. After claims by South Africa that Lesotho was harboring members of the antiapartheid African National Congress, the two countries agreed in 1983 to deny shelter to groups that might damage each other's security. ■

LIBERIA

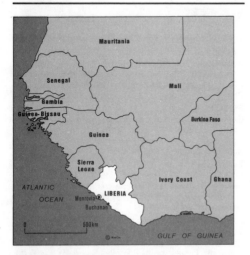

Official name Republic of Liberia
PEOPLE
Population 2,195,000. **Density** 51/mi² (20/km²). **Urban** 33%. **Capital** Monrovia, 243,243. **Ethnic groups** African 95%, descendants of freed American slaves 5%.
Languages English, indigenous. **Religions** Indigenous 75%, Muslim 15%, Christian 10%. **Life expectancy** 55 female, 52 male. **Literacy** 24%.

POLITICS
Government Provisional military government. **Parties** None (suspended). **Suffrage** Property owners, over 18. **Memberships** OAU, UN. **Subdivisions** 10 counties.
ECONOMY
GDP $800,000,000. **Per capita** $385. **Monetary unit** U.S. dollar. **Trade partners** U.S., West Germany, other Western European countries. **Exports** Iron ore, natural rubber, diamonds, wood. **Imports** Machinery, petroleum, transportation equipment, food.
LAND
Description Western Africa. **Area** 43,000 mi² (111,369 km²). **Highest point** Mt. Wuteve, 4,528 ft (1,380 m). **Lowest point** Sea level.

People. Most Liberians belong to indigenous black groups, which number about twenty. Few are descended from the freed American slaves who founded modern Liberia, but this group—known as Americo-Liberians—has traditionally been politically dominant. The official language is English, and more than twenty other tongues are also spoken. Most people are farmers and practice traditional animist beliefs, although Islam and Christianity also have adherents. The only black African state to escape colonialism, Liberia works to preserve its cultural heritage.

Economy and the Land. Liberia owes its healthy economy largely to an open-door policy, which has made Liberia's extensive resources attractive to foreign nations. Two of the most important activities, iron-ore mining and rubber production, were developed by Western firms. Large timber reserves have not yet been fully exploited. Liberia also profits from the vast merchant fleet registered under its flag. Land regions include a coastal plain, plateaus, and low mountains. The hot, humid climate is marked by distinct wet and dry seasons.

History and Politics. Early settlers are thought to have migrated from the north and east between the twelfth and seventeenth centuries A.D. Trade between Europeans and coastal groups developed after the Portuguese visited the area in the late 1400s. The American Colonization Society, a private United States organization devoted to resettling freed slaves, purchased land in Liberia, and in 1822 the first settlers landed at the site of Monrovia. The settlers declared their independence in 1847, setting up a government based on the United States model and creating Africa's first independent republic. For the next century the Liberian government endured attempts at colonization by France and Britain as well as internal tribal opposition. The string of Americo-Liberian rulers was broken in 1980, when a small group of soldiers of African descent toppled the government and imposed martial law, subsequently instituting preparations for a return to civilian rule. ■

LIBYA

Official name Socialist People's Libyan Arab Jamahiriya

PEOPLE
Population 3,785,000. **Density** 5.6/mi² (2.2/km²). **Urban** 52%. **Capital** Tripoli, 858,500. **Ethnic groups** Arab-Berber 97%. **Languages** Arabic. **Religions** Sunni Muslim 97%. **Life expectancy** 59 female, 55 male. **Literacy** 50%.

POLITICS
Government Socialist republic. **Parties** None. **Suffrage** Universal adult. **Memberships** AL, OPEC, UN. **Subdivisions** 10 provinces.

ECONOMY
GDP $26,500,000,000. **Per capita** $7,600. **Monetary unit** Pound. **Trade partners** Italy, West Germany, Spain, France. **Exports** Petroleum. **Imports** Machinery, transportation equipment, food, manufactured goods.

LAND
Description Northern Africa. **Area** 679,362 mi² (1,759,540 km²). **Highest point** Bette, 7,434 ft (2,266 m). **Lowest point** Sabkhat Ghuzzayil, 138 ft (42 m) below sea level.

People. The Berbers were the original settlers of Libya, but today the population is largely mixed Arab and Berber. Almost all Libyans live along the coast, although there are some nomadic groups in desert areas. Large migrations from rural areas to the cities have accompanied Libya's oil-based prosperity. Islam is by far the most popular religion, and nearly all Libyans speak Arabic. Traditional social orders still exist, despite centuries of foreign rule.

Economy and the Land. The discovery of oil in 1959 propelled Libya from the ranks of the world's poorest nations to one of its leading oil producers. It has used its revenues to develop industry and agriculture in an effort to diversify the economy. Because most of Libya is covered by the Sahara Desert, agriculture is limited, and it has been further hurt by the exodus of Libyan farmers from the countryside. The climate is desert except for the coast, which has moderate temperatures.

History and Politics. For much of its history Libya was dominated by the empires of the Mediterranean, from the Phoenician and Carthaginian to the Greek and Roman. In the seventh century A.D. the area was taken by Muslim Arabs, whose language and reli-

gion transformed Libyan culture. Although the Ottoman Turks conquered the region in the sixteenth century, local rulers remained virtually autonomous. Italy invaded Libya in 1911, and the country became an Italian colony. Following World War II, British and French forces occupied the area until a United Nations resolution made Libya an independent nation in 1951. A monarchy ruled until 1969, when a military coup established a republic with Colonel Mu'ammar Muhammad al-Qadhafi in control. Under his leadership, Libya has backed Arab unity and the Palestinian cause, opposed foreign influences, and created a welfare system. ∎

LIECHTENSTEIN

Official name Principality of Liechtenstein
PEOPLE
Population 27,000. **Density** 435/mi² (169/km²). **Capital** Vaduz, 4,980. **Ethnic groups** Alemannic 95%, Italian and others 5%. **Languages** German. **Religions** Roman Catholic 83%, Protestant 7%. **Literacy** 100%.

POLITICS
Government Constitutional monarchy. **Parties** Fatherland Union, Progressive Citizens'. **Suffrage** Universal adult male, limited adult female. **Memberships** None. **Subdivisions** 11 communes.

ECONOMY
GDP $439,400,000. **Per capita** $16,900. **Monetary unit** Swiss franc. **Trade partners** Switzerland, other Western European countries. **Exports** Metal products, precision instruments, artificial teeth.

LAND
Description Central Europe, landlocked. **Area** 62 mi² (160 km²). **Highest point** Vorder-Grauspitz, 8,527 ft (2,599 m). **Lowest point** Ruggelles Riet, 1,411 ft (430 m).

People. In spite of its location at the crossroads of Europe, Liechtenstein has retained a largely homogeneous ethnicity. Almost all Liechtensteiners are descended from the Alemanni, a Germanic tribe, and many speak the Alemanni dialect. German, however, is the official language. Roman Catholicism is the most widely practiced religion, but a Protestant minority also exists. Most of the country is mountainous, and population is concentrated on the fertile plains adjacent to the Rhine River, which forms the country's western boundary. Most Liechtensteiners work in factories or in trades.

Economy and the Land. The last few decades have seen the economy shift from agricultural to highly industrialized. Despite this growth in industry, Liechtenstein has not experienced a serious pollution problem, and the government continues its work to prevent the problem from occurring. An economic alliance with Switzerland dating from 1923 has been profoundly beneficial to Liechtenstein: the two nations form a customs union and use the same currency. Other important sources of revenue are tourism, the sale of postage stamps, and taxation of foreign businesses headquartered here. Most of Liechtenstein, one of the world's smallest nations, is covered by the Alps; nonetheless, its climate is mild.

History and Politics. Early inhabitants of what is now Liechtenstein included the Celts, Romans, and Alemanni, who arrived about A.D. 500. The area became part of the empire of the Frankish king Charlemagne in the late 700s, and following Charlemagne's death, it was divided into the lordships of Vaduz and Schellenberg. By 1719, when the state became part of the Holy Roman Empire, the Austrian House of Liechtenstein had purchased both lordships, uniting them as the Imperial Principality of Liechtenstein. The nation's independence dates from the abolition of the empire by France's Napoleon Bonaparte in 1806. Liechtenstein was neutral in both world wars and has remained unaffected by European conflicts. The government is a hereditary constitutional monarchy; the prince is the head of the House of Liechtenstein, thus chief of state, and the prime minister is the head of government. Women gained limited suffrage in 1984. ∎

LUXEMBOURG

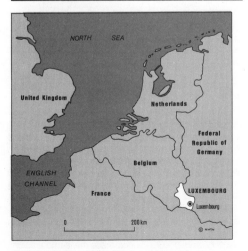

Official name Grand Duchy of Luxembourg

PEOPLE
Population 365,000. **Density** 366/mi² (141/km²). **Urban** 78%. **Capital** Luxembourg, 78,924. **Ethnic groups** Mixed Celtic, French, and German. **Languages** Luxembourgish, French, German. **Religions** Roman Catholic 97%. **Life expectancy** 76 female, 71 male. **Literacy** 100%.

POLITICS
Government Constitutional monarchy. **Parties** Christian Socialist, Liberal, Socialist Workers'. **Suffrage** Universal, over 18. **Memberships** NATO, OECD, UN. **Subdivisions** 3 districts.

ECONOMY
GNP $3,400,000,000. **Per capita** $9,289. **Monetary unit** Franc. **Trade partners** West Germany, Belgium, France. **Exports** Steel, plastic, and rubber products. **Imports** Coal, petroleum, consumer goods.

LAND
Description Western Europe, landlocked. **Area** 998 mi² (2,586 km²). **Highest point** 1,834 ft (559 m). **Lowest point** 427 ft (130 m).

People. Luxembourg's population bears the imprint of foreign influences, yet retains an individual character. Most Luxembourgers are a blend of Celtic, French, and German stock. German and French are official languages, as is Luxembourgish, an indigenous German dialect. Roman Catholicism is observed by virtually all the population. There are significant communities of guest workers from several European nations.

Economy and the Land. Luxembourg's steel industry forms the basis of its economy, and the country has compensated for a worldwide drop in the steel market by developing financial services, notably banking. Manufacturing of plastics and chemicals is also important, as is tourism. Luxembourg's trade benefits from the country's membership in the European Community and the Benelux union. Luxembourg has two distinct regions: the mountainous, wooded north and the open, rolling south, known as Bon Pays. The climate is temperate but somewhat cool and rainy.

History and Politics. The present city of Luxembourg developed from a castle built in A.D. 963 by Count Siegfried of Ardennes. Several heavily fortified towns grew up around the castle, and the area became known as the Gibraltar of the North because of those fortifications. The duchy remained semiautonomous until the Burgundians conquered the area in 1443. Various European powers ruled Luxembourg for most of the next four centuries, and in 1815 the duchy was elevated to a grand duchy. It became autonomous in 1839 and was recognized in 1867 as an independent state. Despite its declaration of neutrality, Luxembourg was occupied by Germany in both world wars. The country maintains a pro-Western, pan-European stance in its foreign relations. ∎

MACAO

Official name Macao

PEOPLE
Population 310,000. **Density** 51,667/mi² (19,375/km²).
Urban 97%. **Capital** Macao, 253,376. **Ethnic groups**
Chinese 98%, Portuguese 2%. **Languages** Portuguese,
Chinese dialects. **Religions** Buddhist, Roman Catholic.
Literacy Portuguese and Macanese 100%.

POLITICS
Government Overseas province (Portugal). **Parties**
None. (Civic associations are represented in legislature.)
Suffrage Portuguese, Chinese, and foreign residents,
over 18. **Memberships** None. **Subdivisions** 2 districts.

ECONOMY
GNP $640,000,000. **Per capita** $2,246. **Monetary unit**
Pataca. **Trade partners** Hong Kong, China, West
Germany, France. **Exports** Textiles, clothing. **Imports**
Food, consumer goods.

LAND
Description Eastern Asia (islands and peninsula on
China's southeastern coast). **Area** 6 mi² (16 km²).
Highest point Coloane Alto, 571 ft (174 m). **Lowest
point** Sea level.

People. Situated on the southeastern China coast,
17 miles (27.4 kilometers) west of Hong Kong, Macao
is populated almost entirely by Chinese. An overseas province of Portugal, minorities include people
of Portuguese and mixed Chinese-Portuguese descent. Several Chinese dialects are widely spoken,
and Portuguese is the official language. Buddhism
is Macao's principal religion, and a very small
percentage of its population practices Roman
Catholicism.

Economy and the Land. Tourism, gambling, and
light industry help make up Macao's economy; however, its leading industries are clothing and textiles,
which employ the majority of the labor force. Macao
has been likened to Hong Kong because of its textile
exports, yet it remains a heavy importer, relying on
China for drinking water and much of its food supply.
The province consists of the city of Macao, located
on a peninsula, and the nearby islands of Taipa and
Coloane. The climate is maritime tropical, with cool
winters and warm summers.

History and Politics. Macao became a Portuguese
trading post in 1557. It flourished as the midpoint for
trade between China and Japan but declined when
Hong Kong became a trading power in the mid-
1800s. Macao remained a neutral port during World
War II and was economically prosperous. Although
the government is nominally directed by Portugal,
any policies relating to Macao are subject to China's
approval. Macao is the oldest European settlement
in the Far East. ∎

MADAGASCAR

Official name Democratic Republic of
Madagascar
PEOPLE
Population 9,775,000. **Density** 43/mi² (17/km²). **Urban**
18%. **Capital** Antananarivo, 484,000. **Ethnic groups** 18
Malagasy groups. **Languages** Malagasy, French.
Religions Indigenous 52%, Christian 41%, Muslim 7%.
Life expectancy 49 female, 46 male. **Literacy** 53%.

POLITICS
Government Socialist republic. **Parties** Advance Guard
of the Revolution, Congress for Independence. **Suffrage**
Universal, over 18. **Memberships** OAU, UN.
Subdivisions 6 provinces.

ECONOMY
GDP $3,200,000,000. **Per capita** $360. **Monetary unit**
Franc. **Trade partners** France, U.S., West Germany,
Japan, Italy. **Exports** Coffee, vanilla, sugar, cloves.
Imports Consumer goods, food, machinery, petroleum,
fertilizer.

LAND
Description Western Indian Ocean island. **Area** 226,658
mi² (587,041 km²). **Highest point** Maromokotro, 9,436 ft
(2,876 m). **Lowest point** Sea level.

People. Most of the population is of mixed African
and Indonesian descent. Those who live on the
coast, the *cotiers,* are of predominantly African origin, while those on the inland plateau have Asian
roots. There is a long-standing rivalry between the
cotiers and the inland groups, most of whom belong
to the Merina people. The official languages are
French and Malagasy. Sizable Christian communities exist, but most Malagasy practice indigenous
beliefs that involve ancestor worship.

Economy and the Land. Madagascar is chiefly an
agricultural nation, with the majority of the work force
engaged in farming or herding. Overpopulation and
outmoded cultivation have recently cut into yields of
rice, an important crop, and other products. Varied
mineral resources, including oil, point to possible expansion. The climate is tropical on the coastal plains
and moderate in the inland highlands.

History and Politics. Madagascar's first settlers
are thought to be Indonesians, who brought African
wives and slaves around two thousand years ago.
Arab traders established themselves on the coast in
the seventh century. The Portuguese first sighted the
island in the 1500s, and other Europeans followed.
The Merina kingdom, based in the central plateau,
gained control over most of the island in the 1790s.
French influence grew throughout the nineteenth
century, and in 1896 France made the island a colony
after subduing the Merina. Resentment of French

rule continued, culminating in an armed revolt in 1947. Moves were made toward autonomy, and full independence came in 1960. After twelve years of rule by the same president, a coup placed the military in power. A new constitution was adopted in 1975 that established the Democratic Republic of Madagascar, a highly centralized socialist state. ∎

MADEIRA ISLANDS

See PORTUGAL.

MALAWI

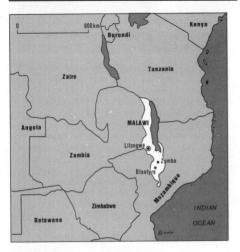

Official name Republic of Malawi
PEOPLE
Population 6,940,000. **Density** 152/mi² (59/km²). **Urban** 8%. **Capital** Lilongwe, 98,718. **Ethnic groups** Chewa, Nyanja, Tumbuka, Yao, Lomwe, others. **Languages** Chichewa, English. **Religions** Protestant 55%, Roman Catholic 20%, Muslim 20%. **Life expectancy** 45 female, 43 male. **Literacy** 25%.
POLITICS
Government Republic. **Parties** Congress. **Suffrage** Universal, over 18. **Memberships** CW, OAU, UN. **Subdivisions** 3 regions.
ECONOMY
GDP $1,340,000,000. **Per capita** $213. **Monetary unit** Kwacha. **Trade partners** South Africa, U.K., U.S., West Germany. **Exports** Tobacco, tea, sugar, peanuts. **Imports** Manufactured goods, machinery, fuels, motor vehicles.
LAND
Description Southern Africa, landlocked. **Area** 45,747 mi² (118,484 km²). **Highest point** Sapitwa, 9,849 ft (3,002 m). **Lowest point** 120 ft (37 m).

People. Almost all Malawians are black Africans descended from Bantu peoples. The Chewa constitute the majority in the central area, while the Nyanja are dominant in the south and the Tumbuka in the north. Chichewa and English are official languages. The majority of the population is rural, and traditional village customs are prevalent. For the most part, the

society is matriarchal. Many Malawians combine Christian or Muslim beliefs with African religious practices.

Economy and the Land. A landlocked nation with limited resources and a largely unskilled work force, Malawi relies almost entirely on agriculture. A recent series of poor harvests, combined with a doubling of population between 1945 and 1966, has contributed to the decline in agricultural output. Among the main exports are tea and tobacco. Many Malawians work part of the year as miners in South Africa, Zambia, and Zimbabwe. Malawi, situated along the Great Rift Valley, has a varied terrain with highlands, plateaus, and lakes. The climate is subtropical, and rainfall varies greatly from north to south.

History and Politics. Archaeological findings indicate that Malawi has been inhabited for at least fifty thousand years. Bantu-speaking peoples, ancestors of the Malawians, immigrated from the north around A.D. 1400 and soon formed centralized kingdoms. In the 1830s other Bantu groups, involved in the slave trade, invaded the region. The arrival of Scottish missionary David Livingstone in 1859 signaled the start of British influence, and in 1891 the territory became the British protectorate of Nyasaland. For about ten years, beginning in 1953, Nyasaland was part of the larger Federation of Rhodesia and Nyasaland. Shortly after attaining independence in 1964, Malawi became a republic with nationalist leader Dr. H. Kamuzu Banda as its first president. Banda was made president-for-life by the Malawi Congress party in 1970. ∎

MALAYSIA

Official name Malaysia
PEOPLE
Population 15,500,000. **Density** 121/mi² (47/km²). **Urban** 30%. **Capital** Kuala Lumpur, 937,817. **Ethnic groups** Malay 50%, Chinese 36%, Indian 10%. **Languages** Malay, Chinese dialects, Tamil. **Religions** Muslim, Buddhist, Hindu, Confucian, Christian. **Life expectancy** 67 female, 63 male. **Literacy** 70%.

POLITICS

Government Constitutional monarchy. **Parties** Berjaya, Democratic Action, Islamic, National Front. **Suffrage** Universal, over 20. **Memberships** CW, UN. **Subdivisions** 13 states.

ECONOMY

GNP $25,100,000,000. **Per capita** $1,750. **Monetary unit** Ringgit. **Trade partners** Japan, U.S., Singapore, Western European countries. **Exports** Petroleum, natural rubber, wood, palm oil, tin. **Imports** Machinery, food, transportation equipment, manufactured goods.

LAND

Description Southeastern Asia. **Area** 128,430 mi² (332,632 km²). **Highest point** Mt. Kinabalu, 13,455 ft (4,101 m). **Lowest point** Sea level.

People. Malaysia's location at one of Southeast Asia's maritime crossroads has left it with a diverse population, including Malays, Chinese, Indians, and native non-Malay groups. The mostly rural Malays dominate politically, while the predominantly urban Chinese are very active in economic life. Considerable tension exists between the two groups. Although most Malays speak Malay and practice Islam, Malaysia's ethnic groups have resisted assimilation; Chinese, Indian, and Western languages and beliefs are also part of the culture. Most Malaysians live in Peninsular Malaysia.

Economy and the Land. The economy is one of the healthiest in the region, supported by multiple strengths in agriculture, mining, forestry, and fishing. The nation is one of the world's leading producers of rubber, palm oil, and tin, and one of the Far East's largest petroleum exporters. Manufacturing is being developed. Malaysia consists of the southern portion of the Malay Peninsula and the states of Sarawak and Sabah on northern Borneo. The land is characterized by swampy areas, mountains, and rain forests. The climate is tropical and very humid.

History and Politics. The Malay Peninsula has been inhabited since the late Stone Age. Hindu and Buddhist influences were widespread from the ninth through the fourteenth centuries A.D., after which Islam was introduced. In 1511 the Portuguese seized Melaka, a trading center, but were soon replaced, first by the Dutch in 1641 and then by the British in 1795. By the early 1900s Britain was in control of present-day Malaysia and Singapore, the areas which were occupied by Japan during World War II. Following the war, the Federation of Malaya was created, a semiautonomous state under British authority. A guerrilla war ensued, waged by Chinese Communists and others who opposed the British. Full independence was gained in 1963 with the unification of Malaysia. Singapore seceded in 1965. In 1969 riots between Malays and Chinese resulted in a suspension of parliamentary democracy lasting almost two years. ∎

MALDIVES

Official name Republic of Maldives

PEOPLE

Population 175,000. **Density** 1,522/mi² (587/km²). **Urban** 21%. **Capital** Male, Male I., 29,555. **Ethnic groups** Mixed Sinhalese, Dravidian, Arab, black. **Languages** Divehi. **Religions** Sunni Muslim. **Literacy** 36%.

POLITICS

Government Republic. **Parties** None. **Suffrage** Universal, over 21. **Memberships** CW, UN. **Subdivisions** 19 districts.

ECONOMY

GDP $74,000,000. **Per capita** $462. **Monetary unit** Rufiyaa. **Trade partners** Japan, Sri Lanka, Thailand. **Exports** Fish products, clothing. **Imports** Food, manufactured goods, machinery, petroleum.

LAND

Description Indian Ocean islands. **Area** 115 mi² (298 km²). **Highest point** 80 ft (24 m). **Lowest point** Sea level.

People. Most Maldivians are descended from Sinhalese peoples from Sri Lanka; southern Indians, or Dravidians; and Arabs. Nearly all Maldivians are Sunni Muslims and speak Divehi. The population is concentrated on Male, the capital island.

Economy and the Land. The nation draws on its advantages as a union of 1,200 islands to fuel its economy: tourism, shipping, and fishing are the mainstays. Because of limited arable land and infertile soil, agriculture is marginal. The Maldives are flat coral islands, grouped into a chain of nineteen atolls. Seasonal monsoons mark the tropical climate.

History and Politics. The Maldives are believed to have been originally settled by southern Indian peoples. Arab sailors brought Islam to the islands in the twelfth century A.D. Although a Muslim sultanate remained in power, with two interruptions, from 1153 until 1968, the Portuguese and Dutch controlled the islands intermittently between the 1500s and the 1700s. The Maldives were a British protectorate from 1887 to 1965, when they achieved independence. A republic was declared three years later. The Republic of Maldives is nonaligned and maintains close ties with other Islamic nations. ∎

MALI

Official name Republic of Mali
PEOPLE
Population 7,650,000. **Density** 16/mi² (6.2/km²). **Urban** 17%. **Capital** Bamako, 404,022. **Ethnic groups** Mande 50%, Fulani 17%, Voltaic 12%, Songhai 6%. **Languages** French, Bambara, indigenous. **Religions** Muslim 90%, indigenous 9%, Christian 1%. **Life expectancy** 46 female, 43 male. **Literacy** 10%.

POLITICS
Government Republic. **Parties** Democratic Union. **Suffrage** Universal, over 21. **Memberships** OAU, UN. **Subdivisions** 7 regions.

ECONOMY
GDP $1,000,000,000. **Per capita** $138. **Monetary unit** Franc. **Trade partners** France, Ivory Coast, China, Senegal, U.K., West Germany. **Exports** Cotton, livestock, dried fish, peanuts. **Imports** Food, machinery, vehicles, petroleum, chemicals and pharmaceuticals.

LAND
Description Western Africa, landlocked. **Area** 478,766 mi² (1,240,000 km²). **Highest point** Hombori Mtn., 3,789 ft (1,155 m).

People. The majority of Malians belong to one of several black groups, although there is a small non-black nomadic population. Most Malians are farmers who live in small villages. The official language is French, but most people communicate in Bambara, a market language. The population is concentrated in the basins of the Niger and Senegal rivers, in the south. Heirs of three ancient empires, Malians have produced a distinct culture.

Economy and the Land. One of the world's poorest nations, Mali depends primarily on agriculture but is limited by a climate that produces drought and a terrain that is almost half desert. Mineral reserves have not been exploited because of poor transportation and power facilities. Food processing and textiles account for most industry. Mali, a landlocked country, faces a growing national debt due to its dependence on foreign goods. The climate is hot and dry, with alternating dry and wet seasons.

History and Politics. Parts of present-day Mali once belonged to the Ghana, Mali, and Songhai empires. These wealthy empires, which ruled from about A.D. 300 to 1600, traded with the Mediterranean world and were centers of Islamic learning. Fierce native resistance delayed colonization by the French until 1904, when French Sudan, as the area was called, was made part of French West Africa. In 1959 it joined Senegal to form the Federation of Mali. Senegal soon withdrew from the union, and French Sudan declared itself the Republic of Mali in 1960. The republic, a socialist state, was overthrown in 1968 by a military coup. Civilian rule was reestablished in 1979. ∎

MALTA

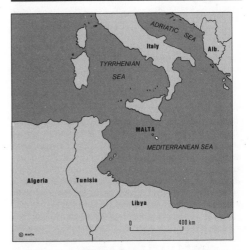

Official name Republic of Malta
PEOPLE
Population 360,000. **Density** 2,951/mi² (1,139/km²). **Urban** 83%. **Capital** Valletta, 13,962. **Ethnic groups** Mixed Arab, Sicilian, Norman, Spanish, Italian, English. **Languages** Maltese, English. **Religions** Roman Catholic 98%. **Life expectancy** 74 female, 70 male. **Literacy** 83%.

POLITICS
Government Republic. **Parties** Labor, Nationalist. **Suffrage** Universal, over 18. **Memberships** CW, UN. **Subdivisions** 13 electoral districts.

ECONOMY
GDP $1,140,000,000. **Per capita** $3,499. **Monetary unit** Pound. **Trade partners** West Germany, Italy, U.K. **Exports** Clothing, textiles, petroleum products. **Imports** Manufactured goods, machinery, food, petroleum.

LAND
Description Mediterranean island. **Area** 122 mi² (316 km²). **Highest point** 829 ft (253 m). **Lowest point** Sea level.

People. Malta's diverse population reflects centuries of rule by Arabs, Normans, and the British. The official languages are English and Maltese, the latter a blend of Arabic and a Sicilian dialect of Italian.

Roman Catholicism is practiced by the majority of residents. Malta is one of the world's most densely populated nations.

Economy and the Land. Situated strategically between Europe and Africa, Malta became an important military site for foreign powers with the opening of the Suez Canal in 1869. Its economy was thus shaped by the patterns of war and peace in the Mediterranean but has recently turned toward commercial shipbuilding, construction, manufacturing, and tourism. Its soil is poor and rocky, and most food is imported. Although there are many natural harbors and hundreds of miles of coastline, fishing is not a major source of income. Malta, with its hilly terrain, is subtropical in summer and temperate the rest of the year.

History and Politics. The Phoenicians and Carthaginians first colonized the island of Malta between 1000 and 600 B.C. Malta was made part of the Roman and Byzantine empires and then was ruled successively by Arabs, Normans, and various feudal lords. In the 1500s the Holy Roman Emperor Charles V ceded Malta to the Knights of St. John of Jerusalem, an order of the Roman Catholic church. The Knights' reign, marked by cultural and architectural achievements, ended with surrender to France's Napoleon Bonaparte in 1798. The Maltese resisted French rule, however, and offered control to Britain, becoming part of the United Kingdom in 1814. Throughout the two world wars Malta was a vital naval base for the Allied forces. It achieved independence from Britain in 1964 and became a republic ten years later. In 1979 the last British and North Atlantic Treaty Organization (NATO) military forces departed, and Malta declared its neutrality and nonalignment. ∎

MARSHALL ISLANDS

See UNITED STATES.

MARTINIQUE

See FRANCE.

MAURITANIA

Official name Islamic Republic of Mauritania
PEOPLE
Population 1,640,000. **Density** 4.1/mi² (1.6/km²). **Urban** 23%. **Capital** Nouakchott, 150,000. **Ethnic groups** Moor-black 40%, Moor 30%, black 30%. **Languages** Arabic, French. **Religions** Muslim. **Life expectancy** 46 female, 43 male. **Literacy** 17%.
POLITICS
Government Provisional military government. **Parties** None (suspended). **Suffrage** Universal adult.

Memberships AL, OAU, UN. **Subdivisions** 12 regions, 1 capital district.
ECONOMY
GNP $720,000,000. **Per capita** $460. **Monetary unit** Ouguiya. **Trade partners** France, other Western European countries, Senegal, U.S. **Exports** Iron ore, processed fish. **Imports** Food, machinery, petroleum, consumer goods.
LAND
Description Western Africa. **Area** 397,955 mi² (1,030,700 km²). **Highest point** Mt. Jill, 3,002 ft (915 m). **Lowest point** Sebkha de Ndrhamcha, 10 ft (3 m) below sea level.

People. Most Mauritanians are Moors, descendants of Arabs and Berbers, or of mixed Arab, Berber, and black descent. The Moors, who speak Arabic, are mostly nomadic herdsmen. The remainder of the population is composed of black Africans, who speak several languages and farm in the Senegal River valley. Virtually all Mauritanians are Muslim. Proportionally, the nomadic population has declined recently because of long periods of drought, although overall population is increasing.

Economy and the Land. Mauritania's economy is based on agriculture, with many farmers producing little more than subsistence-level outputs. Crop production, confined chiefly to the Senegal River valley, has recently fallen because of drought and outmoded cultivation methods. Mining of high-grade iron-ore deposits is the primary industrial activity, although fishing and fish processing are also important. Inadequate transportation and communication systems and a war with Western Sahara have virtually crippled the economy. Besides the river valley, land regions include a northern desert and southeastern grasslands. Mauritania has a hot, dry climate.

History and Politics. Berbers began settling in parts of the area around A.D. 300 and established a network of caravan trading routes. From this time until the late 1500s, sections of the south were dominated by the Ghana, the Mali, and finally the Songhai empires. Contact with Europeans grew between the 1600s and 1800s, and in 1920 France made Mauritania a colony. Mauritania attained independence in 1960, although Morocco claimed the area and did not recognize the state until 1970. During the late seventies Mauritania became embroiled in a war with the Polisario Front, a Western Saharan nationalist group, and Morocco for control of Western Sahara. Mauritania withdrew its claim to the area in 1979. A coup in 1978 ended seventeen years of presidential rule and established a military government that, except for a brief period of civilian authority, has ruled continuously. The Western Sahara conflict continues to dominate foreign policy. ∎

MAURITIUS

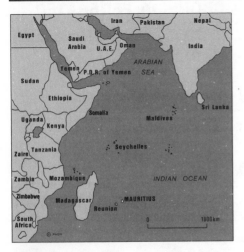

Official name Mauritius
PEOPLE
Population 1,025,000. **Density** 1,297/mi² (501/km²).
Urban 43%. **Capital** Port Louis, 147,386. **Ethnic groups**
Indo-Mauritian 68%, Creole 27%, Sino-Mauritian 3%,
Franco-Mauritian 2%. **Languages** English, French.
Religions Hindu 51%, Christian 30%, Muslim 17%. **Life**
expectancy 68 female, 64 male. **Literacy** 61%.

POLITICS
Government Parliamentary state. **Parties** Labor, Militant
Movement, Militant Socialist Movement, Social
Democratic. **Suffrage** Universal, over 18. **Memberships**
CW, OAU, UN. **Subdivisions** 9 subdivisions.

ECONOMY
GDP $960,000,000. **Per capita** $890. **Monetary unit**
Rupee. **Trade partners** U.K., France, South Africa, U.S.
Exports Sugar, clothing, molasses. **Imports** Food,
petroleum products, capital equipment.

LAND
Description Indian Ocean island. **Area** 790 mi² (2,045
km²). **Highest point** Piton de la Petite Rivière Noire,
2,717 ft (828 m). **Lowest point** Sea level.

People. Mauritius's diverse ethnicity is largely the
product of its past as a sugar-producing colony: Creoles are descendants of African slaves and European plantation owners, while the Indian community traces its roots to laborers who replaced the Africans

after slavery was abolished. There are also people of Chinese and French descent. Franco-Mauritians now compose most of the nation's elite. English is the official tongue, but French, a French creole, and many other languages are also spoken. Religious activity is similarly varied and includes followers of Hinduism, Christianity, and Islam.

Economy and the Land. Sugar remains fundamental to the economy. Almost all arable land is covered by sugarcane, and sugar and its by-products make up the majority of exports. Attempts have been made at diversification, with tea and tobacco recent introductions. Inflation, unemployment, overpopulation, and low sugar prices cloud the economic outlook. Mauritius is a volcanic island, with a central plateau surrounded by mountains. Cyclones sometimes strike the island, which has a tropical climate.

History and Politics. Although visited by Arab, Malay, and Portuguese sailors between the tenth and sixteenth centuries A.D., Mauritius was uninhabited until 1598, when the Dutch claimed it. They abandoned the island in 1710 and were followed five years later by the French, who made it a colony. During the 1700s the French used Mauritius, which they called Île de France, as a naval base and established plantations worked by imported slaves. The British ousted the French in 1810 and outlawed slavery soon afterward. In the nineteenth century indentured workers from India replaced the plantation slaves. Mauritius began its history as an independent state in 1968 with a system of parliamentary democracy. A labor party was in power for fourteen years and was succeeded in 1982 by the Mauritian Militant Movement. ∎

MAYOTTE

See COMOROS.

MEXICO

Official name United Mexican States
PEOPLE
Population 78,670,000. **Density** 103/mi² (40/km²).
Urban 67%. **Capital** Mexico City, 9,373,400. **Ethnic groups** Mestizo 60%, Amerindian 30%, white 9%.
Languages Spanish. **Religions** Roman Catholic 97%,
Protestant 3%. **Life expectancy** 68 female, 64 male.
Literacy 74%.
POLITICS
Government Republic. **Parties** Institutional Revolutionary,
National Action, Unified Socialist. **Suffrage** Universal,
over 18. **Memberships** OAS, UN. **Subdivisions** 31
states, 1 federal district.
ECONOMY
GDP $168,000,000,000. **Per capita** $2,273. **Monetary unit** Peso. **Trade partners** U.S., Western European
countries, Japan. **Exports** Petroleum, cotton, coffee,
minerals. **Imports** Machinery, industrial vehicles,
intermediate goods.
LAND
Description Southern North America. **Area** 761,604 mi²
(1,972,547 km²). **Highest point** Volcán Citlaltépetl,
18,701 ft (5,700 m). **Lowest point** Laguna Salada, 26 ft
(8 m) below sea level.

People. Most Mexicans are mestizos, descended
from Indians and the Spaniards who conquered
Mexico in the 1500s. Spanish is spoken by most
inhabitants, and Roman Catholicism is the most
popular religion. Another major ethnic group is comprised of indigenous Indians, or Amerindians, some
of whom speak only Indian languages and hold traditional religious beliefs. Mexico's rapid population
growth has contributed to poverty among rural dwellers, spurring a migration to the cities. A mild climate
and fertile soils create a concentration of population
on Mexico's central plateau.

Economy and the Land. Mexico is a leading producer of petroleum and silver, a growing manufacturer of iron, steel, and chemicals, and an exporter
of coffee and cotton. Foreign visitors—drawn by archaeological sites and warm, sunny weather—make
tourism an important activity. Despite vast gains
made since the mid-1900s in agriculture and industry, the economy has recently been troubled by inflation, declining oil prices, unemployment arising
from the population boom, and a trade deficit that
has grown with the need for imported materials. In
recent years the peso has been significantly devalued, and banks have been nationalized to help reduce a massive international debt. Austerity plans
and foreign aid are expected to help revitalize the
economy. Terrain and climate are greatly varied,
ranging from tropical jungles along the coast to desert plains in the north. A temperate central plateau
is bounded by rugged mountains in the south, east,
and west.

History and Politics. Farm settlements grew up in
the Valley of Mexico between 6500 and 1500 B.C.,
and during the subsequent three thousand years the
area gave birth to the great civilizations of the Ol-
mec, Maya, Toltec, and Aztec Indians. The Aztec
Empire was overthrown by the Spanish in 1521, and
Mexico became the viceroyalty of New Spain. Although there was much dissatisfaction with Spanish
rule, rebellion did not begin until 1810. Formal independence came in 1821. Mexico lost considerable
territory, including Texas, to the United States during
the Mexican War, from 1846 to 1848. During subsequent years power changed hands frequently as
liberals demanding social and economic reforms
battled conservatives. A brief span of French imperial rule, from 1864 to 1867, interrupted the struggle.
Following a revolution that started in 1910, a new
constitution was adopted in 1917, and progress
toward reform began, culminating in the separation
of church and state and the redistribution of land.
Mexico maintains close relations with the United
States and is anxious to help mediate a peace in
Central America.   ■

MICRONESIA, FEDERATED STATES OF

See UNITED STATES.

MIDWAY ISLANDS

See UNITED STATES.

MONACO

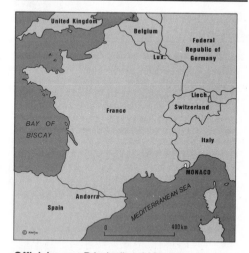

Official name Principality of Monaco
PEOPLE
Population 28,000. **Density** 46,667/mi² (18,667/km²).
Urban 100%. **Capital** Monaco, 25,000. **Ethnic groups**
French 58%, Monegasque 19%, Italian 17%. **Languages**
French, Monegasque, Italian, English. **Religions** Roman
Catholic 95%. **Literacy** 99%.
POLITICS
Government Constitutional monarchy. **Parties** National
and Democratic Union, Socialist. **Suffrage** Universal
adult. **Memberships** None. **Subdivisions** 4 *quartiers.*

ECONOMY
Monetary unit French franc.

LAND
Description Southern Europe. **Area** 0.6 mi² (1.5 km²).
Highest point 459 ft (140 m). **Lowest point** Sea level.

People. Monaco is inhabited mostly by French citizens. Monegasques, citizens of indigenous descent, and Italians form the rest of the population. Many foreigners have taken up residence, drawn by the country's tax benefits. French is the official language. Monegasque, a blend of French and Italian, is also spoken, as are Italian and English. Most residents are Roman Catholic.

Economy and the Land. Monaco's beautiful seaside location, mild Mediterranean climate, and famous gambling casino in Monte Carlo make it a popular tourist haven. Consequently, tourism forms the backbone of the economy. Production of chemicals, food products, and perfumes, among other light industries, are additional sources of income. Monaco also profits from many foreign businesses, attracted by the favorable tax climate, that are headquartered in the principality. France and Monaco form a customs union for a mutually beneficial trade system; the French franc is Monaco's official currency. The world's second smallest independent state in area—after Vatican City—Monaco has four regions: the old city of Monaco-Ville, site of the royal palace; Monte Carlo, the resort and major tourist center; La Condamine, the port area; and Fontvieille, the rapidly growing industrial section.

History and Politics. Known to the Phoenicians, Greeks, and Romans, the region became a Genoese colony in the twelfth century A.D. Around the turn of the fourteenth century, the area was granted to the Grimaldi family of Genoa. France, Spain, and Sardinia had intermittent control of Monaco from 1400 until 1861, when its autonomy was recognized by the Franco-Monegasque Treaty. Another treaty, providing for French protection of Monaco, was signed in 1918. The absolute rule of Monaco's princes ended with the 1911 constitution. ■

MONGOLIA

Official name Mongolian People's Republic
PEOPLE
Population 1,885,000. **Density** 3.1/mi² (1.2/km²). **Urban** 51%. **Capital** Ulan Bator, 435,400. **Ethnic groups** Mongol 90%, Kazakh 4%, Chinese 2%, Russian 2%. **Languages** Khalkha Mongol. **Religions** Tibetan Buddhist, Muslim 4%. **Life expectancy** 65 female, 61 male. **Literacy** 80%.

POLITICS
Government Socialist republic. **Parties** People's Revolutionary. **Suffrage** Universal, over 18. **Memberships** UN. **Subdivisions** 18 provinces, 3 autonomous cities.

ECONOMY
GDP $1,200,000,000. **Per capita** $860. **Monetary unit** Tugrik. **Trade partners** U.S.S.R. **Exports** Livestock, animal products, wool, hides, minerals. **Imports** Machinery, petroleum, clothing, construction materials.

LAND
Description Central Asia, landlocked. **Area** 604,250 mi² (1,565,000 km²). **Highest point** 14,350 ft (4,374 m). **Lowest point** Höh Lake, 1,814 ft (553 m).

People. Mongols, a central Asian people, make up the vast majority of Mongolia's population. Several Mongol groups exist, the largest of which is the Khalkha; Khalkha Mongol is the predominant language. Turkic-speaking Kazakhs as well as Russians and Chinese comprise minorities. Tibetan Buddhism was once the most common religion; however, the government now discourages religious practice. The traditional nomadic way of life is becoming less common as recent government policies have led to urbanization and settled agriculture.

Economy and the Land. Mongolia's economy, long based on the raising of livestock, has been shaped by the ideal grazing land found in most of the country. But significant economic changes have occurred since 1924, including the collectivization and modernization of farming, the introduction of industry, and the exploitation of mineral resources. Although dependent on Soviet aid, Mongolia has made considerable progress toward diversifying and developing its economy. Mongolia's terrain varies from mountains in the north and west to steppe in the east and desert in the south. Located in the heart of Asia, remote from any moderating body of water, Mongolia has a rigorous continental climate with little precipitation.

History and Politics. Mongolian tribes were united under the warlord Genghis Khan around A.D. 1200, and he and his successors built one of history's largest land empires. In 1691 the Manchu dynasty of China subdued Outer Mongolia, as the area was then known, but allowed the Mongol rulers autonomy. Until the Mongols ousted the Chinese in 1911, Outer Mongolia remained a Chinese province. In 1912 the state accepted Russian protection but was unable to prevent a subsequent Chinese advance, and in 1919 Outer Mongolia again became a Chinese province. In 1921 a combined Soviet and Mongolian force defeated Chinese and Belorussian, or White

Russian, troops, and the Mongolian People's Republic was declared in 1924. A mutual-assistance pact was signed by Mongolia and Russia in 1966. Today Mongolia continues to support Soviet foreign policy, and Soviet troops are stationed throughout the land. ∎

MONTSERRAT

See UNITED KINGDOM.

MOROCCO

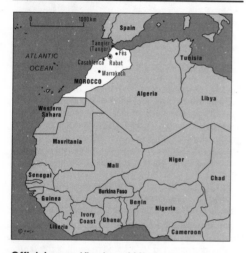

Official name Kingdom of Morocco
PEOPLE
Population 21,750,000. **Density** 126/mi² (49/km²). **Urban** 42%. **Capital** Rabat, 367,620. **Ethnic groups** Arab-Berber 99%. **Languages** Arabic, Berber dialects, French. **Religions** Muslim 99%. **Life expectancy** 59 female, 55 male. **Literacy** 28%
POLITICS
Government Constitutional monarchy. **Parties** Istiqlal, National Assembly of Independents, Popular Movement, Socialist Union of Popular Forces. **Suffrage** Universal, over 20. **Memberships** AL, UN. **Subdivisions** 35 provinces, 2 prefectures.
ECONOMY
GNP $15,200,000,000. **Per capita** $640. **Monetary unit** Dirham. **Trade partners** France, Spain, Saudi Arabia, West Germany. **Exports** Phosphates, food, consumer goods. **Imports** Petroleum, food, machinery.
LAND
Description Northern Africa. **Area** 172,414 mi² (446,550 km²). **Highest point** Jebel Toubkal, 13,665 ft (4,165 m). **Lowest point** Sebkha Tah, 180 ft (55 m) below sea level. *The above information exludes Western Sahara.*

People. Moroccans are virtually homogeneous in race and culture; most are a mixture of Arab and Berber stocks and speak Arabic. A few Berber dialects are spoken in rural mountain areas, and

French and Spanish, the colonial tongues, are common in business and government. The majority of people are Sunni Muslim. The population is concentrated west of the Atlas Mountains, which border the Sahara Desert. Migrations from rural areas to cities, where the standard of living is higher, have been the trend.

Economy and the Land. Although agriculture employs much of the work force and is an important activity, the nation depends on mining for most of its income. Morocco is a leading exporter of phosphates and has other mineral reserves. Fishing and tourism are growing sources of revenue. Such recent developments as severe drought, rising dependency on imported oil, and a costly war in Western Sahara have slowed productivity, while investment by Arab countries has bolstered the economy. Morocco, with its varied terrain of desert, forests, and mountains, has an equally varied climate that is semitropical along the coast, and desert beyond the Atlas Mountains.

History and Politics. In ancient times Morocco was a province of Carthage and Rome. Vandals and Byzantine Greeks, the subsequent rulers, were followed in the A.D. 700s by Arabs, who brought Islam. Morocco's strategic position awakened the interest of colonial powers in the 1800s, and by 1912 the area was divided into French and Spanish protectorates. A nationalist movement began in the twenties, occasionally bringing violence, but not until 1956 did Morocco become independent from France. The last of Spain's holdings in Morocco were returned in 1969. War broke out in 1976, when Morocco claimed the northern part of Western Sahara and was challenged by the Saharan nationalist Polisario Front. Although Mauritania, which had been involved in the war and had been fighting for southern Western Sahara, surrendered its claim in 1979, Morocco has continued to battle the Polisario Front. ∎

MOZAMBIQUE

Official name People's Republic of Mozambique
PEOPLE
Population 13,700,000. **Density** 45/mi² (17/km²). **Urban** 15%. **Capital** Maputo, 739,077. **Ethnic groups** African 99%. **Languages** Portuguese, indigenous. **Religions** Indigenous 60%, Christian 30%, Muslim 10%. **Life expectancy** 48 female, 44 male. **Literacy** 14%.
POLITICS
Government Socialist republic. **Parties** Liberation Front. **Suffrage** Universal adult. **Memberships** OAU, UN. **Subdivisions** 10 provinces.
ECONOMY
GNP $1,500,000,000. **Per capita** $150. **Monetary unit** Metical. **Trade partners** Portugal, South Africa, U.S., West Germany, U.K. **Exports** Cashews, shrimp, sugar, tea, cotton. **Imports** Machinery, petroleum, motor vehicles, electrical equipment.
LAND
Description Southern Africa. **Area** 302,329 mi² (783,030 km²). **Highest point** Monte Binga, 7,992 ft (2,436 m). **Lowest point** Sea level.

People. Black Africans belonging to about ten groups compose the vast majority of the population. Most black Mozambicans live in rural areas, while small European and Asian minorities live primarily in urban centers. Traditional African religions are followed by a majority, but Islam and Christianity also have adherents. Although Portuguese is the official language, most blacks speak Bantu tongues.

Economy and the Land. Mozambique's underdeveloped economy is largely the product of its colonial past, during which its human and natural resources were neglected. Recent political developments in southern Africa have created more economic woes, as lucrative trade agreements with racially divided neighbors have ceased. The mainstays of the economy are agriculture and transport services. Fishing and mining are being developed, and the Marxist government has allowed some private enterprise. Foreign aid is important. The climate is tropical or subtropical along the coastal plain that covers nearly half of the country, with cooler conditions in the western high plateaus and mountains.

History and Politics. Bantu-speaking peoples settled in present-day Mozambique around the first century A.D. Subsequent immigrants included Arab traders in the 800s and the Portuguese in the late 1400s. European economic interest in the area was hindered by lucrative trading with other colonies, and Mozambique wasn't recognized as a Portuguese colony until 1885. Policies instituted by the Portuguese benefited European settlers and Portugal while overlooking the welfare of Mozambique and its native inhabitants. Opposition to foreign rule crystallized with the formation in the early 1960s of the Mozambique Liberation Front, a Marxist nationalist group that initiated an armed campaign against the Portuguese. In 1975 Mozambique became an independent state dedicated to eliminating white-minority rule in the area. Nevertheless, Mozambique has economic ties to South Africa, and in 1984 the two nations pledged to deny refuge to each other's foes. ∎

NAMIBIA

Official name Namibia
PEOPLE
Population 1,095,000. **Density** 3.4/mi² (1.3/km²). **Urban** 45%. **Capital** Windhoek, 88,700. **Ethnic groups** Black 86%, white 7%, mixed 7%. **Languages** Afrikaans, indigenous. **Religions** Christian, indigenous. **Life expectancy** 53 female, 50 male. **Literacy** 100% whites, 28% nonwhites.
POLITICS
Government Under South African administration. **Parties** Action Front for the Preservation of the Turnhalle Principles, Democratic Turnhalle Alliance, South West Africa People's Organization. **Suffrage** Universal adult. **Memberships** None. **Subdivisions** 10 homelands, 16 districts.
ECONOMY
GNP $2,010,000,000. **Per capita** $1,879. **Monetary unit** South African rand. **Trade partners** South Africa, West Germany, U.K., U.S. **Exports** Diamonds, copper, lead, cattle, fish products. **Imports** Food, construction materials, manufactured goods.
LAND
Description Southern Africa. **Area** 318,261 mi² (824,292 km²). **Highest point** Brandberg, 8,445 ft (2,574 m). **Lowest point** Sea level.
The above information excludes Walvis Bay.

People. The largest ethnic group is black African, composed of many indigenous peoples. South Africans, Britons, and Germans constitute the white minority. Black Namibians speak various native dialects, while the majority of whites speak Afrikaans. Traditional customs and religions are still followed by blacks, but a considerable number have converted to Christianity. Whites control economic and political life in Namibia, which is governed by South Africa.

Economy and the Land. Namibia's economy rests on the mining of diamonds, copper, lead, and other minerals. Agriculture makes a marginal contribution, but livestock raising is important. Manufacturing remains undeveloped because of an unskilled work force, and Namibia imports most of its finished goods from South Africa, its partner in a customs union. A variety of factors, including continuing drought and political instability, have held back economic growth. Namibia consists of a high plateau that encompasses the Namib Desert and part of the Kalahari Desert. The climate is subtropical.

History and Politics. Bushmen were probably the area's first inhabitants, followed by other African peoples. European exploration of the coast began in the A.D. 1500s, but the coastal desert prevented foreign penetration. In 1884 Germany annexed all of the territory except for the coastal enclave of Walvis Bay, which had been claimed by Britain in 1878. After South African troops ousted the Germans from the area during World War I, the League of Nations mandated Namibia, then known as South West Africa, to South Africa. Following World War II the United Nations requested that the territory become a trusteeship. South Africa refused to cooperate. In 1966 the United Nations revoked South Africa's mandate, yet South Africa kept control of Namibia. Beginning in the sixties the South West Africa People's Organization, a Namibian nationalist group with Communist support, made guerrilla raids on South African forces from bases in Zambia and, later, from Angola. In 1978 a United Nations plan provided for the withdrawal of South African troops but was unsuccessful. Negotiations for independence continued in the early 1980s. ∎

NAURU

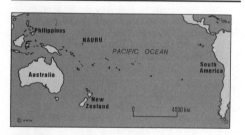

Official name Republic of Nauru
PEOPLE
Population 7,800. **Density** 951/mi² (371/km²). **Capital** Yaren District. **Ethnic groups** Nauruan 58%, other Pacific Islander 26%, Chinese 8%, European 8%. **Languages** Nauruan, English. **Religions** Protestant 67%, Roman Catholic 33%. **Literacy** 99%.
POLITICS
Government Republic. **Parties** Governing faction (not a formal party), Nauru (the opposition). **Suffrage** Universal adult. **Memberships** CW. **Subdivisions** 14 districts.
ECONOMY
GNP $155,400,000. **Per capita** $21,400. **Monetary unit** Australian dollar. **Trade partners** Australia, New Zealand. **Exports** Phosphates. **Imports** Food, fuels, water.
LAND
Description South Pacific island. **Area** 8.2 mi² (21 km²). **Highest point** 213 ft (65 m). **Lowest point** Sea level.

People. Indigenous Nauruans are a mix of Polynesian, Micronesian, and Melanesian stock, and many

residents are from other Pacific islands. Nauruan is the language of most inhabitants, but English is widely spoken. Nearly all Nauruans are Christian.

Economy and the Land. The economy rests entirely on phosphates, the sole resource. Agriculture is very limited; thus Nauruans must import nearly all their food. Nauru is one of the smallest countries in the world. Most of the coral island is a plateau, and the climate is tropical.

History and Politics. Nauru was most likely settled by castaways from nearby islands. Noted by a British explorer in 1798, Nauru remained autonomous until it came under German control in 1881. In 1914 Germany surrendered the island, and it was subsequently mandated to Australia, Britain, and New Zealand. World War II brought occupation by Japan. Nauru reverted to Australian rule in 1947 as a trusteeship. It became independent in 1968 and gained control of European interests in the phosphate industry in 1970. ∎

NEPAL

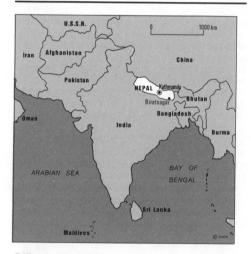

Official name Kingdom of Nepal
PEOPLE
Population 16,785,000. **Density** 299/mi² (115/km²). **Urban** 5%. **Capital** Kathmandu, 235,160. **Ethnic groups** Brahman, Chetri, Gurung, Magar, others. **Languages** Nepali. **Religions** Hindu 88%, Buddhist. **Life expectancy** 44 female, 45 male. **Literacy** 20%.
POLITICS
Government Constitutional monarchy. **Parties** None. **Suffrage** Universal, over 21. **Memberships** UN. **Subdivisions** 14 zones.
ECONOMY
GDP $2,300,000,000. **Per capita** $149. **Monetary unit** Rupee. **Trade partners** India. **Exports** Rice, food, jute, wood. **Imports** Consumer goods, fuels, machinery, fertilizer, food.
LAND
Description Southern Asia, landlocked. **Area** 56,135 mi² (145,391 km²). **Highest point** Mt. Everest, 29,028 ft (8,848 m). **Lowest point** 197 ft (60 m).

People. Nepal's mixed population results from migrations over the centuries from India, Tibet, and central Asia. Most of Nepal's ruling families have been of Indian descent, and Nepali, the official language, is derived from Sanskrit, an ancient Indian language. Although the majority of the population practices Hinduism, Nepal is the birthplace of Buddha and has been greatly influenced by Buddhism as well. The importance of both religions is reflected in the more than 2,700 shrines in the Kathmandu Valley. Most Nepalese are rural farmers.

Economy and the Land. Because of geographic remoteness and a political policy of isolation lasting until the 1950s, Nepal's economy is one of the least developed in the world. Agriculture, concentrated chiefly in the south, is the most significant activity, even though most of Nepal is covered by the Himalayas, the world's highest mountains. This range—which includes Mount Everest, the world's highest peak—has made tourism increasingly lucrative. Nepal has potential in hydroelectricity and forestry, but inadequate transportation routes, overpopulation, and deforestation present obstacles to development. Nepal has received financial aid from many nations, partly because of its strategic location between India and China. The climate varies from subtropical in the flat, fertile south to temperate in the central hill country. Himalayan summers are cool and winters severe.

History and Politics. Several small Hindu-Buddhist kingdoms had emerged in the Kathmandu Valley by about A.D. 300. These states were unified in the late 1700s by the founder of the Shah dynasty. The Rana family wrested control from the Shahs in 1846 and pursued an isolationist course, which thwarted foreign influence but stunted economic growth. Opposition to the Ranas mounted during the 1930s and 1940s, and in 1951 the Shah monarchy was restored by a revolution. In 1962 the king established a government that gave the crown dominance and abolished political parties. A 1980 referendum narrowly upheld this system. ∎

NETHERLANDS

Official name Kingdom of the Netherlands
PEOPLE
Population 14,465,000. **Density** 910/mi² (351/km²).
Urban 88%. **Capital** Amsterdam (constitutional), 687,397; The Hague (seat of government), 449,338. **Ethnic groups** Dutch 99%, Indonesian and others 1%.
Languages Dutch. **Religions** Roman Catholic 40%, Protestant 31%. **Life expectancy** 78 female, 74 male.
Literacy 99%.
POLITICS
Government Constitutional monarchy. **Parties** Christian Democratic Appeal, Democrats '66, Labor, Liberal.
Suffrage Universal, over 18. **Memberships** NATO, OECD, UN. **Subdivisions** 11 provinces.
ECONOMY
GNP $137,300,000,000. **Per capita** $9,807. **Monetary unit** Guilder. **Trade partners** West Germany, Belgium, France, U.S., U.K. **Exports** Food, machinery, chemicals,

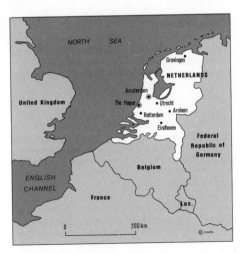

petroleum products. **Imports** Machinery, petroleum, transportation equipment, food.
LAND
Description Western Europe. **Area** 15,892 mi² (41,160 km²). **Highest point** Vaalserberg, 1,053 ft (321 m).
Lowest point Prins Alexander polder, 22 ft (6.7 m) below sea level.

People. The major ethnic group is the Dutch, for the most part a mixture of Germanic peoples. There are small minorities from the former Dutch possessions of Indonesia and Suriname. Dutch is the official language, but many Netherlanders also speak English or German. Although most Dutch are Christian, the nation has a history of religious tolerance that has drawn countless refugees.

Economy and the Land. A variety of manufacturing strengths—notably the metal, chemical, and food-processing industries—fuels the prosperous economy. Tourism and the production of natural gas are also important. A lack of natural resources obliges the Netherlands to import many goods. The country benefits from its strategic position and has enjoyed success in shipping and trade. Much of the Netherlands, including most farmland, has been reclaimed from the sea through artificial drainage. The land is almost uniformly flat, and proximity to the sea produces a mild, damp climate. The Kingdom of the Netherlands includes the Netherland Antilles, two groups of Caribbean islands.

History and Politics. The Germanic tribes of the area were conquered in 58 B.C. by the Romans, who were driven out in the A.D. 400s by the Franks. As part of the Low Countries with Belgium and Luxembourg, the Netherlands was dominated successively by Charlemagne, the dukes of Burgundy, the Hapsburgs, and rulers of Spain. Spanish persecution of Dutch Protestants led to a revolt that in 1581 created the Republic of the United Netherlands. In the 1600s the Netherlands became a maritime as well as a colonial power and produced many masterpieces in painting. But a series of wars with England and France ending in 1714 spelled the end of Dutch influence, and the nation fell to France in

Places and Possessions of the Netherlands

Entity	Status	Area	Population	Capital / Population
Aruba (Caribbean island)	Division of Netherlands Antilles	75 mi² (93 km²)	65,000	Oranjestad, 14,700
Curaçao (Caribbean island)	Division of Netherlands Antilles	171 mi² (444 km²)	165,000	Willemstad, 43,547
Netherlands Antilles— Aruba, Bonaire, Curaçao, Saba, St. Eustatius, St. Maarten (Caribbean islands)	Self-governing territory	383 mi² (993 km²)	250,000	Willemstad, 43,547

1795. With the defeat of Napoleon Bonaparte of France in 1815, the Netherlands was united with Belgium and became an independent kingdom. Belgium seceded in 1830. The Netherlands declared its neutrality in both world wars but was occupied by Germany from 1940 to 1945. The war cost the country many lives and much of its economic strength. Membership in several international economic unions aided recovery. Since the war the Netherlands has abandoned neutrality and now maintains a pro-Western stance in foreign affairs. ∎

NETHERLANDS ANTILLES

See NETHERLANDS.

NEW CALEDONIA

Official name Territory of New Caledonia and Dependencies
PEOPLE
Population 149,000. **Density** 20/mi² (7.8/km²). **Urban** 60%. **Capital** Nouméa, New Caledonia I., 56,078. **Ethnic groups** Melanesian 42%, French 40%, Vietnamese, Indonesian, Chinese, Polynesian. **Languages** French, Malay-Polynesian languages. **Religions** Roman Catholic 60%, Protestant 30%.
POLITICS
Government Overseas territory (France). **Parties** Federation for a New Society, Rally for the Republic, Union Calédonienne. **Suffrage** Universal adult. **Memberships** None. **Subdivisions** 4 divisions.
ECONOMY
GNP $637,000,000. **Per capita** $4,000. **Monetary unit** CFP franc. **Trade partners** France. **Exports** Nickel. **Imports** Fuels, minerals, machinery, electrical equipment.
LAND
Description South Pacific islands. **Area** 7,358 mi² (19,058 km²). **Highest point** Mont Panié, New Caledonia I., 5,341 ft (1,628 m). **Lowest point** Sea level.

People. The largest ethnic group in New Caledonia, a group of Pacific islands northeast of Australia, is the Melanesians, or Kanaks. People of French descent make up the second largest group, with

Asians and Polynesians composing significant minorities. New Caledonia's status as an overseas French territory is reflected in its languages, which include French as well as regional dialects, and in a population that is largely Christian.

Economy and the Land. The principal economic activity, the mining and smelting of nickel, has fallen off in recent years. Small amounts of coffee and copra are exported, and tourism is important in the capital. Possessing few resources, New Caledonia imports almost all finished products from France. The main island, also called New Caledonia, is mountainous and accounts for almost 90 percent of the territory's land area. Smaller islands include the Isle of Pines and the Loyalty and Bélep islands. The climate is tropical.

History and Politics. New Caledonia was settled by Melanesians about 2000 B.C. The main island was first reached by Europeans in 1774, when Captain James Cook of Britain gave it its present name. In 1853 France annexed New Caledonia and used the main island as a penal colony until the turn of the century. During World War II the islands served as a base for the United States military. Officially a French territory since 1946, New Caledonia experienced violence in the 1980s, stemming from the desire of the Kanak population for independence. ∎

NEW ZEALAND

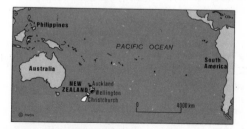

Official name New Zealand
PEOPLE
Population 3,155,000. **Density** 30/mi² (12/km²). **Urban** 83%. **Capital** Wellington, North I., 134,900. **Ethnic groups** European 87%, Maori 9%, Pacific Islander 2%.

Places and Possessions of New Zealand

Entity	Status	Area	Population	Capital / Population
Cook Islands (South Pacific)	Self-governing territory	91 mi² (236 km²)	*16,000*	Avarua, *9,525*
Niue (South Pacific island)	Self-governing territory	102 mi² (263 km²)	*2,900*	Alofi
Tokelau (South Pacific islands)	Island territory	3.9 mi² (10 km²)	*1,500*	None

Languages English, Maori. **Religions** Anglican 29%, Presbyterian 18%, Roman Catholic 15%, others 38%. **Life expectancy** 76 female, 72 male. **Literacy** 98%.
POLITICS
Government Parliamentary state. **Parties** Labor, National, New Zealand, Social Credit Political League. **Suffrage** Universal, over 18. **Memberships** CW, OECD, UN. **Subdivisions** 92 counties.
ECONOMY
GNP $25,390,000,000. **Per capita** $7,947. **Monetary unit** Dollar. **Trade partners** Australia, U.S., Japan, U.K. **Exports** Wool, meat and dairy products, wood products. **Imports** Machinery, manufactured goods, petroleum, motor vehicles, chemicals.
LAND
Description South Pacific islands. **Area** 103,515 mi² (268,103 km²). **Highest point** Mt. Cook, South I., 12,349 ft (3,764 m). **Lowest point** Sea level.

People. The majority of New Zealanders are descended from Europeans, mostly Britons, who arrived in the 1800s. Of Polynesian descent, the indigenous Maori form the largest minority. After a period of decline following the arrival of the Europeans, the Maori population has been increasing. The major languages are English, the official tongue, and Maori. Most New Zealanders live on North Island. Christian religions are observed by many residents, and the Maori have incorporated some Christian elements into their beliefs.

Economy and the Land. Success in agriculture and trade has allowed New Zealand to overcome its small work force, remoteness from major markets, and relative lack of natural resources. A terrain with much ideal grazing land and a climate that is temperate year-round have encouraged cattle and sheep farming. Manufacturing—including the food-processing and paper industries—is an expanding sector, as is tourism. The scenic terrain is greatly varied, ranging from fjords and mountains to a volcanic plateau. New Zealand consists of two large islands—North Island and South Island—and many smaller islands scattered throughout the South Pacific. The nation administers several island territories.

History and Politics. The Maori, the original settlers, are thought to have arrived around A.D. 1000. In 1642 they fought off the Dutch, the first Europeans to reach the area. Captain James Cook of Britain charted the islands in the late 1700s. Soon after, European hunters and traders, drawn by the area's whales, seals, and forests, began to arrive. Maori chiefs signed the 1840 Treaty of Waitangi, establishing British sovereignty, and British companies began to send settlers to New Zealand. Subsequent battles between settlers and Maori ended with the Maori's defeat in 1872, but European diseases and weapons continued to reduce the Maori population. In 1907 New Zealand became a self-governing dominion of Britain; formal independence came forty years later. New Zealand supported Britain in both world wars, but foreign policy has recently focused on Southeast Asia and the South Pacific. Advancing Maori rights has become a priority. ∎

NICARAGUA

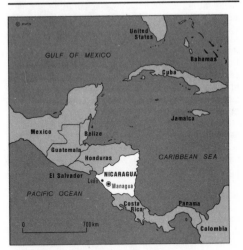

Official name Republic of Nicaragua
PEOPLE
Population 2,970,000. **Density** 59/mi² (23/km²). **Urban** 53%. **Capital** Managua, 644,588. **Ethnic groups** Mestizo 69%, white 17%, black 9%, Indian 5%. **Languages** Spanish, English. **Religions** Roman Catholic 95%. **Life expectancy** 59 female, 55 male. **Literacy** 66%.
POLITICS
Government Republic. **Parties** Sandinista National Liberation Front. **Memberships** OAS, UN. **Subdivisions** 16 departments.
ECONOMY
GDP $2,500,000,000. **Per capita** $846. **Monetary unit** Córdoba. **Trade partners** Western European countries, Central American countries. **Exports** Cotton, coffee,

sugar, meat. **Imports** Food, chemicals and pharmaceuticals, transportation equipment, machinery, petroleum.

LAND
Description Central America. **Area** 50,193 mi² (130,000 km²). **Highest point** Pico Mogotón, 6,913 ft (2,107 m). **Lowest point** Sea level.

People. Nicaraguan society closely reflects the nation's history as a Spanish colony: most of its inhabitants are Spanish speaking, Roman Catholic, and mestizo, a mix of Indian and European stocks. Indian and black communities are found mostly in the Caribbean region.

Economy and the Land. Nicaragua is chiefly an agricultural nation, relying on the production of cotton, coffee, and sugar. Years of instability before a 1979 revolution, a large foreign debt inherited from the previous regime, and a continuing civil war have severely hindered economic prosperity. The nation also suffers from a reliance on imported goods. In 1985 the currency was sharply devalued, and the United States, formerly a chief trading partner, announced a trade embargo. Basic consumer goods are in short supply. The terrain includes a low-lying Pacific region, central highlands, and a flat Caribbean area. The climate is tropical.

History and Politics. Spanish conquistadores, who came via Panama in 1522 to what is now Nicaragua, found a number of independent Indian states. Nicaragua was ruled by Spain as part of Guatemala until it became independent in 1821. In 1823 the former Spanish colonies of the region formed the Federation of Central America, a union which collapsed in 1838, resulting in the independent Republic of Nicaragua. For the next century Nicaragua was the stage both for conflict between the Liberal and Conservative parties and for United States military and economic involvement. Members of the Somoza family, who had close ties to America, directed a repressive regime from 1936 to 1979, when the widely supported Sandinistas overthrew the government. The Sandinistas, who have implemented agrarian reform and improved health care and education, are opposed by Nicaraguans linked to the Somoza administration and by others. Known as contras, these United States–backed insurgents are fighting the Sandinistas from within Nicaragua and from Honduras. ∎

NIGER

Official name Republic of Niger
PEOPLE
Population 6,390,000. **Density** 13/mi² (5/km²). **Urban** 13%. **Capital** Niamey, 362,800. **Ethnic groups** Hausa 56%, Djerma 22%, Fulani 9%, Taureg 8%, Beriberi 4%. **Languages** French, Hausa, indigenous. **Religions** Muslim 80%, indigenous, Christian. **Life expectancy** 46 female, 43 male. **Literacy** 5%.

POLITICS
Government Provisional military government. **Parties** None (banned). **Suffrage** Universal adult. **Memberships** OAU, UN. **Subdivisions** 7 departments.

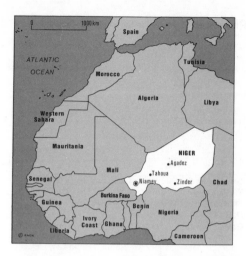

ECONOMY
GDP $2,000,000,000. **Per capita** $425. **Monetary unit** CFA franc. **Trade partners** France, other Western European countries, Nigeria. **Exports** Uranium, livestock, vegetables. **Imports** Petroleum, machinery, motor vehicles, food.

LAND
Description Western Africa, landlocked. **Area** 489,191 mi² (1,267,000 km²). **Highest point** 6,634 ft (2,022 m).

People. Nearly all Nigeriens are black Africans belonging to culturally diverse groups. The Hausa and the Djerma constitute the two largest, and they live mostly in the south and are farmers. The remainder of Nigeriens are nomadic herdsmen who inhabit the northern desert regions. Although the official language is French, most inhabitants speak indigenous tongues. Islam is the most commonly observed religion, but some Nigerians follow indigenous and Christian beliefs.

Economy and the Land. Niger's economy is chiefly agricultural, although arable land is scarce and drought common. The raising of livestock, grain, beans, and peanuts accounts for most farming activity. Uranium mining, a growing industry, has become less productive recently due to a slump in the world uranium market. Most of northern Niger is covered either by mountains or the Sahara Desert, while the south is savanna. The climate is hot and dry.

History and Politics. Because of its central location in northern Africa, Niger was a crossroads for many peoples during its early history and was dominated by several African empires before European explorers arrived in the 1800s. The area was placed within the French sphere of influence in 1885, but not until 1922 did France make Niger a colony of French West Africa. Gradual moves toward autonomy were made during the forties and fifties, and Niger became fully independent in 1960. Unrest caused in part by a prolonged drought led to a coup in 1974 and the establishment of a military government. Civilians now have some part in the political system. Niger maintains close ties to France. ∎

NIGERIA

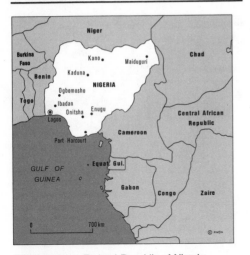

Official name Federal Republic of Nigeria
PEOPLE
Population 89,650,000. **Density** 251/mi² (97/km²).
Urban 28%. **Capital** Lagos, 1,404,000. **Ethnic groups**
Hausa-Fulani, Yoruba, Ibo, others. **Languages** English,
Hausa, Yoruba, Ibo, others. **Religions** Muslim 47%,
Christian 34%, indigenous 18%. **Life expectancy**
51 female, 48 male. **Literacy** 25–30%.
POLITICS
Government Republic. **Parties** None (banned). **Suffrage**
None. **Memberships** CW, OAU, UN. **Subdivisions**
19 states, 1 capital territory.
ECONOMY
GDP $74,000,000,000. **Per capita** $827. **Monetary unit**
Naira. **Trade partners** U.K., other Western European
countries, U.S. **Exports** Petroleum, cocoa, palm products.
Imports Machinery, transportation equipment,
manufactured goods, food.
LAND
Description Western Africa. **Area** 356,669 mi² (923,768
km²). **Highest point** Dimlang, 6,700 ft (2,042 m).
Lowest point Sea level.

People. Nigeria, Africa's most populous nation, contains more than two hundred distinct black African
groups. The largest groups are the Hausa-Fulani,
who dominate the north; the Yoruba, found primarily
in the southwest; and the Ibo, who live in the southeast and have historically been active in government
and trade. Most Hausa-Fulani are Muslim, and the
sizable Christian community is found mainly in the
south. Nigerians commonly combine traditional beliefs with Islam or Christianity. Indigenous tongues
are more widely spoken than English, the official language. Competition among Nigeria's many ethnic
groups has threatened national unity.

Economy and the Land. Nigeria's economy is
based on mining and agriculture. Petroleum is very
important to the Nigerian economy, but a number of
factors—including unskilled labor, poor power facilities, and the worldwide dip in oil prices—have silenced the oil boom of the 1970s and slowed
development in other areas. In 1983 and 1985 the

government expelled millions of illegal aliens in an
effort to revive the economy. The terrain is diverse,
encompassing tropical forest, savanna, and semidesert. The climate is predominantly tropical.

History and Politics. From around 500 B.C. to
about A.D. 200 the region was home to the sophisticated Nok civilization. Later cultures that dominated parts of the area included the Hausa, Fulani,
and Yoruba. The Portuguese arrived in the 1400s,
but the British gained control over the following centuries, uniting the region in 1914 as the Colony and
Protectorate of Nigeria. Nigerian calls for self-rule
culminated in independence in 1960. Internal tensions began to wrack the new nation, and in 1966
two military coups took place. After subsequent
massacres of Ibo, that group declared eastern Nigeria the autonomous state of Biafra. A three-year
civil war followed, ending in 1970 with Biafra's surrender. Economic recovery was speeded by the oil
boom and government development. A civilian government came to power in 1979 but was overthrown
by the military in 1983.   ∎

NIUE

See NEW ZEALAND.

NORFOLK ISLAND

See AUSTRALIA.

NORTHERN MARIANA ISLANDS

See UNITED STATES.

NORWAY

Official name Kingdom of Norway
PEOPLE
Population 4,150,000. **Density** 28/mi² (11/km²). **Urban** 70%. **Capital** Oslo, 448,747. **Ethnic groups** Germanic, Lappish. **Languages** Norwegian, Lappish. **Religions** Lutheran 94%. **Life expectancy** 79 female, 74 male. **Literacy** 100%.
POLITICS
Government Constitutional monarchy. **Parties** Center, Christian People's, Conservative, Labor, Progressive, Socialist Left. **Suffrage** Universal, over 18. **Memberships** NATO, OECD, UN. **Subdivisions** 19 counties.
ECONOMY
GNP $56,200,000,000. **Per capita** $13,600. **Monetary unit** Krone. **Trade partners** U.K., West Germany, Sweden, U.S. **Exports** Petroleum, natural gas, metals, paper and wood pulp, chemicals, fish products. **Imports** Machinery, transportation equipment, food, iron and steel, textiles, clothing.
LAND
Description Northern Europe. **Area** 149,158 mi² (386,317 km²). **Highest point** Glittertinden, 8,110 ft (2,472 m). **Lowest point** Sea level.

People. Because of its relatively remote location in far northern Europe, Norway has seen few population migrations and possesses a virtually homogeneous population, which is predominantly Germanic, Norwegian speaking, and Lutheran. Small communities of Lapps and Finns live in the far north, while most Norwegians live in the south and along the coast. Two mutually intelligible forms of the Norwegian language are taught in schools.

Economy and the Land. Norway's economy, based on shipping, trade, and the mining of offshore oil and natural gas, takes its shape from the nation's proximity to several seas. Shipbuilding, fishing, and forestry are also important activities. Norway is a leading producer of hydroelectricity. Combined with some government control of the economy, these lucrative activities have given the nation a high standard of living and fairly low unemployment. Most of Norway is a high plateau covered with mountains. The Gulf Stream gives the nation a much milder climate than other places at the same latitude.

History and Politics. Parts of present-day Norway were inhabited by about 9000 B.C. Germanic tribes began immigrating to the area about 2000 B.C. Between A.D. 800 and 1100 Viking ships from Norway raided coastal towns throughout Western Europe and also colonized Greenland and Iceland. Unified around 900, Norway was subsequently shaken by civil war, plague, and the end of its royal line. It entered a union with Denmark in 1380, becoming a Danish province in 1536. Around the end of the Napoleonic Wars, in 1814, Norway became part of Sweden. A long struggle against Swedish rule ended in 1905 as Sweden recognized Norwegian independence, and a Danish prince was made king. Norway was neutral in World War I but endured German occupation during World War II. In 1967 the government initiated a wide-ranging social-welfare system. Norway retains relations with Western nations and the Soviet Union but does not allow foreign military bases or nuclear arms on its soil. ∎

OMAN

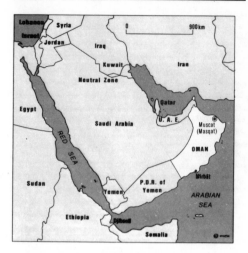

Official name Sultanate of Oman
PEOPLE
Population 1,025,000. **Density** 12/mi² (4.8/km²). **Urban** 8%. **Capital** Muscat, 6,000. **Ethnic groups** Arab, Baluchi, Zanzibari, Indian. **Languages** Arabic, Farsi. **Religions** Ibadite Muslim 75%, Sunni Muslim, Shiite Muslim, Hindu. **Life expectancy** 50 female, 48 male. **Literacy** 20%.
POLITICS
Government Monarchy. **Parties** None. **Suffrage** None. **Memberships** AL, UN. **Subdivisions** 1 province, 2 governorates, numerous districts.
ECONOMY
GNP $6,300,000,000. **Per capita** $6,828. **Monetary unit** Rial. **Trade partners** Japan, United Arab Emirates, U.K., other Western European countries. **Exports** Petroleum. **Imports** Machinery, transportation equipment, manufactured goods, food.
LAND
Description Southwestern Asia. **Area** 82,030 mi² (212,457 km²). **Highest point** Jabal ash Shām, 9,957 ft (3,035 m). **Lowest point** Sea level.

People. Most of Oman's population is Arab, Arabic speaking, and belongs to the Ibadite sect of Islam. Other forms of Islam are also practiced. There is a significant foreign community that includes Indians, Pakistanis, and East African blacks. Many of them are guest workers in the oil industry.

Economy and the Land. Although oil production is the economic mainstay, Oman's reserves are not as vast as those of some other Arab states, and the government is seeking to diversify. The mining of natural gas and copper is being developed, as are agriculture and fishing. A central position in the politically volatile Persian Gulf and revolutionary internal strife have led Oman to devote a considerable portion of its budget to defense. Land regions include a coastal plain and interior mountains and desert. Oman's land borders are undefined and in dispute. A desert climate prevails over most areas except the coast, which has humid conditions.

History and Politics. Islam came to Muscat and Oman, as the nation was known before 1970, in the seventh century A.D. The Portuguese gained control of parts of the coast in 1508 but were driven out in 1650 by the Arabs. At about this time the hereditary sultanate—which absorbed the political power formerly held by the Ibadite religious leaders, or imams—was founded. Close relations with Britain were cemented in a 1798 agreement and subsequent treaties and have continued to the present. Conflicts between the sultan and Omanis who wanted to be ruled exclusively by their imam erupted intermittently after 1900, and in 1959 the sultan defeated the rebels with British help and outlawed the office of imam. Marxist insurgency was put down in 1975. Sultan Qaboos bin Said, who overthrew his father's regime in 1970, has liberalized some policies and worked to modernize the nation. Oman is a moderate, pro-Western Arab state. ∎

ORKNEY ISLANDS

See UNITED KINGDOM.

PACIFIC ISLANDS, TRUST TERRITORY OF THE

See UNITED STATES.

PAKISTAN

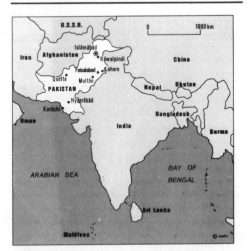

Official name Islamic Republic of Pakistan
PEOPLE
Population 101,300,000. **Density** 298/mi² (115/km²).
Urban 28%. **Capital** Islāmābād, 201,000. **Ethnic groups**
Punjabi, Sindhi, Pushtun, Baluchi. **Languages** Urdu,
English, Punjabi, Sindhi. **Religions** Muslim 97%. **Life**
expectancy 50 female, 51 male. **Literacy** 24%.

POLITICS
Government Republic. **Parties** None (suspended).
Suffrage Universal, over 18. **Memberships** UN.
Subdivisions 4 provinces, 1 capital territory.
ECONOMY
GNP $33,020,000,000. **Per capita** $348. **Monetary unit**
Rupee. **Trade partners** Japan, U.S., U.K., West
Germany, Kuwait. **Exports** Rice, cotton, textiles, light
manufactures. **Imports** Petroleum, transportation
equipment, raw materials, consumer goods.
LAND
Description Southern Asia. **Area** 339,732 mi² (879,902
km²). **Highest point** K², 28,250 ft (8,611 m). **Lowest**
point Sea level.

People. Pakistan's varied ethnicity is the product of centuries of incursions by different racial types. Today each people is concentrated in a different region and speaks its own language; Urdu, the official language, is not widely spoken. The Punjabis compose the largest ethnic group and have traditionally been influential in government and commerce. Virtually all the people of Pakistan, which was created as a Muslim homeland, follow Islam. Spurred by poor living conditions and a lack of jobs, many Pakistanis work abroad.

Economy and the Land. Despite recent progress in manufacturing, agriculture remains the economic mainstay. Improvement in farming techniques has increased productivity. Government planning and foreign assistance have aided all sectors, but Pakistan remains troubled by high population growth, unskilled labor, a trade deficit, and an influx of refugees fleeing the civil war in Afghanistan. Pakistan's terrain includes mountains, fertile plains, and desert. The climate is continental, with extreme variations in temperature.

History and Politics. Around 2500 B.C. the Indus Valley civilization flourished in the area of modern Pakistan. Various empires and immigrants followed, including Aryans, Persians, and Greeks. Invading Arabs introduced Islam to the region in the A.D. 700s. In the 1500s the Mogul Empire of Afghanistan came to include nearly all of present-day Pakistan, India, and Bangladesh, and as that empire declined, various peoples ruled the area. Through wars and treaties, the British presence in Asia expanded, and by the early twentieth century British India included all of modern Pakistan. Because of hostilities between British India's Muslims and Hindus, the separate Muslim nation of Pakistan was created when British India gained independence in 1947. With its boundaries drawn around the Muslim population centers, Pakistan was formed from the northeastern and northwestern parts of India, and its eastern region was separated from the west by more than 1,000 miles (1,600 kilometers). East Pakistanis felt that power was unfairly concentrated in the west, and in 1971 a civil war erupted. Aided by India, East Pakistan won the war and became the independent nation of Bangladesh. Subsequent political activity in Pakistan has included martial law and accusations of government corruption. A dispute with India over ownership of the Kashmir region continues. ∎

PALAU

See UNITED STATES.

PANAMA

Official name Republic of Panama
PEOPLE
Population 2,155,000. **Density** 72/mi² (28/km²). **Urban**
49%. **Capital** Panamá, 388,638. **Ethnic groups** Mestizo
70%, West Indian 14%, white 10%, Indian 6%.
Languages Spanish, English. **Religions** Roman Catholic
93%, Protestant 6%. **Life expectancy** 73 female,
69 male. **Literacy** 85%.
POLITICS
Government Republic. **Parties** Christian Democratic,
Democratic Revolutionary, Liberal, Panameñista. **Suffrage**
Universal, over 18. **Memberships** OAS, UN.
Subdivisions 9 provinces, 1 territory.
ECONOMY
GNP $3,945,000,000. **Per capita** $1,934. **Monetary unit**
Balboa. **Trade partners** U.S., Venezuela, Western
European countries, Japan. **Exports** Petroleum products,
bananas, sugar, shrimp. **Imports** Manufactured goods,
petroleum, machinery, transportation equipment, food.
LAND
Description Central America. **Area** 29,762 mi² (77,082
km²). **Highest point** Volcán Barú, 11,401 ft (3,475 m).
Lowest point Sea level.

People. Most Panamanians are mestizos, a mixture
of Spanish and Indian stocks. Indigenous Indians,
blacks from the West Indies, and whites form the
rest of the population. Former Spanish rule is reflected by the official language, Spanish, and the
predominance of Roman Catholicism. Most people
live in the area around the Panama Canal. A wealthy
white elite has traditionally directed the government
and economy.

Economy and the Land. Because of its strategic
location, Panama has long been a center for trade

and transportation. The 1914 opening of the Panama
Canal, connecting the Atlantic and Pacific oceans,
accentuated these strengths and has provided additional revenue and jobs; the canal area is now Panama's most economically developed region. Agriculture is another important activity. Oil refining,
along with food processing and fishing, is a developing industry, and financial services contribute to
the economy as well. Panama will have to adjust to
the economic and technical losses that will accom-
pany the end of United States operation of the canal
in 1999. Panama has a mountainous interior and a
tropical climate.

History and Politics. Originally inhabited by Indians, Panama became a Spanish colony in the early
1500s and served as a vital transportation center. In
1821 it overcame Spanish rule and entered the Republic of Greater Colombia. After Colombia vetoed
a United States plan to build a canal across the
narrow isthmus, Panama, encouraged by the United
States, seceded from the republic and became independent in 1903. Eleven years later America completed the canal and established control over it and
the Panama Canal Zone. Dissatisfaction with this
arrangement resulted in several anti-American riots
in the fifties and sixties. A 1968 coup placed the
Panamanian National Guard in power, and the
movement to end American control of the Canal
Zone gained momentum. In 1979 the sovereignty of
the Canal Zone was transferred to Panama; it will
gain control of the canal in 1999. Some representation has been returned to civilians, but the military
continues to exercise considerable control. ∎

PAPUA NEW GUINEA

Official name Papua New Guinea
PEOPLE
Population 3,400,000. **Density** 19/mi² (7.3/km²). **Urban**
13%. **Capital** Port Moresby, New Guinea I., 116,952.

Ethnic groups Melanesian, Papuan, Negrito, Micronesian, Polynesian. **Languages** English, Papuan and Negrito languages. **Religions** Roman Catholic, Lutheran, indigenous. **Life expectancy** 52 female, 50 male. **Literacy** 32%.

POLITICS

Government Parliamentary state. **Parties** Melanesian Alliance, National, Pangu, Papua Besena, People's Progress, United. **Suffrage** Universal adult. **Memberships** CW, UN. **Subdivisions** 19 provinces.

ECONOMY

GNP $2,000,000,000. **Per capita** $650. **Monetary unit** Kina. **Trade partners** Australia, Japan, Singapore. **Exports** Copper, coffee beans, coconut products. **Imports** Machinery, manufactured goods, petroleum, food.

LAND

Description South Pacific islands. **Area** 178,703 mi² (462,840 km²). **Highest point** Mt. Wilhelm, New Guinea I., 14,793 ft (4,509 m). **Lowest point** Sea level.

People. Almost all inhabitants are Melanesians belonging to several thousand culturally diverse and geographically isolated communities. More than seven hundred languages are spoken, but most people also speak Motu or a dialect of English to communicate with other groups. The most commonly observed religion is Christianity, brought by European missionaries; diverse faiths based on spirit and ancestor worship are also followed. The traditions of village life remain strong.

Economy and the Land. The economic mainstays are agriculture, which employs most of the work force, and the mining of copper and gold. Papua New Guinea has other mineral resources, as well as potential for forestry. The nation consists of the eastern half of New Guinea Island, plus New Britain, New Ireland, Bougainville, and six hundred smaller islands. Terrain includes mountains, volcanoes, broad valleys, and swamps; the climate is tropical.

History and Politics. Settlers from Southeast Asia are thought to have arrived as long as fifty thousand years ago. Isolated native villages were found by the Spanish and Portuguese in the early 1500s. In 1884 Germany annexed the northeastern part of the island of New Guinea and its offshore islands, and Britain took control of the southeastern section and its islands. Australia assumed administration of the British territory, known as Papua, in 1906 and seized the German regions, or German New Guinea, during World War I. The League of Nations granted Australia a mandate to New Guinea in 1920. After being occupied by Japan in World War II, Papua and New Guinea were united as an Australian territory from 1945 to 1946. The independent nation of Papua New Guinea came into being in 1975. The island of Bougainville seceded a few months later but rejoined the nation in 1976. Papua New Guinea maintains close ties with Australia and a moderate foreign policy. ∎

PARAGUAY

Official name Republic of Paraguay

PEOPLE

Population 3,230,000. **Density** 21/mi² (7.9/km²). **Urban** 39%. **Capital** Asunción, 455,517. **Ethnic groups** Mestizo 95%. **Languages** Spanish, Guarani. **Religions** Roman Catholic 97%, Mennonite. **Life expectancy** 67 female, 63 male. **Literacy** 81%.

POLITICS

Government Republic. **Parties** Colorado, Febrerista, Liberal, Radical Liberal. **Suffrage** Universal adult. **Memberships** OAS, UN. **Subdivisions** 20 departments.

ECONOMY

GDP $5,800,000,000. **Per capita** $1,411. **Monetary unit** Guaraní. **Trade partners** Brazil, Argentina, West Germany, Japan, U.S. **Exports** Cotton, soybeans, wood products. **Imports** Machinery, fuels, motor vehicles, food.

LAND

Description Central South America, landlocked. **Area** 157,048 mi² (406,752 km²). **Highest point** 2,625 ft (800 m). **Lowest point** 151 ft (46 m).

People. Paraguay's population displays a homogeneity unusual in South America; most people are a mix of Spanish and Guarani Indian ancestry, are Roman Catholic, and speak both Spanish and Guarani. The small number of unassimilated Guarani live mostly in western Paraguay, known as the Chaco. There are some foreign communities, mostly German, Japanese, and Brazilian. Culture combines Spanish and Indian traditions.

Economy and the Land. Agriculture—based on cotton, soybeans, and cattle—forms the keystone of the economy. Forestry also contributes significantly to Paraguay's exports. The lack of direct access to the sea, unskilled labor, and a history of war and instability have resulted in an underdeveloped economy; manufacturing in particular has suffered. There is great potential for hydroelectric power, and it is already under exploitation. Paraguay has two distinct regions, divided by the Paraguay River: the semiarid Chaco plains in the west, and the temperate, fertile east, where most farming takes place.

History and Politics. The indigenous Guarani formed an agricultural society centered around what is now Asunción. Portuguese and Spanish explorers arrived in the early 1500s, and the region subsequently gained importance as the center of Spanish holdings in southern South America. During the 1700s Jesuit missionaries worked to convert thousands of Indians to Roman Catholicism. After gaining independence in 1811, Paraguay was ruled until 1870 by three successive dictators: José Gaspar Rodríguez de Francia, who held power from 1814 to 1840 and sealed Paraguay off from foreign influence; Carlos Antonio López, who reversed this isolationism during his rule from 1841 to 1862; and his son,

Francisco Solano López, who led Paraguay into a disastrous war against Uruguay, Argentina, and Brazil that cost the nation half its population. A war against Bolivia from 1932 to 1935 increased Paraguay's territory but further weakened its stability. Alternating weak and repressive regimes followed until 1954, when General Alfredo Stroessner came to power. Having restricted almost all opposition, he has since ruled continuously. ∎

PERU

Official name Republic of Peru
PEOPLE
Population 19,520,000. **Density** 39/mi² (15/km²). **Urban** 65%. **Capital** Lima, 371,122. **Ethnic groups** Indian 45%, mestizo 37%, white 15%. **Languages** Spanish, Quechua, Aymara. **Religions** Roman Catholic. **Life expectancy** 60 female, 56 male. **Literacy** 72%.
POLITICS
Government Republic. **Parties** American Popular Revolutionary Alliance, Popular Action, Popular Christian, United Left. **Suffrage** Universal, over 18. **Memberships** OAS, UN. **Subdivisions** 23 departments, 1 constitutional province.
ECONOMY
GNP $19,200,000,000. **Per capita** $1,018. **Monetary unit** Sol. **Trade partners** U.S., Japan, Western European countries. **Exports** Copper, silver, petroleum, lead, zinc, fish products. **Imports** Machinery, transportation equipment, food, manufactured goods.
LAND
Description Western South America. **Area** 496,224 mi² (1,285,216 km²). **Highest point** Nevado Huascarán, 22,205 ft (6,768 m). **Lowest point** Sea level.

People. Peru's Indian population constitutes the nation's largest ethnic group and the largest Indian concentration in North or South America. Although whites make up the third largest group after Indians and mestizos, they have historically controlled much of the wealth. The Indians are often geographically and culturally remote from the ruling classes and generally live in poverty. Most Peruvians practice Roman Catholicism, a Spanish inheritance.

Economy and the Land. Considerable natural resources have made Peru a leader in the production of minerals—notably copper, lead, and silver—and in fishing. The food-processing, textile, and oil-refining industries also contribute. Productivity has been slowed by a mountainous terrain that impedes transport and communication, earthquakes and other natural disasters, a largely unskilled work force, and years of stringent military rule. Climate varies from arid and mild in the coastal desert to temperate but cool in the Andean highlands and hot and humid in the eastern jungles and plains.

History and Politics. Several sophisticated Indian cultures arose in the region between 900 B.C. and A.D. 1200, the last of which was the Incan. Builders of an empire stretching from Colombia to Chile, the Inca were conquered by the Spanish by 1533. For almost the next three hundred years Peru was a harshly ruled Spanish colony and center for colonial administration. Independence from Spain, which came in 1821, was achieved largely through the efforts of José de San Martín of Argentina and Simón Bolívar of Venezuela. Spain did not formally recognize Peruvian independence until 1879. Peru was ruled by military officers for the rest of the century. In 1883 it was defeated by Chile and Bolivia in the War of the Pacific and lost its valuable southern nitrate region. A reform party, despite being banned by the government, gained momentum in the 1930s and 1940s. Fernando Belaúnde Terry, a moderate reformer, was elected in 1963. A military junta ousted him in 1968, nationalizing some industries and instituting land reform. Inflation and unemployment caused dissatisfaction, and a 1980 election returned Belaúnde to the presidency. The stability of the civilian government has been threatened by strikes and other expressions of internal unrest. ∎

PHILIPPINES

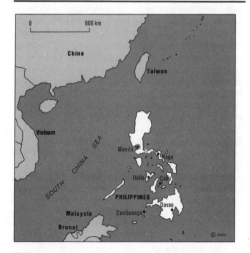

Official name Republic of the Philippines
PEOPLE
Population 55,140,000. **Density** 476/mi² (184/km²).

Urban 37%. **Capital** Manila, Luzon I., 1,626,249. **Ethnic groups** Christian Malay 92%, Muslim Malay 4%, Chinese 2%. **Languages** Pilipino, Spanish, English, Malay-Polynesian languages. **Religions** Roman Catholic 83%, Protestant 9%, Muslim 5%, Buddhist and others 3%. **Life expectancy** 65 female, 61 male. **Literacy** 88%.

POLITICS
Government Republic. **Parties** Laban, Liberal, Nacionalista, New Society. **Suffrage** Universal adult. **Memberships** UN. **Subdivisions** 72 provinces, 61 chartered cities.

ECONOMY
GNP $39,000,000,000. **Per capita** $760. **Monetary unit** Peso. **Trade partners** U.S., Japan, Western European countries, Hong Kong. **Exports** Coconut products, sugar, wood, textiles, copper concentrates. **Imports** Petroleum, industrial equipment, transportation equipment, wheat.

LAND
Description Southeastern Asian islands. **Area** 115,831 mi^2 (300,000 km^2). **Highest point** Mt. Apo, Mindanao I., 9,692 ft (2,954 m). **Lowest point** Sea level.

People. Nearly all Filipinos are descended from Malay peoples. The majority population is Roman Catholic, a reflection of centuries under Spanish rule. A Muslim minority has begun agitating for autonomy. Although nearly ninety native languages and dialects are spoken, Pilipino, English, and Spanish are the official languages. The wide gap between rich and poor was inherited from a plantation economy that concentrated wealth in the hands of the landowners.

Economy and the Land. The Philippines is a primarily agricultural nation, relying on rice, sugar, coconuts, and wood. Fishing is an important activity. Considerable reserves of copper, nickel, and chromite make mining important. Manufacturing is developing through government incentives. A dependence on imported goods, along with inadequate but growing power and transport systems, has hampered growth. The archipelago of more than seven thousand islands is marked by mountains, volcanoes, forests, and inland plains. The climate is tropical and includes a typhoon season.

History and Politics. The islands are thought to have been settled by Negritos about thirty thousand years ago. Beginning about 3000 B.C. Malay immigrants arrived. By 1565 the area was under Spanish control, and the Roman Catholic church had considerable influence throughout the Spanish period. In the late 1800s a movement for independence developed but was put down first by the Spanish and then by the United States, which gained the islands in 1898 after defeating Spain in the Spanish-American War. During World War II Japan occupied the Philippines. Independence came in 1946 and was followed by a rebellion by Communists demanding land reform; the rebels were defeated in 1954. Ferdinand Marcos was elected president in 1965 and, in the face of opposition from many quarters, declared martial law in 1972. Although Marcos lifted martial law in 1981, a 1973 constitution had consolidated his power, allowing continued restrictions on civil liberties. The regime is threatened by increasingly active Communist guerrillas, the Muslim insurgency, and

implications of government involvement in the 1983 assassination of Marcos's chief political rival. Foreign policy features strong ties with the United States. ∎

PITCAIRN

See UNITED KINGDOM.

POLAND

Official name Polish People's Republic
PEOPLE
Population 37,055,000. **Density** 307/mi^2 (119/km^2). **Urban** 59%. **Capital** Warsaw, 1,628,900. **Ethnic groups** Polish 99%. **Languages** Polish. **Religions** Roman Catholic 95%. **Life expectancy** 75 female, 70 male. **Literacy** 98%.

POLITICS
Government Socialist republic. **Parties** United Workers'. **Suffrage** Universal, over 18. **Memberships** COMECON, UN, Warsaw Pact. **Subdivisions** 49 provinces.

ECONOMY
GNP $186,800,000,000. **Per capita** $5,160. **Monetary unit** Złoty. **Trade partners** U.S.S.R., Eastern European countries, West Germany. **Exports** Machinery, equipment, fuels, manufactured goods, textiles, food. **Imports** Machinery, petroleum, raw materials, food.

LAND
Description Eastern Europe. **Area** 120,728 mi^2 (312,683 km^2). **Highest point** Rysy, 8,199 ft (2,499 m). **Lowest point** Raczki Elbląskie, 5.9 ft (1.8 m) below sea level.

People. Poland's homogeneous population is partially a result of Nazi persecution during World War II, which virtually obliterated the Jewish community and led to the emigration of most minorities. Roman Catholicism, practiced by almost all Poles, remains a unifying force. The urban population has risen in the postwar period because of government emphasis on industrialization.

Economy and the Land. Government policies since the war have transformed Poland from an agricultural nation into an industrial one. It is a leading producer of coal and has several metal-processing industries. Machinery and textiles are important products. Although most industries are government controlled, the majority of farms are privately owned. Poland's poor soil and short growing season have kept it from achieving agricultural self-sufficiency. Shortages in consumer goods have been chronic since the 1970s, when debts to the West were compounded by the failure of Polish goods in world markets. Poland has a mostly flat terrain—except for mountains in the south—and a temperate climate.

History and Politics. Slavic tribes inhabited the region of modern Poland several thousand years ago. The Piast dynasty began in the A.D. 900s and established Roman Catholicism as the official religion. In the sixteenth century the Jagiellonian dynasty guided the empire to its height of expansion. A subsequent series of upheavals and wars weakened Poland, and from the 1770s to the 1790s it was partitioned three times, finally disappearing as an independent state. In 1918, following the Allies' World War I victory, Poland regained its independence and, through the 1919 Treaty of Versailles, much of its former territory. World War II began with Germany's invasion of Poland in 1939. With the end of the war Poland came under Communist control and Soviet domination. Antigovernment strikes and riots, some spurred by rising food prices, erupted periodically, and following the formation of the trade union Solidarity, the government imposed martial law in 1981. Although martial law was lifted in 1982, many restrictions and tensions remain. ∎

PORTUGAL

Official name Portuguese Republic
PEOPLE
Population 10,065,000. **Density** 283/mi² (109/km²).
Urban 30%. **Capital** Lisbon, 807,200. **Ethnic groups**
Mediterranean, African. **Languages** Portuguese.
Religions Roman Catholic 97%. **Life expectancy**
75 female, 70 male. **Literacy** 80%.
POLITICS
Government Republic. **Parties** Communist, Social
Democratic, Social Democratic Center, Socialist.
Suffrage Universal, over 18. **Memberships** NATO,
OECD, UN. **Subdivisions** 18 districts, 2 autonomous
regions.

ECONOMY
GNP $23,400,000,000. **Per capita** $2,328. **Monetary
unit** Escudo. **Trade partners** U.K., West Germany, other
Western European countries, U.S. **Exports** Clothing,
textiles, cork and cork products, wood, food and wine.
Imports Petroleum, industrial machinery, transportation
equipment, cotton, chemicals.
LAND
Description Southern Europe. **Area** 35,516 mi² (91,985
km²). **Highest point** Ponta do Pico, 7,713 ft (2,351 m).
Lowest point Sea level.

People. Although many invaders have been drawn by Portugal's long coastline throughout past centuries, today the population is relatively homogeneous. One group of invaders, the Romans, laid the basis for the chief language, Portuguese, which developed from Latin. The only significant minority is composed of black Africans from former colonies. Most Portuguese are rural and belong to the Roman Catholic church, which has had a strong influence on society.

Economy and the Land. The mainstays of agriculture and fishing were joined in the mid-1900s by manufacturing, chiefly of textiles, clothing, cork products, metals, and machinery. A variety of social and political ills have contributed to Portugal's status as one of Europe's poorest nations: past wars with African colonies, an influx of colonial refugees, and intraparty violence. Tourism has declined slightly, and agriculture has suffered from outdated techniques and a rural-to-urban population shift. The terrain is mostly plains and lowlands, with some mountains; the climate is mild and sunny.

Places and Possessions of Portugal

Entity	Status	Area	Population	Capital / Population
Azores (North Atlantic islands)	Autonomous region	868 mi² (2,247 km²)	255,000	Ponta Delgada, 21,200
Madeira Islands (northwest of Africa)	Autonomous region	307 mi² (794 km²)	260,000	Funchal, 44,100

History and Politics. Inhabited by an Iberian people about five thousand years ago, the area was later visited by Phoenicians, Celts, and Greeks before falling to the Romans around the first century B.C. The Romans were followed by Germanic Visigoths and in A.D. 711 by North African Muslims, who greatly influenced Portuguese art and architecture. Spain absorbed Portugal in 1094, and Portugal declared its independence in 1143. About one hundred years later the last of the Muslims were expelled. Portugal's golden age—during which its navigators explored the globe and founded colonies in South America, Africa, and the Far East—lasted from 1385 to the late 1500s. Rival European powers soon began to seize Portuguese holdings, and in 1580 Spain invaded Portugal, ruling until 1640, when the Spanish were driven out and independence reestablished. After the 1822 loss of Brazil, Portugal's most valuable colony, and decades of opposition, a weakened monarchy was overthrown in 1910. The subsequent parliamentary democracy, marked by rapid power shifts and economic instability, proved a failure, and in 1926 it gave way to a military coup. Antonio Salazar became prime minister in 1932, ruling as a virtual dictator until 1968. Salazar's favored treatment of the rich and his refusal to relinquish Portugal's colonies aggravated the economic situation. A 1974 coup toppled Salazar's successor and set up a military government, events that sparked violence among political parties. Almost all Portuguese colonies gained independence during the next two years. A democratic government was adopted in 1976, and since then the nation has been ruled by differing coalitions. Portugal has close ties to the West and has sought to improve relations with the Third World. ∎

PUERTO RICO

Official name Commonwealth of Puerto Rico
PEOPLE
Population 3,350,000. **Density** 953/mi² (368/km²).

Urban 67%. **Capital** San Juan, 422,701. **Languages** Spanish, English. **Religions** Roman Catholic 85%. **Life expectancy** 78 female, 71 male. **Literacy** 92%.
POLITICS
Government Commonwealth (U.S.). **Parties** Independence, New Progressive, Popular Democratic, Socialist. **Memberships** None. **Subdivisions** 78 municipalities.
ECONOMY
GNP 12,140,000,000. **Per capita** $3,713. **Monetary unit** U.S. dollar. **Trade partners** U.S., Venezuela, Netherlands Antilles, Virgin Islands. **Exports** Clothing, textiles, electrical equipment, sugar, tobacco. **Imports** Petroleum, food.
LAND
Description Caribbean island. **Area** 3,515 mi² (9,103 km²). **Highest point** Cerro de Punta, 4,390 ft (1,338 m). **Lowest point** Sea level.

People. Puerto Rico's chief language, Spanish, and religion, Roman Catholicism, reflect this American Commonwealth's past under Spanish rule. Most of the population is descended from Spaniards and black African slaves. A rising population has caused poverty, housing shortages, and unemployment. Many Puerto Ricans live in the United States, mostly in New York City.

Economy and the Land. Once dependent on such plantation crops as sugar and coffee, Puerto Rico is now a manufacturing nation, specializing in food products and electrical equipment. This transformation was aided by Commonwealth incentives for foreign investors after World War II, also known as Operation Bootstrap. Foreign visitors, attracted by the tropical climate, make tourism another important activity. Economic development has been hurt by a paucity of natural resources and by sensitivity to fluctuations of the United States economy. The island's terrain is marked by mountains, lowlands, and valleys.

History and Politics. The original inhabitants, the Arawak Indians, were wiped out by Spanish colonists, who first settled the island in 1508. Despite successive attacks by the French, the English, and the Dutch, Puerto Rico remained under Spanish control until 1898, when the United States took possession after the Spanish-American War. A civil government under a United States governor was set up in 1900; seventeen years later Puerto Ricans were made United States citizens. In 1952 the island became a self-governing Commonwealth. Commonwealth status was upheld in a referendum in 1967, but fierce, occasionally violent internal debate continues over whether Puerto Rico should opt for statehood, continued Commonwealth status, or independence. ∎

QATAR

Official name State of Qatar
PEOPLE
Population 280,000. **Density** 65/mi² (25/km²). **Urban** 87%. **Capital** Doha, 190,000. **Ethnic groups** Arab 40%,

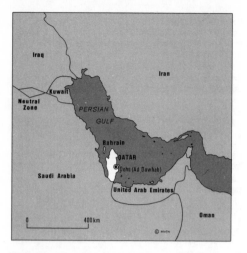

Pakistani 18%, Indian 18%, Iranian 10%. **Languages** Arabic, English. **Religions** Muslim 95%. **Life expectancy** 60 female, 56 male. **Literacy** 40%.

POLITICS
Government Monarchy. **Parties** None. **Suffrage** None. **Memberships** AL, OPEC, UN. **Subdivisions** None.

ECONOMY
GDP $7,900,000,000. **Per capita** $27,790. **Monetary unit** Riyal. **Trade partners** U.K., Japan, other Western European countries, U.S. **Exports** Petroleum. **Imports** Machinery, transportation equipment, manufactured goods, food.

LAND
Description Southwestern Asia. **Area** 4,247 mi² (11,000 km²). **Highest point** Abā al-Bawl Hill, 344 ft (105 m). **Lowest point** Sea level.

People. Qatar's population is distinguished by a relatively high proportion of Iranians, Pakistanis, and Indians, who began arriving during the oil boom of the 1950s. Most Qataris are Sunni Muslims and live in or near Doha, the capital. In recent years the government has encouraged the nomadic Bedouins to take up settled life-styles. Despite a political trend toward a modern welfare state, Qatar retains many elements of a traditional Islamic society.

Economy and the Land. Oil provides the great majority of Qatar's income. Extensive reserves of natural gas await exploitation. The government has made moves toward economic diversification, investing in agriculture and industry; fertilizer and cement are important new products. Most of Qatar is stony desert, and the climate is hot and arid.

History and Politics. No strong central government existed in Qatar before Saudi Muslims gained control in the late eighteenth century. Ottoman Turks occupied the region from 1872 to 1916, when Qatar became a British protectorate. Although oil was discovered in 1940 on the western side of Qatar's peninsula, the outbreak of World War II postponed exploitation for another nine years. Qatar became independent in 1971 after failing to agree on the terms of a union with eight Persian Gulf sheikdoms—today the United Arab Emirates and Bahrain. Oil revenues have been used to improve

housing, transportation, and public health. Qatar maintains friendly relations with the West and neighboring Arab states. ∎

REUNION

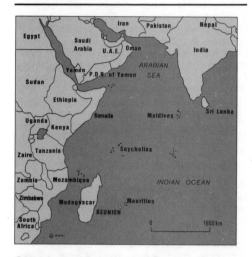

Official name Department of Réunion
PEOPLE
Population 545,000. **Density** 562/mi² (217/km²). **Urban** 41%. **Capital** Saint-Denis, 84,400. **Ethnic groups** Mixed French, African, Malagasy, Chinese, Pakistani, Indian. **Languages** French. **Religions** Roman Catholic 94%. **Life expectancy** 62 female, 56 male. **Literacy** 80%.

POLITICS
Government Overseas department (France). **Parties** Communist, Popular Movement for Liberation, Rally for the Republic, Socialist, Union for Democracy. **Suffrage** Universal adult. **Memberships** None. **Subdivisions** 4 districts.

ECONOMY
Monetary unit French franc. **Trade partners** France, Mauritius. **Exports** Sugar, rum and molasses, perfume essences. **Imports** Manufactured goods, food, machinery, transportation equipment, petroleum.

LAND
Description Indian Ocean island. **Area** 969 mi² (2,510 km²). **Highest point** Piton des Neiges, 10,069 ft (3,069 m). **Lowest point** Sea level.

People. Réunion has a racially mixed population, mainly descended from French settlers, African slaves, and Asian laborers. French is the official language, but most inhabitants speak a creole dialect. The mainly Roman Catholic population is densely concentrated in the lowland areas along the coast. Social stratification is rigid.

Economy and the Land. Réunion's traditional sugar crop continues as its economic mainstay, and sugar by-products such as rum and molasses are also important. Unemployment is a problem, and the island remains dependent upon French aid. The mountainous terrain is marked by one active and several extinct volcanoes. The tropical climate is subject to occasional cyclones and trade winds, which bring high rainfall to the south and southeast.

History and Politics. Although known to the Arabs and the Portuguese, Réunion was uninhabited when French settlement began in the 1660s. First called Île Bourbon, the island originally served as a stopover on the French shipping route to India. The French soon developed coffee and sugar plantations, bringing slaves from Africa to work them. British-French rivalry for control of the area led to brief British rule during the early 1800s. The name was changed to Réunion in 1848, and after the abolition of slavery, indentured laborers were brought from Indochina, India, and eastern Africa. Réunion was a French colony until 1946, when it became an overseas department. ∎

ROMANIA

Official name Socialist Republic of Romania
PEOPLE
Population 22,860,000. **Density** 249/mi² (96/km²).
Urban 50%. **Capital** Bucharest, 1,929,360. **Ethnic groups** Romanian 88%, Hungarian 8%. **Languages** Romanian. **Religions** Romanian Orthodox 80%, Roman Catholic 6%. **Life expectancy** 74 female, 69 male. **Literacy** 98%.
POLITICS
Government Socialist republic. **Parties** Communist. **Suffrage** Universal, over 18. **Memberships** COMECON, UN, Warsaw Pact. **Subdivisions** 41 counties.
ECONOMY
GNP $104,800,000,000. **Per capita** $4,238. **Monetary unit** Leu. **Trade partners** U.S.S.R., West Germany, East Germany. **Exports** Machinery, fuels, textiles, wood products, food. **Imports** Machinery, fuels, iron ore, motor vehicles.
LAND
Description Eastern Europe. **Area** 91,699 mi² (237,500 km²). **Highest point** Moldoveanu, 8,343 ft (2,543 m). **Lowest point** Sea level.

People. The majority population of Romania belongs to the Romanian Orthodox church and traces its roots to Latin-speaking Romans, Thracians, Slavs, and Celts. Minorities, concentrated in Transylvania and areas north and west of Bucharest, are mainly Roman Catholic Hungarians and Germans. Other minorities include Gypsies, Serbs, Croats, Ukrainians, Greeks, Turks, and Armenians. Almost all inhabitants speak Romanian, although other languages are often spoken by minority groups.

Economy and the Land. When Romania became a Communist country in the 1940s, the government began programs to turn the country from agriculture to industry. The economy is now based on industry, and products include oil, wood, and natural gas. Although Romania remains less developed than many other European countries, it has experienced postwar growth in its gross national product. Most agriculture is collectivized, and corn and wheat are major crops. The terrain is marked by a low-lying south-to-northeast plateau that curves around several mountain ranges, including the Carpathians, found in the northern and central regions. The climate is continental, with cold, snowy winters and warm summers.

History and Politics. First colonized by the Dacians, a Thracian tribe, around the fourth century B.C., the area became the Roman province of Romania in the second century A.D. Invading Bulgars, Goths, Huns, Magyars, Slavs, and Tartars followed the Romans. Between 1250 and 1350 the independent Romanian principalities of Walachia and Moldavia emerged. In the fifteenth and sixteenth centuries Ottoman Turks conquered the principalities, and following a Russian-Turkish war, Russians occupied the states. In 1861 Walachia and Moldavia were united as Romania, in 1878 they gained independence, and in 1881 Romania was proclaimed a kingdom. The nation's government was marked by oppression and a concentration of land and wealth among the aristocracy, and a 1907 rebellion was quelled by the army. In 1919, after a World War I alliance with the Allies, Romania gained Transylvania and other territories. Instability and dissatisfaction, spurred by worldwide economic depression, continued through the 1930s. With the cooperation of Romanian leadership, Germany occupied the country in World War II. In 1944 Soviet troops entered Romania, and the nation subsequently joined the Allies. A Communist government was established in 1945, and in 1947 the king was forced to abdicate and Romania officially became a Communist country. Initially Romania's policies were closely tied to those of the Soviet Union, but renewed nationalism in the sixties led to several independent policy decisions. ∎

RWANDA

Official name Rwanda
PEOPLE
Population 5,935,000. **Density** 584/mi² (225/km²).
Urban 5%. **Capital** Kigali, 156,700. **Ethnic groups** Hutu 85%, Tutsi 14%, Twa 1%. **Languages** Kinyarwanda,

French. **Religions** Roman Catholic 65%, indigenous 25%, Protestant 9%, Muslim 1%. **Life expectancy** 47 female, 44 male. **Literacy** 37%.

POLITICS
Government Republic. **Parties** National Revolutionary Movement for Development. **Suffrage** Universal adult. **Memberships** OAU, UN. **Subdivisions** 10 prefectures.

ECONOMY
GDP $1,388,000,000. **Per capita** $270. **Monetary unit** Franc. **Trade partners** Belgium, Kenya, West Germany, France, U.S. **Exports** Coffee, tea, cassiterite, wolfram. **Imports** Food, clothing, machinery, transportation equipment, petroleum.

LAND
Description Eastern Africa, landlocked. **Area** 10,169 mi² (26,338 km²). **Highest point** Volcan Karisimbi, 14,787 ft (4,507 m).

People. Most Rwandans are Hutu, mainly farmers of Bantu stock. Minorities include the Tutsi, a pastoral people that dominated politically until a Hutu rebellion in 1959, and the Twa, Pygmies descended from the original population. Both French and Kinyarwanda are official languages, but most speak Kinyarwanda, a Bantu tongue. Roman Catholicism is the major religion, and minority groups practice indigenous beliefs as well as Protestantism and Islam. Rwanda is characterized by a high population density and a high birthrate.

Economy and the Land. Agriculture is the major activity, although plagued by the erosion and overpopulation of arable land. Many Rwandans practice subsistence farming, while coffee and tea are major export crops. The production and export of minerals such as cassiterite and wolfram, partly fueled by foreign investment, is also important. Economic growth has been hindered by Rwanda's landlocked position and underdeveloped transportation system. The terrain consists mainly of grassy uplands and hills, with volcanic mountains in the west and northwest. The climate is mild.

History and Politics. The Twa, the region's original inhabitants, were followed by the Hutu. The Tutsi most likely arrived about the fourteenth century, subjugating the weaker Hutu and becoming the region's

dominant force. The areas of present-day Rwanda and Burundi became part of German East Africa in the 1890s. In 1919, following World War I, the region was mandated to Belgium as Ruanda-Urundi, and following World War II, Ruanda-Urundi was made a United Nations trust territory under Belgian administration. In 1959 a Hutu revolt against Tutsi domination resulted in the death of many Tutsi and the flight of many more. Independence was gained in 1962, and the former territory split into the countries of Rwanda and Burundi. The military overthrew the nation's first president in 1973, and a civilian government was subsequently installed. ∎

ST. CHRISTOPHER AND NEVIS

Official name Federation of St. Christopher and Nevis

PEOPLE
Population 45,000. **Density** 433/mi² (167/km²). **Urban** 34%. **Capital** Basseterre, St. Christopher I., 14,725. **Ethnic groups** Black. **Languages** English. **Religions** Anglican, other Protestant, Roman Catholic. **Literacy** 80%.

POLITICS
Government Parliamentary state. **Parties** Labor, People's Action Movement, Reformation. **Suffrage** Universal adult. **Memberships** CW, OAS, UN. **Subdivisions** 10 districts.

ECONOMY
GNP $41,600,000. **Per capita** $920. **Monetary unit** East Caribbean dollar. **Trade partners** U.K., other Western European countries, U.S. **Exports** Sugar, molasses. **Imports** Food, manufactured goods, fuels.

LAND
Description Caribbean islands. **Area** 104 mi² (269 km²). **Highest point** Mt. Misery, St. Christopher I., 3,792 ft (1,156 m). **Lowest point** Sea level.

People. Most of the inhabitants of the islands of St. Christopher, often called St. Kitts, and Nevis are of black African descent. The primarily rural population is concentrated along the coast. English is spoken throughout the islands, and most people are Protestant, especially Anglican, evidence of former British rule.

Economy and the Land. Agriculture and tourism are the economic mainstays of St. Christopher and Nevis. Sugarcane is a major crop, cultivated mainly on St. Christopher, while Nevis produces cotton, fruits, and vegetables. Agriculture also provides for sugar processing, the major industrial activity. A tropical climate, beaches, and a scenic mountainous terrain provide for tourism.

History and Politics. The islands were first inhabited by Arawak Indians, who were displaced by the warlike Caribs. In 1493 Christopher Columbus sighted the islands, and in the 1600s British settlement of both islands began, along with French settlement on St. Christopher. Sugar plantations were soon established, and slaves imported from Africa. Britain's control of the islands was recognized by the 1783 Treaty of Paris, and for a time St. Christopher, Nevis, and Anguilla were ruled as a single colony. Anguilla was officially made a separate dependency of Britain in 1980, and St. Christopher and Nevis became independent in 1983. ∎

ST. HELENA

See UNITED KINGDOM.

ST. LUCIA

Official name St. Lucia

PEOPLE
Population 120,000.
Density 504/mi² (195/km²). **Urban** 40%. **Capital** Castries, 47,600. **Ethnic groups** Black 90%, mixed 6%. **Languages** English, French. **Religions** Roman Catholic 90%, Anglican 3%, other Protestant 7%. **Life expectancy** 72 female, 67 male. **Literacy** 78%.

POLITICS
Government Parliamentary state. **Suffrage** Universal, over 18. **Memberships** CW, OAS, UN. **Subdivisions** 16 parishes.

ECONOMY
GDP $121,500,000. **Per capita** $980. **Monetary unit** East Caribbean dollar. **Trade partners** U.K., U.S., Trinidad and Tobago, Barbados. **Exports** Bananas, cocoa. **Imports** Food, machinery, petroleum, fertilizer.

LAND
Description Caribbean island. **Area** 238 mi² (616 km²). **Highest point** Mt. Gimie, 3,117 ft (950 m). **Lowest point** Sea level.

People. St. Lucia's population is composed mainly of descendants of black African slaves, and minority groups include people of African-European descent, whites, and East Indians. During the colonial period the island frequently shifted from British to French control, and its culture reflects both British and French elements. Although English is widely spoken, many St. Lucians speak a dialect of French. Roman Catholicism is the main religion, and the Protestant minority includes Anglicans.

Economy and the Land. Agriculture remains important, and principal crops include bananas and cocoa. Tax incentives and relative political stability have caused an increase in industrial development and foreign investment, mainly from the United States. Tourism is becoming increasingly important, with visitors drawn by the tropical climate, scenic mountainous terrain, and beaches.

History and Politics. Arawak Indians arrived between the A.D. 200s and 400s and were conquered by the Caribs between the ninth and eleventh centuries. Dutch, French, and British rivalry for control began in the seventeenth century, but at first the Europeans were unable to subdue the Caribs. The first successful settlement was established by the French in 1651. After many years of alternating French and British control, St. Lucia came under British rule through the 1814 Treaty of Paris. The island gained full independence in 1979. ∎

ST. PIERRE AND MIQUELON

See FRANCE.

ST. VINCENT AND THE GRENADINES

Official name St. Vincent and the Grenadines

PEOPLE
Population 140,000.
Density 933/mi² (360/km²). **Urban** 14%. **Capital** Kingstown, St. Vincent I., 23,959. **Ethnic groups** Black. **Languages** English. **Religions** Anglican, Methodist, Roman Catholic. **Life expectancy** 60 female, 58 male. **Literacy** 82%.

POLITICS
Government Parliamentary state. **Parties** Labor, New Democratic. **Suffrage** Universal, over 18. **Memberships** CW, OAS, UN.

ECONOMY
GNP $69,200,000. **Per capita** $539. **Monetary unit** East Caribbean dollar. **Trade partners** U.K., Trinidad and Tobago, Canada, U.S. **Exports** Bananas, arrowroot, copra. **Imports** Food, machinery, fertilizer, fuels.

LAND
Description Caribbean islands. **Area** 150 mi² (389 km²). **Highest point** Soufrière, St. Vincent I., 4,048 ft (1,234 m). **Lowest point** Sea level.

People. The people of St. Vincent are mainly descended from black African slaves. The colonial influences of Britain and France are evidenced by the languages and religions: English is the official language and a French patois is also spoken, and most people are either Anglican or Roman Catholic.

Economy and the Land. St. Vincent's economy is based on agriculture, especially banana production. Tourism also plays a role, both on the main island of St. Vincent and in the Grenadines. St. Vincent is the largest island, and about one hundred smaller islands make up the Grenadines. The terrain is mountainous, with coastlines marked by sandy beaches, and the climate is tropical.

History and Politics. The indigenous Arawak Indians were conquered by the Caribs about 1300. Christopher Columbus most likely reached the area in 1498. Although the Caribs fought European occupancy, the British began settling St. Vincent in the 1760s. A period of French control began in 1779, and the islands were returned to the British in 1783. St. Vincent and the Grenadines remained a British dependency until independence was gained in 1979. ∎

SAN MARINO

Official name Republic of San Marino
PEOPLE
Population 23,000. **Density** 958/mi² (377/km²). **Urban** 74%. **Capital** San Marino, 4,623. **Ethnic groups** San Marinese. **Languages** Italian. **Religions** Roman Catholic. **Literacy** 97%.
POLITICS
Government Republic. **Parties** Christian Democratic, Communist, Socialist, Unitary Socialist. **Suffrage** Universal adult. **Memberships** None. **Subdivisions** 9 castles.
ECONOMY
Monetary unit Italian lira. **Trade partners** Italy. **Exports** Construction materials, textiles, wine, postage stamps. **Imports** Consumer goods, petroleum, gold.
LAND
Description Southern Europe, landlocked. **Area** 24 mi²

(61 km²). **Highest point** Monte Titano, 2,425 ft (739 m). **Lowest point** 174 ft (53 m).

People. San Marino is completely surrounded by Italy; thus the San Marinese are ethnically similar to Italians, combining Mediterranean, Alpine, Adriatic, and Nordic roots. Italian is the main language, and Roman Catholicism the major religion. Despite San Marino's similarities to Italy, its long tradition of independence has given its citizens a strong national identity.

Economy and the Land. San Marino and Italy's close economic relationship has resulted in a mutually beneficial customs union; San Marino has no customs restrictions at its borders and receives annual budget subsidiary payments from Italy. Most San Marinese are employed in agriculture; livestock raising is a main activity, and crops include wheat and grapes. Tourism and the sale of postage stamps are major economic contributors, as is industry, which produces construction materials and textiles for export. Located in the Apennine Mountains, San Marino has a rugged terrain and a generally moderate climate.

History and Politics. San Marino is considered the world's oldest republic. Tradition has it that Marinus, a Christian stonecutter seeking religious freedom in a time of repressive Roman rule, founded the state in the fourth century A.D. Partly because of the protection afforded by its mountainous terrain, San Marino has been able maintain continuous independence despite attempted invasions. In the 1300s the country became a republic, and the pope recognized its independent status in 1631. San Marino signed its first treaty of friendship with Italy in 1862. In its foreign relations, the country maintains a distinct identity and status. ∎

SAO TOME AND PRINCIPE

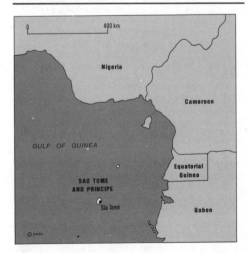

Official name Democratic Republic of São Tomé and Príncipe

PEOPLE
Population 89,000. **Density** 239/mi² (92/km²). **Urban** 32%. **Capital** São Tomé, São Tomé I., 17,380. **Ethnic groups** Mixed African, Portuguese-African. **Languages** Portuguese, indigenous. **Religions** Roman Catholic, Protestant, Seventh Day Adventist. **Literacy** 50%.

POLITICS
Government Republic. **Parties** Movement for Liberation. **Suffrage** Universal, over 18. **Memberships** OAU, UN. **Subdivisions** 7 counties.

ECONOMY
GDP $30,000,000. **Per capita** $300. **Monetary unit** Dobra. **Trade partners** Netherlands, Portugal, U.S., West Germany. **Exports** Cocoa, copra, palm oil. **Imports** Food, machinery, electrical equipment, fuels.

LAND
Description Western African islands. **Area** 372 mi² (964 km²). **Highest point** Pico de São Tomé, São Tomé I., 6,640 ft (2,024 m). **Lowest point** Sea level.

People. Descendants of African slaves and people of Portuguese-African heritage compose most of São Tomé and Príncipe's population. Colonial rule by Portugal is evidenced by the predominance of the Portuguese language and Roman Catholicism. The majority of the population lives on São Tomé.

Economy and the Land. Cocoa dominates São Tomé and Príncipe's economy. Copra and palm-oil production is also important, and fishing plays an economic role as well. Through the development of vegetable crops, the government hopes to diversify agricultural output; much food must now be imported. Part of an extinct volcanic mountain range, São Tomé and Príncipe have a mostly mountainous terrain. The climate is tropical.

History and Politics. When Portuguese explorers arrived in the 1400s, São Tomé and Príncipe were uninhabited. Early settlers included Portuguese convicts and exiles. Cultivation of the land and importation of slaves led to a thriving sugar economy by the mid-1500s. In the 1800s, following slave revolts and the decline of sugar production, coffee and cocoa became the islands' mainstays, and soon large Portuguese plantations called *rocas* were established. Slavery was abolished by Portugal in 1876, but an international controversy arose in the early 1900s when it was found that Angolan contract workers were being treated as virtual slaves. Decades of unrest led to the 1953 Batepa Massacre, in which Portuguese rulers killed several hundred rioting African workers. A movement for independence began in the late 1950s, and following a 1974 change of government in Portugal, São Tomé and Príncipe became independent in 1975. The country has established ties with other former Portuguese colonies in northern Africa since independence. ∎

SAUDI ARABIA

Official name Kingdom of Saudi Arabia
PEOPLE
Population 10,970,000. **Density** 13/mi² (5.1/km²). **Urban** 70%. **Capital** Riyadh, 1,000,000. **Ethnic groups** Arab

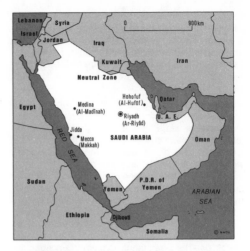

90%, Afro-Asian 10%. **Languages** Arabic. **Religions** Muslim. **Life expectancy** 56 female, 53 male. **Literacy** 52%.

POLITICS
Government Monarchy. **Parties** None. **Suffrage** None. **Memberships** AL, OPEC, UN. **Subdivisions** 14 districts.

ECONOMY
GDP $120,000,000,000. **Per capita** $14,117. **Monetary unit** Riyal. **Trade partners** Japan, U.S., Western European countries. **Exports** Petroleum, petroleum products. **Imports** Manufactured goods, transportation equipment, construction materials, food.

LAND
Description Southwestern Asia. **Area** 830,000 mi² (2,149,690 km²). **Highest point** 10,279 ft (3,133 m). **Lowest point** Sea level.

People. Saudi Arabia is inhabited primarily by Arab Muslims descended from Semitic peoples who settled in the region several thousand years ago. The petroleum industry has attracted a sizable minority of Arabs from other nations, Europeans, and non-Arab Muslims from Africa and Asia. The country's official language is Arabic, although English is used among educated Saudis in business and international affairs. Islam dominates Saudi life, and nearly all the people belong to the religion's Sunni branch. Various forms of Christianity and traditional religions are practiced among foreign workers and indigenous minority groups. Most live in urban areas, but some Bedouin tribes preserve their nomadic way of life.

Economy and the Land. The economy of Saudi Arabia has been shaped by its vast deserts and huge petroleum reserves. The hot, mostly arid climate has prevented agricultural abundance and stability: the country must import nearly all its food. Oil was discovered in the 1930s, but the country did not begin rapid economic development until the reserves were aggressively exploited following World War II. Saudi Arabia is the world's leading exporter of petroleum, possessing the largest concentration of known oil reserves in the world. The government is seeking to diversify the economy, improve transportation and communication lines, and build agricultural output. Private enterprise and foreign investment are encouraged. Saudi Arabia is divided into the western highlands bordering the Red Sea, a central plateau, northern deserts, the huge Rub al Khali desert in the south, and the eastern lowlands. Only the coastal regions receive appreciable rainfall, and some inland desert areas may go without rain for several years.

History and Politics. Even though what is now Saudi Arabia established prosperous trade routes thousands of years ago, its history begins with the founding of Islam by Muhammad in the early 600s A.D. By the end of that century Mecca and Medina were established as political and religious centers of Islam and remain so today. The territory split into numerous states that warred among themselves for over a thousand years. The Ottoman Turks gained control over the coastal region of Hejaz in the early 1500s, while Britain set up protectorates along the southern and eastern coasts of Arabia during the 1800s. The Saud family dynasty, founded in the 1400s, managed to remain a dominant religious and political force. Members of the dynasty fought to establish the supremacy of Islamic law and unite the various clans into one nation. In 1932 Ibn Saud proclaimed the Kingdom of Saudi Arabia and established a Saud monarchy that has continued despite dissension within the royal family. Since the 1960s Saudi Arabia has aggressively sought to upgrade local governments, industry, education, the status of women, and the standard of living while maintaining Islamic values and traditions. Saudi Arabia is a dominant member of the Organization of Petroleum Exporting Countries (OPEC). Despite disagreements with the West and continuing conflicts with Israel, the country maintains strong diplomatic and economic ties with the United States and nations of Western Europe. ∎

SENEGAL

Official name Republic of Senegal

PEOPLE
Population 6,650,000. **Density** 88/mi² (34/km²). **Urban** 34%. **Capital** Dakar, 979,000. **Ethnic groups** Wolof 36%, Fulani 17%, Serer 16%, Toucouleur 9%, Diola 9%, Mandingo 7%. **Languages** French, Wolof, indigenous. **Religions** Muslim 75%, indigenous 20%, Christian 5%. **Life expectancy** 45 female, 43 male. **Literacy** 10%.

POLITICS
Government Republic. **Parties** Assembly, Democratic, Democratic National, Socialist. **Suffrage** Universal adult. **Memberships** OAU, UN. **Subdivisions** 10 regions.

ECONOMY
GDP $2,500,000,000. **Per capita** $410. **Monetary unit** CFA franc. **Trade partners** France, other Western European countries, U.S., Japan. **Exports** Peanuts and peanut products, phosphate rock, canned fish. **Imports** Food, consumer goods, machinery, petroleum, transportation equipment.

LAND
Description Western Africa. **Area** 75,955 mi² (196,722 km²). **Highest point** 1,906 ft (581 m). **Lowest point** Sea level.

People. Most Senegalese are black Africans from many ethnic groups, each with its own customs and language. The country also has many immigrants from other African nations, France, and Lebanon. While French is the official language, Wolof is widely spoken. Most people are Muslim, and the rest are Christian or followers of traditional African beliefs. Senegal is primarily a rural nation of subsistence farmers.

Economy and the Land. The mainstays of the economy are agriculture, fishing, and mining. Tourism is a rapidly growing new industry. Peanuts and peanut products, phosphates, and fish products rank as Senegal's primary exports. Agricultural output is often hurt by irregular weather patterns, and the country must import nearly all its energy. Senegal has one of the finest transportation systems in Africa. The terrain, which is mainly flat, is highlighted by small plateaus, low massifs, marshy swamps, and a sandy coast. The climate is marked by dry and rainy seasons, with differing precipitation patterns in the south and the more arid north.

History and Politics. The area that is now Senegal has been inhabited by black Africans since prehistoric times. When Europeans first established trade ties with the Senegalese in the mid-1400s, the country had been divided into several independent kingdoms. By the early 1800s France had gained control of the region and in 1895 made Senegal part of French West Africa. In 1959 Senegal joined with French Sudan, or present-day Mali, to form the Federation of Mali, which became independent in 1960. However, Senegal withdrew from the federation later in the year to found the independent Republic of Senegal. The new parliamentary government was plagued by coup attempts and an economy crippled by the severe droughts of the late 1960s and early 1970s. In 1982 Senegal formed a union with the Gambia, called the Confederation of Senegambia, to strengthen economic and military ties between the two countries. Senegal has maintained close ties to France and follows a pro-Western foreign policy. ∎

SEYCHELLES

Official name Republic of Seychelles
PEOPLE
Population 66,000. **Density** 386/mi² (149/km²). **Urban** 37%. **Capital** Victoria, Mahé I., 15,559. **Ethnic groups** Mixed Asian, African, European. **Languages** English, French. **Religions** Roman Catholic 90%. **Life expectancy** 71 female, 65 male. **Literacy** 60%.
POLITICS
Government Republic. **Parties** People's Progressive Front. **Suffrage** Universal adult. **Memberships** CW, OAU, UN.
ECONOMY
GDP $128,000,000. **Per capita** $1,330. **Monetary unit** Rupee. **Trade partners** U.K., South Africa, Japan, Singapore. **Exports** Copra, cinnamon, vanilla, fish. **Imports** Food, manufactured goods, machinery, petroleum, transportation equipment.
LAND
Description Indian Ocean islands. **Area** 171 mi² (443 km²). **Highest point** Morne Seychellois, Mahé I., 2,970 ft (905 m). **Lowest point** Sea level.

People. The majority of Seychellois are of mixed African and European ancestry, while the remainder are Chinese or Indian. The islands' culture combines French and African elements, and although the official languages of French and English are widely spoken, most also speak a creole dialect of French. Many of the more than one hundred islands are coral atolls, unable to support human life, and the population is concentrated on Mahé, the largest island. The remainder live mainly on Praslin and La Digue islands.

Economy and the Land. The basis of the economy is tourism, with foreign visitors attracted by the tropical climate, white-sand beaches, and exotic flora and wildlife found on the granite islands. The granite islands also contain fertile soils, producing cinnamon and coconuts for copra. The terrain of the granite islands is characterized by a mountainous and rocky interior and narrow coastal strip, while the coral islands are mainly flat.

History and Politics. The Portuguese reached the uninhabited islands in the early 1500s, and for more than two hundred years the islands served as little more than pirates' havens. France claimed them in 1756, and by the 1770s white planters and African slaves had begun settlement of Mahé. Following a French-English war, the islands were ceded to Britain in 1814. Seychelles achieved independence in 1976. ■

SHETLAND ISLANDS

See UNITED KINGDOM.

SIERRA LEONE

Official name Republic of Sierra Leone
PEOPLE
Population 3,855,000. **Density** 138/mi² (53/km²). **Urban** 25%. **Capital** Freetown, 300,000. **Ethnic groups** Temne 30%, Mende 30%, Creole 2%, others. **Languages** English, Krio, indigenous. **Religions** Indigenous 70%, Muslim 25%, Christian 5%. **Life expectancy** 49 female, 46 male. **Literacy** 15%.
POLITICS
Government Republic. **Parties** All People's Congress. **Suffrage** Universal, over 21. **Memberships** CW, OAU, UN. **Subdivisions** 3 provinces, 1 capital district.
ECONOMY
GDP $1,200,000,000. **Per capita** $291. **Monetary unit** Leone. **Trade partners** U.K., other Western European countries, U.S., Japan. **Exports** Diamonds, palm kernels, coffee, cocoa, iron ore. **Imports** Machinery, food, petroleum, transportation equipment, manufactured goods.
LAND
Description Western Africa. **Area** 27,925 mi² (72,325 km²). **Highest point** Bintimani, 6,381 ft (1,945 m). **Lowest point** Sea level.

People. The population of Sierra Leone is divided into nearly twenty main ethnic groups. The two major groups are the Temne in the north and west and the Mende in the south. Descendants of freed slaves, who settled in Freetown on the coast, make up a sizable Creole minority. English is the official language, but most of the people speak local African tongues. The Creoles speak Krio, a dialect of English. Most people practice various local religions, a significant minority is Muslim, and a small number are Christian.

Economy and the Land. Sierra Leone is one of the world's largest producers of industrial and commercial diamonds. The nation also mines iron ore and rutile. Poor soil and its management, a fluctuating tropical climate, and traditional farming methods keep crop yields low. Rice, coffee, and cocoa are important crops. To improve agricultural production, the government is clearing some of the coastal mangrove swamplands. The interior of Sierra Leone is marked by a broad coastal plain in the north and by mountains and plateaus that rise along the country's northern and eastern borders. During the wet season Sierra Leone receives heavy rainfall in the Freetown area and significantly less in the north.

History and Politics. When the Portuguese reached the region in 1460, they found the area inhabited by the Temne. The British followed the Portuguese in the 1500s. Europeans took slaves from the area for the New World until Britain abolished the slave trade. In 1787 the Englishman Granville Sharp settled nearly four hundred freed black American slaves in what is now Freetown. Britain declared the peninsula a colony in 1808 and a protectorate in 1896. In 1961 Sierra Leone became an independent nation with a constitution and parliamentary form of government. A military takeover in 1967 was short lived, and the constitution was rewritten in 1971 to make the country a republic. Though officially nonaligned, Sierra Leone maintains close ties to Britain and other Western nations. ∎

SINGAPORE

Official name Republic of Singapore
PEOPLE
Population 2,545,000. **Density** 11,361/mi² (4,380/km²). **Urban** 100%. **Capital** Singapore, 2,502,000. **Ethnic groups** Chinese 77%, Malay 15%, Indian 6%. **Languages** English, Chinese, Malay, Tamil. **Religions** Buddhist, Taoist, Muslim, Hindu, Christian. **Life expectancy** 74 female, 70 male. **Literacy** 85%.
POLITICS
Government Republic. **Parties** People's Action. **Suffrage** Universal, over 20. **Memberships** CW, UN.
ECONOMY
GDP $14,200,000,000. **Per capita** $5,745. **Monetary unit** Dollar. **Trade partners** Malaysia, U.S., Japan, Saudi Arabia. **Exports** Petroleum products, electrical machinery, telecommunications equipment, natural rubber. **Imports** Machinery, petroleum, manufactured goods, rice.
LAND
Description Southeastern Asian island. **Area** 224 mi² (581 km²). **Highest point** Timah Hill, 545 ft (166 m). **Lowest point** Sea level.

People. Singapore is one of the most densely populated nations in the world. Most of the population is Chinese. A significant minority is Malay, and the remainder is European or Indian. Singapore's languages include Chinese, English, Malay, and Tamil. The main religions—Buddhism, Taoism, Islam, Hinduism, and Christianity—reflect the cultural diversity of the nation. Singapore's society is characterized by a mixture of Western and traditional customs and dress. Nearly all the population lives in the city of Singapore on Singapore Island.

Economy and the Land. Singapore is a leading Asian economic power. The city of Singapore is well known as a financial center and major harbor for trade. The nation's factories produce a variety of goods, such as chemicals, electronic equipment, and machinery, and are among the world leaders in petroleum refining. Singapore has few natural resources, however, and little arable land. Most agricultural output is consumed domestically; Singapore must import much of its raw materials and food. The nation consists of one main island, which is characterized by wet lowlands, and many small offshore islets. Cool sea breezes and a tropical climate make Singapore an attractive spot for tourists.

History and Politics. Present-day Singapore has been inhabited since prehistoric times. From the 1100s to the 1800s Singapore served mainly as a trading center and refuge for pirates. The British East India Company, the major colonial force in India, realized Singapore's strategic importance to British trade and gained possession of the harbor in 1819. All Singapore became a crown colony in 1826. As the port prospered, the island's population grew rapidly. Following World War II the people of Singapore moved from internal self-government to independence in 1965. The government continues to work in partnership with the business community to further Singapore's growth. In foreign policy, the nation remains nonaligned, but as a small country dependent on trade, Singapore is interested in maintaining wide contacts. ∎

SOLOMON ISLANDS

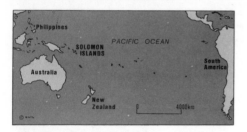

Official name Solomon Islands
PEOPLE
Population 270,000. **Density** 23/mi² (9.1/km²). **Urban** 9%. **Capital** Honiara, Guadalcanal I., 16,125. **Ethnic groups** Melanesian 93%, Polynesian 4%. **Languages** English, Malay-Polynesian languages. **Religions** Anglican, Roman Catholic, Methodist, other Christian. **Literacy** 60%.
POLITICS
Government Parliamentary state. **Parties** National Democratic, People's Alliance, United. **Suffrage** Universal, over 21. **Memberships** CW, UN. **Subdivisions** 4 districts.
ECONOMY
GNP $110,000,000. **Per capita** $460. **Monetary unit** Dollar. **Trade partners** Japan, Australia, U.K., Singapore. **Exports** Copra, wood, fish, palm oil. **Imports** Machinery, transportation equipment, food, fuels.
LAND
Description South Pacific islands. **Area** 11,506 mi² (29,800 km²). **Highest point** Mt. Makarakomburu, Guadalcanal I., 8,028 ft (2,447 m). **Lowest point** Sea level.

People. Over 90 percent of the people are Melanesian, and the remainder are Polynesian, European, Chinese, and Micronesian. English is the official language, but some ninety local languages are also spoken. The dominant religion is Protestantism, and religious minorities include Roman Catholics and followers of local traditions. The population is primarily rural, and much of its social structure is patterned on traditional village life.

Economy and the Land. The economy is based on subsistence farming and exports of fish, wood, copra, and some spices and palm oil. Food, machinery, gasoline, and manufactured goods must be imported. Terrain ranges from forested mountains to low-lying coral atolls. The climate is warm and moist, with heavy annual rainfall.

History and Politics. Hunter-gatherers lived on the islands as early as 1000 B.C. Because of disease and native resistance, early attempts at colonization failed, and Europeans did not firmly establish themselves until the mid-1800s. Britain declared the islands a protectorate in 1893. The area was the site of fierce battles between the Japanese and Allied forces during World War II, and following the war, moves were made toward independence. A constitution was adopted, creating a parliamentary democracy, and the Solomon Islands became a sovereign nation in 1978. ∎

SOMALIA

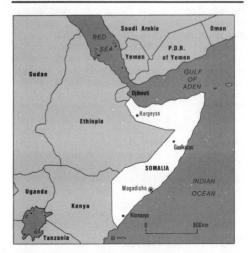

Official name Somali Democratic Republic
PEOPLE
Population 6,465,000. **Density** 26/mi² (10/km²). **Urban** 30%. **Capital** Mogadisho, 400,000. **Ethnic groups** Somali 99%. **Languages** Somali, Arabic, English, Italian. **Religions** Sunni Muslim 99%. **Life expectancy** 39 female, 38 male. **Literacy** 60%.
POLITICS
Government Socialist republic. **Parties** Revolutionary Socialist. **Suffrage** Universal, over 18. **Memberships** AL, OAU, UN. **Subdivisions** 15 regions.
ECONOMY
GDP $1,875,000. **Per capita** $375. **Monetary unit** Shilling. **Trade partners** Saudi Arabia, Italy, U.S., U.K. **Exports** Livestock, bananas, hides and skins. **Imports** Food, petroleum products, transportation equipment.
LAND
Description Eastern Africa. **Area** 246,200 mi² (637,657 km²). **Highest point** Surud Ad, 7,897 ft (2,407 m). **Lowest point** Sea level.

People. Unlike the population in many African nations, the people of Somalia are remarkably homogeneous in their language, culture, and identity. Most are nomadic or seminomadic herders; only a quarter of the people have settled in permanent communities in southern Somalia. While Somali is the official language, Arabic, English, and Italian are also spoken. Nearly all the Somali people are Sunni Muslims. They band together in large family groups, observing a way of life that has endured for centuries.

Economy and the Land. Somalia is a developing country that has not exploited its rich deposits of iron ore and gypsum. There is little manufacturing. The economy is agricultural, though activity is restricted to the vicinity of the rivers and certain coastal districts. Economic development is hampered by a lack of railroads and paved highways and by a hot climate with recurring droughts. The terrain ranges from flatlands to hills.

History and Politics. Ancestors of the Somalis who settled the region were converted by Arabs to Islam in the A.D. 800s and 900s. They fought many religious wars with the Christian kingdom of Ethiopia between the 1300s and 1500s. The British, Italians, and French arrived in the region in the latter half of the 1800s and divided the Somali territory among themselves, with Ethiopia seizing Ogaden in the west. After World War II Italy was made administrator of its former colony to prepare it for independence. In 1960 British Somaliland and Italian Somalia joined to form an independent republic. Since that time, Somalia has had many border clashes with Kenya and Ethiopia over the rights of Somalis living in these countries to determine their own destiny. Military leaders staged a successful coup in 1969. They subsequently changed the nation's name to Somali Democratic Republic and abolished all political parties; the Somali Revolutionary Socialist party was created in 1976. The country remains nonaligned in foreign affairs. ■

SOUTH AFRICA

Official name Republic of South Africa
PEOPLE
Population 26,855,000. **Density** 62/mi² (24/km²). **Urban** 53%. **Capital** Pretoria (administrative seat), 435,100; Cape Town (seat of legislature), 859,940; Bloemfontein (seat of judiciary), 102,600. **Ethnic groups** African 70%, white 18%, Colored 9%, Asian 3%. **Languages** Afrikaans, English, indigenous. **Religions** Christian. **Life expectancy** 56 female, 51 male. **Literacy** 70%.
POLITICS
Government Republic. **Parties** Conservative, National, Progressive Federal. **Suffrage** Whites, over 18 (17 in Natal province). **Memberships** UN. **Subdivisions** 4 provinces.
ECONOMY
GDP $73,600,000,000. **Per capita** $2,500. **Monetary unit** Rand. **Trade partners** U.S., West Germany, Japan, U.K. **Exports** Gold, wool, diamonds. **Imports** Motor vehicles, machinery, metals.
LAND
Description Southern Africa. **Area** 433,680 mi² (1,123,226 km²). **Highest point** eNjesuthi, 11,306 ft

(3,446 m). **Lowest point** Sea level.
The above information includes Walvis Bay.

People. The government of South Africa classifies the country's population into four main groups: black, white, Colored, and Asian. Various black African groups make up the majority population. Whites compose a minority and are either Afrikaners—of Dutch, German, and French descent—or British. Coloreds, people of mixed white, black, and Asian heritage, and Asians, primarily from India, make up the remaining population. Afrikaans and English are the official languages, although the blacks, Coloreds, and Asians speak their own languages as well. The dominant religions are Christian; however, many groups follow traditional practices. The South African government enforces apartheid, a policy of racial segregation widely criticized for violating the rights of blacks, Coloreds, and Asians.

Economy and the Land. The discovery of gold and diamonds in South Africa in the late 1800s shaped the nation's prosperous economy. Revenues from mining promoted industry, and today South Africa is one of the richest and most highly developed countries in Africa. Mining remains a mainstay, as does agriculture; the nation is almost self-sufficient in food production. Many effects of apartheid, including discriminatory systems of education and job reservation, have kept the majority population from the benefits of national prosperity. The varied landscape features coastal beaches, plateaus, mountains, and deep valleys. The climate is temperate. The Republic of South Africa includes the enclave of Walvis Bay, situated on Africa's southwest coast.

History and Politics. Southern Africa has been inhabited for many thousands of years. Ancestors of the area's present African population had settled by the time Portuguese explorers reached the Cape of Good Hope in the late 1400s. The first white settlers, ancestors of today's Afrikaners, established colonies in the seventeenth century. Britain gained control of the area in the late eighteenth century, and relations between Afrikaners and the British soon became strained. To escape British rule, many Afrikaners migrated northward to lands occupied by black Africans. The discovery of gold and diamonds in the late 1800s brought an influx of Europeans and further strained relations between Afrikaners and the British, with both groups striving for control of valuable mineral deposits. Two wars broke out, and in 1902 the British defeated the Afrikaners, or Boers, and incorporated the Boer territories into the British Empire. Black Africans were also subdued by the British, and in 1910 the white-controlled Union of South Africa was formed. Afrikaner nationalism grew in the early twentieth century and led to the formation of the National party, which gained control in 1924 and again in 1948. The party began the apartheid system of separation of the races in the late forties, and subsequent decades saw apartheid legislation and increasing racial tension. Apartheid continued in the eighties, despite violent conflicts and foreign pressure to abolish the system. ■

SOUTH GEORGIA

See UNITED KINGDOM.

SOVIET UNION

Official name Union of Soviet Socialist Republics
PEOPLE
Population 275,590,000. **Density** 32/mi² (12/km²).
Urban 64%. **Capital** Moscow, 8,202,000. **Ethnic groups**
Russian 52%, Ukrainian 16%, others 32%. **Languages**
Russian; other Slavic, Altaic, and Indo-European
languages. **Religions** Russian Orthodox 18%, Muslim
9%. **Life expectancy** 75 female, 70 male.
Literacy 100%.
POLITICS
Government Socialist republic. **Parties** Communist.
Suffrage Universal, over 18. **Memberships** COMECON,
UN, Warsaw Pact. **Subdivisions** 15 Soviet Socialist
Republics.
ECONOMY
GNP $1,715,000,000,000. **Per capita** $6,352. **Monetary
unit** Ruble. **Trade partners** Eastern European countries,
Finland, West Germany, France. **Exports** Petroleum,
petroleum products, natural gas, machinery, manufactured
goods, metals. **Imports** Food, machinery, steel products,
consumer goods.
LAND
Description Eastern Europe and northern Asia. **Area**
8,600,383 mi² (22,274,900 km²). **Highest point**
Communism Pk., 24,590 ft (7,495 m). **Lowest point**
Vpadina Karagiye, 433 ft (132 m) below sea level.

People. The varied population of the Soviet Union
is composed of more than one hundred distinct
groups. Nearly three-quarters of the people are
Eastern Slavs, and more than 70 percent of this
group are Russians. The remaining Slavs are
Ukrainians and Belorussians. The rest of the population belongs to Turkic, Finno-Urgic, Caucasian,
other Indo-European groups, and a mixture of peoples including Inuit. Each group speaks its own language, although Russian is the most widely used.
Religious practice is discouraged by the state, and

churches have no legal status, although Russian Orthodox, Islam, Catholicism, Protestantism, and other
religions are actively practiced.

Economy and the Land. As an industrial power,
the Soviet Union ranks second only to the United
States. Mining, steel production, and other heavy
industries predominate. The economy is controlled
by the state, and economic policies are administered
through a series of five-year plans, which emphasize
industrial and technological growth. The Soviet
economy is suffering from low productivity, energy
shortages, and a lack of skilled labor, problems the
government hopes can be alleviated by increased
use of technology and science. The Soviet Union
trades primarily with members of the Council for Mutual Economic Assistance (COMECON), although
trade with the West has risen sharply in the past few
years. Geographically, the Soviet Union is the largest
nation in the world. Its terrain is widely varied and
richly endowed with minerals. Though the country
contains some of the world's most fertile land,
long winters and hot, dry summers keep many crop
yields low.

History and Politics. Inhabited as early as the
Stone Age, what is now the Soviet Union was much
later invaded successively by Scythians, Sarma-
tians, Goths, Huns, Bulgars, Slavs, and others. By
A.D. 989 Byzantine cultural influence had become
predominant. Various groups and regions were
slowly incorporated into a single state. In 1547 Ivan
IV was crowned czar of all Russia, beginning a tradition of czarist rule that lasted until the 1917 Russian Revolution, when the Bolsheviks came to power
and named Vladimir Ilyich Lenin as head of the first
Soviet government. The Bolsheviks established a
Communist state and weathered a bitter civil war.
Joseph Stalin succeeded Lenin as head of state in
1924 and initiated a series of political purges that
lasted through the 1930s. The Soviet Union became
embroiled in World War II, siding with the Allies,
losing over twenty million people, and suffering widespread destruction of its cities and countryside. It
emerged from the war with extended influence, however, having annexed part of Finland and several
Eastern European nations. Following Stalin's death
in 1953, the Soviet Union experienced a liberalization of policies under Nikita Krushchev. In 1964 Leonid Brezhnev worked to consolidate and strengthen
the power of the Secretariat and Politburo of the
Communist party. Mikhail S. Gorbachev, the youngest Soviet leader in decades, took office in 1985. ∎

SPAIN

Official name Spanish State
PEOPLE
Population 38,515,000. **Density** 198/mi² (76/km²). **Urban**
91%. **Capital** Madrid, 3,188,297. **Ethnic groups** Mixed
Mediterranean and Nordic. **Languages** Spanish.
Religions Roman Catholic 99%. **Life expectancy**
76 female, 72 male. **Literacy** 97%.
POLITICS
Government Constitutional monarchy. **Parties** Popular

has declined to about half of peak production and employment. Spain's terrain is mainly composed of a dry plateau area; mountains cover the northern section, and plains extend down the country's eastern coast. Climate in the eastern and southern regions is Mediterranean, while the northwest has more rainfall and less sunshine throughout the year.

History and Politics. Spain is among the oldest inhabited regions in Europe. For centuries a Roman province, Spain was conquered by the Visigoths in the A.D. 500s, only to change hands again in the 700s when the Arab-Berbers, or Moors, seized control of all but a narrow strip of northern Spain. Christian kings reclaimed the country from the eleventh to the fourteenth centuries. Spain, controlled by the three kingdoms of Navarre, Aragon, and Castile, was united in the late 1400s under King Ferdinand and Queen Isabella. At the height of its empire, Spain claimed territory in North and South America, northern Africa, Italy, and the Canary Islands. However, a series of wars burdened Spain financially, and in the 1500s, under King Philip II, the country entered a period of decline. Throughout the 1700s and 1800s, the nation lost most of its colonial possessions through treaty or revolution. In 1936 a bitter civil war erupted between factions supporting the monarchy and those wishing to establish a republic. General Francisco Franco, leader of the successful monarchist army, ruled as dictator of Spain from the end of the war until his death in 1975. Spain enjoyed phenomenal economic growth during the 1950s and 1960s; however, that growth declined in the 1970s. Since Franco's death, King Juan Carlos has led the country toward a more democratic form of government. ∎

Alliance, Popular Democratic, Socialist Workers'. **Suffrage** Universal, over 18. **Memberships** NATO, OECD, UN. **Subdivisions** 50 provinces.

ECONOMY
GNP $179,700,000,000. **Per capita** $4,746. **Monetary unit** Peseta. **Trade partners** France, U.S., West Germany, Italy, U.K. **Exports** Iron and steel products, machinery, food, automobiles, footwear. **Imports** Fuels, machinery, chemicals, iron and steel, food.

LAND
Description Southern Europe. **Area** 194,882 mi² (504,741 km²). **Highest point** Pico de Teide, Tenerife, Canary Is., 12,188 ft (3,715 m). **Lowest point** Sea level.

People. The population of Spain is a mixture of ethnic groups from northern Europe and the area surrounding the Mediterranean Sea. Spanish is the official language; however, several regional dialects of Spanish are commonly spoken. The Basque minority, one of the oldest surviving ethnic groups in Europe, lives mainly in the Pyrenees in northern Spain, preserving its own language and traditions. Since the 1978 constitution, Spain has not had an official religion, yet nearly all its people are Roman Catholic. Spain has a rich artistic tradition, blending Moorish and Western cultures.

Economy and the Land. Despite the effects of the general worldwide recession of the 1970s, Spain has benefited greatly from an economic-restructuring program that began in the 1950s. The nation has concentrated on developing industry, which now employs over 30 percent of the population. Exploitation of natural-gas deposits is also being explored, with the hope of reducing Spain's dependence on oil imports. The agricultural contribution to the economy

SRI LANKA

Official name Democratic Socialist Republic of Sri Lanka
PEOPLE
Population 16,070,000. **Density** 644/mi² (249/km²). **Urban** 22%. **Capital** Colombo, 585,776. **Ethnic groups** Sinhalese 74%, Tamil 18%, Moor 7%. **Languages** Sinhala, Tamil, English. **Religions** Buddhist 69%, Hindu 15%, Christian 8%, Muslim 8%. **Life expectancy** 72 female, 67 male. **Literacy** 85%.
POLITICS
Government Socialist republic. **Parties** All Ceylon Tamil Congress, Freedom, Janatha Vimukthi Peramuna, United National. **Suffrage** Universal, over 18. **Memberships** CW, UN. **Subdivisions** 9 provinces.

Places and Possessions of Spain

Entity	Status	Area	Population	Capital / Population
Balearic Islands (Mediterranean Sea)	Province	1,936 mi² (5,014 km²)	695,000	Palma, 304,422
Canary Islands (northwest of Africa)	Part of Spain	2,808 mi² (7,273 km²)	1,475,000	None

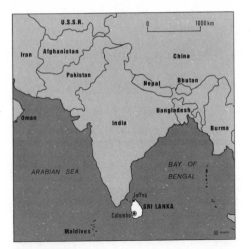

SUDAN

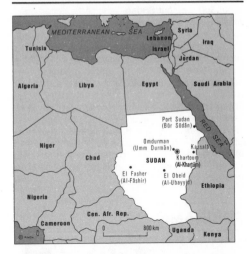

ECONOMY
GDP $4,400,000,000. **Per capita** $286. **Monetary unit** Rupee. **Trade partners** U.S., Saudi Arabia, Japan, U.K., West Germany. **Exports** Tea, natural rubber, petroleum products, textiles. **Imports** Petroleum, machinery, transportation equipment, sugar.

LAND
Description Indian Ocean island. **Area** 24,962 mi² (64,652 km²). **Highest point** Pidurutalagala, 8,281 ft (2,524 m). **Lowest point** Sea level.

People. The two principal groups in Sri Lanka are the majority Sinhalese and the Tamils. Other minorities include the Moors; Burghers, who are descendants of Dutch, Portuguese, and British colonists; Malays; and Veddah aborigines. Sinhala is the official language, though Tamil and English are also widely spoken. Most Sinhalese are Buddhist, most Tamils are Hindu, and the majority of the Moors and Malays are Muslims.

Economy and the Land. Sri Lanka's economy is based on agriculture, which employs nearly half the people in producing tea, rubber, and coconuts. Sri Lanka also hopes to become self-sufficient in rice, thus reducing imports of this staple. Industrial production has increased, and major exports include graphite and textile products. Sri Lanka is also sponsoring several internal-development programs. However, continuing high government subsidy and welfare policies threaten economic growth. Most of Sri Lanka is composed of a low coastal plain, and the southern interior is mountainous and forested. The climate is tropical.

History and Politics. The Sinhalese dynasty was founded by a prince from northern India in about 500 B.C. Later, the Tamils from southern India settled in the north of Sri Lanka. European control began in the 1500s, when the island was ruled by the Portuguese and Dutch. It became the British colony of Ceylon in 1802 and the independent nation of Ceylon in 1948. In 1972 the name was changed to Sri Lanka, and the nation has pursued a nonaligned policy in foreign relations. Tensions between the ruling Sinhalese and the minority Tamils has often erupted in violence. ∎

Official name Democratic Republic of the Sudan
PEOPLE
Population 21,390,000. **Density** 22/mi² (8.5/km²). **Urban** 21%. **Capital** Khartoum, 333,921. **Ethnic groups** Black African 52%, Arab 39%, Beja 6%. **Languages** Arabic, indigenous, English. **Religions** Sunni Muslim 70%, indigenous 20%, Christian 5%. **Life expectancy** 48 female, 45 male. **Literacy** 20%.

POLITICS
Government Republic. **Parties** None (outlawed). **Suffrage** Universal adult. **Memberships** AL, OAU, UN. **Subdivisions** 8 regions.

ECONOMY
GDP $7,100,000,000. **Per capita** $345. **Monetary unit** Pound. **Trade partners** U.K., West Germany, Italy, U.S., Saudi Arabia, France. **Exports** Cotton, gum arabic, peanuts, sesame. **Imports** Petroleum products, machinery, textiles, transportation equipment, food.

LAND
Description Eastern Africa. **Area** 967,500 mi² (2,505,813 km²). **Highest point** Kinyeti, 10,456 ft (3,187 m). **Lowest point** Sea level.

People. Sudan's population is composed of two distinct cultures—black African and Arab. African blacks of diverse ethnicity are a majority and are concentrated in the south, where they practice traditional life-styles and beliefs and speak indigenous languages. Arabic-speaking Muslims belonging to several ethnic groups live mainly in northern and central regions.

Economy and the Land. The economy is based on agriculture, and irrigation has made arid Sudan a leading producer of cotton. Forests provide for production of gum arabic, used in making candy and perfumes, and other crops include peanuts and sesame seeds. Economic activity is concentrated near the Nile River and its branches and near water holes and wells. The mostly flat terrain is marked by eastern and western mountains, and southern forests and savanna give way to swampland, scrubland, and northern desert. The climate varies from desert in the north to tropical in the south.

History and Politics. Egypt mounted repeated invasions of what is now northern Sudan beginning about 300 B.C., but Sudan remained a collection of small independent states until 1821, when Egypt conquered and unified the northern portion. Egypt was unable to establish control over the south, which was often subject to attacks by slave raiders. In 1881 a Muslim leader began uniting various groups in a revolt against Egyptian rule, and success came four years later. His successor ruled until 1898, when British and Egyptian forces reconquered the land. Renamed the Anglo-Egyptian Sudan, the region was ruled jointly by Egypt and Britain, with British administration dominating. Sudan became independent in 1956. A series of military coups since that time has marked the country with political and economic instability. ∎

SURINAME

Official name Republic of Suriname
PEOPLE
Population 375,000. **Density** 5.9/mi² (2.3/km²). **Urban** 66%. **Capital** Paramaribo, 67,718. **Ethnic groups** East Indian 37%, Creole 31%, Javanese 15%, Bush Negro 10%, Amerindian 3%. **Languages** Dutch, English, Hindi, Sranang Tongo, Javanese. **Religions** Hindu, Muslim, Roman Catholic, Moravian, others. **Life expectancy** 71 female, 67 male. **Literacy** 80%.
POLITICS
Government Republic. **Parties** 25 February National Unity Movement. **Suffrage** None (suspended).
Memberships OAS, UN. **Subdivisions** 9 districts.
ECONOMY
GDP $1,044,000,000. **Per capita** $2,916. **Monetary unit** Guilder. **Trade partners** U.S., Netherlands, other Western European countries, Trinidad and Tobago. **Exports** Alumina, bauxite, aluminum, wood and wood products, rice. **Imports** Capital equipment, petroleum, iron and steel, food.
LAND
Description Northern South America. **Area** 63,037 mi² (163,265 km²). **Highest point** Juliana Top, 3,749 ft (1,230 m). **Lowest point** Sea level.

People. Suriname's diverse ethnicity was shaped by the importation of black African slaves and contract laborers from the East. Descendants of East Indians and Creoles, of European–black African heritage, compose the two major groups. Other peoples include the Javanese; Bush Negroes, a black group; Amerindians, descendants of Arawak and Caribs; Chinese; and Europeans. Dutch is the official language, but most groups have preserved their distinct language, culture, and religion.

Economy and the Land. The economy is based on mining and metal processing, and bauxite and alumina account for the major exports. Agriculture plays an economic role as well and, together with fishing and forestry, offers potential for expansion. The terrain is marked by a narrow coastal swamp, central forests and savanna, and southern jungle-covered hills. The climate is tropical.

History and Politics. Prior to the arrival of Europeans, present-day Suriname was inhabited by indigenous Indians. Christopher Columbus sighted the coast in 1498, but Spanish and Portuguese exploration was slowed by the area's lack of gold. The British established the first settlement in 1651, and in 1665 Jews from Brazil erected the first synagogue in the Western Hemisphere. In 1667 the British traded the area to the Netherlands in exchange for the Dutch colony of New Amsterdam—present-day Manhattan, New York. Subsequent wars and treaties caused ownership of Suriname to shift among the British, French, and Dutch until 1815, when the Netherlands regained control. In 1954 Suriname became an autonomous part of the Netherlands, with status equal to that of the Netherlands and the Netherlands Antilles. Independence was gained in 1975. In 1980 the military seized power, and a joint military-civilian government was subsequently established. The nation pursues a policy of nonalignment but maintains relations with many countries. ∎

SWAZILAND

Official name Kingdom of Swaziland
PEOPLE
Population 660,000. **Density** 98/mi² (38/km²). **Urban**
15%. **Capital** Mbabane, 33,000. **Ethnic groups** African
96%, European 3%, mulatto 1%. **Languages** English,
siSwati. **Religions** Christian 57%, indigenous 43%. **Life
expectancy** 56 female, 51 male. **Literacy** 65%.
POLITICS
Government Monarchy. **Parties** None. **Suffrage**
Universal adult. **Memberships** CW, OAU, UN.
Subdivisions 4 districts.
ECONOMY
GDP $500,000,000. **Per capita** $880. **Monetary unit**
Lilangeni. **Trade partners** South Africa, U.K., U.S.
Exports Sugar, asbestos, wood products, electronics,
fruits. **Imports** Motor vehicles, petroleum products,
machinery, food, chemicals.
LAND
Description Southern Africa, landlocked. **Area** 6,704 mi²
(17,364 km²). **Highest point** Emlembe, 6,109 ft (1,862 m).
Lowest point 70 ft (21 m).

People. At least 90 percent of the people of Swaziland are black Africans called Swazi. Very small minorities of white Europeans and people of mixed European and African descent also live in the country. The two official languages are English and siSwati. Government and official business is conducted primarily in English. More than half the Swazi belong to Christian churches, while others practice traditional African religions.

Economy and the Land. Most Swazi are subsistence farmers. Cattle are highly prized for their own sake but are being used increasingly for milk, meat, and profit. Europeans own nearly half the land in Swaziland and raise most of the cash crops, including fruits, sugar, tobacco, cotton, and wood. About half the nation's income comes from European-owned mining operations. Major exports include asbestos and iron ore. Swaziland also has desposits of coal, pottery clay, gold, and tin. The country's mountains and forests have brought a growing tourist industry. The climate is temperate.

History and Politics. According to legend, the Swazi originally came from the area near Maputo. British traders and Dutch farmers from South Africa first reached Swaziland in the 1830s. More whites came in the 1880s when gold was discovered. Swazi leaders unknowingly granted many concessions to the whites at this time. After the Boer War, Britain assumed administration of Swaziland and ruled until 1967. Swaziland became independent in 1968. The British designed a constitution, but many Swazi thought it disregarded their traditions and interests. In 1973, King Sobhuza abolished this constitution, suspended the legislature, and appointed a commission to produce a new constitution. ■

SWEDEN

Official name Kingdom of Sweden
PEOPLE
Population 8,335,000. **Density** 48/mi² (19/km²). **Urban**

83%. **Capital** Stockholm, 649,686. **Ethnic groups** Swedish, Lappish. **Languages** Swedish. **Religions** Lutheran 94%. **Life expectancy** 79 female, 75 male. **Literacy** 99%.
POLITICS
Government Constitutional monarchy. **Parties** Center, Communist, Moderate Coalition, People's, Social Democratic. **Suffrage** Universal, over 18. **Memberships** OECD, UN. **Subdivisions** 24 counties.
ECONOMY
GDP $81,000,000,000. **Per capita** $10,285. **Monetary unit** Krona. **Trade partners** West Germany, U.K., Norway, U.S., Denmark, Finland. **Exports** Machinery, motor vehicles, wood pulp, paper products, iron and steel products. **Imports** Machinery, petroleum, petroleum products, chemicals, food.
LAND
Description Northern Europe. **Area** 173,780 mi² (450,089 km²). **Highest point** Kebnekaise, 6,926 ft (2,111 m). **Lowest point** Sea level.

People. The most significant minorities in the largely urban Swedish population are Swedes of Finnish origin and a small number of Lapps. Sweden is also the home of immigrants from other Nordic countries and Yugoslavia, Greece, and Turkey. Swedish is the main language, although Finns and Lapps often speak other tongues. English is the leading foreign language, especially among students and younger people.

Economy and the Land. Sweden has one of the highest standards of living in the world. Taxes are also high, but the government provides exceptional benefits for most citizens, including free education and medical care, pension payments, four-week vacations, and payments for child care. The nation is industrial and bases its economy on its three most important natural resources—timber, iron ore, and water power. More than a fourth of its exports are lumber or wood products. The iron and steel industry produces high-quality steel used in ball bearings, precision tools, agricultural machinery, aircraft, automobiles, and ships. Swedish farmers rely heavily on dairy products and livestock, and most farms are part of Sweden's agricultural-cooperative movement. Sweden's varied terrain includes mountains, forests, plains, and sandy beaches. The climate is temperate, with cold winters in the north. Northern Sweden lies in the Land of the Midnight Sun and experiences periods of twenty-four hours of daylight in summer and darkness in winter.

History and Politics. Inhabitants of what is now Sweden began to trade with the Roman Empire about 50 B.C. Successful sailing expeditions by Swedish Vikings began about A.D. 800. In the fourteenth century the kingdom came under Danish rule but left the union in 1523 and declared its independence. The Swedish king offered protection to the followers of Martin Luther, and Lutheranism was soon declared the state religion. By the late 1660s Sweden had become one of the great powers of Europe; it suffered a military defeat by Russia in 1709, however, and gradually lost most of its European possessions. An 1809 constitution gave most of the executive power of the government to the king. Despite this, the power of the Parliament gradually increased, and parliamentary rule was adopted in 1917. A 1975 constitution reduced the king's role to a ceremonial one. Sweden remained neutral during both world wars.   ■

SWITZERLAND

Official name Swiss Confederation
PEOPLE
Population 6,485,000. **Density** 408/mi² (157/km²).
Urban 58%. **Capital** Bern, 145,300. **Ethnic groups**
German 65%, French 18%, Italian 10%, Romansch 1%.
Languages German, French, Italian. **Religions** Roman
Catholic 49%, Protestant 48%. **Life expectancy**
78 female, 74 male. **Literacy** 99%.
POLITICS
Government Republic. **Parties** Christian Democratic
People's, People's, Radical Democratic, Social
Democratic. **Suffrage** Universal, over 20. **Memberships**
OECD. **Subdivisions** 23 cantons.
ECONOMY
GNP $95,600,000,000. **Per capita** $14,270. **Monetary**

unit Franc. **Trade partners** West Germany, France, Italy,
U.S., U.K. **Exports** Machinery, electric appliances,
chemicals, precision instruments, watches, textiles.
Imports Machinery, metals and metal products,
petroleum, motor vehicles, iron and steel, food, chemicals.
LAND
Description Central Europe, landlocked. **Area** 15,943 mi²
(41,293 km²). **Highest point** Monte Rosa (Dufourspitze),
15,203 ft (4,634 m). **Lowest point** Lago Maggiore, 633 ft
(193 m).

People. About seven hundred years ago, the Swiss began joining together for mutual defense but were able to preserve their regional differences in language and customs. The country has three official languages—German, French, and Italian—and a fourth language, Romansch, is spoken by a minority. Dialects often differ from community to community. The population is concentrated on a central plain located between mountain ranges.

Economy and the Land. The Alps and Jura Mountains cover nearly 70 percent of Switzerland, making much of the land unsuited for agriculture but providing the basis for a thriving tourist industry. The central plain contains rich cropland and holds Switzerland's major cities and manufacturing facilities, many specializing in high-quality, precision products. Switzerland is also an international banking and finance center. Straddling the ranges of the central Alps, Switzerland has a terrain of mountains, hills, and plateaus. The climate is temperate but varies with altitude.

History and Politics. Helvetic Celts inhabited the area of present-day Switzerland when Julius Caesar conquered the region, annexing it to the Roman Empire. As the Roman Empire declined, northern and western Germanic tribes began a series of invasions, and in the 800s the region became part of the empire of the Frankish king Charlemagne. In 1291 leaders of the three Swiss cantons, or regions, signed an agreement declaring their freedom and promising mutual aid against any foreign ruler. The confederation was the beginning of modern Switzerland. Over the next few centuries Switzerland became a military power, expanding its territories until 1515, when it was defeated by France. Soon after, Switzerland adopted a policy of permanent neutrality. The country was again conquered by France during the French Revolution; however, after Napoleon's final defeat in 1815, the Congress of Vienna guaranteed Switzerland's neutrality, a guarantee that has never been broken.   ■

SYRIA

Official name Syrian Arab Republic
PEOPLE
Population 10,485,000. **Density** 147/mi² (57/km²).
Urban 48%. **Capital** Damascus, 1,201,000. **Ethnic
groups** Arab 90%, Kurdish, Armenian, Circassian,
Turkish. **Languages** Arabic. **Religions** Sunni Muslim
74%, other Muslim 16%, Christian 10%. **Life expectancy**
67 female, 64 male. **Literacy** 50%.

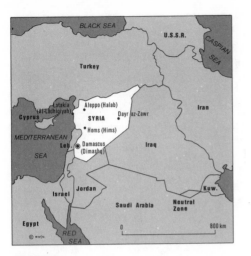

and ruled by several empires, including the Phoenician, Assyrian, Babylonian, Persian, and Greek, before coming under Roman rule in 64 B.C. During subsequent years Christianity arose in the part of Greater Syria called Palestine. In 636 the region fell to Arab Muslims, who governed until 1260, when Egypt gained control. In 1516 Syria became part of the Turkish Ottoman Empire, and during World War I Syria aided Britain in defeating the Turks and Germans in return for independence. After the war, however, the League of Nations divided Greater Syria into four states—Syria, Lebanon, Palestine, and Transjordan—and placed Syria under French control. When Syria gained independence in 1946, many Syrians wanted to reunite Greater Syria. The United Nations instead made part of Palestine into the Jewish state of Israel. Tension between Israel and Syria continued into the 1980s and in 1967 and 1973 erupted in war.   ■

POLITICS
Government Socialist republic. **Parties** Arab Socialist, Arab Socialist Resurrectionist, Arab Socialist Union, Communist, Socialist Unionist Movement. **Suffrage** Universal, over 18. **Memberships** AL, UN. **Subdivisions** 13 provinces, 1 capital district.

ECONOMY
GDP $18,400,000,000. **Per capita** $1,957. **Monetary unit** Pound. **Trade partners** Italy, France, Iraq, Saudi Arabia, Romania, West Germany. **Exports** Petroleum, textiles, cotton, fruits, vegetables. **Imports** Machinery, fuels, metal products, textiles, food.

LAND
Description Southwestern Asia. **Area** 71,498 mi² (185,180 km²). **Highest point** Mt. Hermon, 9,232 ft (2,814 m). **Lowest point** 655 ft (200 m) below sea level.

People. Most Syrians are Arabic-speaking descendants of Semites, a people who settled the region in ancient times. The majority is Sunni Muslim, and Islam is a powerful cultural force. Only a small percentage is Christian. Non-Arab Syrians include Kurds and Armenians, who speak their own languages and maintain their own customs. French is widely understood, and English is spoken in larger cities. The population is evenly divided between urban and rural settlements.

Economy and the Land. Syria is a developing country with great potential for economic growth. Textile manufacturing is a major industry, and oil, the main natural resource, provides for expanding activity in oil refining. The plains and river valleys are fertile, but rainfall is irregular and irrigation is necessary to sustain agriculture. Most farms are small, with cotton and wheat the major products. The terrain is marked by mountains, the Euphrates River valley, and a semiarid plateau. The climate is hot and dry, with relatively cold winters.

History and Politics. Syria was the site of one of the world's most ancient civilizations, and Damascus and other Syrian cities were centers of world trade as early as 2500 B.C. Greater Syria, as the area was called until the end of World War I, originally included much of modern Israel, Jordan, Lebanon, and parts of Turkey. The region was occupied

TAIWAN

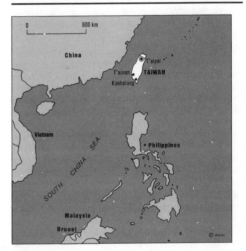

Official name Taiwan
PEOPLE
Population 19,090,000. **Density** 1,373/mi² (530/km²). **Urban** 66%. **Capital** T'aipei, 2,270,983. **Ethnic groups** Taiwanese 84%, Chinese 14%, aborigine 2%. **Languages** Chinese dialects. **Religions** Buddhist, Confucian, and Taoist 93%; Christian 5%. **Life expectancy** 75 female, 70 male. **Literacy** 90%.

POLITICS
Government Republic. **Parties** Kuomintang. **Suffrage** Universal, over 20. **Memberships** None. **Subdivisions** 16 counties, 5 cities, 2 special municipalities.

ECONOMY
GNP $49,800,000,000. **Per capita** $2,673. **Monetary unit** New Taiwan dollar. **Trade partners** U.S., Japan, Hong Kong. **Exports** Textiles, electrical machinery, plastics, metal products, plywood, canned food. **Imports** Petroleum, machinery, chemicals, food, base metals.

LAND
Description Eastern Asian island. **Area** 13,900 mi² (36,002 km²). **Highest point** Mt. Yu 13,113 ft (3,997 m). **Lowest point** Sea level.

People. The majority of Taiwan's inhabitants are descendants of Chinese who migrated from the coast of China in the eighteenth and nineteenth centuries. In 1949, when the Communists came to power on the mainland following a civil war, many business, bureaucratic, and military people arrived, coming from all parts of the mainland. A small group of aborigines lives in the mountains in central Taiwan and are most likely of Malay-Polynesian origin. Most religious practices combine Buddhist and Taoist beliefs with the Confucian ethical code.

Economy and the Land. Since World War II, Taiwan's economy has changed from agriculture to industry. A past emphasis on light industry, producing mainly consumer goods, has shifted to technology and heavy industry. Although only one-quarter of the island is arable, farmland is intensely cultivated, with some areas producing two and three crops a year. Rice, sugarcane, fruits, and tea are important crops. Fishing is also important; however, much food must be imported. The island's terrain is marked by steep eastern mountains sloping to a fertile western region. The capital of T'aipei administers the Penghu Islands and about twenty offshore islands as well as the island of Taiwan. The climate is maritime subtropical.

History and Politics. Chinese migration to Taiwan began as early as A.D. 500. Dutch traders claimed the island in 1624 and used it as a base for trade with China and Japan. It was ruled by China's Manchu dynasty from 1683 until 1895, when China ceded Taiwan to Japan after the first Sino-Japanese war. Following fifty years of Japanese rule, China regained possession of Taiwan after World War II. A civil war in mainland China between Nationalist and Communist forces ended with the victory of the Communists in 1949, and Nationalist leader Chiang Kai-shek fled to Taiwan, proclaiming T'aipei the provisional capital of Nationalist China. Both the People's Republic of China and Nationalist China consider Taiwan a province of the mainland, and both consider themselves to be the legitimate ruler of all China. ∎

TANZANIA

Official name United Republic of Tanzania
PEOPLE
Population 21,525,000. **Density** 59/mi² (23/km²). **Urban** 13%. **Capital** Dar-es-Salaam, 757,346. **Ethnic groups** African 99%. **Languages** Swahili, English, indigenous. **Religions** Christian 35%, Muslim 35%, indigenous 30%. **Life expectancy** 53 female, 50 male. **Literacy** 66%.
POLITICS
Government Republic. **Parties** Chama Cha Mapinduzi. **Suffrage** Universal, over 18. **Memberships** CW, OAU, UN. **Subdivisions** 25 regions.
ECONOMY
GDP $5,200,000,000. **Per capita** $281. **Monetary unit** Shilling. **Trade partners** West Germany, U.K., U.S., other Western European countries. **Exports** Coffee, cotton, sisal, cashews, diamonds, cloves. **Imports** Manufactured goods, machinery, transportation equipment, textiles, petroleum.

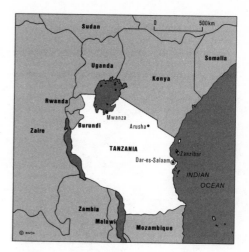

LAND
Description Eastern Africa. **Area** 364,900 mi² (945,087 km²). **Highest point** Kilimanjaro, 19,340 ft (5,895 m). **Lowest point** Sea level.

People. The largely rural African population of Tanzania consists of more than 130 ethnic groups, most speaking a distinct language. Religious beliefs are nearly evenly divided among Christian, Muslim, and traditional religions.

Economy and the Land. Agriculture accounts for the greatest portion of export earnings and employs 80 percent of the work force. Two-thirds of the land cannot be cultivated, however, because of lack of water and tsetse-fly infestation. The mainland farmers grow cassava, corn, and beans. Zanzibar and Pemba islands are well known as sources of cloves. Other cash crops include coffee and cashews. Diamonds, salt, and iron are important mineral resources. Mainland Tanzania, or Tanganyika, is characterized by hot and humid coastal plains, an arid central plateau, and temperate lake and highland areas. Climate is equatorial and characterized by monsoons.

History and Politics. The northern mainland has fossil remains of some of humanity's earliest ancestors. Subsequent early inhabitants were gradually displaced by Bantu farmers and Nilotes. Arabs were trading with coastal groups as early as the eighth century, and by the early 1500s the Portuguese had claimed the coastal region. They were displaced in the 1700s by Arabs, who subsequently established a lucrative slave trade. Germans began colonizing the coast in 1884 and six years later signed an agreement with Great Britain that secured German dominance along the coast and made Zanzibar a British protectorate. After World War I Britain received part of German East Africa from the League of Nations as a mandate and renamed it Tanganyika. The area became a trust territory under the United Nations following World War II. Nationalist movements soon emerged throughout East Africa, and the first Tanganyikan political party was organized in 1954. The country achieved independence in 1961.

Zanzibar received its independence in 1963 as a constitutional monarchy under the sultan. A 1964 revolt by the African majority overthrew the sultan, and Zanzibar and Tanganyika subsequently united and became known as Tanzania. ∎

TASMANIA

See AUSTRALIA.

THAILAND

Official name Kingdom of Thailand
PEOPLE
Population 52,220,000. **Density** 264/mi² (102/km²).
Urban 17%. **Capital** Bangkok, 5,153,902. **Ethnic groups**
Thai 75%, Chinese 14%. **Languages** Thai. **Religions**
Buddhist 95%, Muslim 4%. **Life expectancy** 65 female,
61 male. **Literacy** 84%.
POLITICS
Government Constitutional monarchy. **Suffrage**
Universal, over 20. **Memberships** UN. **Subdivisions**
73 provinces.
ECONOMY
GNP $38,400,000,000. **Per capita** $800. **Monetary unit**
Baht. **Trade partners** Japan, Western European
countries, U.S. **Exports** Rice, natural rubber, sugar,
tapioca, corn, tin. **Imports** Machinery, transportation
equipment, petroleum, chemicals, base metals.
LAND
Description Southeastern Asia. **Area** 198,115 mi² (513,115
km²). **Highest point** Inthanon, 8,530 ft (2,600 m).
Lowest point Sea level.

People. Thailand's society is relatively homogeneous. More than 85 percent of its people speak varying dialects of Thai and share a common culture and common religion, Buddhism. Malay-speaking Muslims and Chinese immigrants compose small minorities. Thai society is rural, with most people living in the rice-growing regions. The government has sponsored a successful family-planning program, which has greatly reduced the annual population growth rate.

Economy and the Land. With an economy based on agriculture, Thailand exports large quantities of rice each year. Forests produce teak and rattan, and tin is another valuable natural resource. Future industrialization may hinge on deposits of coal and natural gas. The cost of feeding, clothing, and sheltering hundreds of thousands of refugees from Vietnam, Laos, and Kampuchea has been a major drain on the Thai economy. A mountainous and heavily forested nation, Thailand has a tropical climate, dominated by monsoons, high temperatures, and humidity.

History and Politics. Thai communities were established as early as 4000 B.C., although a Thai kingdom founded in the thirteenth century A.D. began the history of modern Thailand. In the late 1700s Burmese armies overwhelmed the kingdom. Rama I, founder of the present dynasty, helped to drive the invaders from the country in 1782. He subsequently renamed the nation Siam and established a capital at Bangkok. Siam allowed Europeans to live within its borders during the period of colonial expansion, but the nation never succumbed to foreign rule. As a result, Siam was the only South and Southeast Asian country never colonized by a European power. In 1932 a revolt changed the government from an absolute monarchy to a constitutional monarchy. Military officers assumed control in 1938, and the nation reverted to its former name, Thailand, in 1939. The country was invaded by Japan in World War II. Following the war Thailand was ruled by military officers until 1973, when civilians seized control and instigated a period of democracy that ended in 1976, when the military again took control. ∎

TOGO

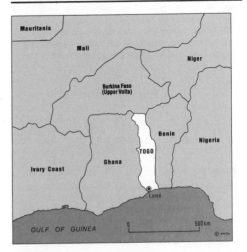

Official name Republic of Togo
PEOPLE
Population 2,965,000. **Density** 135/mi² (52/km²). **Urban**
17%. **Capital** Lomé, 235,000. **Ethnic groups** Ewe, Mina,
Kabyè, others. **Languages** French, indigenous.

Religions Indigenous 70%, Christian 20%, Muslim 10%. **Life expectancy** 50 female, 46 male. **Literacy** 18%.

POLITICS

Government Republic. **Parties** Rally of the People. **Suffrage** Universal adult. **Memberships** OAU, UN. **Subdivisions** 21 circumscriptions.

ECONOMY

GNP $950,000,000. **Per capita** $340. **Monetary unit** CFA franc. **Trade partners** France, other Western European countries. **Exports** Phosphates, cocoa, coffee, palm kernels. **Imports** Consumer goods, fuels, machinery, food.

LAND

Description Western Africa. **Area** 21,925 mi² (56,785 km²). **Highest point** Pic Baumann, 3,235 ft (986 m). **Lowest point** Sea level.

People. Almost all the people of Togo are black Africans, coming primarily from the Ewe, Mina, and Kabyè ethnic groups. Most of the population lives in the south and practices traditional religions. There are, however, significant Christian and Muslim minorities.

Economy and the Land. Togo is an agricultural country, but productive land is scarce. Fishing is a major industry in the coastal areas. Togo has one of the world's largest phosphate reserves. Much of Togo is mountainous, with a sandy coastal plain. The climate is hot and humid.

History and Politics. Togo's original inhabitants were probably the ancestors of the present-day central mountain people. Ewes entered the south in the 1300s, and refugees from war-torn northern countries settled in the north between the 1500s and 1800s. For two hundred years European ships raided the coastal region in search of slaves. In 1884 Germany claimed the territory. After World War I Togoland became a League of Nations mandate governed by Britain and France. The mandate was made a United Nations trust territory following World War II and remained under British and French administration. British Togoland voted to join the Gold Coast and nearby British-administered territories in 1957 and became the independent nation of Ghana. French Togoland voted to become a republic in 1956 with internal self-government within the French Union, although the United Nations did not accept this method of ending the trusteeship. Togo peacefully severed its ties with France in 1960 and became independent the same year. Internal political strife and military dominance of the government have characterized Togo's years of independence. ∎

TOKELAU

See NEW ZEALAND.

TONGA

Official name Kingdom of Tonga

PEOPLE

Population 107,000. **Density** 396/mi² (153/km²). **Urban** 28%. **Capital** Nuku'alofa, Tongatapu I., 18,312. **Ethnic groups** Tongan 98%. **Languages** Tongan, English.

Religions Christian. **Life expectancy** 58 female, 58 male. **Literacy** 93%.

POLITICS

Government Constitutional monarchy. **Parties** None. **Suffrage** Literate adults, over 21 (males must be taxpayers). **Memberships** CW. **Subdivisions** 3 island groups.

ECONOMY

GNP $50,000,000. **Per capita** $520. **Monetary unit** Pa'anga. **Trade partners** Australia, New Zealand, U.S. **Exports** Copra, bananas, coconut products. **Imports** Food, machinery, petroleum.

LAND

Description South Pacific islands. **Area** 270 mi² (699 km²). **Highest point** 3,380 ft (1,030 m). **Lowest point** Sea level.

People. Almost all Tongans are Polynesian and follow the Wesleyan Methodist religion. About two-thirds of the population lives on the main island of Tongatapu.

Economy and the Land. Tonga's economy is dominated by both subsistence and plantation agriculture. Manufacturing is almost nonexistent. Most of the islands are coral reefs; many have fertile soil. The climate is subtropical.

History and Politics. Tonga has been settled since at least 500 B.C. In the late 1700s a civil war broke out among three lines of kings who sought to establish rulership. In 1822 Wesleyan Methodist missionaries converted one of the warring kings to Christianity. His faction prevailed, and he ruled as George Tupou I, founder of the present dynasty. Tonga came under British protection in 1900 but retained its autonomy in internal matters. The nation became fully independent in 1970 and maintains close relations with Great Britain as well as its Pacific neighbors. ∎

TRINIDAD AND TOBAGO

Official name Republic of Trinidad and Tobago

PEOPLE

Population 1,240,000. **Density** 626/mi² (242/km²). **Urban** 49%. **Capital** Port of Spain, Trinidad I., 65,906. **Ethnic groups** Black 43%, East Indian 40%, mixed 14%, white 1%, Chinese 1%. **Languages** English. **Religions** Roman Catholic 36%, Hindu 23%, Protestant 13%, Muslim 6%. **Life expectancy** 74 female, 70 male. **Literacy** 89%.

POLITICS

Government Republic. **Parties** Democratic Action Congress, People's National Movement, United Labor Front. **Suffrage** Universal, over 18. **Memberships** CW, OAS, UN. **Subdivisions** 8 counties.

ECONOMY
GNP $7,316,000,000. **Per capita** $6,651. **Monetary unit** Dollar. **Trade partners** U.S., Saudi Arabia, U.K., Indonesia. **Exports** Petroleum, petroleum products, amonia, fertilizer, food. **Imports** Petroleum, machinery, transportation equipment, food, manufactured goods.

LAND
Description Caribbean islands. **Area** 1,980 mi² (5,128 km²). **Highest point** El Cerro Del Aripo, Trinidad I., 3,085 ft (940 m). **Lowest point** Sea level.

People. The two islands of Trinidad and Tobago form a single country, but Trinidad has nearly all the total land mass and population. About a third of all Trinidadians are black African, a third are East Indian, and a third are European, Chinese, and of mixed descent. Most Tobagonians are black African. The official language is English, and Christianity, Islam, and Hinduism are the major religions.

Economy and the Land. Agriculture and tourism are important, but the economy is based on oil, which accounts for about 80 percent of the nation's exports. Trinidad is also one of the world's chief sources of natural asphalt and possesses supplies of natural gas. The islands are characterized by tropical rain forests, scenic beaches, and fertile farmland.

History and Politics. Trinidad was occupied by Arawak Indians when Christopher Columbus arrived and claimed the island for Spain in 1498. The island remained under Spanish rule until 1797, when the British captured it and ruled for more than 150 years. Tobago changed hands among the Dutch, French, and British until 1814, when Britain took control. In 1888 Trinidad and Tobago became a single British colony and achieved independence in 1962. A separatist movement on Tobago has caused the government to give that island more control over its internal affairs. ∎

TUNISIA

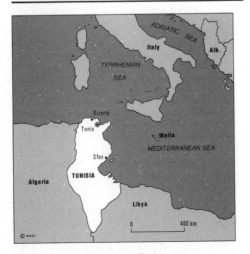

Official name Republic of Tunisia

PEOPLE
Population 7,295,000. **Density** 115/mi² (45/km²). **Urban** 52%. **Capital** Tunis, 550,404. **Ethnic groups** Arab 98%, European 1%. **Languages** Arabic, French. **Religions** Muslim 98%, Christian 1%. **Life expectancy** 63 female, 59 male. **Literacy** 62%.

POLITICS
Government Republic. **Parties** Communist, Destourian Socialist, Movement of Popular Unity, Social Democrats. **Suffrage** Universal, over 21. **Memberships** AL, OAU, UN. **Subdivisions** 23 governorates.

ECONOMY
GNP $8,700,000,000. **Per capita** $1,183. **Monetary unit** Dinar. **Trade partners** France, Italy, West Germany, Greece, U.S. **Exports** Petroleum, textiles, phosphates, olive oil. **Imports** Machinery, petroleum, transportation equipment, food, consumer goods.

LAND
Description Northern Africa. **Area** 63,170 mi² (163,610 km²). **Highest point** Mt. Chambi, 5,066 ft (1,544 m). **Lowest point** Chott el Rharsa, 70 ft (23 m) below sea level.

People. Tunisians are descended from indigenous African ethnic groups and from Arab groups. Nearly all Tunisians are Muslim. Arabic is the official language, and French is widely spoken. Tunisia is a leader in the Arab world in promoting rights for women, and its society is marked by a large middle class and equitable land distribution.

Economy and the Land. Tunisia is an agricultural country; wheat, barley, citrus fruits, and olives are important crops. Oil from deposits discovered in the 1960s supplies domestic needs and serves as a major export, along with phosphates. Tourism is a growing industry, and despite an unemployment problem, Tunisia has a more balanced economy than many of its neighbors. Tunisia's terrain ranges from a well-watered and fertile northern area to more arid central and southern regions.

History and Politics. Phoenicians began the Carthaginian Empire in Tunisia about 1100 B.C. In 146 B.C. Romans conquered Carthage and ruled Tunisia for six hundred years. Arab Muslims from the Middle East gained control of most of North Africa in the seventh century, influencing the religion and overall culture of the region. Tunisia became part of the Turkish Ottoman Empire in the late 1500s, and in 1881 France succeeded in establishing a protectorate in the area. Nationalistic calls for Tunisian independence began before World War I and gained momentum by the 1930s. When Tunisia gained independence in 1956, more than half of the European population emigrated, severely damaging the economy. A year later Tunisia abolished its monarchy and became a republic. The nation maintains a nonaligned stance and has established friendly relations with East and West. ∎

TURKEY

Official name Republic of Turkey

PEOPLE
Population 50,730,000. **Density** 169/mi² (65/km²).

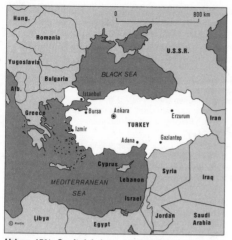

Urban 45%. **Capital** Ankara, 1,877,755. **Ethnic groups** Turkish 85%, Kurdish 12%. **Languages** Turkish, Kurdish. **Religions** Muslim 98%. **Life expectancy** 64 female, 60 male. **Literacy** 70%.

POLITICS
Government Republic. **Parties** Motherland, Nationalist Democracy, Populist. **Suffrage** Universal, over 21. **Memberships** NATO, OECD, UN. **Subdivisions** 67 provinces.

ECONOMY
GNP $53,800,000,000. **Per capita** $1,096. **Monetary unit** Lira. **Trade partners** Iraq, West Germany, U.S., Libya, other Western European countries. **Exports** Cotton, tobacco, fruits, nuts, food, textiles. **Imports** Petroleum, machinery, transportation equipment, metals, fertilizer.

LAND
Description Southeastern Europe and southwestern Asia. **Area** 300,948 mi² (779,452 km²). **Highest point** Mt. Ararat, 16,804 ft (5,122 m). **Lowest point** Sea level.

People. Turkey's majority group is Turkish, descended from an Asian people who migrated from Russia and Mongolia around A.D. 900. About half the Turkish population lives in cities and half in rural areas. Kurds, the largest minority group, live in the country's mountainous regions. Arabs and whites compose smaller minorities. Nearly all the population is Sunni Muslim. The changing status of women and the extent of Islamic influence on daily life are key issues in Turkish society.

Economy and the Land. More than half the workers in this developing country are farmers, but industrialization has increased greatly since 1950. The most productive lands are in the mild coastal regions, although wheat and barley are grown in the desertlike plateau area. The government owns or controls many important industries, transportation services, and utilities, while most small farms and manufacturing companies are privately owned.

History and Politics. Hittites began to migrate to the area from Europe or central Asia around 2000 B.C. Successive dominant groups included Phrygians, Greeks, Persians, and Romans. Muslims and Christians battled in the area during the Crusades of the eleventh and twelfth centuries. In the 1300s

Ottoman Turks began to build what would become a vast empire. The Republic of Turkey was founded by Mustafa Kemal in 1923, after the collapse of the six-hundred-year-old Ottoman Empire. In 1960 the Turkish government was overthrown by Turkish military forces, who subsequently set up a provisional government, adopted a new constitution, and held free elections. In the sixties and seventies disputes with Greece over Cyprus, populated by majority Greeks and minority Turks, flared into violence, and radical groups committed terrorist acts against the government, which changed hands several times. Turkey's generals assumed power in 1980 and restored order to the country. The government returned to civilian rule in 1983. ∎

TURKS AND CAICOS ISLANDS

See UNITED KINGDOM.

TUVALU

Official name Tuvalu
PEOPLE
Population 8,200. **Density** 820/mi² (315/km²). **Capital** Funafuti, Funafuti I., 2,191. **Ethnic groups** Polynesian 96%. **Languages** Tuvaluan, English. **Religions** Christian. **Life expectancy** 60 female, 57 male. **Literacy** 50%.
POLITICS
Government Parliamentary state. **Parties** None. **Memberships** CW.
ECONOMY
GNP $4,000,000. **Per capita** $570. **Monetary unit** Australian dollar. **Trade partners** U.K., Australia. **Exports** Copra. **Imports** Food, fuels.
LAND
Description South Pacific islands. **Area** 10 mi² (26 km²). **Highest point** 15 ft (5 m). **Lowest point** Sea level.

People. The small island nation of Tuvalu has a largely Polynesian population centered in rural villages. Tuvaluans speak the Tuvaluan language, derived from Polynesian, and because of historical ties to Great Britain, many Tuvaluans also speak English.

Economy and the Land. The soil of the Tuvaluan coral-reef islands is poor, and there are few natural resources other than coconut palms. Copra is the primary export, and many Tuvaluans weave mats and baskets for export. Tuvalu has minimal manufacturing and no mining. The nation consists of nine islands, most of them atolls surrounding lagoons. The climate is tropical.

History and Politics. Tuvalu's first inhabitants were probably Samoan immigrants. The islands were not seen by Europeans until 1568 and came under British control in the 1890s. Then called the Ellice Islands by Europeans, they were combined with the nearby Gilbert Islands in 1916 to form the Gilbert and Ellice Islands Colony. The island groups were separated in 1975, and the Ellice Islands were renamed Tuvalu, which became independent in 1978. ∎

UGANDA

Official name Republic of Uganda
PEOPLE
Population 14,505,000. **Density** 159/mi² (61/km²). **Urban** 7%. **Capital** Kampala, 458,423. **Ethnic groups** African 99%. **Languages** English, Swahili, Luganda, indigenous. **Religions** Roman Catholic 33%, Protestant 33%, Muslim 16%, indigenous. **Life expectancy** 49 female, 46 male. **Literacy** 52%.
POLITICS
Government Republic. **Parties** Democratic, Uganda Patriotic Movement, Uganda People's Congress. **Suffrage** Universal adult. **Memberships** CW, OAU, UN. **Subdivisions** 10 provinces.
ECONOMY
GDP $4,800,000,000. **Per capita** $357. **Monetary unit** Shilling. **Trade partners** Kenya, U.S., U.K. **Exports** Coffee, cotton, tea. **Imports** Petroleum products, machinery, textiles, metals, transportation equipment.
LAND
Description Eastern Africa, landlocked. **Area** 91,134 mi² (236,036 km²). **Highest point** Margherita Pk., 16,763 ft (5,109 m). **Lowest point** 2,000 ft (650 m).

People. Uganda is a predominantly rural nation with a largely African population composed of various ethnic groups. Numerous differences divide Uganda's varied groups and have traditionally inspired conflict. Though English is the official language of Uganda, Luganda and Swahili are widely used, as well as indigenous Bantu and Nilotic languages. Most Ugandans are Christian; Muslims and followers of traditional beliefs compose significant minorities.

Economy and the Land. Despite attempts to diversify the economy, the country remains largely agricultural. Uganda is able to meet most of its own food needs, and coffee, cotton, and tea are grown commercially. Copper deposits account for most mining activity. Though Uganda straddles the equator, temperatures are modified by altitude. Most of the country is plateau, and Uganda benefits from proximity to several major lakes.

History and Politics. Arab traders who traveled to the interior of Uganda in the 1830s found sophisticated kingdoms that had developed over several centuries. British explorers tracking the source of the Nile River arrived in the 1860s and were followed by European missionaries. Britain quickly became a dominant force in eastern Africa, and part of modern Uganda became a British protectorate in 1894. Subsequent border adjustments brought Uganda to its present boundaries in 1926. After increasing demands for independence, moves toward autonomy began in the mid-1950s. Independence came in 1962 and was followed by internal conflicts and power struggles. In 1971 Major General Idi Amin Dada led a successful coup against President Obote and declared himself president. His dictatorship was rife with corruption, economic decline, and disregard for human rights. Amin was driven from Uganda by a force of Tanzanian troops and Ugandan exiles in 1979. President Obote returned to power in 1980 but was forced from office in a 1985 military coup. Uganda adheres to a nonaligned foreign policy. ■

UNITED ARAB EMIRATES

Official name United Arab Emirates
PEOPLE
Population 1,600,000. **Density** 50/mi² (19/km²). **Urban** 81%. **Capital** Abū Dhabi, 100,000. **Ethnic groups** Emirian 19%, other Arab 23%, South Asian 50%. **Languages** Arabic, Farsi, English. **Religions** Muslim 96%. **Life expectancy** 65 female, 61 male. **Literacy** 56%.
POLITICS
Government Federation of monarchs. **Parties** None. **Suffrage** None. **Memberships** AL, OPEC, UN. **Subdivisions** 7 emirates.
ECONOMY
GDP $30,000,000,000. **Per capita** $30,000. **Monetary unit** Dirham. **Trade partners** Japan, Western European countries, U.S. **Exports** Petroleum. **Imports** Machinery, consumer goods, food.

LAND

Description Southwestern Asia. **Area** 32,278 mi² (83,600 km²).

People. The United Arab Emirates is a predominantly urban federation of seven independent states, each with its own ruling emir. The indigenous population is mostly Arab and Muslim, but only a small percentage of residents are U.A.E. citizens. Other groups include foreigners attracted by jobs in industry, especially Asians and Western Europeans. Arabic is the official language, but Farsi and English are widely spoken. The people of U.A.E. enjoy one of the highest per capita incomes in the world, with free medical and educational facilities.

Economy and the Land. Most of the United Arab Emirates is desert, which explains agriculture's small economic role. However, the federation is rich in oil, and major deposits, primarily in Abū Dhabi, account for nearly all of the Emirian national budget. The United Arab Emirates has tried to diversify its economy through production of natural gas, ammonia, and building materials. To attract tourists, airport expansion and hotel development are also on the rise.

History and Politics. Centuries ago Arab rulers gained control of the region, formerly called the Trucial Coast, and Islam spread to the area in the A.D. 600s. In 1820 Arabian emirs signed the first of a number of treaties with the United Kingdom. Mutual self-interest led to an 1892 treaty that granted Britain exclusive rights to Trucial territory and government activity in return for military protection. Britain formally withdrew from Trucial affairs in 1971, and six of the Trucial emirates entered into a loose federation called the United Arab Emirates, which included Abū Dhabi, Dubai, Ash Shāriqah, 'Ajmān, Umm al Qaywayn, and Al Fujayrah. The seventh, Ra's al Khaymah, joined in early 1972. Because each emirate has a great deal of control over its internal affairs and economic development, the growth of federal powers has been slow. Defense spending is on the increase, however, and growing Arab nationalism may lead to a more centralized government.   ∎

UNITED KINGDOM

Official name United Kingdom of Great Britain and Northern Ireland

PEOPLE

Population 56,040,000. **Density** 596/mi² (230/km²). **Urban** 76%. **Capital** London, England, 6,851,400. **Ethnic groups** English 81%, Scottish 10%, Irish 2%, Welsh 2%, Ulster 2%. **Languages** English. **Religions** Anglican, Roman Catholic, Presbyterian. **Life expectancy** 76 female, 72 male. **Literacy** 99%.

POLITICS

Government Constitutional monarchy. **Parties** Conservative, Labor, Liberal, Social Democratic. **Suffrage** Universal, over 18. **Memberships** CW, NATO, OECD, UN. **Subdivisions** 6 metropolitan counties, 48

nonmetropolitan counties, 9 regions, 3 island areas, 26 local government districts.

ECONOMY

GNP $482,700,000,000. **Per capita** $8,620. **Monetary unit** Pound sterling. **Trade partners** U.S., West Germany, other Western European countries. **Exports** Machinery, transportation equipment, petroleum, manufactured goods. **Imports** Machinery, food, crude materials, manufactured goods.

LAND

Description Northwestern European islands. **Area** 94,092 mi² (243,694 km²). **Highest point** Ben Nevis, Scotland, 4,406 ft (1,343 m). **Lowest point** Holme Fen, England, 9 ft (3 m) below sea level.

People. The ancestry of modern Britons reflects many centuries of invasions and migrations from Scandinavia and the European continent. Today Britons are a mixture of Celtic, Roman, Anglo-Saxon, Norse, and Norman influences. English is the official language, although Celtic languages such as Welsh and Scottish Gaelic are also spoken. Anglican is the dominant religion in England, while many Scots practice Presbyterianism. A sizable minority is Roman Catholic. The population is primarily urban and suburban, with a significant percentage living in the southeastern corner of England.

Economy and the Land. A land of limited natural resources, the United Kingdom has relied on trading and, more recently, manufacturing to achieve its stature as a world power. Access to the sea is a traditional economic and political asset: the country maintains a large merchant fleet, which at one time dominated world trade. The industrial revolution developed quickly in Great Britain, and the country continues to be a leading producer of transportation equipment, metal products, and other manufactured goods. Agriculture is hindered by climate and limited suitable land, but intensive, mechanized farming methods have allowed the nation to produce half of its food supply. Livestock raising is especially important. Extensive deposits of coal and iron ore make mining important and have contributed to industry. London maintains its position as an international financial center. The United Kingdom includes Scotland, England, Wales, Northern Ireland, and several offshore islands. The varied terrain is marked by several mountain ranges, moors, rolling hills, and plains. The climate is tempered by proximity to the sea but is subject to frequent changes. Great Britain administers many overseas possessions.

History and Politics. Little is known of the earliest inhabitants of Britain, but evidence such as Stonehenge indicates the existence of a developed culture before the Roman invasion in the 50s B.C. Britain began to interact with the rest of Europe while under Roman rule, and the Norman period after A.D. 1066 fostered the establishment of many cultural and political traditions that continue to be reflected in British

life. Scotland came under the British Crown in 1603, and in 1707 England and Scotland agreed to unite as Great Britain. Ireland had been conquered by the early seventeenth century, and the 1801 British Act of Union established the United Kingdom of Great Britain and Ireland. Colonial and economic expansion had taken Great Britain to the Far East, America, Africa, and India, but the nation's influence began to diminish at the end of the nineteenth century as the industrial revolution strengthened other nations. World War I significantly weakened the United Kingdom, and after the war the British Empire lost several components, including southern Ireland in 1921. The period following World War II saw the demise of the empire, with many former colonies gaining independence. ∎

Places and Possessions of the United Kingdom

Entity	Status	Area	Population	Capital / Population
Anguilla (Caribbean island)	Associated state	35 mi² (91 km²)	7,000	The Valley, 760
Ascension (South Atlantic island)	Dependency of St. Helena	34 mi² (88 km²)	1,400	Georgetown
British Indian Ocean Territory (Indian Ocean islands)	Colony	23 mi² (60 km²)	None	None
Cayman Islands (Caribbean Sea)	Colony	100 mi² (259 km²)	22,000	Georgetown, 7,617
Channel Islands (northwest of Europe)	Dependency	75 mi² (195 km²)	132,000	None
Guernsey and dependencies (islands northwest of Europe)	Bailiwick of Channel Islands	30 mi² (77 km²)	78,000	St. Peter Port, 16,982
Isle of Man (northwest of Europe)	Self-governing territory	227 mi² (588 km²)	67,000	Douglas, 20,262
Jersey (island northwest of Europe)	Bailiwick of Channel Islands	45 mi² (117 km²)	54,000	St. Helier, 24,941
Montserrat (Caribbean island)	Colony	40 mi² (103 km²)	12,000	Plymouth, 1,568
Orkney Islands (northwest of Europe)	Part of Scotland	376 mi² (974 km²)	19,000	Kirkwall, 5,713
Pitcairn and dependencies (South Pacific islands)	Colony	19 mi² (49 km²)	50	Adamstown
St. Helena and dependencies (South Atlantic islands)	Colony	162 mi² (419 km²)	6,900	Jamestown, 1,516
Shetland Islands (northwest of Europe)	Part of Scotland	551 mi² (1,427 km²)	29,000	Lerwick, 6,333
South Georgia and dependencies (South Atlantic islands)	Dependency of Falkland Islands	1,580 mi² (4,092 km²)	22	None
Turks and Caicos Islands (Caribbean Sea)	Colony	166 mi² (430 km²)	8,100	Grand Turk, 3,146
Virgin Islands, British (Caribbean islands)	Colony	59 mi² (153 km²)	13,000	Road Town, 2,479

UNITED STATES

Official name United States of America

PEOPLE

Population 237,640,000. **Density** 65/mi² (25/km²).
Urban 74%. **Capital** Washington D.C., 618,400. **Ethnic groups** White 80%, black 11%, Spanish 6%. **Languages** English. **Religions** Protestant, Roman Catholic, Jewish, others. **Life expectancy** 78 female, 73 male.
Literacy 100%.

POLITICS

Government Republic. **Parties** Democratic, Republican.

Suffrage Universal, over 18. **Memberships** NATO, OAS, OECD, UN. **Subdivisions** 50 states, 1 federal district.

LAND

GNP $3,363,300,000,000. **Per capita** $12,530. **Monetary unit** Dollar. **Trade partners** Canada, Japan, Western European countries, Mexico. **Exports** Machinery, chemicals, transportation equipment, food. **Imports** Petroleum, machinery, transportation equipment.

LAND

Description Central North America. **Area** 3,679,245 mi² (9,529,200 km²). **Highest point** Mt. McKinley, 20,320 ft (6,194 m). **Lowest point** Death Valley, 282 ft (86 m) below sea level.

People. The diverse population of the United States is mostly composed of whites, many descended from eighteenth- and nineteenth-century immigrants; blacks, mainly descended from African slaves; peoples of Spanish and Asian origin; and indigenous Indians, Inuit, and Hawaiians. Religions encompass the world's major faiths; predominating are Protestantism, Roman Catholicism, and Judaism. English is the official language, though Spanish is spoken by many, and other languages are often found in ethnic enclaves.

Economy and the Land. The United States is an international economic power, and all sectors of the economy are highly developed. Soils are fertile, and farm output is high, with much land under cultivation. Mineral output includes petroleum and natural gas, coal, copper, lead, and zinc, but high consumption makes the United States dependent on foreign oil. The country is also a leading manufacturer, and the

Places and Possessions of the United States

Entity	Status	Area	Population	Capital / Population
American Samoa (South Pacific islands)	Unincorporated territory	77 mi² (199 km²)	35,000	Pago Pago, 3,075
Guam (North Pacific island)	Unincorporated territory	209 mi² (541 km²)	116,000	Agana, 896
Marshall Islands (North Pacific)	Part of Trust Territory of the Pacific Islands	70 mi² (181 km²)	34,000	Majuro
Micronesia, Federated States of (North Pacific islands)	Part of Trust Territory of the Pacific Islands	271 mi² (702 km²)	80,000	Kolonia, 5,549
Midway Islands (North Pacific)	Unincorporated territory	2 mi² (5.2 km²)	500	None
Northern Mariana Islands (North Pacific)	Part of Trust Territory of the Pacific Islands	184 mi² (477 km²)	19,000	Saipan
Pacific Islands, Trust Territory of the (North Pacific)	UN trusteeship under United States administration	717 mi² (1,857 km²)	146,000	Saipan
Palau (North Pacific islands)	Part of Trust Territory of the Pacific Islands	192 mi² (497 km²)	13,000	Koror, 6,222
Virgin Islands, United States (Caribbean Sea)	Unincorporated territory	133 mi² (344 km²)	105,000	Charlotte Amalie, 11,842
Wake Island (North Pacific)	Unincorporated territory	3 mi² (7.8 km²)	300	None

service sector is developed as well. The terrain is marked by mountains, prairies, woodlands, and deserts. The climate varies regionally, from mild year-round along the Pacific coast and in the South to temperate in the Northeast and Midwest. In addition to forty-eight contiguous states, the country includes the subarctic state of Alaska, northwest of Canada, and the tropical state of Hawaii, an island group in the Pacific.

History and Politics. Thousands of years ago Asiatic peoples, ancestors of American Indians, crossed the Bering Strait land bridge and spread across North and South America. Vikings reached North America around A.D. 1000, and Christopher Columbus arrived in 1492. Early explorations by Portugal and Spain were followed in 1607 by England's establishment of a colony at Jamestown, Virginia. Thirteen British colonies waged a successful war of independence against England from 1775 to 1783, although America had declared its independence in 1776. United States expansion continued westward throughout the nineteenth century. The issues of black slavery and states' rights led to the American Civil War from 1861 to 1865, a struggle that pitted the North against the South and resulted in the end of slavery. Opportunities for prosperity accompanied the industrial revolution in the late nineteenth century and led to a large influx of immigrants. From 1917 to 1918 the country joined with the Allies in World War I. A severe economic depression began in 1929, and the United States did not really recover until military spending during World War II stimulated industry and the economy in general. Allied victory came in 1945. Postwar conflicts included the Korean War of the early fifties and the Vietnam War, which involved the United States from the late 1950s to 1973. ∎

URUGUAY

Official name Oriental Republic of Uruguay

PEOPLE
Population 2,930,000. **Density** 43/mi² (17/km²). **Urban** 84%. **Capital** Montevideo, 1,229,748. **Ethnic groups** White 85–90%, mestizo 5–10%, black 3–5%. **Languages** Spanish. **Religions** Roman Catholic 66%, Protestant 2%, Jewish 2%, others 30%. **Life expectancy** 74 female, 69 male. **Literacy** 94%.

POLITICS
Government Republic. **Parties** Colorado, National. **Suffrage** Universal, over 18. **Memberships** OAS, UN. **Subdivisions** 19 departments.

ECONOMY
GDP $9,400,000,000. **Per capita** $3,201. **Monetary unit** Nuevo peso. **Trade partners** Brazil, Argentina, U.S.,

West Germany, other Western European countries. **Exports** Wool, hides, meat, textiles, leather products. **Imports** Petroleum, machinery, transportation equipment, chemicals, metals.

LAND
Description Southern South America. **Area** 68,037 mi² (176,215 km²). **Highest point** Cerro de las Ánimas, 1,644 ft (501 m). **Lowest point** Sea level.

People. Most Uruguayans are white descendants of nineteenth- and twentieth-century immigrants from Spain, Italy, and other European countries. Mestizos, of Spanish-Indian ancestry, and blacks round out the population. Spanish is the official language, and Roman Catholicism is the major religion, with small Protestant and Jewish minorities. Many Uruguayans claim to follow no religion.

Economy and the Land. Uruguay's fertile soil, grassy plains, and temperate climate provide the basis for agriculture and are especially conducive to livestock raising. The country has virtually no mineral resources, and petroleum exploration has been unrewarding. However, refinement of imported fuel is a major industry, and Uruguay has significant hydroelectric potential.

History and Politics. Uruguay's original inhabitants were Indians. The first European settlement was established by the Portuguese in the 1680s, followed by a Spanish settlement in the 1720s. By the 1770s Spain had gained control of the area, but in the 1820s Portugal once again came to power, annexing present-day Uruguay to Brazil. Nationalistic feelings in the early nineteenth century led to an 1828 war by Uruguayan patriots and Argentina against Brazil, and independence was achieved. Political instability continued until progressive programs were established in the early twentieth century, leading to increased immigration from Mediterranean Europe. Political unrest, caused in part by economic depression, resurfaced in the 1970s, leading to military intervention in the government. ∎

VANUATU

Official name Republic of Vanuatu

PEOPLE
Population 130,000. **Density** 23/mi² (8.8/km²). **Urban** 18%. **Capital** Port Vila, Efate I., 10,158. **Ethnic groups** Melanesian 90%, French 8%. **Languages** Bislama, English, French. **Religions** Christian. **Literacy** 10–20%.

POLITICS
Government Republic. **Parties** National. **Memberships** CW, UN. **Subdivisions** 4 districts.

ECONOMY
Monetary unit Vatu. **Trade partners** Australia, France, Japan. **Exports** Copra, frozen fish, meat. **Imports** Food, manufactured goods, fuels.

LAND
Description South Pacific islands. **Area** 5,714 mi² (14,800 km²). **Highest point** Mt. Tabwémasana, Espíritu Santo I., 6,165 ft (1,879 m). **Lowest point** Sea level.

People. The majority of Vanuatuans are Melanesian. Asians, Europeans, and Polynesians compose minorities. Languages include English and French, the languages of former rulers; and Bislama, a mixture of English and Melanesian. Most Vanuatuans are Christian, and indigenous religions are also practiced.

Economy and the Land. The economy is based on agriculture, and copra is the primary export crop. Fishing is also important, as is the growing tourist business. The more than eighty islands of Vanuatu are characterized by narrow coastal plains, mountainous interiors, and a mostly hot, rainy climate.

History and Politics. In 1606 Portuguese explorers encountered indigenous Melanesian inhabitants on islands that now compose Vanuatu. Captain James Cook of Britain charted the islands in 1774 and named them the New Hebrides after the Hebrides islands of Scotland. British and French merchants and missionaries began to settle the islands in the early 1800s. To resolve conflicting interests, Great Britain and France formed a joint naval commission to oversee the area in 1887 and a condominium government in 1906. Demands for autonomy began in the 1960s, and the New Hebrides became the independent Republic of Vanuatu in 1980. ∎

VATICAN CITY

Official name State of the Vatican City
PEOPLE
Population 700. **Density** 3,500/mi² (1,750/km²). **Urban** 100%. **Capital** Vatican City, 700. **Ethnic groups** Italian. **Languages** Italian, Latin. **Religions** Roman Catholic. **Literacy** 100%.
POLITICS
Government Ecclesiastical state. **Parties** None. **Suffrage** Roman Catholic cardinals less than 80 years old. **Memberships** None. **Subdivisions** None.
ECONOMY
Monetary unit Italian lira.
LAND
Description Southern Europe, landlocked (within the city of Rome, Italy). **Area** 0.2 mi² (0.4 km²). **Highest point** 245 ft (75 m). **Lowest point** 62 ft (19 m).

People. The Vatican City, the smallest independent state in the world, is the administrative and spiritual center of the Roman Catholic church and home to the pope, the church's head. The population is composed of administrative and diplomatic workers of more than a dozen nationalities; Italians and Swiss predominate. A military corps known as the Swiss Guard is also in residence. Roman Catholicism is the only religion. The official language is Italian, although official acts of the Holy See are drawn up in Latin.

Economy and the Land. The Vatican City does not engage in commerce per se; however, it does issue its own coins and postage stamps. In addition, it is the destination of thousands of tourists and pilgrims each year. Lying on a hill west of the Tiber River, the Vatican City is an urban enclave in northwestern Rome, Italy. The Vatican City enjoys a mild climate moderated by the Mediterranean Sea.

History and Politics. For centuries the popes of the Roman Catholic church ruled the Papal States, an area across central Italy, which included Rome. The popes' temporal authority gradually was reduced to the city of Rome, which itself was eventually annexed by the Kingdom of Italy in 1870. Denying these rulings, the pope declared himself a prisoner in the Vatican, a status that lasted fifty-nine years. The Vatican City has been an independent sovereign state since 1929, when Italy signed the Treaty of the Lateran in return for papal dissolution of the Papal States. The pope heads all branches of government, though day-to-day responsibilities are delegated to staff members. ∎

VENEZUELA

Official name Republic of Venezuela
PEOPLE
Population 16,040,000. **Density** 46/mi² (18/km²). **Urban** 76%. **Capital** Caracas, 3,041,000. **Ethnic groups** Mestizo 67%, white 21%, black 10%, Indian 2%. **Languages** Spanish. **Religions** Roman Catholic 96%, Protestant 2%. **Life expectancy** 70 female, 66 male. **Literacy** 86%.
POLITICS
Government Republic. **Parties** Democratic Action, Movement Toward Socialism, Social Christian. **Suffrage** Universal, over 18. **Subdivisions** 20 states, 2 federal territories, 1 federal district.
ECONOMY
GDP $69,300,000,000. **Per capita** $4,716. **Monetary unit** Bolívar. **Trade partners** U.S., Canada, West Germany, Japan, Italy. **Exports** Petroleum, iron ore. **Imports** Machinery, transportation equipment, manufactured goods, chemicals, food.
LAND
Description Northern South America. **Area** 352,144 mi² (912,050 km²). **Highest point** Pico Bolívar, 16,427 ft (5,007 m). **Lowest point** Sea level.

People. Spanish colonial rule of Venezuela is reflected in its predominantly mestizo population, of Spanish-Indian blood, and its official language of Spanish. Minorities include Europeans, blacks, and

Indians, who generally speak local languages. Nearly all Venezuelans are Roman Catholic, further evidence of former Spanish domination. Protestants and lesser numbers of Jews and Muslims compose small minorities, and traditional religious practices continue among some Indians.

Economy and the Land. Since the expansion of the petroleum industry in the 1920s, Venezuela has experienced rapid economic growth, but the economy has been hampered by unevenly distributed wealth, a high birthrate, and fluctuations in the price of oil. Partly because of the emphasis on oil production, agriculture has declined; its contribution to the gross national product is minimal, and Venezuela must import much of its food. Manufacturing and hydroelectric power are being developed. The varied Venezuelan landscape is dominated by the Andes Mountains, a coastal zone, high plateaus, and plains, or llanos. The climate is tropical, but temperatures vary with altitude. Most of the country experiences rainy and dry seasons.

History and Politics. The original inhabitants of modern Venezuela included Arawak and Carib Indians. In 1498 Christopher Columbus was the first European to visit Venezuela. The area became a colony of Spain and was briefly under German rule. Independence was achieved in 1821 under the guidance of Simón Bolívar, Venezuela's national hero. Venezuela became a sovereign state in 1830. The nineteenth century saw political instability and revolutionary fervor, followed by a succession of dictators in the twentieth century. Since 1958 Venezuela has tried to achieve a representational form of government and has held a number of democratic elections. ∎

VIETNAM

Official name Socialist Republic of Vietnam
PEOPLE
Population 58,930,000. **Density** 463/mi² (179/km²).
Urban 19%. **Capital** Hanoi, 819,913. **Ethnic groups**
Vietnamese 85–90%, Chinese 3%. **Languages**

Vietnamese. **Religions** Buddhist, Confucian, Taoist, Roman Catholic, animist, Muslim. **Life expectancy** 54 female, 51 male. **Literacy** 78%.
POLITICS
Government Socialist republic. **Parties** Communist. **Suffrage** Universal, over 18. **Memberships** UN. **Subdivisions** 39 provinces.
ECONOMY
GNP $10,700,000,000. **Per capita** $189. **Monetary unit** Dông. **Trade partners** U.S.S.R., Eastern European countries, Japan. **Exports** Agricultural products, handicrafts, coal, minerals. **Imports** Petroleum, steel products, railroad equipment, chemicals, medicines.
LAND
Description Southeastern Asia. **Area** 127,242 mi² (329,556 km²). **Highest point** Fan Si Pan, 10,312 ft (3,143 m). **Lowest point** Sea level.

People. Despite centuries of foreign invasion and domination, the people of Vietnam remain remarkably homogeneous; ethnic Vietnamese compose the majority of the population. Chinese influence is seen in the major religions of Taoism, Confucianism, and Buddhism. The official language is Vietnamese, but a history of foreign intervention is reflected in wide use of French, English, Chinese, and Russian.

Economy and the Land. The Vietnamese economy has struggled to overcome the effects of war and the difficulties inherent in unifying the once-divided country. Agriculture, centered in the fertile southern plains, continues to employ nearly 70 percent of the people. Vietnam intends to expand its war-damaged mining industry, which has been slowed by lack of skilled personnel and a poor transportation network. Vietnam's economic picture is not likely to improve until the country can resolve its political and social problems. The landscape of Vietnam ranges from mountains to plains, and the climate is tropical.

History and Politics. The first Vietnamese lived in what is now northern Vietnam. After centuries of Chinese rule, Vietnam finally became independent in the 1400s, but civil strife continued for nearly two centuries. French missionary activity began in the early seventeenth century, and by 1883 all of present-day Vietnam, Kampuchea, and Laos were under French rule. When Germany occupied France during World War II, control of French Indochina passed to the Japanese, until their defeat in 1945. The French presence continued until 1954, when Vietnamese Communists led by Ho Chi Minh gained control of North Vietnam. United States aid to South Vietnam began in the 1950s and ended after years of conflict with a cease-fire in 1973. Communist victory and unification of the country as the Socialist Republic of Vietnam was achieved in 1975. Vietnamese military policy has resulted in armed conflict with China and the occupation of Kampuchea, and the country remains dependent on the Soviet Union. ∎

VIRGIN ISLANDS, BRITISH

See UNITED KINGDOM.

VIRGIN ISLANDS, UNITED STATES

See UNITED STATES.

WAKE ISLAND

See UNITED STATES.

WALLIS AND FUTUNA

See FRANCE.

WESTERN SAHARA

Official name Western Sahara
PEOPLE
Population 170,000. **Density** 1.7/mi² (0.6/km²). **Capital**
El Aaiún, 20,000. **Ethnic groups** Arab, Berber.
Languages Arabic. **Religions** Muslim. **Literacy**
Saharans, 5%; Moroccans, 20%.
POLITICS
Government Occupied by Morocco. **Parties** Polisario
Front. **Memberships** OAU.
ECONOMY
Monetary unit Moroccan dirham, Mauritanian ouguiya.
Trade partners Controlled by Morocco. **Exports**
Phosphates. **Imports** Fuels, food.
LAND
Description Northwestern Africa. **Area** 102,703 mi²
(266,000 km²). **Highest point** 2,300 ft (701 m). **Lowest
point** Sea level.

People. Most Western Saharans are nomadic Arabs or Berbers. Because these nomads often cross
national borders in their wanderings, the population
of Western Sahara is in a constant state of flux.
Islam is the principal religion, and Arabic is the dominant language.

Economy and the Land. Most of Western Sahara
is barren, rocky desert, with a sandy soil that severely limits agriculture. Mining of major phosphate
deposits began in 1972; phosphates are now the
primary export. Western Sahara is almost completely arid; rainfall is negligible except along the
coast.

History and Politics. By the fourth century B.C.
Phoenicians and Romans had visited the area.
Spain explored the region in the sixteenth century
and gained control of the region in 1860. Spanish
Sahara was designated a province of Spain in 1958.
Spanish control ceased in 1976, and the area became known as Western Sahara. Mauritania and
Morocco subsequently divided the territory, and Morocco gained control of valuable phosphate deposits.
Fighting soon broke out between an independence
movement, the Polisario Front, and troops from Morocco and Mauritania. In 1979 Mauritania gave up
its claim to the area and withdrew. Morocco claimed
the territory that Mauritania had given up; fighting
between Morocco and the Polisario Front continued
into the 1980s.   ■

WESTERN SAMOA

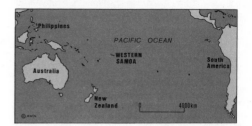

Official name Independent State of Western
Samoa
PEOPLE
Population 160,000. **Density** 146/mi² (56/km²). **Urban**
21%. **Capital** Apia, Upolu I., 33,784. **Ethnic groups**
Samoan, Euronesian. **Languages** Samoan, English.
Religions Christian. **Life expectancy** 64 female,
61 male. **Literacy** 90%.
POLITICS
Government Constitutional monarchy. **Parties** None.
Suffrage 45 members of Legislative Assembly elected by
matais, 2 elected by adults without traditional family ties.
Memberships CW, UN. **Subdivisions** 24 districts.
ECONOMY
GNP $130,000,000. **Per capita** $770. **Monetary unit**
Talà. **Trade partners** New Zealand, U.S., Australia, West
Germany. **Exports** Copra, cocoa, wood, bananas.
Imports Food, manufactured goods, petroleum,
machinery.
LAND
Description South Pacific islands. **Area** 1,097 mi² (2,842
km²). **Highest point** Mt. Silisili, Savai'i I., 6,096 ft (1,858
m). **Lowest point** Sea level.

People. Most Western Samoans are of Polynesian
descent, and a significant minority are of mixed Samoan and European heritage. Most of the population
is Christian and practices a variety of faiths introduced by European missionaries and traders. Samoan and English are the principal languages.

Economy and the Land. The tropical climate of
Western Samoa is suited for agriculture, which is
the country's chief economic reliance. Bananas, coconuts, and tropical fruits are the most important
crops.

History and Politics. Polynesians settled the Samoan islands more than two thousand years ago.
Dutch explorers visited the islands in the early
1700s, and English missionaries arrived in 1830. Rivalry between the islands' royal families increased,
along with competition for influence among the
United Kingdom, the United States, and Germany.
In 1900 the United States annexed Eastern Samoa,
and Germany obtained Western Samoa. By the end
of World War I New Zealand had gained control of
Western Samoa. Growing demand for independence
led to United Nations intervention, and gradual steps
toward self-government were taken. The islands became fully independent in 1962. The nation maintains friendly relations with New Zealand and neighboring Pacific islands.   ■

YEMEN

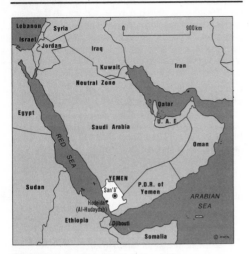

Official name Yemen Arab Republic
PEOPLE
Population 5,985,000. **Density** 79/mi² (31/km²). **Urban** 12%. **Capital** San'ā', 277,800. **Ethnic groups** Arab 90%, Afro-Arab 10%. **Languages** Arabic. **Religions** Muslim. **Life expectancy** 44 female, 42 male. **Literacy** 15%.

POLITICS
Government Republic. **Parties** General People's Congress. **Memberships** AL, UN. **Subdivisions** 11 provinces.

ECONOMY
GNP $3,800,000,000. **Per capita** $740. **Monetary unit** Riyal. **Trade partners** P.D.R. Yemen, China, U.S.S.R., Saudi Arabia, Japan. **Exports** Khat, cotton, coffee, hides. **Imports** Manufactured goods, petroleum products, textiles, food.

LAND
Description Southwestern Asia. **Area** 75,290 mi² (195,000 km²). **Highest point** Mt. Nabi Shuayb, 12,336 ft (3,760 m). **Lowest point** Sea level.

People. Nearly all the inhabitants of the Yemen Arab Republic, or North Yemen, are Arab and Arabic speaking. The predominant religion is Islam, and the population is nearly equally divided into Shiite and Sunni Muslims. The Shiites populate the north, central, and east, and the Sunni community is found in the south and southwest. Most Yemenis are farmers.

Economy and the Land. Yemen has a terrain suited for agriculture, which is the mainstay of the nation's economy. However, ineffective agricultural techniques often combine with regional instability to present obstacles to increased production. Industrial activity is growing slowly, with production based on domestic resources, but exploitation of oil, iron ore, and salt deposits is financially prohibitive at this time. The landscape of the Yemen Arab Republic varies from arid lowlands to the fertile, well-cultivated highlands that dominate the country's center. The climate is temperate inland and hot and dry along the coast.

History and Politics. From earliest times Yemen has been occupied by trade empires, and it was part of the Kingdom of Sheba in the 900s B.C. Christian and Jewish societies thrived in the pre-Islamic period, and the region's flourishing economy made it a focal point in the development of Islam. The Ottoman Empire ruled Yemen from the sixteenth century until 1918, when the Turkish military withdrew and gave control to the highland Zaidis. In 1962 the Yemeni army deposed the Imam Badr and established the Yemen Arab Republic. Civil unrest continued until a reconciliation of royalists and republicans in 1968, but a 1970 constitution was suspended in 1974 and military leaders assumed control. ∎

YEMEN, PEOPLE'S DEMOCRATIC REPUBLIC OF

Official name People's Democratic Republic of Yemen
PEOPLE
Population 2,180,000. **Density** 17/mi² (6.5/km²). **Urban** 38%. **Capital** Aden, 271,600. **Ethnic groups** Arab. **Languages** Arabic. **Religions** Sunni Muslim. **Life expectancy** 47 female, 44 male. **Literacy** 25%.

POLITICS
Government Socialist republic. **Parties** Socialist. **Suffrage** Universal, over 18. **Memberships** AL, UN. **Subdivisions** 6 governorates.

ECONOMY
GNP $792,000,000. **Per capita** $430. **Monetary unit** Dinar. **Trade partners** Yemen, U.K., Japan, Persian Gulf countries, U.S.S.R. **Exports** Petroleum products, fish products, hides and skins. **Imports** Petroleum, food, machinery, transportation equipment.

LAND
Description Southwestern Asia. **Area** 128,560 mi² (332,968 km²). **Highest point** 8,255 ft (2,516 m). **Lowest point** Sea level.

People. Most inhabitants of the People's Democratic Republic of Yemen, or South Yemen, are Arab, with small minorities of Indians, Pakistanis, and East Africans. Islam is the dominant religion, and nearly all South Yemenis belong to the Sunni sect. Small numbers of Christians, Hindus, and Jews also exist. Arabic is the official language, but Semitic variations are heard in the eastern part of the country, and English is widely understood. More than a third of the population lives in or near urban areas, particularly the capital city, Aden.

Economy and the Land. Arable land is limited by South Yemen's arid climate, although most Yemenis are subsistence farmers and nomadic herders. Petroleum products are South Yemen's major industrial export. However, both crude oil and food must be imported for the population, and the diminished oil market is a continuing problem. The terrain is marked by a mountainous interior and a flat, sandy coast. The climate is hot and dry.

History and Politics. Between 1200 B.C. and A.D. 525 the area of present-day Yemen was at the center of the Minaean, Sabaean, and Himyarite cultures.

Christian Ethiopians and Persians also proliferated before the introduction of Islam in the seventh century. Yemen's coastal area came under the control of the British in 1839, and Aden became an important center of trade. Regional instability caused Britain to expand eastward and establish the protectorate of Aden in the 1930s. By the mid-1960s Aden had become the focus of Arab nationalists, and in 1967 Britain granted independence to the People's Republic of South Yemen. After a coup directed by a Marxist faction in 1970, the country was renamed the People's Democratic Republic of Yemen. During the 1970s border clashes erupted with the Yemen Arab Republic, but the governments of both North and South Yemen continue to express a wish to unify Yemen.   ∎

YUGOSLAVIA

Official name Socialist Federal Republic of Yugoslavia

PEOPLE
Population 23,075,000. **Density** 234/mi² (90/km²). **Urban** 39%. **Capital** Belgrade, 936,200. **Ethnic groups** Serb 36%, Croatian 20%, Bosnian 9%, Slovene 8%, Albanian 8%, Macedonian 6%, Montenegrin 3%, Hungarian 2%. **Languages** Serbo-Croatian, Slovene, Macedonian. **Religions** Serbian Orthodox 41%, Roman Catholic 32%, Muslim 12%. **Life expectancy** 73 female, 69 male. **Literacy** 85%.

POLITICS
Government Socialist republic. **Parties** League of Communists. **Suffrage** Universal, over 18. **Memberships** OECD, UN. **Subdivisions** 6 republics, 2 autonomous provinces.

ECONOMY
GNP $53,900,000,000. **Per capita** $2,370. **Monetary unit** Dinar. **Trade partners** U.S.S.R., West Germany, Italy, U.S., Czechoslovakia. **Exports** Food, leather goods and shoes, machinery, textiles, wood products. **Imports** Machinery, petroleum, iron and steel, chemicals.

LAND
Description Eastern Europe. **Area** 98,766 mi² (255,804 km²). **Highest point** Triglav, 9,396 ft (2,864 m). **Lowest point** Sea level.

People. The population of Yugoslavia is one of the most diverse in Eastern Europe, composed of nearly twenty distinct ethnic groups in addition to the main Serbian and Croatian groups. Serbo-Croatian, Slovene, and Macedonian are major languages, and religions are diverse as well, often dividing along ethnic lines. Most Yugoslavs work in industry, resulting in a steady urban shift since World War II and a corresponding rise in the standard of living.

Economy and the Land. Since 1945 Yugoslavia's economy has made a successful transition from agriculture to industry. Once modeled on that of the Soviet Union, the economy today is somewhat decentralized, based on the theory of workers' self-management. Decisions on production, prices, and income are made to benefit society as a whole, though wealth has tended to concentrate in the highly industrialized north, resulting in increasing social tension. Agriculture also plays a part in the economic picture, and farming is helped by the moderate climate along the coast of the Adriatic Sea, with stronger seasonal variations in the mountainous inland regions.

History and Politics. Yugoslavia has been inhabited for at least 100,000 years, its peoples including Illyrians, Thracians, Greeks, Celts, and Romans. In A.D. 395 the Roman Empire was divided into the West Roman Empire and the Byzantine Empire, with the dividing line through present-day Yugoslavia. People in the western region became Roman Catholic and used the Roman alphabet, while Byzantines adopted the Eastern Orthodox faith and the Cyrillic alphabet. Slavic migrations led to the establishment of independent Slavic states such as Serbia and Croatia, and calls for Slavic unity began in the early 1800s. In 1914 a Slavic patriot assassinated Archduke Ferdinand of Austria-Hungary and triggered World War I. The Kingdom of Serbs, Croats, and Slovenes was formed in 1918, but infighting encouraged King Alexander I to declare himself dictator in 1929 and change the new country's name to Yugoslavia, which was retained after Alexander's assassination in 1934. Germany and the other Axis powers invaded Yugoslavia during World War II and were opposed by a partisan army organized by Josip Broz Tito, who assumed leadership when Yugoslavia became a Communist republic in 1945. Tito's policy of nonalignment, the cornerstone of Yugoslavia's foreign policy, caused Russia to break off diplomatic relations from 1948 to 1955. United States aid from the 1940s to the 1960s encouraged a shift toward Western trade and broadened political and cultural exchanges as well. Tito's course of independence and interaction with non-aligned nations continued after his death in 1980.   ∎

ZAIRE

Official name Republic of Zaire
PEOPLE
Population 32,625,000. **Density** 36/mi² (14/km²). **Urban**

History and Politics. The earliest inhabitants of modern Zaire were probably Pygmies who settled in the area thousands of years ago. By the A.D. 700s sophisticated civilizations had developed in what is now southeastern Zaire. Portuguese explorers visited a coastal kingdom in the 1480s. In the early 1500s the Portuguese began the forced emigration of black Africans for slavery. Other Europeans came to the area as the slave trade grew, but the interior remained relatively unexplored until the 1870s. Belgian king Leopold II realized the potential value of the region, and in 1885 his claim was recognized. Belgium took control from Leopold in 1908, renaming the colony the Belgian Congo. Nationalist sentiment grew until rioting broke out in 1959. Independence was granted in 1960, and a weak government assumed control of what was by then called the Congo. Violent civil disorder, provincial secession, and political assassination characterized the next five years. The country stabilized under the rule of President Mobutu Sese Seko, a former army general. Zaire took its present name in 1971. ∎

34%. **Capital** Kinshasa, 2,700,000. **Ethnic groups** Mongo, Luba, Kongo, Mangbetu-Azande, others. **Languages** French, Lingala, Swahili, Kikongo, Tshiluba. **Religions** Roman Catholic 50%, Protestant 20%, Kimbanguist 10%, Muslim 10%, indigenous 10%. **Life expectancy** 52 female, 48 male. **Literacy** 15% female, 40% male.

POLITICS
Government Republic. **Parties** Popular Movement of the Revolution. **Suffrage** Universal, over 18. **Memberships** OAU, UN. **Subdivisions** 8 regions, 1 federal district.

ECONOMY
GDP $3,400,000,000. **Per capita** $570. **Monetary unit** Zaïre. **Trade partners** Belgium, U.S., West Germany. **Exports** Copper, cobalt, diamonds, petroleum, coffee. **Imports** Petroleum products, food, machinery, consumer goods, transportation equipment.

LAND
Description Central Africa. **Area** 905,567 mi² (2,345,409 km²). **Highest point** Margherita Pk., 16,763 ft (5,109 m). **Lowest point** Sea level.

People. The diverse population of Zaire is composed of more than two hundred African ethnic groups, with Bantu peoples accounting for the majority. Belgian settlers introduced French, but hundreds of indigenous languages are more widely spoken. Much of the population is Christian, another result of former European rule. Many non-Christians practice traditional or syncretic faiths such as Kimbanguism. The majority of Zairians are rural farmers.

Economy and the Land. Zaire is rich in mineral resources, particularly copper, cobalt, diamonds, and petroleum; mining has supplanted agriculture in economic importance and now dominates the economy. Agriculture continues to employ most Zairians, however, and subsistence farming is practiced in nearly every region. Industrial activity—especially petroleum refining and hydroelectric production—is growing. Zaire's terrain is composed of mountains and plateaus. The climate is equatorial, with hot and humid weather in the north and west, and cooler and drier conditions in the south and east.

ZAMBIA

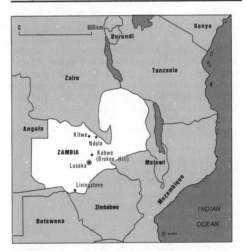

Official name Republic of Zambia
PEOPLE
Population 6,660,000. **Density** 23/mi² (8.8/km²). **Urban** 43%. **Capital** Lusaka, 538,469. **Ethnic groups** African 99%. **Languages** English, indigenous. **Religions** Christian 50–75%, Muslim and Hindu 1%, indigenous. **Life expectancy** 52 female, 49 male. **Literacy** 54%.
POLITICS
Government Republic. **Parties** United National Independence. **Suffrage** Universal, over 18. **Memberships** CW, OAU, UN. **Subdivisions** 9 provinces.
ECONOMY
GDP $2,900,000,000. **Per capita** $476. **Monetary unit** Kwacha. **Trade partners** U.K., South Africa, Japan, West Germany, Saudi Arabia. **Exports** Copper, cobalt, zinc, lead, tobacco. **Imports** Machinery, transportation equipment, fuels, manufactured goods, food.

LAND
Description Southern Africa, landlocked. **Area** 290,586 mi² (752,614 km²). **Highest point** 7,100 ft (2,164 m). **Lowest point** 1,081 ft (329 m).

People. Virtually all Zambians are black Africans belonging to one of more than seventy Bantu-speaking ethnic groups. Besides the indigenous Bantu languages, many speak English, a reflection of decades of British influence. Although most Zambians are Christian, small minorities are Hindu, Muslim, or hold indigenous beliefs. Most Zambians are subsistence farmers in small villages; however, the mining industry has caused many people to move to urban areas, where wages are rising.

Economy and the Land. The economy is based on copper, Zambia's major export. The government is interested in diversifying the economy and has emphasized the development of agriculture to decrease dependence on food imports and achieve an acceptable balance of trade. Zambia is a subtropical nation marked by high plateaus and great rivers.

History and Politics. European explorers arriving in the nineteenth century found an established society of Bantu-speaking inhabitants. In 1888 Cecil Rhodes and the British South Africa Company obtained a mineral-rights concession from local chiefs, and Northern and Southern Rhodesia, now Zambia and Zimbabwe, came within the British sphere of influence. Northern Rhodesia became a British protectorate in 1924. In 1953 Northern Rhodesia was combined with Southern Rhodesia and Nyasaland, now Malawi, to form a federation, despite African-nationalist opposition to the European minority-controlled government in Southern Rhodesia. The federation was dissolved in 1963, and Northern Rhodesia became the independent Republic of Zambia in 1964. Zambia follows a foreign policy of nonalignment. ∎

ZIMBABWE

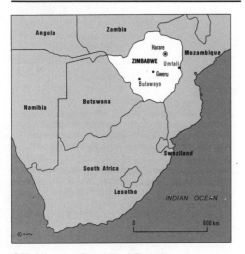

Official name Republic of Zimbabwe

PEOPLE
Population 8,190,000. **Density** 54/mi² (21/km²). **Urban** 23%. **Capital** Harare, 656,011. **Ethnic groups** Shona 77%, Ndebele 19%, European 3%. **Languages** English, ChiShona, Si Ndebele. **Religions** Syncretic 50%, Christian 25%, indigenous 24%. **Life expectancy** 57 female, 53 male. **Literacy** 45–55%.
POLITICS
Government Republic. **Parties** African National Union, African People's Union, Republican Front, United African National Council. **Suffrage** Universal, over 18 (whites, mixed, and Asians vote separately for 20 seats in House of Assembly). **Memberships** CW, OAU, UN. **Subdivisions** 8 provinces.
ECONOMY
GDP $7,100,000,000. **Per capita** $880. **Monetary unit** Dollar. **Trade partners** South Africa, U.K., U.S., West Germany. **Exports** Tobacco, asbestos, copper, tin, chrome, gold, nickel. **Imports** Machinery, petroleum products, transportation equipment.
LAND
Description Southern Africa, landlocked. **Area** 150,804 mi² (390,580 km²). **Highest point** Inyangani, 8,504 ft (2,592 m). **Lowest point** 530 ft (162 m).

People. The great majority of Zimbabweans are black Africans of Bantu descent, with a small but economically significant minority of white Europeans. Most Zimbabweans are subsistence farmers who live in small villages. The influence of British colonization can be seen in the official language, English, and in the influence of Christianity.

Economy and the Land. Zimbabwe's natural mineral resources have played a key role in the country's sustained economic growth. The subtropical climate supports the exportation of many agricultural products and makes large-scale cattle ranching feasible. Though primarily a landlocked country of high plateaus, transportation of goods is facilitated by an excellent system of paved roads and railways.

History and Politics. Zimbabwe was populated by Bantu groups until European exploration in the nineteenth century. British influence began in 1888, when Cecil Rhodes and the British South Africa Company obtained mineral rights to the area from local chiefs, and eventually the region was divided under British rule as Southern Rhodesia, or present-day Zimbabwe, and Northern Rhodesia, or modern Zambia. In 1953 Southern Rhodesia, Northern Rhodesia, and Nyasaland, now Malawi, formed a federation that ended in discord after ten years; Zambia and Malawi gained their independence, and Southern Rhodesia, which remained under British control, became Rhodesia. In response to British pressure to accept black-majority rule, Rhodesian whites declared independence from the United Kingdom in 1965, which led to economic sanctions imposed by the United Nations. These sanctions and years of antigovernment violence finally forced agreement to the principle of black-majority rule. In 1980 the Zimbabwe African National Union–Patriotic Front won a majority of seats in the House of Representatives, and Rhodesia became independent Zimbabwe. Despite Zimbabwe's move toward stability since independence, some internal unrest continues. ∎

World Atlas

Reference Map Legend

CULTURAL FEATURES

Political Boundaries

▬▬▬▬ International

────── Secondary (State, province, etc.)

────── County

Populated Places

Cities, towns, and villages

•••••● Symbol size represents population of the place

Chicago
Gary
Racine
Glenview
Edgewood
Type size represents relative importance of the place

Corporate area of large U.S. and Canadian cities and urban area of other foreign cities

Major Urban Area
Area of continuous commercial, industrial, and residential development in and around a major city

○ Community within a city

⊛ Capital of major political unit

☆ Capital of secondary political unit

⊙ Capital of U.S. state or Canadian province

• County Seat

▲ Military Installation

⊙ Scientific Station

Miscellaneous

National Park

National Monument

Provincial Park

Indian Reservation

△ Point of Interest

∴ Ruins

■ ⚑ Buildings

Race Track

────── Railroad

─┼──┼── Tunnel

---------- Underground or Subway

Dam

Bridge

Dike

LAND FEATURES

Passes =

Point of Elevation above sea level + 8,520 FT.

WATER FEATURES

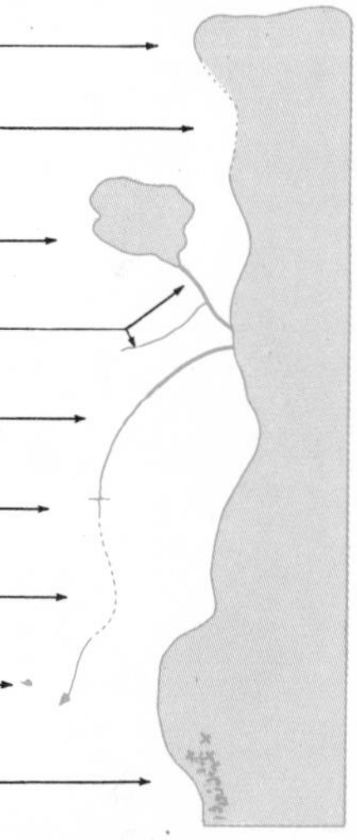

Coastlines and Shorelines ──────→

Indefinite or Unsurveyed Coastlines and Shorelines ──────→

Lakes and Reservoirs ──────→

Canals ──────→

Rivers and Streams ──────→

Falls and Rapids ──────

Intermittent or Unsurveyed Rivers and Streams ──────→

Directional Flow Arrow ──────

Rocks, Shoals and Reefs ──────→

TYPE STYLES USED TO NAME FEATURES

ASIA	Continent
DENMARK CANADA	Country, State, or Province
BÉARN	Region, Province, or Historical Region
CROCKETT	County
PANTELLERIA (ITALY)	Country of which unit is a dependency in parentheses
SRI LANKA (CEYLON)	Former or alternate name
Rome (Roma)	Local or alternate city name
Naval Air Station	Military Installation
MESA VERDE SAN XAVIER	National Park or Monument, Provincial Park, Indian Res.,
UINTA DESERT	Major Terrain Features
MT. MORIAH	Individual Mountain
STROMBOLI NUNIVAK	Island or Coastal Feature
Ocean Lake River Canal	Hydrographic Features

Note: Size of type varies according to importance and available space. Letters for names of major features are spread across the extent of the feature.

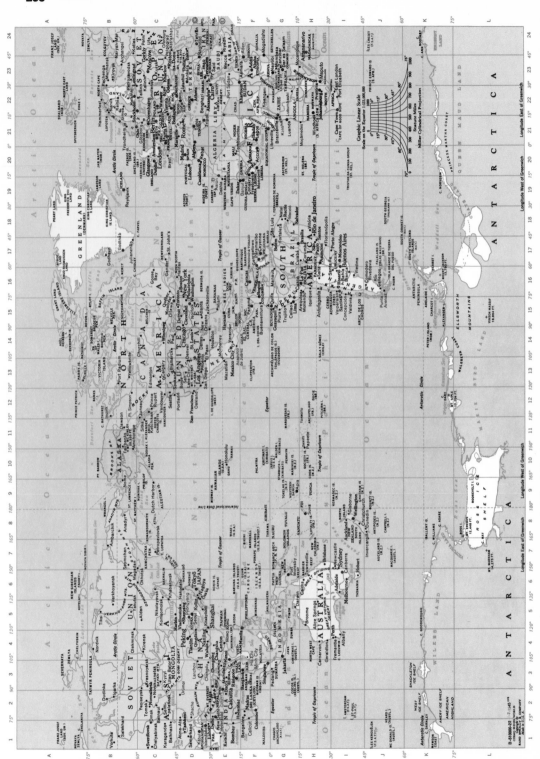

Statute Miles
Kilometers

Longitude West of Greenwich

Longitude East of Greenwich

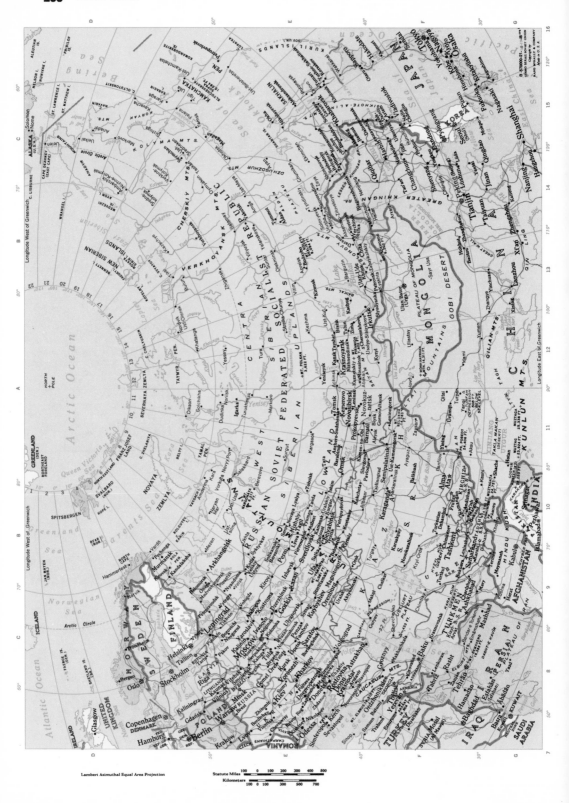

Lambert Azimuthal Equal Area Projection

Statute Miles
100 0 100 200 300 400 500

Kilometers
100 0 100 300 500 700

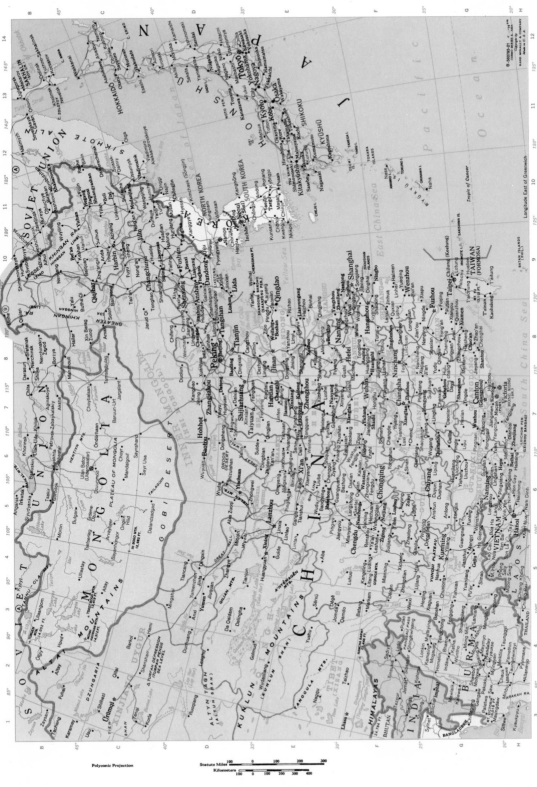

Polyconic Projection

Statute Miles

Kilometers

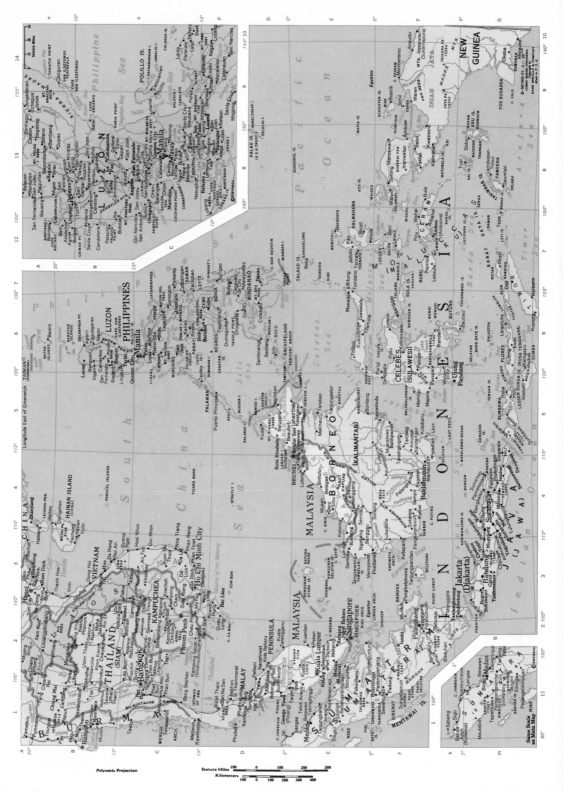

Polyconic Projection

Statute Miles 100 0 100 200 300

Kilometers 100 0 100 200 300 400

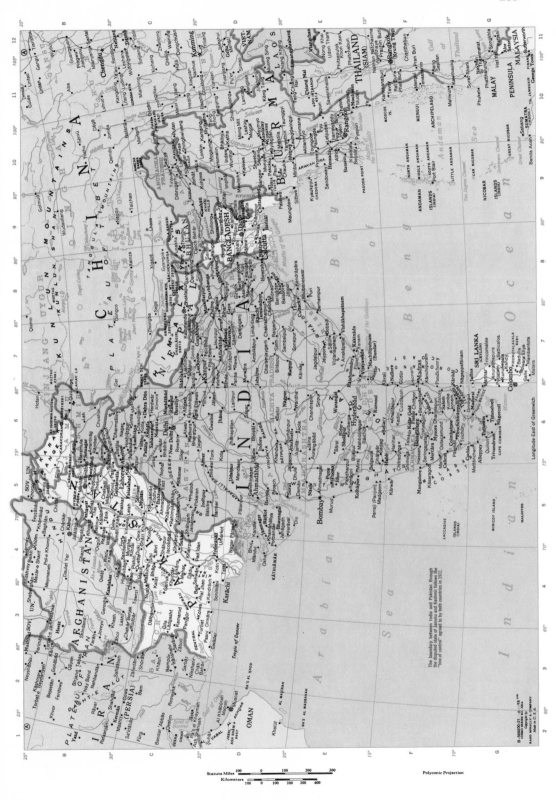

Statute Miles

Kilometers

Polyconic Projection

The boundary between India and Pakistan through
the disputed state of Jammu and Kashmir follows the
"line of control" agreed to by both countries in 1972.

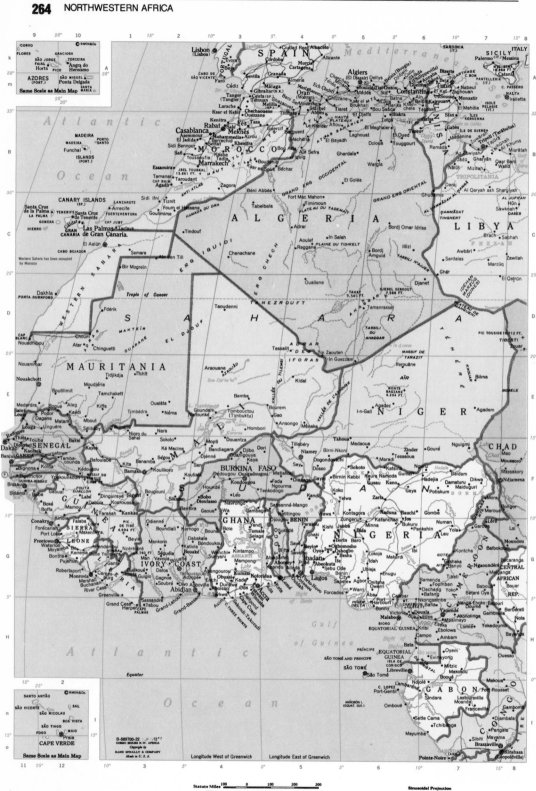

Statute Miles 100 0 100 200 300

Kilometers 100 0 100 200 300 400

Sinusoidal Projection

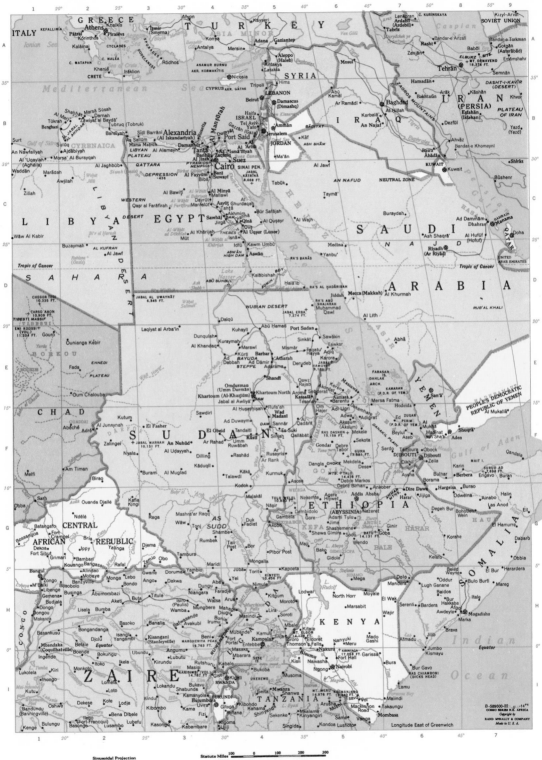

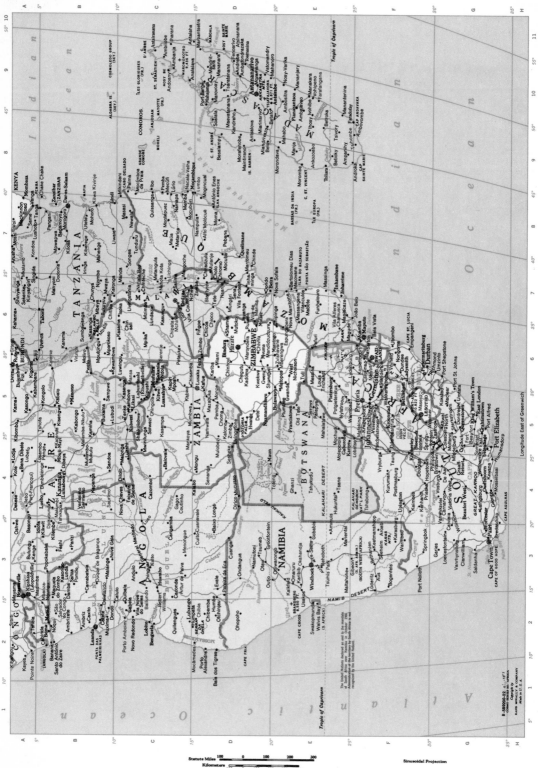

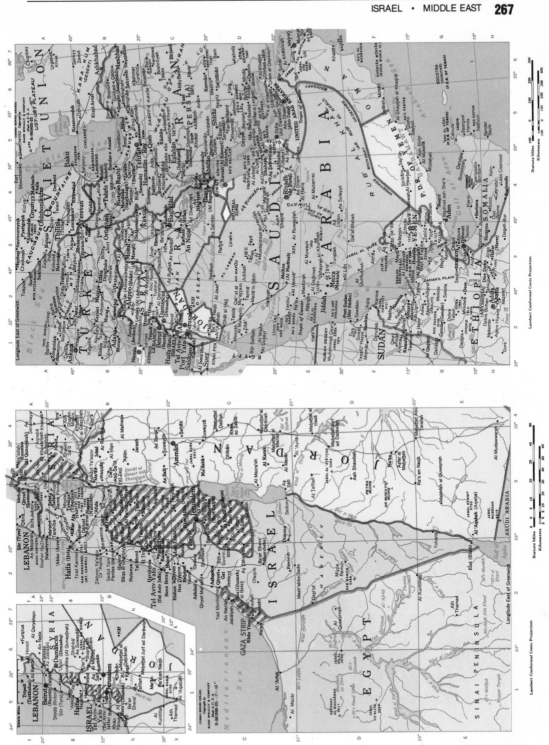

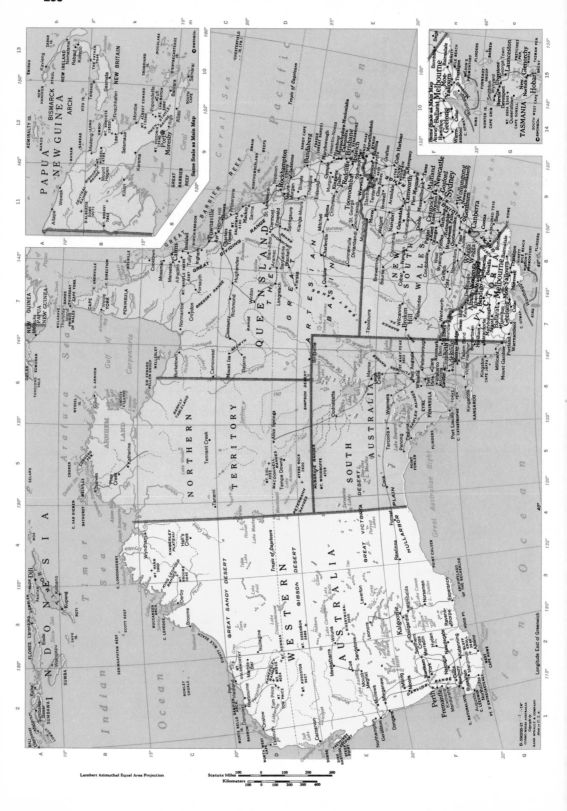

Lambert Azimuthal Equal Area Projection

Statute Miles
Kilometers

NEW ZEALAND

NORTH ISLAND

SOUTH ISLAND

AUSTRALIA

QUEENSLAND

NEW SOUTH WALES

VICTORIA

SOUTH AUSTRALIA

GREAT ARTESIAN BASIN

GREAT DIVIDING RANGE

GREAT BARRIER REEF

Tropic of Capricorn

Indian Ocean

Tasman Sea

Bass Strait

Great Australian Bight

Brisbane, Sydney, Melbourne, Adelaide, Newcastle, Wollongong, Rockhampton, Gladstone, Bundaberg, Maryborough, Toowoomba, Dalby, Roma, Charleville, Longreach, Blackall, Emerald, Canterbury, Betoota, Birdsville, Farina, Quorn, Port Augusta, Port Pirie, Whyalla, Port Lincoln, Broken Hill, Wentworth, Mildura, Swan Hill, Echuca, Bendigo, Ballarat, Geelong, Warrnambool, Hamilton, Portland, Horsham, Stawell, Shepparton, Wagga Wagga, Albury, Wodonga, Wangaratta, Benalla, Seymour, Goulburn, Canberra, Orange, Bathurst, Dubbo, Parkes, Forbes, Cowra, Young, Cooma, Bega, Bombala, Eden, Nowra, Moruya, Bourke, Cobar, Nyngan, Narromine, Condobolin, Griffith, Deniliquin, Hay, Balranald, Ivanhoe, Cunnamulla, Thargomindah, Quilpie, Windorah, Bedourie

Auckland, Wellington, Christchurch, Dunedin, Invercargill, Napier, Hastings, Gisborne, New Plymouth, Palmerston North, Hamilton, Rotorua, Tauranga, Whangarei, Nelson, Blenheim, Greymouth, Westport, Hokitika, Timaru, Oamaru, Ashburton, Queenstown, Wanaka, Gore, Milton, Balclutha, Kaikoura, Picton

NORTH ISLAND

SOUTH ISLAND

Cook Strait

Bay of Plenty

CAPE KARIKARI, NORTH CAPE, CAPE REINGA, CAPE MARIA VAN DIEMEN, THREE KINGS ISLANDS, CAPE EGMONT, CAPE FAREWELL, CAPE FOULWIND, CAPE CAMPBELL, CAPE PALLISER, CAPE KIDNAPPERS, EAST CAPE, MAHIA PENINSULA, BANKS PENINSULA, STEWART ISLAND (OBAN), SOUTH CAPE, SOUTH WEST CAPE, PORT CHALMERS, OTAGO PENINSULA, CASCADE POINT, SECRETARY I., BOUNTY ISLANDS, THE SNARES, THE TRAPS

MT. COOK 12,349 FT., MT. ASPIRING 9,959 FT., MT. TASMAN 11,475 FT., MT. EGMONT 8,260 FT., MT. RUAPEHU 9,175 FT., MT. COOPERNOOK, MT. KOSCIUSKO 7,316 FT., MT. BOGONG 6,508 FT., MT. OSSA 5,305 FT.

Lambert Conformal Conic Projection

Statute Miles
50 0 50 100 150

Kilometers
50 0 50 100 200

Longitude East of Greenwich

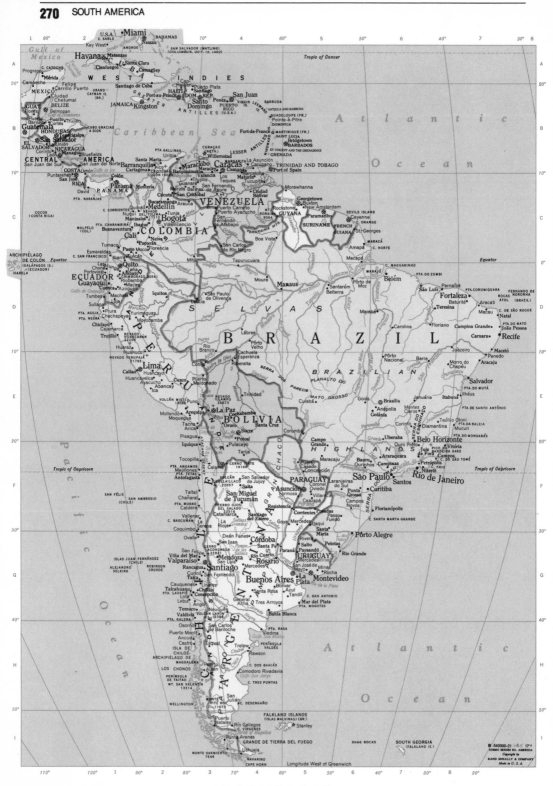

Sinusoidal Projection

Statute Miles
100 0 100   300   500   700

Kilometers
100 0 100 300 500 700 900 1100

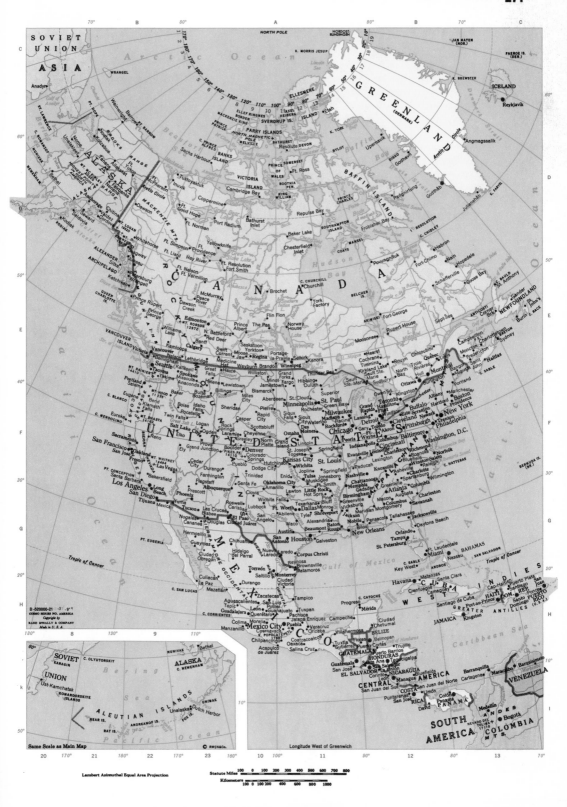

Lambert Azimuthal Equal Area Projection

Statute Miles

Kilometers

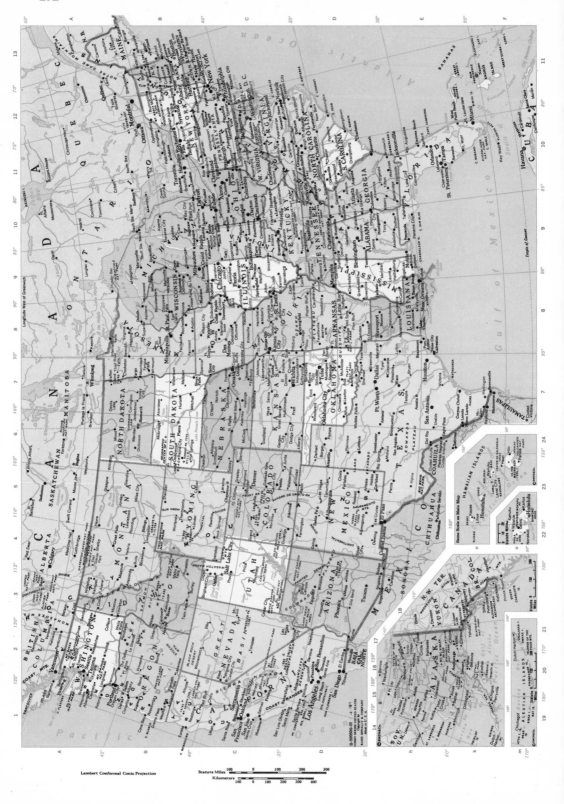

Lambert Conformal Conic Projection

Statute Miles
Kilometers